Date Due

AMERICAN WRITERS SERIES

★

HARRY HAYDEN CLARK
General Editor

★

★ AMERICAN WRITERS SERIES ★

Volumes of representative selections, prepared by American scholars under the general editorship of Harry Hayden Clark, University of Wisconsin

WILLIAM CULLEN BRYANT, *Tremaine McDowell, University of Minnesota*

JAMES FENIMORE COOPER, *Robert E. Spiller, University of Pennsylvania*

JONATHAN EDWARDS, *Clarence H. Faust, University of Chicago, and Thomas H. Johnson, Lawrenceville School*

RALPH WALDO EMERSON, *Frederic I. Carpenter, formerly of Harvard University*

BENJAMIN FRANKLIN, *Frank Luther Mott, University of Missouri, and Chester E. Jorgenson, Wayne University*

ALEXANDER HAMILTON AND THOMAS JEFFERSON, *Frederick C. Prescott, Cornell University*

BRET HARTE, *Joseph B. Harrison, University of Washington*

NATHANIEL HAWTHORNE, *Austin Warren, University of Iowa*

OLIVER WENDELL HOLMES, *S. I. Hayakawa, Illinois Institute of Technology, and Howard Mumford Jones, Harvard University*

WASHINGTON IRVING, *Henry A. Pochmann, University of Wisconsin*

HENRY JAMES, *Lyon Richardson, Western Reserve University*

HENRY WADSWORTH LONGFELLOW, *Odell Shepard, Trinity College*

JAMES RUSSELL LOWELL, *Norman Foerster, formerly of University of Iowa, and Harry H. Clark, University of Wisconsin*

HERMAN MELVILLE, *Willard Thorp, Princeton University*

JOHN LOTHROP MOTLEY, *Chester P. Higby and B. T. Schantz, University of Wisconsin*

THOMAS PAINE, *Harry H. Clark, University of Wisconsin*

FRANCIS PARKMAN, *Wilbur L. Schramm, University of Iowa*

EDGAR ALLAN POE, *Margaret Alterton, late of University of Iowa, and Hardin Craig, Stanford University*

WILLIAM HICKLING PRESCOTT, *William Charvat, Ohio State University, and Michael Kraus, College of the City of New York*

SOUTHERN POETS, *Edd Winfield Parks, University of Georgia*

SOUTHERN PROSE WRITERS, *Gregory Paine, University of North Carolina*

HENRY DAVID THOREAU, *Bartholow Crawford, University of Iowa*

MARK TWAIN, *Fred Lewis Pattee, Rollins College*

WALT WHITMAN, *Floyd Stovall, North Texas State Teachers College*

Pen drawing by Kerr Eby

JAMES RUSSELL LOWELL

James Russell Lowell

REPRESENTATIVE SELECTIONS, WITH
INTRODUCTION, BIBLIOGRAPHY, AND NOTES

BY

HARRY HAYDEN CLARK

Professor of English
University of Wisconsin

AND

NORMAN FOERSTER

Director of the School of Letters
University of Iowa, 1930–1944

AWS

AMERICAN BOOK COMPANY

New York · Cincinnati · Chicago
Boston · Atlanta · Dallas · San Francisco

E.P.I.
Clark and Foerster's James Russell Lowell
Made in U. S. A.

PREFACE

We have aimed, so far as the scope of one volume permits, to interpret and reprint selections representing Lowell's *development* as an unusually versatile man-of-letters, using a multitude of forms, from youth to old age. It is hoped that the first half of the Introduction will help to show that he was not as inconsistent as some readers suppose, and that within broad periods, corresponding to trends in American life, he wrote in the light of certain reasonably unified patterns of ideas. Perhaps what is sometimes condemned in Lowell as inconsistency can be better defined as open-mindedness and the courage to modify attitudes which did not seem to him justified by the results. If his versatility did not enable him to concentrate his complete powers so as to achieve supreme eminence in any one form or activity, this tendency also has its good (and perhaps distinctively American?) aspect: he kept measure with his people, tried to meet their changing needs, was not above trying to put his idealistic theories into practice, and especially as ambassador and commentator on public affairs he used the torch of learning to light the way of our citizens in their various worldly and political affairs. When his career is viewed *as a whole* what stands out is his inclusiveness and his uniting of opposites: although not always in the same period, he unites in his total career social reform and self-reform, ardent humanitarianism and the ideal of a natural aristocracy of virtue and wisdom, of social responsibility and stewardship; he unites nationalism and cosmopolitan internationalism, and concern with the present guided by lessons learned from a critical winnowing of the past; his fervent moral seriousness is leavened by racy humor; and his bookishness is leavened by a zestful devotion to the speech of the rustic, rooted in the soil. A good case could be made out for Lowell, all things considered, as the most completely representative spokesman of the New England mind. If wholesomeness, integrity, social consciousness and idealism are his chief qualities, these are made lovable by his curiously unique individuality and "personality," especially as revealed in his letters.

Some of the earlier parts of Mr. Clark's portion of the present Introduction are based on an article of his in *Studies in Philology*, for the use of which he thanks the editors of that journal. This earlier interpretation has been much amplified and modified, however, and the section dealing with Lowell's final mature period is almost entirely new, including much fresh material on Lowell's neglected but essentially sympathetic attitude toward science and the mild form of socialism advocated by Howells, whom he befriended so warmly. The annotated bibliography and the notes are based on Mr. Clark's *Major American Poets* (American Book Company, 1936), with changes to bring them up to date. Our choice of Lowell's letters has been guided by that of Professor Byron J. Rees in his *Nineteenth Century Letters* (1919), and is here used with permission of the publishers, Charles Scribner's Sons. Mr. Foerster's part of the Introduction is taken from his *American Criticism* (1928), with the kind permission of the Houghton Mifflin Company. We are also grateful to the Houghton Mifflin Company as publishers of Lowell's complete works for permission to use the selections comprising the body of this volume.

H. H. C.
N. F.

CONTENTS

vii

INTRODUCTION

I. LOWELL'S MENTAL GROWTH

Before one attempts an appraisal of Lowell, it is well to try to envisage the whole man as he lived from 1819 to 1891 and responded to the successive political, religious, social, and literary trends of the nineteenth century in his versatile capacities as poet, editor, familiar essayist, literary critic, nature writer, letter-writer, humorist, professor, ambassador, and philosopher. Lowell had roots deep in the New England past, symbolized by ancestral Elmwood, his Cambridge home where he was born and where he died; as he grew, his interests broadened and extended from kin to kind, and he owed much to the stimulus of many friends. "I would rather be loved than anything else in the world," he once remarked. "I always thirst for affection . . . I have never lost a friend."[1] He insisted that, after having been wined and dined by Europe's great while he was ambassador, he had never known such choice company as he knew in his formative years in the old Cambridge days of The Saturday Club, Longfellow's Dante Club, and the contributors to *The Atlantic Monthly* which Lowell founded in 1857 and made the mouthpiece of the most gifted writers of the age. He wore his great learning lightly, and tempered ethical fervor with boyish vivacity. "What are we good for," he once exclaimed, "if our natural temperament doesn't now and then take the bit in its

---

[1] *The Complete Writings of James Russell Lowell.* Elmwood Edition. Sixteen Volumes. Cambridge, Mass. 1904. XV, 277. Hereafter in the present study volume numbers standing alone refer to this edition. In cases where *Writings* are cited, the reference is to the Riverside Edition of 1890. When the term *Letters* is used, reference is made to the two-volume edition; XIV, XV, XVI refer to the three-volume edition (Elmwood).

teeth and scamper till our hair bristles in the wind?"[2] President
Eliot thought that Lowell did his best teaching when he had a
few gifted students such as Henry James or Barrett Wendell in
his book-lined study where the dancing fire-light symbolized
the free play of his fancy and thought. While Emerson gleaned
for his journals the harvest of a quiet eye in solitary and gravely
reflective walks about Concord, Lowell profited by the stimula-
tion of congenial companionship and conversation. He had a
way of salvaging the best thoughts so inspired, of putting them
into his letters, and then polishing them for inclusion in his
essays, where they have the quality of seasoned timber. Prizing
absolute integrity, Lowell has something of Emerson's aversion
to dealing with topics on which he has nothing original or
fresh to say, and to enslaving himself to a logical sequence with
high-lighted transitions merely for the sake of orderly comprehensiveness. Of course orderliness is desirable, but many
writers of golden thoughts have survived without it; and perhaps we should not deplore Lowell's deficiency in this respect
too much, for it gave a greater latitude to his rich insights and
zestful individuality.

It may be well, however, to resist the temptation to deal with
his personality, attractive as that is, and to return to the problem of the growth of his mind. Broadly speaking, one can distinguish in this three successive patterns of ideas. Until about
1850 he was a *humanitarian*, devoted to advancing mankind by
revolting from the "blood-rusted" past and by emancipation,
institutional reform (especially abolition of slavery), and an appeal to the sympathetic heart rather than the head. Second,
from about 1850 to about 1867 he was a *nationalist* who thought
that abolition was subordinate to the preservation of the Union,
to "nationality" as the parent of authoritative order as opposed
to secession and anarchy; he hoped that the mutable Many
might find worthy perpetuation in the immutable One, a coer-

[2] XV, 320.

cive Union, and that inevitably "a strong nation begets strong citizens."[3] Third, from about 1867 to the end, he became what Jefferson[4] meant by a *natural aristocrat* who is socially responsible. The political and financial corruption after the War led him to think that "popular government is not in itself a panacea, is no better than any other form except as the virtue and wisdom of the people [as individuals] make it so," and that the long-range "interest of the many" could be best insured "by bringing the influence [through education] of the more cultivated to bear with greater energy and directness on the less cultivated . . ."[5] In this period he thought that charity of heart and institutional reform needed to be supplemented by the head, and by wisdom, *and* by the virtuous self-reform of individuals guided by a winnowing of mankind's whole heritage

[3] VI, 345.

[4] Jefferson, the father of democracy, wrote John Adams, the Federalist, on Oct. 28, 1813, "I agree with you that there is a natural aristocracy among men. The grounds of this are virtue and talents," as opposed to "wealth and birth" which are the grounds of an "artificial aristocracy." "The natural aristocracy I consider," said Jefferson, "as the most precious gift of nature, for the instruction, the trusts, and government of society . . . May we not even say, that that form of government is the best, which provides the most effectually for a pure selection of these natural aristoi into the offices of government?" And after framing bills to eliminate primogeniture (laying "the ax to the foot of pseudo-aristocracy") and to insure religious freedom, Jefferson regarded his plan for free education of students who won in competition in successive schools as "the keystone of the arch of our government," as the best means of qualifying the people "to select the veritable aristoi, for the trusts of government." By such a plan, Jefferson thought, "worth and genius would thus have been sought out from every condition of life, and completely prepared by education for defeating the competition of wealth and birth for public trusts," for the "election and separation of the aristoi from the pseudo-aristoi, of wheat from the chaff. In general they [the people, properly educated] will elect the really good and wise."

[5] I, 326 ("Condescension in Foreigners," 1869); VIII, 157 ("Progress of the World," 1886); VII, 206 ("Harvard Anniversary Address," 1886).

of experience in the past, by what has proved to be valuable in
both science and the Humanities. Let us hasten to add that
these three ideals do not represent air-tight compartments but
rather centers of relative emphasis: in this constant expansion
of his horizon Lowell did not so much reject his earlier ideals
as transcend them by including them in a larger outlook. For
example, he never ceased to be proud that he had contributed
to the abolition of slavery and had advocated charity of heart;
during his last period, if he emphasized self-reform, he also
took an active part (as presidential elector, ambassador to Spain
and to England, and as a crusader for Civil Service Reform and
for "The Independent in Politics") in institutional reform and
in striving to make the nation strong. The evidence to be cited
would seem to indicate clearly, however, that he recognized
thankfully that his life was steadily being "changed and renewed" by a "broadening of the mind," and that he placed his
emphasis successively upon humanitarianism, nationalism, and
a natural aristocracy of virtue and wisdom dedicated to "a
wider and wiser humanity."[6] Let us now trace his attempt to
keep measure with his people through these three periods as he
rounded "a whole life to the circle fair of orbed fulfillment."[7]

[6] XV, 360 ("Letters," 1875); VII, 37. Looking back in 1875 to
the period of 1838 when abolition had been his chief interest and he
had proclaimed "I am fast becoming ultra-democratic" (XIV, 41),
Lowell said humorously that he "was as great an ass as every brayed
and thought it singing" (XV, 351).
[7] This is the phrase Lowell used to describe Washington's disciplined development "in perfect symmetry of self-control" (XIII,
92). The "Three Memorial Poems" (XIII, 70–108), dedicated to
E. L. Godkin "in cordial acknowledgement of his eminent service in
heightening and purifying the tone of our political thought," represent Lowell's best poetic expression of the natural aristocracy of his
third period. He says that *The Nation*, which Godkin edited from
1865 to 1881, has "done more good and influenced opinion more than
any other agency" (XV, 175).

A. THE HUMANITARIAN

Humanitarian Influences in Youth.

It is important to remember that Lowell's youth coincided with the full flush of the humanitarian movement, which may perhaps be traced back to Locke's doctrine that man is the product of his environment and which had been heralded and made the basis of humanitarian hopefulness in the Old World by such men as Shaftesbury, Thomson, Cowper, Blake, Rousseau, Wordsworth, Coleridge, and Shelley, and in the New World by men as diverse as Franklin, Woolman, Jefferson, Barlow, Paine, and Freneau. The more radical believed that, since man is the product of outer forces, himself naturally good, he could be perfected by a modification of these outer forces, especially by emancipation from tyranny and tradition. In place of the Puritans' "vertical" love of man for God, a stress on perfecting one's higher self, there appeared a "horizontal" love of man for man, a stress on perfecting one's neighbors. Franklin, who read Shaftesbury and Collins, and confessed that he "became a thorough deist," had proclaimed that "the most acceptable service of God was the doing good to man." Quakerism, Unitarianism, and Transcendentalism deepened the sense of the dignity of man inherited from the Enlightenment. After 1833, when Garrison and Whittier helped to form the American Anti-Slavery Society, the cause of Abolition attracted in different degrees such different personalities as Wendell Phillips, Mrs. Maria W. Chapman, Mrs. Lydia M. Child, Channing, Emerson, Thoreau, Parker, and Longfellow.[8]

[8] On backgrounds consult Mary S. Locke, *Anti-Slavery in America . . . (1619–1808)* (Boston, 1901); Lorenzo D. Turner, *Anti-Slavery Sentiment in America Prior to 1865* (Washington, D.C. 1929); Wm. L. Mathieson, *British Slavery and Its Abolition, 1823–1838* (London, 1926); J. T. Adams, *New England in the Republic* (Boston, 1926) Ch. XVII; and A. H. Abel and F. J. Klingberg, *A Side-Light on Anglo-American Relations, 1839–1858*, a study involving the corre-

Even Lowell's background was not so conservative as sometimes supposed, for his grandfather had been an early abolitionist. And Lowell's Class Poem at Harvard in 1838 is not so
much an attack on all abolitionists as an attempt to distinguish
between the "canting fanatics" who in following the extremist
Garrison wanted "to bring Millennium by force," and the
milder portion of the party of whom Lowell approved. "It is
too late in the day now," according to one of his notes to the
poem, "to *sneer* at Abolitionists . . . For I suppose that there
is not a man in New England who is not an Abolitionist at
heart." Lowell's appeal in this period is not to force or to the
head but to the heart[9]:

> Not mine the heart that would not keenly feel
> A fellow's moan 'neath slavery's iron heel,
> Nor mine the eye which could unquivering see
> Oppression grind the weak that clasp his knee.

"I am fast becoming ultra-democratic," he exclaimed in November of the same year. "Liberty is now no longer a cant word in
the mouths of knaves and fools."[10] News of a Manchester
meeting of distressed workmen, "a vast multitude starved,"
"almost brings tears." Of the present extant parties, he wrote
in 1839, the "Abolitionists are the only ones with whom I

---

spondence of Lewis Tappan and others with the British and Foreign
Anti-Slavery Society (Lancaster, 1927). For the other side of the
argument, see W. S. Jenkins, *Pro-Slavery Thought in the Old South*
(Chapel Hill, N.C., 1935).

[9] T. W. Higginson (*Old Cambridge*, New York, 1900, p. 175) quotes
Lowell in this period as saying, "I go out sometimes with my heart so
full of yearning toward my fellows that the indifferent look with
which even entire strangers pass brings tears into my eyes." Higginson, himself an abolitionist who loved Lowell, remarks (p. 173)
that Lowell was "secretly over-sensitive, pensive, and given to anxiety
and despair" during this early period. His 1843 volume of *Poems*
had berated the later conservative Wordsworth as "an old man faith-
less to Humanity." Lowell in the "Fable for Critics" had said that
Poe's "heart somehow seems all squeezed out by the mind."

[10] *Letters*, I, 33–34.

sympathize."[11] Thenceforth Lowell's sympathy for the oppressed and his hatred for slavery found voice in poems which he published in such Journals as the *Knickerbocker Magazine* and the *Southern Literary Messenger*. These were collected in 1841 in a book called *A Year's Life*, dedicated to the spirituelle reformer Maria White to whom he became engaged in 1840. She was the Una whose loveliness threw enchantment over abolition, and Lowell fared forth as her Red Cross Knight to succor the oppressed. His "perfect love" must lead to "wide love for all,"· and "elevate into a holy bond of brotherhood all earthly things." After graduating from the Harvard Law School in 1840, he championed all reforms, spoke at anti-slavery and temperance conventions, tried to found *The Pioneer*[12] magazine dedicated to reform. He was finally married in 1844. He contributed much humanitarian writing during this period to such journals as the *Anti-Slavery Standard* (to which he was a regular contributor from 1846 to 1850), the *Pennsylvania Freeman*, *The Broadway Journal*, and the Boston *Courier* in which most of the First Series of "Biglow Papers"[13] appeared from 1846 to 1848.

[11] *Ibid.*, I, 34–35.

[12] For an account of this magazine see E. D. Mead, "Lowell's *Pioneer*," *New England Magazine*, n.s., V, 235–248 (Oct., 1891); J. Albree (ed.), *Whittier Correspondence from the Oak Knoll Collection, 1830–1892* (Salem, 1911), p. 84; and S. T. Pickard, *Life and Letters of John Greenleaf Whittier* (Boston, 1894), I, 289, which quotes Lowell's letter regarding his plans. *The Pioneer* was a monthly magazine edited by Lowell and R. Carter. Only three issues appeared, in January, February, and March, 1843. Among the contributors were Hawthorne, Poe, Elizabeth Barrett (Browning), Jones Very, W. W. Story, and Whittier. Its most interesting notice, says Mead, 245, is a notice of Longfellow's "Poems on Slavery" containing "an account of the strong words on the anti-slavery reform, into which Lowell was already throwing himself." See also Frank Luther Mott, *A History of American Magazines, 1741–1850* (New York, 1930), pp. 735–738.

[13] The first paper appeared in the Boston *Courier*, June 17, 1846, and the others appeared in that paper and the *Anti-Slavery Standard*

Literature the Handmaid of Reform.

Consistent with his central belief that the hope of the world lay in bettering the outward lot of mankind generally, Lowell during this period made literature the handmaid of reform.[14] In the "Ode" of 1842 he censures the contemporary poet as an "empty rhymer" whose aestheticism is "misnamed Art." He demands that a poet confront even "the shadow of wrong" in his own time, convinced that there lies

> beneath the foulest faces lurking,
> One God-built shrine of reverence and love;
>
> . . . God and Heaven's great deeps are nearer
> Him to whose heart his fellow-man is nigh.

In his spirited opening editorial in *The Pioneer* (1843) he repudiates the widespread demand of his time for a *national* literature[15] and asks instead for a *natural*, that is, a humanitarian literature:

> any literature, as far as it is national,
> is diseased, inasmuch as it appeals to some climactic
> peculiarity, rather than to the universal nature.
> Morever, everything that tends to encourage the
> sentiment of caste, to widen the boundary between
> races, and put further off the hope of one great

---

until Sept., 1848. The papers were first published in book form in 1848. For discussion see Walter Blair's *Native American Humor*, New York, 1937.

[14] Cf. Whittier who wrote in 1841: "Poetry that won't speak and ring is worse than none. Poetry is the match, the torch of our little field piece, and if it is not fiery, if there is no ignition in it, no explosion, we might as well put an icicle to our priming," for true poetry must be

> A hate of tyranny intense
> And hearty in its vehemence.

Quoted by F. L. Pattee, *The First Century of American Literature, 1770–1870* (New York, 1935), p. 557.

[15] See B. T. Spencer, "A National Literature, 1837–1855," *American Literature*, VIII, 125–159 (May, 1936).

brotherhood, should be steadily resisted by all good
men. But we do long for a *natural* literature.[16]

In 1844 Whittier begged Lowell to write the "Liberty song"
which "shall be to our cause what the song of Rouget de Lisle
was to the French Republicans."[17] And two years later, Lowell
himself, now completely enrolled in the cause of humanity,
tried to enlist the pen of Holmes on the side of abolition,
temperance, the claims of the poor, pacificism, and reforms and
reformers in general.[18]

[16] Quoted by Scudder, *Lowell*, I, 103. In 1841, in the poem "L'En-
voi," Lowell had come out for a literature of universal human sentiment in preference to nationalism:

> They tell us that our land was made for song,
> With its huge rivers and sky-piercing peaks, . . .
> But Poesy springs not from rocks and woods;
> Her womb and cradle are the human heart.

In his review of Longfellow's "Kavanagh," *North American Review*,
LXIX, 196–215 (July, 1849), he treats nationality in literature at
great length. Following Longfellow, he ridicules literary nationalism
as only a wider form of provincialism and urges our writers instead to
be "thoroughly impregnated with humane and manly sentiment."
"Poets, however valuable in their own esteem, are not, after all, the
most important productions of a nation. If we can frame a commonwealth in which it shall not be a misfortune to be born, in which there
shall never be a pair of hands nor a mouth too much, we shall be as
usefully employed as if we should flower with a Dante or so, and
remain a bony stalk forever after" (p. 199).

[17] Quoted by Ferris Greenslet, *James Russell Lowell* (Boston, 1905),
p. 64. See also Albree, *op. cit.*, p. 91.

[18] See Holmes' letter of reply in John T. Morse, *Life and Letters of
Oliver Wendell Holmes* (New York, 1896), I, 295–303, where he gives
specific reasons for not taking part in each of Lowell's listed reforms.
See also another letter to Lowell two years later, II, 108, in which he
says good-humoredly that he tries in his poetry to set forth the *whole*
of the "crystalline order of things," but that Lowell always comes
in with "temperance sand" and "abolition grit" and rubs the polish
off. In his review of Macaulay's *Lays* in *The Pioneer* (I, 93–94,
Jan., 1843), Lowell pleaded for "poetry which awakens the gentle
and deeper feelings" and "spurs the soul to overcome hatred with
love, and violence with meekness . . ."

Suiting deed to word, the early poetry of Lowell attacks the
traditional past as tyrannical, expresses a firm faith in progress,
and sees in America the Utopian hope of the world. Inspired
by the fine fervor of his humanitarian bride,[19] the ardent young
poet goes comrading forth with Prometheus, Columbus, and
Cromwell—the crusaders and liberators of the race. In "Prometheus" the overthrow of Jove, symbolizing tyranny and ob-
scurantism, is foretold by the hero, who symbolizes oppressed
humanity to be set free by Truth, Beauty, "free love and peace,"
and "love of human kind." "With a far-spread gush of hope,"
he beholds afar "the sunrise of that Beauty" which is to hallow
Utopia. Lowell says that, although Shelley "handled the subject," "I have looked at it from a somewhat new point of view.
I have made it *radical*, and I believe that no poet in this age can
write much that is good unless he give himself up to this
tendency. For radicalism . . . has never till now been seen to
be one of the great wings that upbear the universe." Another
typical poem of this period, "Columbus," proclaims that "the
old world is effete," "Europe's world reels on to judgment,"
and the true hero is he who voyages through strange seas in
the solitude of a high resolve to found an "untried world," aspiring to a "large Humanity"

> To which by natural instinct every man
> Pays loyalty exulting.

In "A Glance Behind the Curtain," Cromwell, the hero—
dreamer and emancipator, crusader against king and priests—
scorns "the laws that in our fathers' day were best," rejoices
that his soul "is not a palace of the past," and is enthralled with
the "promise of the future," the promise of "Utopia." "The
Present Crisis" urges the nation to liberate "the slave, where'er

---

[19] See Hope J. Vernon, *The Poems of Maria Lowell, with Unpublished Letters and a Biography* (Providence, 1936), p. 96. Incidentally,
Lowell was an abolitionist before he met Maria and he continued
to be for some time after her death.

he cowers," since abolition is the "great cause, God's new
Messiah," allegiance to which parts the sheep from the goats.
Since "Humanity sweeps onward," and "Time makes ancient
good uncouth," we should not "attempt the Future's portal
with the Past's blood-rusted key."[20] W. G. Jenkins, who has
examined minutely his political thought, says that from "his
early years to the end of his life Lowell affirmed his belief in
progress,"[21] but that in his early days he did not yet see that
this was based on the past.[22] He criticized Calhoun in *The
Biglow Papers* as the opponent of progress, the spirit of the
age.[23] And looking back from 1856 he wrote Dr. Estes Howe
that out of American conditions of that time "a finer plant of
freedom is to grow." His rejection of tradition combined with
his enchanted vision of illimitable progress for mankind, on
one hand, and of a high-missioned future for America, on the
other, underlies Lowell's fervent Americanism in "A Fable for
Critics"[24] (1848) which was one of the early enthusiastic "sur-

---

[20] Cf. "The Sower" (1848) and its vision of a decrepid sower sowing
the seeds of past truths, but each "germ of truth"

> Was mated with a dragon's tooth
> Whence there sprang up an armed man.

See also the companion poems "To the Past" and "To the Future"
(1845) and "The Pioneer" (1847).
[21] "Lowell's Criteria of Political Values," *New England Quarterly*
(March, 1934), VII, 116. On p. 116 ff. Jenkins gives a full discussion
of Lowell's belief in progress; and Low, *op. cit.*, pp. 317–318, many
years ago noticed that Lowell "did honestly believe in Progress,
whether it was the progress of nations toward freedom and justice
or the progress of the individual on the stepping-stones of his own
dead self to higher things."
[22] Jenkins, *op. cit.*, p. 119. In a letter to Edward M. Davis in 1845
Lowell asserted that in the internal motives of life man has made
"steady progress."
[23] First Series, V.
[24] It should be noted here that the "Fable" probably marks
Lowell's turn from the sentimental to the critical temper with the
realization of the peril to himself in his "isms."

veys" of our native literature.[25]   America is urged to cut loose
from the past, to exploit her material resources:

> Forget Europe wholly, your veins throb with blood,
> To which the dull current in hers is but mud . . .
>
> By the scale of the hemisphere shape your designs,
> Be true to yourselves and this new nineteenth age . . .
>
> Plough, sail, forge, build, carve, paint, make all over new,
> To your own New-World instincts contrive to be true,
> Keep your ears open wide to the Future's first call.

"I am the first poet who has endeavored to express the American
Idea," he said later, "and I shall be popular by and by."[26]

Concurrently with Lowell's revolt from tradition and his
rose-tinted Americanism runs his tendency to sentimentalize
Christianity, to substitute outer for inner working.   Thus in
"The Search" Lowell seeks Christ in vain in Nature, "mid power
and wealth," and finally finds "his throne is with the outcast
and the weak."[27]   "Rhoecus" (1843) resembles the humanitarian
theme of "The Rime of the Ancient Mariner": a youth wounds
a bee, and the moral is expounded that

> He who scorns the least of Nature's works
> Is thenceforth exiled and shut out from all.

In the *Conversations on Some of the Old Poets* (1845) he has
John object to religion being a "gloomy turnpike to heaven,"
convinced that he is "upon the right path" whenever he comes
to "love man, and therefore God, the more."[28]   The best il-

[25] For the backgrounds of such surveys see E. C. Hassold, *American
Literary History Before the Civil War* (Chicago, 1935).

[26] *Letters*, I, 148.

[27] *Writings*, VII, 178.

[28] (Boston, 1893; 3rd ed. enlarged), p. 73.   P. 293 says God is
"most easily" beheld in "humble and common" people.   This edition
contains seven essays as follows: "Chaucer," "The Old Dramatists"
(2), "Chapman," "Ford," "Middleton," and "Song-Writing."

lustration, however, of Lowell's early humanitarian religion is "The Vision of Sir Launfal"[29] (1845) in which the quest for Christ is realized only in giving "a mouldy crust of bread" to a leper—who thereupon "stood before him glorified" in the person of Christ:

> Thou hast spent thy life for the Holy Grail;
> Behold it is here, . . .
> Who gives himself with his alms feeds three,
> Himself, his hungering neighbour, and me.

H. E. Scudder remarked that here Lowell "in the broadest interpretation of democracy, sang of the levelling of all ranks in a common humanity. There is a subterranean passage connecting the 'Biglow Papers' with 'Sir Launfal'; it is the holy zeal which attacks slavery issuing in this fable of a beautiful charity, Christ in the guise of a beggar."[30]

---

[29] During this early period Lowell was something of an emotional mystic. He claimed that occasionally Christ appeared to him in a vision. See *Letters*, I, 117, where he calls himself "mystic" and "enthusiast."

[30] H. E. Scudder, *James Russell Lowell: A Biography* (Boston, 1901), I, 268. Lowell's faith that goodness "is native in the simple heart of all" appears especially in his poem on Burns entitled "An Incident in a Railroad Car" (1842). In *Conversation on Some of the Old Poets* (1845), as in the paragraphs above, Lowell expresses many aspects of the literary, social, and philosophical radicalism of the early 19th century. He is ultra-sentimental (44, 246); likes Chaucer for his "simple choking words sobbed out" (14). He places humanitarian love of man above the love of God (73); expresses his faith in abolition and attacks the church as pro-slavery (74–77); and believes in a progress based on a reformed past cleared of its "poisonous rottenness" (245–246). Nature rather than theology is the way to God, the leaf of a tree having more of "the love of God . . . than a leaf of Taylor or Barrow" (71–72). He rejects reason for intuition; when "we are in the right, we can never reason, but only assert" (82, 125–126). His critical theory rejects literary nationalism for a sentimental universality based on the human heart; the center of past and future "is the living heart of man" (195–196). True literature therefore has a humanitarian instead of a national purpose, something "to make us wiser and better" (5) and is good as it advances "the

Abolitionism.

"The Anti-Slavery Papers"[31] contributed to the *Pennsylvania Freeman* and the *National Anti-Slavery Standard* between 1844 and 1850 contain the fullest exposition of Lowell's early humanitarian principles. More than has generally been realized, slavery was to Lowell only one of many external evils which he attacked in the world at large. "The aim of the true abolitionist," he wrote in his first paper, "is not only to put an end to negro slavery in America; he is equally the sworn foe of tyranny throughout the world."[32] Looking closely at any social wrong shows "its inextricable connection with all others."[33] There-

refinement . . . of mankind" (291). He scorns the "kennel standard of poetry" of the neo-classics (6), rejects all "rules" (224), dismisses judicial criticism because our arbitrary tastes "forbid the establishment of a code of criticism" (47, 49, 95), and denies the validity of literary tradition (130). In place of these objective guides he puts his faith in romantic subjectivity; hence the great poet "borrows not from without, but . . . from within" (81). He accepts most of the key ideas of romantic critical theory: (i) belief in nature as guide; every thought and feeling "unpremeditatedly takes its proper metre" (81); (ii) belief in inspiration, "those precious inner promptings to truth and love" (289); (iii) a yearning for the antiquarian past, for Chaucer who becomes dearer "the farther I can throw him back into the past" (20) and for the glory of the Renaissance (218); (iv) a desire for the melancholy romantic, for songs which have "some tinge of mysterious sadness in them" (174, 262); (v) a liking for the naturalness of Burns (223), the simplicity of Wordsworth (69, 71), and sensuous description of Keats (94) and Chaucer (71–72); (vi) a preference for the "commonplace" (98, 156) expressed in "plain words" (75) and not the language "over-purified" with the "Gallicisms" which have corrupted with politeness our "Saxon-sprung New England" (163).

[31] *The Anti-Slavery Papers of James Russell Lowell* (Boston, 1902) in 2 volumes. According to the unsigned introduction, p. vi, "The two volumes contain more than fifty articles; the first five contributed during 1844 to the 'Pennsylvania Freeman'; the rest, between 1845 and 1850, to the 'National Anti-Slavery Standard,' of which he was for two of these years titular associate editor." None of these papers are in Lowell's collected works; though not published until 1902, they are indispensable to any full estimate of the man.

[32] *Anti-Slavery Papers*, I, 6.   [33] *Anti-Slavery Papers*, I, 14.

fore Lowell attacked America's indifference to the French Revolution of 1848 which he regarded as an attempt to emancipate
the poor and as having its fundamental cause in the policy of
"considering dollars and not man as the foundation" of social
justice.[34]   He deplored American apathy toward the insurrection
in Rome in 1849 which he saw as another attack on the "hereditary privilege which binds the nations of Europe hand and
foot."[35]   He sympathized with the revolt of the Irish peasants[36]
and the cause of Kossuth against the inhumanity of the Turks.[37]
He urged a more just recognition of an equitable social contract
between labor and the dominant class.   Since labor no longer
feels the need of being protected by feudal lords, it "has begun
to demand a new settlement, in which its claims shall be duly
regarded."[38]   In "An Imaginary Conversation" between Calhoun, Foote, and Cass he classes Northern capitalist with
Southern slaveholder and makes Calhoun satirize both as the
exploiters of labor.   It "hardly seems more unnatural," says
Calhoun, that capital "should own the laborer outright, than
that it should buy the use of him at the cheapest rate.   If labor
may come into the market, why not the laborer himself?"[39]
Thus Lowell warned the reformers that though "chattel slavery"
is the "most odious shape in which oppression presents itself,"
the abolition of it is not to be considered an end, but merely "a
step toward a more perfect organization of society."[40]

   Lowell's recognition of the need for a far-flung reform move-

---

[34] *Ibid.*, I, 117.   "His Ode to France" (1848), *Writings*, VII, 252–
258, attacks "the yellow blood of Trade" and France's "Broker-King"
at strife with the humanitarian "Spirit of the Age"; he also pities
"the oppressed, their darkness and their woe."   In "The Ghost Seer"
(1845) he attributes sin to "want."

[35] *Ibid.*, II, 107.   [36] *Ibid.*, I, 100.
[37] *Ibid.*, II, 158.   [38] *Ibid.*, II, 116.
[39] *Anti-Slavery Papers*, I, 79.   Cf. also I, 10: "The system of labor
and of its reward at the North we sincerely believe to be but little
better than at the South."
[40] *Ibid.*, I, 195.

ment led him, unlike the great mass of abolitionists, to attack slavery through religion and not through politics.[41] He believed that the preference of the abolitionists for a political attack on slavery was ruining their whole movement. Their affiliation, for instance, with the Free Soil movement had done infinite harm. "Political parties have their crises of enthusiasm. Their zeal rises before an election and as naturally subsides after it." Moreover, "an unsuccessful election contest ... is a defeat, and defeat is discouragement."[42] On the other hand, if the abolitionists win the election and abolish slavery politically, "the power of the abolitionist will extend no further. No tall moral beacon-fire will be kindled, flinging its light into the unwilling recesses and hideous caverns of other oppressions."[43] Finally Lowell argues against political abolition because the forces of evil and wrong "can wield the cunning weapons of political management more adroitly than we."[44] Turning from politics, Lowell advocates the use of *true* religion. It is idle, he thinks, to attempt to use both politics and religion,—"to defeat our enemies with carnal weapons, and then strive to maintain and improve our victory with spiritual ones!"[45] Besides its consistency, the religious approach has other advantages. A "pure Ethical Idea can never be defeated" as can a political party. It "cannot be brought into conflict with material organizations,

[41] This is undoubtedly similar to the point of view of the greater part of the "Transcendental" abolitionists. Thoreau and Emerson took a similar view. It should be noted here that in recognizing the universality of evil in the world and in his attack on it through religion, Lowell already is on his way to the position he finally takes in his third period with Emerson and Thoreau that "the only reform is the inner reform." He had first, however, to go through the fire of the Civil War and the consequent corruption and disillusion before he centered his attention on self-reform.

[42] *Anti-Slavery Papers*, II, 46.   [43] *Ibid.*, I, 6–7.

[44] *Ibid.*, I, 7.

[45] *Ibid.*, I, 7. In *Conversations*, p. 76, he said there are no nations "so wicked as those which profess Christianity ... The church has corrupted Christianity."

but only applied to them as an impartial test."[46] The crushing
defeat inflicted on the abolition-minded political parties in 1848
and 1849 convinced Lowell of the "absolute necessity of a distinctly moral organization against slavery."[47] In contrast to
this crushing failure of the political approach he points to the
revolution which the abolitionists have brought about by putting the pro-slavery forces in contact "with the moral sentiment
of the whole world," making "their opponents feel that behind
them lie encamped the great moving forces which have given
every forward impulse to man."[48]

The attack from the religious point of view gave the abolitionists a tremendous superiority in Lowell's view. To the
transcendentalist thinker, a "moral idea never changes"[49] and
is immanent in the minds of all men. The consequence of the
religious approach, then, was that the abolitionist could ask of
every program, Is it right, or is it merely made right by expediency, on one hand, or by constitutional sanction or by the
Biblical sanction of organized religion, on the other? These
were two ways by which tradition supported slavery in the pre-
Civil War days. Lowell's attitude thus puts the abolitionists
on the side of high moral principle and puts the pro-slavery
advocates on the side of either personal selfishness or tradition.
He explained the pro-slavery opposition partly on the basis of
mere expediency because, for them, "Righteousness and expediency turn out in the end to be identical."[50] The constitutional
argument for slavery was equally false, since our "statutes are
subject to revision in that higher Congress where the laws of
Nature are enacted."[51] As for the religious basis professed by
pro-slavery people, Lowell undermines that by making a distinction between "religion" and the "church," the latter being

[46] *Ibid.*, II, 47.   [47] *Ibid.*, II, 48.   [48] *Ibid.*, II, 56.
[49] Charles Eliot Norton, "American Political Ideas," *North American Review* (Oct., 1865), CI, 563.
[50] *Anti-Slavery Papers*, II, 170.
[51] *Ibid.*, II, 175.

only " a task ceremony to be gone through with, and not a principle of life itself."[52]   The prayers there go up for the prosperous only; "as if God had ordained our pride of caste and our
distinctions of color."[53]

Attack on Traditionalism in Government and Church.

  The result of Lowell's stand is an attack on tradition in the
form of the Constitution and the organized churches. He sees in
them an instance of the temporary, the local, and the individual
setting themselves against the timeless, universal principles
based on the intuitions of the human heart. "We did not get
rid of George III," he says, "to enthrone a Constitution as pig-
headed as he."[54]   The poem "Anti-Apis," written in 1848, appeals to the higher law as against man-made law:

> Law is holy: aye, but what law? Is there nothing more divine
> Than the patched-up broils of Congress, venal, full of meat
>   and wine?

Lowell concludes sadly that we have come to "consider the law
of man as paramount to the laws of God . . . so that even in our
churches, the Constitution has taken the place of the Deca-
logue."[55]   He is equally emphatic in denouncing the tyranny
of the church. "The Church needs reforming now as much as
in Luther's time. . . . Christ scourged the sellers of doves out
of the temples; we invite the sellers of men and women in."[56]
He makes clear that his own appeal to religion is "not that of
which the churches and clergy of the land are the present expo-
nents."[57]   He ends by renouncing any reliance whatever on the

---

[52] *Conversations*, p. 75.   [53] *Ibid.*, pp. 77–78.

[54] *Anti-Slavery Papers*, II, 108. See also "The Sacred Parasol,"
I, 85–92, in which he lauds the Declaration of Independence and
condemns the Constitution as a "sacréd symbol" and "miraculous
parchment" without life.

[55] *Ibid.*, I, 12.

[56] *Conversations*, p. 74. See also p. 121; *Letters*, I, 98: and *Anti-
Slavery Papers*, I, 23–34; II, 17.   [57] *Anti-Slavery Papers*, I, 26.

past. "Freedom of autochthonic development is our peculiar privilege and safeguard, and the touch of Europe brings only disease and vice to us as to the islanders of the South Sea."[58]

Turning from established law and tradition, Lowell asks for a direct democracy.[59] At the present time our "government is as absolutely a distinct thing from the people as that of [Czar] Nicholas,"[60] for "we have never been more than nominal republicans."[61] The basis of Lowell's direct democracy is the divinity immanent in the consciences of all men, that "inward consciousness which distinguishes right from wrong as infallibly as the electric spark selects the iron and shuns the glass."[62] Lowell was quick to refute the accusation that the besiegers of Rome in 1849 were no better than a lawless mob. The people "are always politically consistent. Theirs is the consistency of the needle in its loyalty to the pole."[63] Direct democracy, however, is not the whole solution for Lowell. Out of it should come a universal public philanthropy. This is *the* solution. All who desire a "universal remedy," he says, should throw "no obstacle in the way of individual and immediate philanthropy," but their *chief hope* "is to combine the fragmentary benevolence into a system which shall render private philanthropy useless by removing its objects."[64] Such a system goes beyond Church and Constitution and takes its guidance directly from the

[58] *Ibid.*, II, 197.

[59] Lowell gives additional reasons for a direct democracy. In the present system the separation of politics and religion is very dangerous. It is a precept "which had its origin in the unprincipled self-interest of politicians" (*Anti-Slavery Papers*, II, 18). In the same place (I, 52–53) he tries to show an unholy alliance between government and property. Such poems as "The Heritage" (1840), "Hunger and Cold" (1843), and "The Ghost Seer" (1845) are hostile to the rich. They give the background for "The Vision of Sir Launfal."

[60] *Anti-Slavery Papers*, I, 56–57.

[61] *Ibid.*, I, 57.   [62] *Ibid.*, I, 109.   [63] *Ibid.*, II, 109.

[64] *Ibid.*, I, 121. One cannot help noticing in this an approach to the ideal of a benevolent nationalism which Lowell was soon to adopt as his next ideal.

original source of truth in the world, the divinely inspired sympathetic human heart.

Social and Racial Equalitarianism.

From here Lowell's thought leads directly to equalitarianism, social and racial. His first argument comes from the science of ethnology which he says, has proved that the differences between races are due to climatic and other purely external conditions.[65] Hence the supposed innate inferiority of the Negro race is a pure fiction. Lowell's other argument for equalitarianism has much greater implications. He takes it from a politico-sociological study of the present and past social conditions in Europe. The mid-century revolutions in Europe have a dual nature, "resulting from the effort of races to establish their national individuality, and of classes to acquire privileges long . . . and as unjustly usurped."[66] It is in the class distinctions that the individual "will take the deepest interest." An examination, he says, of the June Rebellion in Paris shows an astonishing variety in its ranks. This proves that the dissatisfaction was widespread and that always when a social revolution becomes inevitable, "the armies of the extremest left will be recruited from nearly all ranks of society."[67] On the other hand, he sees many instances in Europe where race distinctions exist. It is this "spirit of race," continually fostered by further oppression, which prevents the assimilation of the Jews, Poles, and Irish. Applying this to America, he finds that we have both race and class distinctions, for slavery degrades the non-slaveholding whites as well as Negroes. The result is that in America at present "there is a natural union of all except the highest class, not only against that highest class, but against the system whose necessary tendency is to divide men at last into a highest and a lowest with no intermediate grade."[68] Lowell concludes from

[65] *Anti-Slavery Papers*, II, 31.   [66] *Ibid.*, I, 197.
[67] *Ibid.*, I, 198.   [68] *Ibid.*, I, 200.

this that only where "all are admitted to equal privileges," can these imaginary boundary-lines be "rapidly obliterated."[69]

And this leads Lowell to his main problem—the function of the abolitionist. Believing in progress, he finds in European history "a movement of the general mind tending steadily in one direction." It shows "as distinctly the lines which indicate the successive subsidences of Privilege as the surface of the earth does those of ancient sea-levels."[70] The basis of the social state has been "a crude idea of Partnership," but as the average of "popular intelligence" rises gradually higher and higher, a readjustment of the terms of the partnership becomes necessary.[71] It is for this reason that in this great forward movement of the world-mind, slavery has become an *anachronism*. To Lowell the laws by which the social state evolves are transcendentally inevitable and rest upon "a system as harmonious and as subject to eternal principles as that of the planets." Hence all that is necessary is "to allow the laws of social gravitation to act unimpeded."[72] This fact defines the function of the abolitionist. He need only call the attention of all men to slavery's violation of the natural social law, and slavery will be doomed.

The Biglow Papers.

Having such a theory, Lowell in the "Biglow Papers" (1846) found a superb instrument for calling the attention of the world to human wrong.[73] How deeply he was impressed by the ef-

---

[69] *Anti-Slavery Papers*, I, 198–199.   [70] *Ibid.*, II, 115.

[71] *Ibid.*, II, 115–116.   [72] *Ibid.*, II, 116–117. See also II, 196.

[73] The popularity of the "Biglow Papers" has become legendary. J. R. Dennett, *Nation* (Nov. 15, 1866), III, 387, called them "a complete success from the beginning." The First Series, in covers, sold 1500 copies during one week and went through at least ten editions in America by 1876. Lowell himself in the Introduction to the Second Series, *Writings*, VIII, 157, records his first realization of the significance of his new invention: "The success of my experiment soon began not only to astonish me, but to make me feel the responsibility

fectiveness of his new weapon, he confesses shortly after beginning the series: "It seems as if my heart would break in pouring out a glorious song that should be the gospel of Reform, full of consolation and strength to the oppressed . . ." As he explained in the Introduction to the Second Series, he wrote the first "Biglow Papers" thinking "the Mexican war, as I think it still, a national crime committed in behoof of Slavery, our common sin."[74] "If I put on the cap and bells and made myself one of the court-fools of King Demos, it was less to make his majesty laugh than to win a passage to his royal ears for certain things which I had deeply at heart."[75] Indeed, one may say that Lowell's humor—suggesting an adjustive power in the interest of equilibrium rare in humanitarians—was his most important contribution to reform; as his fellow-abolitionist Whittier said, "the world-wide laugh" caused by Hosea Biglow was alone enough to "have shaken half the walls of Slavery down."[76] Lowell refracts himself dramatically through the character of Hosea, embodying "homely common-sense vivified and heated by conscience"; Birdofredum Sawin, the "incarnation . . . of national recklessness as to right and wrong"; and the Rev. Mr. Wilbur, "who should express the more cau-

of knowing that I held in my hand a weapon instead of the mere fencing-stick I had supposed." The causes of the work's great popularity are still something of an enigma in the literary world. Blair, p. 47, says that "Various elements which made Sam Slick and Jack Downing popular in the forties gave to the Yankees of Lowell's First Series such popularity that Lowell was astonished." See also Constance Rourke, *American Humor: A Study of National Character* (N.Y., 1931), p. 22 ff., and the Notes in H. H. Clark's *Major American Poets* (N.Y., 1936), pp. 869–872. The "Biglow Papers" have a sort of timeless appeal; on one side, they combine elements of native American humor; on another, their dialect and realism anticipate the realistic and critical attitude of recent American writing.

[74] *Writings*, VIII, 155.   [75] *Ibid.*, VIII, 157.

[76] See Jeannette Tandy, "The Biglow Papers" in *Crackerbox Philosophers in American Humor and Satire* (N.Y., 1925), pp. 43–64, who says "Lowell's range and penetration in satirical portraiture are unsurpassed in America."

tious element of the new England character and its pedantry."
In using the Yankee dialect Lowell said that he was merely
using his "mother tongue," that he was simply carried back
"to long-ago noonings in my father's hay-fields, and to the talk
of Sam and Job over their jug of *blackstrap* under the shadow
of the ashtree."[77]   The First Series of the "Biglow Papers"
deals mainly with pacifistic humanitarianism, with a satire on
contemporary politics, and with the collision in Congress
between the North and the South.   Hosea, "kind o' prest
with Hayin'," declines to enlist in the Mexican War to assist
his loving countryman, "the one-eyed Slarterer, the bloody
Birdofredum," in "pullin' o'triggers to extend the aree of
abusin' the niggers," in disseminating vital religion by "skewer-
ing the infidels upon his apostolical lance!"   The Mexican War
might well be condemned on other grounds, but Lowell condemns it in the name of universal pacifism: "Ez fer war, I call it
murder."   "We kind o' thought Christ went agin war an'
pillage."   Birdofredum complains that "ninepunce a day fer
killin' folks comes kind o' low fer murder."   "The war is a war
fer the spreadin' o' slavery," for "stealin' bigger pens to cram
with slaves."   The poet pours dire sarcasm on the "Demmer-
crats" who "sucked us right into a mis'able war," and upon the
Whigs who betray their "constitoounts."   He ironically urges the
election of General Scott, since he "has blown to pieces . . .
more Mexicans than any other commander," and he ridicules
the Whigs' nomination of a candidate "ef on all pints at issoo
he'd stay unintelligible."   "Direct taxation" is revealed as a
means of converting "the money we expend for tea" into
"Mexican blood."   And he ridicules log-cabin politics and
agrarianism, being unable to discover "the precise connection
between agricultural pursuits and statesmanship."   Later papers,
such as "The Debate in the Sennit," direly ironical in nursery
rime, satirize Calhoun's appeal to the Constitution—"Free-

[77] *Writings,* VIII, 208.

dom's Keystone is Slavery"—and Webster's vacillation. Elsewhere at this time he glorifies the Declaration of Independence
written by Jefferson, of whom he said "I doubt if we have produced a better thinker," and he accuses the Federalist Fathers
of creating a "Sacred Parasol,"[78] "a stout machine of parchment, . . . a Constitution" to be interposed "wherever there
seemed to be danger from the hostile incursions of light."[79]
It is well to remember that the later Unionist urged disunion in
this humanitarian period, urged us "to disown the tradoocers
of our people"; "we should go to work an' part." He makes
merry with the troubles of enforcing the Fugitive Slave Law,
lamenting the fact that, while all riches have wings, Southern
possessions have "legs," and "a kind of brute instinct . . . to
use them in a northerly direction."[80] The First Series concludes with Birdofredum's depression because an escaped slave,
whom he had captured and was about to sell, stole his wooden
leg and made him "larn him readin'":

> I vow I didn't b'lieve there wuz a decent alligatur
> Thet hed a heart so destitoot o' common human natur.

Since Lowell's later indifference to abolition has been attributed to the absence of his wife's influence[81] following her

---

[78] *Anti-Slavery Papers*, I, 85–92.
[79] *Ibid.*, I, 86.
[80] Quoted by Scudder, *op. cit.*, I, 215–216.
[81] In her first extant letter to Lowell late in 1840 she expressed her
intense, almost painful, sympathy with human suffering. "I felt
sorrowful for days and days after I read 'Chartism'." Recalling that
Lowell once said that men ought to pass their lives in *self culture*, she
replied: "Is not *self culture* most noble as it involves the thought of
the culture of others? There are enough of the pure and good in live
[sic] to leaven the whole lump of wretchedness and crime. But they
steal away to one chosen circle where nothing offends their taste and
sensibility," Vernon, *op. cit.*, p. 96. In the light of this it seems
indeed probable that the relaxation of her influence should have allowed the more conservative elements in Lowell's nature to come to
the fore. Such a conclusion, however, disregards the possibility of
Mrs. Lowell herself becoming more conservative. Her later letters,

death in 1853, it is important to observe that his growing dissatisfaction with Garrison's faction of the abolition movement began as early as 1848, five years before her death, when
he confessed he did "not agree with the abolitionists in their
disunion and non-voting theories." In the same letter, however, he calls Garrison "a great and extraordinary man," and
agrees to write a year for the *Anti-Slavery Standard*.[82] Later
in 1848, we find him disparaging his "contributions to the
Standard." "It is not the place for me. It *fags* me to deal with
particulars. The tendency of my mind is too reflective. I can
interest myself in general ideas (such as include the particulars),
but weary of their application to the present."[83] He had begun
that growth which was to transcend humanitarianism by including it in an infinitely more comprehensive system. He is
looking in the direction of centrality and self-mastery. In May,
1849, he complains of the vain attempt to please two masters.
"In writing for the *Standard*, I have felt that I ought in some
degree to admit the whole Executive Committee into my workshop, and defer as much as possible to the opinion of persons
whose opinions (however valuable on a point of morals) would
not properly weigh a pin with me on an aesthetic question. I
have felt that I ought to work in my own way, and yet I have
also felt that I ought to *try* to work in *their* way, so that I have
failed of working in either."[84] He goes on to explain his growing conviction that "the world must be healed by degrees," not
so much by direct outer means as by an appeal to man's inner
aspiration. "Let us sow the best seed we have, my dear Sydney,
and convert other men by our crops, not by drubbing them
with our hoes. . . . Let us not *preach* about the bright side of
human nature and *look* always at the dark. . . . We all revolve

---

after the birth of her children, show almost no interest in current
reforms, her energy apparently being completely absorbed by
domestic affairs.

[82] *Letters*, I, 125.   [83] *Ibid.*, I, 134.   [84] *Ibid.*, I, 156.

xxxvi — James Russell Lowell

around God with larger or lesser orbits, but we all likewise turn
upon our own axes. . . ."[85]   Thus, even as early as 1849, does
he dimly recognize the doctrine of centrality, the necessity of
organic poise, of revolving on one's own axis.[86]   "Accordingly,"
speaking of his relations with the *Anti-Slavery Standard*, he says,
"I throw up our engagement altogether."   Later, in 1850, he
confesses "there never has been a oneness of sentiment between
me and the Society."[87]   In a letter of January 23, 1850, he presents his "mental and moral latitude and longitude," convinced
that he is "farther eastward or nearer morning than ever
hitherto":

> I begin to feel that I must enter on a new year of my appren-
> ticeship.   My poems have thus far had a regular and natural
> sequence.   First, Love and the mere happiness of existence
> beginning to be conscious of itself, then Freedom—both being
> the sides of Beauty presented to me—and now I am going to try
> more wholly after Beauty herself.[88]   Next, if I live, I shall try
> to present Life as I have seen it.   In the "Nooning" I shall have
> not even a glance towards Reform . . .   Certainly I shall not
> grind for any Philistines, whether Reformers or Conservatives.
> I find that Reform cannot take up the whole of me, and I am
> sure that eyes were given us to look about us with sometimes,
> and not to be always looking forward.[89]

[85] *Letters*, I, 159.   Cf. I, 158, where he expresses his dislike for the
purely vituperative attacks of the abolitionists and asks that they
treat the slaveholders more fairly because even "*they* are human."

[86] He confesses that his heart is out of tune with abolition-writing:
"My own house has too many vitreous points about it to allow me to
think of throwing any stones."   *Letters*, I, 149.

[87] *Letters*, I, 181.   Also XIV, 210, 231–233, 238–239; Scudder I, 232.

[88] Cf. his earlier statement in *Conversations*, p. 292: "That which
alone can make men truly happy and exalted in nature is freedom;
and freedom of spirit, without which mere bodily liberty is but vilest
slavery, can only be achieved by cultivating men's sympathy with
the beautiful."

[89] *Letters*, I, 172–173.   In *A Fable for Critics* (1848) Lowell had
(anonymously) described his earlier work as "a whole bale of *isms*
tied together with rhyme," and he had said that he could not succeed

In 1839 Lowell had said, "I shall let my fate be governed by circumstance and influence. . . . A man should not only regard what is *in* him, but also what is *without* acting on that within."[90] This humanitarian concern with outer working, however, does not seem to have given him happiness, for he says in 1850, longing to go to Italy, "the farther I can get from American Slavery the better I shall feel. Such enormities as the Slave Law weigh me down without rebound, make me unhappy and too restless to work well in my own special vineyard."[91] In later years he confessed, "I remember in '39 putting a cocked pistol to my forehead—and being afraid to pull the trigger."[92] One is reminded of Wordsworth's early humanitarian yearning for the "dawn" when "all institutes" would be "forever blotted out," and his subsequent account of how he "yielded up moral questions in despair." However, if humanitarianism led Lowell to despair, he—like Wordsworth—decided to adopt an experimental attitude toward another view of life. He did not completely repudiate reform; rather, he subordinated it to somewhat wider interests.

B. The Nationalist

Effect of His European Sojourn.

In order to understand Lowell's growing devotion to his controlling concept from 1850 to 1867—the concept of nationality[93]—one must note with care the influence of his sojourn in Europe from 1851 to 1852 in deepening and broadening his respect for the organic continuity of tradition, for a sharing of a permanence which inspires peace. In "Leaves from My Jour-

---

as a poet until he learned "the distinction 'twixt singing and preaching'."

[90] *Letters*, I, 48.   [91] *Ibid.*, I, 188.   [92] *Ibid.*, I, 375.

[93] For studies of Lowell's political theories see J. F. Jameson, "Lowell and Public Affairs," *Review of Reviews*, IV, 287–291 (Oct., 1891) and W. G. Jenkins, "Lowell's Criteria of Political Values," *New England Quarterly*, VII, 115–141 (March, 1934).

nal in Italy"[94] he reports that, since he has come "from a country
where everything seems shifting like quicksand," "the sense of
permanence, unchangeableness, and repose which Italy gives
us is delightful."   Throughout this period, especially in his
criticism of America, we find his constant preoccupation with
this theme: the necessity of finding some changeless unity amid
an ever-changing multiplicity.   Although he seldom formulated
logically his intuitive attitude toward a science which, then as
now, threatened to overleap its limits, it is clear that he recognized the dangers of scientific monism, scepticism, and rational-
ism, and the attempt to disregard changeless human values in
the name of natural "undeniable evidence" which was ever
changing.   He complains that modern travelers "take science
(or nescience) with them," that "all their senses are sceptics and
doubters, materialists reporting things for other sceptics to
doubt still further upon."   "Analysis is carried into everything.
Even Deity is subjected to chemic tests."   Already a devout
student of Dante and mediaevalism, he recognizes the positive
values of the dualism of Catholicism:—"she has never lost sight
of the truth" that man is "composed of the sum of flesh and
spirit"; she is "the only church that has been loyal to the heart
and soul of man, that has clung to her faith in the imagination,"
with a wholesome recognition of the perils of surrendering
everything to "the iconoclast Understanding."[95]   Scion of the
Puritans as he was, he confesses that "Protestantism . . . made
a blunder in trusting herself to the intellect alone," and he confesses "a singular sympathy with what are known as the Middle
Ages," finding it more difficult "to bridge over the gulf to
Paganism."

And furthermore, the disenchanted abolitionist who in his
"regular and natural sequence" of living was "going to try

---

[94] Published in *Graham's Monthly*, April to June, 1854. Repub-
lished in *Fireside Travels* (1864).

[95] *Writings*, I, 195.

more *wholly* after Beauty herself"—although he was later distracted by the War—began to perceive the organic relation between art and national background, between the individual imagination and the social imagination. "What we always feel the artistic want of at home is background. . . . Surely, in all that concerns aesthetics, Europeans have us at an immense advantage. They start at a point which we arrive at after weary years, for literature is not shut up in books, nor art in galleries: both are taken in by unconscious absorption through the pores of mind and character in the atmosphere of society. We are not yet out of our Crusoe-hood. . . ."[96] He recognizes the danger of too-rapid social change, and wants instead

> to hev all *we* gain stick,
> An' not to start Millenium too quick.[97]

The Search for Stability.

He, who once thought that abolition was the most necessary reform, now recognizes that the problems of reform are immensely larger and more difficult than he had thought; the "black man's right" is no longer the "hardest question":

> The trouble is to 'mancipate the white;
> One's chained in body an' can be sot free,
> But t'other's chained in soul to an idee.[98]

Though Lowell had not yet come to see that evil was too universal to be conquered by outer reform alone and still spoke at times of relying "more wholly on nature," yet he was coming

[96] *Ibid.*, I, 113.

[97] *Ibid.*, VIII, 340. See also Parson Wilbur's fable, "Festina Lente," *Writings*, VIII, 298–300, where the reform party in the frog pond cut off the tails of the tadpoles to hasten their growth into frogs and succeed only in killing them. The moral points the danger of hasty action contrary to nature's slow evolutionary laws.

[98] *Writings*, VIII, 340. Cf. Emerson's similar view in his "Ode to W. H. Channing; also M. M. Moody, "The Evolution of Emerson as an Abolitionist," *American Literature*, XVII, 1–21 (March, 1945).

slowly to see that if there is to be any permanence, any unity, any immutable one in the present, it must evolve slowly from the best in the past:

> Young folks are smart, but all ain't good thet's new:
> I guess the gran'thers they knowed sunthin', tu.[99]

Even at the height of his anti-British feeling in the Civil War days,[100] while hoping that the present estrangement would "make us more independent of British twaddle," Lowell saw clearly that in any shutting "ourselves out from the advantages of English culture, the loss will be ours, and not theirs."[101]

It is significant that on Lowell's return home in 1853 he first published *A Moosehead Journal*, a rather idyllic account— "floating on the current of reverie"[102]—of a vacation trip to a Maine lake, which deals in part with the influence of the frontier on the American attitude and character. He laments indifference to culture, conscious that "till our struggle with nature is over, till this shaggy hemisphere is tamed and subjugated, the work shop will be the college whose degrees will be most valued. . . . I suppose we must wait, for we are a great bivouac as yet, rather than a nation on the march from the Atlantic to the Pacific, and pitch tents instead of building houses. Our very villages seem to be in motion, following westward the bewitching music of some Pied Piper of Hamelin."[103] However, if the frontier was indifferent toward culture and permanence, Lowell was not oblivious of its moulding of self-reliant manhood. After watching the manual dexterity of the Maine loggers, he concludes that "an aristocracy is evolved from this democracy

---

[99] *Writings*, VIII, 265, *Biglow Papers*, Second Series, which should be constantly distinguished from the First Series.
[100] For Lowell's sharp sense of England's betrayal in aiding the South during the Civil War see the poem, "Jonathan to John," *Writings*, VIII, 266–270.
[101] *Writings*, VIII, 250–251.
[102] *Ibid.*, I, 34.
[103] *Ibid.*, I, 6–7.

of the woods," for M., "a famous river-driver," was "a man really educated,—that is, with all his aptitudes *drawn out* and ready for use." After his breakfast with the loggers and hay-makers following a fruitless all-night hunt for a moose, he says, "If their hospitality lacked anything of hard external polish, it had all the deeper grace which springs from sincere manliness. . . . I have never seen a finer race of men."[104] It does not appear that the man accused of being a snobbish and "genteel" Brahmin was unable to appreciate the finer qualities of Hosea Biglow's rustic common sense or the "spice-lands of character" he found among the Maine loggers.

Growing Regard for the Past.

Next year, 1854, Lowell's fireside pilgrimage to *Cambridge Thirty Years Ago* reveals the roots of his somewhat conservative heritage in this rather idyllic and glamorous view, through the soft haze of retrospect, of the essentially "English village, quiet, unspeculative, without enterprise, sufficing to itself,"[105] where people still lived "who regretted the late unhappy separation from the mother island."[106] Colorful and beautiful and well-seasoned as this lyric essay is, one suspects that as yet the past was for Lowell more of a romantic bower of dreams than a stern school of experience. In this Lamb-like picture of the external oddities of Old Cambridge he says "a man who uses the eyes of his heart may find here also pretty bits of what may be called the social picturesque, and little landscapes over which that Indian-summer atmosphere of the Past broods as sweetly and tenderly as over a Roman ruin."[107] Here again he languidly resents the tendency toward eternal change and instability. So rapid are "our changes in America that the transition from old to new, the shifting from habits and associations to others entirely different, is as rapid almost as the passing in

---

[104] *Writings*, I, 38. [105] *Ibid.*, I, 55.
[106] *Ibid.*, I, 56. [107] *Ibid.*, I, 53.

of one scene and the drawing out of another on the stage."[108]
"Things were established then," and he says that "hurry and
competition seem to have quite unhung the modulating pendulum of steady thrift and competent training. . . . Life flowed
in recognized channels, narrower perhaps, but with all the more
individuality and force."[109] "There was an aristocracy such as
is healthful in a well-ordered community, founded on public
service, and hereditary so long as the virtue which was its
patent was not escheated."[110] The seaboard Brahmin recognized, as a book on *The Frontier in American Literature* (1927)
by Mrs. Lucy Hazard has recognized, that "pioneering involved
a break with the past," a disregard for "the sense of continuity,
of permanence, which makes of the present a bridge between a
past of revered memories and a future of assured anticipations;
the beauty and sentiment which hallow traditions; the tenderness
and sympathy which are flowers of slow growth, possible only
when man stands in definite and continuous relations to his
fellowmen." Lowell is convinced that "an orbed and balanced
life would revolve between the Old and the New Worlds as
opposite, but not antagonistic poles, the true equator lying
somewhere midway between them."[111] In this period, then,
it is Lowell's faith that the ideal lies "midway" between Old
World tradition and New World practice that determined after
1855 his endeavors as a Harvard professor to integrate the past
and the present, to render available for the guidance of his
countrymen the experience of the race. Doubtless this ideal
determined also in part his growing veneration for the hitherto
scorned Constitution, "the most remarkable monument of
political wisdom known to history," erected by pioneer Federal-
ists who had "a great respect for authority in all its manifestations; for the law first of all, for age, for learning, and for experience."[112] They were "led astray by no theories of what

108 *Writings*, I, 52.   109 *Ibid.*, I, 58–59.   110 *Ibid.*, II, 290.
111 *Ibid.*, I, 43.   112 *Ibid.*, VI, 206.

might be good, but clave closely to what experience had demonstrated to *be* good."[113]

Just as Lowell had come to respect the past he had before scorned, so now he who had pleaded for freedom came to exalt control, as illustrated in the "Ode to Happiness" (1861).[114] This *Ode* is somewhat analogous to Wordsworth's "Ode to Duty" in his recognition of the inadequacy of the humanitarianism of the French Revolution; sorrowing at the death of his brother John, Wordsworth is tired by "this unchartered freedom," confesses that he has "too blindly" reposed his trust, and supplicates for "a repose that ever is the same," for the "control" of the "Stern Lawgiver." So Lowell, following his disillusionment with outward reform and his grief at the death of his two children and his wife, is confident that although the capricious "half-earthly" happiness of boyhood has fled, Tranquillity, her "elder sister," "born of the immortals," will come to him who matches impulse with control,

> Who, dowered with every gift of passion,
> In that fierce flame can forge and fashion
> Of sin and self the anchor strong;
> Can thence compel the driving force
> Of daily life's mechanic course,
> Nor less the nobler energies
> Of needful toil and culture wise;
> Whose soul is worth the tempter's lure
> Who can renounce, and yet endure,
> To him I come, not lightly wooed,
> But won by silent fortitude.

It was in this mood, then, with some increase of respect for tradition, permanence, and inner control, that Lowell entered upon his fruitful career as professor at Harvard (1857–1877), as editor of the *Atlantic Monthly* (1857–1861), and as co-editor of

---

[113] *Ibid.*, VI, 206.
[114] Published in the *Atlantic Monthly*, VIII, (Sept., 1861).

The North American Review (1863–1872). During these crucial years which span the turmoil of the Civil War his main concern was with the destiny of the nation, as manifested in the substantial twelve papers which he later collected in the volume called *Political Essays*. Professional historians like James Ford Rhodes have testified to his weighty influence in moulding the mind of the North during this era of conflict.[115] The first two papers are merely transitional. *The American Tract Society* (1858) recognizes that "the Anti-slavery question . . . is in no sense political," but pleads for its discussion as a moral issue. "The Election in November" (1860) points out that the Republican party—with which Lowell was loosely affiliated—merely wishes to hem slavery "within its present limits," to exclude it from the territories; "the object of the Republican party is not the abolition of African slavery." Not until 1861, however, in the noble essay "E Pluribus Unum," does he envisage the true character of the conflict—a conflict for nationality to which he subordinates abolition. "Slavery is no longer the matter in debate, and we must beware of being led off upon that side-issue. The matter now in hand is the reëstablishment of order, the reaffirmation of national unity."[116] It is not "a commonplace war, a prosaic and peddling quarrel about cotton" and slavery, but "a question of national existence": "the faith of a nation in its own manhood" is threatened with "the formless void of anarchy." Looking back in 1876, he says, "The war was fought through for nationality. . . . Emancipation was a very welcome incident of the war and nothing more,"[117] a fact

[115] Rhodes states that during the Civil War Lowell spoke for a large number of the people, especially men of thought and culture, that he was one of the first of the Brahmins to recognize Lincoln and later Cleveland, and that during the Republican political graft in the 1870's he was one of the first to call for reform. (Rhodes' *History of the United States* (N.Y., 1906), II, 132, 252, 253, 472, 486; VII, 190–191.)

[116] *Writings*, V, 71.
[117] *Letters*, II, 174.

which he had dwelt upon in the essay on "Abraham Lincoln"
(1864–1865).

The Civil War.

The Civil War led Lowell to consider the broad problems of
coercion and authority. The war, he thought, was essentially
a "struggle between Law and Anarchy"[118] in which "the very
germinating principle of our nationality was at stake,"[119] the
real question being "whether the principle of legitimate authority or that of wanton insurrection against it should prevail."[120]
As a result, in place of his earlier humanitarian pacifism, his view
that "war is murder," we see a growing defense of the use of
righteous force when other means fail. Even as early as 1858
he had come to recognize that while "Peace is an excellent
thing, . . . principle and pluck are better."[121] In 1861 he wrote
that "War has no evil comparable in its effect on national character to that of a craven submission to manifest wrong, the
postponement of moral to material interests."[122] In the Second
Series of the "Biglow Papers" (1862),[123] whose quality he

---

[118] "Pickens-and-Stealin's Rebellion" (1861), *Writings*, V, 82.

[119] "McClellan or Lincoln?" (1864), *ibid.*, V, 167.

[120] *Writings*, V, 158.

[121] *Ibid.*, V, 9. He thought that Lincoln did not pursue the war
vigorously enough in its early days. "Mr. Lincoln seems to have a
theory of carrying on war without hurting the enemy. He is incapable, apparently, of understanding that they ought to be hurt."
Scudder, *op. cit.*, II, 29.

[122] *Ibid.*, V, 88.

[123] William Dean Howells in his review of the *Biglow Papers*,
Atlantic Monthly, XIX, 123–125 (Jan., 1867), praises their characterization, fiction, and satire. Artemus Ward and Nasby "are of a
stuff wholly different from Hosea Biglow, who is the type of a civilization, and who expresses in a genuine vernacular, the true feeling, the
racy humor, and the mother-wit of Yankeeland." "The First and
Second Series form a creative fiction of unique excellence." "There
never was political satire so noble before." In tone it is as "full and
rich as the best talk of Montaigne and Cervantes." English review-
ers were equally enthusiastic. *Littell's Living Age* (March 16, 1867),

thought "more permanent"[124] than that of the First Series, he exclaims:

> We want some more o' Gideon's sword, I jedge,
> For proclamations ha'n't no gret of edge;
> There's nothin' for a cancer but the knife . . .
> Why, law an' order, honor, civil right,
> Ef they *ain't* wuth it, wut *is* wuth a fight?[125]

And in the "Commemoration Ode" he holds that when "the soft Ideal we wooed" is "foe-beset,"

> To front a lie in arms and not to yield,
> This shows, methinks, God's plan . . .[126]

"Rebellion smells no sweeter because it is called Secession, nor does Order lose its divine precedence in human affairs because a knave may nickname it Coercion. Secession means chaos, and Coercion the exercise of legitimate authority."[127] He holds that that authority was given under an irrevocable social contract and had become "a common stock of Power to be wielded for the common protection, and from which no minority or majority of partners can withdraw its contribution under any conditions . . ."[128] In this period he turns away from the romanticists, "a society of cripples undertaking to teach the

---

XCII, 681, says that "the crowning quality of Lowell's humor is, that it was found at home, his book is a national birth." The *British Quarterly Review* (Oct., 1870), LII, 332, says the *Papers* "hold a very high place in literature of this class, for their humorous satire is based on the most clear conviction of justice and its opposite." *The Cornhill Magazine* (Jan., 1875), XXXI, 66, praises the variety of the *Papers:* "the combination of deep and generous sympathy with a keen perception of the ludicrous is the substratum of the finest kind of humor; and it is that which enables Biglow to pass without any sense of discord from pure satire into strains of genuine poetry."
    [124] *Letters*, II, 331.   [125] *Writings*, VIII, 264.   [126] *Ibid.*, X, 22.
    [127] *Ibid.*, V, 53. Bibliographical guidance to the Southern argument will be found in A. C. Cole's *The Irrepressible Conflict* (New York, 1934).
    [128] *Writings*, V, 71-72.

new generation how to walk,"[129] to Burke,[130] who "left him some of the profoundest aphorisms of political wisdom,"[131] who had said that "society cannot exist unless a controlling power upon will and appetite be placed somewhere, and the less of it there is within, the more there must be without." Like Burke, he had come to prefer "Anglo-Saxon soundness of understanding" which allows "institutions to be formulated gradually, by custom, convenience, or necessity" and which prefers "the practical comfort of a system that works, to the French method of a scientific machinery of perpetual motion, demonstrably perfect in all its parts, and yet refusing to go."[132]

Yet coercion, "the assertion of constituted and acknowledged authority," is merely a means of safe-guarding a common liberty, of insuring "every man his right, and not only that, but the permanence of it." In other words, just as Lowell had found that in the case of the individual the greatest poise and satisfaction are possible only when desires are restrained which would prevent the gratification of other desires equally essential for happiness, so now, in the case of the nation, he finds coercion, grim as it is, justified when other means fail in "the neutralization of numberless individual ambitions" which, if gratified, would imperil a common equality of opportunity for happiness. In his opinion, the South wished to substitute for the "right of all men to the pursuit of happiness the more practical privilege of some men to pursue their own negro."

If one glances ahead for a moment to ascertain the basis for his belief, one finds him distinguishing sharply between the quality of a Rousseauistic-Jeffersonian liberty and that of a

---

[129] *Ibid.*, II, 159.

[130] Lowell's regard for Burke rose higher as he grew older. In 1885 he wrote that Burke liberates the young student of politics "from narrow views and merely contemporaneous judgments" (*Writings*, VI, 79). In 1887 he called him the greatest political thinker since Aristotle (*Writings*, VI, 197).

[131] *Writings*, II, 234.   [132] *Ibid.*, V, 218.

Puritan liberty. He recognizes that absolute liberty destroys itself when universalized by individuals in a social community, that true liberty is possible only when the expansive, acquisitive tendency of the individual is curbed—whether outwardly or inwardly—in the interest of a common good. Thus in "The Rebellion: Its Causes and Consequences" (1864) he sees the chief cause of the alleged rebellion as the Southerners' "faith that secession is not only their right but the only safeguard of their freedom," a faith which he traces to the "dexterous leger-demain" and the "unhappy ingenuity of Mr. Jefferson," whom he formerly had exalted as our best thinker.[133] It was Jefferson who, in framing the Kentucky Resolutions in 1799, "devised that theory of strict construction which would enable any State to profit by the powers of the Constitution so long as it was for her interest or convenience, and then, by pleading its want of powers, to resolve the helpless organization once more into the incoherence of confederacy."[134] Lowell sees the Civil War as a conflict essentially "between law and license,"[135] chiefly caused by the "absence" of "the principle of coercion," and the "inability of its [the North's] representatives to say *No*, when policy as well as conscience made it imperative."[136]

Later, in "Rousseau and the Sentimentalists" (1867), he asserts that Rousseau,[137] who "professed and evidently felt deeply a faith in the goodness both of man and of God,"—in Rousseau's own words, a faith that "man is naturally good and

---

[133] Quoted by Scudder, *op. cit.*, I, 218.   [134] *Writings*, V, 148.

[135] *Ibid.*, V, 149.   [136] *Ibid.*, V, 146.

[137] Later in 1890 Lowell expressed his strong dislike for Rousseau, *Letters*, II, 424: "He is always the victim of a fine phrase—a monstrous liar, but always the first dupe of his own lie." Conversely, Lowell held in 1864 that "Fielding is the greatest creative artist who has written in English since Shakespeare" (*Function of the Poet*, etc., 169–170). It will be recalled that Fielding has one of his mouthpieces say that there is only one objection to the theory of natural altruism: it isn't true. He also satirized the sentimentalism of Richardson which Rousseau turned to new uses.

that it is by our institutions alone that men become wicked"—
had "so deep and lasting an influence" as to be "the father . . .
in politics of Jefferson and Thomas Paine."[138] Whether or not
one can accept this derivation after reading Professor Chinard's
Thomas Jefferson, it would appear that Lowell is right in per-
ceiving a distinction between the liberty of the Declaration of
Independence, based on natural rights, and that of the Constitution, based on "checks and balances," a distinction between the
liberty of the Jeffersonian and that of the semi-Puritan Federalist. And certainly a central difference is that regarding the
attitude toward a principle of control. In "New England Two
Centuries Ago" (1865)[139] Lowell asserted that "Puritanism,
believing itself quick with the seed of religious liberty, laid,
without knowing it, the egg of democracy," an idea to which

[138] *Writings*, II, 237. For some parallels see H. H. Clark's "Thomas
Paine's Relation to Voltaire and Rousseau," *Revue Anglo-Americaine*,
IX, 305-318; 393-405 (April and June, 1932).

[139] The essay is one of the most appreciative defenses of Puritanism
ever made. Through the mouth of Parson Wilbur, Lowell earlier
paid tribute to the Puritans: "I am a more hearty admirer of the
Puritans than seems now to be the fashion, and believe . . . they
showed remarkable sagacity as statesmen and founders . . . we cannot settle the great political questions which are now presenting themselves to the nation by the opinions of Jeremiah or Ezekiel. . . . At
the same time I could wish that their habit of subordinating the
actual to the moral, the flesh to the spirit, and this world to the other,
were more common." (*Writings*, II, 329.) See also *The Function of
the Poet*, p. 128. Later in his "Harvard Anniversary Address" (1886)
Lowell contended that the early New England Puritans "were children of the most splendid intellectual epoch that England has ever
known." (*Writings*, VI, 144.) He wrote three essays on the Puritan
Milton: "Milton" in *Lectures on English Poets* (1855); a review of
Masson's *Life of Milton* (1872), (*Writings*, IV, 58-117); and a Pref-
ace to the Grolier edition of Milton's *Areopagitica* (1890), (*Latest
Literary Essays and Addresses*, pp. 94-110). R. C. Pettigrew,
"Lowell's Criticism of Milton," *American Literature* (Jan., 1932),
III, 463-464, concludes that Lowell's "contribution to the Miltonic
tradition consists chiefly in his ability to kindle our enthusiasm for
Milton."

much attention has been given in recent research.[140] "Simple manhood is to have a chance to play his stake against Fortune with honest dice, uncogged by those three hoary sharpers, Prerogative, Patricianism, and Priestcraft."[141] While many of "our national characteristics . . . are traceable to the influences of Puritan descent,"[142] the Puritans gave us "the one great strength of democracy," the ideal—in Winthrop's words—of "a Civil, a Moral, a Federal Liberty, which is the proper End and Object of *Authority*." The Puritans, according to Lowell, "knew that liberty in the hands of feeble-minded and unreasoning persons . . . means nothing less, therefore, than downright chaos."[143] "Sober, earnest, and thoughtful men," the Puritans sought "no Utopia, no New Atlantis, no realization of a splendid dream, which they had at heart, but the establishment of the divine principle of Authority on the common interest and the common consent; the making, by a contribution from the free-will of all, a power which could curb and guide the free-will of each for the general good."[144]

The Need for Established Law.

Now, to return to Lowell's argument in "E Pluribus Unum" (1861), the submission required is not to an individual or a

[140] *Writings*, II, 12–13. See *The Puritans* (New York: 1938) by Perry Miller and T. H. Johnson, especially pp. 181–280 and bibliography, pp. 792–798; Lindsay Swift, "The Massachusetts Election Sermon: An Essay in Descriptive Bibliography," *Publications of the Colonial Society of Massachusetts*, I (1894), pp. 388–451; R. W. G. Vail, "A Check-List of New England Election Sermons," *Proceedings of the American Antiquarian Society*, XLV (1935); Alice Baldwin, *The New England Clergy and the American Revolution*. Durham, N.C., 1928.   [141] *Ibid.*, II, 4.   [142] *Ibid.*, II, 14.   [143] *Ibid.*, II, 10.
[144] *Writings*, II, 9–10. Cf. *ibid.*, II, 3, where Lowell says of Puritan polity: "Extrinsically, it is prosaic and plebeian; intrinsically, it is poetic and noble; for it is, perhaps, the most perfect incarnation of an idea the world has ever seen. That idea was not to found a democracy, . . . They had no faith in the Divine institution of a system which gives Teague, because he can dig, as much influence as Ralph, because he can think, nor in personal at the expense of general freedom."

faction, but "to the laws and to the benign intentions of the Constitution, as they were understood by its framers." The rebel from the past, who had derided the Constitution as a "Sacred Parasol," now honors its framers, who were mindful of "the folly of breaking with the past," mindful of "the value of tradition and habit as the great allies of permanence and stability." He who had tended to sentimentalize religion now sees temporal law as sanctioned by eternal law, an eternal law—like Emerson's Oversoul—which we can co-operate with for our happiness or violate for our misery. "Every human government is bound to make its laws so far resemble His that they shall be uniform, certain, and unquestionable in their operation; and this it can do only by a timely show of power, and by an appeal to that authority which is of divine right, inasmuch as its office is to maintain that order which is the single attribute of the Infinte Reason."[145] In his essay on Lincoln he wrote that undoubtedly "the highest function of statesmanship is by degrees to accommodate the conduct of communities to ethical laws, and to subordinate the conflicting self-interests of the day to higher and more permanent concerns."[146] The maintenance of civil order, then, is motivated by a passion for that ideal and finely-adjusted balance which to Plato was Justice and to Lowell, "the eternal harmony which we call God."[147]

This is the idealistic mood which inspired "The Washers of the Shroud" (1861) with its impassioned conviction that America's doom depends not on "Opinion's wind" but on an

[145] *Writings*, V, 74. Cf. Emerson's conclusion in his *New England Reformers* (*Works*, III, 268): the great man "shall not take counsel of flesh and blood, but shall rely on the Law alive and beautiful which works over our hands and under our feet. Pitiless, it avails itself of our success when we obey it, and of our ruin when we contravene it." For full discussion see Raymer McQuiston's "The Relation of Ralph Waldo Emerson to Public Affairs," *Bulletin of the University of Kansas*, XXIV, No. 8, Humanistic Studies, III, No. I, April, 1923, pp. 7–63.

[146] *Writings*, V, 195.   [147] *Ibid.*, II, 144.

intelligent and purposeful obedience to "the Law before all time":

> Three roots bear up Dominion: Knowledge, Will—
> These twain are strong, but stronger yet the third,—
> Obedience.

The former pacifist now knows that "the sheathed blade may rust with darker sin," and as he thinks proudly of his nephews, the "dear ones by Potomac's side" who even then had donned "Death's royal purple in the foeman's lines," he prays,

> God, give us peace! not such as lulls to sleep,
> But sword on thigh, and brow with purpose knit!
> And let our Ship of State to harbor sweep,
> Her ports all up, her battle-lanterns lit
> And her leashed thunders gathering for their leap!

Perils of an Unqualified Democracy.

The humanitarian Utopian who had urged "the levelling of all ranks in a common humanity," who had recoiled from unlocking "The Future's portal with the Past's blood-rusted key," now recognizes the perils of an unqualified democracy which relies upon votes to "turn biled kebbage into brain,"[148] which disregards the fact that "Time Was unlocks the riddle of Time Is." The former sentimentalist recognizes that "this is no time for sentimentalisms," and he praises Lincoln because he distrusts "holiday enthusiasms," because he "always addresses himself to the reason of the American People."[149] It is "on the understanding, and not on the sentiment, of a nation that all safe legislation must be based."[150] Later, in "Reconstruction" (1865) Lowell rendered timely service in insisting that "the public mind should be made up as to what are the essential conditions of real and lasting peace, before it is subjected to the sentimental delusions of the inevitable era of good feeling."[151]

[148] *Writings*, VIII, 296.   [149] *Ibid.*, V, 206.   [150] *Ibid.*, V, 195–196.
[151] *Ibid.*, V, 237.

He condemned any general confiscation of Rebel property as "unthrifty housekeeping," and favored instead an equal tax on North and South "as the most prudent way" of establishing "our national solvency."[152] He praises Lincoln's "singularly masculine intelligence" which "taught him that precedent is only another name for embodied experience, and that it counts for even more in the guidance of communities of men than in that of the individual life."[153] Lincoln was no humanitarian Utopian, no doctrinaire, no believer in the shifting sands of human sentiment; for his "faith in God was qualified by a very well-founded distrust of the wisdom of man."[154]

A permanent nationality, the mutable Many embraced by an immutable One, "the radiant image of something better and nobler and more enduring than we" [155]—that is the thought which lends moral and imaginative splendour to the "Commemoration Ode" (1865). The sensuous life of the individual is "dream-footed as the shadow of a cloud," and yet man craves a changeless peace, "a high immunity from Night."

> Our slender life runs rippling by, and glides
>   Into the silent hollow of the past;
>   What is there that abides . . . ?
> What ever 'scaped Oblivion's subtle wrong . . .
>   Where nought abiding is but only Change . . . ?

Then he glimpses "some more noble permanence" born of man's aspiration and of man's sacrifice for the organic continuity of the Nation as an imaginative and vital reality:

>   'Tis no Man we celebrate,
>   By his country's victories great,
>   A hero half, and half the whim of Fate,
>   But the pith and marrow of a Nation
>   Drawing force from all her men . . .

---

[152] *Writings*, V, 226.   [153] *Ibid.*, V, 194.
[154] *Ibid.*, V, 194–195.   [155] *Ibid.*, VI, 221.

The Many who have laid down their lives for the perpetuation of the One, the Union, are "secure from change in their high-hearted ways":

> Ah, there is something here
> Unfathomed by the cynic's sneer,
> Something that gives our feeble light
> A high immunity from Night . . .
> A conscience more divine than we,
> A gladness fed with secret tears,
> A vexing, forward-reaching sense
> Of some more noble permanence;
> A light across the sea,
> Which haunts the soul and will not let it be,
> Still beaconing from the heights of undegenerate years.

In this noble poem, then, Lowell has enshrined his devotion in those stirring times to that abiding organic continuity of national tradition, to what his master Burke called "the great primeval contract of eternal society, linking the lower with the higher natures, connecting the visible and invisible world," "an idea of continuity, which extends in time as well as in numbers and in space, . . . a partnership not only between those who are living, but between those who are living, those who are dead, and those who are to be born."

It was largely by this standard of value that Lowell judged contemporary events in this period. He attacked Douglas and Breckenridge in 1860 because, in surrendering all to Capital, they violated the necessary unity and continuity of the social life. "Both of them mean that Labor has no rights which Capital is bound to respect,—that there is no higher law than human interest and cupidity."[156] It was this breadth of spirit that enabled Lowell, after the Civil War, to see the Southern point of view, to sympathize with "men who sacrificed everything even to a bad cause which they could see only the good

[156] *Writings*, V, 24.

side of," and to understand, as unfortunately very few of his contemporaries did, that the North could never "reconstruct the South except through its own leading men."[157]

Noble as is Lowell's thought in this period, nobly as he kept "measure with his people,"[158] it is important that we should not disregard his tendency even now toward a somewhat complacent reliance upon the power of a nationalistic state to remake mankind, upon a faith in a temporal order little stronger than the sum of its parts because it minimized the larger extra-national experience of the race. Instead of relying on "the best that has been thought and said in the world," Lowell still tended to feel that that "best" had been produced in America itself, from the early days of our Puritan traditions. His ideal man was Lincoln, "a man whom America made, as God made Adam, out of the very earth, unancestried, unprivileged, unknown," and he ends his volume of *Political Essays* on a note of complacency: "We have only to be unswervingly faithful to what is the true America of our hope and belief, and whatever is American will rise from one end of the country to the other instinctively to our side, with more than ample means of present succor and of final triumph."[159] Thus the nationalist in 1867, like the humanitarian up to 1850, tended to rely, though much more sternly, upon an outward, temporal order.

A National Literature.

It is important to notice, also, that the powerful influence of the Civil War changed Lowell's literary theories and made him (until about 1867) reject his earlier idea that a nationalistic literature is "diseased" and to uphold the idea that the War had for the first time given Americans "that conscious feeling of nationality," a sense of having an "ideal abstract of history and

---

[157] *Letters*, II, 5.   [158] *Ibid.*, I, 412.
[159] *Writings*, V, 326–327. (On his ardent faith in nationalism see also the Elmwood Edition, VI, 266, 299–300.)

tradition" of our own, which are necessary in addition to nature
to inspire literature.[160]   Thus in reviewing Whittier's "In War
Time" and "Home Ballads" in 1860–1864 Lowell praises him as
"the most American of our poets," gifted with "a fire of warlike
patriotism," and (Quaker as he is) "more deeply imbued with
the spirit of the Puritans than even their own lineal representatives."   Indeed Lowell added that while in the Old World the
Puritans had no "deliberate forethought" of democracy although they "brought over its seed, but unconsciously"; yet it
was "the kindly nature of the soil and climate that was to give it
the chance to propagate and disperse itself."   Lowell especially
values Whittier's "intense home-feeling" and the fact that "he
is the most indigenous of our poets."[161]   Almost at the same time
Lowell came to the full maturity of his philological knowledge,[162] and realized, as every true philologist knows, that language is kept most alive among the common people; he realized

[160] *Writings*, V, 211, 216.

[161] *The Function of the Poet*, pp. 127–139.

[162] Lowell's thorough knowledge of language was the result of the
widespread interest of his day.   As a result of English contempt for
the English language as it was spoken in America, a vigorous controversy developed in the days before and during the Civil War between
English and American students and patriots as to the place and importance of the "American" language.   Protagonists of each side
were found in both countries and in America the controversy centered around the famous "War of the Dictionaries" of Webster and
Worcester.   The result as Blair, *op. cit.*, p. 52, points out was that
interest in "the language of Americans" was "greatly stimulated in
the forties and fifties."   See the contemporary studies by John Russell Bartlett, *Dictionary of Americanisms* (first issued in 1848, with a
third edition in 1860); J. O. Halliwell-Philips, *A Dictionary of Archaisms and Provincialisms. Containing Words Now Obsolete in England,
All of Which Are Familiar and in Common Use in America* (1847,
2nd ed., 1850); Charles A. Bristed, "The English Language in
America," *Cambridge Essays* (London, 1855), pp. 58–78; and A. L.
Elwyn, *Glossary of Supposed Americanisms* (Philadelphia, 1859).   For
an expert analysis of the controversy by a modern scholar see George
H. McKnight's chapter, "Beginnings of American Speech," in his
Modern English in the Making (N.Y., 1928), pp. 460–494.

fully for the first time the dignity, variety, and literary power of the Yankee dialect.[163]   Both of these tendencies, his ardent war nationalism and his studies in dialect, underlie his long Introduction to the Second Series of the "Biglow Papers" (1867). The Introduction (1) calls for a national literature,[164] (2) proves

[163] He wrote in 1854 that he considered himself "a good taster of dialects" (*Writings*, I, 115). Brooks, *op. cit.*, p. 313, says: "With his philological instinct, a natural Cambridge trait, he liked to trace the origins of words, the earliest use of phrases, the history of archaisms and colloquialisms; and this had led him to study the Yankee speech, which he knew as Tennyson knew the 'northern farmer's'."
   The authenticity of the Biglow dialect has never been questioned, not even in its own day.   Francis Lieber, *Stranger in America* (London, 1834), I, 256, testifies that the Yankee dialect consists as much in peculiarity of "thought and pronunciation" as in "peculiar words," "words used in a peculiar sense," "peculiar mode of expression," and "strange metaphors."   He says also that in 1834 true blue Yankees said that Jack Downing did "not write classical Yankee."   Two years before the appearance of the first *Biglow Papers*, C. C. Felton, in a review of Haliburton, *North American Review*, LVIII, 211–227 (Jan., 1844), while asserting that New England character had "never yet been portrayed . . . in a work of fiction" and that Sam Slick's expressions were false Yankee, being simply "the coinage of the provincial writer's own brain," almost predicted Lowell: ". . . in the terse peculiarities of the New England idiom," he said, "the grave far-reaching sense of the Massachusetts farmer, the humorous, sly, and quaint expressions in which his thought is uttered, the delineator of manners, had he the discerning eye, might find the rich elements of varied character almost wholly new to the world of letters. But the attempt will never be successfully made, until some native writer, of genius to create, and culture to represent characters with the true national stamp, shall set aside foreign models . . . in order to study the humors and peculiarities of American life" (212).   Bristed, in 1855 said, *op. cit.*, p. 66, that the *Biglow Papers* were better than the "two Jack Downings," that they "represent the language of the masses," and that the glossary at the end of the *Biglow Papers* is mostly in sober earnest.
[164] F. L. Pattee, *Century Readings in the American Short Story*, New York, 1927, p. 117, says that Lowell as editor of the *Atlantic* exerted an enormous influence in nationalizing the American short story. "Lowell preferred native themes and native tangs and actuality in our native fiction and knowing this the younger writers for *The Atlantic* unconsciously began to write more naturally and more

that a distinct American speech exists,[165] (3) proves that that
speech is a legitimate one based on English traditions,[166] and

---

spontaneously." Pattee, *First Century*, p. 591, quotes his letter to
Mrs. Stowe, advising her to "stick to Nature and avoid what people
commonly call the ideal; for that, and beauty, and pathos, and success, all lie in the simply natural." F. L. Mott, *A History of American
Magazines*, Cambridge, Mass., 1938, Vol. II, p. 501, also asserts that
he "made his magazine a great force for the more realistic, vital fiction
by printing the work of Rose Terry, Rebecca Harding Davis, and
other honest writers." Mr. Mott (p. 173) says he "went counter to
the general honeyed stickiness" current at the time.

[165] In the application and combination of words, he says, the language of my countrymen seems "to me full of humor, invention,
quickness of wit, and that sense of subtle analogy which needs only
refining to become fancy and imagination" (*Writings*, VIII, 198).
He thinks the Yankee "a new phenomenon" which places you in
"the age and country in which you are born" (*Ibid.*, VIII, 203).
McKnight, *op. cit.*, p. 472, in our day bears out Lowell's contention
that there was at that time a distinct American speech; in the "third
decade of the nineteenth century American use of words in colloquial
speech had come to deviate to an appreciable extent from the use
current in England."

[166] Lowell refuted the English charge that American speech was
vulgar by proving that "we have the countenance of very good com-
pany" for our vulgarisms, their source often being the English of
Shakespeare (*Writings*, VIII, 202). Elwyn, *op. cit.*, p. iii, says in 1859
that the purpose of his *Glossary* was to show how much remains of
the language and customs brought here by "our remotest ancestry."
Many words "that we have been ridiculed for using are good old
English; . . . and nearly all to be heard at this day in England . . ."
In Elwyn's review of the dictionaries of Webster and Worcester,
Atlantic Monthly, V, 631–637 (May, 1860), while deprecating Webster's attempt "to regulate, and not to *record*" the language, he com-
mended him because he "stoutly maintained the right of English as
spoken in America to all the privileges of a living language." Modern
scholars have borne out and praised Lowell's defense of an "American" language. A. C. Baugh, *A History of the English Language*
(N.Y., 1935), p. 457, says that up to the Civil War the prevailing
attitude in this country was deference to English usage and Lowell's
Introduction was "one of the most important contributions to the
controversy over Americanisms. While it had often been recognized
that many of the distinctive features of American English were sur-
vivals of the older English of England, no one had been at the pains
to bring together the enormous mass of evidence on the subject. . . .

(4) defends its capacity as a literary vehicle.[167] Even though American life is "utterly orphaned of the solemn inspiration of antiquity," he concluded, "the ordinary talk of unlettered men among us" will surpass in vividness "that of any other people."[168] He tended at this time to attach great importance to a fresh vigorous language as the deciding factor in the creative process. Dialect was the antidote for the corrupting influences of the current "literary" language, and only "by turning into one of our narrow New England lanes"[169] could we hope to have an "original literature" which would "suck up the feeding juices secreted for it in the rich mother-earth of common

Since the appearance of this essay, the legitimacy of one large class of Americanisms has not been questioned." Baugh says Lounsbury and Brander Matthews take Lowell as a point of departure in their defense of American English. McKnight, *op. cit.*, p. 462, also says that Lowell's conclusions have largely been "confirmed by later studies," especially C. H. Grandgent's article, "From Franklin to Lowell. A Century of New England Pronunciation," *PMLA*, XIV, (n.s., VII), 207–239 (1899).

[167] McKnight, *op. cit.*, p. 490, says that American dependence on England in Lowell's time "was particularly apparent in the literary language." Even Lowell himself was guilty in his early days of imitating the style of Tennyson; see E. C. Stedman, *Poets of America* (Boston, 1894), p. 310. One form which the current controversy took was to reject the "literary" for the "living" language. Bartlett, in his long Introduction, *op. cit.*, pp. xxxi–xxxii, condemns vigorously our "literary dialect" and praises the vernacular as the vehicle for a literature of beauty and merit. Lowell, reviewing Bartlett in the *Atlantic Monthly*, IV, 638–643 (Nov., 1859), agrees that it "is only from the roots that a language can be refreshed." "The first postulate of an original literature is, that a people use their language as if they owned it. . . . Vulgarisms are often only poetry in the egg." He says that he chose the Yankee dialect with forethought. The great "vice of American writing was a studied want of simplicity . . . we were in danger of coming to look on our mother-tongue as a dead language" (*Writings*, VIII, 158). He praises the speech of Lincoln as "a truly masculine English." References to his preference at this time for the vernacular as the proper medium of literature are widespread. See *Writings*, III, 6, 15, 17, 237; VIII, 203.

[168] *Writings*, VIII, 198–199.

[169] *Ibid.*, VIII, 203.

folk."[170]   Thus in both political and literary matters, the idea which Lowell emphasized during this period from about 1850 to 1867 was that inevitably "a strong nation begets strong citizens."[171]

C. The Natural Aristocrat.

We come now to Lowell's third phase, after about 1867, during which he emphasized the hope which might lie in a natural aristocracy of virtue and wisdom dedicated to the welfare of all the people.   The main document bridging his period of nationalism and the beginning of the third period is his "Condescension in Foreigners" (1869), in which he retains a considerable measure of nationalistic hostility toward foreigners and traditions older than ours, but recognizes (as we have seen) that "popular government is not itself a panacea, is no better than any other form except as the virtue and wisdom of the people make it so."   He says that in choosing our leaders a "reaction" has begun not toward "the old notion, which paid too much regard to birth and station," but "towards fitness either from natural aptitude or special training," as opposed to

---

[170] *Writings*, VIII, 159.   Since some literary historians have tried to make it appear that there is a deep chasm between New England Brahmins such as Lowell and the down-to-earth realism of the West and South, it may be well to remember that Eggleston, author of *The Hoosier Schoolmaster* (1871) emphasizing dialect, confessed that "Mr. Lowell has been my master more than anyone else.   He showed me how to combine a genuine Americanism with a scholarly catholicity, a rare and piquant humor with dignity and refinement" (*The Critic*, XIV, 92).   Far from ignoring Mark Twain, Lowell said that "real humor is of the same nature in Aristophanes and Mark Twain" (VIII, 282), and we know he admired Lowell's "Biglow Papers." And the creator of Uncle Remus and Br'er Rabbit concluded his tribute to Lowell as follows: "there is no one more indebted to him for the happy stimulus which his works impart, nor one who more heartily admires his character as a man than Joel Chandler Harris." (*The Critic*, XI, n.s., 105, March 2, 1889).

[171] *Ibid.*, V, 281.

"putting the highest of human functions up at auction to be bid for by any creature capable of going upright on two legs."[172]

Post-War Corruption of Democracy.

However, before we elaborate the ideas Lowell emphasized in this period, it may be well to suggest the basic reasons for his new emphasis. Did our life after the Civil War justify his nationalistic faith that, with the Union preserved, "a strong nation begets strong citizens," and that "whatever is American will rise . . . instinctively to our side, with more than ample means of present succor and of final triumph?"[173] The answer is obvious, if we remember how Mark Twain sketched "The Gilded Age," how Parrington painted it as "The Great Barbecue,"[174] how the historian Allan Nevins traced in sober detail from 1865 to 1873 "The Moral Collapse in Government and Business,"[175] how even the optimistic Walt Whitman[176] was obliged to confess in "Democratic Vistas" (1871) that:

"Society in these States, is canker'd, crude, superstitious, and rotten . . . New World democracy . . . is, so far, an almost complete failure in its social aspects, and in really grand religious, moral, literary, and esthetic results," because "in any vigor, the element of the moral conscience, the most important, the verteber to State or man, seems to me either entirely lacking,

[172] I, 326, 311.   [173] VI, 398.

[174] V. L. Parrington, *The Beginnings of Critical Realism in America, 1860–1920* (New York, 1930), pp. 23 ff. Although Parrington is unsympathetic toward Lowell, the whole book is valuable in helping us to understand the current evils in our political life that Lowell tried to correct.

[175] Allan Nevins, *The Emergence of Modern America, 1865–1878* (New York, 1927), Chapter VII, with bibliography in the rear.

[176] The most elaborate discussion is Newton Arvin's semi-socialistic *Whitman* (New York, 1939). If Whitman saw the merits of both individualism and brotherhood and said "the two are contradictory, but our task is to reconcile them," the evidence would seem to suggest that Lowell himself in befriending Howells was traveling in the same direction.

or seriously enfeebled or outgrown." He had described "seven eighths" of the members of an earlier political convention as "the meanest kind of bawling and blowing office-holders, office-seekers, pimps, malignants, conspirators, murderers, . . . kept-editors, . . . scarr'd inside with vile disease, gaudy outside with gold chains made from the people's money and harlot's money twisted together; crawling, serpentine men, the lousy combings and born freedom-sellers of the earth."

If Whitman is recognized as our most ardent champion of democracy, it seems unfair to condemn Lowell for being undemocratic (as many critics do) because he merely observed the same facts, and tried to suggest a program for improvement. Carlyle and Lowell's friend Ruskin were of course equally critical of the actual operation of laissez-faire doctrines in England during the same period.[177] In America, sanctioned by the spread of deterministic evolutionary doctrines of the struggle for existence and the survival of the fittest, a nation-wide conflict between the financial-industrial interests on the one hand and the labor-agricultural interests on the other, in the midst of the vast economic resources of a frontier land, resulted in an era of gross materialism, political corruption, and indifference toward the sanctity of the individual personality.

There is nothing very unexpected, then, in the fact that Lowell as a high-minded idealist became convinced that the current *practice* of democracy was corrupt, although his exposure of the results of laissez-faire may have aided socialism. "The power of 'Rings' in our politics," he writes in 1869, "is becoming enormous. Men buy their seats in the Senate, and of course, expect a profit on their investment . . . We are becoming a huge stock-jobbery, and Republicans and Democrats are names for bulls and bears."[178] Later, his sense of civic dignity outraged by the Crédit Mobilier scandal, by

---

[177] See F. W. Roe, *The Social Philosophy of Carlyle and Ruskin* (New York, 1921).   [178] XV, 203 ("Letters," 1869).

western railway and land speculations, and Boss Tweed's political domination via Tammany Hall, Lowell voiced his indigna-
tion in *The Nation* (which led the idealistic reformers) in such
poems as "The World's Fair, 1876," and "Tempora Mutantur."
Like most other contemporaries, and not merely as an expression
of personal pessimism, Lowell read "the festering news" of

> "public scandal, private fraud,
> Crime flaunting scot-free while the mob applaud,
> Office made vile to bribe unworthiness."[179]

Just as he had earlier used words as a weapon against slavery,
so now, as he writes to encourage G. W. Curtis in his efforts
at Civil Service Reform in 1874, Lowell disdains "the pleasures
of retreat" and says

> "I must twist my little gift of words
> Into a scourge of rough and knotted cords
> Unmusical, that whistle as they swing
> To leave on shameless backs their purple sting."

Does this sound as if Lowell were in this period an escapist (as
he is often charged with being), indifferent to his country's
plight? The poem to Curtis continues with "three instances"
of corruption which are enough "to stir a pigeon's gall":

> "Office a fund for ballot-brokers made
> To pay the drudges of their gainful trade;
> Our cities taught what conquered cities feel
> By aediles chosen that they might safely steal;
> And gold, however got, a title fair
> To such respect as only gold can bear.
> I seem to see this; how shall I gainsay
> What all our journals tell me every day?"[180]

[179] XIII, 112 ("Agassiz," 1874).
[180] XIII, 153–154. He also satirized an instance of "a jury chosen
by the thief." (XV, 373). See especially his long letter to Joel Benton
(XV, 373–378), who had defended "Mr. Lowell's Recent Political
Verse" in the *Christian Union* of Dec. 15, 1875.

Lowell thought that in the midst of such corruption his "duty was plain . . . That I hit the mark I aimed at is proved by the attacks," some of which originated from the anti-British Tammany Hall and took the form of insinuating that Lowell "had been corrupted by association with foreign aristocracies!" "If I am not an American, who ever was?" he exclaims. What troubled him especially was "the degradation of the moral tone," but he adds, "I am no pessimist, nor ever was." He thinks that the moral tone can be improved by recalling the people to a sense of duty and the fact that "it is honor, justice, culture, that make liberty invaluable, else worse than worthless if it mean only freedom to be base and brutal. . . . Let us all work together (and the task will need us all) to make Democracy possible. It certainly is no invention to go of itself any more than the perpetual motion."[181]

Self-Reform of the Individual.

Since corruption and materialism were wide-spread, in spite of the humanitarian and institutional reform of slavery and the preservation of the united nation, Lowell thought that there must be deeper sources of evil, and he concluded that these are within the individual and are to be overcome only by self-reform. Ultimately, he was convinced, public corruption is the result of private evil.[182] Thus from about 1865 on, Lowell occasionally satirizes those who have "a mission (with a capital M) to attend to everybody else's business," and the kind of humanitarian who thinks that utopias can be ushered in merely by some quick external change, "so soon as hooks and eyes should be substituted for buttons." If he is distrustful of social panaceas,[183] comparing them to applying "plasters to a

[181] XV, 376–378.

[182] V, 64 ("Dante," 1872); VII, 36 ("Democracy").

[183] II, 132 ("Thoreau," 1865); Lowell smiles at those who stood ready "at a moment's notice to reform everything but themselves." Also VII, 111; VIII, 142–143.

single pustule of the smallpox with a view of driving out the disease," that is because Lowell has come to think that external reforms and remedies for evil "are partial and palliative merely" *unless* they are *combined* (as he wishes them to be) with the individual's own efforts "to extirpate the germs" of evil by self-reform and the reinforcement of "honor, justice, culture."[184] It is probable that in his new emphasis on the need of supplementing institutional reform by self-reform and personal integrity he was influenced by the similar view of Emerson, to whom Lowell dedicated his second series of *Among My Books* in 1875 as a token of "a love and honor which more than thirty years have deepened," and as a "public acknowledgement of a debt I can never repay."[185] And in the later Wordsworth Lowell traced a development somewhat similar to his own, for the author of *The Prelude* had as a youthful radical hoped for the "gregarious regeneration of man" through the humanitarian principles of the French Revolution; but he had eventually decided that the most effectual "remedy" for the evils that beset man are "those moral influences that build up and buttress the personal character": it is "the individual that should and could be leavened, and through the individual the lump [society]. To reverse the process was to break the continuity of history."

[184] VII, 36; XV, 378.

[185] See Emerson's *Letters* (ed. R. L. Rusk, New York, 1939), VI, 506, for a whole column of index references to their correspondence and mutual respect. Although he, like Lowell, had been an abolitionist, he gently satirized "New England Reformers," and concluded that "the criticism and attack on institutions, which we have witnessed, has made one thing plain, that society gains nothing whilst a man, not himself renovated, attempts to renovate things around him: . . . hypocrisy and vanity are often the disgusting result" (*Works*, III, 261). Emerson only wanted to "draw individuals out of" the masses, whom he regarded as "rude, lame, unmade, pernicious in their demands . . ." Emerson also saw great defects in both parties and sought "the considerate vote of single men spoken on their honor and their conscience" (*Works*, VI, 249). See A. I. Ladu, "Emerson: Whig or Democrat," *New England Quarterly*, XIII, 419–441 (Sept., 1940).

Lowell praised Wordsworth's aim "to make men better by opening to them the sources of an unalterable well-being; to make them free, in a sense higher than political, by showing them that these sources are within them, and that no contrivance of man can permanently emancipate narrow natures and depraved minds."[186] This is an excellent summary of Lowell's own central conviction during his last period. Among other influences which in varying degrees helped to mould Lowell's growing faith in a natural aristocracy of virtue and wisdom are Dante, Shakespeare,[187] Puritanism,[188] Burke,[189] Federalism,[190] Carlyle,[191] Darwinism,[192] Holmes, Arnold,[193] Godkin,[194] and Norton.[195]

---

[186] *Writings*, VI, 103, IV, 366.   [187] V, 147–148.

[188] See this book, pp. xlix–l, and Lowell's three essays on Milton, and praise of his doctrine that freedom is "not to be won from without, but from within . . ." (VIII, 123).

[189] See this book, p. xlvii, and Lowell's review of Burke in the *North American Review*, CII, 634–637 (April, 1866).

[190] See this book, pp. xlix, lxviii.

[191] Despite his cool essay on the author of "Hero-Worship," Lowell admitted "a secret partiality" toward him (XV, 276).

[192] See this book, pp. lxxviii ff.

[193] Cf. Arnold's American lecture on "Numbers" and the saving remnant. Lowell had reviewed Arnold's "On Translating Homer" appreciatively in *The Atlantic* (IX, 142–144, Jan., 1862). And when he followed him as President of the Wordsworth Society, he spoke of Arnold's essay on that poet as a "finished model" by a man "who always has the art of saying what all of us would be glad to say if we could" (VII, 123). He occasionally diverged from his opinions but set "a high value on Mr. Arnold and his poetic gift" (II, 172).

[194] On Godkin and Holmes see this book, pp. xiv, lxxx.

[195] Lowell told Godkin that Norton kept him "writing political articles" for the *North American Review* (XV, 129), which they edited together after 1864. Norton's *Recent Social Theories* parallels Lowell at many points. He wrote Lowell (Norton's *Letters*, 1913, I, 385) in 1870 "that simply to cultivate one's-self, is perhaps the best service an American can render," and in the *New Princeton Review* (VI, 24, 1888) Norton concluded that if "our civilization is to be prevented from degenerating," it is only by the "steady improvement" of our institutions of highest learning. He also thought that institutional reform would be ineffectual without individual "moral restraining."

The great problem to which Lowell now addressed himself was this: how can we keep what is sound in democracy, eradicate what has caused it to degenerate, and prevent base men (such as Boss Tweed) from dominating? First, let us note carefully what Lowell regards as "the real essence" of democracy: it is that form of society "in which every man had a chance and knew that he had it."[196] American democracy "means education, equality before the law, and every upward avenue of life made as free to one man as another."[197] "We would not rob you," he writes the British Leslie Stephen, "of a single one of your valuable institutions—state church, peerage, pauperage —so long as you like 'em and like to pay for 'em . . . I don't understand your English taste for what you call 'respectability,' . . . thinking, as I do, that the one thing worth striving for in this world is a state founded on pure manhood, where everybody has a chance given him to better himself, and where the less costume and the more reality there is, the better."[198] It should be noted that Lowell distinguishes carefully between equality of opportunity and equality of actual ability and virtue. The democrat does not try to fortify himself against his rivals in free competition, allowing merit to be the creator of its own reward. On the other hand, Lowell insists, as James Fenimore Cooper did, that "we cannot equalize conditions and fortunes any more than we can equalize the brains of men," although (as we shall see later) he sought to "do something to correct those methods and influences that lead to enormous inequalities and to prevent their growing more enormous."[199] Lowell thought universal suffrage essential to a democracy, and thought

[196] VII, 32 ("Democracy," 1884).

[197] VI, 341 ("The President on the Stump," 1866).

[198] XV, 119 ("Letters," 1866). Lowell thinks that President Hayes represents true Americanism, which involves "not thinking yourself either better or worse than your neighbors by reason of any artificial distinction" (XVI, 15).

[199] VII, 34 ("Democracy").

that giving the Negro the vote would be an incentive to the
whites to educate him, even though this attitude angered his
friend E. L. Godkin. For Lowell insisted, as Jefferson did, that
suffrage "is of advantage to the commonwealth only in proportion as it is intelligently exercised. Then, indeed, its constant
exercise should train the faculties of forethought and judgment better, and should give men a keener sense of their own
value than perhaps anything else can do."[200] And in addition
to universal suffrage and equality of opportunity, Lowell emphasized the fact that democracy's "ideal is to substitute the
interest of the many for that of the few as the test of what is
wise in polity and administration."[201]

But since in actual practice democracy had grown corrupt
and base leaders had risen so that materialism was rampant,
Lowell rejected the other assumption of the Civil War era, the
assumption that a democracy must substitute the judgment and
"the opinion of the many for that of the few as the rule of conduct in public affairs." In so doing, however, Lowell kept
within our historical framework and merely insisted that "we
have got to work back from a democracy to our original institution as a republic again,"[202] to the traditional Federalistic doc-

[200] VII, 255–256 ("Independent in Politics," 1888); VI, 280–281,
371; VII, 26–27.

[201] VIII, 157 ("The Progress of the World," 1886).

[202] XV, 380 ("Letters," 1876). He told Guizot that America will
endure "so long as the ideas of its founders continue to be dominant . . . I naturally explained that by 'ideas' I meant also the traditions of their race in government and morals" (XVI, "Letters,"
1890). He remarks that our "War of Independence, though it gave
the first impulse to that awful riot of human nature turned loose upon
first principles, was but the reassertion of established precedents and
traditions, and essentially conservative in its aim, however deflected
in its course. It is true that, to a certain extent, the theories of the
French doctrinaires gave a tinge to the rhetoric of our patriots, but it
is equally true that they did not perceptibly affect the conclusions of
our Constitution-makers. Nor had those doctrinaires themselves
any suspicion of the explosive mixture that can be made by the conjunction of abstract theory with brutal human instinct."

trine of checks and balances guided by the light of historical experience.

Leadership of Men of Virtue and Wisdom.

Lowell's problem, then, was how America could keep universal suffrage, concern for the interest of the many, and equality of opportunity and before the law, while at the same time preventing the dominance of bad men and materialistic forces. Briefly, he thought the solution lay in our being able to increase the virtue and wisdom of the people by securing leaders who were pre-eminent in these two qualities. He is of special interest in his third period in his view that wholesale equality as a "cure-all"[203] is inadequate, his frank acceptance of the inequality of virtue and wisdom, as well as ability, and in his frank avowal that ways and means must be found by which the few best men can help to guide the many for their own long-range interest. He was a perfectionist, standing for quality: "it is one of the prime weaknesses of a democracy to be satisfied with the second-best"; "democracy must show its capacity for producing, not a higher average man, but the highest possible types of manhood in all its manifold varieties, or it is a failure."[204] And, like Jefferson, he was confident that the many, the people, properly educated, would select the few best leaders. "If there be one thing steadfast and of favorable omen, one thing to make optimism distrust its own obscure distrust, it is the rooted instinct in men to admire what is better and more beautiful than themselves. The touchstone of political and

[203] XIII, 67 ("The Cathedral").
[204] VII, 204–206 ("Harvard Anniversary Address"). In "Democracy" VII, 17) Lowell strives to refute the common charge that it will "reduce all mankind to a dead level of mediocrity in character and culture, . . . vulgarize men's conceptions of life, and therefore their code of morals, manners, and conduct." In the public libraries of a democracy Lowell says all the people have free access to "a select society of all the centuries," (VII, 102) and he urges emphasis on "the supreme books" as ladders to wisdom.

social institutions is their ability to supply them with worthy objects of this sentiment, which is the very tap-root of civilization and progress."[205]   Lowell's "Harvard Anniversary Address," 1886, is his most eloquent formulation of his reliance upon the "cultivated few":

"What we need more than anything else," he said, "is to increase the number of our highly cultivated men and thoroughly trained minds; for these, wherever they go, are sure to carry with them, consciously or not, the seeds of sounder thinking and of higher ideals.   The only way in which our civilization can be maintained even at the level it has reached, the only way in which that level can be made more general and be raised higher, is by bringing the influence of the more cultivated to bear with greater energy and directness on the less cultivated, and by opening more inlets to those indirect influences which make for refinement of mind and body."[206]

Lowell's view is given added interest by the fact that he served as the spokesman of a considerable group, especially in New England, who shared, with minor variations, his faith in natural aristocracy.   Mr. Parrington subtitles his unsympathetic essay on Lowell the "Cambridge Brahmin" and admits that he "was certainly the ablest and most distinguished of the old Cambridge breed"; he was "of the true Brahmin line of Josiah Quincy and Edward Everett and Oliver Wendell Holmes —men of sound culture who could serve God valiantly in the social station in which He had placed them . . ."[207]   To these names might be added C. E. Norton, Henry Adams, E. L. Godkin, G. W. Curtis, Francis Parkman, G. L. Motley, W. H. Prescott, Barrett Wendell, George Woodberry, and others. With the rise of equalitarianism the views of this group have become increasingly unpopular, and they have been dubbed by

[205] VII, 31; also 28.   [206] VII, 206; see also VIII, 141.

[207] V. L. Parrington, *The Romantic Revolution in America*, New York, 1927, p. 460.

such names as "The Genteel Tradition," the snobs, or regarded
as hypocritical apologists for parasitical capitalism. Regardless
of one's personal bias, however, Lowell's views are roughly
representative of an influential group and did much to shape
the public opinion which crystallized in governmental trends
and traditions which have been of far-reaching importance,
whether for good or evil. It behooves us, therefore, to try to
understand objectively precisely what it was that Lowell advocated in his third period, if only the better to understand what
radicalism has had to fight. The more intelligent radicals will
surely realize that little is gained in the long run by misrepre-
senting or under-estimating the concepts of their opponents.

Training in Virtue.

But let us return to our problem and begin by defining what
Lowell meant by virtue or character (to the lack of which he
attributed the degeneration of democracy) with reference to his
concept of the gentleman—"a profession," he remarked, "of
greater consequence than is generally conceived."[208] Indeed,
he held that the highest aim of culture must be the training of
the gentleman,[209] whose "first quality," Lowell held, must be

---

[208] See Lowell's "Tribute to Hon. John P. Kennedy," *Proc. Mass.
Hist. Soc.*, XI, 365–367 (Sept. 1870). He said Kennedy made the
"strongest impression" as a thorough-going gentleman. In *The
Function of the Poet*, p. 167, Lowell said he hated shams and loved
manliness and especially "gentlemanliness as its highest type." For
other references to the concept of the gentleman see: I, 36, 318; XV,
294, 297, 298; XVI, 136.

[209] VII, 212–213. Many critics of Lowell convey the impression
that he was a man of wealth. It may be well to mention, therefore,
that most of his life he was actually poor. As late as 1871 he gave
Howells heartfelt thanks for securing him a fee a bit larger than expected for "The Cathedral," because he will have money to buy his
wife "a new gown—a luxury she has not had these three years"
(XV, 240). In 1871, to be sure, he did manage to sell some land so
that he had an annual income of $5000; but since he relinquished his
professorship the next year his income must have been far from
plutocratic!

his ability to stand "squarely on his own feet,"[210] to forego all
hereditary or artificial distinctions, to expect no rewards beyond
those which one's own ability or service merited; while Lowell
admired this kind of basic gentleman-like quality in Westerners,
he found it most fully developed in the personal dignity, self-
respect, and "self-centered poise" of the Federalist Josiah
Quincy,[211] and especially in Emerson as our ideal spokesman
and exemplar of "self-culture and the independent development of the individual man"[212] whose self-reliance was essentially "reliance on God."[213] The gentleman is obedient to
divine law, to conscience, to God—who is to Lowell "so far
above, yet in and of me," revealed to man in every inward impulse "that liberates and lifts."[214] Lowell's work is shot
through with the earnest conviction that "the great motors of
the race are moral, not intellectual, and their force lies ready to
the use of the poorest and weakest of us all,"[215] just as Emerson
thought that the highest type, "God's gentleman," was such
because he opened his heart to the influx of the divine "law

[210] XVI, 76 ("Letters," 1880).

[211] II, 20, 46. See his whole appreciative essay on Quincy (II,
3–49), "A Great Public Character," who represented "an aristocracy
such as is healthful in a well-ordered community, founded on public
service, and hereditary so long as the virtue which was its patent was
not escheated" (II, 24).

[212] II, 138 ("Thoreau," 1865). Like Arnold, Lowell thought Emerson greater than Carlyle. Lowell said that Emerson is America's
conclusive answer to the problem of "whether democracy could produce a gentleman."

[213] Emerson's *Works*, XI, 236; X, 65–66; the climax of Emerson's
central essay on "Self-Reliance" is as follows: "High be his heart,
faithful his will, clear his sight, that he may in good earnest be doctrine, society, law, to himself, that a simple purpose may be to him as
strong as iron necessity is to others" (*Works*, II, 75).

[214] XIII, 54, 68 ("The Cathedral," 1869).

[215] V, 160 ("Dante"). In this passage Lowell rejects Buckle's
thesis that the advance of mankind is "in the direction of science,
and not in morals"; he wants a balance of the two.

alive and beautiful."[216] Christ was "the first true gentleman" and "the first true democrat."[217] The gentleman combines fruitfully the common-sense Understanding and the higher, and imaginative Reason,[218] the head and the heart. The gentleman respects conventions.[219] He is "a man of culture, a man of intellectual resource," who is guided not only by his own meagre experience but by the winnowed experience of all mankind, by tradition.[220] Lowell's gentleman uses culture as a means of developing a quality on which much emphasis is placed, on "many-sided versatility,"[221] and the ability by the exercise of the vicarious imagination to enter into and sympathize with the experiences of all sorts of different people.[222] The gentleman must possess symmetry and balance and harmonious development.[223] He must exemplify good taste, refinement, and courtesy.[224] And last, as the crown of all, con-

---

[216] Emerson's *Works*, III, 283.   [217] VII, 18 ("Democracy").

[218] II, 212–213; VII, 84–85. He would combine the best characteristics of Franklin and Goethe (XV, 134).

[219] XV, 302 ("Letters," 1873). Lowell objects to Leslie Stephen's lumping *"shams* and *conventions* too solidly together. All conventions are not shams by a good deal, and we should soon be Papuans without them."

[220] VII, 212–213 ("Harvard Anniversary Address"); see also V, 138; II, 210.

[221] VII, 202, 211, 329, 333, 336.

[222] In *The Function of the Poet* (p. 59) Lowell said that except for his one mania Don Quixote was a "true gentleman, such a gentleman as only purity, disinterestedness, generosity, and fear of God can make."   [223] VII, 213.

[224] II, 29, 23; XV, 295–296; XVI, 71; VII, 213. Lowell regards Gray as a "finished gentleman" of the early eighteenth century "in which decorum was religion." (VIII, 20–21.) No doubt it is inevitable that one's views of what constitutes a gentleman, while garnished with historical illustrations, should be partly autobiographical. Thus the personal impression that Lowell himself made (as recorded by Moses Coit Tyler who visited him in 1882 while he was ambassador to England) fulfills Lowell's own blue-prints of the gentleman as regards poise and graciousness: "My first impression," says Tyler, who incidentally looked like Lowell, "was of the gracefulness and

scious of having free-will and hence responsibility, the gentleman will make thought whole with deed and will practise the
Christian doctrine of love for one's neighbor and of charity of
heart toward the less fortunate.[225]   Lowell had a deep affection

---

graciousness of the man; his elegance in dress and form; his manly
beauty. As he told me, he is sixty-two years old; his dark auburn
hair still abundant and rich, just touched with silver and parted
in the middle. His whiskers are more whitened. His eyes bright;
his whole face mobile, aristocratic, refined. The perfect courtier and
man of the world, dashed by scholarship, wit, genius, consciousness
of reputation, and success. His voice was very pleasant and sweet;
his tones indescribably pleasant, a pronunciation not copied from the
English, and as pure and melodious as theirs at the best. His fluency
in words perfect, his diction neat, pointed, with merry implications
and fine turns. He is an immense success in England, in society and
public meetings; petted and flattered like a prince; admired by men
and worshipped by women. He has the pick and run of the best society in the kingdom. His manners have the ease, poise, facility, and
polish of one who has got used to courts and palaces. I must say I
never saw a more perfect gentleman." (Quoted from Tyler's journal
by J. B. Hubbell, *American Life in Literature*, New York, 1936, I,
384.) Lowell himself, while admiring the *"lofty*-minded" R. H. Dana,
his "life-long" friend, said that he could have been a Senator or
Minister to England had it not been for "a quality of character
pushed to excess": Dana "could not meet his fellows on such terms
(nowise degrading) as is needful for success in a democracy" (XVI,
97, "Letters," 1882). In contrast to this "weakness" of Dana is
Lowell's admiration for the "assured ease and dignified familiarity
of a thorough gentleman" (VIII, 239), which he himself tried to
exemplify.

[225] VII, 54 (on Dean Stanley's charity); VII, 42, 213; on Howells,
the socialist: XVI, 269–270, and a host of references in the index of
"Letters," XVI, 353. Lowell even admired the humanitarian "motive" though not the practicability of Henry George and Karl Marx
(VII, 34; VIII, 160), and while he thought Marxian or "State Socialism would cut off the very roots in personal character—self-help,
forethought, and frugality—which nourish and sustain the trunk
and branches of every vigorous commonwealth," he held that
[Christian?] "Socialism means, or wishes to mean, cooperation and
community of interests, sympathy, and giving to the hands not so
large a share as the brains, but a larger share than hitherto in the
wealth they must combine to produce—means, in short, the practical
application of Christianity to life, and has in it the secret of an orderly

for Howells (as we shall see later) and his mildly socialistic ideals of brotherhood and co-operation as opposed to rugged individualism.[226]

In summary, Lowell told his Harvard anniversary audience, which included the President of the United States, that the great hope of university education was to train "not a conventional gentleman, but [one who should be] a man of culture, a man of intellectual resource, a man of public spirit, a man of refinement, with that good taste which is the conscience of the mind, and that conscience which is the good taste of the soul . . . We cannot do this for all, at best,—perhaps only for a few; but the influence for good of a highly trained intelligence and a harmoniously developed character is incalculable; for though it be subtle and gradual in its operation, it is pervasive as it is subtle."[227] Virtuous character as embodied in the gentleman meant to Lowell a gracious, poised personality devoted to the practice of the two primary Christian principles: the love of divine perfection (along with the free-willed attempt to reform one's self in the light of this perfection) and the love of one's neighbor. In the face of the charges against him it is well to

---

and benign reconstruction" (VII, 35). See also H. E. Scudder, *Lowell*, II, 378, 315; and Lowell's *New Letters*, 153, 347, where he admits, referring to Howells as "the sweetest socialist that ever was," that "there is a good deal of that leaven in me, but it struggles vainly against my common sense."

[226] XVI, 269–270. Since many students of Lowell have thought of him as completely hostile to the French Revolution, it is well to recall that even in 1886 he viewed it as caused by the upper class "forgetfulness that the world existed for any but a single class in it, and this carelessness of the comfort of others" (VIII, 24).

[227] VII, 212–213. The British Leslie Stephen testified that Lowell's patriotic democracy was never "blunted by the cajolery of the British aristocracy or other evil-disposed persons" (Lowell, XVI, 334). Dr. Edwin Cady's doctoral dissertation, which I directed, on *The Concept of the Gentleman in Representative American Authors*, 1943, has comprehensive chapters on John Adams, Jefferson, Cooper, Emerson, Holmes, and Howells, which provide useful orientation for Lowell, although the latter is not included in the study.

remember his keen sense of the gentleman's responsibility to
the less fortunate, and his reiterated exclamation, "How I hate
snobs!"[228]

Training in Wisdom.

Having now sketched what Lowell meant by the first of his
remedies for the current corruption of democracy, virtuous
character as embodied in gentlemen, "the cultivated few," let
us turn to his second remedy, which is wisdom. It is true that
he prized, like Holmes, innate intellectuality and emphasized
"the supreme fact that intellect is the divinely appointed lieutenant of God in the government of this World, and in the ordering of man's place in it and of his relations towards it."[229]
Despite his protestations of indolence, Lowell himself was a
hard worker who often studied fifteen hours a day. In the
study of Puritanism vs. witchcraft and of older literature such
as that of Chaucer he helped to set the pace for masterful factual scholars such as G. L. Kittredge and Francis Child, his
close friend.[230] It is very significant that Lowell was honored

---

[228] XVI, 76. So far as the charge of snobbery has any basis at all,
it appears to rest on a passage in Howells' very sympathetic account
of him in which he remarked that Lowell could "snub" people whom
he thought guilty of "presumption," and that after his return from
his ambassadorships to Cambridge Lowell occasionally wore "a high
hat" and gloves! Howells' *Literary Friends and Acquaintance*,
Library ed., 1911, 230, 232.

[229] VIII, 161-162 ("The Progress of the World").

[230] See Lowell's studies of "Witchcraft" (III, 115-211), Puritanism
("N.E. Two Centuries Ago," IV, 1-88), and his close and hard-
hitting textual criticism in "Library of Old Authors" (II, 271-388).
Cf. Lowell's insistence that Puritanism was not responsible for the
witchcraft delusion (IV, 14) and G. L. Kittredge's monumental
Witchcraft in Old England and New, Cambridge, Mass., 1929. In
many other ways Lowell paved the way for and arrived at generalizations which have been substantiated by modern interpreters of
Puritanism such as K. B. Murdock and Perry Miller. Lowell and
Child were boon companions and admired the scholarship of one
another (see index to XVI); Lowell said that Child's *Observations on*

with the presidency of the Modern Language Association in 1889 after the Germanic-historical scholarship of Johns Hopkins (where Lowell lectured and was greatly respected) had been flourishing for thirteen years. "Mr. Longfellow [whom Lowell succeeded in 1855 as Smith Professor, serving thirty-one years] is not," Lowell remarks, "a scholar in the German sense of the word,—that is to say, he is no pedant; but he certainly is a scholar in another and perhaps a higher sense; I mean in range of acquirement and the flavor that comes of it."[231] The interpretation applies equally well to Lowell, although he admitted in regard to the rigorous methods of German scholars that "no one is more indebted to them than I."[232] It is interesting, incidentally, to note that Professor Bliss Perry, speaking at Lowell's anniversary in 1919 flanked by such world-renowned scholars as Kittredge, Ford, and Grandgent, confessed "it is certain that if our Division of Modern Languages were called upon to produce a volume of essays matching in human interest one of Lowell's volumes drawn from these various fields [Dante, Old French, Chaucer, Shakespeare], we should be obliged, first, to organize a syndicate, and second, to accept defeat with as good grace as possible."[233] No, it will not do to question Lowell's position in his own day as a significant and thorough pioneer in hard factual scholarship

---

the Language of Chaucer (1862) and other studies had "done more for the great poet's memory than any man since Tyrwhitt" (II, 191). Lowell was also a pioneer in demonstrating that the pronunciations of Yankeeisms "are mostly archaisms [going back to Elizabethan and Puritan Britain] and not barbarisms" as generally thought in his day (XV, 253, and Introduction to the "Biglow Papers," XI, 5–79). See the authoritative C. H. Grandgent's "From Franklin to Lowell. A Century of New England Pronunciation," *Publications of the Modern Language Association*, XIV, 207–239 (1899).

[231] XV, 160.

[232] VII, 184.

[233] Bliss Perry, *The Praise of Folly and Other Essays* (Boston, 1924), p. 144.

aerated by well-founded intuition, and not without the flavor
of a delightful personality.

But Lowell himself insisted that firm and full knowledge
should be assimilated into one's own personality, that it be
vitalized by imagination and ethical purpose, and used as a
guide to the conduct of life for the people as a whole—in other
words that knowledge should be transmuted into "that temperance and serenity of mind" which is "the ripest fruit of
Wisdom,"[234] the "widener of our intellectual sympathies."[235]
Of course his own training was primarily in literature, in the
Humanities, and naturally he cherished these most although he
saw them not "as the antithesis of Science but as her elder or
fairer sister."[236]

Science.

Lowell thought that science should reinforce the Humanities
and be supplemented at some points by them. V. L. Parrington
concluded in his essay on Lowell that "science he would have
none of,"[237] and Bernard Smith concluded that his awareness
"of evolutionary theories [was] practically non-existent."[238]
Such a view might seem justified if one takes a playful passage
in his letters as telling the whole story about science: "I hate it
as a savage hates writing, because I fear it will hurt me somehow." But if one examines the contexture even of this passage,
it will be found that it is followed by an assurance to Mrs.
W. E. Darwin that "I have a great respect for Mr. Darwin, as
almost the only perfectly disinterested lover of truth I ever
encountered"[239]; and Lowell requests permission to present her

[234] VII, 104 ("Books and Libraries," 1885).
[235] VII, 108.   [236] VII, 112.
[237] Parrington, *The Romantic Revolution in America*, New York,
1927, p. 461.
[238] Bernard Smith, *Forces in American Criticism*, New York, 1939,
p. 238.
[239] XVI, 55 ("Letters," 1878). Once he spoke of the evolutionists'
theory of "protoplasm" as a "mush," a "poor substitute for the Rock

with a translation he has made to spread a knowledge of Darwin's life in Spain. If Lowell had been a hater of Darwinism it is unlikely that he would have been chosen (or would have accepted the choice) as one of the eight pall-bearers along with "dear and admirable Huxley" at Darwin's funeral in 1882 in Westminster Abbey.[240] Since science played such a large part in shaping the religious and ethical views of Lowell's day, and his own attitude toward science has been neglected if not distorted, it may be well to pause here to examine the complex evidence in some detail, and to view it in relation to his political and religious thought as a whole. If Lowell reserved a place for faith and intuition, it is well to remember that supposedly more advanced thinkers such as Whitman and Burroughs did also.

Exalting intellect, and urging that it be discovered among the people at large by educational competition ("a practical application of the doctrine of Natural Selection"), Lowell inevitably values science, which he held should be more widely taught in our schools, as not the antithesis but the "sister" of art as an important guide to physical well-being, to political and social justice, and to religious truth. For intellectual science liberates and is of God, who is in all "that liberates and lifts."[241] Lowell does recognize certain dangers of science: in truncated form it might be misunderstood so as to foster the triad materialism, determinism, and anti-humanitarianism. But since in the long run "nature insists above all things upon balance" and "contrives to maintain a harmony between the material and spiritual," he was confident that "science cannot, if it would, disengage itself

---

of Ages—by which I mean a certain set of higher instincts"; (XVI, 73) but he admitted repeatedly that "Science has scuttled the old Ship of Faith" (Scudder, II, 175); and that these higher instincts could have originated by evolution (XVI, 72).

[240] Francis Darwin, *The Life and Letters of Charles Darwin*, New York, 1897, II, 532.

[241] VIII, 161–162; VII, 101–102, 203, 112, 194; XII, 54; XIII, 54–55.

from human nature" and "the moral and imaginative part of
man." He was thus confident that eventually science could be
used to reinforce, not the dangerous triad mentioned, but
spirituality, free-willed responsibility, and the effective practice
of charity of heart.[242] Rightly considered, evolution will mean
"a reinforcement of optimism, a renewal of courage and hope,"
while Theology will "exchange a man who fell in Adam for a
man risen out of nonentity," a view heartily shared by Lowell's
good friend Holmes.[243]

Lowell was also friendly with Agassiz (a disciple of Hum-
boldt, who came between Newton and Darwin); Emerson;
Asa Gray (whose three essays reconciling Darwinism and the
theistic argument from design Lowell accepted as editor of *The
Atlantic* in 1860); Jeffries Wyman, his "old friend," the pro-
Darwinian comparative. anatomist; Norton, who had been
Darwin's sympathetic neighbor; Henry Adams; the Rev. M. J.
Savage, author of the conciliatory *Religion of Evolution*, 1876,
with which he said Lowell confessed agreement; A. D. White,
President of Cornell and later author of *The Warfare of Science
with Theology;* and Leslie Stephen,[244] whose trenchant ethical

[242] XIII, 55, 248. ("The Cathedral" and "Credidimus Jovem
Regnare" both begin by suggesting the dangers of materialism but
end with the affirmation of hopefulness in the larger and democratic
scientific vision). See also V, 70; *Round Table*, 70–71; VII, 21; *The
Function of the Poet*, 19–23; XIII, 288; VI, 378.

[243] XIII, 250 (Eventually, Lowell decides, our descendants will be
"as much superior to us" as we are to the dog-faced baboon); VIII,
146–147; Holmes' *Writings*, Riverside edition, III, 304–306.

[244] See Lowell's poetic tribute to Agassiz, XIII, 111–129, in which
he says that while Agassiz could not share orthodox "habitudes of
faith" he "fain would spare" them; XVI, index on Agassiz; H. M.
Jones, *Ideas in America*, Cambridge, 1944, pp. 134, 288 ff. on Humboldt as standing for the dynamic and organic, poetic insight, intuition, majesty in nature, etc.; Joseph LeConte's *Evolution*, 1888,
Chapter II, which argues that while Agassiz opposed Darwinism he
actually paved the way for it by establishing three
of the laws on which it was based—laws of "Differentiation," "Progress of the Whole," and of "Cyclical Movement," involving the suc-

thought owed much to Darwin. After reading Stephen's work on *Free-Thinking*, Lowell said he had been "emancipated" long ago, and he allowed "no distinction between natural and supernatural,"[245] although he did recognize an inward conflict between natural instinct and aspiration.

Lowell urges the use of the inductive scientific method which rests interpretation on an assembly on all the facts available.[246]

---

cession of organic form; *Leading American Men of Science*, ed. D. S. Jordan, New York, 1910, on Agassiz' idea of the unity of species as evidence of a divine plan, natural law presupposing a divine lawgiver, pp. 168 ff.; H. H. Clark, "Emerson and Science," *Philological Quarterly*, X, 225–260 (July, 1931); Asa Gray, in *Atlantic*, VI, 109–116, 229–239, 406–425 (July, Aug., Oct., 1860); for Lowell's poetic tribute to Gray, his neighbor and associate, see Scudder, II, 325; for tribute to Wyman, also Lowell's personal physician, XIII, 140–141, XVI, 265, and D. S. Jordan, *op. cit.*, 171–210; Norton's *Letters*, index; Henry Adams, XVI, index, and *New Letters*, 196–201, 245 ff. Lowell and Adams were ship-mates in 1872 after they had just served two years together as co-editors of the *North American Review;* see Savage's "The Religion of Lowell's Poems," *The Arena*, IX, 721 (May, 1894), also Savage's "A Morning with Lowell," *The Arena*, XV, 1–12 (Dec. 1895); A. D. White and Stephen, index to "Letters," XVI. Stephen visited Lowell in 1863 and 1868, and they saw much of each other in England.

[245] Scudder, II, 175. For general discussion see L. M. Shea, *Lowell's Religious Outlook* (Washington, D.C., 1926), Chapter VIII, "Faith and Science," as interpreted by a Catholic; and for orientation, B. J. Loewenberg, "The Controversy over Evolution in New England, 1859–1873," *New England Quarterly*, VIII, 232–257, and his "Reactions of American Scientists to Darwinism," *American Historical Review*, XXXVIII, 687–701 (dealing with Lowell's friend Agassiz among others); W. H. Roberts, *The Reaction of American Protestant Churches to the Darwinian Philosophy, 1860–1900*, Chicago, 1936; and H. W. Schneider, "The Influence of Darwin and Spencer on American Philosophical Theology," *Journal of the History of Ideas*, VI, 3–18 (Jan., 1945).

[246] See articles (in bibliography) by Grandgent and Russel Nye. In reviewing Max Müller's *Lectures on the Science of Language* (*Atlantic Monthly*, IX, 141–142, Jan., 1862) Lowell wrote: "As regards originality of treatment of a purely scientific subject, a good deal depends on the meaning we attach to the term. If we understand by it striking conclusions drawn from theoretic premises . . ., clever

Although he himself was a pioneer in linguistic science,[247] he regarded government, political science, as "the highest of all sciences," and "nobler even than astronomy, for it deals with the mutual repulsions and attractions, not of inert masses, but of bodies endowed with thought and will, calculates moral forces and reckons the orbits of God's purposes toward mankind . . ."[248] Lowell thought that such scientific inventions as the telegraph and inexpensive printing were valuable means by which the fruits of practical science and better ways of doing things could be shared by all the people.[249] He holds that the physical betterment of the lives of the people as a whole by

generalizations from fortuitous analogies and coincidences insufficiently weighed . . . or . . . speculations suggestive of thought . . . we vainly seek for such originality in Mr. Müller's lectures. But if we take it to mean, as we most certainly do, safety of conclusion founded on thorough knowledge and comparison, clear statement guarded on all sides by long intimacy with the subject, and theory the result of legitimate deduction and judicial weighing of evidence, we shall find enough in the book to content us."

[247] In the opinion of the judicious W. P. Trent (*American Literature*, New York, 1903, p. 439), Lowell "was probably better equipped in this [linguistic] particular, as well as in the older portions of the Romance literatures, than any other of the chief English-speaking critics."

[248] VII, 210; VI, 388. Lowell was confident that political science would find "nobler teachers and students," and he warned his Harvard audience in 1886 that "the better mind" of the country ought not to continue to be "alienated" from this science. It is interesting to recall that Theodore Roosevelt, the conservationist who learned much about political science from Huxley, (*The Foes of Our Own Household*, New York, 1917, pp. 141–142), had graduated from Harvard only six years before and was in 1886 striving to become mayor of New York. It is likely that Lowell helped to inspire such men to enter politics. In a tribute to Lowell (*The Critic*, XI, 86–87, Feb. 23, 1889) T. R. Roosevelt said that, although he did "not forget" Shelley or Keats or Tennyson or Browning, "on the whole I think that of all the poets of the Nineteenth Century we could least afford to lose Lowell," for the author of the "Biglow Papers" and the "Commemoration Ode" is essentially and characteristically a national and American poet."

[249] VI, 299–302.

means of science is a necessary preliminary basis for any cultural or spiritual flowering.[250]   Although he respected Hosea Biglow the rustic, Lowell sees much hope in the application of scientific inventions in industrialism, transportation, and urban life,[251] just as striking changes have been wrought gradually in the geological[252] and biological realms.

If Lowell's mature thought is permeated with the idea that our salvation is found in free-willed obedience (duty's "taproot") to divine law and "immutable decree,"[253] it is important to recognize that, as in the case of his master Emerson,[254] his concept of divine and immutable laws was mirrored and proved by parallel and immutable physical laws discovered by such men as his good friend Agassiz who, in thinking the divine lawgiver's thoughts after him, made a religion of science.[255]   Thus

[250] V, 159–160; VIII, 164.

[251] VI, 40. Here he remarks that trade "is developed only by communities where education induces refinement, where the facility of communication stimulates invention and variety of enterprise, where newspapers make every man's improvement in tools, machinery, or culture of the soil an incitement to all, and bring all the thinkers of the world to teach in the cheap university of the people."

[252] VI, 53.

[253] XIII, 5, 107–108. He insists repeatedly that ultimately the salvation of a state depends upon the extent to which the democratic "Many's plaudits" can be made to harmonize with these immutable divine laws; to Lowell it was one of the chief functions of the "cultivated few" (including the wiser scientists) to lead the Many to see the imperative need for such harmony, such obedience to divine law, mirrored by scientific laws. For his insistence on free will see V, 141, 148; *Writings*, X, 87 and III, 315.

[254] Emerson's *Works* (Centenary edition), I, 32–33: "The laws of moral nature answer to those of matter as face to face in a glass. . . . The axioms of physics translate the laws of ethics." Also I, 141, 151. In speaking of "the Law alive and beautiful which works over our heads and under our feet," Emerson says (III, 283), "pitiless, it avails itself of our success when we obey it, and of our ruin when we contravene it." For detailed analysis, see H. H. Clark's "Emerson and Science" in Bibliography.

[255] See Lowell's ardent poetic tribute to Agassiz, whom he "liked better" as he grew older (XIII, 111–129, XV, 322 ff.), in connection

in Lowell's sympathetic essay on evolution he says roundly that "the course of this moral thing we call the World is controlled by laws as certain and immutable . . . as those which govern with such exquisite precision that of the physical thing we call the Earth, could we but find them out. It has ever been the business of wise men to trace and to illustrate them, of prudent men to allow for and to seek alliance with them, of good men to conform their lives with them."[256] Man is capable of making the laws of evolution ("Natural Selection, Survival of the Fittest, and Heredity") his "partners."[257] Like Emerson,[258] Lowell disliked only what he regarded as half-way scientists who stopped short with materialism and merely physical laws, who did not combine the Understanding with the intuitive Reason and help us understand the *implications* of the new scientific discoveries in the realm of ethics and religion. Thus in "The Cathedral," while Lowell recognizes that half-way science threatens to "make thought physical," he thinks Faith could place its dependence upon science if science would avail itself of the transcendental "weapons of the time," show us that "Man cannot be God's outlaw if he would" (since both outward nature and man's psychological "upward impulses" are "messages of splendor from that Source"[259]) and show us that purposeful physical laws help us to see a divine

---

with LeConte's discussion (*Evolution* . . ., 1897, pp. 37–38, 11–29) of the way in which Agassiz paved the way for the future acceptance of evolution by proving three immutable scientific laws.

[256] VIII, 138.   [257] VIII, 163.

[258] Cf. Emerson, *Works*, I, 67: "Empirical science is apt to cloud the sight, and by the very knowledge of functions and processes to bereave the student of the manly contemplations of the whole." Cf. Lowell's "The Function of the Poet" in regard to the futile tendency of half-way science to become "too grimly intellectual," when "divorced from the moral and imaginative part of man."

[259] In this passage, and especially in the first hundred lines of "The Cathedral" Lowell shows his allegiance to the later transcendental Wordsworth who disliked the scientist who would "peep and botanize upon his mother's grave" but who held that "the remotest dis-

> "Purpose gleaming through
> The secular confusions of the world."[260]

Lowell says that he is an "Intuitionalist" and inclined "to shut my eyes resolutely in certain speculative directions" (i.e., sceptical materialism); yet he insists that "there is something in the flesh that is superior to the flesh, something that can in finer moments abolish matter and pain," and in this very passage he admits the possibility that this "something" may be "the result of long and laborious evolution," just as evolutionary theories of heredity (to which his friend Holmes was devoted in *The Guardian Angel* and other works) helped him explain his own rigorous conscience as "a case of *reversion*, I suppose, to some Puritan ancestor.[261] Since Lowell accepts limited free-will and emphasizes personality and moral forces, he does not wholly accept the deterministic ideas of Buckle and Taine; but he was familiar with their doctrines and (as Dr. R. D. Altick [262] has shown) he tempered judicial criticism with considerable attention to the way in which a given place

---

coveries of the chemist, the botanist, or the mineralogist will be . . . proper objects of the poet's art" if they can be related to men as "enjoying and suffering beings." See Lowell's two essays on Wordsworth; it is likely that Wordsworth's later idea that "The child is father of the man" and that "our days are bound each to each by natural piety" (especially as later applied to institutions and tradition) may have reinforced Lowell's Darwinian ideas of heredity and continuity.

[260] XIII, 41–72.

[261] XVI, 72–73 ("Letters," 1879); XV, 385 (He goes on to speak of his "great sympathy" for Jonathan Edwards except in his idea of physical damnation). If Lowell speaks of the evolutionists' emphasis at that time on the "fetich of their protoplasm" as a "poor substitute" for "a certain set of higher instincts which mankind have found solid under their feet in all weathers" (XVI, 73) it is well to remember that Lowell's "dear and admirable Huxley" (who had made the most of protoplasm) eventually himself repudiated what he called the "gladiatorial" theory of existence and emphasized the need for "a tender conscience," respect for others, and self-restraint.

[262] See Altick, Bibliography, for full assembly of evidence.

and time and race had fostered certain literary works and helped
them to evolve.

Darwinism was of much interest to Lowell in part because,
broadly conceived, its emphasis on the ruthlessness of man's
struggle for existence and of the survival of the fittest (as
opposed to natural altruism and equalitarianism) seemed to
reinforce his ancestral Calvinism and Federalism, with their
emphasis on depravity and the elect.[263]   Since in his essay on
evolution Lowell saw that man's inherited animal instincts
"are always there and ready to take the bit in their teeth at the
first chance,"[264] it seems probable that Darwinism (as in the
case of his friend Howells) [265] helped to convince him that, if the

---

[263] It is significant than Lowell's admiring student, Barrett Wendell, elaborated the parallels between Calvinism and Darwinism in
some detail; see his *Temper of the Seventeenth Century* (New York,
1904, pp. 217–221), his *Literary History of America* (New York, 1900,
pp. 16–17), and "Mr. Lowell as a Teacher" in *Stelligeri* (New York,
1893, pp. 205–217).   Also G. F. Wright, "Some Analogies between
Calvinism and Darwinism," *Bibliotheca Sacra*, XXXVII (1880),
76 ff.   [264] VIII, 142; 157.

[265] In 1890, although Lowell did not share Howells' view of the
Chicago Haymarket trial of alleged communists, he called Howells
"one of the chief honors of our literature" (XVI, 264), and he had
told A. D. White earlier that Howells was "almost the only one of
our younger authors in whom I have faith, for almost alone of them
he has an earnest purpose and a hunger after excellence" (*New Letters*, 153).   And in 1890 Lowell had urged his friends to read Howells'
socialistic *Hazard of New Fortunes* (1889): "A noble sentiment per-
vades it, and it made my inherited comforts here at Elmwood dis-
comforting to me in a salutary way.   I felt in reading some parts of
it as I used when the slave would not let me sleep.   I don't see my
way out of the labyrinth except with the clue of cooperation" (XVI,
269–270).   What was this "noble sentiment" which so moved Lowell?
It was Howells' conviction that a mild cooperative socialism is necessary because the unrestrained competition of ruthless capitalists who
crush laborers represents an "evolution from grub to beetle" and
makes life for everyone a matter of "pushing and pulling, climbing
and crawling, thrusting aside and trampling underfoot, lying, cheat-
ing, stealing . . . covered with blood and dirt and sin and shame . . .
to a palace of our own, or the poor-house, which is about the only

democratic welfare of the many is to be protected against the
rapaciousness of supermen who live by the law of the jungle,
there must be both governmental and ethical control, including
the state's interference with private enterprise. (It will be
recalled that in 1871 Huxley had attacked Herbert Spencer's
unbridled individualism, his "Administrative Nihilism," [266] and
that in 1883, before Lowell made his last great addresses, Spencer's American follower, W. G. Sumner of Yale, had used
Darwinism to glorify rapacious individualism and had written
a book entitled *What the Social Classes Owe Each Other*, to
which question Sumner had answered nothing is owed.) [267]

---

possession we can claim in common with our brother-man" (*A
Hazard*, ed. 1911, pp. 259, 507). In *A Traveler from Altruria* (ed.
1900, pp. 14–15) Howells attacked the fatalism of "the process of
natural selection" in our economic-social life. For an able analysis
of Howells' economic ideas, see W. F. Taylor's *The Economic Novel
in America* (Chapel Hill, N.C., 1942), pp. 214–281. It is significant
that in his crusade for realism in *Criticism and Fiction* (1891) Howells
called the author of the "Biglow Papers" "almost the greatest and
finest realist who ever wrought in verse" (p. 256; see also *My Literary
Passions*, ed. 1895, on Lowell, pp. 45, 81, 82, 134, 154, 176; and the
index to the collected letters by both men. Howells' faith in Lowell
is also shown in his being mainly responsible for Lowell's appoint-
ment by President Hayes, his wife's brother, as Ambassador to Spain.
See Lyon N. Richardson, "Men of Letters and the Hayes Administration," *New England Quarterly*, XV, 110–141 (March, 1942), for
many hitherto unpublished letters; and of course Howells' essay on
Lowell in *Literary Friends and Acquaintance*, edition of 1911, p. 273,
where he calls him "a blend of those patrician qualities and democratic principles which made Lowell anomalous even to himself."
In Howells' *Letters* (New York, 1928, II, 1) he refers to himself and
his wife as "theoretical socialists, and practical aristocrats," and
therefore he would appear to be "anomalous" also, although in a
slighter degree.

[266] T. H. Huxley, *Methods and Results*, New York, 1896, pp. 251–
289.

[267] See Richard Hofstadter's *Social Darwinism*, Philadelphia, 1944,
pp. 37–51 and passim, for an excellent analysis of Sumner's extreme
individualism, followed by an analysis of Lester Ward who reacted
to Darwinism much as Howells did and used it to show the need for
socialized control.

No wonder, then, Lowell, as an earlier champion of the slave and of social justice for all, worried, the year after Sumner's book, about "the effect of Darwinism as a disintegrator of humanitarianism," [268] and sought ways and means "to mitigate natural laws" derived from the animal world, [269] to reduce unethical inequalities between classes,[270] and to temper ruthless competition by "co-operation."

Evolution and its doctrines of heredity and inexorable continuity strengthened Lowell's reliance in part upon slow growth and gradual transformations based on the constant adaptation of social and political institutions to our geographical environment, to one's own time and place in which he thought it important that one should have deep roots as a means of fostering primal associations and steady habits.[271] Lowell never went to the extreme of Wordsworth in favoring a politically-established church and monarchy; but he did attribute to the British poet in his later conservatism emphasis on "the conditions, whether of time or place, under which alone it [freedom] can be beneficent, . . . insisting that it must be an evolution and not a manufacture, and that it should coordinate itself with the prior claims of society and civilization, . . . that tradition, habitude, and heredity are great forces, whether for impulse or restraint."[272] On the other hand, it is interesting to notice that Lowell recognized long *before* F. J. Turner that much of our "distinctive Americanism"—our emphasis on self-reliance, anti-traditionalism, equality, and optimism—had been moulded and inspired by the adaptation of our western people to a frontier environment which "destroyed all artificial distinctions" and made pos-

[268] VII, 21. In the very late poem, "St. Michael the Weigher" (XIII, 287–288), he develops the idea that "all the glories of our race," including "skill in science," are outweighed by charity of heart.

[269] VIII, 163.   [270] VII, 34.

[271] VI, 35, XV, 360, 369, 350, 321, 330, 299–300, 188, 338, VII, 116.

[272] VII, 124, 128.

sible democracy as a "pure evolution from the nature of man in a perfectly free medium." [273] Since the trend from a privileged aristocracy to a more humanitarian and equalitarian democracy seemed to Lowell inevitable, he urges us "to make the transition gradual and easy" by educating all the people so that they will not spell what ought to be "evolution with an initial 'R.' "[274]

Thus it would appear that Lowell's reflections on science and evolution helped considerably to motivate one of the most interesting aspects of his significance (in neglecting which the liberal critics have done their own cause a disservice): his significance as a very influential spokesman of the *transition* from Emersonian laissez-faire individualism to the mild socialism of Howells,[275] involving a belief in the beneficence of increased state interference with private enterprise. For Lowell sought "to correct those methods and influences that lead to enormous inequalities"[276]; he attacked "exceptional consideration" being given to property while "poverty pays with its person · the chief expense of war, pestilence, and famine."[277] He uncompromisingly exposed financial and political corrup-

[273] VII, 249; XV, 389–390; VI, 204; VII, 248–250. See Turner's famous address, "The Significance of the Frontier in American History," in the *Annual Report of the American Historical Association for 1893*, where he applies Darwinism to history: "Behind institutions . . . lie the vital forces which call these organs into life and shape them to meet changing conditions," the "European germs" of these institutions being adapted to a new environment. "This country will yet be viewed and reviewed as an organism of historic growth, developing from minute germs from the very protoplasm of state-life" (pp. 199, 201). For Lowell's further comment on the West in this connection see V, 192; 93–94; XIV, 325; XV, 169, 173, 248; and especially his tribute to Lincoln's anti-traditional democracy as bred by the West (XIII, 23–24), a tribute which Turner repeatedly quoted with admiration.

[274] VII, 16; VI, 268.

[275] See "Lowell and Howells," *Harper's Weekly*, XLVI, 101 ff. (1902); and Viola P. Franklin, "Lowell's Appreciation of Howells," *Methodist Review*, LXII, 112 ff. Also footnotes 123, 225, 265.

[276] VII, 34.   [277] VII, 24.

tion, "Rings," political parties bribed by wealth, and reinforced the multitude of current movements dedicated to similar exposure and to social justice[278]; like his friend Ruskin[279] who influenced American Christian socialists such as Henry D. Lloyd and W. D. P. Bliss, Lowell insisted that "humanity" makes "by far the most important part of political economy,"[280] and he thought that the innate tendency toward ruthlessness, proved by Darwinism, demonstrated the crying need for ways of counteracting this tendency by education, reason, and charity of heart. He constantly preached the need for the individual's responsibility to society and to future generations; and since he regarded democracy as the result of humanity's long struggle upward, of the "evolution of things," he had faith that "human nature" can be "reshaped by the slow influences of a long future." [281]

A few concrete illustrations may serve to clarify Lowell's trend toward Howells' kind of mild socialism. Even as early as 1864 he had reviewed *Man and Nature, or Physical Geography as Modified by Human Action*, an epoch-making book by George P. Marsh, now venerated as virtually the father of the conservation movement which did not win much governmental sanction until the Forest Reserve Act of 1891. Lowell praised

[278] See bibliography in Allan Nevins, *Emergence of Modern America, 1865–1878* (1928), and in Arthur Schlesinger, *The Rise of the City, 1878–1898* (1933); also W. F. Taylor, *The Economic Novel in America* (1942), and C. C. Regier, *The Era of the Muckrakers* (1932).

[279] Ruskin and Lowell were introduced in 1873 by C. E. Norton. Lowell pleaded with Ruskin to contribute to *The Atlantic*. Ruskin wrote that from "my dear friend and teacher," from "Lowell, I have myself received more help than from any other writer whatsoever" (Ruskin's *Works*, ed. Cook and Wedderburn, 1907, VII, 451; XXXVIII, 330). Of Lowell's "Cathedral" Ruskin wrote, "the main substance of the poem is most precious to me" (Scudder, *Lowell*, II, 140). See index to Lowell's *Letters* and *New Letters* for many comments, and for Ruskin's criticism of individualistic democracy see B. Lippincott, *Victorian Critics of Democracy* (Minneapolis, 1938).

[280] VII, 34.   [281] VII, 14.

the work of this eminent scientist: "Some of the facts cited by
Mr. Marsh to show the wasteful and short-sighted energy of
man as a destroying agent, almost seem to justify the old
cynical view of the race as a tribe of ants ... We are ... led,
as Mr. Marsh ... pointedly hints, to reflect upon the rights and
duties of government, as preventive and advisory, and to feel
that there is a common interest which vastly transcends the
claims of individual freedom and action."[282] Lowell vigorously attacked the spoils system and advocated civil service
reform as one antidote to municipal and governmental corruption.[283] It is interesting to note that Lowell early advocated
pure food inspection by the government ("supervision of a
thoroughly scientific character"[284]), a cause to which the ardent
socialist Upton Sinclair later devoted himself, his humanitarian
plans being violently opposed by the Darwinian W. G. Sum-

[282] *North American Review*, XCIX, 318–320 (July, 1864). Incidentally, Lowell's friend C. E. Norton wrote such articles as "Dwelling Houses for the Poor," *North American Review*, LXIV, 464–489
(1852), and (like Ruskin) he helped establish in Boston evening
schools for workingmen. Lowell said that "only when the bodily
appetites of man are satisfied does he become first conscious of a
spiritual hunger" (VIII, 164), and that history teaches the "close
relation between the moral and the physical well being of man"
(VIII, 139).

[283] In pleading for "The Independent in Politics" (1888) to form
a high-minded group "large enough to moderate between both
[parties] and make them cautious in the choice of candidates and in
the use of evil practices," Lowell says that "our first aim should
be ... the reform of our civil service, for that is the fruitful mother
of all our [political] ills" (VII, 258, 260). Scudder, II, 377, quotes
from a speech he made at a civil service dinner: "it is a better
world" because of the "increased demands made upon it by those
who were once dumb and helpless and for their increasing power to
enforce those demands." See also his tribute to G. W. Curtis, one
of the founders in 1881 of the National Civil Service Reform League,
XIII, 148–157; the poem exposes "ballot-brokers," thieving city
officials, and the false aristocracy of ill-gotten wealth.

[284] Cited by R. C. Beatty, *Lowell*, p. 266. He is discussing shipping
cattle to and from England.

ner.[285]   And Lowell also did much to awaken public sentiment in favor of international copyright laws to protect the rights of hard working authors to the fruits of their labor.[286]

Perhaps, however, Lowell paved the way for a mild socialism most effectively by revolting against the Republican party [287] at a time when it was coming under the domination of "big money"; he called for "The Independent in Politics" (1888) who would be free to join with other high-minded individuals to vote as their consciences dictated regardless of parties, the theory being that if the two traditional parties were about evenly balanced such a group free to throw its support toward any good candidate could carry his election.   Thus W. P. Trent praises Lowell especially for being "an effective and stimulating leader in the movement for purer and more independent politics that marked the decade from 1880 to 1890."[288]

[285] See Sumner's "Reply to a Socialist," 1904, in answer to Sinclair's "The Socialist Party: Its Aims in the Present Campaign," *Collier's* XXXIV (Oct., 1904).   See also Sumner's characteristic "The Absurd Effort to Make the World Over," 1894.   Lowell's attitude in the later period has much more in common with that of Richard T. Ely, author of *French and German Socialism* (1883) and *Social Aspects of Christianity* (1889); Ely, a powerfully influential economist, was one of the founders of the American Economic Association in 1885 opposed to Spencer's economic individualism and laissez-faire and dedicated to mild state regulation in the interest of Christian ethics. Incidentally Robert Ingersoll was trying to convince people that Christianity was outmoded and the enemy of humanitarian progress.

[286] XIV, 115; XVI, 95–96; 278–282; Scudder, II, 326–332.

[287] The most intensive study of this subject is a University of Wisconsin doctoral dissertation by E. A. White entitled *The Republican Party in National Politics, 1888–1891* (1940).   He shows that the Republican "National Committee raised $3,300,000 for the campaign, an amount so far in excess of previous campaign funds that the election of 1888 marked a turning point in American political history. Private industrial organizations such as the American Iron and Steel Association and the American Protective Tariff League assisted the party by flooding the West with tariff propaganda and making financial contributions to the local campaigns."

[288] W. P. Trent, *American Literature* (New York, 1903), p. 430. See Lowell, VII, 233–268, and "Tariff Reform," VII, 219–229.

Of course Lowell's greatest social service was in the interest
of higher education dedicated to ethical elevation and the provision for a more intelligent and social-minded leadership in
our democracy. He insists that education should include a
proportionate emphasis on "science that ennobles life and makes
it generous," for to him "the noblest definition of Science is
that breadth and impartiality of view which liberates the mind
from specialities, and enables it to organize whatever we learn,
so that it become real Knowledge by being brought into true
and helpful relation with the rest."[289]

Humane Letters.

Now let us turn to Lowell's view of the Humanities, of
literature, as another guide to virtue and wisdom. For science
herself in seeking breadth of view and in deducing "theory from
the amplest possible comparison and correlation of facts, . . .
from recorded experience,"[290] would lead one inevitably to
study the age-long history of man's highest and most distinctively human achievements which constitute tradition.
Lowell had at first been scornful of tradition as having sanctioned some social evils such as slavery. However, he eventually

---

While he is often thought of as representing the industrial East,
Lowell opposed protection of wealth by means of tariff and trusts as
an unfair kind of class legislation. See Riverside Edition, VI, 191
and 216–217. If Lowell was unsympathetic toward labor organizations (XV, 219–223), it was because he feared they might misuse
universal suffrage to promote "class-legislation to escape which we
left the Old World" (VII, 211). He thought enlightened statesmanship involved looking out for the rights of *all* classes, and he opposed
special privileges for *both* labor and capital.

[289] VII, 193–194.

[290] VII, 236. Lowell praises Burke for his "pregnant lessons in the
science of how to look at things" inductively (VII, 241). See A.T.
Hadley, "The Influence of Charles Darwin upon Historical and
Political Thought" (*Psychological Review*, XVI, n.s., 143–151, May
1909) on the evolutionary "attitude of mind as having been foreshadowed in the works of Edmund Burke" (p. 149).

came to see that, properly winnowed for what is "perdurable,"[291] tradition can give the individual perspective and can
act as a steadying and quickening power, for "the collective
thought, the faith, the desire of a nation or a race, is the cumulative result of many ages, is something organic, and is wiser
and stronger than any single person . . ."[292] "Mankind in the
aggregate is always wiser than any single man, because its experience is derived from a larger range of observation and experience, and because the springs that feed it drain a wider
region both of time and of space."[293] Since God has "made
Good infinitely and eternally lovely to the soul of man,"
throughout history "every high example of virtue, though it led
to the stake or scaffold, becomes part of the reserved force of
humanity, and from generation to generation summons kindred natures to a standard of righteousness as with the sound
of a trumpet."[294] If our universities are to fulfill their "chief
function" and to develop character and elevate the conduct of
life by "bringing the influence of the more cultivated to bear
with greater energy and directness on the less cultivated,"
Lowell thought that the study of science needed to be balanced
by the study of those masterpieces of literature (to which
philological science is but a "ladder") which "have overcome
death by reason of their wisdom and of the beauty in which it
is incarnated, such parts as are universal by reason of their civilizing properties, their power to elevate and fortify the mind. . . .
Leave in their traditional preëminence those arts that were

[291] XV, 230–231, where Lowell gives a young correspondent some
interesting directions on how to read literature. Much as he admired the ancient Greeks, he recognized that their attitude toward
democracy could not be accepted by an American who knew it not
"merely from books" but "by rubbing shoulders with it lifelong"
(VI, 223).

[292] V, 138 ("Dante").

[293] II, 210 ("Chaucer"). See also on tradition VIII, 141; VII, 20,
234; V, 5, 271; VI, 16, 134.

[294] VI, 160.

rightly called liberal; those studies that kindle the imagination, and through it irradiate the reason; those studies that manumitted the modern mind; those in which the brains of finest temper have found alike their stimulus and their repose, taught by them that power of intellect is heightened in proportion as it is made gracious by measure and symmetry."[295] Since "the mind sinks or rises to the level of its habitual society," as he said in "Books and Libraries," 1885, each of us can by identifying ourselves with the spirit of the best books elevate ourselves by living in "a select society of all the centuries" and profit by "the company of saint and sage, of the wisest and wittiest at their wisest and wittiest moment."[296]

Lowell had something of his master Emerson's doctrine in "History" that, beyond surface variety of costume and of local and contemporary mannerisms, "the mind of man is one" in basic motives throughout the ages; and Lowell's disciple, George Woodberry, in his essay on "Man and the Race" (1905) elaborated Lowell's idea of "literature as an organ of the race-mind,

---

[295] VII, 191, 193. In "The Function of the Poet," the address which had won him his professorship, he had urged a devotion to art "not as an amusement, not as a mere ornament," but for "its humanizing and ennobling energy, for its power of making men better by arousing in them a perception of their own instincts for what is beautiful, and therefore sacred and religious, and an eternal rebuke of the base and worldly . . ." In holding that "Good taste . . . is one of the most powerful factors of civilization" (VIII, 202), Lowell essentially continued and illustrated with more scholarly knowledge Emerson's Platonic idea that "The Beautiful is the highest," and that "Beauty is the mark God sets upon virtue." He was a strong influence on his student Henry James (whose work he praised in *The Function of the Poet*, 105-115) who developed in still more artistic form the doctrine that taste is an index to character. It will be recalled that in her formative years Willa Cather thought no one so "wonderful" as Henry James and that she censures her "Lost Lady" not because she has violated a moral scruple but "an aesthetic principle": hers is the sophisticated teaching that evil is to be avoided because it is ugly, while goodness is beautiful.

[296] VII, 102-104.

and of education as the process by which the individual enters
into the race-mind [he means the mind of the human race], and
becomes more and more man . . ."[297]   Like Emerson,[298] however, Lowell emphasized the fact that mere passive reading or
listening to lectures will hardly enable us to profit by literary
masterpieces, by tradition; even this "living emanation of the
Eternal Mind, organically operative in history, becomes a dead
formula" unless the individual reader assimilates it, re-creates
it in his own imagination, relives in his own life the vision of
the author, and has "realized a tradition of the memory into a
conviction of the understanding and the soul."[299]   Unlike
mathematical truths such as two and two make four, "every
truth of morals must be redemonstrated in the experience of
the individual man before he is capable of utilizing it as a con-
stituent of character or a guide in action."[300]

[297] *American Critical Essays*, ed. N. Foerster (Oxford, 1930), p. 234.
Woodberry adds, "I conceive of history as a single process in which
through century after century in race after race the soul of man proceeds in a progressive comprehension of the universe and evolution
of its own humanity, and passes to each new generation its accumulated knowledge and developed energies in their totality and without
loss, at the acme of achievement."   See Woodberry's ardent essay on
Lowell, *Makers of Literature* (New York, 1901).

[298] Lowell's theory is similar to Emerson's.   A great book being
the organic expression of one who has risen above his own uniqueness
and that of his age, Emerson valued not so much an antiquarian concern with the unique and mutable particulars of literary history as
the perception of the extent to which the book reveals "the universal
mind," the "law for man."   He urged "creative reading"; genius being "a larger imbibing of the common heart," he said that rightly read
"the great poet makes *us* feel our *own* wealth" and *we* are "born into
the great, the *universal* mind."   (Emerson's *Works*, I, 108; II, 38;
I, 89, I, 93; II, 288–289; *Journals*, II, 296.)

[299] VI, 45.

[300] V, 160–161.   Lowell illustrates his point by Dante's treatment
of the mystery of the incarnation.   "The divine reason must forever
manifest itself anew in the lives of men, and that as individuals.   This
atonement with God, this identification of the man with the truth,
so that right action shall not result from the lower reason of utility,

It will be recalled that at the end of his address on "Democracy" Lowell said that fundamentally "our healing" is not in outward forms of government, however "palliative" the best of them may be, but rather in the individual's obedience "to the conscience and the heart, prompting us to a wider and wiser humanity," and that he said elsewhere that "we have an instinct to prefer the good, other things being equal, and in exact proportion to our culture we know better what is good, and prefer it more habitually."[301] As path-finder for the Modern Language Association in his address in 1889 as an early president, Lowell argued that literature, when studied in the Emersonian manner, can "liberalize us as only an acquaintance with the infinite diversity of men's mind and judgment can do . . . It is only through this record of Man's joys and sorrows, of his aspirations and failures, of his thought, his speculation, and his dreams, that we can become complete man, and learn both what he is and what he may be, for it is the unconscious autobiography of mankind."[302] Literature not only helps to develop that "many-sidedness" and breadth of sympathy which he regarded as "the very essence of culture," not only reveals to us our own kinship with the wisest men of all times and the rich resources and potentialities of the human spirit as it has encountered crises through the ages, but through the universality of literature in its higher trans-national reaches it can do much to obliterate the idea of alien or enemy races and by making us all citizens of "an invisible and holier fatherland" it can do much to promote international understanding, brotherhood, and peace. Indeed, broadly considered, Lowell's

---

but from the higher of a will so purified of self as to sympathize by instinct with the eternal laws, is not something that can be done once for all, that can become historic and traditional, a dead flower pressed between the leaves of the family Bible, but must be renewed in every generation, and in the soul of every man, that it may be valid."

[301] *Letters* (2 vol. edition), II, 14.

[302] VII, 329, 333, 336.

literary nationalism, intense as it was in the period of the *Biglow Papers*, was but a kind of detour caused by the influence on him of the Civil War, for during his final period he essentially reinforced the emotional universalism of his first period by much more knowledge of and respect for traditions of many different times and lands.

Thus on the threshold of his third period he had concluded in 1867 that literature "tends more and more to become a vast commonwealth, with no dividing lines of nationality."[303] From 1870, devoted to five "cosmopolitan" authors (Virgil, Dante, Cervantes, Shakespeare, and Goethe),[304] Lowell had "little faith in that quality in literature which is commonly called nationality. . . . To tell you when you cannot fully taste a book that it is because it is so thoroughly national, is to condemn the book. To say it of a poem is even worse, for it is to say that what should be true of the whole compass of human nature is true only to some north-and-by-east-half-east point of it. . . . All great poetry must smack of the soil, for it must be rooted in it, must suck life and substance from it, but it must do so with the aspiring instinct of the pine and climb forever toward diviner air, and not in the grovelling fashion of the potato. Any verse that makes you and me foreigners is not only not great poetry, but no poetry at all."[305] · Thus, as in the case of institutional vs. personal reform, Lowell now harmonized the counter-claims of literary roots-in-a-national-soil vs. literary universalism. · After his extravagant claims for

[303] See the whole important passage of which this is a part in Lowell's essay on Percival, II, 114–117. It is here that he says appreciatively that "the struggle of Goethe's whole life was to emancipate himself from Germany, and fill his lungs for once with a more universal air. (II, 115.) See Wurfl (Bibliography), pp. 74–82 on Lowell's debt to Goethe's doctrine of universality.

[304] VII, 131. He says these authors "have stood the supreme test of being translated into all tongues, because the large humanity of their theme, and their handling of it, needed translation into none."

[305] IV, 227 ("Spenser," 1875).

dialect in 1862, he now thinks that an "American lingo" of our provincial making would be "artificial and wearisome" unless "some man with a truly lyrical genius could breathe life into the rigid formula."[306] American English has evolved from other national languages, rests especially on "its admirable mixture of Saxon and Latin" which give it "strength and sonorousness," and thus "the purity, the elegance, the decorum, the chastity of our mother tongue are a sacred trust in our hands. I am tired of hearing the foolish talk of an American variety of it."[307]

Contrary to the general supposition, Lowell did write (according to G. W. Cooke's *Bibliography*) about thirty essays on American and contemporary authors; but he especially prized the "select company" of the great masters chiefly for their universality and their testimony to the essential oneness and brotherhood of man. "This is why the study of them is fitly called a liberal education, because it emancipates the mind from every narrow provinciality whether of egotism or tradition, and is the apprenticeship that every one must serve before becoming a free brother of the guild which passes the torch of life from age to age. . . . Their vitality is the vitality not of one or another blood or tongue, but of human nature; their truth is not topical and transitory, but of universal acceptation . . ."[308] Thus, while Lowell was a pioneer in linguistic science and knew much of the deep historical roots of words, he warned us of the dangers of mere "pedantry,"[309] and he had a sublime vision of how, by bringing the past "to bear with all its plastic force upon our wholly new conditions of life and thought," the study of literature might serve with a new worthi-

---

[306] *Writings*, III, 308. He comes to emphasize *both* the need for freshness of language *and* a writer's native genius.

[307] VIII, 202 ("The Old English Dramatists," 1887). On the matter of changing attitudes toward the use of dialect, see the evidence assembled by Russel Nye (Bibliography).

[308] III, 250–251 ("Shakespeare Once More," 1868).

[309] VII, 184.

ness in promoting the brotherhood of all mankind. And who shall say that this, perhaps Lowell's master-idea, does not offer timely promise in the midst of our own problems of healing the wounds of warring nations, promoting international understanding, and paving the way for a more enduring peace based on a sense of humanity's essential unity?

The discipline, however, by which we avail ourselves of the winnowed resources of literature is criticism, and it is time to turn now to Lowell's practice as a critic.

H. H. C.

II. LOWELL AS CRITIC [310]

A. GENERAL

In no other American of the nineteenth century has the critical spirit manifested itself so comprehensively as in James Russell Lowell. Despite the fact that he leaves an impression of comparative superficiality and futility—shortcomings to which we are keenly sensitive today, perhaps because they are our own—he must still be regarded as our most distinguished literary critic. While there is far more of original vigor in both Poe and Emerson, he was free of the special purposes that limited their achievement as critics. The bulk of Poe's work was journalism, book-reviewing, ephemeral commentary on the books of the day; Emerson, at the other extreme, characteristically chose for his literary essays themes that are timeless; Lowell, however, attempted rounded portraits and estimates of so many authors of the past that he virtually wrote a critical history of literature from Dante to his own age.[311] As this con-

[310] Reprinted, with the consent of the publishers, Houghton Mifflin Company, from Norman Foerster's *American Criticism*, Chapter III, pp. 111–150.

[311] For convenient reference I will arrange his subjects in chronological order: 1. Dante (*Prose Works*, vol. IV); 2. Chaucer (III);

trast might imply, Poe read little outside his times; Emerson read widely but transcendentally; while Lowell was a good deal of the detached scholar. Again, Poe in his most memorable work was concerned with technique; Emerson, as Lowell phrases it, with "the profounder ethics of art"; and Lowell himself with both. Poe extolled beauty and fought the heresy of the didactic; Emerson, though eager for beauty, could not long lay aside his ministerial function; it remained for Lowell to mediate, with fair success, between the two. Poe and Emerson were at their best in critical theory; Lowell, wanting their turn for speculation, excelled in practice. Poe and Emerson have certain aesthetic doctrines associated with their names; but the name of Lowell suggests nothing of the kind, suggests, rather, gusto and flashes of insight, the free play of feeling and intelligence.

From what has just been said—that aesthetic doctrines are so inconspicuous in Lowell, and that he excelled in practice rather than theory—it might reasonably be inferred that he was an impressionist, that the center of interest in his essays is the man himself, a delightful personality, blending such qualities as warmth of sympathy, infectious enthusiasm, an active imagination and fancy, irrepressible wit and humor, fundamental sanity and common sense. In substantiation of this inference, it

---

3. Don Quixote (VI); 4. Spenser (IV); 5. Marlowe (VII); 6. Shakespeare Once More (III); 7. Shakespeare's *Richard III* (VII); 8. Beaumont and Fletcher (VII); 9. Webster (VII); 10. Chapman (VII); 11. Massinger and Ford (VII); 12. Milton (IV); 13. Milton's *Areopagitica* (VII); 14. Walton (VII); 15. Dryden (III); 16. Pope (IV); 17. Rousseau (II); 18. Fielding (VI); 19. Gray (VII); 20. Lessing (II); 21. Wordsworth (IV); 22. Wordsworth (VI); 23. Coleridge (VI); 24. Keats (I); 25. Landor, Some Letters of (VII); 26. Carlyle (II); 27. Swinburne's Tragedies (II); 28. Percival, Life and Letters of (II); 29. Emerson the Lecturer (I); 30. Thoreau (I). (In this list I have disregarded *Lowell's Early Prose Writings, The Function of the Poet and Other Essays,* and *Letters of James Russell Lowell.*) An edition of Lowell's literary essays, thus arranged, would render a service to lovers of books.

might be urged that we read his literary essays much as we read his charming letters—for their personal qualities—and that if we subtracted these personal qualities the essays would dissolve into nothingness, while in the case of Poe and Emerson the skeleton of ideas would remain. At a glance, one has reason to say of Lowell: his criteria are negligible, the man is all, he was an impressionist.

Such, I say, is the conclusion to which we are quickly drawn if we follow what Poe, with his one-track mind, somewhat haughtily termed ratiocination, or what Emerson, with his trackless mind, disparaged as mere logic or understanding. Yet surely the weakness of logic resides less in the thing itself than in the ease of its abuse by those who, indulging an emotional bias, disregard important facts and arrive at a predetermined conclusion. In the present instance, the important facts are twofold. In the first place is the obvious fact that the impressionist is not a critic without criteria, but a critic who refuses to delimit his criteria by deliberate formulation and application. To call Lowell an impressionist is not to dispose of his criteria. In the second place, a thorough scrutiny of Lowell's criticism would show that his criteria, far from being negligible, are really distinct and impressive. It could probably be demonstrated, indeed, that his weakness was the very reverse of that which is commonly alleged; that, instead of having insignificant criteria and effective personal qualities, he possessed a set of controlling ideas that wanted only the impetus of great personal qualities to make them in the highest degree significant and useful.

This is a large claim, necessitating a careful study both of his theory of criticism and literary art, and of his personal endowment and attainment.

B. Task of the Critic

Books and the Man—in the commerce of the two lies the whole story of criticism. While Emerson defined the scholar or critic as Man Thinking, and, though a great reader, never lost himself in his books, Lowell might almost have defined the critic as Man Reading, since his habitual occupation was so much more passive than active, receptive than creative. In his commerce with books, Lowell's imports far exceeded his exports. From childhood to old age he read voraciously, in the fine library of his father, in the library of Harvard College, and in his own accumulating collection of books. Not long before his death he came to the conclusion that "the problem of the scholar was formerly how to acquire books; for us it is how to get rid of them." He spoke of Cotton Mather as book-suffocated, an epithet that perhaps describes himself quite as justly. From the greatest of English Puritans he selected, with unconscious irony, the following motto for one of his "Elizabethan Dramatists":

> . . . Who reads
> Incessantly, and to his reading brings not
> A spirit and judgment equal or superior,
> . . . .
> Uncertain and unsettled still remains,
> Deep versed in books and shallow in himself.

As a professor of literature, aware of the *gründliche* Germans, he read with a kind of monastic zeal; but even then, as well as before and after, he must have been largely an epicurean browser. In one of his essays he tells of his magical hours in the old library in Harvard Hall, where he read undisturbed save by the sun, which drew him to a north or south window according to the season, and by his conscience, which reproached his truancy from the tasks of the day. "It was the merest browsing, no doubt, as Johnson called it, but how delightful it was!" Though I do not know just what he refers to in Johnson or Boswell, I do know that "His Majesty having observed to him that he supposed he must have read a great deal; Johnson answered, that he thought more than he read"—a quotation quite as damaging to Lowell as the above motto from Milton. He was under no delusion as to his intellectual indolence. From his own experience he realized that the profusion of books makes men "depend on their shelves rather than on their brains; it has supplanted a strenuous habit of thinking with a loose indolence of reading which relaxes the muscular fiber of the mind." In his "Moosehead Journal" he confesses "how tyrannical the habit of reading is, and what shifts we make to escape thinking." His weakness in this regard is but one instance of the fact that his enthusiasms were far greater than his strenuosities—a fact, one suspects, even in his moral nature, in which ideals counted for more than standards. However that may be, his literary essays, despite fluency of style, are inferior to Emerson's in fundamental brain-work, in the "mere logic" of the brain as well as in its bolder movements. There is scant evidence that he really exerted himself to overcome the tendency he deplored, though one might find some suggestion of his effort, and his defeat, in his definition of man as "the only animal that thinks he is thinking when he is merely ruminating!"

Intellectually indolent, Lowell was attracted to impressionism. Although in his best years he appealed to standards, he was always, late and early, something of an impressionist. As late as 1883, speaking of Fielding, he affirmed the vanity of seeking to weigh a man's work by fixed standards, "when each of us stamps his own weights, and warrants the impartiality of his own scales." More than once he urges skepticism as a primary attribute of the critic, meaning an independence of tradition: a self-reliance that he himself practiced most markedly, as one would expect, in his early romantic criticism written under the influence of Charles Lamb. Thus, he praised the Elizabethan poets for having no creed, for knowing nothing of "'established principles'—which seem, indeed, to be little better than scarecrows set up by one half of the world for the other half to pelt with mud. They knew that to be a slave in one thing is to be a

slave in all. . . . Freedom is the only law which genius knows."
There being no established principles, the critic is to record his
"impressions, which may be valuable or not, according to the
greater or less ductility of the senses on which they are made.
Charles Lamb, for instance, came to the old English dramatists
with the feeling of a discoverer. He brought with him an alert
curiosity, and everything was delightful simply because it was
strange. . . . He had the great advantage . . . of not thinking
it needful to make them square with any Westminster Cate-
chism of aesthetics." Here is that "very air of a Columbus"
which Browning observed in the young American critic, and
which clung to him even in his maturity. Whatever else he may
have become, he remained in large measure the discoverer, the
adventurer in the realms of gold, full of zest and waywardness,
recording impressions on senses not a little remarkable for
ductility. As an impressionist of the romantic and not of our
realistic age, he was concerned with the culling of beauties. "I
string together a few at random," he says, a few being seventeen,
but "I shall excuse myself from giving any instances" of the
author's faults. Instead of regarding quotations as a documentation and illumination of purposeful discourse, he tended to
look upon himself as a kind of showman, displaying this, that,
and the other, with comments expressing his own pleasure in
the objects. Thus, in a comment on Spenser that promises to
develop into purposeful discourse, he suddenly breaks off with
the remark, "But I am keeping my readers from the sweetest
idealization that love ever wrought," and reprints two entire
pages of the "Faërie Queene" which could presumably be
found in any edition of that poem. Having skipped this long
quotation, the reader is proudly asked whether "there is any
passage in any poet"—stimulating challenge to an unread
audience!—"that so ripples and sparkles with simple delight?"
We like it, adds the showman, because—well, because we like
similar things in Sidney and Dante; and presently he is heading

toward another long quotation with the information that Ben
Jonson spent a whole night "looking to his great toe." Nor is
he nonplused when a fine exhibit is suddenly missing, but quite
equal to the occasion, as when, in an essay on winter writers,
he turns to the "excellent snow scenery in Judd's 'Margaret,'
but some one has confiscated my copy of that admirable book,
and, perhaps, Homer's picture of a snow-storm is the best yet,"
and so offers that instead.

Delightful, yes, these divagations, but at the same time in-
dicative of an irresponsibility of mood that vitiates high achievement. We shall concede to him, as he concedes to Walton, a
genius for rambling; but we must also hold against him, as he
does *not* hold against Lessing, the tendency of his thoughts "to
want connection." When he tells us that enthusiasm has led
him astray from his purpose, we cannot but doubt of the purpose itself: Was it really clear to him? Was it a serious purpose?
Was it a purpose at all or an assortment of velleities? Of the
three processes that enter into a serious purpose, namely, acquisition, organization, and explication, only the first interested
him. We should have known, without his express statement,
that he was capable of vast drudgery in acquisition but impatient in communication; significantly, he wholly omits from his
statement the intermediate step of mental organization, the
process of thinking the chaos of impressions into a luminous
coherence. Even as an impressionist, he fell short of the ideal,
which is surely not to express the first or second but rather the
final impression resulting from repeated and protracted reflection. For the ideal impressionist is not intellectually indolent,
but by hard thinking integrates his intuitions into a final impression and achieves a firm unity, and is never content, as Lowell
sometimes was, with a mere congeries of intuitions. Wanting
the command of wholes, he relied upon the parts; he expressed
wonderfully the fragmentary intuitions that came to him during

his reading or writing, as a single instance will show. It is the well-known remark that "Pope's proverbial verse,

'True wit is Nature to advantage drest,'

unpleasantly suggests Nature under the hands of a ladies'-maid." This is perfect insight, perfect criticism of not only a verse but an entire age of European culture. Deriving his intuition from the word "drest," Lowell perceives that lady's-maids are indeed eminently desirable for the adornment of social manners, but that when they bestow their art upon the great Mother, upon all that is sublime in *Natura naturans*, they surpass their charming province.[312] Perhaps this expresses quite as much as Arnold's elegant recognition that the age of social life and manners, of prose and reason, was after all "indispensable," or as much as Carlyle's eloquent mouthings over "the putrid Eighteenth Century, such an Ocean of sordid nothingness, shams, and scandalous hypocrisies as never weltered in the world before." Yet Lowell introduces his remark almost parenthetically; it is a "happy thought," a sudden flash that illuminates, and while he was always capable of vivid coruscations he proceeded most of the time in a soft-fluttering illumination that reminds one of what is called heat lightning. If to succeed be to burn steadily, as Pater has it, with a hard, gemlike flame, to maintain a state of ecstasy, Lowell was a most inadequate impressionist.

But it is time to say plainly that Lowell was not content to be an impressionist; that, on the contrary, he strove to possess himself of universal principles of criticism. While we may say of his work, as of that of most modern critics, that it manifests various impressionistic tendencies—recurrent skepticism,

[312] To be just to Pope we should remember that, three verses above, he extols
          "The naked Nature and the living Grace"
and that he is the author of that other proverbial verse:
          "And snatch a Grace beyond the Reach of Art."

random expression of intuitions, complaisance with a rambling
mood as if it were a kind of wise passiveness—it is clear that by
the time he entered upon his most successful activity he had
already formulated a set of criteria. "Subjective criticism" he
held to be "as untrustworthy as it is fascinating." In the very
passage I have quoted, in which he praises Lamb as an impressionist, Lowell asserts that "unless we admit certain principles
as fixed beyond question, we shall be able to render no adequate
judgment, but only to record our impressions." Impressions,
to be sure, we must have, fresh and keen as our faculties permit;
for if we lack "the capacity to admire" we cannot do justice to
an author's strongest side—cannot "measure" him fairly, which
is our real object. A critic like Leigh Hunt has the "feminine
temperament" that gives "acute perceptions at the expense of
judgment." While granting that the feminine virtue of openness to impressions is indispensable, Lowell is certain as a *man*
can be that the sovereign virtue of a fertile criticism is judgment
or measurement.

Rejecting subjective criticism as untrustworthy, he found his
standards in three forms of supposedly objective criticism, viz.,
historical, aesthetic, and didactic criticism.[313]

---

[313] Lowell had no real leaning to the kind of criticism termed "expressionistic." It is true that he quoted approvingly, from one of
its alleged prophets, a passage regarded by J. E. Spingarn as containing the essence of the expressionist system. Goethe, he says,
contrasts "a destructive criticism and a productive." For the former,
the critic "has only to set up in his mind any standard, any model,
however narrow," and damn a work that does not conform. "Productive criticism is a great deal more difficult; it asks, What did the
author propose to himself? Is what he proposes reasonable and
comprehensible? and how far has he succeeded in carrying it out?"
(III, 67.) But this is a summary of the expressionistic position only
if one misrepresents Goethe by omitting the second of his three questions, as Mr. Spingarn does in *Creative Criticism*, p. 20. Restoring
the question in his translation of *Goethe's Literary Essays*, Mr. Spingarn renders it, "Was his plan reasonable and sensible?" To ask this
question is to invite all those hordes of intellectualistic and moralistic

When Lowell speaks of "that breadth which comes only of thorough knowledge and sympathy," he refers to the two indispensable preliminaries of judgment—vivid impressions and historical understanding. Comparatively neglected before the Romantic Movement, they had been well exemplified in Europe before Lowell came to his task, but in America he himself was the first distinguished critic-scholar adequately to indicate their importance. If he may be regarded as the forerunner of the impressionistic critics who today abound outside the universities, he may with better reason be viewed as the chief American ancestor of the historical critics and scholars who abound within the universities. Poe had neither the learning nor the flexibility implied in the historical approach; Emerson sensed in a general way the relation of an author to his times, as when he pointed out how heavily indebted Shakespeare was; it remained for Lowell to state more clearly the nature of historical criticism, to exemplify it in studies of a series of great writers, and to demonstrate its value as a preparation for literary criticism in its highest form.

Historical criticism, he pointed out, measures an author "relatively to his position in the literary history of his country and the conditions of his generation." Although an author's positive merit is to be measured by a higher standard, "a perfectly fair judgment" must indeed consider not only "what he was, but what, under the given circumstances, it was possible for him to be." While it is not essential that we should *explain* him by means of his circumstances,[314] it is essential that we should *understand* him by these means. Warning us of the danger of falling into anachronism, understanding requires us to win our way back to the author's generation. It is true that "the principles of art are immutable," but it is also true that

criteria which are forever breaking, like barbarian hosts, upon the beautifully simple empire of Croce and his lieutenants.

[314] Acquainted with the pseudo-science of Taine, Lowell was influenced more by earlier critics, especially Goethe.

"their application must accommodate itself to the material supplied to them by the time and by the national character and
traditions." Behind this conception lies, as Lowell knew, the
idea of the organic—the idea that literature is not a manufacture
but a growth. The creative artist dooms himself to relative
failure if he merely copies models instead of letting the "genetic
principle" of his land and time work through him; and, similarly,
the critic who does not seek to understand the genetic principle
in the writers of the past is incapable of a complete criticism.
By study and imagination the critic must be able to *expatriate*
himself; he will not commit the error, for example, of judging
Rousseau "after our blunt English fashion" and condemning
him "on the finding of a jury of average householders." He
must be able likewise to *ex-temporate* himself; instead of mis-
representing the Puritans of New England, he will make it his
business to become "contemporary with, and therefore able to
understand" them.

Nowhere has Lowell so clearly exemplified the nature and
value of historical criticism as in his attitude toward the eighteenth century, the literature of which meant so little to Poe,
Emerson, Whitman, and the Romantics generally. With becoming diffidence he recognized that a thoroughgoing extem-
poration was necessary for the understanding of Pope. "I was
brought up in the old superstition that he was the greatest
poet that ever lived"; then, as the romantic revolt developed in
America, came an "ardent desire for smashing the idols I had
been brought up to worship. . . . There was a time when I
could not read Pope." Lowell always retained, as he had reason
to do, a measure of disapprobation of "the classicism of red
heels and periwigs," of "the lullaby seesaw of the couplet," of a
poetry so remote from the simple that "everybody ceremoni-
ously took a bushel-basket to bring a wren's nest to market in."
He was justified in preferring his Dante and Chaucer. Yet he
managed to deal with the literature of that alien age more justly,

on the whole, than any other romantic critic. He loved his "Dear Dr. Johnson," "gruff old Ursa Major," and he was one of the first to discover the real Fielding and to discredit the traditional view of the man; but the most instructive example is his return to Pope. He came to perceive that "it is a school-boy blunder in criticism to deny one kind of perfection because it is not another"; that Pope had unquestionably achieved one kind of perfection, the representation of conventional life, as Chaucer had represented actual life, Spenser imaginative life, Shakespeare ideal life, and Milton interior life; and that he had written "one perfect work," unsurpassed "for wit, fancy, invention, keeping," and for power of "pure entertainment," viz., "The Rape of the Lock." How did Lowell attain this conclusion? Through historical understanding and historical judgment. "Pope," he argues, "had one of the prime qualities of a great poet in exactly answering the intellectual needs of the age in which he lived, and in reflecting its lineaments." In the hands of Pope the artificial style was not mechanical but "living and powerful, because he used it to express artificial modes of thinking and an artificial state of society." Under the given circumstances, it was not possible for Pope to achieve the modes of perfection that we have in Chaucer, or Spenser, or Shakespeare, or Milton. He used, as every successful artist must, the materials offered him in his own time, and used them supremely well. He is the greatest of English poets in his own kind—this is the verdict of historical criticism, and it is very different from the old superstition that Pope was the greatest poet who ever lived.

The verdicts of historical criticism, however, while final within their jurisdiction, are not the ultimate verdicts of literary claims. That Pope reached perfection in his special department does not mean to Lowell that he was a greater writer than those who fell somewhat short of perfection in higher departments. In a comprehensive estimate of a writer we must estimate also the department chosen for him by the time-spirit. "Is the department of Milton," for example, "no higher than that of Butler?" This is a question which common sense requires us to ask, and which historical criticism is incompetent to answer. While historical criticism has indeed a certain objectivity in forcing the critic to apply standards more authoritative than his personal likes and dislikes, it none the less falls short of an ultimate verdict. If impressionistic criticism is relative to the critic, historical criticism is relative to the age, and an absolute criticism is yet to seek.

Speaking of Dante, Lowell says that in the end a poet must be judged by his poetic qualities, and that "he must be judged by them absolutely, with reference, that is, to the highest standard, and not relatively to the fashions and opportunities of the age in which he lived." Passing beyond the domain of historical criticism, we must endeavor to plant ourselves "on the aesthetic point of view"—as British critics have rarely done. For example, Wordsworth, says Lowell to a British audience, "has too commonly been estimated rather as philosopher or teacher than as poet. The value of what he said has had more influence with the jury than the way in which he said it. There are various methods of criticism, but I think we should all agree that literary work is to be judged from the purely literary point of view." Lowell means, I take it, from the purely aesthetic point of view. When we rise above the fascinations of impressionistic and the learning of historical criticism and seek to estimate the absolute value of a work of art, the questions that confront us are of a higher mood: Is it in truth a work of art, and why? To what extent is it beautiful or ugly—what quantity or degree of beauty does it possess? Such are the questions that Lowell, as we shall see, feels that he must ask and attempt to answer. But they are not all. "I believe we should judge a book," he says, "rather by its total effect than by the adequacy of special parts, and is not this effect moral as well as aesthetic?" For, observing that a work of art has effects on man's moral as well as his aesthetic nature, and reasoning, like Aristotle, from effects to causes, Lowell maintains that it possesses ethical qualities, excellent or inferior, and that these ethical qualities must play a coefficient part, along with aesthetic qualities, in the determination of value. By way of illustration he points to the "Chanson de Roland," which is "certainly not to be named with the 'Iliad' for purely literary charms" but is "equipped with the same moral qualities" that we respond to in Homer. To employ again terms I have found useful, we may say that the "Chanson" is distinguished for its *quality* rather than its *quantity* of beauty, whereas the "Iliad" is distinguished for both. Nor does Lowell merely place the two—quality and quantity—side by side as parallel considerations in the criticism of poem or poet; they should be brought into relation in a "comparative criticism" that "teaches us that moral and aesthetic defects are more nearly related than is commonly supposed." It teaches us that "faults of style and of thought" (and, correspondingly, merits) are not fortuitous, but have "their root in character and temperament" and have "their necessary relation to, and dependence on, each other."

Such, then, is Lowell's comprehensive vision of the task of the critic. It involves sensitiveness to impressions, historical understanding, and an aesthetic-ethical judgment. Upon these he bases his placement of the great authors—a habit of his more naïve than dogmatic—ranking Homer, Æschylus, Dante, and Shakespeare as the four supreme poets, and Wordsworth as "fifth in the succession of the great English Poets." Of Donne he said that he "wrote more profound verses than any other English poet save one only"—not telling us whom he meant by the one. It must be admitted that Lowell was a little childish in his love of superlatives. But it must also be admitted (to apply a superlative to Lowell himself) that beneath all his surface caprices lies a literary creed, aesthetic and moral, that is the most representative of man's artistic experience through the ages yet attained in America. This creed has never been given sufficiently serious attention, presumably because Lowell, with his genius for rambling, formulated it only in fragments. It will be our task to put the fragments together.

C. Form and the Ideal

The unifying principle in the artistic and literary creed of Lowell lies in his attempt to use the best ideas offered by the two great critical traditions, the classic and the romantic. His favorite examples, however, he found neither in the ancient world nor in the nineteenth century, but in the Middle Ages and the Renaissance, Dante, Chaucer, Shakespeare, Cervantes, Calderón, and other of the early "moderns."[315]

In one of his essays he assures us that he is not going to renew the Battle of the Books; yet he did repeatedly renew it, fighting sometimes on one side, sometimes on the other, sometimes viewing the battle from the safe vantage-point of a neutral, and giving in the end the impression of a struggle waged inconclusively within his own mind. At one time it is a question of taste, not to be authoritatively settled; at another, it appears that both the ancients and the moderns are necessary, to clarify each other; now it is plain that the moderns have the better of it, giving us examples of form and the grand style in addition to their own special excellences; and again it is just as plain that the ancients are victorious, speaking to us with a clearer voice than that of any living language, through a literature "rammed with life" and "as contemporary with today as with the ears it first enraptured." The key to this confusion in strategy is

---

[315] Such moderns had also been the center of interest to the Schlegel brothers, who presented them as examples of the *romantisch*, of *eine eigentümlich moderne, nicht nach den Mustern des Altertums gebildete Poesie*. To Lowell, however, they were examples of principles that appear in both ancient and modern literature and must appear in all literature that is "classic" in the sense of "best."

doubtless to be found in Lowell's reaction from the tyrannical "formula which prescribed the Greek and Latin Classics as the canonical books of that infallible Church of Culture outside of which there could be no salvation." "I was a great while emancipating myself," he says, from this formula—"indeed, I am not sure that I have wholly emancipated myself even yet" (this as late as 1889). Having the Protestantism of the Protestant religion, Lowell balks at receiving anything on authority; truth itself, on these terms, ranks as superstition. That on the whole he regarded the supremacy of the ancients to be truth is the final impression left by a consideration of the drift of all his passages bearing on the Battle of the Books. Even in his address to the Modern Language Association, as a teacher speaking to teachers, he confides his pleasure that his grandson is "taking kindly to his Homer," for "I had rather he should choose Greek than any modern tongue," a language that taxes the sinews of the climber but leads him at last to the summits; while in favor of the modern languages he merely concedes that it may be prudent to allow them as avenues to literature in the case of minds "of softer fibre, and less eager of emprise" than the commendable grandson aforesaid.

While Lowell with a characteristic inner disunion gave his heart to the older moderns and his head to the ancient Greeks, within the sphere of art his recognition of the supremacy of the Greeks was almost constant. His most serious discontent with their art (stated but once, I believe) is that their tragic agents "seem to be commonly rather types than individuals," wanting "that exquisite analysis of complex motives" which reached its height in Cervantes and Shakespeare; yet while this is so, he observes in the same passage, it is likewise true that the simplicity of Greek tragedy "is by no means that of expression, but of form merely." And in respect to form—"to those laws of grace, of proportion, of design"—he remarks in the same essay (that on Shakespeare, one of his best)—in respect to form, which he holds to be virtually synonymous with art, he asserts that its laws are "more clearly to be deduced from the eminent examples of Greek literature than from any other source." He goes on to say:

It is the Greeks who must furnish us with our standard of comparison. Their stamp is upon all the allowed measures and weights of aesthetic criticism. . . . The model is not there to be copied merely [Lowell repeatedly condemns the modern antique], but that the study of it may lead us insensibly to the same processes of thought by which its purity of outline and harmony of parts were attained, and enable us to feel that strength is consistent with repose, that multiplicity is not abundance, that grace is but a more refined form of power, and that a thought is none the less profound that the limpidity of its expression allows us to measure it at a glance. To be possessed with this conviction gives us at least a determinate point of view, and enables us to appeal a case of taste to a court of final adjudicature, whose decisions are guided by immutable principles.

To the Greeks Lowell was indebted for the principles or qualities that constantly guided his aesthetic criticism: *unity, design, proportion, clearness, economy, power, control, repose, sanity, impersonality*, all of which are involved in the conception of self-subsistent form. Among nineteenth-century English critics we think of Matthew Arnold as almost solitary in urging impressively the claims of form as understood by the Greeks; but Lowell was a more frequent champion, who lacked impressiveness largely because his doctrine on this subject as on all subjects was set forth somewhat in the manner of *obiter dicta*, which is to say that he himself was deplorably wanting in that sense of design that he includes among his immutable principles. He preaches the gospel of form the more strenuously because as Anglo-Saxons "we care nothing about Art," and because romanticism led to a criticism "which regards parts rather than wholes, which dwells on the beauty of passages." Passages, he says, are good only "when they lead to something, when they are necessary parts of the building, but they are not good to dwell in." Thus, Carlyle is an ineffective humorist because of his indifference to form, whereas Cervantes "had been trained to authorship in a school where form predominated over substance, and the most convincing proof of the supremacy of art at the highest period of Greek literature is to be found in Aristophanes." Fine passages do not make fine literature, nor do "admiring italics" constitute criticism. In the pseudo-classical eighteenth century, which had nearly all the classical qualities except *power*, as romanticism later had power but was deficient in the rest, Lowell praised writers like Pope and Gray for keeping alive for us the tradition that writing *was* an art; nor did he hesitate to put in the forefront of one of his definitions of form a term dear to pseudo-classicism but anathema to romanticism, the term "decorum": form, he says, is "the artistic sense of decorum controlling the co-ordination of parts and ensuring their harmonious subservience to a common end." And it was for not keeping decorum that he was all but ready to hang William Wordsworth, acquitting him at last only on the plea of a divine insanity.

When speaking of decorum, Lowell is not thinking of an arbitrary standard of propriety and elegance as the grand master-piece to observe, but of "a higher or organic unity." He makes much of that contrast between organic and mechanical form adumbrated by the ancients and brought to clearness by A. W. Schlegel, Coleridge, and Emerson. Emerson himself he attacks for violating the law of life:

Roots, wood, bark, and leaves singly perfect may be,
But, clapt hodge-podge together, they don't make a tree.

One of Lowell's most explicit statements of the contrast is the following passage, written quite in the manner of Aristotle, on the requirement of organic unity in the drama:

In a play we not only expect a succession of scenes, but that each scene should lead, by a logic more or less stringent, if not to the next, at any rate to something that is to follow, and that all should contribute their fraction of impulse towards the inevitable catastrophe. That is to say, the structure should be organic, with a necessary and harmonious connection and relation of parts, and not merely mechanical, with an arbitrary or haphazard joining of one part to another. It is in the former sense alone that any production can be called a work of art.

This use of a biological analogy, he goes on to remark, legitimately implies a principle of *life* or *soul* in a work of art, and elsewhere he reminds us of the Platonic enthusiasm of Spenser for the idea that "Soul is form, and doth the body make." The thought-and-emotion—the intuition of our latter-day expressionists—grows into bodily form, as in "Hamlet," for example, in which the character of the Prince was "the ovum out of which the whole organism was hatched." From the inner life proceed even the rhythm—whether verse or prose— and the very words themselves. "He who is thoroughly possessed of his thought, who imaginatively conceives an idea or image, becomes master of the word that shall most amply and fitly utter it"—hence it was that Shakespeare was not constrained to blot his manuscripts, his language being not the vehicle of his thought but "its very flesh and blood." It follows that translation is essentially impossible, for we soon discover "not only that there is a best way, but that it is the only way." The line from Pope about wit and nature, while itself, as Lowell might have remarked, a capital instance of organic expression, misrepresents the true concept of form, which "is not a garment, but a body." The creative idea and the form created "cannot be divided without endangering the lives of both." For idea and form, substance and expression, matter and style, meaning and music, thought and word, are not two things but merely two aspects of one thing. We may discover a similar correlation between a writer's experience of life and his artistic product. Behind the product lies, or should lie, the writer's experience, "because nothing that has not been living experience can become living expression"; and behind his personal experience of life, furthermore, there lies "the collective thought, the faith, the desire of a nation or a race," which is "the cumulative result of many ages, is something organic, and is wiser and stronger than any single person, and will make a great statesman or a great poet out of any man who can entirely surrender himself to it." Thus it appears that the organic principle is active in the entire functioning of a poet, from the message given him to communicate to the means of expression; and thus does Lowell repeat, in less mystical language, what we have already found in Emerson.

Form, then, is Lowell's primary criterion of a work of art, sometimes conceived in its structural effect, sometimes in its organic cause. So far he may be termed an Aristotelian, an exponent of the "Poetics" and of romantic critical theory that amplified Aristotle's conception of a work of art as an organism. We may next observe that he again follows Aristotle in requiring not merely organic form but *ideal* form, "that sense of ideal form which made the Greeks masters in art to all succeeding generations." Twice in his essay on Shakespeare he defines art essentially in the Greek way, once as "that ideal representation of the great passions" and elsewhere as "Nature as it is ideally reproduced through the imagination." We are here treading on dangerous ground, inasmuch as modern romanticism, while eagerly availing itself of the words *ideal* and *imagination*, has robbed them of their old meaning without offering a definite new meaning (or, at least, a new meaning that the ancients could have accepted). Other passages in Lowell, however, make it quite clear that his own sense of the ideal is substantially that of the Greeks. He agrees with Aristotle as to the relation of poetry and history, asserting that "the proper object of poetry" is ideal nature, and that history, "far from being ideal," is "still farther from an exclusive interest in those heroic or typical figures which answer all the wants of the epic and the drama." "Do we know as much of any authentic Danish prince as of Hamlet?" "Truth to nature," he concludes, "can be reached ideally, never historically." Again, he agrees with Aristotle as to the relation of the ideal and the actual, when he writes: "The true ideal is not opposed to the real [actual], nor is it any artificial heightening thereof, but lies *in* it"; although in some passages his conception of the ideal is akin rather to Plato's. Here we may pause, for it is to this ideality that Lowell assigns the signal excellencies of not only the Greeks but also the greatest of English poets—it is the secret of Shakespeare's supremacy and permanence.

Precisely what, then, in Lowell's mind, is the relation of the actual, the real, and the ideal? "Am I wrong," he asks, "in using the word *realities?* wrong in insisting on the distinction between the real and the actual? in assuming for the ideal an existence as absolute and self subsistent as that which appeals to our senses, nay, so often cheats them, in the matter of fact?" In the type of writer whom he depreciates as "the so-called realist," we do not find "the facts of life" but merely "the accidental and transitory phenomena" of life. Whereas the Greeks in their tragic art removed everything in some degree from "the plane of the actual and the trivial," showing nothing that "could be met in the streets," "we barbarians, on the other hand, take delight precisely in that. We admire the novels of Trollope and the groups of Rogers because, as we say, they are so *real*, while it is only because they are so matter-of-fact, so exactly on the level with our own trivial and prosaic apprehensions." Even on the occasion of the unveiling of the bust of Fielding, Lowell fully expresses what might be called his conscientious scruples with regard to realism. Fielding, he concedes with damnatory parentheses, "has the merit, what-

ever it may be, of inventing the realistic novel, as it is called";
and for the praise of Fielding he is driven to a contrast between
him and "some French so-called realists for whose title-pages
I should be inclined to borrow an inscription from the old
tavern-signs, 'Entertainment for Man—and Beast.'" For if
Fielding painted vice "as a figure in the social landscape, . . .
he at least does not paint the landscape as a mere background
for the naked nymph," nor does he fail to indicate the consequences of sin upon the fortunes of his characters. In his blunt
way he wrote with a serious moral purpose, and his deficiency
lies rather in his literary creed, which calls for exactitude, not
for truth, the actual, not the real. From the same point of view
Lowell deprecates also the detailed exactitude of "what is called
pre-Raphaelite on canvas and in verse," a mode of art which
gives an "uncomfortable feeling of *costume*" and a merely
cluttered landscape, instead of that sense of reality everywhere
present in a true pre-Raphaelite like Dante.

"The real and abiding facts," then, we are to seek, not as the
realist and naturalist affirm, in the transitory phenomena of life,
but in "those everlasting realities of the mind which seem unreal
only because they lie beyond the horizon of the every-day
world." Not even Spenser, with a Platonism that carries him
far from the actual, transports us to a world of unreality—"it
is only a world of unrealism. It is from pots and pans and
stocks and futile gossip and inch-long politics that he emancipates us." The right use of the actual life surrounding an
author, as the examples of Homer, Dante, Shakespeare, and
Goethe suffice to show in all the great ages of literature, is not
to rest content with depiction of it but to "levy" upon it for
images and illustrations in the service of a higher reality.

Thus, while ideality involves a certain remotion from actuality, it at the same time *uses* the actual by drawing upon it in
order to envisage and represent types of human nature. The
true ideal, we have already quoted Lowell as saying, lies *in* the

actual. To take a crucial instance, that of the poet Chaucer, a
close observer of manners who held the mirror to contemporary
life, we perceive that he "reflected life in its large sense as the
life of *men*, from the knight to the ploughman—the life of every
day as it is made up of that curious compound of human nature
with manners." In contrast with a poet like Crabbe, who
scatters rather than deepens "the impression of reality," and
makes us "feel as if every man were a species by himself," a poet
like Chaucer, "never forgetting the essential sameness of human
nature," gives not only the individuality of each character but
his type, which "will continue contemporary and familiar forever." "So wide," Lowell concludes, "is the difference between
knowing a great many men and that knowledge of human nature
which comes of sympathetic insight and not of observation."
Or, to return to the case of Fielding, we must admit that, great
as was his genius, it was a genius "incapable of that ecstasy of
conception" which "produces figures that are typical without
loss of characteristic individuality, as if they were drawn, not
from what we call real life, but from the very source of life
itself."

D. Imagination

Now, the faculty that perceives the essential type and dis-
engages it from accidental particulars, and then reclothes it with
fitting particulars through an ecstasy of conception, is the imagination. Although the Greeks exemplified this and all other
workings of the faculty of imagination, they did not use the
term itself for any of its higher manifestations. From romantic
theorists, Coleridge most of all, Lowell derived a theory of the
imagination that runs everywhere through his writings. This
was true of Emerson likewise, only whereas Emerson preferred
to speak transcendentally of the Reason (a synonym used
sparingly by Lowell) and suffused his doctrine with not a little
of the Coleridgean moonshine, Lowell made a comparatively
successful effort to lay hold of the term with his Understanding

and to distinguish with clearness and consistency the various offices of Imagination. Noting carefully all his important passages on the subject, we shall discover, I think, no fundamental contradictions of the following summary.

Imagination is a faculty that operates in three ways. First, there is a *spiritual imagination*, a power of intuitive insight indispensable for great art yet not specifically aesthetic; secondly, there is a *plastic imagination*, a creative power of shaping materials into organic unity, which is the primary aesthetic imagination; and thirdly, there is an *expressive imagination*, a power of realizing or representing the parts of the whole, which is the secondary aesthetic imagination.

Imagination is, first of all, "the spiritual eye."[316] Lowell is perhaps quite as insistent as Coleridge and Carlyle and Emerson on the insufficiency of the Understanding, without sharing, however, their inclination to brush it hastily aside. While invariably suspicious of cloud castles, he readily concedes that Coleridge was "a main influence in showing the English mind how it could emancipate itself from the vulgarizing tyranny of common sense, and teaching it to recognize in the imagination an important factor not only in the happiness but in the destiny of man." Thus does he describe the spiritual influence of the stimulating mind that, in "The Friend" and "Aids to Reflection," addressed itself to all that lay deepest and unexpressed in the young men of England and America. In his literary essays, however, Lowell is of course not concerned with the direct use of spiritual imagination, the highest reach of human power, but with its indirect use in literary art. It appears, for instance, in the brave translunary things of Donne that "open vistas for the imagination through the blind wall of the senses," and

[316] According to Coleridge, the Reason, as opposed to the Understanding, is "an organ bearing the same relation to spiritual object . . . as the eye bears to material and contingent *phenomena*." (*The Friend*, 144, ed. Shedd.)

among modern English poets it appears most signally in Wordsworth, who, notwithstanding the most egregious artistic weaknesses, "seems to have caught and fixed forever in immutable grace the most evanescent and intangible of our intuitions, the very ripple-marks on the remotest shores of being." In his enthusiasm for "the incomparable Odes to Duty and on Immortality," Lowell was at one with Emerson and the other Transcendentalists. And yet he could not forget that it was only in height and depth that Wordsworth excelled and not also in breadth, that his was "a piecemeal insight," a receptive or feminine imagination; and consequently he refused to allow him "a place beside the few great poets who exalt men's minds, and give a right direction and safe outlet to their passions through the imagination, while insensibly helping them toward balance of character and serenity of judgment by stimulating their sense of proportion, form, and the nice adjustment of means to ends." He is not with Shakespeare; he is not even with Spenser. He could give us only momentary vistas of that ampler realm which the great poets disclose to us—"not the world of abstraction and nonentity, as some conceive, but a world formed out of chaos by a sense of the beauty that is in man and the earth on which he dwells. It is the realm of Might-be, our haven of refuge from the shortcomings and disillusions of life. It is, to quote Spenser, who knew it well—

'The world's sweet inn from care and wearisome turmoil.'"

Divine glimpses Wordsworth could give us of a world more truly real than the world of appearance, but he had not the masculine, creative energy needed to give shape and clarity to that world and make it habitable. He could not reach to the ultimate effect of idealization, which is the creation of a whole world superior to our own (better, in Aristotle's sense) because freed from embarrassing accident and rendered in its pure type.

Thus, in its ultimate reaches the spiritual imagination can

shape a typical cosmos, an approximation to the type intended by nature. This is the achievement, for example, of Dante, "the highest spiritual nature that has expressed itself in rhythmical form," who "has shown us the way by which that country far beyond the stars may be reached, may become the habitual dwelling-place and fortress of our nature."

But the Ineffable is not alone the goal of the spiritual imagination: it has likewise its less aspiring but invaluable aim of envisaging the constitution of man rather than the secret order of the cosmos, and man in his total humanity rather than pure spirituality. Such is the imagination of Homer and the Greeks generally, and of Shakespeare and Cervantes among the moderns —an humanistic or ethical imagination, dwelling upon the ethos or permanent elements in human nature, which resolves the many men into certain types of man. It is the function of this imagination to mark "the outlines and boundaries of character, not by arbitrary lines drawn at this angle or that, according to the whim of the tracer, but by those mountain-ranges of human nature which divide man from man." Alcestis and Antigone, Hamlet and Cordelia, Don Quixote and Sancho Panza are not persons whom we have seen, but persons whom we might see if we were so fortunate, not persons "who have been," but persons who "might have been." Superior to all such types is the "type of what is highest in human nature"; rising supreme over all mountain-ranges of character is the grand form of the loftiest mountain. Whereas Emerson centers his gaze upon this absolute ideal as seen from the plain of the commonplace, seeking to possess it in ecstatic contemplation, Lowell is content to pursue it by the arduous way that leads from range to range toward the summit. Between men as they are and ideal Man are those many-formed types which constitute the chief substance of enduring literature. Lovers of outlines and boundaries, the Greeks delineated these types, and the comprehensive intellect of Shakespeare, adding an "exquisite analysis of complex motives," revealed them with unexampled truth and variety. If Dante, master of the human soul, showed best the capacities of spiritual imagination, Shakespeare, master of men, excelled all other poets in humanistic or ethical imagination.

Imagination, in these activities, is for Lowell the main instrument in the attainment of understanding of life, and of the happiness that springs from understanding. It was consequently natural for him to tend to measure a work of art by the vitality of its ethical or spiritual insight. This would determine its quality of beauty, and quality, he everywhere implies, is the *final* and highest consideration. Explicitly, however, he insists again and again that the *initial* and inescapable consideration in a work of art is quantity, that is, its degree of beauty rather than its kind, since it is this which determines whether indeed it may be called a work of art at all. Accordingly, his primary criterion, as we have already observed, is that of form. Form being the *sine qua non* of art, Lowell maintains that first among all the functions of the imagination is form-giving. Imagination is from this point of view to be defined as "the faculty that shapes, gives unity of design and balanced gravitation of parts"; it is a faculty that "looks before and after" (connecting beginning, middle, and end, as Aristotle would say); and the seat of this presiding faculty "is in the higher reason"—reason, as Wordsworth phrases it, "in its most exalted mood." Of imagination thus conceived as a shaping or creative faculty, Wordsworth himself was "wholly void," for though he owned a rich quarry he could not build a poem. As his "insight" was "piecemeal," so was his "utterance." Approaching, at his finest, the majesty of Milton, he ever lapsed into the diffuse and commonplace. And not only Wordsworth, foremost of the English romantic poets, but virtually all modern writers in Europe and America, Lowell rated as wanting in this *sine qua non* of art because they neglected the whole in their concern for expressive parts; Matthew Arnold's own indictment of modern poetry is not more sweeping. Not occasionally but in nearly every essay that he wrote, Lowell demands of his subjects that they reveal the presence of "the plastic imagination, the shaping faculty," "that shaping imagination which is the highest [primary, rather] criterion of a poet."

Yet expressive parts are, of course, needed to constitute the whole, and although modern criticism makes too much of them, they must be provided for in an adequate aesthetic. Subordinate to the plastic imagination, then, as means are subordinate to an end, the expressive imagination nevertheless plays an essential rôle. It provides the images, the feelings, the concepts, the rhythms, the words that will fitly represent what the writer wishes to convey. Shakespeare has this excellence with all the rest, finding in that teeming mind of his the vehicle for communicating his every intention. A writer like Carlyle, on the other hand, has the power of expression without the plastic sense, stimulating us endlessly without leading us toward any large and luminous object. Lowell might as well have instanced himself as an example; for assuredly his merit as an artist is the modern merit of brilliant piecemeal insight and utterance, both in his poems and in his essays, and his defect is the absence of the shaping faculty and the higher spiritual imagination that makes a cosmos out of chaos. In his capacity of literary critic, however, he did not rest content, as Poe constantly and Emerson sometimes inclined to do, with the judgment of others in accordance with his own merits and defects, but frankly invoked standards that would depreciate himself along with his contemporaries. This argues a disinterestedness and a breadth as rare as they are admirable.

It remains to say that all these kinds of imagination, spiritual, plastic, and expressive—corresponding nearly with the vision, the faculty divine, and the accomplishment of verse required of the poet by Wordsworth—must be authenticated by other human faculties. Possibly having in mind another phrase of

Wordsworth's, "emotion recollected in tranquillity," Lowell
speaks of profound poetry as "very passion of very soul sobered
by afterthought and embodied in eternal types by imagination."
Before passion is fit to be embodied, it must be worked upon
by the mind in its reflective and contemplative activity, which
deepens and enriches while it tranquillizes, and, melting away
the dross of egoism, begets "that concurring instinct of all the
faculties which is the self-forgetting passion of the entire man."
The essence of this selfless passion is not the superficial excitement of the emotions, nor even the "fine madness" of the soul,
but that "something even finer than that fine madness," viz.,
"the imperturbable sanity" that characterizes the great poets.
This Lowell everywhere insists upon, under a variety of names:
"reserve," "restraint," "sobriety," "repose," and the like.   In
his enthusiasm for imagination, which in his day had only re-
cently been made the central term in literary criticism, and had
not yet fallen into the limbo of the trite where it now dwells
not without hope of restoration, Lowell contrived to maintain
his critical equilibrium by steadily insisting upon the ineluctable
claims of its "less showy and more substantial allies."   "There
must be wisdom," he writes, "as well as wit, sense no less than
imagination, judgment in equal measure with fancy, and the
fiery rocket must be bound fast to the poor wooden stick that
gives it guidance if it would mount and draw all eyes."   The
image, to be sure, is romantically derogatory to the allies,
making them only a poor wooden stick; yet, after all, the stick
that gives guidance is indispensable for right aspiration toward
the heavens.   A more ordinary but juster image appears in the
essay on Percival, whose verse "carries every inch of canvas
that diction and sentiment can crowd, but the craft is leaky, and
we miss that deep-grasping keel of reason which alone can
steady and give direction."   The most enlightening example,
however, is that of Dante, who in his "Vita Nuova" enables
us to see in some sort "how, from being the slave of his imagi-

native faculty, he rose by self-culture and force of will to that mastery of it which is art." For Dante attained the harmony of his faculties, imaginative, moral, and intellectual, essential to his great poetic achievement, and his aspiration toward the heavens was not a flight into the inane but a steady climb "to that supersensual region where the true, the good, and the beautiful blend in the white light of God." Platonist by nature, Aristotelian by training, and the very avatar of the Christian idea, "his feet keep closely to the narrow path of dialectics, because he believed it the safest, while his eyes are fixed on the stars." Allowing no "divorce between the intellect and the soul in its highest sense," he makes "reason and intuition work together to the same end of spiritual perfection." Though of aspiration all compact, he will not, like so many moderns, trust himself to the thin air without guidance, but will follow the leading of reason till it can lead no more:

> What Reason seeth here
> Myself [Virgil] can tell thee; beyond that await
> For Beatrice, since 'tis a work of Faith.

These are lines quoted by Lowell himself; and they may be taken to have expressed for him his conviction that in literature no less than in life the value of imagination, the aspiring and creative power, is determined by its relation to reason, the power of guidance.

E. FUNCTION OF LITERATURE

In the foregoing attempt to summarize with some degree of system Lowell's innumerable brief discussions of form and of imagination, we have repeatedly touched upon but never formulated his position in regard to the immemorial problem of the function of literature. Possibly the problem itself received its final statement in the well-worn words of Horace: Should poetry, should literature, instruct or delight, or instruct and delight at the same time? How did Lowell deal with this question?

His attitude is surprisingly definite and consistent; and it is an attitude that forbids our continuing to set him down as a Puritan whose didacticism was ill concealed with romantic gusto and random insight. We have too often accepted as truth his satiric portrait of himself in "A Fable for Critics," forgetting that it is a portrait of the immature Lowell, still in his twenties, still burdened with the *isms* of his sentimental and Transcendental period, not the Lowell who returned from Europe a few years later with a larger vision of the values of life. There is not only self-condemnation but also prophecy in his recognition that

> The top of the hill he will ne'er come nigh reaching
> Till he learns the distinction 'twixt singing and preaching.

He *saw* the distinction in 1848; he *learned* it a few years later under the tutelage of European experience and an inner compulsion; he exemplified it well enough in the best of his later poetry; and he stated it in its significant nuances in his literary criticism.

"The first duty of the Muse," he says with ample candor, "is to be delightful." While this is not the whole duty of the poet, it is his primary and fundamental obligation, just as the plastic imagination, while not the only kind of imagination, is the first kind that we look for in his work. A poem is an aesthetic, not a moral or intellectual performance; its special concern is with beauty, not with goodness or truth. Lowell plainly enough denounces "that invasion of the aesthetic by the moral" and by the intellectual, "which has confused art by dividing its allegiance." In a passage in which he is apparently combating the didactic tendencies of Arnold's conception of the grand style, of culture, and of the value of poetry, he deplores a recent disposition "to value literature and even poetry for their usefulness as courses of moral philosophy or metaphysics, or as exercises to put and keep the mental muscles in training." Elsewhere, he complains of Wordsworth that he regarded poetry "as an exercise rather of the intellect than as a nepenthe of the imagination." Lowell also tells us that late in life he re-read the whole of the "Arabian Nights" "with as much pleasure as when I was a boy, perhaps with more. For it appears to me that it is the business of all imaginative literature to offer us a sanctuary from the world of the newspapers, in which we have to live, whether we will or no." He thus allows ample room for what he terms "literature as holiday," literature "as a charmer of leisure," literature suited to "our hours of relaxation." He was well aware, like Aristotle long before him, of a merely recreative function of literature; and he was equally well aware, as Aristotle had been, of a higher function, in which the principle of pleasure reappears, so to speak, on a higher plane, in vital relation with moral and intellectual values. It is the function of imaginative literature not only to give mere pleasure ($\pi\rho\grave{o}\varsigma$ $\dot{\eta}\delta o\nu\acute{\eta}\nu$), but also to give rational enjoyment ($\pi\rho\grave{o}\varsigma$ $\delta\iota\alpha\gamma\omega\gamma\acute{\eta}\nu$): not only to give the pleasure of pastime which prepares us for work, but also to give what might better be called happiness, an end and not a means, a serious working of the soul and not a sportive activity. If it is necessary to relate to some tradition Lowell's view of the end of literature, let us refrain from the facile and false assumption that he was a "Puritan" (as was Milton for that matter) and instead label him an "Aristotelian." In a dozen passages he protests, as outspokenly as Poe, against the heresy of the didactic involved in the deliberate teaching of morals through literature—it is gravel in strawberries and cream. The primary object in tragedy, for example, "is not to inculcate a formal moral"; and yet the moral is there, for, "representing life, it teaches, like life, by indirection." From Shakespeare we may no doubt derive many lessons, as he himself very likely realized, "but I do not believe that he

wrote his plays with any such didactic purpose. . . . He did not
mean his great tragedies for scarecrows. . . . He loves the
hawk-nature as well as the hen-nature; and if he is unequaled in
anything, it is in that sunny breadth of view, that impregnability of reason, that looks down on all ranks and conditions of
men, all fortune and misfortune, with the equal eye of the artist."
If this is the morality of the most comprehensive of intellects,
what shall we say of the morality of the highest spiritual nature,
Dante? It is possible to reconcile the "Divine Comedy,"
with the idea that the primary function of art is to delight and
not to teach?

Lowell is exceptionally systematic in his approach to the
answer. A poet, he says, must not be judged historically,
relatively to his age; but absolutely, according to the artistic
qualities of his work and according to the man's genius and his
vision. "We may reckon up pretty exactly," says Lowell, "a
man's advantages and defects as an artist; these he has in common with others, and they are to be measured by a recognized
standard." The quantity of beauty, we might say, can be measured with fair accuracy. But the quality eludes our makeshift
instruments: "there is something in his *genius* that is incalculable." If we compare say Æschylus and Euripides, we cannot but feel that "the latter, though in some respects a better
dramatist, was an infinitely lighter weight. Æschylus stirs
something in us far deeper than the sources of mere pleasurable
excitement." Instead of mere pleasure, he gives us happiness,
rousing that which is "most sacred in us." For "the man
behind the verse is far greater than the verse itself." And so of
Dante: it is not for his purely aesthetic excellence, "but it is for
his power of inspiring and sustaining, it is because they find in
him a spur to noble aims, a secure refuge in that defeat which
the present always seems, that they prize Dante who know and
love him best. He is not merely a great poet, but an influence,
part of the soul's resources in time of trouble." The qualifica-

tion of beauty is here determined by the romantic conception of genius and personality. But in the next paragraph, the culminating one in the long essay on Dante, emphasis shifts from the man to his vision, from the idiosyncratic to the universal. "All great poets have their message to deliver us, from something higher than they. . . . In the company of the epic poets there was a place left for whoever should embody the Christian idea of a triumphant life, outwardly all defeat, inwardly victorious, who should make us partakers of that cup of sorrow in which all are communicants with Christ." And Dante has done this. If the normal method of the poets, even of the great poets, is to teach like life by indirection, nevertheless the high cunning of Dante showed that it is possible to combine "poesy with doctrine" without loss of power in either, but rather enhancement. While Emerson, impatient of the labor of removing the historical barriers to an understanding of the "Divine Comedy," never paid due homage to Dante, but looked to the future for his type of the poet-priest, Lowell by dint of "twenty years of assiduous study" (as he himself tells us) arrived at the conclusion that the type had been for once realized, and not merely foreshadowed, in Dante himself.

If Lowell found his highest happiness in Dante, his debt to some of the "moderns" was not much less. In the more strictly modern ages, from Milton down to his own time, he found, to be sure, nothing that stirred the whole of his nature to passion, and he gave excellent reasons for not being stirred deeply.[317] Toward the ancients, at the other extreme chronologically, his prevailing attitude was one of admiration rather than love, an attitude that would probably not have been reversed if he had bestowed twenty years of study to the Greeks.

---

[317] Most of these reasons have been brought together and interpreted by Harry Hayden Clark in an article on "Lowell's Criticism of Romantic Literature." (*Publications of the Modern Language Association*, XLI [1926], pp. 209–228).

In the halfway moderns, however, above all in Dante, Cervantes, Calderón, and Shakespeare, he found the function of literature achieved with a warmth of energy that kindled his utmost enthusiasm. Conceding the supremacy of the Greeks in respect to form, and consequently in respect to imagination in its plastic activity, he held that the best of the moderns had a sufficient sense of form along with a richness of ethical and spiritual imagination wanting in the ancients. This was true even of Calderón, "with his tropical warmth and vigor of production," who won a place close to Lowell's heart (see, for instance, "The Nightingale in the Study"), but who, because he was *Spanish* rather than broadly human, could not be ranked critically with Cervantes and the others. In "Don Quixote" the imagination of Cervantes is not so much Spanish as "universal and cosmopolitan"; his book is "a *human* book in the fullest sense of the word," next to Shakespeare in innate understanding of human nature, in the power of embodying "generic types rather than individuals," so that "Don Quixote and Sancho, like the men and women of Shakespeare, are the contemporaries of every generation." These two characters, "who together make a complete man," Lowell found specially significant for consideration of latter-day generations of quixotic romanticists, since, as Coleridge has it, DonQuixote is Reason without common sense, while Sancho is common sense without Reason—both are vital to the integrity of man. The criticism of modern romanticism suggested by Cervantes attracted Lowell the more because it was conveyed in a humorous and satiric vein kindred to his own, a vein, moreover, "thoroughly good-natured," unembittered by the experience of life, sweet and fresh despite a large acquaintance with misfortune and disenchantment, as if "the notion of *Weltschmerz*, or the misery of living and acting in this beautiful world," had never occurred to him.

As for Shakespeare "once more"—"that divine apparition known to mortals as Shakespeare," as Lowell styles him even in his late years—the romantic critics were right, he maintains, in regarding him as a great artist, though it is not for his plastic and expressive imagination that we love him, but rather for his serene and comprehensive humanity. Like Chaucer, Shakespeare delights "in the pageantry of the actual world," and, unlike Dante, essentially holds to "the moral of worldly wisdom," so that his genius is human rather than spiritual; and yet he lifted the human to a plane higher than the actual by means of his typifying or idealizing imagination. Men and women as we know them reappear in his plays shorn of all that is accidental and meaningless, and stand revealed as enduring types of what men and women essentially are. Dante, writing an epic on *Man* instead of a man, had left *men* for Shakespeare: and Shakespeare gladly took them for his theme, not chance individuals but broad types of men, creating beneath the summit of Dante and above the plain of everyday humanity a vast plateau region where the air is fresh and clear—"how serene and high he seems," how grandly he rises above "our self-exploiting nineteenth century, with its melancholy liver-complaint"! As free as Cervantes of egoistic *Weltschmerz*, he elevates us to the region of the eternally human, of *das ewig Weibliche* and *das ewig Männliche*. To know Shakespeare is to know life itself, and in that knowledge to be happy. Only the *destiny* of man remains obscure, and for a vision of that we must climb with Dante, as Lowell unweariedly did, toward the summit and the vision beatific.

F. Creed and Personal Traits

And now, finally, we may proceed to formulate succinctly the conception of literary art and its functions that we have studied in the foregoing pages:

Literature is the ideal representation of human nature. Each literary work must have first of all a self-contained form, possess-

ing such qualities as unity, design, proportion, clearness, power, economy, control, repose, sanity, impersonality. This form is organic; that is, the structure is determined from within by the "soul" or animating conception, and the conception in turn is organic, proceeding from the writer's personal experience and cultural heritage. The faculty that images the whole and the necessary and harmonious relation of the parts is the plastic imagination. Form must be not only organic but ideal; that is, it must embody the real that resides in the actual. The faculty that images the ideal is the spiritual imagination. When the spiritual imagination acts in its ordinary capacity, representing the perdurable types of human nature, and in so doing achieves an elevated breadth, it may be termed the humanistic or ethical imagination. When it acts in its extraordinary capacity, revealing the life of the soul itself, and in so doing achieves height if need be at the expense of breadth, it is the ultimate spiritual imagination. Of this ultimate spiritual imagination, two kinds may be distinguished: an inferior kind that expresses momentary intuitions, and a superior kind that transforms the entire chaos of experience into a vision of the cosmos. In all its activities, the imagination must be guided by other human faculties, most of all by reason.

Form determines quantitatively the beauty of a given work of art; spiritual imagination, guided by reason, determines it qualitatively. In the "possible unity" of the greatest degree and the finest kind of beauty, we may conceive of the perfect work of art.

The function of a work of art is to give delight. Of delight there are two general grades: first, the delight of recreation, when the more serious faculties are resting with a view to future working and the sportive faculties are free to confer charm upon leisure; and secondly, the joyful exercise of the higher faculties, or perhaps of all the faculties of mind and spirit working in harmony and so producing happiness rather than mere pleasure. For the fulfillment of both grades of delight, excellence of form is requisite; but the higher grade demands in addition moral or spiritual excellence—

the contagion of a fine personality or the inspiration of an ideal vision of life.

From the test of a summary Lowell's literary creed issues triumphant. If it were possible for us to lay aside our memory of the personality of Lowell and of the weaknesses of his essays, and to concentrate our minds solely upon the system of ideas outlined above, we should certainly be drawn to the conclusion that we have here the sanest and most comprehensive conception of literature formed in America prior to the twentieth century. Laying aside also our twentieth-century predilections (if we have them) for various limited kinds of art denominated realistic, we are bound to admit the impressiveness of a creed that offers justification, at one and the same time, for Æschylus, for Aristophanes, for the "Arabian Nights," for Dante, for Chaucer, for Cervantes, for Shakespeare, for Milton, and for Wordsworth. As Aristotle based his "Poetics" upon the attainment of the writers before his day, so did Lowell seek his principles in the achievement of an immensely rich past. In so doing, moreover, he was saved from vagueness by the soundness of his discrimination, which forbade his accepting as really excellent everything that happened to be historically necessary. It was easy for him, in his romantic age, to reject the claims of the literature of pseudo-classicism; it was not easy but difficult and admirable for him to deplore the drift of romanticism itself: its tendency to sentimentalism rather than true passion, to egoism rather than impersonality, to excitement rather than repose, to unreality rather than a higher reality, to concern for parts rather than for wholes. Nor did he find room for modern realism, arising in his time and still on trial in ours, since in practice it violated his standards of moral truth and made undue concessions to the spirit and method of science. Banishing from his more serious thought pseudo-classicism, romanticism, and realism, he founded his creed upon the examples of classical art and the masterpieces of the Middle Ages and the Renaissance.

Within these ample limits, he had before him virtually all of the greatest writers of Greek, Italian, Spanish, and English literature. Despite his personal lukewarmness toward the ancients, he believed that he must concede their preëminence in the first essentials of art. As the leading humanist of the renaissance of New England, he made it his twofold task to belittle the specious attractions of the recent moderns, and to establish the high claims of those halfway moderns or halfway ancients, from Dante to Milton, whom the American public had not rightly valued. From the romanticism that resounded about him in his early manhood, he derived chiefly a part of his terminology, notably the term "imagination," which he used with romantic frequency and unromantic caution. The result of his entire procedure (doubtless in the main an unconscious one) was a conception of literature that one would find it perilous to assail, unless with the weapons of a skepticism that logically destroys itself along with everything else. Lowell's creed is almost the unwritten constitution of the republic of letters.

Why is it, then, as we acknowledged at the beginning, that the critical essays of Lowell leave an impression of comparative superficiality and futility? The answer is inescapable: it is not his creed that is weak, but the man himself. Lowell is a capital instance of the fact that it is possible to think both rightly and feebly, just as it is possible to think both wrongly and energetically. Most men of distinction do the latter, espousing with fanatical ardor the errors or the half-truths of their age, exploiting the potentialities of the special tendencies everywhere current round them. Heedless of the fact that in the higher interests of humanity truth is not cumulative as in science, they are hoodwinked by the provincialism of their time and easily convinced that their partial truths are the whole truth. Loyal only to their age, they are rewarded by their age, and also by posterity, on the ground that they have made a distinctive contribution. And so they have; though it is a contribution to truth and not truth itself. A small part of the truth they see steadily, but they do not see steadily the whole or even a large portion of the whole. Such men of distinction were Poe and Whitman. On the other hand, there are occasionally a few men who attain distinction through a vital valuation of their own age and a vital revaluation of tradition, a few men who make all truth their province and who have power sufficient to effect a conquest and settlement of a very large part of the truth. The best modern example is Goethe; the best example in American letters is Emerson. Related with this class are many who share the same impulse but who are far less distinguished because they want the power of conquest. Of limited endowment, they lack the vitality which is the first requisite for greatness, and for which no such qualities as sanity and comprehensiveness are really compensatory. They are neither small tyrants, like the first class, nor great leaders, like the second, but useful lieutenants of the great leaders. Such a man was Lowell.

Poet, scholar, teacher, critic, essayist, editor, abolitionist, patriot, ambassador to the Old World; possessing an extraordinary assortment of qualities—sensuousness, emotionality, imagination and fancy, facility of expression, moral earnestness, common sense and logic, wit and humor—Lowell stood forth among his contemporaries because of his accomplished versatility rather than because of high attainment. Once or twice, as in the "Biglow Papers" and the Harvard "Commemoration Ode," he was able to fuse most of his powers in adequate expression, but the rest of the time he was a man of parts, a man of shreds. Capable of growth—more capable than Poe or even Emerson—he was unhappily incapable of self-mastery, no part of his nature being strong enough to force the rest into submission. Nor did he find help in the age in which he lived, which suffered his own difficulties writ large.

N. F.

CHRONOLOGICAL TABLE

1819   Born in Cambridge, February 22.

1838   Could not read in person the class poem he had written for his graduation from Harvard, since he was rusticated to the care of a Concord minister for misdemeanors at college.

1840   Graduated from Harvard Law School.

1841   *A Year's Life and Other Poems.*

1843   Co-editor with Robert Carter of *The Pioneer: A Literary and Critical Magazine*, which was discontinued after three months.

   Poems. Married to Maria White, who was interested in poetry and the anti-slavery cause. Editorial writer for *Pennsylvania Freeman.*

1845   *Conversations on Some of the Old Poets.*

1845–48 Anti-slavery writing. Connected with the *National Anti-Slavery Standard;* corresponding editor, 1848.

1848   *Poems* (2 vols.). *A Fable for Critics. The Biglow Papers,* first series. *The Vision of Sir Launfal.*

1851–52 Traveled in Europe.

1853   Wife died.

1855   Smith professor of the French and Spanish languages and literatures and professor of belles-lettres at Harvard in succession to Longfellow.

1855–56 Studied in Germany and Italy.

1857–61 Editor, *Atlantic Monthly.* Married Frances Dunlap.

1863–72 Joint-editor of the *North American Review* to 1868 with C. E. Norton; 1868–1870 with E. W. Gurney; 1870–1872 with Henry Adams. *Fireside Travels.*

1865   *Ode Recited at the Harvard Commemoration.*

1867   *Biglow Papers,* second series. (These had previously appeared in *Atlantic Monthly,* 1862–1865.)

1868   *Under the Willows.*

1870   *The Cathedral. Among My Books.*

1871   *My Study Windows.*

1872   Resigned professorship.   Third visit to Europe.

1876   *Among My Books*, second series. Delegate to Republican
       Convention.

1877   *Three Memorial Poems.*   Minister to Spain until 1880.

1880–85   Minister to England.

1884   "Democracy," address.

1885   Wife died.   Diplomatic service ended.

1885–90   Four visits to England.

1886   *Democracy and Other Addresses.*

1888   *Heartsease and Rue.   Political Essays.*

1891   Died at Cambridge, on August 12.   *Latest Literary
       Essays and Addresses.*

1892   *The Old English Dramatists.*

BIBLIOGRAPHY

I. BIBLIOGRAPHY

Campbell, Killis. "Bibliographical Notes on Lowell," *University of Texas Bulletin*, Studies in English, No. 4, pp. 115–119 (1924). (To Lowell's list of published writings, Mr. Campbell adds one poem ["Lover's Drink Song"] and four prose pieces. He gives the first place of publication of ten pieces and calls attention to variant versions of six pieces.)

Chamberlain, J. C., and Livingston, L. S. *First Editions of the Writings of James Russell Lowell.* New York: 1914. (A valuable list of items printed as individual volumes, as pamphlets, or in volumes such as annuals. Does not include items which appeared in magazines or newspapers.)

Cooke, G. W. *A Bibliography of James Russell Lowell.* Boston: 1906. (A masterly compilation, indispensable for all serious students because it gives the date and place of first publication of all Lowell's writings, a great many of which are not included in his collected works, and because it lists all notices and criticisms of his work by others to 1906.)

Joyce, H. E. "A Bibliographical Note on James Russell Lowell," *Modern Language Notes*, XXXV, 249–250 (April, 1920). (To the seven known poems by Lowell in *The Pioneer*, Joyce adds "The Poet and Apollo" in the January issue and the "Song" ["Oh Moonlight deep and tender"] in the February issue.)

Scudder, H. E. *James Russell Lowell: A Biography.* Boston: 1901, II, 421–447. (The pages indicated contain a chronological list of Lowell's writings, with date and place of first publication.)

II. TEXT

Writings. Riverside Edition. Boston: 1890. 11 vols. Prose, I–VII; Poems, VII–X; Latest Essays, XI.

Writings. Standard Library Edition. Boston: 1891. 11 vols.
(Printed from plates of the Riverside Edition, with contents
of individual volumes unchanged. Scudder's *Life* in 2 vols.
added in 1902.)

Complete Writings. Elmwood Edition. Boston: 1904. 16
vols. ("This edition varies from the Riverside Edition of
1890 in the retention of the original titles of the volumes of
prose essays."—Publishers' note in Vol. I. Includes *Letters
of Lowell* [3 vols.], and Scudder's *Life* [2 vols.].)

Complete Poetical Works. Household Edition. Boston: 1895.

Complete Poetical Works, ed. by H. E. Scudder. Cambridge
Edition. Boston: 1897, 1917. (Especially valuable for head-
notes, and for chronology of the poems, pp. 481–484.)

Early Prose Writings, with a prefatory note by Dr. Hale . . .
and an introduction by Walter Littlefield. London: 1902.

Conversations on Some Old Poets. 1845. Revised in 1846.
"Third Edition Enlarged," with an introduction by Robert
Ellis Thompson, Philadelphia; 1893.

The Function of the Poet and Other Essays, collected and edited
by Albert Mordell. Boston: 1920. (Early essays and reviews
throwing important light on the growth of Lowell's mind.)

The Round Table. Boston: 1913. (A title given by an anony-
mous editor to a collection of nine of Lowell's reviews not included in his collected works.)

Lectures on the English Poets. Cleveland: 1897. (The Row-
fant Club here reprints from the Boston *Daily Advertiser*
the Lowell Institute lectures given by Lowell in 1855.)

The Anti-Slavery Papers of James Russell Lowell. Boston:
1902. 2 vols. (According to the unsigned introduction,
p. vi: "The two volumes contain more than fifty articles, the
first five being contributed during 1844 to the 'Pennsylvania
Freeman,' the rest, between 1845 and 1850, to the 'National
Anti-Slavery Standard,' of which he was for two of these
years titular associate editor." None of these papers are in
Lowell's collected works. They are indispensable to any full
and just estimate of the growth of his mind and his political
influence.)

Impressions of Spain. Boston: 1899. Compiled from the Diplomatic Correspondence, by J. B. Gilder, with an Introduction by A. A. Adee.

Papers Relating to the Foreign Relations of the United States, 1877–1885. Washington, D.C. (Contains the record of his diplomatic career.)

Last Poems of James Russell Lowell, ed. by C. E. Norton. Boston: 1895. (Two of the ten poems appeared here for the first time.)

Letters of James Russell Lowell, ed. by C. E. Norton. New York: 1894. Norton says, in his editorial note that he has tried to select letters which will give the work "an autobiographic character.")

Letters of James Russell Lowell, ed. by C. E. Norton. Boston: 1904. 3 vols. (Enlarged from the edition of 1894. Norton says in the first volume: "A number of letters, which have come to me since the original edition of this selection of Mr. Lowell's letters was published, are now included in their respective places in these volumes. They add nothing essential to the image of him presented in the former edition, but serve to fill up some minor parts of its outline with details which strengthen the likeness.")

New Letters of James Russell Lowell, ed. by M. A. DeW. Howe. New York: 1932. (These letters, many of them to Lowell's daughter, serve especially to reveal the more intimate and human aspects of the man, but they contribute little to a history of his ideas.)

(It should be noted that, in addition to 181 poems, a considerable body of Lowell's prose pieces remains uncollected. These may be located in the original magazines and newspapers by referring to G. W. Cooke's *Bibliography* and to notes by Campbell and Joyce, above.)

III. BIOGRAPHY AND CRITICISM

Allen, G. W. "Lowell," in *American Prosody,* New York: 1935, pp. 244–270. (A comprehensive and scholarly survey of the meters and stanzaic forms used by Lowell. Finds that his versification introduced into American poetry a freedom involving "a more varied placing of accents and the combination of different kinds of feet to produce a suggestiveness of tone and cadence" tending toward "a greater emphasis of melody and harmony" [pp. 269–270]).

Altick, R. D. "Was Lowell an Historical Critic?" *American Literature*, XIV, 250–259 (Nov., 1942). (Useful assemblage of evidence, showing that "Lowell was actually abreast of, if not a little ahead of, his times," although he did not use the historical method either consistently or with maximum effectiveness. Possibly more counter-evidence should be cited, such as the (V, 167) passage where Lowell says a poet should be "judged" by his poetic qualities "absolutely, with reference, that is, to the highest standard, and not relatively to the fashions and opportunities of the age in which he lived.")

Bail, H. V. "James Russell Lowell's (Commemoration) Ode," *Papers of the Bibliographical Society of America*, XXXVII, 169–202 (Third Quarter, 1943). (Useful assembly of material bearing on circumstances of composition and delivery. Among those who wrote him praising the poem were G. W. Curtis, S. H. Gay, J. F. Clarke, Richard Grant White, E. E. Hale, T. W. Higginson, and H. E. Scudder.) According to Mr. Bail it is "even America's greatest poem—one of the great occasional poems of the world." (p. 190)

Bailey, E. J. "Lowell," in *Religious Thought in the Greater American Poets*. Boston: 1922, pp. 158–182. (A competent general survey. Concludes that Lowell's "attitude toward many important religious ideas may not unjustly be termed . . . nobly pagan," although he had a profound faith in God. "He could not bring himself to feel that the Church and the Bible speak with authority, yet he was far from sneering at the claims of the former or thrusting the latter aside as valueless." [p. 171.] See Shea, below.)

Beatty, R. C. *James Russell Lowell*. Nashville, Tennessee: 1942. (Latest full-length analysis. Regards his literary criticism as "empty or flabby" [p. 188] compared to his political writing, which is appraised from a militantly southern angle. Thinks he "exploited" God and ethics to support the northern "Cause whose issue was piracy," and that he was "a dupe of the most irresponsible propaganda his age afforded." [pp. 164–165.] By trying to summarize each of Lowell's main essays, Mr. Beatty aims to show that "the central facts" about his mind "were its discursiveness, its self-conscious irrelevance, and inner uncertainty, the compulsion of which was always present to disperse his meditations." Stimulating for a fresh, if prejudiced, view of Lowell's writing regarding the South. Documented, and well written.)

Bernard, E. G. "New Light on Lowell as Editor," *New England Quarterly*, X, 337–341 (June, 1937).

Brenner, Rita. "Lowell," in *Twelve American Poets before 1900*. New York: 1933, pp. 199–228. (Mostly biographical: Superficial.

Brooks, Van Wyck. *The Flowering of New England*. New York: 1936, *passim*. (Strangely bitter toward Lowell, who in his second phase embodied much that Brooks thinks he lacked. Weak on documentation and on Lowell's ideas.)

Brownell, W. C. "Lowell," in *American Prose Masters*, New York: 1909, pp. 271–335. (Probably the best of the general critiques on Lowell. The last section deals with his poetry. Brownell concludes that Lowell's poetry "constitutes, on the whole, the most admirable American contribution to the nature poetry of English literature," and that his *Commemoration Ode* "has the elevation of ecstasy and the splendor of the sublime.")

Campbell, Killis. "Lowell's Uncollected Poems," *Publications of the Modern Language Association*, XXXVIII, 933–937 (Dec., 1923). (A valuable study. Concludes that "Lowell acted wisely in rejecting" from his "final collective edition a total of 181 poems that had hitherto been published." Mr. Campbell thinks that the "sheer immaturity" and "diffuseness and an imperfect focus will sufficiently account for the discarding of most of the rejected longer poems of the early forties.")

Campbell, Killis. "Three Notes on Lowell," *Modern Language Notes*, XXXVIII, 121–122 (Feb., 1923). (Identifies a sonnet by Lowell on Charles Dickens, an advance notice of *A Fable for Critics*, and finds Emersonian influence in "The Sphinx," "To Perdita, Singing," "Ode," "The Landlord," "Bibliolatres," and "The Fountain of Youth.")

Chapman, E. M. "The Biglow Papers Fifty Years After," *Yale Review*, n.s., VI, 120–134 (Oct., 1916). (An interesting appreciation, concluding that *The Biglow Papers* are "always humane, shrewd, and right-minded," that they represent "the complex and sometimes contradictory qualities of New England character," and that they are vitally alive today.)

Cheney, J. V. "Lowell," in *That Dome in Air*. Chicago: 1895, pp. 61–90. (A discursive critique. Finds Lowell inferior to Arnold, although the two sowed the same field. Emphasizes Lowell's deficiency in "primal power of construction," "minor points of technics," "music and passion.")

Chrisman, L. H. "Permanent Values in *The Biglow Papers*," in *John Ruskin, Preacher, and Other Essays*. New York: 1921, pp. 163–176. (Concludes that "no other writer has written in dialect lines so pathetically beautiful and enchantingly melodious" [p. 172], that "in the field of satire we have nothing better to show than Lowell's Biglow Papers" [p. 163], that often in a few sentences he packs "whole chapters of social psychology." An interesting and well-written appreciation.)

Clark, H. H. "Lowell's Criticism of Romantic Literature," *Publications of the Modern Language Association*, XLI, 209–228 (March, 1926). (Attempts to show that Lowell's judgments of the romanticists were based on well-considered philosophic and literary principles. Dissents from the view of J. J. Reilly that Lowell was merely an impressionist.)

Clark, H. H. "Lowell—Humanitarian, Nationalist, or Humanist?" *Studies in Philology*, XXVII, 411–441 (July, 1930). (Attempts to show the development of Lowell's mind through three different philosophies. Stresses the need of the genetic approach.)

The Critic, Feb. 23, 1889. (A special number celebrating

Lowell's seventieth birthday. Of many tributes, that by J. H. Morse, picturing Lowell as a teacher, is especially interesting.)

Curtis, G. W. *James Russell Lowell.* New York: 1892. (A memorial address delivered at the Brooklyn Institute.)

DeMille, G. E. "Lowell," in *Literary Criticism in America.* New York: 1931, pp. 49–85. (A reasonably good, readable essay, somewhat unsympathetic to Lowell. Although Mr. DeMille admits that "Foerster has completely and finally demolished" Reilly's view that Lowell had no critical doctrines, he tends to emphasize what he regards as Lowell's inconsistencies and discursiveness.)

Eliot, C. W. "James Russell Lowell as a Professor," *Harvard Graduates' Magazine,* XXVII, 492–497 (June, 1919). (A charmingly written account. Says Lowell's greatest work as a teacher was done in his evening classes in his own library.)

Flower, B. O. "James Russell Lowell as a Poet of Freedom and Human Rights," *Arena,* XLI, 309–317 (March, 1909). (Lowell "justly holds a foremost place among the American poets of freedom and progress" [p. 310]. Emphasizes the influence of Maria White. Although somewhat vague and grandiloquent, the essay is interesting in showing the continuation of appreciation of Lowell as a radical.)

Foerster, Norman. "Lowell," in *Nature in American Literature.* New York: 1923, pp. 143–175. (A survey of Lowell's treatment of various aspects of nature, followed by an analysis of his philosophic reaction to nature-philosophies. Concludes that in spite of "a confusion of mind and heart" colored by the time-spirit, Lowell increasingly came to see, "however fitfully, the futility of an humanitarianism divorced from both the discipline of humanism and the discipline of religion" [p. 175].)

Foerster, Norman. "Lowell," in *American Criticism.* Boston: 1928, pp. 111–156. (Reprinted, with the omission of the last six pages, in the present book, pp. c–cxxxix.)

Fuess, C. M. "Some Forgotten Political Essays by Lowell," *Massachusetts Historical Society Proceedings,* LXII, 3–12

(Oct., 1928). (A description of uncollected essays in the *Atlantic* on "Mr. Buchanan's Administration," April, 1858; "The Pocket-Celebration of the Fourth," Aug., 1858, attacking Choate as a weak compromiser; and "A Sample of Consistency," Nov., 1858, attacking Cushing as a self-seeking traitor to the North.)

Gibbs, Lincoln. "A Brahman's Version of Democracy," *Antioch Review*, I, 50–62 (Spring, 1941). (Praises his native sagacity and idealism, although he lacked training in the social sciences. Denies that he was a snob who distrusted the people.)

Grandgent, C. H. "From Franklin to Lowell. A Century of New England Pronunciation," *Publications of the Modern Language Association*, XIV, 207–239 (1899). (A scholarly article by a great philologist, especially interesting in its analysis of the linguistic aspects of *The Biglow Papers*.)

Grattan, C. H. "Lowell," *American Mercury*, II, 63–69 (May, 1924). (A good example of the bitter attacks made on Lowell by journalistic radicals during the nineteen-twenties. Based partly on a failure to recognize the extent to which Lowell's thought developed as he grew older.)

Greenslet, Ferris. *James Russell Lowell*. Boston: 1905. American Men of Letters Series. (A good brief biography. Chapter VII, pp. 245–265, deals with "Lowell's Poetry.")

Grubb, Edward. "The Socialism of James Russell Lowell," *New England Magazine*, n.s., VI, 676–678 (July, 1892). (An able article. Concludes, on the basis of convincing evidence, that Lowell was an adherent of socialism when the word is defined as "the practical application of Christianity to life" but that in the political sense of the word he was in no way a socialist.)

Hale, E. E., Jr. *James Russell Lowell and His Friends*. Boston: 1899. (Valuable for personal reminiscences.)

Hale, E. E., Jr. *James Russell Lowell*. Beacon Biographies Series. Boston: 1899. (Very brief.)

Hart, J. M. "James Russell Lowell," *Publications of the Modern Language Association*, VII, 25–31 (1892). (An obituary essay, paying tribute to Lowell as "a truly representative American scholar" worthy of serving "as our model" because "his culture was the broadest and richest that our people has yet exhibited." Lowell was the first president of the Association.)

Harte, Bret. "A Few Words about Mr. Lowell," *New Review*, V, 193–201 (Sept., 1891). (A sensitive and charming appreciation of Lowell's many-sided genius.)

Hatfield, J. T. *Addresses Delivered at the Lowell Commemoration Held in the Architektenhaus*, Berlin, Feb. 19, 1891. (Mr. Hatfield's address, pp. 11–28, although general and brief, is rich, many-sided, deeply appreciative, and aptly illustrated. Brief addresses by Alois Brandl and by Herman Grimm are also printed in this volume, pp. 5–7 and pp. 8–10.)

Heil, J. A. "*Die Volkssprache im Nordosten der Vereinigten Staaten von Amerika, dargestellt auf Grund der Biglow Papers von James Russell Lowell*," in *Giessener Beiträge zur Erforschung der Sprache und Kultur Englands und Nordamerikas*. Breslau, 1927. III, No. 2, 205–311. (A. G. Kennedy, reviewing this work in *American Speech* [III, 426–427, June, 1928], concludes that Heil offers a careful study of the New England dialect by classification and comparison of sounds, inflections, and syntactical peculiarities, and that his comparisons with forms from Middle English lend dignity to Biglow's words as part of the historical development of the English language. Mr. Kennedy indicates frequent textual errors and misprints in Heil's work.)

Henry, H. T. "James Russell Lowell's Moral Intuitions," *Catholic Educational Review*, XXII, 6–17 (Jan., 1924).

Henry, H. T. "Religious Intimations in the Writings of James Russell Lowell," *Catholic Educational Review*, XXI, 398–408 (Sept., 1923).

Henry, H. T. "Music in Lowell's Prose and Verse," *Musical Quarterly*, XXIV, 546–572 (Oct., 1924). (An interesting survey of Lowell's allusions to music, concluding: "in no other writer of any generation who has not written professedly on musical topics, will so many musical ideas and expressions

be found" [p. 572]. Shows that he thought a sense of harmony and a knowledge of music essential to a poet, and that
as a critic he included musical harmony among his criteria in
appraising the poetry of others. This preliminary study
could be much further developed.)

Hicks, Granville. *The Great Tradition. An Interpretation of
American Literature since the Civil War*. New York: 1933.
(A representative and undocumented Marxian attack on
Lowell, pp. 13–20. "To the development of American
literature he contributed almost nothing . . . He made not
the slightest effort to understand the peculiar conditions
under which American writers were working, and did nothing, either by example or counsel, to help the men who were
trying to understand them" [p. 17].)

Howe, M. A. DeW. "Lowell," in *Dictionary of American
Biography*. New York: 1933, XI, 458–464. (The best brief,
up-to-date biography.)

Howells, W. D. "Studies of Lowell," in *Literary Friends and
Acquaintance*. New York: 1900, pp. 212–250. (Invaluable
and charmingly written testimony by a friend regarding
Lowell's tolerance, kindliness, and magnanimity toward a
realist and a socialist. Probably the most vivid presentation
available of Lowell in his habit as he lived. Howells was in-
strumental in having Hayes appoint Lowell minister to Spain,
and he has many interesting comments on his political views.
He concludes that, of all the great men of that period, "Lowell
was of the richest nature I have known.") See also Howells'
comment in *Atlantic Monthly*, XXXIX, 93 ff., (Jan. 1877);
Scribner's Magazine, XXVIII, 363 ff., (Sept. 1900); *Current
Literature*, XXX, 48 ff., (Jan. 1901).

Hudson, W. H. *Lowell and His Poetry*. London: 1914. (A
discursive English view, dealing successively through
Lowell's poetry with his love for Maria White, his nature interests, his patriotism, his academic interests, and his religion.)

James, Henry. "James Russell Lowell," in *Essays in London
and Elsewhere*. New York: 1893, pp. 44–80. (A charming
essay, by a friend, based partly on conversations with Lowell

in London and emphasizing his passionate devotion to America and the republican ideal.)

Jameson, J. F. "Lowell and Public Affairs," *Review of Reviews*, IV, 287–291 (Oct., 1891). (A brief but very judicious survey of an important subject by a distinguished historian. Concludes that as a poet Lowell's "best inspiration was derived from passionate interest in public affairs," as illustrated in *The Biglow Papers* and the *Commemoration Ode*. Finds the former "the best political satires the present century has produced," being comparable to the work of Swift, Dryden, and Butler. "None has ever enjoyed a more brilliant reception" as ambassador to England. Pays high tribute to Lowell as representative of the idealistic man of thought "devoted to the good of the commonwealth," and deplores the growing divergence between traditional idealism and politics. This essay is followed by one by C. T. Winchester on "Lowell as a Man of Letters," one by R. D. Jones on "Lowell and the Public Schools," one by W. T. Stead on "Lowell's Message, and How It Helped Me," and one by Raymond Blathwayt on "A Last Interview.")

Jenkins, W. G. "Lowell's Criteria of Political Values," *New England Quarterly*, VII, 115–141 (March, 1934). (A carefully documented, comprehensive survey supplementing Jameson's study above. Concludes, "To realize the fact that Lowell's political thought was based on moral ideas is of prime importance. The progress in which he believed was a progress toward moral improvement. . . . Increasingly ever as he grew older did he refer to this past as a storehouse of experience and knowledge. Just here was the importance of the statesman as he saw it: he must know the value of the past and should be able to determine the general trend of his people and endeavor to direct opinion toward conformity with ethics" [pp. 140–141]. Although this study may not make quite enough allowance for Lowell's change of opinions as he grew older, it is of fundamental importance.)

Killheffer, Marie. "A Comparison of the Dialect of the 'Biglow Papers' with the Dialect of Four Yankee Plays,"

American Speech, III, 222–236 (Feb., 1928). (The plays are Royall Tyler's *The Contrast*, 1787, David Humphreys's *The Yankey in England*, 1815, Joseph Jones's *The People's Lawyer*, 1839, and Denman Thompson's *The Old Homestead*, 1886. Compared with these authors, Lowell used a higher percentage of low colloquials along with picturesque compounds and phrasings, and he approached dialect from a scientific angle, although he was more concerned with the written than with the spoken word. A scholarly study.)

Kreymborg, Alfred. "The Poet of Too Many Isms," in *Our Singing Strength*. New York: 1929, pp. 116–133. (An interesting impressionistic survey, somewhat condescending. Conventional stress on Lowell's eccentricities, versatility, and his inability to give his poems "the final finish to make them endure.")

Lange, Alexis F. "James Russell Lowell as a Critic," *California University Chronicle*, VIII, 352–364 (1906). (Deals with Lowell's canons of criticism. Thinks his qualifications as interpreter equal to those of Arnold. According to Lowell's "working creed for criticism," literature was purely an "expression of human experience" and "the books . . . always stood for the writers" [p. 355]. He did not neglect artistic form, but viewed it as organic, as "the living thought creating its embodiment" [p. 357]. See Foerster above.)

Lawton, W. C. *The New England Poets*. New York: 1898. (Commonplace.)

Literary World, XVI, 217–226 (June 27, 1885). (A "Lowell Number.")

Lockwood, Ferris. "Mr. Lowell on Art-Principles," *Scribner's Magazine*, XV, 186–189 (Feb., 1894). (A penetrating, succinct, and well-documented exposition of the basis of Lowell's poetry and criticism: his doctrine that the artist must select materials from actual life which are to be "ideally reproduced through the imagination," which not only shapes them into unity of design but inspires style, "a sense of indefinable completeness." Lockwood says these principles "come with especial authority from one who, while he will always stand in the front rank as a critic, was at the same time greater still as an artist" [p. 189].)

Lovett, R. M. "Lowell," in *American Writers on American Literature*, ed. by John Macy. New York: 1931, pp. 177–189. (A felicitous essay, with apt quotations, praising Lowell's early radicalism, and contrasting Concord to Cambridge culture at the expense of the latter. Mr. Lovett's view that Lowell "had no passion for ideas" [p. 186] in his criticism, that he was as critic "nearer to Charles Lamb than to Coleridge or Matthew Arnold" [p. 187], and that his later mature development represented merely a "stiffening of mind and hardening of heart" [p. 188] would seem to require much modification in the light of evidence presented by Foerster and others.)

Low, Sidney. "Lowell and His Poetry," *Fortnightly Review*, LVI, 310–324 (Sept. 1, 1891). (One of the best of the earlier general critiques. Stresses Lowell's New England Calvinism and his didacticism.)

Mabie, H. W. "Lowell's Letters," in *My Study Fire* (Second Series, New York: 1894), pp. 79–85. (Appreciative comment by one of Lowell's more sentimental followers.)

Macy, John. "Lowell," in *The Spirit of American Literature*. New York: 1908. (A spirited and radical nationalist praises *The Biglow Papers* and Lowell's other early radical utterances, and thinks that after 1880 he became "a mere literary man" and "degenerated into a polite conservative statesman." Macy thinks the merits of his prose are "its humanity, audacity, colloquial ease"; its defects, "his amateurishness, capricious responsibility." He says of Lowell's nationalistic *Political Essays*, "no one of the time has left us a better volume of its kind.")

Mead, E. D. "Lowell's *Pioneer*," *New England Magazine*, n.s., V, 235–258 (Oct., 1891).

Mims, Edwin. "Lowell as a Citizen," *South Atlantic Quarterly*, I, 27–40 (Jan., 1902). (An intelligent and sympathetic essay. Unlike the radicals, Mr. Mims sees that one of Lowell's best qualities as a citizen was "his ability to change as conditions changed" [p. 36]. His political writings were not those "of an eager-hearted, narrow reformer, but of a wise, practical statesman—who seemed to have many of the qualities of his hero [Lincoln]—the 'good sense, the good humor, the sagacity, the large-mindedness, and the unselfish honesty'" [p. 36]. "It was his belief that in a democracy every man must do what he can to create right public sentiment" [p. 27].)

Moulton, C. W. *Library of Literary Criticism*. Buffalo: 1905. VIII, 17–42. (Useful assembly of excerpts from criticisms of Lowell enabling one to trace the history of his reputation.)

Nichols, E. J. "Identification of Characters in Lowell's 'A Fable for Critics,'" *American Literature*, IV, 191–194 (May, 1932). (Would substitute Thoreau and Channing for two blanks in "A Fable.")

Norton, C. E. "James Russell Lowell," *Harper's Magazine*, LXXXVI, 846–857 (May, 1893). (By Lowell's closest friend.)

Nye, Russel. "Lowell and American Speech," *Philological Quarterly*, XVII, 249–256 (1939). (Able analysis of his early defence and use of dialect and then his later turn to universality.)

Odgen, R. *Life and Letters of E. L. Godkin*. New York: 1907. 2 vols. (II, 70–95, contain important correspondence with Lowell.)

Palmer, Ray. "James Russell Lowell and Modern Literary Criticism," *International Review*, IV, 264–281 (March, 1877). (A review of Lowell's *Among My Books*, both series, this is by far the ablest of the early essays on Lowell as critic. In contrast to most contemporary critics, with whom Mr. Palmer compares Lowell, he finds him unique in his fruitful harmonizing of historical, interpretative, and judicial criticism. His essays contain "scholarly accuracy, . . . keenness of perception, . . . comprehensiveness of knowledge . . . esthetic culture, . . . impartial judgment, together with the power of expressing the nicest shades of thought" [p. 267]. He has "attained to a high ideal of what the work of criticism properly involves" [p. 269].)

Parrington, V. L. "Lowell, Cambridge Brahmin," in *The Romantic Revolution in America*. New York: 1927, pp. 460–472. (A prejudiced but stimulating interpretation by a radical economic determinist. Repeats the conventional charge that Lowell showed an "inveterate unwillingness to think. He never speculated widely or analyzed critically. Ideas, systems of thought, intellectual and social movements, he had no interest in; he was content to remain a bookish amateur in letters . . . History remained a blank to him" [p. 461]. For different views supported by evidence, see Foerster, Jenkins, Pritchard, and Clark.)

Parsons, E. S. "Lowell's Conception of Poetry," *Colorado College Publications*, Language Series, II, 67–84 (Sept., 1908). (An able and sympathetic interpretation, well buttressed by evidence.)

Perry, Bliss. "Lowell," in *The Praise of Folly and Other Papers*. Boston: 1923, pp. 130–150. (An appreciative survey, delightfully written. Emphasizes Lowell's distinction as "an inheritor and an enricher of the Great Tradition," devoted to "the common interests of all" and to "civic responsibility.")

Pettigrew, R. C. "Lowell's Criticism of Milton," *American Literature*, III, 457–464 (Jan., 1932). (A scholarly article, concluding that, while Lowell offers a "really excellent discussion of Milton's metrics," his utterances on Milton in general [Lowell's *Works*, IV, 58–117, and VII, 94–110] reveal him "as one whose critical powers are largely impressionistic," largely devoted in this case to kindling our enthusiasm.)

Phelps, W. L. "Lowell," in *Howells, James, Bryant, and Other Essays*. New York: 1924, pp. 96–122. (Discursive and appreciative.)

Poe, E. A. "Poems of Lowell," *Graham's Magazine*, XXIV, 142–143 (March, 1844); and "A Fable for Critics," *Southern Literary Messenger* (March, 1849). The first is reprinted in Poe's *Complete Works*, edited by J. A. Harrison, XI, 243–249; the second in *ibid.*, XIII, 165–175. (In the review mentioned, Poe praises "The Legend of Brittany" as one of our best poems. In the second he was prejudiced because Lowell was "one of the most rabid of the Abolitionist fanatics" and because he had characterized Poe as "two fifths sheer fudge." Attacks *A Fable* as "essentially 'loose'—ill-conceived and feebly executed as well in detail as in general," as wanting "artistic finish . . . especially in its versification," and as malevolent, especially toward Margaret Fuller. Yet he concludes that Lowell and Longfellow are "upon the whole, perhaps our best" poets. A very sharp and influential essay by a shrewd critic.)

Pollak, Gustav. "Lowell: Patriot and Cosmopolitan," in *International Perspective in Criticism: Goethe, Grillparzer, Sainte-Beuve, Lowell*. New York: 1914, pp. 58–83. (Compares the views of the four critics regarding the same authors. An important study, concluding that Lowell ranks favorably with the critics named and that "his outlook on life and literature was that of the serene philosopher and the cosmopolitan critic" [p. 59].)

Pollak, Gustav. "Lowell: Patriot and Cosmopolitan," in *International Minds and the Search for the Restful*. New York: 1919, pp. 68–80.

Pound, Louise. "Lowell's 'Breton Legend,'" *American Literature*, XII, 348–350 (1940). (Suggests Emile Souvestre as source for "Washers of the Shroud.")

Pritchard, J. P. "Lowell's Debt to Horace's *Ars Poetica*," *American Literature*, III, 259–276 (November, 1931). (A valuable scholarly study casting much light on Lowell's literary theory and its kinship with that of classicism. Lowell referred intelligently to Horace's *Ars Poetica* throughout life. The two theorizers agreed that poetry should give profitable pleasure; that it springs from genius and careful study, from knowledge of men supplementing knowledge of books. They agreed that a poet should await inspiration; should select and combine materials to achieve unity of effect; should accept originality as a fresh vision of the familiar; should carefully attend to criticism and to execution. They agreed as to the need of attention to diction and metre and the need of guarding against the prosaic and the temptation to be unworthily popular for the moment by disregarding the rules based on the unity of memory and taste common to the centuries.)

Pritchard, J. P. "Aristotle's *Poetics* and Certain American Literary Critics," *Classical Weekly*, XXVII, 81–85; 89–93; 97–99 (1934). (The critics are Poe, Lowell, and Stedman. Lowell is treated in the issue for Jan. 15, 1934, pp. 89–93. An able classical scholar here gives a fine, documented analysis of Lowell's references and probable debt to Aristotle. Shows his deep interest and "first-hand information"; concludes that his critical position is "based largely upon his knowledge of the principles advocated by Aristotle in the *Poetics*, and his adherence to them." These two valuable studies by Pritchard supplement and reinforce the interpretation by Foerster. See also Pritchard's *Return to the Fountains*. Durham, N.C.: 1942, pp. 99–118, and *passim*.)

Quayle, W. A. *Modern Poets and Christian Teaching: Lowell*. New York: 1906. (Somewhat vague and fanatical chapters on Lowell's relation to Christianity, the moral atmosphere, love, and humor shown in his work. The best chapter is XII, dealing with "The Cathedral." Concludes that Lowell "lacked the divine, contagious faith . . . and did not know that Christ was God" [p. 155]. See Bailey, Shea, and Strong.)

Reilly, J. J. *James Russell Lowell as a Critic*. New York: 1915. (An extensive, elaborately documented, but prejudiced book, with bibliography. Chapters on the man and writer; his range of knowledge; the breadth and limitations of his sympathy; relation to the judicial attitude; penetration; type of mind; the critic and his criticism. Concludes, "If Lowell is to survive, it must be frankly as an impressionist. For so far as criticism approaches a science, so far as it depends to any serious extent on ultimate principles, so far, in a word, as it is something more fundamental and abiding than the *ipse dixit* of an appreciator, Lowell is not a critic" [p. 214]. While Foerster is now generally regarded as having presented evidence of Lowell's advocacy and practice of judicial criticism which refutes Reilly's conclusion, this book nevertheless contains much that is of value along the way.)

Review of "The Biglow Papers," *New Englander*, o.s., VII, 63–72 (1849). (Appreciative. Says that twenty years hence the dialect will seem to readers "more expressive than the most courtly English.")

Rice, Wallace. "Lowell on Human Liberty," *Dial*, XXXIV, 14–16 (January 1, 1903). (An interesting review of Lowell's *Anti-Slavery Papers*. Concludes that "The theme of the collection is something greatly broader and deeper than the mere abolition of chattel slavery in the southern United States", that it can be applied to any nation in any age.)

Roberts, R. E. "James Russell Lowell: A British Estimate," *Living Age*, CCCI, 231–235 (April 26, 1919). (Reprinted from the London *Bookman*, LV, 185–187, March, 1919. An unbiased, sane and richly appreciative essay showing that the British loved Lowell chiefly because they thought him spiritually "healthy." Although much of Lowell's poetry was anti-British and democratic, this British critic says Lowell's place in British affections depends wholly on his poetry and its sense of brotherhood and political equality. Compares him to Dickens and Lamb in his humanity. Praises him as a critic for his breadth of sympathy, quick insight, commonsense, and generous enthusiasm for beauty and honor.)

Robertson, J. M. "Lowell as a Critic," *North American Review*, CCIX, 246–262 (Feb., 1919). (Starts out to refute Reilly's conclusion that "Lowell is not 'a critic,'" then comes to a rather lame and partial agreement. Claims that criticism is also creation, that "Lowell 'creates' . . . getting his impressions less judicially, more spontaneously, trusting his 'intuitions' until further knowledge moves him tacitly to discard them" [p. 255]. "Impressionist and 'expressionist,' his function was to expatiate, not to compare notes, or to reason reciprocally" [p. 257]. A rather disappointing essay.)

Savage, Rev. M. J. "The Religion of Lowell's Poems," *Arena*, IX, 705–722 (May, 1894). (Appreciative but vague. Superseded by Bailey, Shea, Strong, and Voigt.)

Scudder, H. E. *James Russell Lowell: A Biography*. Boston: 1901. 2 vols. (This is the most extensive biography—a competent conservative work. For his political interests see especially "In the Anti-Slavery Ranks," I, 151–237; "Lowell and the War for the Union," II, 1–73; "Politics," II, 185–220; "The Spanish Mission," II, 221–258; "The English Mission," II, 259–321. Reviewed in *Atlantic Monthly*, LXXXIX, 253–264 [Feb., 1902.]; by W. M. Payne, *Dial*, XXXI, 312 ff., [Nov. 1, 1901]; by J. W. Chadwick, *Nation*, LXXIII, 416 ff. [Nov. 28, 1901]; *The Critic*, XL, 121 ff. [Feb., 1902].)

Scudder, H. E. "Mr. Lowell as a Teacher," *Scribner's Magazine*, X, 645–649 (Nov., 1891). (See also Eliot and Wendell.)

Shea, L. M. *Lowell's Religious Outlook*. Washington, D.C.: 1926. (A scholarly dissertation done at The Catholic University of America and distinguished for precision, elaborate documentation, and detachment. Includes analysis of Lowell's view of God, providence, immortality, and science. The best treatment of the subject, although to be supplemented in parts by Bailey and Strong.)

Smalley, G. W. "Mr. Lowell in England," *Harper's*, XCII, 788–801 (April, 1896).

Smith, Bernard. *Forces in American Criticism*. New York: 1939, pp. 235–242, *passim*. (This leading Marxist critic claims that after abolition Lowell "lost most of his intellectual contacts with the world in which the mass of mankind worked and fought" and that he knew "nothing" of Darwin [p. 238]. See present Introduction on Lowell vs. Howells and Darwinism, pp. lxxviii–xcii.)

Smith, F. D. "Mr. Wilbur's Posthumous Macaronics," *Quarterly Journal of the University of North Dakota*, X, 436–443 (1920). (A scholarly analysis of No. VIII of the second series of *The Biglow Papers*.)

Stedman, E. C. "James Russell Lowell," in *Poets of America*. Boston: 1885, pp. 304–348. (A comprehensive general essay, considering Lowell as our "representative man of letters" devoted to culture, to idealism, to the republican idea, and to catholicity of taste. Finds that his "irregular ear" occasionally left "technical blemishes" in his poems, and that his fine passages are not infrequently marred by "odd conceits, mixed metaphors, and licenses . . ." Concludes that he is "a poet who is our most brilliant and learned critic, and . . . has given us our best native idyll, our best and most complete work in dialectic verse, and the noblest heroic ode that America has produced,—each and all ranking with the first of their kinds in English literature of the modern time" [pp. 347–348]. A judicious and influential essay.)

Strong, A. H. "James Russell Lowell," in *American Poets and Their Theology*. Philadelphia: 1916, pp. 265–317. (Although somewhat garrulous, didactic, and confessedly partisan, Strong's work is of value because he supports his conclusions with considerable evidence, and it serves as a partial supplement to "economic" interpretations. Views Lowell as distinctively our chief poetical moralist, whose ethics vitalized his patriotism and his criticism. As a Calvinist, Strong finds Lowell's chief "error" [p. 297] in his ignoring "man's sin and perversity" and his disregard for a miraculous revelation of a transcendent God. Attacks Lowell's humanistic idea in "The Cathedral" that each man is able to redeem himself in the light of divine perfection inwardly revealed, and that Christ is not divine but one of many admirable traditional guides. Yet Strong admits that "the good in his poetry rests on an inherited Christian faith." Probably in his later work on Puritanism and Dante Lowell recognized the conflict between good and evil within the individual much more than Strong indicates.)

Swift, Lindsay. "Our Literary Diplomats: Part IV," *Book-Buyer*, n.s., XXI, 90–98 (Sept., 1900). (A rather general and superficial review of Lowell's diplomatic career. Concludes that he "performed all of . . .[the] exactions according to his lights, which were excellent.")

Tandy, Jeannette. "The Biglow Papers," in *Crackerbox Philosophers in American Humor and Satire*. New York: 1925, pp. 43–64. (An admirable scholarly study. "Lowell's range and penetration in satirical portraiture are unsurpassed in

America." Interesting proof that the supposed academic eastern snob was a pioneer and master in a field in which the West and South are popularly supposed to have had a monopoly—in the humorous and dialectical presentation of the common man.)

Taylor, Bayard. "Lowell," in *Critical Essays and Literary Notes*. New York: 1880, pp. 298–301. (Brief but discriminating appreciation by a fellow poet. "No one of our poets shows a richer or wider range of thought than Mr. Lowell: no one a greater variety of expression in verse." Yet he "seems hostile to that quality which compels each conception to shape itself into clear symmetry." Concludes that "The Cathedral" best represents Lowell's virtues and vices.)

Thayer, W. R. "James Russell Lowell as a Teacher: Recollections of His Last Pupil," *Scribner's Magazine*, LXVIII, 473–480 (Oct., 1920). (An interesting account of Lowell's methods as a teacher, by one of his former students.)

Thorndike, A. H. "Lowell," in *The Cambridge History of American Literature*. New York: 1918, II, 245–257. (A brief but judicious survey, emphasizing Lowell's great function as a critic in teaching "a new people to guide their steps by the great men and the great ideas of the past.")

Traill, H. D. "Mr. J. R. Lowell," *Fortnightly Review*, n.s., XXXVIII, 79–89 (July, 1885). (An amusing and excellent appreciation by a representative English critic. Discusses "the homage so effusively paid to him . . . by his English admirers," and concludes that "the contrast . . . between a somewhat far-fetched thought and its nobly simple expression . . . is the *ism* which really prevented him from scaling Parnassus" [p. 85–86].)

Traubel, H. L. "Lowell—Whitman: A Contrast," *Poet-Lore*, IV, 22–31 (Jan. 15, 1892). (An ardent champion of Whitman disparages Lowell as a critical and scholarly "conservator" who "ploughs along accomplished ways," while Whitman is a "creator" with "vital pluck out of nature's heart; . . . in his soul are illuminating fires, hot with the glow of immortal meaning." See also Portia Barker, "Walt Whitman and

The Atlantic Monthly," *American Literature,* VI, 283–301, especially pp. 287–288.)

Underwood, F. H. *James Russell Lowell: A Biographical Sketch.* Boston: 1882.

Underwood, F. H. *The Poet and the Man: Recollections and Appreciations of James Russell Lowell.* Boston: 1893.

Voigt, G. P. "Lowell," in *The Religious and Ethical Element in the Major American Poets.* Bulletin of the University of South Carolina, The Graduate School, June 1, 1925, pp. 100–123. (Generally judicious, especially in his recognition that Lowell "felt an increasingly strong inclination towards some of the doctrines of Calvinism" [p. 104], such as predestination, the sovereignty of God, and the moral earnestness of the Puritans, although he abandoned some of their other beliefs such as that in original sin. Supplements Bailey and Strong.)

Voss, A. W. M. "The Evolution of Lowell's 'The Courtin,'" *American Literature,* XV, 42–50 (1943). (Good study of sources and date of each stanza.)

Warren, Austin. "Lowell on Thoreau," *Studies in Philology* XXVII, 442–461 (July, 1930). (An exhaustive and judicious study of the development of Lowell's hostile attitude towards Thoreau and a statement of the points at final issue between the two men. Throws important light on a transitional period in Lowell's critical thought and practice.)

Watson, William. "Lowell as a Critic," in *Excursions in Criticism.* London: 1893, pp. 89–96. (An appreciative and shrewd English view; brief and discursive. Lowell is America's "most brilliant 'all-around' literary representative." His critical prose is "the product of judgment aërated by wit." His "forte is profusion, and his foible prodigality"; his criticism is "delightfully fresh and tonic, with a certain saline shrewdness in it," and his direct method is "picturesque and robust.")

Weber, C. J. "Lowell: Poet and Friendly Critic," *Colby Library Quarterly,* I, 19–23 (1943). (Letters to his niece, published from MSS.)

Wendell, Barrett. "Mr. Lowell as a Teacher," in *Stelligeri and*

Other Essays Concerning America. New York: 1893, pp. 205–217. (Himself a great teacher, Wendell, one of Lowell's former students, charmingly describes his methods and concludes that he was "the most inspiring teacher I had ever had" [p. 217].)

Werner, Dorothy L. *The Idea of Union in American Verse (1776–1876).* Philadelphia: 1932. (A dissertation done at the University of Pennsylvania. See index for many references to Lowell's political poems. A valuable compilation and discussion.)

White, W. "Two Versions of Lowell's 'Function of the Poet,'" *Philological Quarterly,* XX, 587–596 (1941). (Revision shows a "calmer evaluation of the devastating effect of the new science upon the old humanities" and "a more humanistic view than nationalism permits of.")

Wilkinson, W. C. "Mr. Lowell's Poetry," "Mr. Lowell's 'Cathedral,'" and "Mr. Lowell's Prose," in *A Free Lance in the Field of Life and Letters.* New York: 1874, pp. 50–183. (Remarkably sharp judicial criticism, finely detailed, by a critic of classical bias. Thinks that "The Vision of Sir Launfal" shows Lowell's "most perfect felicity" [p. 64], and that "The Commemoration Ode" is among the few "greatest odes in the English language" [p. 67]. In general, however, Wilkinson censures Lowell's *"want of firm and harmonious tone"* [p. 113] as well as his "remarkable incoherencies and inconsistencies." Finds him "in the noblest sense conservative," and thinks that "Puritanism might almost have made Mr. Lowell a lesser Milton" [p. 89]. While Wilkinson attacks "The Cathedral" especially, he thinks that "Mr. Lowell is primarily a poet" [p. 150], and he belittles his criticism, especially on grammatical grounds. Each point is strikingly illustrated by quotations.)

Will, T. E. "A Poet of Freedom," *Arena,* XXXI, 262–271 (March, 1904).

Willson, Beckles. *America's Ambassadors to England (1785–1929).* New York: 1929, pp. 374–388. (An excellent summary of Lowell's diplomatic career in England, with many sidelights upon the questions of international affairs during Lowell's term of office. Lowell was especially troubled by the attempts of Irishmen to secure release from English prisons by fraudulently claiming that they were American citizens entitled to the intervention of our minister.)

Woodberry, G. E. "James Russell Lowell," in *Authors at Home*, ed. by J. L. and J. B. Gilder. New York: 1889, pp. 229–235.

Woodberry, G. E. "James Russell Lowell," in *Makers of Literature*. New York: 1900, pp. 324–349. (An appreciative and generally judicious essay by a discriminating critic who continued in some measure the impressionistic aspect of Lowell's work.)

Wurfl, G. "Lowell's Debt to Goethe," *Pennsylvania State College Studies*, I, 1–89 (1936). (Shows considerable influence on Lowell's critical method. Closely documented.)

For scholarly articles devoted to Lowell published after 1945 one should consult especially the current bibliographies in *American Literature*, *Publications of the Modern Language Association* (American Literature section), *New England Quarterly*, and Grace G. Griffin's *Writings on American History*.

★

Selections from
JAMES RUSSELL LOWELL

★

POEMS

TO THE SPIRIT OF KEATS

Great soul, thou sittest with me in my room,
Uplifting me with thy vast, quiet eyes,
On whose full orbs, with kindly lustre, lies
The twilight warmth of ruddy ember-gloom:
Thy clear, strong tones will oft bring sudden bloom
Of hope secure, to him who lonely cries,
Wrestling with the young poet's agonies,
Neglect and scorn, which seem a certain doom:
Yes! the few words which, like great thunderdrops,
Thy large heart down to earth shook doubtfully,   10
Thrilled by the inward lightning of its might,
Serene and pure, like gushing joy of light,
Shall track the eternal chords of Destiny,
After the moon-led pulse of ocean stops.

1841   1842

"GREAT TRUTHS ARE PORTIONS
OF THE SOUL OF MAN"

Great Truths are portions of the soul of man;
Great souls are portions of Eternity;
Each drop of blood that e'er through true heart ran
With lofty message, ran for thee and me;
For God's law, since the starry song began,
Hath been, and still forevermore must be,
That every deed which shall outlast Time's span
Must spur the soul to be erect and free;
Slave is no word of deathless lineage sprung;
Too many noble souls have thought and died,   10
Too many mighty poets lived and sung,
And our good Saxon, from lips purified
With martyr-fire, throughout the world hath rung
Too long to have God's holy cause denied.

1841   1842

3

"I ASK NOT FOR THOSE THOUGHTS,
THAT SUDDEN LEAP"

I ask not for those thoughts, that sudden leap
From being's sea, like the isle-seeming Kraken,
With whose great rise the ocean all is shaken
And a heart-tremble quivers through the deep;
Give me that growth which some perchance deem sleep,
Wherewith the steadfast coral-stems uprise,
Which, by the toil of gathering energies,
Their upward way into clear sunshine keep,
Until, by Heaven's sweetest influences,
Slowly and slowly spreads a speck of green   10
Into a pleasant island in the seas,
Where, 'mid tall palms, the cane-roofed home is seen,
And wearied men shall sit at sunset's hour,
Hearing the leaves and loving God's dear power.

1841   1843

"MY LOVE, I HAVE NO FEAR THAT
THOU SHOULDST DIE"

My Love, I have no fear that thou shouldst die;
Albeit I ask no fairer life than this,
Whose numbering-clock is still thy gentle kiss,
While Time and Peace with hands enlockèd fly;
Yet care I not where in Eternity
We live and love, well knowing that there is
No backward step for those who feel the bliss
Of Faith as their most lofty yearnings high:
Love hath so purified my being's core,
Meseems I scarcely should be startled, even,   10
To find, some morn, that thou hadst gone before;
Since, with thy love, this knowledge too was given,
Which each calm day doth strengthen more and more,
That they who love are but one step from Heaven.

1841   1843

"BELOVED, IN THE NOISY CITY HERE"

Beloved, in the noisy city here,
The thought of thee can make all turmoil cease;
Around my spirit, folds thy spirit clear
Its still, soft arms, and circles it with peace;
There is no room for any doubt or fear
In souls so overfilled with love's increase,
There is no memory of the bygone year
But growth in heart's and spirit's perfect ease:
How hath our love, half nebulous at first,
Rounded itself into a full-orbed sun!   10
How have our lives and wills (as haply erst
They were, ere this forgetfulness begun)
Through all their earthly distances outburst,
And melted, like two rays of light in one!

1842   1843

"OUR LOVE IS NOT A FADING EARTHLY FLOWER"

Our love is not a fading earthly flower:
Its wingèd seed dropped down from Paradise,
And, nursed by day and night, by sun and shower,
Doth momently to fresher beauty rise:
To us the leafless autumn is not bare,
Nor winter's rattling boughs lack lusty green.
Our summer hearts make summer's fulness, where
No leaf, or bud, or blossom may be seen:
For nature's life in love's deep life doth lie,
Love,—whose forgetfulness is beauty's death,   10
Whose mystic key these cells of Thou and I
Into the infinite freedom openeth,
And makes the body's dark and narrow grate
The wide-flung leaves of Heaven's own palace-gate.

1842   1843

· SONG

O moonlight deep and tender,
  A year and more agone,
Your mist of golden splendor
  Round my betrothal shone!

O elm-leaves dark and dewy,
  The very same ye seem,
The low wind trembles through ye,
  Ye murmur in my dream!

O river, dim with distance,
  Flow thus forever by,   10
A part of my existence
  Within your heart doth lie!

O stars, ye saw our meeting,
  Two beings and one soul,
Two hearts so madly beating
  To mingle and be whole!

O happy night, deliver
  Her kisses back to me,
Or keep them all, and give her
  A blissful dream of me!   20

1842   1843

THE SHEPHERD OF KING ADMETUS

There came a youth upon the earth,
  Some thousand years ago,
Whose slender hands were nothing worth,
Whether to plough, or reap, or sow.

Upon an empty tortoise-shell
  He stretched some chords, and drew
Music that made men's bosoms swell
Fearless, or brimmed their eyes with dew.

Then King Admetus, one who had
    Pure taste by right divine,   10
Decreed his singing not too bad
To hear between the cups of wine:

And so, well pleased with being soothed
    Into a sweet half-sleep,
Three times his kingly beard he smoothed,
And made him viceroy o'er his sheep.

His words were simple words enough,
    And yet he used them so,
That what in other mouths was rough
In his seemed musical and low.   20

Men called him but a shiftless youth,
    In whom no good they saw;
And yet, unwittingly, in truth,
They made his careless words their law.

They knew not how he learned at all,
    For idly, hour by hour,
He sat and watched the dead leaves fall,
Or mused upon a common flower.

It seemed the loveliness of things
    Did teach him all their use,   30
For, in mere weeds, and stones, and springs,
He found a healing power profuse.

Men granted that his speech was wise,
    But, when a glance they caught
Of his slim grace and woman's eyes,
They laughed, and called him good-for-naught.

Yet after he was dead and gone,
    And e'en his memory dim,
Earth seemed more sweet to live upon,
More full of love, because of him.   40

And day by day more holy grew
    Each spot where he had trod,
Till after-poets only knew
    Their first-born brother as a god.

                   1842

AN INCIDENT IN A RAILROAD CAR

He spoke of Burns: men rude and rough
Pressed round to hear the praise of one
Whose heart was made of manly, simple stuff,
    As homespun as their own.

And, when he read, they forward leaned,
    Drinking, with thirsty hearts and ears,
His brook-like songs whom glory never weaned
    From humble smiles and tears.

Slowly there grew a tender awe,
    Sun-like, o'er faces brown and hard,   10
As if in him who read they felt and saw
    Some presence of the bard.

It was a sight for sin and wrong
    And slavish tyranny to see,
A sight to make our faith more pure and strong
    In high humanity.

I thought, these men will carry hence
    Promptings their former life above,
And something of a finer reverence
    For beauty, truth, and love.   20

God scatters love on every side
    Freely among his children all,
And always hearts are lying open wide,
    Wherein some grains may fall.

There is no wind but soweth seeds
    Of a more true and open life,
Which burst, unlooked for, into high-souled deeds,
        With wayside beauty rife.

We find within these souls of ours
    Some wild germs of a higher birth,   30
Which in the poet's tropic heart bear flowers
        Whose fragrance fills the earth.

Within the hearts of all men lie
    These promises of wider bliss,
Which blossom into hopes that cannot die,
        In sunny hours like this.

All that hath been majestical
    In life or death, since time began,
Is native in the simple heart of all,
        The angel heart of man.   40

And thus, among the untaught poor,
    Great deeds and feelings find a home,
That cast in shadow all the golden lore
        Of classic Greece and Rome.

O mighty brother-soul of man,
    Where'er thou art, in low or high,
Thy skyey arches with exulting span
        O'er-roof infinity!

All thoughts that mold the age begin
    Deep down within the primitive soul,   50
And from the many slowly upward win
        To one who grasps the whole:

In his wide brain the feeling deep
    That struggled on the many's tongue
Swells to a tide of thought, whose surges leap
        O'er the weak thrones of wrong.

All thought begins in feeling,—wide
  In the great mass its base is hid,
And, narrowing up to thought, stands glorified,
    A moveless pyramid.   60

Nor is he far astray, who deems
  That every hope, which rises and grows broad
In the world's heart, by ordered impulse streams
    From the great heart of God.

God wills, man hopes: in common souls
  Hope is but vague and undefined,
Till from the poet's tongue the message rolls
    A blessing to his kind.

Never did Poesy appear
  So full of heaven to me, as when   70
I saw how it would pierce through pride and fear
    To the lives of coarsest men.

It may be glorious to write
  Thoughts that shall glad the two or three
High souls, like those far stars that come in sight
    Once in a century;—

But better far it is to speak
  One simple word, which now and then
Shall waken their free nature in the weak
    And friendless sons of men;   80

To write some earnest verse or line,
  Which, seeking not the praise of art,
Shall make a clearer faith and manhood shine
    In the untutored heart.

He who doth this, in verse or prose,
  May be forgotten in his day,
But surely shall be crowned at last with those
    Who live and speak for aye.

1842   1842

STANZAS ON FREEDOM

Men! whose boast it is that ye
Come of fathers brave and free,
If there breathe on earth a slave,
Are ye truly free and brave?
If ye do not feel the chain,
When it works a brother's pain,
Are ye not base slaves indeed,
Slaves unworthy to be freed?

Women! who shall one day bear
Sons to breathe New England air,   10
If ye hear, without a blush,
Deeds to make the roused blood rush
Like red lava through your veins,
For your sisters now in chains,—
Answer! are ye fit to be
Mothers of the brave and free?

Is true Freedom but to break
Fetters for our own dear sake,
And, with leathern hearts, forget
That we owe mankind a debt?   20
No! true freedom is to share
All the chains our brothers wear,
And, with heart and hand, to be
Earnest to make others free!

They are slaves who fear to speak
For the fallen and the weak;
They are slaves who will not choose
Hatred, scoffing, and abuse,
Rather than in silence shrink
From the truth they needs must think;   30
They are slaves who dare not be
In the right with two or three.

1843   1843

WENDELL PHILLIPS

He stood upon the world's broad threshold; wide
The din of battle and of slaughter rose;
He saw God stand upon the weaker side,
That sank in seeming loss before its foes:
Many there were who made great haste and sold
Unto the cunning enemy their swords,
He scorned their gifts of fame, and power, and gold,
And, underneath their soft and flowery words,
Heard the cold serpent hiss; therefore he went
And humbly joined him to the weaker part,   10
Fanatic named, and fool, yet well content
So he could be the nearer to God's heart,
And feel its solemn pulses sending blood
Through all the widespread veins of endless good.

                                                      1843

RHŒCUS

God sends his teachers unto every age,
To every clime, and every race of men,
With revelations fitted to their growth
And shape of mind, nor gives the realm of Truth
Into the selfish rule of one sole race:
Therefore each form of worship that hath swayed
The life of man, and given it to grasp
The master-key of knowledge, reverence,
Infolds some germs of goodness and of right;
Else never had the eager soul, which loathes   10
The slothful down of pampered ignorance,
Found in it even a moment's fitful rest.

    There is an instinct in the human heart
Which makes that all the fables it hath coined,
To justify the reign of its belief
And strengthen it by beauty's right divine,

Veil in their inner cells a mystic gift,
Which, like the hazel twig, in faithful hands,
Points surely to the hidden springs of truth.
For, as in nature naught is made in vain,   20
But all things have within their hull of use
A wisdom and a meaning which may speak
Of spiritual secrets to the ear
Of spirit; so, in whatsoe'er the heart
Hath fashioned for a solace to itself,
To make its inspirations suit its creed,
And from the niggard hands of falsehood wring
Its needful food of truth, there ever is
A sympathy with Nature, which reveals,
Not less than her own works, pure gleams of light   30
And earnest parables of inward lore.
Hear now this fairy legend of old Greece,
As full of gracious youth, and beauty still
As the immortal freshness of that grace
Carved for all ages on some Attic frieze.

A youth named Rhœcus, wandering in the wood,
Saw an old oak just trembling to its fall,
And, feeling pity of so fair a tree,
He propped its gray trunk with admiring care,
And with a thoughtless footstep loitered on.   40
But, as he turned, he heard a voice behind
That murmured "Rhœcus!" 'Twas as if the leaves,
Stirred by a passing breath, had murmured it,
And, while he paused bewildered, yet again
It murmured "Rhœcus!" softer than a breeze.
He started and beheld with dizzy eyes
What seemed the substance of a happy dream
Stand there before him, spreading a warm glow
Within the green glooms of the shadowy oak.
It seemed a woman's shape, yet far too fair   50

To be a woman, and with eyes too meek
For any that were wont to mate with gods.

All naked like a goddess stood she there,
And like a goddess all too beautiful
To feel the guilt-born earthliness of shame.
"Rhœcus, I am the Dryad of this tree,"
Thus she began, dropping her low-toned words
Serene, and full, and clear, as drops of dew,
"And with it I am doomed to live and die;
The rain and sunshine are my caterers,   60
Nor have I other bliss than simple life;
Now ask me what thou wilt, that I can give,
And with a thankful joy it shall be thine."

    Then Rhœcus, with a flutter at the heart,
Yet by the prompting of such beauty bold,
Answered: "What is there that can satisfy
The endless craving of the soul but love?
Give me thy love, or but the hope of that
Which must be evermore my nature's goal."
After a little pause she said again,   70
But with a glimpse of sadness in her tone,
"I give it, Rhœcus, though a perilous gift;
An hour before the sunset meet me here."
And straightway there was nothing he could see
But the green glooms beneath the shadowy oak,
And not a sound came to his straining ears
But the low trickling rustle of the leaves,
And far away upon an emerald slope
The falter of an idle shepherd's pipe.

    Now, in those days of simpleness and faith,   80
Men did not think that happy things were dreams
Because they overstepped the narrow bourn
Of likelihood, but reverently deemed
Nothing too wondrous or too beautiful
To be the guerdon of a daring heart.
So Rhœcus made no doubt that he was blest,
And all along unto the city's gate
Earth seemed to spring beneath him as he walked,

The clear, broad sky looked bluer than its wont,
And he could scarce believe he had not wings,   90
Such sunshine seemed to glitter through his veins
Instead of blood, so light he felt and strange.

Young Rhœcus had a faithful heart enough,
But one that in the present dwelt too much,
And, taking with blithe welcome whatsoe'er
Chance gave of joy, was wholly bound in that,
Like the contented peasant of a vale,
Deemed it the world, and never looked beyond.
So, haply meeting in the afternoon
Some comrades who were playing at the dice,   100
He joined them, and forgot all else beside.

The dice were rattling at the merriest,
And Rhœcus, who had met but sorry luck,
Just laughed in triumph at a happy throw,
When through the room there hummed a yellow bee
That buzzed about his ear with down-dropped legs
As if to light. And Rhœcus laughed and said,
Feeling how red and flushed he was with loss,
"By Venus! does he take me for a rose?"
And brushed him off with rough, impatient hand.   110
But still the bee came back, and thrice again
Rhœcus did beat him off with growing wrath.
Then through the window flew the wounded bee,
And Rhœcus, tracking him with angry eyes,
Saw a sharp mountain-peak of Thessaly
Against the red disk of the setting sun,—
And instantly the blood sank from his heart,
As if its very walls had caved away.
Without a word he turned, and, rushing forth,
Ran madly through the city and the gate,   120
And o'er the plain, which now the wood's long shade,
By the low sun thrown forward broad and dim,
Darkened wellnigh unto the city's wall.

Quite spent and out of breath he reached the tree,
And, listening fearfully, he heard once more
The low voice murmur "Rhœcus!" close at hand:
Whereat he looked around him, but could see
Naught but the deepening glooms beneath the oak.
Then sighed the voice, "O Rhœcus! nevermore
Shalt thou behold me or by day or night,   130
Me, who would fain have blessed thee with a love
More ripe and bounteous than ever yet
Filled up with nectar any mortal heart:
But thou didst scorn my humble messenger,
And sent'st him back to me with bruisèd wings.
We spirits only show to gentle eyes,
We ever ask an undivided love,
And he who scorns the least of Nature's works
Is thenceforth exiled and shut out from all.
Farewell! for thou canst never see me more."   140

Then Rhœcus beat his breast, and groaned aloud,
And cried, "Be pitiful! forgive me yet
This once, and I shall never need it more!"
"Alas!" the voice returned, "'tis thou art blind,
Not I unmerciful; I can forgive,
But have no skill to heal thy spirit's eyes;
Only the soul hath power o'er itself."
With that again there murmured "Nevermore!"
And Rhœcus after heard no other sound,
Except the rattling of the oak's crisp leaves,   150
Like the long surf upon a distant shore,
Raking the sea-worn pebbles up and down.
The night had gathered round him: o'er the plain
The city sparkled with its thousand lights,
And sounds of revel fell upon his ear
Harshly and like a curse; above, the sky,
With all its bright sublimity of stars,
Deepened, and on his forehead smote the breeze:

Beauty was all around him and delight,
But from that eve he was alone on earth.   160
                                                            1843

COLUMBUS

The cordage creaks and rattles in the wind,
With whims of sudden hush; the reeling sea
Now thumps like solid rock beneath the stern,
Now leaps with clumsy wrath, strikes short, and falling,
Crumbled to whispery foam, slips rustling down
The broad backs of the waves, which jostle and crowd
To fling themselves upon that unknown shore,
Their used familiar since the dawn of time,
Whither this foredoomed life is guided on
To sway on triumph's hushed, aspiring poise   10
One glittering moment, then to break fulfilled.

How lonely is the sea's perpetual swing,
The melancholy wash of endless waves,
The sigh of some grim monster undescried,
Fear-painted on the canvas of the dark,
Shifting on his uneasy pillow of brine!
Yet night brings more companions than the day
To this drear waste; new constellations burn,
And fairer stars, with whose calm height my soul
Finds nearer sympathy than with my herd   20
Of earthen souls, whose vision's scanty ring
Makes me its prisoner to beat my wings
Against the cold bars of their unbelief,
Knowing in vain my own free heaven beyond.
O God! this world, so crammed with eager life,
That comes and goes and wanders back to silence
Like the idle wind, which yet man's shaping mind
Can make his drudge to swell the longing sails
Of highest endeavor,—this mad, unthrift world,
Which, every hour, throws life enough away   30
To make her deserts kind and hospitable,

Lets her great destinies be waved aside
By smooth, lip-reverent, formal infidels,
Who weigh the God they not believe with gold,
And find no spot in Judas, save that he,
Driving a duller bargain than he ought,
Saddled his guild with too cheap precedent.
O Faith! if thou art strong, thine opposite
Is mighty also, and the dull fool's sneer
Hath ofttimes shot chill palsy through the arm   40
Just lifted to achieve its crowning deed,
And made the firm-based heart, that would have quailed
The rack or fagot, shudder like a leaf
Wrinkled with frost, and loose upon its stem.
The wicked and the weak, by some dark law,
Have a strange power to shut and rivet down
Their own horizon round us, to unwing
Our heaven-aspiring visions, and to blur
With surly clouds the Future's gleaming peaks,
Far seen across the brine of thankless years.   50
If the chosen soul could never be alone
In deep mid-silence, open-doored to God,
No greatness ever had been dreamed or done;
Among dull hearts a prophet never grew;
The nurse of full-grown souls is solitude.

The old world is effete; there man with man
Jostles, and, in the brawl for means to live,
Life is trod underfoot,—Life, the one block
Of marble that's vouchsafed wherefrom to carve
Our great thoughts, white and godlike, to shine down   60
The future, Life, the irredeemable block,
Which one o'er-hasty chisel-dint oft mars,
Scanting our room to cut the features out
Of our full hope, so forcing us to crown
With a mean head the perfect limbs, or leave
The god's face glowing o'er a satyr's trunk,
Failure's brief epitaph.

Yes, Europe's world
Reels on to judgment; there the common need,
Losing God's sacred use, to be a bond
'Twixt Me and Thee, sets each one scowlingly   70
O'er his own selfish hoard at bay; no state,
Knit strongly with eternal fibres up
Of all men's separate and united weals,
Self-poised and sole as stars, yet one as light,
Holds up a shape of large Humanity
To which by natural instinct every man
Pays loyalty exulting, by which all
Mould their own lives, and feel their pulses filled
With the red, fiery blood of the general life,
Making them mighty in peace, as now in war   80
They are, even in the flush of victory, weak,
Conquering that manhood which should them subdue.
And what gift bring I to this untried world?
Shall the same tragedy be played anew,
And the same lurid curtain drop at last
On one dread desolation, one fierce crash
Of that recoil which on its makers God
Lets Ignorance and Sin and Hunger make,
Early or late? Or shall that commonwealth
Whose potent unity and concentric force   90
Can draw these scattered joints and parts of men
Into a whole ideal man once more,
Which sucks not from its limbs the life away,
But sends it flood-tide and creates itself
Over again in every citizen,
Be there built up? For me, I have no choice;
I might turn back to other destinies,
For one sincere key opes all Fortune's doors;
But whoso answers not God's earliest call
Forfeits or dulls that faculty supreme   100
Of lying open to his genius
Which makes the wise heart certain of its ends.
Here am I; for what end God knows, not I;

Westward still points the inexorable soul:
Here am I, with no friend but the sad sea,
The beating heart of this great enterprise,
Which, without me, would stiffen in swift death;
This have I mused on, since mine eye could first
Among the stars distinguish and with joy
Rest on that God-fed Pharos of the north,   110
On some blue promontory of heaven lighted
That juts far out into the upper sea;
To this one hope my heart hath clung for years,
As would a foundling to the talisman
Hung round his neck by hands he knew not whose;
A poor, vile thing and dross to all beside,
Yet he therein can feel a virtue left
By the sad pressure of a mother's hand,
And unto him it still is tremulous
With palpitating haste and wet with tears,   120
The key to him of hope and humanness,
The coarse shell of life's pearl, Expectancy.
This hope hath been to me for love and fame,
Hath made me wholly lonely on the earth,
Building me up as in a thick-ribbed tower,
Wherewith enwalled my watching spirit burned,
Conquering its little island from the Dark,
Sole as a scholar's lamp, and heard men's steps,
In the far hurry of the outward world,
Pass dimly forth and back, sounds heard in dream.   130
As Ganymede by the eagle was snatched up
From the gross sod to be Jove's cup-bearer,
So was I lifted by my great design:
And who hath trod Olympus, from his eye
Fades not that broader outlook of the gods;
His life's low valleys overbrow earth's clouds,
And that Olympian spectre of the past
Looms towering up in sovereign memory,
Beckoning his soul from meaner heights of doom.
Had but the shadow of the Thunderer's bird,   140

Flashing athwart my spirit, made of me
A swift-betraying vision's Ganymede,
Yet to have greatly dreamed precludes low ends;
Great days have ever such a morning-red,
On such a base great futures are built up,
And aspiration, though not put in act,
Comes back to ask its plighted troth again,
Still watches round its grave the unlaid ghost
Of a dead virtue, and makes other hopes,
Save that implacable one, seem thin and bleak   150
As shadows of bare trees upon the snow,
Bound freezing there by the unpitying moon.

While other youths perplexed their mandolins,
Praying that Thetis would her fingers twine
In the loose glories of her lover's hair,
And wile another kiss to keep back day,
I, stretched beneath the many-centuried shade
Of some writhed oak, the wood's Laocoön,
Did of my hope a dryad mistress make,
Whom I would woo to meet me privily,   160
Or underneath the stars, or when the moon
Flecked all the forest floor with scattered pearls.
O days whose memory tames to fawning down
The surly fell of Ocean's bristled neck!

I know not when this hope enthralled me first,
But from my boyhood up I loved to hear
The tall pine-forests of the Apennine
Murmur their hoary legends of the sea,
Which hearing, I in vision clear beheld
The sudden dark of tropic night shut down   170
O'er the huge whisper of great watery wastes,
The while a pair of herons trailingly
Flapped inland, where some league-wide river hurled
The yellow spoil of unconjectured realms
Far through a gulf's green silence, never scarred
By any but the North-wind's hurrying keels.

And not the pines alone; all sights and sounds
To my world-seeking heart paid fealty,
And catered for it as the Cretan bees
Brought honey to the baby Jupiter,   180
Who in his soft hand crushed a violet,
Godlike foremusing the rough thunder's gripe;
Then did I entertain the poet's song,
My great Idea's guest, and, passing o'er
That iron bridge the Tuscan built to hell,
I heard Ulysses tell of mountain-chains
Whose adamantine links, his manacles,
The western main shook growling, and still gnawed.
I brooded on the wise Athenian's tale
Of happy Atlantis, and heard Björne's keel   190
Crunch the gray pebbles of the Vinland shore:
I listened, musing, to the prophecy
Of Nero's tutor-victim; lo, the birds
Sing darkling, conscious of the climbing dawn
And I believed the poets; it is they
Who utter wisdom from the central deep,
And, listening to the inner flow of things,
Speak to the age out of eternity.

Ah me! old hermits sought for solitude
In caves and desert places of the earth,   200
Where their own heart-beat was the only stir
Of living thing that comforted the year;
But the bald pillar-top of Simeon,
In midnight's blankest waste, were populous,
Matched with the isolation drear and deep
Of him who pines among the swarm of men,
At once a new thought's king and prisoner,
Feeling the truer life within his life,
The fountain of his spirit's prophecy,
Sinking away and wasting, drop by drop,   210
In the ungrateful sands of sceptic ears.
He in the palace-aisles of untrod woods

Doth walk a king; for him the pent-up cell
Widens beyond the circles of the stars,
And all the sceptred spirits of the past
Come thronging in to greet him as their peer;
But in the market-place's glare and throng
He sits apart, an exile, and his brow
Aches with the mocking memory of its crown
Yet to the spirit select there is no choice;   220
He cannot say, This will I do, or that,
For the cheap means putting Heaven's ends in pawn,
And bartering his bleak rocks, the freehold stern
Of destiny's first-born, for smoother fields
That yield no crop of self-denying will;
A hand is stretched to him from out the dark,
Which grasping without question, he is led
Where there is work that he must do for God.
The trial still is the strength's complement,
And the uncertain, dizzy path that scales   230
The sheer heights of supremest purposes
Is steeper to the angel than the child.
Chances have laws as fixed as planets have,
And disappointment's dry and bitter root,
Envy's harsh berries, and the choking pool
Of the world's scorn, are the right mother-milk
To the tough hearts that pioneer their kind,
And break a pathway to those unknown realms
That in the earth's broad shadow lie enthralled;
Endurance is the crowning quality,   240
And patience all the passion of great hearts;
These are their stay, and when the leaden world
Sets its hard face against their fateful thought,
And brute strength, like the Gaulish conqueror,
Clangs his huge glaive down in the other scale,
The inspired soul but flings his patience in,
And slowly that outweighs the ponderous globe,—
One faith against a whole earth's unbelief,
One soul against the flesh of all mankind.

Thus ever seems it when my soul can hear   250
The voice that errs not; then my triumph gleams,
O'er the blank ocean beckoning, and all night
My heart flies on before me as I sail;
Far on I see my lifelong enterprise,
That rose like Ganges 'mid the freezing snows
Of a world's solitude, sweep broadening down,
And, gathering to itself a thousand streams,
Grow sacred ere it mingle with the sea;
I see the ungated wall of chaos old,
With blocks Cyclopean hewn of solid night,   260
Fade like a wreath of unreturning mist
Before the irreversible feet of light;—
And lo, with what clear omen in the east
On day's gray threshold stands the eager dawn,
Like young Leander rosy from the sea
Glowing at Hero's lattice!

                              One day more
These muttering shoalbrains leave the helm to me:
God, let me not in their dull ooze be stranded;
Let not this one frail bark, to hollow which
I have dug out the pith and sinewy heart   270
Of my aspiring life's fair trunk, be so
Cast up to warp and blacken in the sun,
Just as the opposing wind 'gins whistle off
His cheek-swollen pack, and from the leaning mast
Fortune's full sail strains forward!

                              One poor day!—
Remember whose and not how short it is!
It is God's day, it is Columbus's.
A lavish day! One day, with life and heart,
Is more than time enough to find a world.

1844   1847

THE PRESENT CRISIS

When a deed is done for Freedom, through the broad earth's
    aching breast
Runs a thrill of joy prophetic, trembling on from east to west,
And the slave, where'er he cowers, feels the soul within him
    climb
To the awful verge of manhood, as the energy sublime
Of a century bursts full-blossomed on the thorny stem of Time.

Through the walls of hut and palace shoots the instantaneous
    throe,
When the travail of the Ages wrings earth's systems to and fro;
At the birth of each new Era, with a recognizing start,
Nation wildly looks at nation, standing with mute lips apart,
And glad Truth's yet mightier man-child leaps beneath the
    Future's heart.   10

So the Evil's triumph sendeth, with a terror and a chill,
Under continent to continent, the sense of coming ill,
And the slave, where'er he cowers, feels his sympathies with
    God
In hot tear-drops ebbing earthward, to be drunk up by the sod,
Till a corpse crawls round unburied, delving in the nobler clod.

For mankind are one in spirit, and an instinct bears along,
Round the earth's electric circle, the swift flash of right or
    wrong;
Whether conscious or unconscious, yet Humanity's vast frame
Through its ocean-sundered fibres feels the gush of joy or
    shame;—
In the gain or loss of one race all the rest have equal claim.   20

Once to every man and nation comes the moment to decide,
In the strife of Truth with Falsehood, for the good or evil side;

Some great cause, God's new Messiah, offering each the bloom
    or blight,
Parts the goats upon the left hand, and the sheep upon the right,
And the choice goes by forever 'twixt that darkness and that
    light.

Hast thou chosen, O my people, on whose party thou shalt
    stand,
Ere the Doom from its worn sandals shakes the dust against our
    land?
Though the cause of Evil prosper, yet 'tis Truth alone is strong,
And, albeit she wander outcast now, I see around her throng
Troops of beautiful, tall angels, to enshield her from all wrong.

Backward look across the ages and the beacon-moments see,
That, like peaks of some sunk continent, jut through Oblivion's
    sea;   32
Not an ear in court or market for the low foreboding cry
Of those Crises, God's stern winnowers, from whose feet
    earth's chaff must fly;
Never shows the choice momentous till the judgment hath
    passed by.

Careless seems the great Avenger; history's pages but record
One death-grapple in the darkness 'twixt old systems and the
    Word;
Truth forever on the scaffold, Wrong forever on the throne,—
Yet that scaffold sways the future, and, behind the dim un-
    known,
Standeth God within the shadow, keeping watch above his
    own.   40

We see dimly in the Present what is small and what is great,
Slow of faith how weak an arm may turn the iron helm of fate,
But the soul is still oracular; amid the market's din,

List the ominous stern whisper from the Delphic cave within,—
"They enslave their children's children who make compromise
with sin."

Slavery, the earth-born Cyclops, fellest of the giant brood,
Sons of brutish Force and Darkness, who have drenched the
earth with blood,
Famished in his self-made desert, blinded by our purer day,
Gropes in yet unblasted regions for his miserable prey;—
Shall we guide his gory fingers where our helpless children
play?   50

Then to side with Truth is noble when we share her wretched
crust,
Ere her cause bring fame and profit, and 'tis prosperous to be
just;
Then it is the brave man chooses, while the coward stands aside,
Doubting in his abject spirit, till his Lord is crucified,
And the multitude make virtue of the faith they had denied.

Count me o'er earth's chosen heroes,—they were souls that
stood alone,
While the men they agonized for hurled the contumelious stone,
Stood serene, and down the future saw the golden beam incline
To the side of perfect justice, mastered by their faith divine,
By one man's plain truth to manhood and to God's supreme
design.   60

By the light of burning heretics Christ's bleeding feet I track,
Toiling up new Calvaries ever with the cross that turns not
back,
And these mounts of anguish number how each generation
learned
One new word of that grand *Credo* which in prophet-hearts
hath burned
Since the first man stood God-conquered with his face to heaven
upturned.

For Humanity sweeps onward: where today the martyr stands,
On the morrow crouches Judas with the silver in his hands;
Far in front the cross stands ready and the crackling fagots
     burn,
While the hooting mob of yesterday in silent awe return
To glean up the scattered ashes into History's golden urn.   70

'Tis as easy to be heroes as to sit the idle slaves
Of a legendary virtue carved upon our fathers' graves,
Worshippers of light ancestral make the present light a crime;—
Was the Mayflower launched by cowards, steered by men
     behind their time?
Turn those tracks toward Past or Future, that make Plymouth
     Rock sublime?

They were men of present valor, stalwart old iconoclasts,
Unconvinced by axe or gibbet that all virtue was the Past's;
But we make their truth our falsehood, thinking that hath made
     us free,
Hoarding it in mouldy parchments, while our tender spirits flee
The rude grasp of that great Impulse which drove them across
     the sea.   80

They have rights who dare maintain them; we are traitors to
     our sires,
Smothering in their holy ashes Freedom's new-lit altar-fires;
Shall we make their creed our jailer? Shall we, in our haste to
     slay,
From the tombs of the old prophets steal the funeral lamps
     away
To light up the martyr-fagots round the prophets of today?

New occasions teach new duties; Time makes ancient good
     uncouth;
They must upward still, and onward, who would keep abreast
     of Truth;
Lo, before us gleam her camp-fires! we ourselves must Pil-
     grims be,

Launch our Mayflower, and steer boldly through the desperate
    winter sea,
Nor attempt the Future's portal with the Past's blood-rusted
    key. 90
1844 1845

A CONTRAST

Thy love thou sentest oft to me,
    And still as oft I thrust it back;
Thy messengers I could not see
    In those who everything did lack,
    The poor, the outcast and the black.

Pride held his hand before mine eyes,
    The world with flattery stuffed mine ears;
I looked to see a monarch's guise,
    Nor dreamed thy love would knock for years,
    Poor, naked, fettered, full of tears. 10

Yet, when I sent my love to thee,
    Thou with a smile didst take it in,
And entertain'dst it royally,
    Though grimed with earth, with hunger thin,
    And leprous with the taint of sin.

Now every day thy love I meet,
    As o'er the earth it wanders wide,
With weary step and bleeding feet,
    Still knocking at the heart of pride
    And offering grace, though still denied. 20
1845

TO THE DANDELION

Dear common flower, that grow'st beside the way,
Fringing the dusty road with harmless gold,
    First pledge of blithesome May,

Which children pluck, and full of pride uphold,
High-hearted buccaneers, o'erjoyed that they
An Eldorado in the grass have found,
Which not the rich earth's ample round
May match in wealth, thou art more dear to me
Than all the prouder summer-blooms may be.

Gold such as thine ne'er drew the Spanish prow   10
Through the primeval hush of Indian seas,
Nor wrinkled the lean brow
Of age, to rob the lover's heart of ease;
'Tis the Spring's largess, which she scatters now
To rich and poor alike, with lavish hand,
Though most hearts never understand
To take it at God's value, but pass by
The offered wealth with unrewarded eye.

Thou art my tropics and mine Italy;
To look at thee unlocks a warmer clime;   20
The eyes thou givest me
Are in the heart, and heed not space or time:
Not in mid June the golden-cuirassed bee
Feels a more summer-like warm ravishment
In the white lily's breezy tent,
His fragrant Sybaris, than I, when first
From the dark green thy yellow circles burst.

Then think I of deep shadows on the grass,
Of meadows where in sun the cattle graze,
Where, as the breezes pass,   30
The gleaming rushes lean a thousand ways,
Of leaves that slumber in a cloudy mass,
Or whiten in the wind, of waters blue
That from the distance sparkle through
Some woodland gap, and of a sky above,
Where one white cloud like a stray lamb doth move.

My childhood's earliest thoughts are linked with thee;
The sight of thee calls back the robin's song,
    Who, from the dark old tree
Beside the door, sang clearly all day long,   40
    And I, secure in childish piety,
Listened as if I heard an angel sing
    With news from heaven, which he could bring
    Fresh every day to my untainted ears
When birds and flowers and I were happy peers.

How like a prodigal doth nature seem,
When thou, for all thy gold, so common art!
    Thou teachest me to deem
More sacredly of every human heart,
    Since each reflects in joy its scanty gleam   50
Of heaven, and could some wondrous secret show,
    Did we but pay the love we owe,
    And with a child's undoubting wisdom look
On all these living pages of God's book.

1844   1845

From THE BIGLOW PAPERS

FIRST SERIES

No. I

A LETTER

FROM MR. EZEKIEL BIGLOW OF JAALAM TO THE HON. JOSEPH T.
BUCKINGHAM, EDITOR OF THE BOSTON COURIER, INCLOSING A
POEM OF HIS SON, MR. HOSEA BIGLOW

JAYLEM, june 1846.

Mister Eddyter,—Our Hosea wuz down to Boston last week,
and he see a cruetin Sarjunt a struttin round as popler as a hen
with 1 chicking, with 2 fellers a drummin and fifin arter him like
all nater. the sarjunt he thout Hosea hed n't gut his i teeth cut

cos he looked a kindo 's though he 'd jest com down, so he cal'-
lated to hook him in, but Hosy wood n't take none o' his sarse
for all he hed much as 20 Rooster's tales stuck onto his hat and
eenamost enuf brass a bobbin up and down on his shoulders
and figureed onto his coat and trousis, let alone wut nater hed
sot in his featers, to make a 6 pounder out on.

   wal, Hosea he com home considerabal riled, and arter I'd gone
to bed I heern Him a thrashin round like a short-tailed Bull in
fli-time. The old Woman ses she to me ses she, Zekle, ses she,
our Hosee 's gut the chollery or suthin anuther ses she, don't
you Bee skeered, ses I, he 's oneya makin pottery[1] ses i, he 's ollers
on hand at that ere busynes like Da & martin, and shure enuf,
cum mornin, Hosy he cum down stares full chizzle, hare on
eend and cote tales flyin, and sot rite of to go reed his varses to
Parson Wilbur bein he haint aney grate shows o' book larnin
himself, bimeby he cum back and sed the parson wuz dreffle
tickled with 'em as i hoop you will Be, and said they wuz True
grit.

   Hosea ses taint hardly fair to call 'em hisn now, cos the parson
kind o' slicked off sum o' the last varses, but he told Hosee he
did n't want to put his ore in to tetch to the Rest on 'em, being
they wuz verry well As thay wuz, and then Hosy ses he sed
suthin a nuther about Simplex Mundishes or sum sech feller,
but I guess Hosea kind o' did n't hear him, for I never hearn
o' nobody o' that name in this villadge, and I 've lived here man
and boy 76 year cum next tater diggin, and thair aint no wheres
a kitting spryer 'n I be.

   If you print 'em I wish you 'd jest let folks know who hosy's
father is, cos my ant Keziah used to say it 's nater to be curus ses
she, she aint livin though and he 's a likely kind o' lad.

                                                   EZEKIEL BIGLOW.

        Thrash away, you 'll *hev* to rattle
            On them kittle-drums o' yourn,—
        'T aint a knowin' kind o' cattle
            Thet is ketched with moldy corn;

   [1] Aut insanit, aut versus facit. — H. W.

Put in stiff, you fifer feller,
    Let folks see how spry you be,—
Guess you 'll toot till you are yeller
    'Fore you git ahold o' me!

Thet air flag 's a leetle rotten,
    Hope it aint your Sunday's best;—
Fact! it takes a sight o' cotton
    To stuff out a soger's chest:
Sence we farmers hev to pay fer 't,
    Ef you must wear humps like these,
S'posin' you should try salt hay fer 't,
    It would du ez slick ez grease.

'T would n't suit them Southun fellers,
    They're a dreffle graspin' set,
We must ollers blow the bellers
    Wen they want their irons het;
May be it 's all right ez preachin',
    But *my* narves it kind o' grates,
Wen I see the overreachin'
    O' them nigger-drivin' States.

Them thet rule us, them slave-traders,
    Haint they cut a thunderin' swarth
(Helped by Yankee renegaders),
    Thru the vartu o' the North!
We begin to think it 's nater
    To take sarse an' not be riled;—
Who 'd expect to see a tater
    All on eend at bein' biled?

Ez fer war, I call it murder,—
    There you hev it plain an' flat;
I don't want to go no furder
    Than my Testyment fer that;
God hez sed so plump an' fairly,
    It 's ez long ez it is broad,

An' you 've gut to git up airly
  Ef you want to take in God.   40

'T aint your eppyletts an' feathers
  Make the thing a grain more right;
'T aint afollerin' your bell-wethers
  Will excuse ye in His sight;
Ef you take a sword an' dror it,
  An' go stick a feller thru,
Guv'ment aint to answer for it,
  God'll send the bill to you.

Wut 's the use o' meetin'-goin'
  Every Sabbath, wet or dry,   50
Ef it 's right to go amowin'
  Feller-men like oats an' rye?
I dunno but wut it 's pooty
  Trainin' round in bobtail coats,—
But it 's curus Christian dooty
  This 'ere cuttin' folks's throats.

They may talk o' Freedom's airy
  Tell they 're pupple in the face,—
It 's a grand gret cemetary
  Fer the barthrights of our race;   60
They jest want this Californy
  So 's to lug new slave-States in
To abuse ye, an' to scorn ye,
  An' to plunder ye like sin.

Aint it cute to see a Yankee
  Take sech everlastin' pains,
All to get the Devil's thankee
  Helpin' on 'em weld their chains?
Wy, it 's jest ez clear ez figgers,
  Clear ez one an' one make two,   70
Chaps thet make black slaves o' niggers
  Want to make wite slaves o' you.

Tell ye jest the eend I 've come to
  Arter cipherin' plaguy smart,
An' it makes a handy sum, tu,
  Any gump could larn by heart;
Laborin' man an' laborin' woman
  Hev one glory an' one shame.
Ev'y thin' thet 's done inhuman
  Injers all on 'em the same.   80

'T aint by turnin' out to hack folks
  You 're agoin' to git your right,
Nor by lookin' down on black folks
  Coz you 're put upon by wite;
Slavery aint o' nary color,
  'T aint the hide thet makes it wus,
All it keers fer in a feller
  'S jest to make him fill its pus.

Want to tackle *me* in, du ye?
  I expect you 'll hev to wait;   90
Wen cold lead puts daylight thru ye
  You 'll begin to kal'late;
S'pose the crows wun't fall to pickin'
  All the carkiss from your bones,
Coz you helped to give a lickin'
  To them poor half-Spanish drones?

Jest go home an' ask our Nancy
  Wether I 'd be sech a goose
Ez to jine ye,—guess you 'd fancy
  The etarnal bung wuz loose!   100
She wants me fer home consumption,
  Let alone the hay 's to mow,—
Ef you 're arter folks o' gumption,
  You 've a darned long row to hoe.

Take them editors thet 's crowin'
  Like a cockerel three months old,—

Don't ketch any on 'em goin',
    Though they *be* so blasted bold;
Aint they a prime lot o' fellers?
    'Fore they think on 't guess they 'll sprout   110
(Like a peach thet 's got the yellers),
    With the meanness bustin' out.

Wal, go 'long to help 'em stealin'
    Bigger pens to cram with slaves,
Help the men thet 's ollers dealin'
    Insults on your fathers' graves;
Help the strong to grind the feeble,
    Help the many agin the few,
Help the men thet call your people
    Witewashed slaves an' peddlin' crew!   120

Massachusetts, God forgive her,
    She 's akneelin' with the rest,
She, thet ough' to ha' clung ferever
    In her grand old eagle-nest;
She thet ough' to stand so fearless
    W'ile the wracks are round her hurled,
Holdin' up a beacon peerless
    To the oppressed of all the world!

Ha'n't they sold your colored seamen?
    Ha'n't they made your env'ys w'iz?   130
Wut 'll make ye act like freemen?
    Wut 'll git your dander riz?
Come, I' ll tell ye wut I 'm thinkin'
    Is our dooty in this fix,
They 'd ha' done 't ez quick ez winkin'
    In the days o' seventy-six.

Clang the bells in every steeple,
    Call all true men to disown
The tradoocers of our people,
    The enslavers o' their own;   140

Let our dear old Bay State proudly
    Put the trumpet to her mouth,
Let her ring this messidge loudly
    In the ears of all the South:—

"I 'll return ye good fer evil
    Much ez we frail mortils can,
But I wun't go help the Devil
    Makin' man the cus o' man;
Call me coward, call me traiter,
    Jest ez suits your mean idees,—   150
Here I stand a tyrant-hater,
    An' the friend o' God an' Peace!"

Ef I 'd *my* way I hed ruther
    We should go to work an' part,
They take one way, we take t' other,
    Guess it would n't break my heart;
Man hed ough' to put asunder
    Them thet God has noways jined;
An' I should n't gretly wonder
    Ef there 's thousands o' my mind.   160

June 17, 1846

[The first recruiting sergeant on record I conceive to have
been that individual who is mentioned in the Book of Job as
going to and fro in the earth, and walking up and down in it.
Bishop Latimer will have him to have been a bishop, but to me
that other calling would appear more congenial. The sect of
Cainites is not yet extinct, who esteemed the first-born of
Adam to be the most worthy, not only because of that privilege
of primogeniture, but inasmuch as he was able to overcome and
slay his younger brother. That was a wise saying of the famous
Marquis Pescara to the Papal Legate, that *it was impossible for
men to serve Mars and Christ at the same time*. Yet in time past
the profession of arms was judged to be κατ' ἐξοχήν that of a
gentleman, nor does this opinion want for strenuous upholders

even in our day. Must we suppose, then, that the profession of Christianity was only intended for losels, or, at best, to afford an opening for plebeian ambition? Or shall we hold with that nicely metaphysical Pomeranian, Captain Vratz, who was Count Königsmark's chief instrument in the murder of Mr. Thynne, that the Scheme of Salvation has been arranged with an especial eye to the necessities of the upper classes, and that "God would consider *a gentleman* and deal with him suitably to the condition and profession he had placed him in"? It may be said of us all, *Exemplo plus quam ratione vivimus.* —H. W.]

No. III

WHAT MR. ROBINSON THINKS

[A few remarks on the following verses will not be out of place. The satire in them was not meant to have any personal, but only a general, application. Of the gentleman upon whose letter they were intended as a commentary Mr. Biglow had never heard, till he saw the letter itself. The position of the satirist is oftentimes one which he would not have chosen, had the election been left to himself. In attacking bad principles, he is obliged to select some individual who has made himself their exponent, and in whom they are impersonate, to the end that what he says may not, through ambiguity, be dissipated *tenues in auras.* For what says Seneca? *Longum iter per præcepta, breve et efficace per exempla.* A bad principle is comparatively harmless while it continues to be an abstraction, nor can the general mind comprehend it fully till it is printed in that large type which all men can read at sight, namely, the life and character, the sayings and doings, of particular persons. It is one of the cunningest fetches of Satan, that he never exposes himself directly to our arrows, but, still dodging behind this neighbor or that acquaintance, compels us to wound him through them, if at all. He holds our affections as hostages, the while he patches up a truce with our conscience.

Meanwhile, let us not forget that the aim of the true satirist is not to be severe upon persons, but only upon falsehood, and, as Truth and Falsehood start from the same point, and sometimes even go along together for a little way, his business is to follow the path of the latter after it diverges, and to show her floundering in the bog at the end of it. Truth is quite beyond the reach of satire. There is so brave a simplicity in her, that she can no more be made ridiculous than an oak or a pine. The danger of the satirist is, that continual use may deaden his sensibility to the force of language. He becomes more and more liable to strike harder than he knows or intends. He may be careful to put on his boxing-gloves, and yet forget that, the older they grow, the more plainly may the knuckles inside be felt. Moreover, in the heat of contest, the eye is insensibly drawn to the crown of victory, whose tawdry tinsel glitters through that dust of the ring which obscures Truth's wreath of simple leaves. I have sometimes thought that my young friend, Mr. Biglow, needed a monitory hand laid on his arm,—*aliquid sufflaminandus erat.* I have never thought it good husbandry to water the tender plants of reform with *aqua fortis*, yet, where so much is to do in the beds, he were a sorry gardener who should wage a whole day's war with an iron scuffle on those ill weeds that make the garden-walks of life unsightly, when a sprinkle of Attic salt will wither them up. *Est ars etiam maledicendi*, says Scaliger, and truly it is a hard thing to say where the graceful gentleness of the lamb merges in downright sheepishness. We may conclude with worthy and wise Dr. Fuller, that "one may be a lamb in private wrongs, but in hearing general affronts to goodness they are asses which are not lions." —H. W.]

Guvener B. is a sensible man;
   He stays to his home an' looks arter his folks;
He draws his furrer ez straight ez he can,
   An' into nobody's tater-patch pokes;
        But John P.
        Robinson he
     Sez he wunt vote fer Guvener B.

My! aint it terrible? Wut shall we du?
   We can't never choose him o' course,—thet 's flat;
Guess we shall hev to come round, (don't you?)   10
   An' go in fer thunder an' guns, an' all that;
        Fer John P.
        Robinson he
   Sez he wunt vote fer Guvener B.

Gineral C. is a dreffle smart man:
   He 's ben on all sides thet give places or pelf;
But consistency still wuz a part of his plan,—
   He 's ben true to *one* party,—an' thet is himself;—
        So John P.
        Robinson he   20
   Sez he shall vote fer Gineral C.

Gineral C. he goes in fer the war;
   He don't vally principle more 'n an old cud;
Wut did God make us raytional creeturs fer,
   But glory an' gunpowder, plunder an' blood?
        So John P.
        Robinson he
   Sez he shall vote fer Gineral C.

We were gittin' on nicely up here to our village,
   With good old idees o' wut 's right an' wut aint,   30
We kind o' thought Christ went agin war an' pillage,
   An' thet eppyletts worn't the best mark of a saint;
        But John P.
        Robinson he
   Sez this kind o' thing 's an exploded idee.

The side of our country must ollers be took,
   An' Presidunt Polk, you know, *he* is our country.
An' the angel thet writes all our sins in a book
   Puts the *debit* to him, an' to us the *per contry;*
        An' John P.   40
        Robinson he
   Sez this is his view o' the thing to a T.

Parson Wilbur he calls all these argimunts lies;
  Sez they 're nothin' on airth but jest *fee, faw, fum;*
An' thet all this big talk of our destinies
  Is half on it ign'ance, an' t' other half rum;
          But John P.
          Robinson he
  Sez it aint no sech thing; an', of course, so must we.

Parson Wilbur sez *he* never heerd in his life   50
  Thet th' Apostles rigged out in their swaller-tail coats,
An' marched round in front of a drum an' a fife,
  To git some on 'em office, an' some on 'em votes;
          But John P.
          Robinson he
  Sez they didn't know everythin' down in Judee.

Wal, it's a marcy we've gut folks to tell us
  The rights an' the wrongs o' these matters, I vow,—
God sends country lawyers, an' other wise fellers,
  To start the world's team wen it gits in a slough;   60
          Fer John P.
          Robinson he
  Sez the world 'll go right, ef he hollers out Gee!

[The attentive reader will doubtless have perceived in the
foregoing poem an allusion to that pernicious sentiment,—"Our
country, right or wrong." It is an abuse of language to call a
certain portion of land, much more, certain personages, elevated
for the time being to high station, our country. I would not
sever nor loosen a single one of those ties by which we are
united to the spot of our birth, nor minish by a tittle the respect
due to the Magistrate. I love our own Bay State too well to
do the one, and as for the other, I have myself for nigh forty
years exercised, however unworthily, the function of Justice of
the Peace, having been called thereto by the unsolicited kindness of that most excellent man and upright patriot, Caleb
Strong. *Patriæ fumus igne alieno luculentior* is best qualified

with this,—*Ubi libertas, ibi patria.* We are inhabitants of two
worlds, and owe a double, but not a divided, allegiance. In
virtue of our clay, this little ball of earth exacts a certain loyalty
of us, while, in our capacity as spirits, we are admitted citizens
of an invisible and holier fatherland. There is a patriotism of
the soul whose claim absolves us from our other and terrene
fealty. Our true country is that ideal realm which we represent
to ourselves under the names of religion, duty, and the like.
Our terrestrial organizations are but far-off approaches to so
fair a model, and all they are verily traitors who resist not any
attempt to divert them from this their original intendment.
When, therefore, one would have us to fling up our caps and
shout with the multitude,—*"Our country, however bounded!"*
he demands of us that we sacrifice the larger to the less, the
higher to the lower, and that we yield to the imaginary claims
of a few acres of soil our duty and privilege as liegemen of
Truth. Our true country is bounded on the north and the
south, on the east and the west, by Justice, and when she oversteps that invisible boundary-line by so much as a hair's breadth,
she ceases to be our mother, and chooses rather to be looked
upon *quasi noverca.* That is a hard choice when our earthly
love of country calls upon us to tread one path and our duty
points us to another. We must make as noble and becoming
an election as did Penelope between Icarius and Ulysses. Veil-
ing our faces, we must take silently the hand of Duty to follow
her. . . . H. W.]

Nov. 2, 1847

No. V

THE DEBATE IN THE SENNIT

SOT TO A NUSRY RHYME

[The incident which gave rise to the debate satirized in the
following verses was the unsuccessful attempt of Drayton and
Sayres to give freedom to seventy men and women, fellow-
beings and fellow-Christians. Had Tripoli, instead of Washing-

ton, been the scene of this undertaking, the unhappy leaders in
it would have been as secure of the theoretic as they now are of
the practical part of martyrdom. I question whether the Dey
of Tripoli is blessed with a District Attorney so benighted as
ours at the seat of government. Very fitly is he named Key,
who would allow himself to be made the instrument of locking
the door of hope against sufferers in such a cause. Not all the
waters of the ocean can cleanse the vile smutch of the jailer's
fingers from off that little Key. *Ahenea clavis*, a brazen Key
indeed!

Mr. Calhoun, who is made the chief speaker in this burlesque,
seems to think that the light of the nineteenth century is to be
put out as soon as he tinkles his little cow-bell curfew. Whenever slavery is touched, he sets up his scarecrow of dissolving
the Union. This may do for the North, but I should conjecture
that something more than a pumpkin-lantern is required to
scare manifest and irretrievable Destiny out of her path.
Mr. Calhoun cannot let go the apron-string of the Past. The
Past is a good nurse, but we must be weaned from her sooner or
later, even though, like Plotinus, we should run home from
school to ask the breast, after we are tolerably well-grown
youths. It will not do for us to hide our faces in her lap, whenever the strange Future holds out her arms and asks us to come
to her.

But we are all alike. We have all heard it said, often enough,
that little boys must not play with fire; and yet, if the matches
be taken away from us, and put out of reach upon the shelf, we
must needs get into our little corner, and scowl and stamp and
threaten the dire revenge of going to bed without our supper.
The world shall stop till we get our dangerous plaything again.
Dame Earth, meanwhile, who has more than enough household matters to mind, goes bustling hither and thither as a
hiss or a sputter tells her that this or that kettle of hers is boiling over, and before bedtime we are glad to eat our porridge
cold, and gulp down our dignity along with it.

Mr. Calhoun has somehow acquired the name of a great statesman, and, if it be great statesmanship to put lance in rest and

run a tilt at the Spirit of the Age with the certainty of being next moment hurled neck and heels into the dust amid universal laughter, he deserves the title. He is the Sir Kay of our modern chivalry. He should remember the old Scandinavian mythus. Thor was the strongest of gods, but he could not wrestle with Time, nor so much as lift up a fold of the great snake which bound the universe together; and when he smote the Earth, though with his terrible mallet, it was but as if a leaf had fallen. Yet all the while it seemed to Thor that he had only been wrestling with an old woman, striving to lift a cat, and striking a stupid giant on the head.

And in old times, doubtless, the giants *were* stupid, and there was no better sport for the Sir Launcelots and Sir Gawains than to go about cutting off their great blundering heads with enchanted swords. But things have wonderfully changed. It is the giants, nowadays, that have the science and the intelligence, while the chivalrous Don Quixotes of Conservatism still cumber themselves with the clumsy armor of a bygone age. On whirls the restless globe through unsounded time, with its cities and its silences, its births and funerals, half light, half shade, but never wholly dark, and sure to swing round into the happy morning at last. With an involuntary smile, one sees Mr. Calhoun letting slip his pack-thread cable with a crooked pin at the end of it to anchor South Carolina upon the bank and shoal of the Past.—H. W.]

TO MR. BUCKENAM

mr. Editer, As i wuz kinder prunin round, in a little nussry sot out a year or 2 a go, the Dbait in the sennit cum inter my mine An so i took & Sot it to wut I call a nussry rime. I hev made sum onnable Gentlemun speak thut dident speak in a Kind uv Poetikul lie sense the seeson is dreffle backerd up This way

ewers as ushul

HOSEA BIGLOW.

"Here we stan' on the Constitution, by thunder!
   It 's a fact o' wich ther 's bushils o' proofs;
Fer how could we trample on 't so, I wonder,
   Ef 't worn't thet it 's ollers under our hoofs?"
     Sez John C. Calhoun, sez he;
       "Human rights haint no more
       Right to come on this floor,
     No more'n the man in the moon," sez he.

"The North haint no kind o' bisness with nothin',
   An' you 've no idee how much bother it saves;   10
We aint none riled by their frettin' an' frothin',
   We 're *used* to layin' the string on our slaves,"
     Sez John C. Calhoun, sez he;—
       Sez Mister Foote,
       "I should like to shoot
     The holl gang, by the gret horn spoon!" sez he.

"Freedom's Keystone is Slavery, thet ther 's no doubt on,
   It 's sutthin' thet 's—wha' d 'ye call it?—divine,—
An' the slaves thet we ollers *make* the most out on
   Air them north o' Mason an' Dixon's line,"   20
     Sez John C. Calhoun, sez he;—
       "Fer all thet," sez Mangum,
       "'T would be better to hang 'em,
     An' so git red on 'em soon," sez he.

"The mass ough' to labor an' we lay on soffies,
   Thet 's the reason I want to spread Freedom's aree;
It puts all the cunninest on us in office,
   An' reelises our Maker's orig'nal idee,"
     Sez John C. Calhoun, sez he;—
       "Thet 's ez plain," sez Cass,   30
       "Ez thet some one 's an ass,
     It 's ez clear ez the sun is at noon," sez he.

"Now don't go to say I 'm the friend of oppression,
   But keep all your spare breath fer coolin' your broth,

Fer I ollers hev strove (at least thet 's my impression)
   To make cussed free with the rights o' the North,"
      Sez John C. Calhoun, sez he;
        "Yes," sez Davis o' Miss.,
        "The perfection o' bliss
      Is in skinnin' thet same old coon," sez he.   40

"Slavery 's a thing thet depends on complexion,
   It 's God's law thet fetters on black skins don't chafe;
Ef brains wuz to settle it (horrid reflection!)
   Wich of our onnable body 'd be safe?"
      Sez John C. Calhoun, sez he;—
        Sez Mister Hannegan,
        Afore he began agin,
      "Thet exception is quite oppertoon," sez he.

"Gen'nle Cass, Sir, you need n't be twitchin' your collar,
   Your merit 's quite clear by the dut on your knees,   50
At the North we don't make no distinctions o' color;
   You can all take a lick at our shoes wen you please,"
      Sez John C. Calhoun, sez he;—
        Sez Mister Jarnagin,
        "They wun't hev to larn agin,
      They all on 'em know the old toon," sez he.

"The slavery question aint no ways bewilderin',
   North an' South hev one int'rest, it 's plain to a glance;
No'thern men, like us patriarchs, don't sell their childrin,
   But they *du* sell themselves, ef they git a good chance,"   60
      Sez John C. Calhoun, sez he;—
        Sez Atherton here,
        "This is gittin' severe,
      I wish I could dive like a loon," sez he.

"It 'll break up the Union, this talk about freedom,
   An' your fact'ry gals (soon ez we split) 'll make head,
An' gittin' some Miss chief or other to lead 'em,
   'll go to work raisin' permiscoous Ned,"

Sez John C. Calhoun, sez he;—
    "Yes, the North," sez Colquitt,   70
    "Ef we Southeners all quit,
Would go down like a busted balloon," sez he.

"Jest look wut is doin', wut annyky 's brewin'
   In the beautiful clime o' the olive an' vine,
All the wise aristoxy 's atumblin' to ruin,
   An' the sankylots drorin' an' drinkin' their wine,"
     Sez John C. Calhoun, sez he;—
       "Yes," sez Johnson, "in France
       They 're beginnin' to dance
     Beëlzebub's own rigadoon," sez he.   80

"The South 's safe enough, it don't feel a mite skeery,
   Our slaves in their darkness an' dut air tu blest
Not to welcome with proud hallylugers the ery
   Wen our eagle kicks yourn from the naytional nest,"
     Sez John C. Calhoun, sez he;—
       "Oh," sez Westcott o' Florida,
       "Wut treason is horrider
     Then our priv'leges tryin' to proon?" sez he.

"It 's 'coz they 're so happy, thet, wen crazy sarpints
   Stick their nose in our bizness, we git so darned riled;   90
We think it 's our dooty to give pooty sharp hints,
   Thet the last crumb of Edin on airth sha' n't be spiled,"
     Sez John C. Calhoun, sez he;—
       "Ah," sez Dixon H. Lewis,
       "It perfectly true is
     Thet slavery 's airth's grettest boon," sez he.

[It was said of old time, that riches have wings; and, though
this be not applicable in a literal strictness to the wealth of our
patriarchal brethren of the South, yet it is clear that their possessions have legs, and an unaccountable propensity for using
them in a northerly direction. I marvel that the grand jury of

Washington did not find a true bill against the North Star for aiding and abetting Drayton and Sayres. It would have been quite of a piece with the intelligence displayed by the South on other questions connected with slavery. I think that no ship of state was ever freighted with a more veritable Jonah than this same domestic institution of ours. Mephistopheles himself could not feign so bitterly, so satirically sad a sight as this of three millions of human beings crushed beyond help or hope by this one mighty argument,—*Our fathers knew no better!* Nevertheless, it is the unavoidable destiny of Jonahs to be cast overboard sooner or later. Or shall we try the experiment of hiding our Jonah in a safe place, that none may lay hands on him to make jetsam of him? Let us, then, with equal forethought and wisdom, lash ourselves to the anchor, and await, in pious confidence, the certain result. Perhaps our suspicious passenger is no Jonah after all, being black. For it is well known that a superintending Providence made a kind of sandwich of Ham and his descendants, to be devoured by the Caucasian race.

In God's name, let all, who hear nearer and nearer the hungry moan of the storm and the growl of the breakers, speak out! But alas! we have no right to interfere. If a man pluck an apple of mine, he shall be in danger of the justice; but if he steal my brother, I must be silent. Who says this? Our Constitution, consecrated by the callous consuetude of sixty years, and grasped in triumphant argument by the left hand of him whose right hand clutches the clotted slave-whip. Justice, venerable with the undethronable majesty of countless æons, says,— SPEAK! The Past, wise with the sorrows and desolations of ages, from amid her shattered fanes and wolf-housing palaces, echoes,—SPEAK! Nature, through her thousand trumpets of freedom, her stars, her sunrises, her seas, her winds, her cataracts, her mountains blue with cloudy pines, blows jubilant encouragement, and cries,—SPEAK! From the soul's trembling abysses the still, small voice not vaguely murmurs,—SPEAK! But, alas! the Constitution and the Honorable Mr. Bagowind, M. C., say— BE DUMB!

It occurs to me to suggest, as a topic of inquiry in this connection, whether, on that momentous occasion when the goats and the sheep shall be parted, the Constitution and the Honorable Mr. Bagowind, M. C., will be expected to take their places on the left as our hircine vicars.

> *Quid sum miser tunc dicturus?*
> *Quem patronum rogaturus?*

There is a point where toleration sinks into sheer baseness and poltroonery. The toleration of the worst leads us to look on what is barely better as good enough, and to worship what is only moderately good. Woe to that man, or that nation, to whom mediocrity has become an ideal!

Has our experiment of self-government succeeded, if it barely manage to *rub and go?* Here, now, is a piece of barbarism which Christ and the nineteenth century say shall cease, and which Messrs. Smith, Brown, and others say shall *not* cease. I would by no means deny the eminent respectability of these gentlemen, but I confess, that, in such a wrestling-match, I cannot help having my fears for them.

> *Discite justitiam, moniti, et non temnere divos.*

H. W.]

1848

From No. VI

THE PIOUS EDITOR'S CREED

I du believe in Freedom's cause,
  Ez fur away ez Payris is;
I love to see her stick her claws
  In them infarnal Phayrisees;
It's wal enough agin a king
  To dror resolves an' triggers,—
But libbaty 's a kind o' thing
  Thet don't agree with niggers.

I du believe the people want
   A tax on teas an' coffees,   10
Thet nothin' aint extravygunt,—
   Purvidin' I 'm in office;
Fer I hev loved my country sence
   My eye-teeth filled their sockets,
An' Uncle Sam I reverence,
   Partic'larly his pockets.

I du believe in *any* plan
   O' levyin' the texes,
Ez long ez, like a lumberman,
   I git jest wut I axes;   20
I go free-trade thru thick an' thin,
   Because it kind o' rouses
The folks to vote,—an' keeps us in
   Our quiet custom-houses.

I du believe it 's wise an' good
   To sen' out furrin missions,
Thet is, on sartin understood
   An' orthydox conditions;—
I mean nine thousan' dolls. per ann.,
   Nine thousan' more fer outfit,   30
An' me to recommend a man
   The place 'ould jest about fit.

I du believe in special ways
   O' prayin' an' convartin';
The bread comes back in many days,
   An' buttered, tu, fer sartin;
I mean in preyin' till one busts
   On wut the party chooses,
An' in convartin' public trusts
   To very privit uses.   40

I du believe hard coin the stuff
   Fer 'lectioneers to spout on;

The people 's ollers soft enough
    To make hard money out on;
Dear Uncle Sam pervides fer his,
    An' gives a good-sized junk to all,—
I don't care *how* hard money is,
    Ez long ez mine 's paid punctooal.

I du believe with all my soul
    In the gret Press's freedom,   50
To pint the people to the goal
    An' in the traces lead 'em;
Palsied the arm thet forges yokes
    At my fat contracts squintin',
An' withered be the nose thet pokes
    Inter the gov'ment printin'!

I du believe thet I should give
    Wut 's his'n unto Cæsar,
Fer it 's by him I move an' live,
    Frum him my bread an' cheese air;   60
I du believe thet all o' me
    Doth bear his superscription,—
Will, conscience, honor, honesty,
    An' things o' thet description.

I du believe in prayer an' praise
    To him thet hez the grantin'
O' jobs,—in every thin' thet pays,
    But most of all in CANTIN';
This doth my cup with marcies fill,
    This lays all thought o' sin to rest,—   70
I *don't* believe in princerple,
    But oh, I *du* in interest.

I du believe in bein' this
    Or thet, ez it may happen
One way or t' other hendiest is
    To ketch the people nappin';

It aint by princerples nor men
   My preudunt course is steadied,—
I scent wich pays the best, an' then
   Go into it baldheaded.   80

I du believe thet holdin' slaves
   Comes nat'ral to a Presidunt,
Let 'lone the rowdedow it saves
   To hev a wal-broke precedunt;
Fer any office, small or gret,
   I could n't ax with no face,
'uthout I 'd ben, thru dry an' wet,
   Th' unrizzest kind o' doughface.

I du believe wutever trash
   'll keep the people in blindness,—   90
Thet we the Mexicuns can thrash
   Right inter brotherly kindness,
Thet bombshells, grape, an' powder 'n' ball
   Air good-will's strongest magnets,
Thet peace, to make it stick at all,
   Must be druv in with bagnets.

In short, I firmly du believe
   In Humbug generally,
Fer it 's a thing thet I perceive
   To hev a solid vally;   100
This heth my faithful shepherd ben,
   In pasturs sweet heth led me,
An' this 'll keep the people green
   To feed ez they hev fed me.

                               May 4, 1848

From No. VII

A LETTER

FROM A CANDIDATE FOR THE PRESIDENCY IN ANSWER TO SUTTIN
QUESTIONS PROPOSED BY MR. HOSEA BIGLOW, INCLOSED IN A
NOTE FROM MR. BIGLOW TO S. H. GAY. ESQ., EDITOR OF THE
NATIONAL ANTI-SLAVERY STANDARD.

Dear Sir,—You wish to know my notions
　　On sartin pints thet rile the land;
There 's nothin' thet my natur so shuns
　　Ez bein' mum or underhand;
I 'm a straight-spoken kind o' creetur
　　Thet blurts right out wut 's in his head,
An' ef I 've one pecooler feetur,
　　It is a nose thet wunt be led.

So, to begin at the beginnin'
　　An' come direcly to the pint,　　　　　　　10
I think the country's underpinnin'
　　Is some consid'ble out o' jint;
I aint agoin' to try your patience
　　By tellin' who done this or thet,
I don't make no insinooations,
　　I jest let on I smell a rat.

Thet is, I mean, it seems to me so,
　　But, ef the public think I 'm wrong,
I wunt deny but wut I be so,—
　　An', fact, it don't smell very strong;　　　20
My mind 's tu fair to lose its balance
　　An' say wich party hez most sense;
There may be folks o' greater talence
　　Thet can't set stiddier on the fence.

I 'm an eclectic; ez to choosin'
　　'Twixt this an' thet, I 'm plaguy lawth;

I leave a side thet looks like losin',
    But (wile there's doubt) I stick to both;
I stan' upon the Constitution,
    Ez preudunt statesmun say, who 've planned   30
A way to git the most profusion
    O' chances ez to *ware* they 'll stand.

Ez fer the war, I go agin it,—
    I mean to say I kind o' du,—
Thet is, I mean thet, bein' in it,
    The best way wuz to fight it thru;
Not but wut abstract war is horrid,
    I sign to thet with all my heart,—
But civlyzation *doos* git forrid
    Sometimes upon a powder-cart.   40

About thet darned Proviso matter
    I never hed a grain o' doubt,
Nor I aint one my sense to scatter
    So 'st no one could n't pick it out;
My love fer North an' South is equil,
    So I 'll jest answer plump an' frank,
No matter wut may be the sequil,—
    Yes, Sir, I *am* agin a Bank.

Ez to the answerin' o' questions,
    I 'm an off ox at bein' druv,   50
Though I aint one thet ary test shuns
    'll give our folks a helpin' shove;
Kind o' permiscoous I go it
    Fer the holl country, an' the ground
I take, ez nigh ez I can show it,
    Is pooty gen'ally all round.

I don't appruve o' givin' pledges;
    You 'd ough' to leave a feller free,
An' not go knockin' out the wedges
    To ketch his fingers in the tree;   60

Pledges air awfle breachy cattle
   Thet preudunt farmers don't turn out,—
Ez long 'z the people git their rattle,
   Wut is there fer 'm to grout about?

Ez to the slaves, there 's no confusion
   In *my* idees consarnin' them,—
I think they air an Institution,
   A sort of—yes, jest so,—ahem:
Do *I* own any? Of my merit
   On thet pint you yourself may jedge;   70
All is, I never drink no sperit,
   Nor I haint never signed no pledge.

Ez to my princerples, I glory
   In hevin' nothin' o' the sort;
I aint a Wig, I aint a Tory,
   I'm jest a canderdate, in short;
Thet 's fair an' square an' parpendicler
   But, ef the Public cares a fig
To hev me anthin' in particler,
   Wy, I 'm a kind o' peri-Wig.   80

P. S.

Ez we 're a sort o' privateerin',
   O' course, you know, it 's sheer an' sheer,
An' there is sutthin' wuth your hearin'
   I 'll mention in *your* privit ear;
Ef you git *me* inside the White House,
   Your head with ile I 'll kin' o' 'nint
By gittin' *you* inside the Light-house
   Down to the eend o' Jaalam Pint.

An' ez the North hez took to brustlin'
   At bein' scrouged frum off the roost,   90
I 'll tell ye wut 'll save all tusslin'
   An' give our side a harnsome boost,—

Tell 'em thet on the Slavery question
  I'm RIGHT, although to speak I 'm lawth;
This gives you a safe pint to rest on,
  An' leaves me frontin' South by North.

AN INDIAN–SUMMER REVERIE

What visionary tints the year puts on,
When falling leaves falter through motionless air
  Or humbly cling and shiver to be gone!
How shimmer the low flats and pastures bare,
  As with her nectar Hebe Autumn fills
  The bowl between me and those distant hills,
And smiles and shakes abroad her misty, tremulous hair!

No more the landscape holds its wealth apart,
Making me poorer in my poverty,
  But mingles with my senses and my heart;   10
My own projected spirit seems to me
  In her own reverie the world to steep;
  'Tis she that waves to sympathetic sleep,
Moving, as she is moved, each field and hill and tree.

How fuse and mix, with what unfelt degrees,
Clasped by the faint horizon's languid arms,
  Each into each, the hazy distances!
The softened season all the landscape charms;
  Those hills, my native village that embay,
  In waves of dreamier purple roll away,   20
And floating in mirage seem all the glimmering farms.

Far distant sounds the hidden chickadee
Close at my side; far distant sound the leaves;
  The fields seem fields of dream, where Memory
Wanders like gleaning Ruth; and as the sheaves
  Of wheat and barley wavered in the eye
  Of Boaz as the maiden's glow went by,
So tremble and seem remote all things the sense receives.

The cock's shrill trump that tells of scattered corn,
Passed breezily on by all his flapping mates,   30
    Faint and more faint, from barn to barn is borne,
Southward, perhaps to far Magellan's Straits;
    Dimly I catch the throb of distant flails;
    Silently overhead the hen-hawk sails,
With watchful, measuring eye, and for his quarry waits.

The sobered robin, hunger-silent now,
Seeks cedar-berries blue, his autumn cheer;
    The chipmunk, on the shingly shagbark's bough
Now saws, now lists with downward eye and ear,
    Then drops his nut, and, cheeping, with a bound   40
    Whisks to his winding fastness underground;
The clouds like swans drift down the streaming atmosphere.

O'er yon bare knoll the pointed cedar shadows
Drowse on the crisp, gray moss; the ploughman's call
    Creeps faint as smoke from black, fresh-furrowed meadows;
The single crow a single caw lets fall;
    And all around me every bush and tree
    Says Autumn's here, and Winter soon will be,
Who snows his soft, white sleep and silence over all.

The birch, most shy and ladylike of trees,   50
Her poverty, as best she may, retrieves,
    And hints at her foregone gentilities
With some saved relics of her wealth of leaves;
    The swamp-oak, with his royal purple on,
    Glares red as blood across the sinking sun,
As one who proudlier to a falling fortune cleaves.

He looks a sachem, in red blanket wrapt,
Who, mid some council of the sad-garbed whites,
    Erect and stern, in his own memories lapt,
With distant eye broods over other sights,   60
    Sees the hushed wood the city's flare replace,
    The wounded turf heal o'er the railway's trace,
And roams the savage Past of his undwindled rights.

The red-oak, softer-grained, yields all for lost,
And, with his crumpled foliage stiff and dry,
   After the first betrayal of the frost,
Rebuffs the kiss of the relenting sky;
   The chestnuts, lavish of their long-hid gold,
   To the faint Summer, beggared now and old,
Pour back the sunshine hoarded 'neath her favoring eye.   70

The ash her purple drops forgivingly
And sadly, breaking not the general hush;
   The maple-swamps glow like a sunset sea,
Each leaf a ripple with its separate flush;
   All round the wood's edge creeps the skirting blaze
   Of bushes low, as when, on cloudy days,
Ere the rain fall, the cautious farmer burns his brush.

O'er yon low wall, which guards one unkempt zone,
Where vines and weeds and scrub-oaks intertwine
   Safe from the plough, whose rough, discordant stone   80
Is massed to one soft gray by lichens fine,
   The tangled blackberry, crossed and recrossed, weaves
   A prickly network of ensanguined leaves;
Hard by, with coral beads, the prim black-alders shine.

Pillaring with flame this crumbling boundary,
Whose loose blocks topple 'neath the ploughboy's foot,
   Who, with each sense shut fast except the eye,
Creeps close and scares the jay he hoped to shoot,
   The woodbine up the elm's straight stem aspires,
   Coiling it, harmless, with autumnal fires;   90
In the ivy's paler blaze the martyr oak stands mute.

Below, the Charles, a stripe of nether sky,
Now hid by rounded apple-trees between,
   Whose gaps the misplaced sail sweeps bellying by,
Now flickering golden through a woodland screen,
   Then spreading out, at his next turn beyond,
   A silver circle like an inland pond—
Slips seaward silently through marshes purple and green.

Dear marshes! vain to him the gift of sight
Who cannot in their various incomes share,   100
  From every season drawn, of shade and light,
Who sees in them but levels brown and bare;
  Each change of storm or sunshine scatters free
  On them its largess of variety,
For Nature with cheap means still works her wonders rare.

In Spring they lie one broad expanse of green,
O'er which the light winds run with glimmering feet:
  Here, yellower stripes track out the creek unseen,
There, darker growths o'er hidden ditches meet;
  And purpler stains show where the blossoms crowd,   110
  As if the silent shadow of a cloud
Hung there becalmed, with the next breath to fleet.

All round, upon the river's slippery edge,
Witching to deeper calm the drowsy tide,
  Whispers and leans the breeze-entangling sedge;
Through emerald glooms the lingering waters slide,
  Or, sometimes wavering, throw back the sun,
  And the stiff banks in eddies melt and run
Of dimpling light, and with the current seem to glide.

In Summer 'tis a blithesome sight to see,   120
As, step by step, with measured swing, they pass,
  The wide-ranked mowers wading to the knee,
Their sharp scythes panting through the wiry grass;
  Then, stretched beneath a rick's shade in a ring,
  Their nooning take, while one begins to sing
A stave that droops and dies 'neath the close sky of brass.

Meanwhile that devil-may-care, the bobolink,
Remembering duty, in mid-quaver stops
  Just ere he sweeps o'er rapture's tremulous brink,
And 'twixt the winrows most demurely drops,   130
  A decorous bird of business, who provides
  For his brown mate and fledglings six besides,
And looks from right to left, a farmer 'mid his crops.

Another change subdues them in the Fall,
But saddens not; they still show merrier tints,
    Though sober russet seems to cover all;
When the first sunshine through their dewdrops glints,
    Look how the yellow clearness, streamed across,
    Redeems with rarer hues the season's loss,
As Dawn's feet there had touched and left their rosy prints.   140

Or come when sunset gives its freshened zest,
Lean o'er the bridge and let the ruddy thrill,
    While the shorn sun swells down the hazy west,
Glow opposite;—the marshes drink their fill
    And swoon with purple veins, then slowly fade
    Through pink to brown, as eastward moves the shade,
Lengthening with stealthy creep, of Simond's darkening hill.

Later, and yet ere Winter wholly shuts,
Ere through the first dry snow the runner grates,
    And the loath cart-wheel screams in slippery ruts,   150
While firmer ice the eager boy awaits,
    Trying each buckle and strap beside the fire,
    And until bedtime plays with his desire,
Twenty times putting on and off his new-bought skates;—

Then, every morn, the river's banks shine bright
With smooth plate-armor, treacherous and frail,
    By the frost's clinking hammers forged at night,
'Gainst which the lances of the sun prevail,
    Giving a pretty emblem of the day
    When guiltier arms in light shall melt away,   160
And states shall move free-limbed, loosed from war's cramping
    mail.

And now those waterfalls the ebbing river
Twice every day creates on either side
    Tinkle, as through their fresh-spared grots they shiver
In grass-arched channels to the sun denied;

High flaps in sparkling blue the far-heard crow,
  The silvered flats gleam frostily below,
Suddenly drops the gull and breaks the glassy tide.

  But crowned in turn by vying seasons three,
Their winter halo hath a fuller ring;   170
  This glory seems to rest immovably,—
The others were too fleet and vanishing;
  When the hid tide is at its highest flow,
  O'er marsh and stream one breathless trance of snow
With brooding fulness awes and hushes everything.

  The sunshine seems blown off by the bleak wind,
As pale as formal candles lit by day;
  Gropes to the sea the river dumb and blind;
The brown ricks, snow-thatched by the storm in play,
  Show pearly breakers combing o'er their lee,   180
  White crests as of some just enchanted sea,
Checked in their maddest leap and hanging poised midway.

  But when the eastern blow, with rain aslant,
From mid-sea's prairies green and rolling plains
  Drives in his wallowing herds of billows gaunt,
And the roused Charles remembers in his veins
  Old Ocean's blood and snaps his gyves of frost,
  That tyrannous silence on the shores is tost
In dreary wreck, and crumbling desolation reigns.

  Edgewsie or flat, in Druid-like device,   190
With leaden pools between or gullies bare,
  The blocks lie strewn, a bleak Stonehenge of ice;
No life, no sound, to break the grim despair,
  Save sullen plunge, as through the sedges stiff
  Down crackles riverward some thaw-sapped cliff,
Or when the close-wedged fields of ice crunch here and there.

  But let me turn from fancy-pictured scenes
To that whose pastoral calm before me lies:

Here nothing harsh or rugged intervenes;
The early evening with her misty dyes   200
   Smooths off the ravelled edges of the nigh,
   Relieves the distant with her cooler sky,
And tones the landscape down, and soothes the wearied eyes.

There gleams my native village, dear to me,
Though higher change's waves each day are seen,
   Whelming fields famed in boyhood's history,
Sanding with houses the diminished green;
   There, in red brick, which softening time defies,
   Stand square and stiff the Muses' factories;—
How with my life knit up is every well-known scene!   210

Flow on, dear river! not alone you flow
To outward sight, and through your marshes wind;
   Fed from the mystic springs of long-ago,
Your twin flows silent through my world of mind:
   Grow dim, dear marshes, in the evening's gray!
   Before my inner sight ye stretch away,
And will forever, though these fleshly eyes grow blind.

Beyond the hillock's house-bespotted swell,
Where Gothic chapels house the horse and chaise,
   Where quiet cits in Grecian temples dwell,   220
Where Coptic tombs resound with prayer and praise,
   Where dust and mud the equal year divide,
   There gentle Allston lived, and wrought, and died,
Transfiguring street and shop with his illumined gaze.

Virgilium vidi tantum,—I have seen
But as a boy, who looks alike on all,
   That misty hair, that fine Undine-like mien,
Tremulous as down to feeling's faintest call;—
   Ah, dear old homestead! count it to thy fame
   That thither many times the Painter came;—   230
One elm yet bears his name, a feathery tree and tall.

Swiftly the present fades in memory's glow,—
Our only sure possession is the past;
  The village blacksmith died a month ago,
And dim to me the forge's roaring blast;
  Soon fire-new mediævals we shall see
  Oust the black smithy from its chestnut-tree,
And that hewn down, perhaps, the beehive green and vast.

How many times, prouder than king on throne,
Loosed from the village school-dame's A's and B's,   240
  Panting have I the creaky bellows blown,
And watched the pent volcano's red increase,
  Then paused to see the ponderous sledge, brought down
  By that hard arm voluminous and brown,
From the white iron swarm its golden vanishing bees.

Dear native town! whose choking elms each year
With eddying dust before their time turn gray,
  Pining for rain,—to me thy dust is dear;
It glorifies the eve of summer day,
  And when the westering sun half sunken burns,   250
  The mote-thick air to deepest orange turns,
The westward horseman rides through clouds of gold away,

So palpable, I've seen those unshorn few,
The six old willows at the causey's end
  (Such trees Paul Potter never dreamed nor drew),
Through this dry mist their checkering shadows send,
  Striped, here and there, with many a long-drawn thread,
  Where streamed through leafy chinks the trembling red,
Past which, in one bright trail, the hangbird's flashes blend.

Yes, dearer far thy dust than all that e'er,   260
Beneath the awarded crown of victory,
  Gilded the blown Olympic charioteer;
Though lightly prized the ribboned parchments three,
  Yet *collegisse juvat*, I am glad
  That here what colleging was mine I had,—
It linked another tie, dear native town, with thee!

Nearer art thou than simply native earth,
My dust with thine concedes a deeper tie;
   A closer claim thy soil may well put forth,
Something of kindred more than sympathy;   270
   For in thy bounds I reverently laid away
   That blinding anguish of forsaken clay,
That title I seemed to have in earth and sea and sky,

   That portion of my life more choice to me
(Though brief, yet in itself so round and whole)
   Than all the imperfect residue can be;—
The Artist saw his statue of the soul
   Was perfect; so, with one regretful stroke,
   The earthen model into fragments broke,
And without her the impoverished seasons roll.   280
1846   1847

HEBE

   I saw the twinkle of white feet,
   I saw the flash of robes descending;
      Before her ran an influence fleet,
   That bowed my heart like barley bending.

      As, in bare fields, the searching bees
   Pilot to blooms beyond our finding,
      It led me on, by sweet degrees
   Joy's simple honey-cells unbinding.

      Those Graces were that seemed grim Fates;
   With nearer love the sky leaned o'er me;   10
      The long-sought Secret's golden gates
   On musical hinges swung before me.

      I saw the brimmed bowl in her grasp
   Thrilling with godhood; like a lover
      I sprang the proffered life to clasp;—
   The beaker fell; the luck was over.

The Earth has drunk the vintage up;
　What boots it patch the goblet's splinters?
　　Can Summer fill the icy cup,
Whose treacherous crystal is but Winter's?　　　　20

O spendthrift haste! await the Gods;
The nectar crowns the lips of Patience;
　Haste scatters on unthankful sods
The immortal gift in vain libations.

Coy Hebe flies from those that woo,
And shuns the hands would seize upon her;
　Follow thy life, and she will sue
To pour for thee the cup of honor.

1847

ODE TO FRANCE

February, 1848

I

As, flake by flake, the beetling avalanches
　Build up their imminent crags of noiseless snow,
Till some chance thrill the loosened ruin launches
　In unwarned havoc on the roofs below,
So grew and gathered through the silent years
　The madness of a People, wrong by wrong.
There seemed no strength in the dumb toiler's tears,
　No strength in suffering; but the Past was strong:
The brute despair of trampled centuries
　Leaped up with one hoarse yell and snapped its bands, 10
　Groped for its right with horny, callous hands,
And stared around for God with bloodshot eyes.
　What wonder if those palms were all too hard
For nice distinctions,—if that maenad throng—
　They whose thick atmosphere no bard

Had shivered with the lightning of his song,
   Brutes with the memories and desires of men,
   Whose chronicles were writ with iron pen,
     In the crooked shoulder and the forehead low,
     Set wrong to balance wrong,   20
     And physicked woe with woe?

II

They did as they were taught; not theirs the blame,
If men who scattered firebrands reaped the flame:
   They trampled Peace beneath their savage feet,
     And by her golden tresses drew
Mercy along the pavement of the street.
O Freedom! Freedom! is thy morning-dew
     So gory red? Alas, thy light had ne'er
     Shone in upon the chaos of their lair!
They reared to thee such symbol as they knew,   30
     And worshipped it with flame and blood,
     A Vengeance, axe in hand, that stood
Holding a tyrant's head up by the clotted hair.

III

What wrongs the Oppressor suffered, these we know;
   These have found piteous voice in song and prose;
But for the Oppressed, their darkness and their woe,
   Their grinding centuries,—what Muse had those?
Though hall and palace had nor eyes nor ears,
   Hardening a people's heart to senseless stone,
Thou knewest them, O Earth, that drank their tears,   40
   O Heaven, that heard their inarticulate moan!
They noted down their fetters, link by link;
Coarse was the hand that scrawled, and red the ink;
   Rude was their score, as suits unlettered men,
Notched with a headman's axe upon a block:
What marvel if, when came the avenging shock,
   'T was Atë, not Urania, held the pen?

IV

With eye averted, and an anguishing frown,
    Loathingly glides the Muse through scenes of strife,
Where like the heart of Vengeance up and down,   50
    Throbs in its framework the blood-muffled knife;
Slow are the steps of Freedom, but her feet
    Turn never backward: hers no bloody glare;
Her light is calm, and innocent, and sweet,
    And where it enters there is no despair:
Not first on palace and cathedral spire
Quivers and gleams that unconsuming fire;
    While these stand black against her morning skies,
The peasant sees it leap from peak to peak
    Along his hills; the craftsman's burning eyes   60
Own with cool tears its influence mother-meek;
    It lights the poet's heart up like a star;
    Ah! while the tyrant deemed it still afar,
And twined with golden threads his futile snare,
    That swift, convicting glow all round him ran;
'T was close beside him there,
Sunrise whose Memnon is the soul of man.

V

O Broker-King, is this thy wisdom's fruit?
    A dynasty plucked out as 't were a weed
    Grown rankly in a night, that leaves no seed!   70
Could eighteen years strike down no deeper root?
    But now thy vulture eye was turned on Spain;
A shout from Paris, and thy crown falls off,
    Thy race has ceased to reign,
And thou become a fugitive and scoff:
Slippery the feet that mount by stairs of gold,
And weakest of all fences one of steel;
    Go and keep school again like him of old,
The Syracusan tyrant;—thou mayst feel
Royal amid a birch-swayed commonweal!   80

VI

Not long can he be ruler who allows
  His time to run before him; thou wast naught
Soon as the strip of gold about thy brows
  Was no more emblem of the People's thought:
Vain were thy bayonets against the foe
  Thou hadst to cope with; thou didst wage
War not with Frenchmen merely;—no,
  Thy strife was with the Spirit of the Age,
The invisible Spirit whose first breath divine
     Scattered thy frail endeavor,   90
And, like poor last year's leaves, whirled thee and thine
     Into the Dark forever!

VII

  Is here no triumph?   Nay, what though
The yellow blood of Trade meanwhile should pour
  Along its arteries a shrunken flow,
And the idle canvas droop around the shore?
     These do not make a state,
     Nor keep it great;
     I think God made
  The earth for man, not trade;   100
And where each humblest human creature
Can stand, no more suspicious or afraid,
Erect and kingly in his right of nature,
To heaven and earth knit with harmonious ties,—
  Where I behold the exultation
  Of manhood glowing in those eyes
    That had been dark for ages,
    Or only lit with bestial loves and rages,
    There I behold a Nation:
     The France which lies   110
  Between the Pyrenees and Rhine
    Is the least part of France;
I see her rather in the soul whose shine

Burns through the craftsman's grimy countenance,
   In the new energy divine
      Of Toil's enfranchised glance.

VIII

      And if it be a dream,
   If the great Future be the little Past
'Neath a new mask, which drops and shows at last
   The same weird, mocking face to balk and blast,   120
Yet, Muse, a gladder measure suits the theme,
      And the Tyrtæan harp
   Loves notes more resolute and sharp,
Throbbing, as throbs the bosom, hot and fast:
      Such visions are of morning,
      Theirs is no vague forewarning,
The dreams which nations dream come true,
      And shape the world anew;
      If this be a sleep,
      Make it long, make it deep,   130
O Father, who sendest the harvests men reap!
      While Labor so sleepeth,
      His sorrow is gone,
   No longer he weepeth,
   But smileth and steepeth
      His thoughts in the dawn;
   He heareth Hope yonder
      Rain, lark-like, her fancies,
   His dreaming hands wander
      Mid heart's-ease and pansies;   140
   "'T is a dream! 'T is a vision!"
      Shrieks Mammon aghast;
   "The day's broad derision
      Will chase it at last;
   Ye are mad, ye have taken
   A slumbering kraken
      For firm land of the Past!"

Ah! if he awaken,
   God shield us all then,
If this dream rudely shaken   150
   Shall cheat him again!

IX

Since first I heard our North-wind blow,
Since first I saw Atlantic throw
On our grim rocks his thunderous snow,
I loved thee, Freedom; as a boy
The rattle of thy shield at Marathon
   Did with a Grecian joy
   Through all my pulses run;
But I have learned to love thee now
Without the helm upon thy gleaming brow,   160
   A maiden mild and undefiled
Like her who bore the world's redeeming child;
  And surely never did thine altars glance
  With purer fires than now in France;
  While, in their clear white flashes,
   Wrong's shadow, backward cast,
  Waves cowering o'er the ashes
   Of the dead, blaspheming Past,
  O'er the shapes of fallen giants,
   His own unburied brood,   170
  Whose dead hands clench defiance
   At the overpowering Good:
And down the happy future runs a flood
   Of prophesying light;
It shows an Earth no longer stained with blood,
Blossom and fruit where now we see the bud
   Of Brotherhood and Right.

                    1848

THE FIRST SNOW-FALL

The snow had begun in the gloaming,
   And busily all the night

    Had been heaping field and highway
      With a silence deep and white.

Every pine and fir and hemlock
    Wore ermine too dear for an earl,
And the poorest twig on the elm-tree
    Was ridged inch deep with pearl.

From shed new-roofed with Carrara
    Came Chanticleer's muffled crow,   10
The stiff rails softened to swans-down,
    And still fluttered down the snow.

I stood and watched by the window
    The noiseless work of the sky,
And the sudden flurries of snow-birds,
    Like brown leaves whirling by.

I thought of a mound in sweet Auburn
    Where a little headstone stood;
How the flakes were folding it gently,
    As did robins the babes in the wood.   20

Up spoke our own little Mabel,
    Saying, "Father, who makes it snow?"
And I told of the good All-father
    Who cares for us here below.

Again I looked at the snow-fall,
    And thought of the leaden sky
That arched o'er our first great sorrow,
    When that mound was heaped so high.

I remembered the gradual patience
    That fell from that cloud like snow,   30
Flake by flake, healing and hiding
    The scar that renewed our woe.

And again to the child I whispered,
  "The snow that husheth all,
Darling, the merciful Father
  Alone can make it fall!"

Then, with eyes that saw not, I kissed her,
  And she, kissing back, could not know
That *my* kiss was given to her sister,
  Folded close under deepening snow.   40
                                1849

THE VISION OF SIR LAUNFAL

PRELUDE TO PART FIRST

Over his keys the musing organist,
  Beginning doubtfully and far away,
First lets his fingers wander as they list,
  And builds a bridge from Dreamland for his lay:
Then, as the touch of his loved instrument
  Gives hope and fervor, nearer draws his theme,
First guessed by faint auroral flushes sent
  Along the wavering vista of his dream.
  Not only around our infancy
  Doth heaven with all its splendors lie;   10
  Daily, with souls that cringe and plot,
  We Sinais climb and know it not.

Over our manhood bend the skies;
  Against our fallen and traitor lives
The great winds utter prophecies;
  With our faint hearts the mountain strives;
Its arms outstretched, the druid wood
  Waits with its benedicite;
And to our age's drowsy blood
  Still shouts the inspiring sea.   20

Earth gets its price for what Earth gives us;
    The beggar is taxed for a corner to die in,
The priest hath his fee who comes and shrives us,
    We bargain for the graves we lie in;
At the devil's booth are all things sold,
Each ounce of dross costs its ounce of gold;
    For a cap and bells our lives we pay,
Bubbles we buy with a whole soul's tasking:
    'Tis heaven alone that is given away,
'Tis only God may be had for the asking;   30
No price is set on the lavish summer;
June may be had by the poorest comer.

And what is so rare as a day in June?
    Then, if ever, come perfect days;
Then Heaven tries earth if it be in tune,
    And over it softly her warm ear lays;
Whether we look, or whether we listen,
We hear life murmur, or see it glisten;
Every clod feels a stir of might,
    An instinct within it that reaches and towers,   40
And, groping blindly above it for light,
    Climbs to a soul in grass and flowers;
The flush of life may well be seen
    Thrilling back over hills and valleys;
The cowslip startles in meadows green,
    The buttercup catches the sun in its chalice,
And there's never a leaf nor a blade too mean
    To be some happy creature's palace;
The little bird sits at his door in the sun,
    Atilt like a blossom among the leaves,   50
And lets his illumined being o'errun
    With the deluge of summer it receives;
His mate feels the eggs beneath her wings,
And the heart in her dumb breast flutters and sings;
He sings to the wide world, and she to her nest,—
In the nice ear of Nature which song is the best?

Now is the high-tide of the year,
   And whatever of life hath ebbed away
Comes flooding back with a ripply cheer,
   Into every bare inlet and creek and bay;   60
Now the heart is so full that a drop overfills it,
We are happy now because God wills it;
No matter how barren the past may have been,
'Tis enough for us now that the leaves are green;
We sit in the warm shade and feel right well
How the sap creeps up and the blossoms swell;
We may shut our eyes, but we cannot help knowing
That skies are clear and grass is growing;
The breeze comes whispering in our ear,
That dandelions are blossoming near,   70
   That maize has sprouted, that streams are flowing,
That the river is bluer than the sky,
That the robin is plastering his house hard by;
And if the breeze kept the good news back,
For other couriers we should not lack;
   We could guess it all by yon heifer's lowing,—
And hark! how clear bold chanticleer,
Warmed with the new wine of the year,
   Tells all in his lusty crowing!

Joy comes, grief goes, we know not how;   80
Everything is happy now,
   Everything is upward striving;
'Tis as easy now for the heart to be true
As for grass to be green or skies to be blue,—
   'Tis the natural way of living:
Who knows whither the clouds have fled?
   In the unscarred heaven they leave no wake;
And the eyes forget the tears they have shed,
   The heart forgets its sorrow and ache;
The soul partakes the season's youth,   90
   And the sulphurous rifts of passion and woe

Lie deep 'neath a silence pure and smooth,
  Like burnt-out craters healed with snow.
What wonder if Sir Launfal now
Remembered the keeping of his vow?

PART FIRST

I

"My golden spurs now bring to me,
  And bring to me my richest mail,
For tomorrow I go over land and sea
  In search of the Holy Grail;
Shall never a bed for me be spread,   100
Nor shall a pillow be under my head,
Till I begin my vow to keep;
Here on the rushes will I sleep,
And perchance there may come a vision true
Ere day create the world anew."
    Slowly Sir Launfal's eyes grew dim,
    Slumber fell like a cloud on him,
  And into his soul the vision flew.

II

The crows flapped over by twos and threes,
In the pool drowsed the cattle up to their knees,   110
  The little birds sang as if it were
  The one day of summer in all the year,
And the very leaves seemed to sing on the trees:
The castle alone in the landscape lay
Like an outpost of winter, dull and gray:
'Twas the proudest hall in the North Countree,
And never its gates might opened be,
Save to lord or lady of high degree;
Summer besieged it on every side,
But the churlish stone her assaults defied;   120
She could not scale the chilly wall,

Though around it for leagues her pavilions tall
Stretched left and right,
Over the hills and out of sight;
   Green and broad was every tent,
   And out of each a murmur went
Till the breeze fell off at night.

III

The drawbridge dropped with a surly clang,
And through the dark arch a charger sprang,
Bearing Sir Launfal, the maiden knight,   130
In his gilded mail, that flamed so bright
It seemed the dark castle had gathered all
Those shafts the fierce sun had shot over its wall
   In his siege of three hundred summers long,
And, binding them all in one blazing sheaf,
   Had cast them forth: so, young and strong,
And lightsome as a locust-leaf,
Sir Launfal flashed forth in his maiden mail,
To seek in all climes for the Holy Grail.

IV

It was morning on hill and stream and tree,   140
   And morning in the young knight's heart;
Only the castle moodily
Rebuffed the gifts of the sunshine free,
   And gloomed by itself apart;
The season brimmed all other things up
Full as the rain fills the pitcher-plant's cup.

V

As Sir Launfal made morn through the darksome gate,
   He was 'ware of a leper, crouched by the same,
Who begged with his hand and moaned as he sate;
   And a loathing over Sir Launfal came;   150
The sunshine went out of his soul with a thrill,
   The flesh 'neath his armor 'gan shrink and crawl,

And midway its leap his heart stood still
    Like a frozen waterfall;
For this man, so foul and bent of stature,
Rasped harshly against his dainty nature,
And seemed the one blot on the summer morn,—
So he tossed him a piece of gold in scorn.

VI

The leper raised not the gold from the dust:
"Better to me the poor man's crust,   160
Better the blessing of the poor,
Though I turn me empty from his door;
That is no true alms which the hand can hold;
He gives only the worthless gold
    Who gives from a sense of duty;
But he who gives but a slender mite,
And gives to that which is out of sight,
    That thread of the all-sustaining Beauty
Which runs through all and doth all unite,—
The hand cannot clasp the whole of his alms,   170
The heart outstretches its eager palms,
For a god goes with it and makes it store
To the soul that was starving in darkness before."

PRELUDE TO PART SECOND

Down swept the chill wind from the mountain peak,
    From the snow five thousand summers old;
On open wold and hilltop bleak
    It had gathered all the cold,
And whirled it like sleet on the wanderer's cheek;
It carried a shiver everywhere
From the unleafed boughs and pastures bare;   180
The little brook heard it and built a roof
'Neath which he could house him, winterproof;
All night by the white stars' frosty gleams
He groined his arches and matched his beams;

Slender and clear were his crystal spars
As the lashes of light that trim the stars:
He sculptured every summer delight
In his halls and chambers out of sight;
Sometimes his tinkling waters slipt
Down through a frost-leaved forest-crypt,   190
Long, sparkling aisles of steel-stemmed trees
Bending to counterfeit a breeze;
Sometimes the roof no fretwork knew
But silvery mosses that downward grew;
Sometimes it was carved in sharp relief
With quaint arabesques of ice-fern leaf;
Sometimes it was simply smooth and clear
For the gladness of heaven to shine through, and here
He had caught the nodding bulrush-tops
And hung them thickly with diamond drops,   200
That crystalled the beams of moon and sun,
And made a star of every one:
No mortal builder's most rare device
Could match this winter-palace of ice;
'Twas as if every image that mirrored lay
In his depths serene through the summer day,
Each fleeting shadow of earth and sky,
    Lest the happy model should be lost,
Had been mimicked in fairy masonry
    By the elfin builders of the frost.   210

Within the hall are song and laughter,
    The cheeks of Christmas glow red and jolly,
And sprouting is every corbel and rafter
    With lightsome green of ivy and holly;
Through the deep gulf of the chimney wide
Wallows the Yule-log's roaring tide;
The broad flame-pennons droop and flap
    And belly and tug as a flag in the wind;
Like a locust shrills the imprisoned sap,
    Hunted to death in its galleries blind;   220

And swift little troops of silent sparks,
　　Now pausing, now scattering away as in fear,
Go threading the soot-forest's tangled darks
　　Like herds of startled deer.

But the wind without was eager and sharp,
Of Sir Launfal's gray hair it makes a harp,
　　And rattles and wrings
　　The icy strings,
　Singing, in dreary monotone,
　A Christmas carol of its own,   230
　Whose burden still, as he might guess,
　Was "Shelterless, shelterless, shelterless!"
The voice of the seneschal flared like a torch
As he shouted the wanderer away from the porch,
And he sat in the gateway and saw all night
　　The great hall-fire, so cheery and bold,
　　Through the window-slits of the castle old,
Build out its piers of ruddy light
Against the drift of the cold.

PART SECOND

I

There was never a leaf on bush or tree,   240
The bare boughs rattled shudderingly;
The river was dumb and could not speak,
　For the weaver Winter its shroud had spun;
A single crow on the tree-top bleak
　From his shining feathers shed off the cold sun;
Again it was morning, but shrunk and cold,
As if her veins were sapless and old,
And she rose up decrepitly
For a last dim look at earth and sea.

II

Sir Launfal turned from his own hard gate,   250
For another heir in his earldom sate;

An old, bent man, worn out and frail,
He came back from seeking the Holy Grail;
Little he recked of his earldom's loss,
No more on his surcoat was blazoned the cross,
But deep in his soul the sign he wore,
The badge of the suffering and the poor.

III

Sir Launfal's raiment thin and spare
Was idle mail 'gainst the barbèd air,
For it was just at the Christmas time;   260
So he mused, as he sat, of a sunnier clime,
And sought for a shelter from cold and snow
In the light and warmth of long-ago;
He sees the snake-like caravan crawl
O'er the edge of the desert, black and small,
Then nearer and nearer, till, one by one,
He can count the camels in the sun,
As over the red-hot sands they pass
To where, in its slender necklace of grass,
The little spring laughed and leapt in the shade,   270
And with its own self like an infant played,
And waved its signal of palms.

IV

"For Christ's sweet sake, I beg an alms";
The happy camels may reach the spring,
But Sir Launfal sees only the grewsome thing,
The leper, lank as the rain-blanched bone,
That cowers beside him, a thing as lone
And white as the ice-isles of Northern seas
In the desolate horror of his disease.

V

And Sir Launfal said, "I behold in thee   280
An image of Him who died on the tree;

Thou also hast had thy crown of thorns,
Thou also hast had the world's buffets and scorns,
And to thy life were not denied
The wounds in the hands and feet and side:
Mild Mary's Son, acknowledge me;
Behold, through him, I give to thee!"

VI

Then the soul of the leper stood up in his eyes
   And looked at Sir Launfal, and straightway he
Remembered in what a haughtier guise   290
   He had flung an alms to leprosie,
When he girt his young life up in gilded mail
And set forth in search of the Holy Grail.
The heart within him was ashes and dust;
He parted in twain his single crust,
He broke the ice on the streamlet's brink,
And gave the leper to eat and drink,
'Twas a mouldy crust of coarse brown bread,
   'Twas water out of a wooden bowl,—
Yet with fine wheaten bread was the leper fed,   300
   And 'twas red wine he drank with his thirsty soul.

VII

As Sir Launfal mused with a downcast face,
A light shone round about the place;
The leper no longer crouched at his side,
But stood before him glorified,
Shining and tall and fair and straight
As the pillar that stood by the Beautiful Gate,—
Himself the Gate whereby men can
Enter the temple of God in Man.

VIII

His words were shed softer than leaves from the pine, 310
And they fell on Sir Launfal as snows on the brine,

That mingle their softness and quiet in one
With the shaggy unrest they float down upon;
And the voice that was softer than silence said,
"Lo, it is I, be not afraid!
In many climes, without avail,
Thou hast spent thy life for the Holy Grail;
Behold, it is here,—this cup which thou
Didst fill at the streamlet for me but now;
This crust is my body broken for thee,   320
This water his blood that died on the tree;
The Holy Supper is kept, indeed,
In whatso we share with another's need;
Not what we give, but what we share,
For the gift without the giver is bare;
Who gives himself with his alms feeds three,
Himself, his hungering neighbor, and me."

IX

Sir Launfal awoke as from a swound:
"The Grail in my castle here is found!
Hang my idle armor up on the wall,   330
Let it be the spider's banquet-hall;
He must be fenced with stronger mail
Who would seek and find the Holy Grail."

X

The castle gate stands open now,
    And the wanderer is welcome to the hall
As the hangbird is to the elm-tree bough;
    No longer scowl the turrets tall,
The Summer's long siege at last is o'er;
When the first poor outcast went in at the door,
She entered with him in disguise,   340
And mastered the fortress by surprise;
There is no spot she loves so well on ground,
She lingers and smiles there the whole year round;

The meanest serf on Sir Launfal's land
Has hall and bower at his command;
And there's no poor man in the North Countree
But is the lord of the earldom as much as he.
1848   1848

From A FABLE FOR CRITICS

*Reader! walk up at once (it will soon be too late), and buy
at a perfectly ruinous rate*

A FABLE FOR CRITICS:

OR, BETTER,

(I LIKE, AS A THING THAT THE READER'S FIRST FANCY MAY STRIKE,
AN OLD-FASHIONED TITLE-PAGE, SUCH AS PRESENTS A TABULAR
VIEW OF THE VOLUME'S CONTENTS),

A GLANCE AT A FEW OF OUR LITERARY PROGENIES

(MRS. MALAPROP'S WORD)

FROM THE TUB OF DIOGENES;

A VOCAL AND MUSICAL MEDLEY,

THAT IS,

A SERIES OF JOKES

𝔅𝔶 𝔄 𝔚𝔬𝔫𝔡𝔢𝔯𝔣𝔲𝔩 𝔔𝔲𝔦𝔷.

WHO ACCOMPANIES HIMSELF WITH A RUB-A-DUD-DUB, FULL OF
SPIRIT AND GRACE, ON THE TOP OF THE TUB.

*Set forth in October, the 31st day,
In the year '48, G. P. Putnam, Broadway.*

———————

It being the commonest mode of procedure, I premise a few
candid remarks

To the Reader:—

This trifle, begun to please only myself and my own private fancy, was laid on the shelf. But some friends, who had seen it, induced me, by dint of saying they liked it, to put it in print. That is, having come to that very conclusion, I asked their advice when 'twould make no confusion. For though (in the gentlest of ways) they had hinted it was scarce worth the while, I should doubtless have printed it.

I began it, intending a Fable, a frail, slender thing, rhyme-ywinged, with a sting in its tail. But, by addings and alterings not previously planned, digressions chance-hatched, like birds' eggs in the sand, and dawdlings to suit every whimsey's demand (always freeing the bird which I held in my hand, for the two perched, perhaps out of reach, in the tree),—it grew by degrees to the size which you see. I was like the old woman that carried the calf, and my neighbors, like hers, no doubt, wonder and laugh; and when, my strained arms with their grown burthen full, I call it my Fable, they call it a bull.

Having scrawled at full gallop (as far as that goes) in a style that is neither good verse nor bad prose, and being a person whom nobody knows, some people will say I am rather more free with my readers than it is becoming to be, that I seem to expect them to wait on my leisure in following wherever I wander at pleasure, that, in short, I take more than a young author's lawful ease, and laugh in a queer way so like Mephistopheles, that the Public will doubt, as they grope through my rhythm, if in truth I am making fun *of* them or *with* them.

So the excellent Public is hereby assured that the sale of my book is already secured. For there is not a poet throughout the whole land but will purchase a copy or two out of hand, in the fond expectation of being amused in it, by seeing his betters cut up and abused in it. Now, I find, by a pretty exact calculation, there are something like ten thousand bards in the nation, of that special variety whom the Review and Magazine critics call *lofty* and *true*, and about thirty thousand (*this* tribe is increasing) of the kinds who are termed *full of promise* and *pleasing*. The Public will see by a glance at this schedule, that they cannot expect me to be over-sedulous about courting *them*, since it seems I have got enough fuel made sure of for boiling my pot.

As for such of our poets as find not their names mentioned once in my pages, with praises or blames, let them SEND IN THEIR CARDS, without further DELAY, to my friend G. P. PUT-NAM, Esquire, in Broadway, where a LIST will be kept with the strictest regard to the day and the hour of receiving the card. Then, taking them up as I chance to have time (that is, if their names can be twisted in rhyme), I will honestly give each his PROPER POSITION, at the rate of ONE AUTHOR to each NEW EDI-TION. Thus a PREMIUM is offered sufficiently HIGH (as the magazines say when they tell their best lie) to induce bards to CLUB their resources and buy the balance of every edition, until they have all of them fairly been run through the mill.

One word to such readers (judicious and wise) as read books with something behind the mere eyes, of whom in the country, perhaps, there are two, including myself, gentle reader, and you. All the characters sketched in this slight *jeu d'esprit*, though, it may be, they seem, here and there, rather free, and drawn from a somewhat too cynical standpoint, are *meant* to be faithful, for that is the grand point, and none but an owl would feel sore at a rub from a jester who tells you, without any subterfuge, that he sits in Diogenes' tub.

Phœbus, sitting one day in a laurel-tree's shade,
Was reminded of Daphne, of whom it was made,
For the god being one day too warm in his wooing,
She took to the tree to escape his pursuing;
Be the cause what it might, from his offers she shrunk,
And, Ginevra-like, shut herself up in a trunk;
And, though 'twas a step into which he had driven her,
He somehow or other had never forgiven her;
Her memory he nursed as a kind of a tonic,
Something bitter to chew when he'd play the Byronic,   10
And I can't count the obstinate nymphs that he brought over
By a strange kind of smile he put on when he thought of her.
"My case is like Dido's," he sometimes remarked;

"When I last saw my love, she was fairly embarked
In a laurel, as *she* thought—but (ah, how Fate mocks!)
She has found it by this time a very bad box;
Let hunters from me take this saw when they need it,—
You're not always sure of your game when you've treed it.
Just conceive such a change taking place in one's mistress!
What romance would be left?—who can flatter or kiss trees?   20
And, for mercy's sake, how could one keep up a dialogue
With a dull wooden thing that will live and will die a log,—
Not to say that the thought would forever intrude
That you've less chance to win her the more she is wood?
Ah! it went to my heart, and the memory still grieves,
To see those loved graces all taking their leaves;
Those charms beyond speech, so enchanting but now,
As they left me forever, each making its bough!
If her tongue *had* a tang sometimes more than was right,
Her new bark is worse than ten times her old bite."   30

                              *   *   *

    Apollo looked up, hearing footsteps approaching,
And slipped out of sight the new rhymes he was broaching,—
"Good day, Mr. D—, I'm happy to meet
With a scholar so ripe, and a critic so neat,
Who through Grub Street the soul of a gentleman carries;
What news from that suburb of London and Paris
Which latterly makes such shrill claims to monopolize
The credit of being the New World's metropolis?"

    "Why, nothing of consequence, save this attack
On my friend there, behind, by some pitiful hack,   40
Who thinks every national author a poor one,
That isn't a copy of something that's foreign,
And assaults the American Dick—"
                              "Nay, 'tis clear
That your Damon there's fond of a flea in his ear,
And, if no one else furnished them gratis, on tick
He would buy some himself, just to hear the old click;

Why, I honestly think, if some fool in Japan
Should turn up his nose at the 'Poems on Man'
(Which contain many verses as fine, by the bye,
As any that lately came under my eye),   50
Your friend there by some inward instinct would know it,
Would get it translated, reprinted, and show it;
As a man might take off a high stock to exhibit
The autograph round his own neck of the gibbet;
Nor would let it rest so, but fire column after column,
Signed Cato, or Brutus, or something as solemn,
By way of displaying his critical crosses,
And tweaking that poor transatlantic proboscis,
His broadsides resulting (this last there's no doubt of)
In successively sinking the craft they're fired out of.   60
Now nobody knows when an author is hit,
If he have not a public hysterical fit;
Let him only keep close in his snug garret's dim ether,
And nobody'd think of his foes—or of him either;
If an author have any least fibre of worth in him,
Abuse would but tickle the organ of mirth in him;
All the critics on earth cannot crush with their ban
One word that's in tune with the nature of man."

                              *   *   *

  "But stay, here comes Tityrus Griswold, and leads on
The flocks whom he first plucks alive, and then feeds on,—   70
A loud-cackling swarm, in whose feathers warm drest,
He goes for as perfect a—swan as the rest.

  "There comes Emerson first, whose rich words, every one,
Are like gold nails in temples to hang trophies on,
Whose prose is grand verse, while his verse, the Lord knows,
Is some of it pr—No, 'tis not even prose;
I'm speaking of metres; some poems have welled
From those rare depths of soul that have ne'er been excelled;
They're not epics, but that doesn't matter a pin,
In creating, the only hard thing's to begin;   80

A grass-blade's no easier to make than an oak;
If you've once found the way, you've achieved the grand stroke;
In the worst of his poems are mines of rich matter,
But thrown in a heap with a crash and a clatter;
Now it is not one thing nor another alone
Makes a poem, but rather the general tone,
The something pervading, uniting the whole,
The before unconceived, unconceivable soul,
So that just in removing this trifle or that, you
Take away, as it were, a chief limb of the statue;   90
Roots, wood, bark, and leaves singly perfect may be,
But, clapt hodge-podge together, they don't make a tree.

"But, to come back to Emerson (whom, by the way,
I believe we left waiting),—his is, we may say,
A Greek head on right Yankee shoulders, whose range
Has Olympus for one pole, for t'other the Exchange;
He seems, to my thinking (although I'm afraid
The comparison must, long ere this, have been made),
A Plotinus-Montaigne, where the Egyptian's gold mist
And the Gascon's shrewd wit cheek-by-jowl coexist;   100
All admire, and yet scarcely six converts he's got
To I don't (nor they either) exactly know what;
For though he builds glorious temples, 'tis odd
He leaves never a doorway to get in a god.
'Tis refreshing to old-fashioned people like me
To meet such a primitive Pagan as he,
In whose mind all creation is duly respected
As parts of himself—just a little projected;
And who's willing to worship the stars and the sun,
A convert to—nothing but Emerson.   110
So perfect a balance there is in his head,
That he talks of things sometimes as if they were dead;
Life, nature, love, God, and affairs of that sort,
He looks at as merely ideas; in short,
As if they were fossils stuck round in a cabinet,
Of such vast extent that our earth's a mere dab in it;

Composed just as he is inclined to conjecture her,
Namely, one part pure earth, ninety-nine parts pure lecturer;
You are filled with delight at his clear demonstration,
Each figure, word, gesture, just fits the occasion,   120
With the quiet precision of science he'll sort 'em,
But you can't help suspecting the whole a *post mortem.*

"There are persons, mole-blind to the soul's make and style,
Who insist on a likeness 'twixt him and Carlyle;
To compare him with Plato would be vastly fairer,
Carlyle's the more burly, but E. is the rarer;
He sees fewer objects, but clearlier, truelier,
If C.'s as original, E.'s more peculiar;
That he's more of a man you might say of the one,
Of the other he's more of an Emerson;   130
C.'s the Titan, as shaggy of mind as of limb,—
E. the clear-eyed Olympian, rapid and slim;
The one's two thirds Norseman, the other half Greek,
Where the one's most abounding, the other's to seek;
C.'s generals require to be seen in the mass,—
E.'s specialties gain if enlarged by the glass;
C. gives nature and God his own fits of the blues,
And rims common-sense things with mystical hues,—
E. sits in a mystery calm and intense,
And looks coolly around him with sharp common-sense;   140
C. shows you how every-day matters unite
With the dim transdiurnal recesses of night,—
While E., in a plain, preternatural way,
Makes mysteries matters of mere every day;
C. draws all his characters quite *à la* Fuseli,—
Not sketching their bundles of muscles and thews illy,
He paints with a brush so untamed and profuse
They seem nothing but bundles of muscles and thews;
E. is rather like Flaxman, lines strait and severe,
And a colorless outline, but full, round, and clear;—   150
To the men he thinks worthy he frankly accords
The design of a white marble statue in words.

C. labors to get at the centre, and then
Take a reckoning from there of his actions and men;
E. calmly assumes the said centre as granted,
And, given himself, has whatever is wanted.

"He has imitators in scores, who omit
No part of the man but his wisdom and wit,—
Who go carefully o'er the sky-blue of his brain,
And when he has skimmed it once, skim it again;   160
If at all they resemble him, you may be sure it is
Because their shoals mirror his mists and obscurities,
As a mud-puddle seems deep as heaven for a minute,
While a cloud that floats o'er is reflected within it.

"There comes ——, for instance; to see him's rare sport,
Tread in Emerson's tracks with legs painfully short;
How he jumps, how he strains, and gets red in the face,
To keep step with the mystagogue's natural pace!
He follows as close as a stick to a rocket,
His fingers exploring the prophet's each pocket.   170
Fie, for shame, brother bard; with good fruit of your own,
Can't you let Neighbor Emerson's orchards alone?
Besides, 'tis no use, you'll not find e'en a core,—
—— has picked up all the windfalls before.
They might strip every tree, and E. never would catch 'em,
His Hesperides have no rude dragon to watch 'em;
When they send him a dishful, and ask him to try 'em,
He never suspects how the sly rogues came by 'em;
He wonders why 'tis there are none such his trees on,
And thinks 'em the best he has tasted this season.   180

* * *

"There is Bryant, as quiet, as cool, and as dignified,
As a smooth, silent iceberg, that never is ignified,
Save when by reflection 'tis kindled o' nights
With a semblance of flame by the chill Northern Lights.
He may rank (Griswold says so) first bard of your nation
(There's no doubt that he stands in supreme iceolation),

Your topmost Parnassus he may set his heel on,
But no warm applauses come, peal following peal on,—
He's too smooth and too polished to hang any zeal on:
Unqualified merits, I'll grant, if you choose, he has 'em,   190
But he lacks the one merit of kindling enthusiasm;
If he stir you at all, it is just, on my soul,
Like being stirred up with the very North Pole.

"He is very nice reading in summer, but *inter
Nos*, we don't want *extra* freezing in winter;
Take him up in the depth of July, my advice is,
When you feel an Egyptian devotion to ices.
But, deduct all you can, there's enough that's right good in him,
He has a true soul for field, river, and wood in him;
And his heart, in the midst of brick walls, or where'er it is, 200
Glows, softens, and thrills with the tenderest charities—
To you mortals that delve in this trade-ridden planet?
No, to old Berkshire's hills, with their limestone and granite.
If you're one who *in loco* (add *foco* here) *desipis*,
You will get of his outermost heart (as I guess) a piece;
But you'd get deeper down if you came as a precipice,
And would break the last seal of its inwardest fountain,
If you only could palm yourself off for a mountain.
Mr. Quivis, or somebody quite as discerning,
Some scholar who's hourly expecting his learning,   210
Calls B. the American Wordsworth; but Wordsworth
May be rated at more than your whole tuneful herd's worth.
No, don't be absurd, he's an excellent Bryant;
But, my friends, you'll endanger the life of your client,
By attempting to stretch him up into a giant:
If you choose to compare him, I think there are two per-
-sons fit for a parallel—Thomson and Cowper[1];

---

[1] To demonstrate quickly and easily how per-
-versely absurd 'tis to sound this name *Cowper*,
As people in general call him named *super*,
I remark that he rhymes it himself with horse-trooper.
    [Lowell's note.]

I don't mean exactly,—there's something of each,
There's T.'s love of nature, C.'s penchant to preach;
Just mix up their minds so that C.'s spice of craziness   220
Shall balance and neutralize T.'s turn for laziness,
And it gives you a brain cool, quite frictionless, quiet,
Whose internal police nips the buds of all riot,—
A brain like a permanent strait-jacket put on
The heart that strives vainly to burst off a button,—
A brain which, without being slow or mechanic,
Does more than a larger less drilled, more volcanic;
He's a Cowper condensed, with no craziness bitten,
And the advantage that Wordsworth before him had written.

"But, my dear little bardlings, don't prick up your ears   230
Nor suppose I would rank you and Bryant as peers;
If I call him an iceberg, I don't mean to say
There is nothing in that which is grand in its way;
He is almost the one of your poets that knows
How much grace, strength, and dignity lie in Repose;
If he sometimes fall short, he is too wise to mar
His thought's modest fulness by going too far;
'Twould be well if your authors should all make a trial
Of what virtue there is in severe self-denial,
And measure their writings by Hesiod's staff,   240
Which teaches that all has less value than half.

"There is Whittier, whose swelling and vehement heart
Strains the strait-breasted drab of the Quaker apart,
And reveals the live Man, still supreme and erect,
Underneath the bemummying wrappers of sect;
There was ne'er a man born who had more of the swing
Of the true lyric bard and all that kind of thing;
And his failures arise (though he seem not to know it)
From the very same cause that has made him a poet,—
A fervor of mind which knows no separation   250
'Twixt simple excitement and pure inspiration,
As my Pythoness erst sometimes erred from not knowing
If 'twere I or mere wind through her tripod was blowing;

Let his mind once get head in its favorite direction
And the torrent of verse bursts the dams of reflection,
While, borne with the rush of the metre along,
The poet may chance to go right or go wrong,
Content with the whirl and delirium of song;
Then his grammar's not always correct, nor his rhymes,
And he's prone to repeat his own lyrics sometimes,   260
Not his best, though, for those are struck off at white-heats
When the heart in his breast like a trip-hammer beats,
And can ne'er be repeated again any more
Than they could have been carefully plotted before:
Like old what's-his-name there at the battle of Hastings
(Who, however, gave more than mere rhythmical bastings),
Our Quaker leads off metaphorical fights
For reform and whatever they call human rights,
Both singing and striking in front of the war,
And hitting his foes with the mallet of Thor;   270
Anne haec, one exclaims, on beholding his knocks,
Vestis filii tui, O leather-clad Fox?
Can that be thy son, in the battle's mid din,
Preaching brotherly love and then driving it in
To the brain of the tough old Goliath of sin,
With the smoothest of pebbles from Castaly's spring
Impressed on his hard moral sense with a sling?

"All honor and praise to the right-hearted bard
Who was true to The Voice when such service was hard,
Who himself was so free he dared sing for the slave   280
When to look but a protest in silence was brave;
All honor and praise to the women and men
Who spoke out for the dumb and the down-trodden then!
It needs not to name them, already for each
I see History preparing the statue and niche;
They were harsh, but shall *you* be so shocked at hard words
Who have beaten your pruning-hooks up into swords,
Whose rewards and hurrahs men are surer to gain
By the reaping of men and of women than grain?

Why should *you* stand aghast at their fierce wordy war, if   290
You scalp one another for Bank or for Tariff?
Your calling them cut-throats and knaves all day long
Doesn't prove that the use of hard language is wrong;
While the World's heart beats quicker to think of such men
As signed Tyranny's doom with a bloody steel-pen,
While on Fourth-of-Julys beardless orators fright one
With hints at Harmodius and Aristogeiton,
You need not look shy at your sisters and brothers
Who stab with sharp words for the freedom of others;—
No, a wreath, twine a wreath for the loyal and true   300
Who, for sake of the many, dared stand with the few,
Not of blood-spattered laurel for enemies braved,
But of broad, peaceful oak-leaves for citizens saved!

* * *

   "There is Hawthorne, with genius so shrinking and rare
That you hardly at first see the strength that is there;
A frame so robust, with a nature so sweet,
So earnest, so graceful, so lithe and so fleet,
Is worth a descent from Olympus to meet;
'Tis as if a rough oak that for ages had stood,
With his gnarled bony branches like ribs of the wood,   310
Should bloom, after cycles of struggle and scathe,
With a single anemone trembly and rathe;
His strength is so tender, his wildness so meek,
That a suitable parallel sets one to seek,—
He's a John Bunyan Fouqué, a Puritan Tieck;
When Nature was shaping him, clay was not granted
For making so full-sized a man as she wanted,
So, to fill out her model, a little she spared
From some finer-grained stuff for a woman prepared,
And she could not have hit a more excellent plan   320
For making him fully and perfectly man.

* * *

   "Here's Cooper, who's written six volumes to show
He's as good as a lord: well, let's grant that he's so;

If a person prefer that description of praise,
Why, a coronet's certainly cheaper than bays;
But he need take no pains to convince us he's not
(As his enemies say) the American Scott.
Choose any twelve men, and let C. read aloud
That one of his novels of which he's most proud,
And I'd lay any bet that, without ever quitting   330
Their box, they'd be all, to a man, for acquitting.
He has drawn you one character, though, that is new,
One wildflower he's plucked that is wet with the dew
Of this fresh Western world, and, the thing not to mince,
He has done naught but copy it ill ever since;
His Indians, with proper respect be it said,
Are just Natty Bumppo, daubed over with red,
And his very Long Toms are the same useful Nat,
Rigged up in duck pants and sou'wester hat
(Though once in a Coffin, a good chance was found   340
To have slipped the old fellow away underground).
All his other men-figures are clothes upon sticks,
The *dernière chemise* of a man in a fix
(As a captain besieged, when his garrison's small,
Sets up caps upon poles to be seen o'er the wall);
And the women he draws from one model don't vary,
All sappy as maples and flat as a prairie.
When a character's wanted, he goes to the task
As a cooper would do in composing a cask;
He picks out the staves, of their qualities heedful,   350
Just hoops them together as tight as is needful,
And, if the best fortune should crown the attempt, he
Has made at the most something wooden and empty.

"Don't suppose I would underrate Cooper's abilities;
If I thought you'd do that, I should feel very ill at ease;
The men who have given to *one* character life
And objective existence are not very rife;
You may number them all, both prose-writers and singers,
Without overrunning the bounds of your fingers,

And Natty won't go to oblivion quicker   360
Than Adams the parson or Primrose the vicar.

   "There is one thing in Cooper I like, too, and that is
That on manners he lectures his countrymen gratis;
Not precisely so either, because, for a rarity,
He is paid for his tickets in unpopularity.
Now he may overcharge his American pictures,
But you'll grant there's a good deal of truth in his strictures;
And I honor the man who is willing to sink
Half his present repute for the freedom to think,
And, when he has thought, be his cause strong or weak,   370
Will risk t'other half for the freedom to speak,
Caring naught for what vengeance the mob has in store,
Let that mob be the upper ten thousand or lower.

   "There are truths you Americans need to be told,
And it never'll refute them to swagger and scold;
John Bull, looking o'er the Atlantic, in choler
At your aptness for trade, says you worship the dollar;
But to scorn such eye-dollar-try's what very few do,
And John goes to that church as often as you do.
No matter what John says, don't try to outcrow him,   380
'Tis enough to go quietly on and outgrow him;
Like most fathers, Bull hates to see Number One
Displacing himself in the mind of his son,
And detests the same faults in himself he'd neglected
When he sees them again in his child's glass reflected;
To love one another you're too like by half;
If he is a bull, you're a pretty stout calf,
And tear your own pasture for naught but to show
What a nice pair of horns you're beginning to grow.

   "There are one or two things I should just like to hint,   390
For you don't often get the truth told you in print;
The most of you (this is what strikes all beholders)
Have a mental and physical stoop in the shoulders;

Though you ought to be free as the winds and the waves,
You've the gait and the manners of runaway slaves;
Though you brag of your New World, you don't half believe
    in it;
And as much of the Old as is possible weave in it;
Your goddess of freedom, a tight, buxom girl,
With lips like a cherry and teeth like a pearl,
With eyes bold as Herë's, and hair floating free,   400
And full of the sun as the spray of the sea,
Who can sing at a husking or romp at a shearing,
Who can trip through the forests alone without fearing,
Who can drive home the cows with a song through the grass,
Keeps glancing aside into Europe's cracked glass,
Hides her red hands in gloves, pinches up her lithe waist,
And makes herself wretched with transmarine taste;
She loses her fresh country charm when she takes
Any mirror except her own rivers and lakes.

"You steal Englishmen's books and think Englishmen's
    thought,   410
With their salt on her tail your wild eagle is caught;
Your literature suits its each whisper and motion
To what will be thought of it over the ocean;
The cast clothes of Europe your statesmanship tries
And mumbles again the old blarneys and lies;—
Forget Europe wholly, your veins throb with blood,
To which the dull current in hers is but mud:
Let her sneer, let her say your experiment fails,
In her voice there's a tremble e'en now while she rails,
And your shore will soon be in the nature of things   420
Covered thick with gilt drift-wood of castaway kings,
Where alone, as it were in a Longfellow's Waif,
Her fugitive pieces will find themselves safe.
O my friends, thank your god, if you have one, that he
'Twixt the Old World and you set the gulf of a sea;
Be strong-backed, brown-handed, upright as your pines,
By the scale of a hemisphere shape your designs,

Be true to yourselves and this new nineteenth age,
As a statue by Powers, or a picture by Page,
Plough, sail, forge, build, carve, paint, make all over new,   430
To your own New-World instincts contrive to be true,
Keep your ears open wide to the Future's first call,
Be whatever you will, but yourselves first of all,
Stand fronting the dawn on Toil's heaven-scaling peaks,
And become my new race of more practical Greeks."

                              *   *   *

    Here Miranda came up, and said, "Phœbus! you know
That the Infinite Soul has its infinite woe,
As I ought to know, having lived cheek by jowl,
Since the day I was born, with the Infinite Soul;
I myself introduced, I myself, I alone,   440
To my Land's better life authors solely my own,
Who the sad heart of earth on their shoulders have taken,
Whose works sound a depth by Life's quiet unshaken,
Such as Shakespeare, for instance, the Bible, and Bacon,
Not to mention my own works; Time's nadir is fleet,
And, as for myself, I'm quite out of conceit"—

    "Quite out of conceit! I'm enchanted to hear it,"
Cried Apollo aside. "Who'd have thought she was near it?
To be sure, one is apt to exhaust those commodities
One uses too fast, yet in this case as odd it is   450
As if Neptune should say to his turbots and whitings,
'I'm as much out of salt as Miranda's own writings'
(Which, as she in her own happy manner has said,
Sound a depth, for 'tis one of the functions of lead).
She often has asked me if I could not find
A place somewhere near me that suited her mind;
I know but a single one vacant, which she,
With her rare talent that way, would fit to a T.
And it would not imply any pause or cessation
In the work she esteems her peculiar vocation,—   460
She may enter on duty today, if she chooses,
And remain Tiring-woman for life to the Muses."

* * *

"There comes Poe, with his raven, like Barnaby Rudge,
Three fifths of him genius and two fifths sheer fudge,
Who talks like a book of iambs and pentameters,
In a way to make people of common sense damn metres,
Who has written some things quite the best of their kind,
But the heart somehow seems all squeezed out by the
        mind,
Who—But hey-day! What's this? Messieurs Mathews and
        Poe,
You mustn't fling mud-balls at Longfellow so,   470
Does it make a man worse that his character's such
As to make his friends love him (as you think) too much?
Why, there is not a bard at this moment alive
More willing than he that his fellows should thrive;
While you are abusing him thus, even now
He would help either one of you out of a slough;
You may say that he's smooth and all that till you're hoarse,
But remember that elegance also is force;
After polishing granite as much as you will,
The heart keeps its tough old persistency still;   480
Deduct all you can, *that* still keeps you at bay;
Why, he'll live till men weary of Collins and Gray.
I'm not over-fond of Greek metres in English,
To me rhyme's a gain, so it be not to jinglish,
And your modern hexameter verses are no more
Like Greek ones than sleek Mr. Pope is like Homer;
As the roar of the sea to the coo of a pigeon is,
So, compared to your moderns, sounds old Melesigenes;
I may be too partial, the reason, perhaps, o't is
That I've heard the old blind man recite his own rhapsodies,
And my ear with that music impregnate may be,   491
Like the poor exiled shell with the soul of the sea,
Or as one can't bear Strauss when his nature is cloven
To its deeps within deeps by the stroke of Beethoven;
But, set that aside, and 'tis truth that I speak,
Had Theocritus written in English, not Greek,

I believe that his exquisite sense would scarce change a line
In that rare, tender, virgin-like pastoral Evangeline.
That's not ancient nor modern, its place is apart
Where time has no sway, in the realm of pure Art,   500
'Tis a shrine of retreat from Earth's hubbub and strife
As quiet and chaste as the author's own life.

* * *

"What! Irving? thrice welcome, warm heart and fine brain,
You bring back the happiest spirit from Spain,
And the gravest sweet humor, that ever were there
Since Cervantes met death in his gentle despair;
Nay, don't be embarrassed, nor look so beseeching,
I sha'n't run directly against my own preaching,
And, having just laughed at their Raphaels and Dantes,
Go to setting you up beside matchless Cervantes;   510
But allow me to speak what I honestly feel,—
To a true poet-heart add the fun of Dick Steele,
Throw in all of Addison, *minus* the chill,
With the whole of that partnership's stock and good-will,
Mix well, and while stirring, hum o'er, as a spell,
The fine *old* English Gentleman, simmer it well,
Sweeten just to your own private liking, then strain,
That only the finest and clearest remain,
Let it stand out of doors till a soul it receives
From the warm lazy sun loitering down through green leaves,
And you'll find a choice nature, not wholly deserving   521
A name either English or Yankee,—just Irving."

* * *

Here, "Forgive me, Apollo," I cried, "while I pour
My heart out to my birthplace: O loved more and more
Dear Baystate, from whose rocky bosom thy sons
Should suck milk, strong-will-giving, brave, such as runs
In the veins of old Graylock—who is it that dares
Call thee pedler, a soul wrapped in bankbooks and shares?
It is false! She's a Poet! I see, as I write,   •

Along the far railroad the steam-snake glide white,   530
The cataract-throb of her mill-hearts I hear,
The swift strokes of trip-hammers weary my ear,
Sledges ring upon anvils, through logs the saw screams,
Blocks swing to their place, beetles drive home the beams:—
It is songs such as these that she croons to the din
Of her fast-flying shuttles, year out and year in,
While from earth's farthest corner there comes not a breeze
But wafts her the buzz of her gold-gleaning bees:
What though those horn hands have as yet found small time
For painting and sculpture and music and rhyme?   540
These will come in due order; the need that pressed sorest
Was to vanquish the seasons, the ocean, the forest,
To bridle and harness the rivers, the steam,
Making those whirl her mill-wheels, this tug in her team,
To vassalize old tyrant Winter, and make
Him delve surlily for her on river and lake;—
When this New World was parted, she strove not to shirk
Her lot in the heirdom, the tough, silent Work,
The hero-share ever from Herakles down
To Odin, the Earth's iron sceptre and crown: 550
Yes, thou dear, noble Mother! if ever men's praise
Could be claimed for creating heroical lays,
Thou hast won it; if ever the laurel divine
Crowned the Maker and Builder, that glory is thine!
Thy songs are right epic, they tell how this rude
Rock-rib of our earth here was tamed and subdued;
Thou hast written them plain on the face of the planet
In brave, deathless letters of iron and granite;
Thou hast printed them deep for all time; they are set
From the same runic type-fount and alphabet   560
With thy stout Berkshire hills and the arms of thy Bay,—
They are staves from the burly old Mayflower lay.
If the drones of the Old World, in querulous ease,
Ask thy Art and thy Letters, point proudly to these,
Or, if they deny these are Letters and Art,
Toil on with the same old invincible heart;

Thou art rearing the pedestal broad-based and grand
Whereon the fair shapes of the Artist shall stand,
And creating, through labors undaunted and long,
The theme for all Sculpture and Painting and Song!   570

   "But my good mother Baystate wants no praise of mine,
She learned from *her* mother a precept divine
About something that butters no parsnips, her *forte*
In another direction lies, work is her sport
(Though she'll curtsey and set her cap straight, that she will,
If you talk about Plymouth and red Bunker's hill).
Dear, notable goodwife! by this time of night,
Her hearth is swept neatly, her fire burning bright,
And she sits in a chair (of home plan and make) rocking,
Musing much, all the while, as she darns on a stocking,   580
Whether turkeys will come pretty high next Thanksgiving,
Whether flour'll be so dear, for, as sure as she's living,
She will use rye-and-injun then, whether the pig
By this time ain't got pretty tolerable big,
And whether to sell it outright will be best,
Or to smoke hams and shoulders and salt down the rest,—
At this minute, she'd swop all my verses, ah, cruel!
For the last patent stove that is saving of fuel;
So I'll just let Apollo go on, for his phiz
Shows I've kept him awaiting too long as it is."   590

   "If our friend, there, who seems a reporter, is done
With his burst of emotion, why, I will go on,"
Said Apollo; some smiled, and, indeed, I must own
There was something sarcastic, perhaps, in his tone:—

   "There's Holmes, who is matchless among you for wit;
A Leyden-jar always full-charged, from which flit
The electrical tingles of hit after hit;
In long poems 'tis painful sometimes, and invites
A thought of the way the new Telegraph writes,
Which pricks down its little sharp sentences spitefully   600
As if you got more than you'd title to rightfully,

Poems

103

And you find yourself hoping its wild father Lightning
Would flame in for a second and give you a fright'ning.
He has perfect sway of what I call a sham metre,
But many admire it, the English pentameter,
And Campbell, I think, wrote most commonly worse,
With less nerve, swing, and fire in the same kind of verse,
Nor e'er achieved aught in't so worthy of praise
As the tribute of Holmes to the grand *Marseillaise*.
You went crazy last year over Bulwer's New Timon;—   610
Why, if B., to the day of his dying, should rhyme on,
Heaping verses on verses and tomes upon tomes,
He could ne'er reach the best point and vigor of Holmes.
His are just the fine hands, too, to weave you a lyric
Full of fancy, fun, feeling, or spiced with satiric
In a measure so kindly you doubt if the toes
That are trodden upon are your own or your foes'.

   "There is Lowell, who's striving Parnassus to climb
With a whole bale of *isms* together with rhyme,
He might get on alone, spite of brambles and boulders,   620
But he can't with that bundle he has on his shoulders,
The top of the hill he will ne'er come nigh reaching
Till he learns the distinction 'twixt singing and preaching;
His lyre has some chords that would ring pretty well,
But he'd rather by half make a drum of the shell,
And rattle away till he's old as Methusalem,
At the head of a march to the last new Jerusalem."

*   *   *

   Here Miranda came up and began, "As to that—"
Apollo at once seized his gloves, cane, and hat,
And, seeing the place getting rapidly cleared,   630
I too snatched my notes and forthwith disappeared.

1847–48   1848

SHE CAME AND WENT

As a twig trembles, which a bird
  Lights on to sing, then leaves unbent,
So is my memory thrilled and stirred;—
  I only know she came and went.

As clasps some lake, by gusts unriven,
  The blue dome's measureless content,
So my soul held that moment's heaven;—
  I only knew she came and went.

As, at one bound, our swift spring heaps
  The orchards full of bloom and scent,   10
So clove her May my wintry sleeps;—
  I only know she came and went.

An angel stood and met my gaze,
  Through the low doorway of my tent;
The tent is struck, the vision stays;—
  I only know she came and went.

Oh, when the room grows slowly dim,
  And life's last oil is nearly spent,
One gush of light these eyes will brim,
  Only to think she came and went.   20

1847?   1849

ODE TO HAPPINESS

Spirit, that rarely comest now
  And only to contrast my gloom,
  Like rainbow-feathered birds that bloom
A moment on some autumn bough
That, with the spurn of their farewell,
Sheds its last leaves,—thou once didst dwell
  With me year-long, and make intense

To boyhood's wisely vacant days
Their fleet but all-sufficing grace
   Of trustful inexperience,   10
   While soul could still transfigure sense,
And thrill, as with love's first caress,
At life's mere unexpectedness.
   Days when my blood would leap and run
     As full of sunshine as a breeze,
     Or spray tossed up by Summer seas
   That doubts if it be sea or sun!
Days that flew swiftly like the band
   That played in Grecian games at strife,
And passed from eager hand to hand   20
   The onward-dancing torch of life!

Wing-footed! thou abid'st with him
   Who asks it not; but he who hath
   Watched o'er the waves thy waning path,
Shall nevermore behold returning
The high-heaped canvas shoreward yearning!
Thou first reveal'st to us thy face
Turned o'er the shoulder's parting grace,
   A moment glimpsed, then seen no more,—
Thou whose swift footsteps we can trace   30
   Away from every mortal door!

Nymph of the unreturning feet,
   How may I win thee back?   But no,
   I do thee wrong to call thee so;
'Tis I am changed, not thou art fleet:
The man thy presence feels again,
Not in the blood, but in the brain,
Spirit, that lov'st the upper air
Serene and passionless and rare,
   Such as on mountain heights we find   40
   And wide-viewed uplands of the mind;
Or such as scorns to coil and sing

Round any but the eagle's wing
    Of souls that with long upward beat
    Have won an undisturbed retreat
Where, poised like wingëd victories,
They mirror in relentless eyes
    The life broad-basking 'neath their feet,—
Man ever with his Now at strife,
    Pained with first gasps of earthly air,   50
    Then praying Death the last to spare,
Still fearful of the ampler life.

Not unto them dost thou consent
    Who, passionless, can lead at ease
A life of unalloyed content,
    A life like that of land-locked seas,
That feel no elemental gush
Of tidal forces, no fierce rush
    Of storm deep-grasping scarcely spent
    'Twixt continent and continent.   60
Such quiet souls have never known
    Thy truer inspiration, thou
    Who lov'st to feel upon thy brow
Spray from the plunging vessel thrown
    Grazing the tusked lee shore, the cliff
That o'er the abrupt gorge holds its breath,
    Where the frail hair-breadth of an *if*
Is all that sunders life and death:
These, too, are cared-for, and round these
Bends her mild crook thy sister Peace;   70
    These in unvexed dependence lie,
    Each 'neath his strip of household sky;
O'er these clouds wander, and the blue
Hangs motionless the whole day through;
    Stars rise for them, and moons grow large
And lessen in such tranquil wise
As joys and sorrows do that rise
    Within their nature's sheltered marge;

Their hours into each other flit
    Like the leaf-shadows of the vine   80
And fig-tree under which they sit,
    And their still lives to heaven incline
With an unconscious habitude,
    Unhistoried as smokes that rise
From happy hearths and sight elude
    In kindred blue of morning skies.

Wayward! when once we feel thy lack,
'Tis worse than vain to woo thee back!
    Yet there is one who seems to be
Thine elder sister, in whose eyes   90
A faint far northern light will rise
    Sometimes, and bring a dream of thee;
She is not that for which youth hoped,
    But she hath blessings all her own,
Thoughts pure as lilies newly oped,
    And faith to sorrow given alone;
Almost I deem that it is thou
Come back with graver matron brow,
    With deepened eyes and bated breath,
    Like one that somewhere hath met Death.   100
But "No," she answers, "I am she
Whom the gods love, Tranquillity;
    That other whom you seek forlorn
    Half earthly was; but I am born
Of the immortals, and our race
Wear still some sadness on our face:
    He wins me late, but keeps me long,
Who, dowered with every gift of passion,
In that fierce flame can forge and fashion
    Of sin and self the anchor strong;   110
Can thence compel the driving force
Of daily life's mechanic course,
Nor less the nobler energies
Of needful toil and culture wise;

Whose soul is worth the tempter's lure
Who can renounce, and yet endure,
To him I come, not lightly wooed,
But won by silent fortitude."
1854?   1861

THE WASHERS OF THE SHROUD

OCTOBER, 1861

Along a river-side, I know not where,
I walked one night in mystery of dream;
A chill creeps curdling yet beneath my hair,
To think what chanced me by the pallid gleam
Of a moon-wraith that waned through haunted air.

Pale fireflies pulsed within the meadow-mist
Their halos, wavering thistle downs of light;
The loon, that seemed to mock some goblin tryst,
Laughed; and the echoes, huddling in affright,
Like Odin's hounds, fled baying down the night.   10

Then all was silent, till there smote my ear
A movement in the stream that checked my breath:
Was it the slow plash of a wading deer?
But something said, "This water is of Death!
The Sisters wash a shroud,—ill thing to hear!"

I, looking then, beheld the ancient Three
Known to the Greek's and to the Northman's creed,
That sit in shadow of the mystic Tree,
Still crooning, as they weave their endless brede,
One song: "Time was, Time is, and Time shall be."   20

No wrinkled crones were they, as I had deemed,
But fair as yesterday, today, tomorrow,
To mourner, lover, poet, ever seemed;
Something too high for joy, too deep for sorrow,
Thrilled in their tones, and from their faces gleamed.

"Still men and nations reap as they have strawn,"
So sang they, working at their task the while;
"The fatal raiment must be cleansed ere dawn:
For Austria? Italy? the Sea-Queen's isle?
O'er what quenched grandeur must our shroud be drawn?   30

"Or is it for a younger, fairer corse,
That gathered States like children round his knees,
That tamed the wave to be his posting horse,
Feller of forests, linker of the seas,
Bridge-builder, hammerer, youngest son of Thor's?

"What make we, murmur'st thou? and what are we?
When empires must be wound, we bring the shroud,
The time-old web of the implacable Three:
Is it too coarse for him, the young and proud?
Earth's mightiest deigned to wear it,—why not he?"   40

"Is there no hope?" I moaned, "so strong, so fair!
Our Fowler whose proud bird would brook erewhile
No rival's swoop in all our western air!
Gather the ravens, then, in funeral file
For him, life's morn yet golden in his hair?

"Leave me not hopeless, ye unpitying dames!
I see, half seeing. Tell me, ye who scanned
The stars, Earth's elders, still must noblest aims
Be traced upon oblivious ocean-sands?
Must Hesper join the wailing ghosts of names?"   50

"When grass-blades stiffen with red battle-dew,
Ye deem we choose the victor and the slain:
Say, choose we them that shall be leal and true
To the heart's longing, the high faith of brain?
Yet there the victory lies, if ye but knew.

"Three roots bear up Dominion: Knowledge, Will,—
These twain are strong, but stronger yet the third,—

Obedience,—'tis the great tap-root that still,
Knit round the rock of Duty, is not stirred,
Though Heaven-loosed tempests spend their utmost skill.   60

"Is the doom sealed for Hesper? 'Tis not we
Denounce it, but the Law before all time:
The brave makes danger opportunity;
The waverer, paltering with the chance sublime,
Dwarfs it to peril: which shall Hesper be?

"Hath he let vultures climb his eagle's seat
To make Jove's bolts purveyors of their maw?
Hath he the Many's plaudits found more sweet
Than Wisdom? held Opinion's wind for Law?
Then let him hearken for the doomster's feet!   70

"Rough are the steps, slow-hewn in flintiest rock,
States climb to power by; slippery those with gold
Down which they stumble to eternal mock:
No chafferer's hand shall long the sceptre hold,
Who, given a Fate to shape, would sell the block.

"We sing old Sagas, songs of weal and woe,
Mystic because too cheaply understood;
Dark sayings are not ours; men hear and know,
See Evil weak, see strength alone in Good,
Yet hope to stem God's fire with walls of tow.   80

"Time Was unlocks the riddle of Time Is,
That offers choice of glory or of gloom;
The solver makes Time Shall Be surely his.
But hasten, Sisters! for even now the tomb
Grates its slow hinge and calls from the abyss."

"But not for him," I cried, "not yet for him,
Whose large horizon, westering, star by star
Wins from the void to where on Ocean's rim
The sunset shuts the world with golden bar,
Not yet his thews shall fail, his eye grow dim!   90

"His shall be larger manhood, saved for those
That walked unblenching through the trial-fires;
Not suffering, but faint heart, is worst of woes,
And he no base-born son of craven sires,
Whose eye need blench confronted with his foes.

"Tears may be ours, but proud, for those who win
Death's royal purple in the foeman's lines;
Peace, too, brings tears; and 'mid the battle-din,
The wiser ear some text of God divines,
For the sheathed blade may rust with darker sin. 100

"God, give us peace! not such as lulls to sleep,
But sword on thigh, and brow with purpose knit!
And let our Ship of State to harbor sweep,
Her ports all up, her battle-lanterns lit,
And her leashed thunders gathering for their leap!"

So cried I with clenched hands and passionate pain,
Thinking of dear ones by Potomac's side;
Again the loon laughed mocking, and again
The echoes bayed far down the night and died,
While waking I recalled my wandering brain. 110
1861   1861

THE BIGLOW PAPERS

SECOND SERIES

THE COURTIN'

God makes sech nights, all white an' still
    Fur'z you can look or listen,
Moonshine an' snow on field an' hill,
    All silence an' all glisten.

Zekle crep' up quite unbeknown
    An' peeked in thru' the winder,

An' there sot Huldy all alone,
    'ith no one nigh to hender.

A fireplace filled the room's one side
    With half a cord o' wood in—   10
There warn't no stoves (tell comfort died)
    To bake ye to a puddin'.

The wa'nut logs shot sparkles out
    Towards the pootiest, bless her,
An' leetle flames danced all about
    The chiny on the dresser.

Agin the chimbley crook-necks hung,
    An' in amongst 'em rusted
The ole queen's-arm thet gran'ther Young
    Fetched back f'om Concord busted.   20

The very room, coz she was in,
    Seemed warm from floor to ceilin',
An' she looked full ez rosy agin
    Ez the apples she was peelin'.

'Twas kin' o' kingdom-come to look
    On sech a blessed cretur,
A dogrose blushin' to a brook
    Ain't modester nor sweeter.

He was six foot o' man, A 1,
    Clear grit an' human natur';   30
None couldn't quicker pitch a ton
    Nor dror a furrer straighter.

He'd sparked it with full twenty gals,
    He'd squired 'em, danced 'em, druv 'em,
Fust this one, an' then thet, by spells—
    All is, he couldn't love 'em.

But long o' her his veins 'ould run
    All crinkly like curled maple,
The side she breshed felt full o' sun
    Ez a south slope in Ap'il.   40

She thought no v'ice hed sech a swing
    Ez hisn in the choir;
My! when he made Ole Hunderd ring,
    She *knowed* the Lord was nigher.

An' she'd blush scarlit, right in prayer,
    When her new meetin'-bunnet
Felt somehow thru' its crown a pair
    O' blue eyes sot upun it.

Thet night, I tell ye, she looked *some!*
    She seemed to 've gut a new soul,   50
For she felt sartin-sure he'd come,
    Down to her very shoe-sole.

She heered a foot, an' knowed it tu,
    A-raspin' on the scraper,—
All ways to once her feelin's flew
    Like sparks in burnt-up paper.

He kin' o' l'itered on the mat
    Some doubtfle o' the sekle,
His heart kep' goin' pity-pat,
    But hern went pity Zekle.   60

An' yit she gin her cheer a jerk
    Ez though she wished him furder,
An' on her apples kep' to work,
    Parin' away like murder.

"You want to see my Pa, I s'pose?"
    "Wal . . . no . . . I come dasignin'"—
"To see my Ma? She's sprinklin' clo'es
    Agin to-morrer's i'nin'."

To say why gals acts so or so,
   Or don't, 'ould be persumin';   70
Mebby to mean *yes* an' say *no*
   Comes nateral to women.

He stood a spell on one foot fust,
   Then stood a spell on t'other,
An' on which one he felt the wust
   He couldn't ha' told ye nuther.

Says he, "I'd better call agin";
   Says she, "Think likely, Mister":
Thet last word pricked him like a pin,
   An' . . . Wal, he up an' kist her.   80

When Ma bimeby upon 'em slips,
   Huldy sot pale ez ashes,
All kin' o' smily roun' the lips
   An' teary roun' the lashes.

For she was jes' the quiet kind
   Whose naturs never vary,
Like streams that keep a summer mind
   Snowhid in Jenooary.

The blood clost roun' her heart felt glued
   Too tight for all expressin',   90
Tell mother see how metters stood,
   And gin 'em both her blessin'.

Then her red come back like the tide
   Down to the Bay o' Fundy,
An' all I know is they was cried
   In meetin' come nex' Sunday.

From No. II

MASON AND SLIDELL: A YANKEE IDYLL

JONATHAN TO JOHN

It don't seem hardly right, John,
    When both my hands was full,
To stump me to a fight, John,—
    Your cousin, tu, John Bull!
        Ole Uncle S. sez he, "I guess
        We know it now," sez he,
"The lion's paw is all the law,
        Accordin' to J. B.,
        Thet 's fit for you an' me!"

You wonder why we 're hot, John?   10
    Your mark wuz on the guns,
The neutral guns, thet shot, John,
    Our brothers an' our sons:
        Ole Uncle S. sez he, "I guess
        There 's human blood," sez he,
"By fits an' starts, in Yankee hearts,
        Though 't may surprise J. B.
        More 'n it would you an' me."

Ef *I* turned mad dogs loose, John,
    On *your* front-parlor stairs,   20
Would it jest meet your views, John,
    To wait an' sue their heirs?
        Ole Uncle S. sez he, "I guess,
        I on'y guess," sez he,
"Thet ef Vattel on *his* toes fell,
        'T would kind o' rile J. B.,
        Ez wal ez you an' me!"

Who made the law thet hurts, John,
    Heads I win,—ditto tails?

"*J. B.*" was on his shirts, John,   30
 Onless my memory fails.
  Ole Uncle S. sez he, "I guess
  (I'm good at thet)," sez he,
"Thet sauce for goose ain't *jest* the juice
  For ganders with J. B.,
  No more 'n with you or me!"

When your rights was our wrongs, John,
 You did n't stop for fuss,—
Britanny's trident prongs, John,
 Was good 'nough law for us.   40
  Ole Uncle S. sez he, "I guess,
  Though physic's good," sez he,
"It does n't foller thet he can swaller
  Prescriptions signed 'J. B.,'
  Put up by you an' me!"

We own the ocean, tu, John:
 You mus' n' take it hard,
Ef we can't think with you, John,
 It 's jest your own back-yard.
  Ole Uncle S. sez he, "I guess,   50
  Ef *thet* 's his claim," sez he,
"The fencin'-stuff 'll cost enough
  To bust up friend J. B.,
  Ez wal ez you an' me!"

Why talk so dreffle big, John,
 Of honor when it meant
You did n't care a fig, John,
 But jest for *ten per cent?*
  Ole Uncle S. sez he, "I guess
  He 's like the rest," sez he: 60
"When all is done, it 's number one
  Thet 's nearest to J. B.,
  Ez wal ez t' you an' me!"

We give the critters back, John,
    Cos Abram thought 't was right;
It warn't your bullyin' clack, John,
    Provokin' us to fight.
        Ole Uncle S. sez he, "I guess
        We 've a hard row," sez he,
"To hoe jest now; but thet, somehow,   70
        May happen to J. B.,
        Ez wal ez you an' me!"

We ain't so weak an' poor, John,
    With twenty million people,
An' close to every door, John,
    A school-house an' a steeple.
        Ole Uncle S. sez he, "I guess,
        It is a fact," sez he,
"The surest plan to make a Man
        Is, think him so, J. B.,   80
        Ez much ez you or me!"

Our folks believe in Law, John;
    An' it 's for her sake, now,
They 've left the axe an' saw, John,
    The anvil an' the plough.
        Ole Uncle S. sez he, "I guess,
        Ef't warn't for law," sez he,
"There 'd be one shindy from here to Indy;
        An' thet don't suit J. B.
        (When 't ain't 'twixt you an' me!)"   90

We know we 've got a cause, John,
    Thet 's honest, just, an' true;
We thought 't would win applause, John,
    Ef nowheres else, from you.
        Ole Uncle S. sez he, "I guess
        His love of right," sez he,

"Hangs by a rotten fibre o' cotton:
    There 's natur' in J. B.,
    Ez wal 'z in you an' me!"

The South says, "*Poor folks down!*" John,   100
    An' "*All men up!*" say we,—
White, yaller, black, an' brown, John:
    Now which is your idee?
        Ole Uncle S. sez he, "I guess,
        John preaches wal," sez he;
"But, sermon thru, an' come to *du*,
    Why, there 's the old J. B.
    A-crowdin' you an' me!"

Shall it be love, or hate, John?
    It 's you thet 's to decide;   110
Ain't *your* bonds held by Fate, John,
    Like all the world's beside?
        Ole Uncle S. sez he, "I guess
        Wise men forgive," sez he,
"But not forgit; an' some time yit
    Thet truth may strike J. B.,
    Ez wal ez you an' me!"

God means to make this land, John,
    Clear thru, from sea to sea,
Believe an' understand, John,   120
    The *wuth* o' bein' free.
        Ole Uncle S. sez he, "I guess,
        God's price is high," sez he;
"But nothin' else than wut He sells
    Wears long, an' thet J. B.
    May larn, like you an' me!"
December, 1861   February, 1862

From No. IV

A MESSAGE OF JEFF DAVIS IN SECRET SESSION

Conjecturally reported by H. BIGLOW

TO THE EDITORS OF THE ATLANTIC MONTHLY

I sent you a messige, my friens, t' other day,
To tell you I 'd nothin' pertickler to say:
't wuz the day our new nation gut kin' o' stillborn,
So 't wuz my pleasant dooty t' acknowledge the corn,
An' I see clearly then, ef I did n't before,
Thet the *augur* in inauguration means *bore*.
I need n't tell *you* thet my messige wuz written
To diffuse correc' notions in France an' Gret Britten,
An' agin to impress on the poppylar mind
The comfort an' wisdom o' goin' it blind,—   10
To say thet I did n't abate not a hooter
O' my faith in a happy an' glorious futur',
Ez rich in each soshle an' p'litickle blessin'
Ez them thet we now hed the joy o' possessin',
With a people united, an' longin' to die
For wut *we* call their country, without askin' why,
An' all the gret things we concluded to slope for
Ez much within reach now ez ever—to hope for.
We 've gut all the ellerments, this very hour,
Thet make up a fus'-class, self-governin' power: 20
We 've a war, an' a debt, an' a flag; an' ef this
Ain't to be inderpendunt, why, wut on airth is?
An' nothin' now henders our takin' our station
Ez the freest, enlightenedest, civerlized nation,
Built up on our bran'-new politickle thesis
Thet a Gov'ment's fust right is to tumble to pieces,—
I say nothin' henders our takin' our place
Ez the very fus'-best o' the whole human race,
A spittin' tobacker ez proud ez you please

On Victory's bes' carpets, or loafin' at ease   30
In the Tool'ries front-parlor, discussin' affairs
With our heels on the backs o' Napoleon's new chairs,
An' princes a-mixin' our cocktails an' slings,—
Excep', wal, excep' jest a very few things,
Sech ez navies an' armies an' wherewith to pay,
An' gittin' our sogers to run t' other way,
An' not be too over-pertickler in tryin'
To hunt up the very las' ditches to die in.

Ther' are critters so base thet they want it explained
Jes' wut is the totle amount thet we've gained,   40
Ez if we could maysure stupenjious events
By the low Yankee stan'ard o' dollars an' cents:
They seem to forgit, thet, since last year revolved,
We 've succeeded in gittin' seceshed an' dissolved,
An' thet no one can't hope to git thru dissolootion
'thout some kin' o' strain on the best Constitootion.
Who asks for a prospec' more flettrin' an' bright,
When from here clean to Texas it 's all one free fight?
Hain't we rescued from Seward the gret leadin' featurs
Thet makes it wuth while to be reasonin' creaturs?   50
Hain't we saved Habus Coppers, improved it in fact,
By suspendin' the Unionists 'stid o' the Act?
Ain't the laws free to all? Where on airth else d' ye see
Every freeman improvin' his own rope an' tree?
Ain't our piety sech (in our speeches an' messiges)
Ez t' astonish ourselves in the bes'-composed pessiges,
An' to make folks thet knowed us in th' ole state o' things
Think convarsion ez easy ez drinkin' gin-slings?

It's ne'ssary to take a good confident tone
With the public; but here, jest amongst us, I own   60
Things look blacker 'n thunder. Ther' 's no use denyin'
We 're clean out o' money, an' 'most out o' lyin';
Two things a young nation can't mennage without,
Ef she wants to look wal at her fust comin' out;

For the fust supplies physickle strength, while the second
Gives a morril edvantage thet 's hard to be reckoned:
For this latter I' m willin' to du wut I can;
For the former you 'll hev to consult on a plan,—
Though our *fust* want (an' this pint I want your best views on)
Is plausible paper to print I. O. U.s on.   70

Some gennlemen think it would cure all our cankers
In the way o' finance, ef we jes' hanged the bankers;
An' I own the proposle 'ud square with my views,
Ef their lives wuz n't all thet we 'd left 'em to lose.
Some say thet more confidence might be inspired,
Ef we voted our cities an' towns to be fired,—
A plan thet 'ud suttenly tax our endurance,
Coz 't would be our own bills we should git for th' insurance;
But cinders, no metter how sacred we think 'em,
Might n't strike furrin minds ez good sources of income,   80
Nor the people, perhaps, would n't like the eclaw
O' bein' all turned into paytriots by law.
Some want we should buy all the cotton an' burn it,
On a pledge, when we 've gut thru the war, to return it,—
Then to take the proceeds an' hold *them* ez security
For an issue o' bonds to be met at maturity
With an issue o' notes to be paid in hard cash
On the fus' Monday follerin' the 'tarnal All-smash:
This hez a safe air, an', once hold o' the gold,
'ud leave our vile plunderers out in the cold,   90
An' *might* temp' John Bull, ef it warn't for the dip he
Once gut from the banks o' my own Mississippi.
Some think we could make, by arrangin' the figgers,
A hendy home-currency out of our niggers;
But it wun't du to lean much on ary sech staff,
For they 're gettin' tu current a'ready, by half.

One gennleman says, ef we lef' our loan out
Where Floyd could git hold on 't *he* 'd take it, no doubt;
But 't ain't jes' the takin', though 't hez a good look,
We mus' git sunthin' out on it arter it 's took,   100

An' we need now more 'n ever, with sorrer I own,
Thet some one another should let us a loan,
Sence a soger wun't fight, on'y jes' while he draws his
Pay down on the nail, for the best of all causes,
'thout askin' to know wut the quarrel 's about,—
An' once come to thet, why, our game is played out.
It 's ez true ez though I should n't never hev said it,
Thet a hitch hez took place in our system o' credit;
I swear it 's all right in my speeches an' messiges,
But ther' 's idees afloat, ez ther' is about sessiges: 110
Folks wun't take a bond ez a basis to trade on,
Without nosin' round to find out wut it 's made on,
An' the thought more an' more thru the public min' crosses
Thet our Treshry hez gut 'mos' too many dead hosses.
Wut 's called credit, you see, is some like a balloon,
Thet looks while it 's up 'most ez harnsome 'z a moon,
But once git a leak in 't, an' wut looked so grand
Caves righ' down in a jiffy ez flat ez your hand.
Now the world is a dreffle mean place, for our sins,
Where ther' ollus is critters about with long pins   120
A-prickin' the bubbles we 've blowed with sech care,
An' provin' ther' 's nothin' inside but bad air:
They 're all Stuart Millses, poor-white trash, an' sneaks,
Without no more chivverlry 'n Choctaws or Creeks,
Who think a real gennleman's promise to pay
Is meant to be took in trade's ornery way:
Them fellers an' I could n' never agree;
They 're the nateral foes o' the Southun Idee;
I 'd gladly take all of our other resks on me
To be red o' this low-lived politikle 'con'my!   130

Now a dastardly notion is gittin' about
Thet our bladder is bust an' the gas oozin' out,
An' onless we can mennage in some way to stop it,
Why, the thing 's a gone coon, an' we might ez wal drop it.
Brag works wal at fust, but it ain't jes' the thing
For a stiddy inves'ment the shiners to bring,

An' votin' we 're prosp'rous a hundred times over
Wun't change bein' starved into livin' in clover.
Manassas done sunthin' tow'rds drawin' the wool
O'er the green, antislavery eyes o' John Bull: 140
Oh, *warn't* it a godsend, jes' when sech tight fixes
Wuz crowdin' us mourners, to throw double-sixes!
I wuz tempted to think, an' it wuz n't no wonder,
Ther' wuz reely a Providence,—over or under,—
When, all packed for Nashville, I fust ascertained
From the papers up North wut a victory we 'd gained.
't wuz the time for diffusin' correc' views abroad
Of our union an' strength an' relyin' on God;
An', fact, when I 'd gut thru my fust big surprise,
I much ez half b'lieved in my own tallest lies,   150
An' conveyed the idee thet the whole Southun popperlace
Wuz Spartans all on the keen jump for Thermopperlies,
Thet set on the Lincolnites' bombs till they bust,
An' fight for the priv'lege o' dying' the fust;
But Roanoke, Bufort, Millspring, an' the rest
Of our recent starn-foremost successes out West,
Hain't left us a foot for our swellin' to stand on,—
We 've showed *too* much o' wut Buregard calls *abandon*,
For all our Thermopperlies (an' it 's a marcy
We hain't hed no more) hev ben clean vicy-varsy,   160
An' wut Spartans wuz lef' when the battle wuz done
Wuz them thet wuz too unambitious to run.

Oh, ef we had on'y jes' gut Reecognition,
Things now would ha' ben in a different position!
You 'd ha' hed all you wanted: the paper blockade
Smashed up into toothpicks; unlimited trade
In the one thing thet 's needfle, till niggers, I swow,
Hed ben thicker 'n provisional shin-plasters now;
Quinine by the ton 'ginst the shakes when they seize ye;
Nice paper to coin into C. S. A. specie;   170
The voice of the driver 'd be heerd in our land,
An' the univarse scringe, ef we lifted our hand:

Would n't *thet* be some like a fulfillin' the prophecies,
With all the fus' fem'lies in all the fust offices?
't wuz a beautiful dream, an' all sorrer is idle,—
But *ef* Lincoln *would* ha' hanged Mason an' Slidell!
For would n't the Yankees hev found they 'd ketched Tartars,
Ef they 'd raised two sech critters as them into martyrs?
Mason *wuz* F. F. V., though a cheap card to win on,
But t' other was jes' New York trash to begin on;   180
They ain't o' no good in Európean pellices,
But think wut a help they 'd ha' been on their gallowses!
They 'd ha' felt they wuz truly fulfillin' their mission,
An', oh, how dog-cheap we 'd ha' gut Reecognition!

But somehow another, wutever we 've tried,
Though the the'ry 's fust-rate, the facs *wun't* coincide:
Facs are contrary 'z mules, an' ez hard in the mouth,
An' they allus hev showed a mean spite to the South.
Sech bein' the case, we hed best look about
For some kin' o' way to slip *our* necks out: 190
Le' 's vote our las' dollar, ef one can be found,
(An', at any rate, votin' it hez a good sound,)—
Le' 's swear thet to arms all our people is flyin',
(The critters can't read, an' wun't know how we 're lyin',)—
Thet Toombs is advancin' to sack Cincinnater,
With a rovin' commission to pillage an' slahter,—
Thet we 've throwed to the winds all regard for wut 's lawfle,
An' gone in for sunthin' promiscu'sly awfle.
Ye see hitherto, it 's our own knaves an' fools
Thet we 've used, (those for whetstones, an' t' others ez tools,)
An' now our las' chance is in puttin' to test   201
The same kin' o' cattle up North an' out West,—
Your Belmonts, Vallandighams, Woodses, an' sech,
Poor shotes thet ye could n't persuade us to tech,
Not in ornery times, though we 're willin' to feed 'em
With a nod now an' then, when we happen to need 'em;
Why, for my part, I 'd ruther shake hands with a nigger
Than with cusses that load an' don't darst dror a trigger;

They 're the wust wooden nutmegs the Yankees perdooce,
Shaky everywheres else, an' jes' sound on the goose;   210
They ain't wuth a cuss, an' I set nothin' by 'em,
But we 're in sech a fix thet I s'pose we mus' try 'em.
I—But, Gennlemen, here 's a despatch jes' come in
Which shows thet the tide 's begun turnin' agin',—
Gret Cornfedrit success! C'lumbus eevacooated!
I mus' run down an' hev the thing properly stated,
An' show wut a triumph it is, an' how lucky
To fin'lly git red o' thet cussed Kentucky,—
An' how, sence Fort Donelson, winnin' the day
Consists in triumphantly gittin' away.   220

1862

From No. VI

SUNTHIN' IN THE PASTORAL LINE

Once git a smell o' musk into a draw,
An' it clings hold like precerdents in law:
Your gra'ma'am put it there,—when, goodness knows,—
To jes' this-worldify her Sunday-clo'es;
But the old chist wun't sarve her gran'son's wife
(For, 'thout new funnitoor, wut good in life?),
An' so ole clawfoot, from the precinks dread
O' the spare chamber, slinks into the shed,
Where, dim with dust, it fust or last subsides
To holdin' seeds an' fifty things besides;   10
But better days stick fast in heart an' husk,
An' all you keep in 't gits a scent o' musk.

Jes' so with poets: wut they 've airly read
Gits kind o' worked into their heart an' head,
So 's 't they can't seem to write but jest on sheers
With furrin countries or played-out ideers,
Nor hev a feelin', ef it doos n't smack
O' wut some critter chose to feel 'way back:

This makes 'em talk o' daisies, larks, an' things,
Ez though we 'd nothin' here that blows an' sings   20
(Why, I'd give more for one live bobolink
Than a square mile o' larks in printer's ink),—
This makes 'em think our fust o' May is May,
Which 't ain't, for all the almanicks can say.

O little city-gals, don't never go it
Blind on the word o' noospaper or poet!
They 're apt to puff, an' May-day seldom looks
Up in the country ez 't doos in books;
They 're no more like than hornets'-nests an' hives,
Or printed sarmons be to holy lives.   30
I, with my trouses perched on cowhide boots,
Tuggin' my foundered feet out by the roots,
Hev seen ye come to fling on April's hearse
Your muslin nosegays from the milliner's,
Puzzlin' to find dry ground your queen to choose,
An' dance your throats sore in morocker shoes:
I 've seen ye an' felt proud, thet, come wut would,
Our Pilgrim stock wuz pethed with hardihood.
Pleasure doos make us Yankees kind o' winch,
Ez though 't wuz sunthin' paid for by the inch;   40
But yit we du contrive to worry thru,
Ef Dooty tells us thet the thing 's to du,
An' kerry a hollerday, ef we set out,
Ez stiddily ez though 't wuz a redoubt.

I, country-born an' bred, know where to find
Some blooms thet make the season suit the mind,
An' seem to metch the doubtin' bluebird's notes,—
Half-vent'rin' liverworts in furry coats,
Bloodroots, whose rolled-up leaves ef you oncurl,
Each on 'em 's cradle to a baby-pearl,—   50
But these are jes' Spring's pickets; sure ez sin,
The rebble frosts 'll try to drive 'em in;
For half our May 's so awfully like May n't,
't would rile a Shaker or an evrige saint;

Though I own up I like our back'ard springs
Thet kind o' haggle with their greens an' things,
An' when you 'most give up, 'uthout more words
Toss the fields full o' blossoms, leaves, an' birds;
Thet 's Northun natur', slow an' apt to doubt
But when it *doos* git stirred, ther' 's no gin-out!   60

Fust come the blackbirds clatt'rin' in tall trees,
An' settlin' things in windy Congresses,—
Queer politicians, though, for I 'll be skinned
Ef all on 'em don't head aginst the wind.
'fore long the trees begin to show belief,—
The maple crimsons to a coral-reef,
Then saffern swarms swing off from all the willers
So plump they look like yaller caterpillars,
Then gray hossches'nuts leetle hands unfold
Softer 'n a baby's be at three days old: 70
Thet 's robin-redbreast's almanick; he knows
Thet arter this ther' 's only blossom-snows;
So, choosin' out a handy crotch an' spouse,
He goes to plast'rin' his adobe house.

Then seems to come a hitch,—things lag behind,
Till some fine mornin' Spring makes up her mind,
An' ez, when snow-swelled rivers cresh their dams
Heaped-up with ice thet dovetails in an' jams,
A leak comes spirtin' thru some pin-hole cleft,
Grows stronger, fercer, tears out right an' left,   80
Then all the waters bow themselves an' come,
Suddin, in one gret slope o' shedderin' foam,
Jes' so our Spring gits everythin' in tune
An' gives one leap from Aperl into June:
Then all comes crowdin' in; afore you think,
Young oak-leaves mist the side-hill woods with pink;
The catbird in the laylock-bush is loud;
The orchards turn to heaps o' rosy cloud;
Red-cedars blossom tu, though few folks know it,

An' look all dipt in sunshine like a poet;   90
The lime-trees pile their solid stacks o' shade
An' drows'ly simmer with the bees' sweet trade;
In ellum-shrouds the flashin' hangbird clings
An' for the summer vy'ge his hammock slings;
All down the loose-walled lanes in archin' bowers
The barb'ry droops its strings o' golden flowers,
Whose shrinkin' hearts the school-gals love to try
With pins,—they 'll worry yourn so, boys, bimeby!
But I don't love your cat'logue style,—do you?—
Ez ef to sell off Natur' by vendoo;   100
One word with blood in 't 's twice ez good ez two:
'nuff sed, June's bridesman, poet o' the year,
Gladness on wings, the bobolink, is here;
Half-hid in tip-top apple-blooms he swings,
Or climbs aginst the breeze with quiverin' wings,
Or, givin' way to 't in a mock despair,
Runs down, a brook o' laughter, thru the air.

I ollus feel the sap start in my veins
In Spring, with curus heats an' prickly pains,
Thet drive me, when I git a chance, to walk   110
Off by myself to hev a privit talk
With a queer critter thet can't seem to 'gree
Along o' me like most folks,—Mister Me.
Ther' 's times when I 'm unsoshle ez a stone,
An' sort o' suffercate to be alone,—
I 'm crowded jes' to think thet folks are nigh,
An' can't bear nothin' closer than the sky;
Now the wind 's full ez shifty in the mind
Ez wut it is ou'-doors, ef I ain't blind,
An' sometimes, in the fairest sou'west weather,   120
My innard vane pints east for weeks together,
My natur' gits all goose-flesh, an' my sins
Come drizzlin' on my conscience sharp ez pins:
Wal, et sech times I jes' slip out o' sight
An' take it out in a fair stan'-up fight

With the one cuss I can't lay on the shelf,
The crook'dest stick in all the heap,—Myself.

'T wuz so las' Sabbath arter meetin'-time:
Findin' my feelin's would n't noways rhyme
With nobody's, but off the hendle flew   130
An' took things from an east-wind pint o' view,
I started off to lose me in the hills
Where the pines be, up back o' 'Siah's Mills:
Pines, ef you 're blue, are the best friends I know,
They mope an' sigh an' sheer your feelin's so,—
They hesh the ground beneath so, tu, I swan,
You half-forgit you 've gut a body on.
Ther' 's a small school'us' there where four roads meet,
The door-steps hollered out by little feet,
An' side-posts carved with names whose owners grew   140
To gret men, some on 'em, an' deacons, tu;
't ain't used no longer, coz the town hez gut
A high-school, where they teach the Lord knows wut:
Three-story larnin' 's pop'lar now; I guess
We thriv' ez wal on jes' two stories less,
For it strikes me ther' 's sech a thing ez sinnin'
By overloadin' children's underpinnin':
Wal, here it wuz I larned my A B C,
An' it 's a kind o' favorite spot with me.

We 're curus critters: Now ain't jes' the minute   150
Thet ever fits us easy while we 're in it;
Long ez 't wuz futur', 't would be perfect bliss,—
Soon ez it 's past, *thet* time 's wuth ten o' this;
An' yit there ain't a man thet need be told
Thet Now's the only bird lays eggs o' gold.
A knee-high lad, I used to plot an' plan
An' think 't wuz life's cap-sheaf to be a man;
Now, gittin' gray, there's nothin' I enjoy
Like dreamin' back along into a boy:
So the ole school'us' is a place I choose   160
Afore all others, ef I want to muse;

I set down where I used to set, an' git
My boyhood back, an' better things with it,—
Faith, Hope, an' sunthin', ef it is n't Cherrity,
It 's want o' guile, an' thet 's ez gret a rerrity,—
While Fancy's cushin', free to Prince and Clown,
Makes the hard bench ez soft ez milk-weed-down.

Now, 'fore I knowed, thet Sabbath arternoon
When I sot out to tramp myself in tune,
I found me in the school'us' on my seat,   170
Drummin' the march to No-wheres with my feet.
Thinkin' o' nothin', I 've heerd ole folks say
Is a hard kind o' dooty in its way:
It 's thinkin' everythin' you ever knew,
Or ever hearn, to make your feelin's blue.
I sot there tryin' thet on for a spell:
I thought o' the Rebellion, then o' Hell,
Which some folks tell ye now is jest a meterfor
(A the'ry, p'raps, it wun't *feel* none the better for);
I thought o' Reconstruction, wut we 'd win   180
Patchin' our patent self-blow-up agin:
I thought ef this 'ere milkin' o' the wits,
So much a month, warn't givin' Natur' fits,—
Ef folks warn't druv, findin' their own milk fail,
To work the cow thet hez an iron tail,
An' ef idees 'thout ripenin' in the pan
Would send up cream to humor ary man:
From this to thet I let my worryin' creep,
Till finally I must ha' fell asleep.

Our lives in sleep are some like streams thet glide   190
'twixt flesh an' sperrit boundin' on each side,
Where both shores' shadders kind o' mix an' mingle
In sunthin' thet ain't jes' like either single;
An' when you cast off moorin's from Today,
An' down towards Tomorrer drift away,
The imiges thet tengle on the stream
Make a new upside-down'ard world o' dream:

Sometimes they seem like sunrise-streaks an' warnin's
O' wut 'll be in Heaven on Sabbath-mornin's,
An', mixed right in ez ef jest out o' spite,   200
Sunthin' thet says your supper ain't gone right.
I 'm gret on dreams, an' often when I wake,
I 've lived so much it makes my mem'ry ache,
An' can't skurce take a cat-nap in my cheer
'thout hevin' 'em, some good, some bad, all queer.

Now I wuz settin' where I 'd ben, it seemed,
An' ain't sure yit whether I r'ally dreamed,
Nor, ef I did, how long I might ha' slep',
When I hearn some un stompin' up the step,
An' lookin' round, ef two an' two make four,   210
I see a Pilgrim Father in the door.
He wore a steeple-hat, tall boots, an' spurs
With rowels to 'em big ez ches'nut-burrs,
An' his gret sword behind him sloped away
Long 'z a man's speech thet dunno wut to say.—
"Ef your name 's Biglow, an' your given-name
Hosee," sez he, "it 's arter you I came;
I 'm your gret-gran'ther multiplied by three."—
"My *wut?*" sez I.—"Your gret-gret-gret," sez he:
"You would n't ha' never ben here but for me.   220
Two hundred an' three year ago this May
The ship I come in sailed up Boston Bay;
I 'd been a cunnle in our Civil War,—
But wut on airth hev *you* gut up one for?
Coz we du things in England, 't ain't for you
To git a notion you can du 'em tu:
I 'm told you write in public prints: ef true,
It 's nateral you should know a thing or two."—
"Thet air 's an argymunt I can't endorse,—
't would prove, coz you wear spurs, you kep' a horse: 230
For brains," sez I, "wutever you may think,
Ain't boun' to cash the drafs o' pen-an'-ink,—
Though mos' folks write ez ef they hoped jes' quickenin'

The churn would argoo skim-milk into thickenin';
But skim-milk ain't a thing to change its view
O' wut it 's meant for more 'n a smoky flue.
But du pray tell me, 'fore we furder go,
How in all Natur' did you come to know
'bout our affairs," sez I, "in Kingdom-Come?"—
"Wal, I worked round at sperrit-rappin' some,   240
An' danced the tables till their legs wuz gone,
In hopes o' larnin' wut wuz goin' on,"
Sez he, "but mejums lie so like all-split
Thet I concluded it wuz best to quit.
But, come now, ef you wun't confess to knowin',
You 've some conjectures how the thing 's a-goin'."—
"Gran'ther," sez I, "a vane warn't never known
Nor asked to hev a jedgment of its own;
An' yit, ef 't ain't gut rusty in the jints,
It 's safe to trust its say on certin pints: 250
It knows the wind's opinions to a T,
An' the wind settles wut the weather 'll be."
"I never thought a scion of our stock
Could grow the wood to make a weathercock;
When I wuz younger 'n you, skurce more 'n a shaver,
No airthly wind," sez he, "could make me waver!"
(Ez he said this, he clinched his jaw an' forehead,
Hitchin' his belt to bring his sword-hilt forrard.)—
"Jes so it wuz with me," sez I, "I swow,
When *I* wuz younger 'n wut you see me now,—   260
Nothin' from Adam's fall to Huldy's bonnet,
Thet I warn't full-cocked with my jedgment on it;
But now I 'm gittin' on in life, I find
It 's a sight harder to make up my mind,—
Nor I don't often try tu, when events
Will du it for me free of all expense.
The moral question 's ollus plain enough,—
It 's jes' the human-natur' side thet 's tough;
Wut 's best to think may n't puzzle me nor you,—
The pinch comes in decidin' wut to *du;*   270

Ef you *read* History, all runs smooth ez grease,
Coz there the men ain't nothin' more 'n idees,—
But come to *make* it, ez we must today,
Th' idees hev arms an' legs an' stop the way:
It's easy fixin' things in facts an' figgers,—
They can't resist, nor warn't brought up with niggers;
But come to try your the'ry on,—why, then
Your facts an' figgers change to ign'ant men
Actin' ez ugly—" —"Smite 'em hip an' thigh!"
Sez gran'ther, "and let every man-child die!   280

Oh for three weeks o' Crommle an' the Lord!
Up, Isr'el, to your tents an' grind the sword!"—
"Thet kind o' thing worked wal in ole Judee,
But you forgit how long it's ben A. D.;
You think thet's ellerkence,—I call it shoddy,
A thing," sez I, "wun't cover soul nor body;
I like the plain all-wool o' common-sense,
Thet warms ye now, an' will a twelvemonth hence.
You took to follerin' where the Prophets beckoned,
An', fust you knowed on, back come Charles the Second;   290
Now wut I want 's to hev all *we* gain stick,
An' not to start Millennium too quick;
We hain't to punish only, but to keep,
An' the cure 's gut to go a cent'ry deep."
"Wal, milk-an'-water ain't the best o' glue,"
Sez he, "an' so you 'll find afore you 're thru;
Ef reshness venters sunthin', shilly-shally
Loses ez often wut 's ten times the vally.
Thet exe of ourn, when Charles's neck gut split,
Opened a gap thet ain't bridged over yit: 300
Slav'ry 's your Charles, the Lord hez gin the exe—"
"Our Charles," sez I, "hez gut eight million necks.
The hardest question ain't the black man's right,
The trouble is to 'mancipate the white;
One 's chained in body an' can be sot free,
But t' other 's chained in soul to an idee:

It 's a long job, but we shall worry thru it;
Ef bagnets fail, the spellin'-book must du it."
"Hosee," sez he, "I think you 're goin' to fail:
The rettlesnake ain't dangerous in the tail;   310
This 'ere rebellion 's nothing but the rettle,—
You 'll stomp on thet an' think you 've won the bettle;
It 's Slavery thet 's the fangs an' thinkin' head,
An' ef you want selvation, cresh it dead,—
An' cresh it suddin, or you 'll larn by waitin'
Thet Chance wun't stop to listen to debatin'!"—
"God's truth!" sez I,—"an' ef *I* held the club,
An' knowed jes' where to strike,—but there 's the rub!"—
"Strike soon," sez he, "or you 'll be deadly ailin',—
Folks thet 's afeared to fail are sure o' failin';   320
God hates your sneakin' creturs thet believe
He 'll settle things they run away an' leave!"
He brought his foot down fercely, ez he spoke,
An' give me sech a startle thet I woke.

                                                        1862

From No. VII

LATEST VIEWS OF MR. BIGLOW

Ef I a song or two could make
    Like rockets druv by their own burnin',
All leap an' light, to leave a wake
    Men's hearts an' faces skyward turnin'!—
But, it strikes me, 't ain't jest the time
    Fer stringin' words with settisfaction:
Wut 's wanted now 's the silent rhyme
    'Twixt upright Will an' downright Action.

Words, ef you keep 'em, pay their keep,
    But gabble 's the short cut to ruin;   10
It 's gratis (gals half-price), but cheap
    At no rate, ef it henders doin';

Ther' 's nothin' wuss, 'less 't is to set
    A martyr-prem'um upon jawrin':
Teapots git dangerous, ef you shet
    Their lids down on 'em with Fort Warren.

'Bout long enough it 's ben discussed
    Who sot the magazine afire,
An' whether, ef Bob Wickliffe bust,
    'T would scare us more or blow us higher.   20
D' ye s'pose the Gret Foreseer's plan
    Wuz settled fer him in town-meetin'?
Or thet ther' 'd ben no Fall o' Man,
    Ef Adam 'd on'y bit a sweetin'?

Oh, Jon'than, ef you want to be
    A rugged chap agin an' hearty,
Go fer wutever 'll hurt Jeff D.,
    Nut wut 'll boost up ary party.
Here 's hell broke loose, an' we lay flat
    With half the univarse a-singein',   30
Till Sen'tor This an' Gov'nor Thet
    Stop squabblin' fer the garding-ingin.

It 's war we 're in, not politics;
    It 's systems wrastlin' now, not parties;
An' victory in the eend 'll fix
    Where longest will an' truest heart is.
An' wut 's the Guv'ment folks about?
    Tryin' to hope ther' 's nothin' doin',
An' look ez though they did n't doubt
    Sunthin' pertickler wuz a-brewin'.   40

Ther' 's critters yit thet talk an' act
    Fur wut they call Conciliation;
They 'd hand a buff'lo-drove a tract
    When they wuz madder than all Bashan.
Conciliate? it jest means *be kicked*,
    No metter how they phrase an' tone it;

It means thet we 're to set down licked,
    Thet we 're poor shotes an' glad to own it!

A war on tick 's ez dear 'z the deuce,
    But it wun't leave no lastin' traces,   50
Ez 't would to make a sneakin' truce
    Without no moral specie-basis:
Ef greenbacks ain't nut jest the cheese,
    I guess ther' 's evils thet 's extremer,—
Fer instance,—shinplaster idees
    Like them put out by Gov'nor Seymour.

Last year, the Nation, at a word,
    When tremblin' Freedom cried to shield her,
Flamed weldin' into one keen sword
    Waitin' an' longin' fer a wielder: 60
A splendid flash!—but how 'd the grasp
    With sech a chance ez thet wuz tally?
Ther' warn't no meanin' in our clasp,—
    Half this, half thet, all shilly-shally.

More men? More Man! It 's there we fail;
    Weak plans grow weaker yit by lengthenin':
Wut use in addin' to the tail,
    When it 's the head 's in need o' strengthenin'?
We wanted one thet felt all Chief
    From roots o' hair to sole o' stockin',   70
Square-sot with thousan'-ton belief
    In him an' us, ef earth went rockin'!

Ole Hick'ry would n't ha' stood see-saw
    'Bout doin' things till they wuz done with,—
He 'd smashed the tables o' the Law
    In time o' need to load his gun with;
He could n't see but jest one side,—
    Ef his, 't wuz God's, an' thet wuz plenty;
An' so his "*Forrards!*" multiplied
    An army's fightin' weight by twenty.   80

But this 'ere histin', creak, creak, creak,
 Your cappen's heart up with a derrick,
This tryin' to coax a lightnin'-streak
 Out of a half-discouraged hay-rick,
This hangin' on mont' arter mont'
 Fer one sharp purpose 'mongst the twitter,—
I tell ye, it doos kind o' stunt
 The peth and sperit of a critter.

In six months where 'll the People be,
 Ef leaders look on revolution 90
Ez though it wuz a cup o' tea,—
 Jest social el'ments in solution?
This weighin' things doos wal enough
 When war cools down, an' comes to writin';
But while it 's makin', the true stuff
 Is pison-mad, pig-headed fightin'.

Democ'acy gives every man
 The right to be his own oppressor;
But a loose Gov'ment ain't the plan,
 Helpless ez spilled beans on a dresser: 100
I tell ye one thing we might larn
 From them smart critters, the Seceders,—
Ef bein' right 's the fust consarn,
The 'fore-the-fust 's cast-iron leaders.

But 'pears to me I see some signs
 Thet we 're a-goin' to use our senses:
Jeff druv us into these hard lines,
 An' ough' to bear his half th' expenses;
Slavery 's Secession's heart an' will,
 South, North, East, West, where'er you find it, 110
An' ef it drors into War's mill,
 D' ye say them thunder-stones sha'n't grind it?

D' ye s'pose, ef Jeff giv *him* a lick,
 Ole Hick'ry 'd tried his head to sof'n

So 's 't would n't hurt thet ebony stick
    Thet 's made our side see stars so of'n?
"No!" he 'd ha' thundered, "on your knees,
    An' own one flag, one road to glory!
Soft-heartedness, in times like these,
    Shows sof'ness in the upper story!"   120

An' why should we kick up a muss
    About the Pres'dunt's proclamation?
It ain't-a-goin' to lib'rate us,
    Ef we don't like emancipation:
The right to be a cussed fool
    Is safe from all devices human,
It 's common (ez a gin'l rule)
    To every critter born o' woman.

So *we* 're all right, an' I, fer one,
    Don't think our cause 'll lose in vally   130
By rammin' Scriptur in our gun,
    An' gittin' Natur' fer an ally:
Thank God, say I, fer even a plan
    To lift one human bein's level,
Give one more chance to make a man,
    Or, anyhow, to spile a devil!

Not thet I 'm one thet much expec'
    Millennium by express tomorrer;
They *will* miscarry,—I rec'lec'
    Tu many on 'em, to my sorrer: 140
Men ain't made angels in a day,
    No matter how you mould an' labor 'em,
Nor 'riginal ones, I guess, don't stay
    With Abe so of'n ez with Abraham.

The'ry thinks Fact a pooty thing,
    An' wants the banns read right ensuin';
But fact wun't noways wear the ring,
    'Thout years o' settin' up an' wooin'.

Though, arter all, Time's dial-plate
   Marks cent'ries with the minute-finger,   150
An' Good can't never come tu late,
   Though it doos seem to try an' linger.

An' come wut will, I think it 's grand
   Abe's gut his will et last bloom-furnaced
In trial-flames till it 'll stand
   The strain o' bein' in deadly earnest:
Thet 's wut we want,—we want to know
   The folks on our side hez the bravery
To b'lieve ez hard, come weal, come woe,
   In Freedom ez Jeff doos in Slavery.   160

Set the two forces foot to foot,
   An' every man knows who 'll be winner,
Whose faith in God hez ary root
   Thet goes down deeper than his dinner:
Then 't will be felt from pole to pole,
   Without no need o' proclamation,
Earth's biggest Country's gut her soul
   An' risen up Earth's Greatest Nation!

        1863

ODE RECITED AT THE HARVARD COMMEMORATION

JULY 21, 1865

I

Weak-winged is song,
Nor aims at that clear-ethered height
Whither the brave deed climbs for light:
   We seem to do them wrong,
Bringing our robin's-leaf to deck their hearse
Who in warm life-blood wrote their nobler verse,
Our trivial song to honor those who come
With ears attuned to strenuous trump and drum,

And shaped in squadron-strophes their desire,
Live battle-odes whose lines were steel and fire: 10
    Yet sometimes feathered words are strong,
A gracious memory to buoy up and save
From Lethe's dreamless ooze, the common grave
    Of the unventurous throng.

II

Today our Reverend Mother welcomes back
  Her wisest Scholars, those who understood
The deeper teaching of her mystic tome,
    And offered their fresh lives to make it good:
      No lore of Greece or Rome,
No science peddling with the names of things,   20
Or reading stars to find inglorious fates,
      Can lift our life with wings
Far from Death's idle gulf that for the many waits,
      And lengthen out our dates
With that clear fame whose memory sings
In manly hearts to come, and nerves them and dilates:
Nor such thy teaching, Mother of us all!
      Not such the trumpet-call
      Of thy diviner mood,
      That could thy sons entice   30
From happy homes and toils, the fruitful nest
Of those half-virtues which the world calls best,
      Into War's tumult rude;
      But rather far that stern device
The sponsors chose that round thy cradle stood
  In the dim, unventured wood,
    The VERITAS that lurks beneath
    The letter's unprolific sheath,
  Life of whate'er makes life worth living,
Seed-grain of high emprise, immortal food,   40
  One heavenly thing whereof earth hath the giving.

III

Many loved Truth, and lavished life's best oil
   Amid the dust of books to find her,
Content at last, for guerdon of their toil,
    With the cast mantle she hath left behind her.
     Many in sad faith sought for her,
     Many with crossed hands sighed for her;
     But these, our brothers, fought for her,
     At life's dear peril wrought for her,
     So loved her that they died for her,   50
     Tasting the raptured fleetness
     Of her divine completeness:
     Their higher instinct knew
Those love her best who to themselves are true,
And what they dare to dream of, dare to do;
     They followed her and found her
     Where all may hope to find,
Not in the ashes of the burnt-out mind,
But beautiful, with danger's sweetness round her.
     Where faith made whole with deed   60
     Breathes its awakening breath
     Into the lifeless creed,
     They saw her plumed and mailed,
     With sweet, stern face unveiled,
And all-repaying eyes, look proud on them in death.

IV

Our slender life runs rippling by, and glides
   Into the silent hollow of the past;
    What is there that abides
   To make the next age better for the last?
    Is earth too poor to give us   70
   Something to live for here that shall outlive us?
    Some more substantial boon
Than such as flows and ebbs with Fortune's fickle moon?
    The little that we see
    From doubt is never free;

The little that we do
Is but half-nobly true;
With our laborious hiving
What men call treasure, and the gods call dross,
Life seems a jest of Fate's contriving,   80
Only secure in every one's conniving,
A long account of nothings paid with loss,
Where we poor puppets, jerked by unseen wires,
After our little hour of strut and rave,
With all our pasteboard passions and desires,
Loves, hates, ambitions, and immortal fires,
Are tossed pell-mell together in the grave.
But stay! no age was e'er degenerate,
Unless men held it at too cheap a rate,
For in our likeness still we shape our fate.   90
Ah, there is something here
Unfathomed by the cynic's sneer,
Something that gives our feeble light
A high immunity from Night,
Something that leaps life's narrow bars
To claim its birthright with the hosts of heaven;
A seed of sunshine that can leaven
Our earthly dullness with the beams of stars,
And glorify our clay
With light from fountains elder than the Day;   100
A conscience more divine than we,
A gladness fed with secret tears,
A vexing, forward-reaching sense
Of some more noble permanence;
A light across the sea,
Which haunts the soul and will not let it be,
Still beaconing from the heights of undegenerate years.

v

Whither leads the path
To ampler fates that leads?

Not down through flowery meads, 110
 To reap an aftermath
Of youth's vainglorious weeds,
 But up the steep, amid the wrath
And shock of deadly-hostile creeds,
 Where the world's best hope and stay
By battle's flashes gropes a desperate way,
And every turf the fierce foot clings to bleeds.
 Peace hath her not ignoble wreath,
 Ere yet the sharp, decisive word
Light the black lips of cannon, and the sword 120
 Dreams in its easeful sheath;
But some day the live coal behind the thought,
 Whether from Baäl's stone obscene,
 Or from the shrine serene
 Of God's pure altar brought,
Bursts up in flame; the war of tongue and pen
Learns with what deadly purpose it was fraught,
And, helpless in the fiery passion caught,
Shakes all the pillared state with shock of men:
Some day the soft Ideal that we wooed 130
Confronts us fiercely, foe-beset, pursued,
And cries reproachful: "Was it, then, my praise,
And not myself was loved? Prove now thy truth;
I claim of thee the promise of thy youth;
Give me thy life, or cower in empty phrase,
The victim of thy genius, not its mate!"
 Life may be given in many ways,
 And loyalty to Truth be sealed
As bravely in the closet as the field,
 So bountiful is Fate; 140
 But then to stand beside her,
 When craven churls deride her,
To front a lie in arms and not to yield,
 This shows, methinks, God's plan
 And measure of a stalwart man,
 Limbed like the old heroic breeds,

Who stands self-poised on manhood's solid earth,
   Not forced to frame excuses for his birth,
Fed from within with all the strength he needs.

VI

Such was he, our Martyr-Chief,   150
      Whom late the Nation he had led,
      With ashes on her head,
Wept with the passion of an angry grief:
Forgive me, if from present things I turn
To speak what in my heart will beat and burn,
And hang my wreath on his world-honored urn.
      Nature, they say, doth dote,
      And cannot make a man
      Save on some worn-out plan,
      Repeating us by rote.   160
For him her Old-World moulds aside she threw,
      And choosing sweet clay from the breast
      Of the unexhausted West,
With stuff untainted shaped a hero new,
Wise, steadfast in the strength of God, and true.
      How beautiful to see
Once more a shepherd of mankind indeed,
Who loved his charge, but never loved to lead;
One whose meek flock the people joyed to be,
      Not lured by any cheat of birth,   170
      But by his clear-grained human worth,
And brave old wisdom of sincerity!
      They knew that outward grace is dust;
      They could not choose but trust
In that sure-footed mind's unfaltering skill,
      And supple-tempered will
That bent like perfect steel to spring again and thrust.
      His was no lonely mountain-peak of mind,
      Thrusting to thin air o'er our cloudy bars,
      A sea-mark now, now lost in vapors blind;   180

Broad prairie rather, genial, level-lined,
Fruitful and friendly for all human kind,
Yet also nigh to heaven and loved of loftiest stars.
Nothing of Europe here,
Or, then, of Europe fronting mornward still,
Ere any names of Serf and Peer
Could Nature's equal scheme deface
And thwart her genial will;
Here was a type of the true elder race,
And one of Plutarch's men talked with us face to face. 190
I praise him not; it were too late;
And some innative weakness there must be
In him who condescends to victory
Such as the Present gives, and cannot wait,
Safe in himself as in a fate.
So always firmly he:
He knew to bide his time,
And can his fame abide,
Still patient in his temple faith sublime,
Till the wise years decide.   200
Great captains, with their guns and drums,
Disturb our judgment for the hour,
But at last silence comes;
These all are gone, and, standing like a tower,
Our children shall behold his fame.
The kindly-earnest, brave, foreseeing man,
Sagacious, patient, dreading praise, not blame,
New birth of our new soil, the first American.

VII

Long as man's hope insatiate can discern
Or only guess some more inspiring goal   210
Outside of Self, enduring as the pole,
Along whose course the flying axles burn
Of spirits bravely-pitched, earth's manlier brood;
Long as below we cannot find
The meed that stills the inexorable mind;

So long this faith to some ideal Good,
Under whatever mortal names it masks,
Freedom, Law, Country, this ethereal mood
That thanks the Fates for their severer tasks,
    Feeling its challenged pulses leap,   220
    While others skulk in subterfuges cheap,
And, set in Danger's van, has all the boon it asks,
    Shall win man's praise and woman's love,
    Shall be a window that we set above
All other skills and gifts to culture dear,
    A virtue round whose forehead we inwreathe
    Laurels that with a living passion breathe
When other crowns grow, while we twine them, sear.
    What brings us thronging these high rites to pay,
And seal these hours the noblest of our year,   230
    Save that our brothers found this better way?

VIII

We sit here in the Promised Land
    That flows with Freedom's honey and milk;
But 'twas they won it, sword in hand,
Making the nettle danger soft for us as silk.
    We welcome back our bravest and our best;—
    Ah me! not all! some come not with the rest,
Who went forth brave and bright as any here!
I strive to mix some gladness with my strain,
        But the sad strings complain,   240
        And will not please the ear:
I sweep them for a pæan, but they wane
        Again and yet again
Into a dirge, and die away, in pain.
In these brave ranks I only see the gaps,
Thinking of dear ones whom the dumb turf wraps,
Dark to the triumph which they died to gain:
    Fitlier may others greet the living,
    For me the past is unforgiving;

I with uncovered head   250
     Salute the sacred dead,
Who went, and who return not.—Say not so!
'Tis not the grapes of Canaan that repay,
But the high faith that failed not by the way;
Virtue treads paths that end not in the grave;
No ban of endless night exiles the brave;
     And to the saner mind
We rather seem the dead that stayed behind.
Blow, trumpets, all your exultations blow!
For never shall their aureoled presence lack: 260
I see them muster in a gleaming row,
With ever-youthful brows that nobler show;
We find in our dull road their shining track;
     In every nobler mood
We feel the orient of their spirit glow,
Part of our life's unalterable good,
Of all our saintlier aspiration;
     They come transfigured back,
Secure from change in their high-hearted ways,
Beautiful evermore, and with the rays   270
Of morn on their white Shields of Expectation!

IX

     But is there hope to save
     Even this ethereal essence from the grave?
     What ever 'scaped Oblivion's subtle wrong
Save a few clarion names, or golden threads of song?
     Before my musing eye
     The mighty ones of old sweep by,
Disvoicèd now and insubstantial things,
As noisy once as we; poor ghosts of kings,
Shadows of empire wholly gone to dust,   280
And many races, nameless long ago,
To darkness driven by that imperious gust
Of ever-rushing Time that here doth blow:

O visionary world, condition strange,
  Where naught abiding is but only Change,
Where the deep-bolted stars themselves still shift and range!
  Shall we to more continuance make pretence?
Renown builds tombs; a life-estate is Wit;
        And, bit by bit,
The cunning years steal all from us but woe;   290
  Leaves are we, whose decays no harvest sow.
        But, when we vanish hence,
  Shall they lie forceless in the dark below,
Save to make green their little length of sods,
Or deepen pansies for a year or two,
Who now to us are shining-sweet as gods?
Was dying all they had the skill to do?
That were not fruitless: but the Soul resents
Such short-lived service, as if blind events
Ruled without her, or earth could so endure;   300
She claims a more divine investiture
Of longer tenure than Fame's airy rents;
Whate'er she touches doth her nature share;
Her inspiration haunts the ennobled air,
        Gives eyes to mountains blind,
Ears to the deaf earth, voices to the wind,
And her clear trump sings succor everywhere
By lonely bivouacs to the wakeful mind;
For soul inherits all that soul could dare:
        Yea, Manhood hath a wider span   310
And larger privilege of life than man.
The single deed,the private sacrifice,
So radiant now through proudly-hidden tears,

Is covered up erelong from mortal eyes
With thoughtless drift of the deciduous years;
But that high privilege that makes all men peers,
That leap of heart whereby a people rise
        Up to a noble anger's height,
And, flamed on by the Fates, not shrink, but grow more bright,

That swift validity in noble veins,   320
    Of choosing danger and disdaining shame,
        Of being set on flame
    By the pure fire that flies all contact base
But wraps its chosen with angelic might,
        These are imperishable gains,
    Sure as the sun, medicinal as light,
    These hold great futures in their lusty reins
And certify to earth a new imperial race.

                        x

        Who now shall sneer?
    Who dare again to say we trace   330
    Our lines to a plebeian race?
        Roundhead and Cavalier!
Dumb are those names erewhile in battle loud;
Dream-footed as the shadow of a cloud,
        They flit across the ear:
That is best blood that hath most iron in 't,
To edge resolve with, pouring without stint
        For what makes manhood dear.
        Tell us not of Plantagenets,
Hapsburgs, and Guelfs, whose thin bloods crawl   340
Down from some victor in a border-brawl!
    How poor their outworn coronets,
Matched with one leaf of that plain civic wreath
Our brave for honor's blazon shall bequeath,
    Through whose desert a rescued Nation sets
Her heel on treason, and the trumpet hears
Shout victory, tingling Europe's sullen ears
    With vain resentments and more vain regrets!

                        XI

    Not in anger, not in pride,
    Pure from passion's mixture rude   350
    Ever to base earth allied,

But with far-heard gratitude,
    Still with heart and voice renewed,
To heroes living and dear martyrs dead,
The strain should close that consecrates our brave.
    Lift the heart and lift the head!
        Lofty be its mood and grave,
        Not without a martial ring,
        Not without a prouder tread
        And a peal of exultation: 360
        Little right has he to sing
        Through whose heart in such an hour
        Beats no march of conscious power,
        Sweeps no tumult of elation!
        'Tis no Man we celebrate,
        By his country's victories great,
    A hero half, and half the whim of Fate,
        But the pith and marrow of a Nation
        Drawing force from all her men,
        Highest, humblest, weakest, all,   370
        For her time of need, and then
        Pulsing it again through them,
Till the basest can no longer cower,
Feeling his soul spring up divinely tall,
Touched but in passing by her mantle-hem.
Come back, then, noble pride, for 'tis her dower!
        How could poet ever tower,
        If his passions, hopes, and fears,
        If his triumphs and his tears,
        Kept not measure with his people?   380
Boom, cannon, boom to all the winds and waves!
Clash out, glad bells, from every rocking steeple!
Banners, advance with triumph, bend your staves!
        And from every mountain-peak
        Let beacon-fire to answering beacon speak,
        Katahdin tell Monadnock, Whiteface he,
And so leap on in light from sea to sea,
            Till the glad news be sent

Across a kindling continent,
Making earth feel more firm and air breathe braver: 390
"Be proud! for she is saved, and all have helped to save her!
   She that lifts up the manhood of the poor,
   She of the open soul and open door,
   With room about her hearth for all mankind!
   The fire is dreadful in her eyes no more;
   From her bold front the helm she doth unbind,
   Sends all her handmaid armies back to spin,
   And bids her navies, that so lately hurled
   Their crashing battle, hold their thunders in,
   Swimming like birds of calm along the unharmful shore.
   No challenge sends she to the elder world,   401
   That looked askance and hated; a light scorn
   Plays o'er her mouth, as round her mighty knees
   She calls her children back, and waits the morn
Of nobler day, enthroned between her subject seas."

XII

Bow down, dear Land, for thou hast found release!
   Thy God, in these distempered days,
   Hath taught thee the sure wisdom of His ways,
And through thine enemies hath wrought thy peace!
   Bow down in prayer and praise!   410
No poorest in thy borders but may now
Lift to the juster skies a man's enfranchised brow.
O Beautiful! my Country! ours once more!
Smoothing thy gold of war-dishevelled hair
O'er such sweet brows as never other wore,
   And letting thy set lips,
   Freed from wrath's pale eclipse,
The rosy edges of their smile lay bare,
What words divine of lover or of poet
Could tell our love and make thee know it,   420
Among the Nations bright beyond compare?
   What were our lives without thee?

What all our lives to save thee?
We reck not what we gave thee;
We will not dare to doubt thee,
But ask whatever else, and we will dare!
1865   1865

THE CATHEDRAL

Far through the memory shines a happy day,
Cloudless of care, down-shod to every sense,
And simply perfect from its own resource,
As to a bee the new campanula's
Illuminate seclusion swung in air.
Such days are not the prey of setting suns,
Nor ever blurred with mist of after-thought;
Like words made magical by poets dead,
Wherein the music of all meaning is
The sense hath garnered or the soul divined,   10
They mingle with our life's ethereal part,
Sweetening and gathering sweetness evermore,
By Beauty's franchise disenthralled of time.

I can recall, nay, they are present still,
Parts of myself, the perfume of my mind,
Days that seem farther off than Homer's now
Ere yet the child had loudened to the boy,
And I, recluse from playmates, found perforce
Companionship in things that not denied
Nor granted wholly; as is Nature's wont,   20
Who, safe in uncontaminate reserve,
Lets us mistake our longing for her love,
And mocks with various echo of ourselves.

These first sweet frauds upon our consciousness,
That blend the sensual with its imaged world,
These virginal cognitions, gifts of morn,
Ere life grow noisy, and slower-footed thought
Can overtake the rapture of the sense,

To thrust between ourselves and what we feel,
Have something in them secretly divine. 30
Vainly the eye, once schooled to serve the brain,
With pains deliberate studies to renew
The ideal vision: second-thoughts are prose;
For Beauty's acme hath a term as brief
As the wave's poise before it break in pearl.
Our own breath dims the mirror of the sense,
Looking too long and closely: at a flash
We snatch the essential grace of meaning out,
And that first passion beggars all behind,
Heirs of a tamer transport prepossessed. 40
Who, seeing once, has truly seen again
The gray vague of unsympathizing sea
That dragged his Fancy from her moorings back
To shores inhospitable of eldest time,
Till blank foreboding of earth-gendered power,
Pitiless seignories in the elements,
Omnipotences blind that darkling smite,
Misgave him, and repaganized the world?
Yet, by some subtler touch of sympathy,
These primal apprehensions, dimly stirred, 50
Perplex the eye with pictures from within.
This hath made poets dream of lives foregone
In worlds fantastical, more fair than ours;
So Memory cheats us, glimpsing half-revealed.
Even as I write she tries her wonted spell
In that continuous redbreast boding rain:
The bird I hear sings not from yonder elm;
But the flown ecstasy my childhood heard
Is vocal in my mind, renewed by him,
Haply made sweeter by the accumulate thrill 60
That threads my undivided life and steals
A pathos from the years and graves between.

I know not how it is with other men,
Whom I but guess, deciphering myself;

For me, once felt is so felt nevermore.
The fleeting relish at sensation's brim
Had in it the best ferment of the wine.
One spring I knew as never any since:
All night the surges of the warm southwest
Boomed intermittent through the shuddering elms,   70
And brought a morning from the Gulf adrift,
Omnipotent with sunshine, whose quick charm
Startled with crocuses the sullen turf
And wiled the bluebird to his whiff of song:
One summer hour abides, what time I perched,
Dappled with noonday, under simmering leaves,
And pulled the pulpy oxhearts, while aloof
An oriole clattered and the robins shrilled,
Denouncing me an alien and a thief:
One morn of autumn lords it o'er the rest,   80
When in the lane I watched the ash-leaves fall,
Balancing softly earthward without wind,
Or twirling with directer impulse down
On those fallen yesterday, now barbed with frost,
While I grew pensive with the pensive year:
And once I learned how marvellous winter was,
When past the fence-rails, downy-gray with rime,
I creaked adventurous o'er the spangled crust
That made familiar fields seem far and strange
As those stark wastes that whiten endlessly   90
In ghastly solitude about the pole,
And gleam relentless to the unsetting sun:
Instant the candid chambers of my brain
Were painted with these sovran images;
And later visions seem but copies pale
From those unfading frescos of the past,
Which I, young savage, in my age of flint,
Gazed at, and dimly felt a power in me
Parted from Nature by the joy in her
That doubtfully revealed me to myself.   100
Thenceforward I must stand outside the gate;

And paradise was paradise the more,
Known once and barred against satiety.

What we call Nature, all outside ourselves,
Is but our own conceit of what we see,
Our own reaction upon what we feel;
The world 's a woman to our shifting mood,
Feeling with us, or making due pretence;
And therefore we the more persuade ourselves
To make all things our thought's confederates,   110
Conniving with us in whate'er we dream.
So when our Fancy seeks analogies,
Though she have hidden what she after finds,
She loves to cheat herself with feigned surprise.
I find my own complexion everywhere:
No rose, I doubt, was ever, like the first,
A marvel to the bush it dawned upon,
The rapture of its life made visible,
The mystery of its yearning realized,
As the first babe to the first woman born;   120
No falcon ever felt delight of wings
As when, an eyas, from the stolid cliff
Loosing himself, he followed his high heart
To swim on sunshine, masterless as wind;
And I believe the brown Earth takes delight
In the new snowdrop looking back at her,
To think that by some vernal alchemy
It could transmute her darkness into pearl;
What is the buxom peony after that,
With its coarse constancy of hoyden blush?   130
What the full summer to that wonder new?

But, if in nothing else, in us there is
A sense fastidious hardly reconciled
To the poor makeshifts of life's scenery,
Where the same slide must double all its parts,
Shoved in for Tarsus and hitched back for Tyre.

I blame not in the soul this daintiness,
Rasher of surfeit than a humming-bird,
In things indifferent by sense purveyed;
It argues her an immortality   140
And dateless incomes of experience,
This unthrift housekeeping that will not brook
A dish warmed-over at the feast of life,
And finds Twice stale, served with whatever sauce.
Nor matters much how it may go with me
Who dwell in Grub Street and am proud to drudge
Where men, my betters, wet their crust with tears:
Use can make sweet the peach's shady side,
That only by reflection tastes of sun.

But she, my Princess, who will sometimes deign   150
My garret to illumine till the walls,
Narrow and dingy, scrawled with hackneyed thought
(Poor Richard slowly elbowing Plato out),
Dilate and drape themselves with tapestries
Nausikaa might have stooped o'er, while, between,
Mirrors, effaced in their own clearness, send
Her only image on through deepening deeps
With endless repercussion of delight,—
Bringer of life, witching each sense to soul,
That sometimes almost gives me to believe   160
I might have been a poet, gives at least
A brain desaxonized, an ear that makes
Music where none is, and a keener pang
Of exquisite surmise outleaping thought,—
Her will I pamper in her luxury:
No crumpled rose-leaf of too careless choice
Shall bring a northern nightmare to her dreams,
Vexing with sense of exile; hers shall be
The invitiate firstlings of experience,
Vibrations felt but once and felt lifelong: 170
Oh, more than half-way turn that Grecian front
Upon me, while with self-rebuke I spell,

On the plain fillet that confines thy hair
In conscious bounds of seeming unconstraint,
The *Naught in overplus*, thy race's badge!

One feast for her I secretly designed
In that Old World so strangely beautiful
To us the disinherited of eld,—
A day at Chartres, with no soul beside
To roil with pedant prate my joy serene   180
And make the minster shy of confidence.
I went, and, with the Saxon's pious care,
First ordered dinner at the pea-green inn,
The flies and I its only customers.
Eluding these, I loitered through the town,
With hope to take my minster unawares
In its grave solitude of memory.
A pretty burgh, and such as Fancy loves
For bygone grandeurs, faintly rumorous now
Upon the mind's horizon, as of storm   190
Brooding its dreamy thunders far aloof,
That mingle with our mood, but not disturb.
Its once grim bulwarks, tamed to lovers' walks,
Look down unwatchful on the sliding Eure,
Whose listless leisure suits the quiet place,
Lisping among his shallows homelike sounds
At Concord and by Bankside heard before.
Chance led me to a public pleasure-ground,
Where I grew kindly with the merry groups,
And blessed the Frenchman for his simple art   200
Of being domestic in the light of day.
His language has no word, we growl, for Home;
But he can find a fireside in the sun,
Play with his child, make love, and shriek his mind,
By throngs of strangers undisprivacied.
He makes his life a public gallery,
Nor feels himself till what he feels comes back
In manifold reflection from without;

While we, each pore alert with consciousness,
Hide our best selves as we had stolen them,   210
And each bystander a detective were,
Keen-eyed for every chink of undisguise.

So, musing o'er the problem which was best,—
A life wide-windowed, shining all abroad,
Or curtains drawn to shield from sight profane
The rites we pay to the mysterious I,—
With outward senses furloughed and head bowed
I followed some fine instinct in my feet,
Till, to unbend me from the loom of thought,
Looking up suddenly, I found mine eyes   220
Confronted with the minster's vast repose.
Silent and gray as forest-leaguered cliff
Left inland by the ocean's slow retreat,
That hears afar the breeze-borne rote and longs,
Remembering shocks of surf that clomb and fell,
Spume-sliding down the baffled decuman,
It rose before me, patiently remote
From the great tides of life it breasted once,
Hearing the noise of men as in a dream.
I stood before the triple northern port,   230
Where dedicated shapes of saints and kings,
Stern faces bleared with immemorial watch,
Looked down benignly grave and seemed to say,
Ye come and go incessant; we remain
Safe in the hallowed quiets of the past;
Be reverent, ye who flit and are forgot,
Of faith so nobly realized as this.
I seem to have heard it said by learnèd folk
Who drench you with æsthetics till you feel
As if all beauty were a ghastly bore,   240
The faucet to let loose a wash of words,
That Gothic is not Grecian, therefore worse;
But, being convinced by much experiment
How little inventiveness there is in man,

Grave copier of copies, I give thanks
For a new relish, careless to inquire
My pleasure's pedigree, if so it please,
Nobly, I mean, nor renegade to art.
The Grecian gluts me with its perfectness,
Unanswerable as Euclid, self-contained,   250
The one thing finished in this hasty world,
Forever finished, though the barbarous pit,
Fanatical on hearsay, stamp and shout
As if a miracle could be encored.
But ah! this other, this that never ends,
Still climbing, luring fancy still to climb,
As full of morals half-divined as life,
Graceful, grotesque, with ever new surprise
Of hazardous caprices sure to please,
Heavy as nightmare, airy-light as fern,   260
Imagination's very self in stone!
With one long sigh of infinite release
From pedantries past, present, or to come,
I looked, and owned myself a happy Goth.
Your blood is mine, ye architects of dream,
Builders of aspiration incomplete,
So more consummate, souls self-confident,
Who felt your own thought worthy of record
In monumental pomp! No Grecian drop
Rebukes these veins that leap with kindred thrill,   270
After long exile, to the mother-tongue.

Ovid in Pontus, puling for his Rome
Of men invirile and disnatured dames
That poison sucked from the Attic bloom decayed,
Shrank with a shudder from the blue-eyed race
Whose force rough-handed should renew the world,
And from the dregs of Romulus express
Such wine as Dante poured, or he who blew
Roland's vain blast, or sang the Campeador
In verse that clanks like armor in the charge,—   280

Homeric juice, though brimmed in Odin's horn.
And they could build, if not the columned fane
That from the height gleamed seaward many-hued,
Something more friendly with their ruder skies:
The gray spire, molten now in driving mist,
Now lulled with the incommunicable blue;
The carvings touched to meanings new with snow,
Or commented with fleeting grace of shade;
The statues, motley as man's memory,
Partial as that, so mixed of true and false,   290
History and legend meeting with a kiss
Across this bound-mark where their realms confine;
The painted windows, freaking gloom with glow,
Dusking the sunshine which they seem to cheer,
Meet symbol of the senses and the soul;
And the whole pile, grim with the Northman's thought
Of life and death, and doom, life's equal fee,—
These were before me: and I gazed abashed,
Child of an age that lectures, not creates,
Plastering our swallow-nests on the awful Past,   300
And twittering round the work of larger men,
As we had builded what we but deface.
Far up the great bells wallowed in delight,
Tossing their clangors o'er the heedless town,
To call the worshippers who never came,
Or women mostly, in loath twos and threes.
I entered, reverent of whatever shrine
Guards piety and solace for my kind
Or gives the soul a moment's truce of God,
And shared decorous in the ancient rite   310
My sterner fathers held idolatrous.
The service over, I was tranced in thought:
Solemn the deepening vaults, and most to me,
Fresh from the fragile realm of deal and paint,
Or brick mock-pious with a marble front;
Solemn the lift of high-embowered roof,
The clustered stems that spread in boughs disleaved,

Through which the organ blew a dream of storm,—
Though not more potent to sublime with awe
And shut the heart up in tranquillity,   320
Than aisles to me familiar that o'erarch
The conscious silences of brooding woods,
Centurial shadows, cloisters of the elk:
Yet here was sense of undefined regret,
Irreparable loss, uncertain what:
Was all this grandeur but anachronism,—
A shell divorced of its informing life,
Where the priest housed him like a hermit-crab,
An alien to that faith of elder days
That gathered round it this fair shape of stone?   330
Is old Religion but a spectre now,
Haunting the solitude of darkened minds,
Mocked out of memory by the sceptic day?
Is there no corner safe from peeping Doubt,
Since Gutenberg made thought cosmopolite
And stretchèd electric threads from mind to mind?
Nay, did Faith build this wonder? or did Fear,
That makes a fetish and misnames it God
(Blockish or metaphysic, matters not),
Contrive this coop to shut its tyrant in,   340
Appeased with playthings, that he might not harm?

I turned and saw a beldame on her knees;
With eyes astray, she told mechanic beads
Before some shrine of saintly womanhood,
Bribed intercessor with the far-off Judge:
Such my first thought, by kindlier soon rebuked,
Pleading for whatsoever touches life
With upward impulse: be He nowhere else,
God is in all that liberates and lifts,
In all that humbles, sweetens, and consoles: 350
Blessèd the natures shored on every side
With landmarks of hereditary thought!
Thrice happy they that wander not lifelong

Beyond near succor of the household faith,
The guarded fold that shelters, not confines!
Their steps find patience in familiar paths,
Printed with hope by loved feet gone before
Of parent, child, or lover, glorified
By simple magic of dividing Time.
My lids were moistened as the woman knelt,   360
And—was it will, or some vibration faint
Of sacred Nature, deeper than the will?—
My heart occultly felt itself in hers,
Through mutual intercession gently leagued.

Or was it not mere sympathy of brain?
A sweetness intellectually conceived
In simpler creeds to me impossible?
A juggle of that pity for ourselves
In others, which puts on such pretty masks
And snares self-love with bait of charity?   370
Something of all it might be, or of none:
Yet for a moment I was snatched away
And had the evidence of things not seen;
For one rapt moment, then it all came back,
This age that blots out life with question-marks,
This nineteenth century with its knife and glass
That make thought physical, and thrust far off
The Heaven, so neighborly with man of old,
To voids sparse-sown with alienated stars.

'Tis irrecoverable, that ancient faith,   380
Homely and wholesome, suited to the time,
With rod or candy for child-minded men:
No theologic tube, with lens on lens
Of syllogism transparent, brings it near,—
At best resolving some new nebula,
Or blurring some fixed-star of hope to mist.
Science was Faith once; Faith were Science now,
Would she but lay her bow and arrows by

And arm her with the weapons of the time.
Nothing that keeps thought out is safe from thought. 390
For there's no virgin-fort but self-respect,
And Truth defensive hath lost hold on God.
Shall we treat Him as if He were a child
That knew not His own purpose? nor dare trust
The Rock of Ages to their chemic tests,
Lest some day the all-sustaining base divine
Should fail from under us, dissolved in gas?
The armëd eye that with a glance discerns
In a dry blood-speck between ox and man,
Stares helpless at this miracle called life, 400
This shaping potency behind the egg,
This circulation swift of deity,
Where suns and systems inconspicuous float
As the poor blood-disks in our mortal veins.
Each age must worship its own thought of God,
More or less earthy, clarifying still
With subsidence continuous of the dregs;
Nor saint nor sage could fix immutably
The fluent image of the unstable Best,
Still changing in their very hands that wrought: 410
Today's eternal truth Tomorrow proved
Frail as frost-landscapes on a window-pane.
Meanwhile Thou smiledst, inaccessible,
At Thought's own substance made a cage for Thought,
And Truth locked fast with her own masterkey;
Nor didst Thou reck what image man might make
Of his own shadow on the flowing world;
The climbing instinct was enough for Thee.
Or wast Thou, then, on ebbing tide that left
Strewn with dead miracle those eldest shores, 420
For men to dry, and dryly lecture on,
Thyself thenceforth incapable of flood?
Idle who hopes with prophets to be snatched
By virtue in their mantles left below;
Shall the soul live on other men's report,

Herself a pleasing fable of herself?
Man cannot be God's outlaw if he would,
Nor so abscond him in the caves of sense
But Nature still shall search some crevice out
With messages of splendor from that Source   430
Which, dive he, soar he, baffles still and lures.
This life were brutish did we not sometimes
Have intimation clear of wider scope,
Hints of occasion infinite, to keep
The soul alert with noble discontent
And onward yearnings of unstilled desire;
Fruitless, except we now and then divined
A mystery of Purpose, gleaming through
The secular confusions of the world,
Whose will we darkly accomplish, doing ours.   440
No man can think nor in himself perceive,
Sometimes at waking, in the street sometimes,
Or on the hillside, always unforewarned,
A grace of being, finer than himself,
That beckons and is gone,—a larger life
Upon his own impinging, with swift glimpse
Of spacious circles luminous with mind,
To which the ethereal substance of his own
Seems but gross cloud to make that visible,
Touched to a sudden glory round the edge.   450
Who that hath known these visitations fleet
Would strive to make them trite and ritual?
I, that still pray at morning and at eve,
Loving those roots that feed us from the past,
And prizing more than Plato things I learned
At that best academe, a mother's knee,
Thrice in my life perhaps have truly prayed,
Thrice, stirred below my conscious self, have felt
That perfect disenthralment which is God;
Nor know I which to hold worst enemy,—   460
Him who on speculation's windy waste
Would turn me loose, stript of the raiment warm

By Faith contrived against our nakedness,
Or him who, cruel-kind, would fain obscure,
With painted saints and paraphrase of God,
The soul's east-window of divine surprise.
Where others worship I but look and long;
For, though not recreant to my fathers' faith,
Its forms to me are weariness, and most
That drony vacuum of compulsory prayer, 470
Still pumping phrases for the Ineffable,
Though all the valves of memory gasp and wheeze.
Words that have drawn transcendent meanings up
From the best passion of all bygone time,
Steeped through with tears of triumph and remorse,
Sweet with all sainthood, cleansed in martyr-fires,
Can they, so consecrate and so inspired,
By repetition wane to vexing wind?
Alas! we cannot draw habitual breath
In the thin air of life's supremer heights, 480
We cannot make each meal a sacrament,
Nor with our tailors be disbodied souls,—
We men, too conscious of earth's comedy,
Who see two sides, with our posed selves debate,
And only for great stakes can be sublime!
Let us be thankful when, as I do here,
We can read Bethel on a pile of stones,
And, seeing where God *has* been, trust in Him.

Brave Peter Fischer there in Nuremberg,
Moulding Saint Sebald's miracles in bronze, 490
Put saint and stander-by in that quaint garb
Familiar to him in his daily walk,
Not doubting God could grant a miracle
Then and in Nuremberg, if so He would;
But never artist for three hundred years
Hath dared the contradiction ludicrous
Of supernatural in modern clothes.
Perhaps the deeper faith that is to come

Will see God rather in the strenuous doubt,
Than in the creed held as an infant's hand   500
Holds purposeless whatso is placed therein.

Say it is drift, not progress, none the less,
With the old sextant of the fathers' creed,
We shape our courses by new-risen stars,
And, still lip-loyal to what once was truth,
Smuggle new meanings under ancient names,
Unconscious perverts of the Jesuit, Time.
Change is the mask that all Continuance wears
To keep us youngsters harmlessly amused;
Meanwhile, some ailing or more watchful child,   510
Sitting apart, sees the old eyes gleam out,
Stern, and yet soft with humorous pity too.
Whilere, men burnt men for a doubtful point,
As if the mind were quenchable with fire,
And Faith danced round them with her war-paint on,
Devoutly savage as an Iroquois;
Now Calvin and Servetus at one board
Snuff in grave sympathy a milder roast,
And o'er their claret settle Comte unread.
Fagot and stake were desperately sincere.   520
Our cooler martyrdoms are done in types;
And flames that shine in controversial eyes
Burn out no brains but his who kindles them.
This is no age to get cathedrals built:
Did God, then, wait for one in Bethlehem?
Worst is not yet: lo, where his coming looms,
Of Earth's anarchic children latest born,
Democracy, a Titan who hath learned
To laugh at Jove's old-fashioned thunderbolts,—
Could he not also forge them, if he would?   530
He, better skilled, with solvents merciless,
Loosened in air and borne on every wind,
Saps unperceived: the calm Olympian height
Of ancient order feels its bases yield,

And pale gods glance for help to gods as pale.
What will be left of good or worshipful,
Of spiritual secrets, mysteries,
Of fair Religion's guarded heritage,
Heirlooms of soul, passed downward unprofaned
From eldest Ind? This Western giant coarse,   540
Scorning refinements which he lacks himself,
Loves not nor heeds the ancestral hierarchies,
Each rank dependent on the next above
In orderly gradation fixed as fate.
King by mere manhood, nor allowing aught
Of holier unction than the sweat of toil;
In his own strength sufficient; called to solve,
On the rough edges of society,
Problems long sacred to the choicer few,
And improvise what elsewhere men receive   550
As gifts of deity; tough foundling reared
Where every man's his own Melchisedek,
How make him reverent of a King of kings?
Or Judge self-made, executor of laws
By him not first discussed and voted on?
For him no tree of knowledge is forbid,
Or sweeter if forbid. How save the ark,
Or holy of holies, unprofaned a day
From his unscrupulous curiosity
That handles everything as if to buy,   560
Tossing aside what fabrics delicate
Suit not the rough-and-tumble of his ways?
What hope for those fine-nerved humanities
That made earth gracious once with gentler arts,
Now the rude hands have caught the trick of thought
And claim an equal suffrage with the brain?

The born disciple of an elder time,
(To me sufficient, friendlier than the new,)
Who in my blood feel motions of the Past,
I thank benignant nature most for this,—   570

A force of sympathy, or call it lack
Of character firm-planted, loosing me
From the pent chamber of habitual self
To dwell enlarged in alien modes of thought,
Haply distasteful, wholesomer for that,
And through imagination to possess,
As they were mine, the lives of other men.
This growth original of virgin soil,
By fascination felt in opposites,
Pleases and shocks, entices and perturbs.   580
In this brown-fisted rough, this shirt-sleeved Cid,
This backwoods Charlemagne of empires new,
Whose blundering heel instinctively finds out
The goutier foot of speechless dignities,
Who, meeting Cæsar's self, would slap his back,
Call him "Old Horse," and challenge to a drink,
My lungs draw braver air, my breast dilates
With ampler manhood, and I front both worlds,
Of sense and spirit, as my natural fiefs,
To shape and then reshape them as I will.   590
It was the first man's charter; why not mine?
How forfeit? when deposed in other hands?

Thou shudder'st, Ovid?   Dost in him forbode
A new avatar of the large-limbed Goth,
To break, or seem to break, tradition's clue,
And chase to dreamland back thy gods dethroned?
I think man's soul dwells nearer to the east,
Nearer to morning's fountains than the sun;
Herself the source whence all tradition sprang,
Herself at once both labyrinth and clue.   600
The miracle fades out of history,
But faith and wonder and the primal earth
Are born into the world with every child.
Shall this self-maker with the prying eyes,
This creature disenchanted of respect
By the New World's new fiend, Publicity,

Whose testing thumb leaves everywhere its smutch,
Not one day feel within himself the need
Of loyalty to better than himself,
That shall ennoble him with the upward look?   610
Shall he not catch the Voice that wanders earth,
With spiritual summons, dreamed or heard,
As sometimes, just ere sleep seals up the sense,
We hear our mother call from deeps of Time,
And, waking, find it vision,—none the less
The benediction bides, old skies return,
And that unreal thing, preëminent,
Makes air and dream of all we see and feel?
Shall he divine no strength unmade of votes,
Inward, impregnable, found soon as sought,   620
Not cognizable of sense, o'er sense supreme?
Else were he desolate as none before,
His holy places may not be of stone,
Nor made with hands, yet fairer far than aught
By artist feigned or pious ardor reared,
Fit altars for who guards inviolate
God's chosen seat, the sacred form of man.
Doubtless his church will be no hospital
For superannuate forms and mumping shams,
No parlor where men issue policies   630
Of life-assurance on the Eternal Mind,
Nor his religion but an ambulance
To fetch life's wounded and malingerers in,
Scorned by the strong; yet he, unconscious heir
To the influence sweet of Athens and of Rome,
And old Judæa's gift of secret fire,
Spite of himself shall surely learn to know
And worship some ideal of himself,
Some divine thing, large-hearted, brotherly,
Not nice in trifles, a soft creditor,   640
Pleased with his world, and hating only cant.
And, if his Church be doubtful, it is sure
That, in a world, made for whatever else,

Not made for mere enjoyment, in a world
Of toil but half-requited, or, at best,
Paid in some futile currency of breath,
A world of incompleteness, sorrow swift
And consolation laggard, whatsoe'er
The form of building or the creed professed,
The Cross, bold type of shame to homage turned,   650
Of an unfinished life that sways the world,
Shall tower as sovereign emblem over all.

The kobold Thought moves with us when we shift
Our dwelling to escape him; perched aloft
On the first load of household-stuff he went;
For, where the mind goes, goes old furniture.
I, who to Chartres came to feed my eye
And give to Fancy one clear holiday,
Scarce saw the minster for the thoughts it stirred
Buzzing o'er past and future with vain quest.   660
Here once there stood a homely wooden church,
Which slow devotion nobly changed for this
That echoes vaguely to my modern steps.
By suffrage universal it was built,
As practised then, for all the country came
From far as Rouen, to give votes for God,
Each vote a block of stone securely laid
Obedient to the master's deep-mused plan.
Will what our ballots rear, responsible
To no grave forethought, stand so long as this?   670
Delight like this the eye of after days
Brightening with pride that here, at least, were men
Who meant and did the noblest thing they knew?
Can our religion cope with deeds like this?
We, too, build Gothic contract-shams, because
Our deacons have discovered that it pays,
And pews sell better under vaulted roofs
Of plaster painted like an Indian squaw.
Shall not that Western Goth, of whom we spoke,

So fiercely practical, so keen of eye,   680
Find out, some day, that nothing pays but God,
Served whether on the smoke-shut battle-field,
In work obscure done honestly, or vote
For truth unpopular, or faith maintained
To ruinous convictions, or good deeds
Wrought for good's sake, mindless of heaven or hell?
Shall he not learn that all prosperity,
Whose bases stretch not deeper than the sense,
Is but a trick of this world's atmosphere,
A desert-born mirage of spire and dome,   690
Or find too late, the Past's long lesson missed,
That dust the prophets shake from off their feet
Grows heavy to drag down both tower and wall?
I know not; but, sustained by sure belief
That man still rises level with the height
Of noblest opportunities, or makes
Such, if the time supply not, I can wait.
I gaze round on the windows, pride of France,
Each the bright gift of some mechanic guild
Who loved their city and thought gold well spent   700
To make her beautiful with piety;
I pause, transfigured by some stripe of bloom,
And my mind throngs with shining auguries,
Circle on circle, bright as seraphim,
With golden trumpets, silent, that await
The signal to blow news of good to men.

Then the revulsion came that always comes
After these dizzy elations of the mind:
And with a passionate pang of doubt I cried,
"O mountain-born, sweet with snow-filtered air   710
From uncontaminate wells of ether drawn
And never-broken secrecies of sky,
Freedom, with anguish won, misprized till lost,
They keep thee not who from thy sacred eyes
Catch the consuming lust of sensual good

And the brute's license of unfettered will.
Far from the popular shout and venal breath
Of Cleon blowing the mob's baser mind
To bubbles of wind-piloted conceit,
Thou shrinkest, gathering up thy skirts, to hide   720
In fortresses of solitary thought
And private virtue strong in self-restraint.
Must we too forfeit thee misunderstood,
Content with names, nor inly wise to know
That best things perish of their own excess,
And quality o'er-driven becomes defect?
Nay, is it thou indeed that we have glimpsed,
Or rather such illusion as of old
Through Athens glided menadlike and Rome,
A shape of vapor, mother of vain dreams   730
And mutinous traditions, specious plea
Of the glaived tyrant and long-memoried priest?"

I walked forth saddened; for all thought is sad,
And leaves a bitterish savor in the brain,
Tonic, it may be, not delectable,
And turned, reluctant, for a parting look
At those old weather-pitted images
Of bygone struggle, now so sternly calm.
About their shoulders sparrows had built nests,
And fluttered, chirping, from gray perch to perch,   740
Now on a mitre poising, now a crown,
Irreverently happy. While I thought
How confident they were, what careless hearts
Flew on those lightsome wings and shared the sun,
A larger shadow crossed; and looking up,
I saw where, nesting in the hoary towers,
The sparrow-hawk slid forth on noiseless air,
With sidelong head that watched the joy below,
Grim Norman baron o'er this clan of Kelts.
Enduring Nature, force conservative,   750
Indifferent to our noisy whims! Men prate

Of all heads to an equal grade cashiered
On level with the dullest, and expect
(Sick of no worse distemper than themselves)
A wondrous cure-all in equality;
They reason that Tomorrow must be wise
Because Today was not, nor Yesterday,
As if good days were shapen of themselves,
Not of the very lifeblood of men's souls;
Meanwhile, long-suffering, imperturbable,   760
Thou quietly complet'st thy syllogism,
And from the premise sparrow here below
Draw'st sure conclusion of the hawk above,
Pleased with the soft-billed songster, pleased no less
With the fierce beak of natures aquiline.

Thou beautiful Old Time, now hid away
In the Past's valley of Avilion,
Haply, like Arthur, till thy wound be healed,
Then to reclaim the sword and crown again!
Thrice beautiful to us; perchance less fair   770
To who possessed thee, as a mountain seems
To dwellers round its bases but a heap
Of barren obstacle that lairs the storm
And the avalanche's silent bolt holds back
Leashed with a hair,—meanwhile some far-off clown,
Hereditary delver of the plain,
Sees it an unmoved vision of repose,
Nest of the morning, and conjectures there
The dance of streams to idle shepherds' pipes,
And fairer habitations softly hung   780
On breezy slopes, or hid in valleys cool,
For happier men. No mortal ever dreams
That the scant isthmus he encamps upon
Between two oceans, one, the Stormy, passed,
And one, the Peaceful, yet to venture on,
Has been that future whereto prophets yearned
For the fulfilment of Earth's cheated hope,

Shall be that past which nerveless poets moan
As the lost opportunity of song.

O Power, more near my life than life itself   790
(Or what seems life to us in sense immured),
Even as the roots, shut in the darksome earth,
Share in the tree-top's joyance, and conceive
Of sunshine and wide air and wingèd things
By sympathy of nature, so do I
Have evidence of Thee so far above,
Yet in and of me! Rather Thou the root
Invisibly sustaining, hid in light,
Not darkness, or in darkness made by us.
If sometimes I must hear good men debate   800
Of other witness of Thyself than Thou,
As if there needed any help of ours
To nurse Thy flickering life, that else must cease,
Blown out, as 'twere a candle, by men's breath,
My soul shall not be taken in their snare,
To change her inward surety for their doubt
Muffled from sight in formal robes of proof:
While she can only feel herself through Thee,
I fear not Thy withdrawal; more I fear,
Seeing, to know Thee not, hoodwinked with dreams 810
Of signs and wonders, while, unnoticed, Thou,
Walking Thy garden still, commun'st with men,
Missed in the commonplace of miracle.
1869   1869

AGASSIZ

Come
Dicesti *egli ebbe?* non viv' egli ancora?
Non fiere gli occhi suoi lo dolce lome?

I

1.

The electric nerve, whose instantaneous thrill
Makes next-door gossips of the antipodes,

Confutes poor Hope's last fallacy of ease,—
The distance that divided her from ill:
Earth sentient seems again as when of old
            The horny foot of Pan
Stamped, and the conscious horror ran
Beneath men's feet through all her fibres cold:
Space's blue walls are mined; we feel the throe
From underground of our night-mantled foe: 10
            The flame-winged feet
Of Trade's new Mercury, that dry-shod run
Through briny abysses dreamless of the sun,
            Are mercilessly fleet,
            And at a bound annihilate
Ocean's prerogative of short reprieve;
            Surely ill news might wait,
And man be patient of delay to grieve:
            Letters have sympathies
            And tell-tale faces that reveal,   20
            To senses finer than the eyes,
Their errand's purport ere we break the seal;
They wind a sorrow round with circumstance
To stay its feet, nor all unwarned displace
The veil that darkened from our sidelong glance
            The inexorable face:
            But now Fate stuns as with a mace;
The savage of the skies, that men have caught
            And some scant use of language taught,
            Tells only what he must,—   30
The steel-cold fact in one laconic thrust.

                                2.

So thought I, as, with vague, mechanic eyes,
I scanned the festering news we half despise
            Yet scramble for no less,
And read of public scandal, private fraud,
Crime flaunting scot-free while the mob applaud,

Office made vile to bribe unworthiness,
    And all the unwholesome mess
The Land of Honest Abraham serves of late
    To teach the Old World how to wait,   · 40
        When suddenly,
As happens if the brain, from overweight
      Of blood, infect the eye,
Three tiny words grew lurid as I read,
And reeled commingling: *Agassiz is dead.*
As when, beneath the street's familiar jar,
An earthquake's alien omen rumbles far,
Men listen and forebode, I hung my head,
    And strove the present to recall,
As if the blow that stunned were yet to fall.   50

3.

    Uprooted is our mountain oak,
That promised long security of shade
And brooding-place for many a wingèd thought;
    Not by Time's softly-cadenced stroke
With pauses of relenting pity stayed,
But ere a root seemed sapt, a bough decayed,
From sudden ambush by the whirlwind caught
And in his broad maturity betrayed!

4.

Well might I, as of old, appeal to you,
    O mountains, woods, and streams,   60
To help us mourn him, for ye loved him too;
    But simpler moods befit our modern themes,
And no less perfect birth of nature can,
Though they yearn tow'rd him, sympathize with man,
Save as dumb fellow-prisoners through a wall;
    Answer ye rather to my call,
Strong poets of a more unconscious day,
When Nature spake nor sought nice reasons why,

Too much for softer arts forgotten since
That teach our forthright tongue to lisp and mince, 70
And drown in music the heart's bitter cry!
Lead me some steps in your directer way,
Teach me those words that strike a solid root
      Within the ears of men;
Ye chiefly, virile both to think and feel,
Deep-chested Chapman and firm-footed Ben,
For he was masculine from head to heel.
Nay, let himself stand undiminished by
With those clear parts of him that will not die.
Himself from out the recent dark I claim 80
To hear, and, if I flatter him, to blame;
To show himself, as still I seem to see,
A mortal, built upon the antique plan,
Brimful of lusty blood as ever ran,
And taking life as simply as a tree!
To claim my foiled good-by let him appear,
Large-limbed and human as I saw him near,
Loosed from the stiffening uniform of fame:
And let me treat him largely: I should fear
(If with too prying lens I chanced to err, 90
Mistaking catalogue for character,)
His wise forefinger raised in smiling blame.
Nor would I scant him with judicial breath
And turn mere critic in an epitaph;
I choose the wheat, incurious of the chaff
That swells fame living, chokes it after death,
And would but memorize the shining half
Of his large nature that was turned to me:
Fain had I joined with those that honored him
With eyes that darkened because his were dim, 100
And now been silent: but it might not be.

II

1.

In some the genius is a thing apart,
        A pillared hermit of the brain,
Hoarding with incommunicable art
                Its intellectual gain;
            Man's web of circumstance and fate
            They from their perch of self observe,
Indifferent as the figures on a slate
            Are to the planet's sun-swung curve
            Whose bright returns they calculate;   110
            Their nice adjustment, part to part,
Were shaken from its serviceable mood
By unpremeditated stirs of heart
            Or jar of human neighborhood:
Some find their natural selves, and only then,
In furloughs of divine escape from men,
And when, by that brief ecstasy left bare,
            Driven by some instinct of desire,
They wander worldward, 'tis to blink and stare,
Like wild things of the wood about a fire,   120
Dazed by the social glow they cannot share;
            His nature brooked no lonely lair,
But basked and bourgeoned in copartnery,
Companionship, and open-windowed glee:
                He knew, for he had tried,
            Those speculative heights that lure
The unpractised foot, impatient of a guide,
            Tow'rd ether too attenuately pure
For sweet unconscious breath, though dear to pride,
            But better loved the foothold sure   130
Of paths that wind by old abodes of men
Who hope at last the churchyard's peace secure,
And follow time-worn rules, that them suffice,
Learned from their sires, traditionally wise,
Careful of honest custom's how and when;

His mind, too brave to look on Truth askance,
No more those habitudes of faith could share,
But, tinged with sweetness of the old Swiss manse,
Lingered around them still and fain would spare.
Patient to spy a sullen egg for weeks,   140
The enigma of creation to surprise,
His truer instinct sought the life that speaks
Without a mystery from kindly eyes;
In no self-spun cocoon of prudence wound,
He by the touch of men was best inspired,
And caught his native greatness at rebound
From generosities itself had fired;
Then how the heat through every fibre ran,
Felt in the gathering presence of the man,
While the apt word and gesture came unbid!   150
Virtues and faults it to one metal wrought,
      Fined all his blood to thought,
And ran the molten man in all he said or did.
All Tully's rules and all Quintilian's too
He by the light of listening faces knew,
And his rapt audience all unconscious lent
Their own roused force to make him eloquent;
Persuasion fondled in his look and tone;
Our speech (with strangers prudish) he could bring
To find new charm in accents not her own;   160
Her coy constraints and icy hindrances
Melted upon his lips to natural ease,
As a brook's fetters swell the dance of spring.
Nor yet all sweetness: not in vain he wore,
Nor in the sheath of ceremony, controlled
By velvet courtesy or caution cold,
That sword of honest anger prized of old,
      But, with two-handed wrath,
If baseness or pretension crossed his path,
      Struck once nor needed to strike more.   170

2.

His magic was not far to seek,—
He was so human! Whether strong or weak,
Far from his kind he neither sank nor soared,
But sate an equal guest at every board:
No beggar ever felt him condescend,
No prince presume; for still himself he bare
At manhood's simple level, and where'er
He met a stranger, there he left a friend.
How large an aspect! nobly unsevere,
With freshness round him of Olympian cheer,   180
Like visits of those earthly gods he came;
His look, wherever its good-fortune fell,
Doubled the feast without a miracle,
And on the hearthstone danced a happier flame;
Philemon's crabbed vintage grew benign;
Amphitryon's gold-juice humanized to wine.

III

1.

The garrulous memories
Gather again from all their far-flown nooks,
Singly at first, and then by twos and threes,
Then in a throng innumerable, as the rooks   190
        Thicken their twilight files
Tow'rd Tintern's gray repose of roofless aisles:
Once more I see him at the table's head
When Saturday her monthly banquet spread
        To scholars, poets, wits,
All choice, some famous, loving things, not names,
And so without a twinge at others' fames;
Such company as wisest moods befits,
Yet with no pedant blindness to the worth
        Of undeliberate mirth,   200
Natures benignly mixed of air and earth,

Now with the stars and now with equal zest
Tracing the eccentric orbit of a jest.

2.

I see in vision the warm-lighted hall,
The living and the dead I see again,
And but my chair is empty; 'mid them all
'Tis I that seem the dead: they all remain
Immortal, changeless creatures of the brain:
Wellnigh I doubt which world is real most,
Of sense or spirit, to the truly sane;   210
In this abstraction it were light to deem
Myself the figment of some stronger dream;
They are the real things, and I the ghost
That glide unhindered through the solid door,
Vainly for recognition seek from chair to chair,
And strive to speak and am but futile air,
As truly most of us are little more.

3.

Him most I see whom we most dearly miss,
        The latest parted thence,
His features poised in genial armistice   220
And armed neutrality of self-defence
Beneath the forehead's walled preëminence,
While Tyro, plucking facts with careless reach,
Settles off-hand our human how and whence;
The long-trained veteran scarcely wincing hears
The infallible strategy of volunteers
Making through Nature's walls its easy breach,
And seems to learn where he alone could teach.
Ample and ruddy, the board's end he fills
As he our fireside were, our light and heat,   230
Centre where minds diverse and various skills
Find their warm nook and stretch unhampered feet;
I see the firm benignity of face,

Wide-smiling champaign, without tameness sweet,
The mass Teutonic toned to Gallic grace,
The eyes whose sunshine runs before the lips
While Holmes's rockets curve their long ellipse,
    And burst in seeds of fire that burst again
        To drop in scintillating rain.

4.

There too the face half-rustic, half-divine,   240
Self-poised, sagacious, freaked with humor fine,
Of him who taught us not to mow and mope
About our fancied selves, but seek our scope
In Nature's world and Man's, nor fade to hollow trope,
    Content with our New World and timely bold
    To challenge the o'ermastery of the Old;
    Listening with eyes averse I see him sit
    Pricked with the cider of the Judge's wit
    (Ripe-hearted homebrew, fresh and fresh again),
    While the wise nose's firm-built aquiline   250
        Curves sharper to restrain
    The merriment whose most unruly moods
    Pass not the dumb laugh learned in listening woods
        Of silence-shedding pine:
Hard by is he whose art's consoling spell
Hath given both worlds a whiff of asphodel,
His look still vernal 'mid the wintry ring
Of petals that remember, not foretell,
The paler primrose of a second spring.

5.

And more there are: but other forms arise   260
And seen as clear, albeit with dimmer eyes:
First he from sympathy still held apart
By shrinking over-eagerness of heart,
    Cloud charged with searching fire, whose shadow's sweep
    Heightened mean things with sense of brooding ill,

And steeped in doom familiar field and hill,—
New England's poet, soul reserved and deep,
November nature with a name of May,
Whom high o'er Concord plains we laid to sleep,
While the orchards mocked us in their white array   270
And building robins wondered at our tears,
Snatched in his prime, the shape august
That should have stood unbent 'neath fourscore years,
The noble head, the eyes of furtive trust,
  All gone to speechless dust.
  And he our passing guest,
Shy nature, too, and stung with life's unrest,
Whom we too briefly had but could not hold,
Who brought ripe Oxford's culture to our board,
  The Past's incalculable hoard,   280
Mellowed by scutcheoned panes in cloisters old,
Seclusions, ivy-hushed, and pavements sweet
With immemorial lisp of musing feet;
Young head time-tonsured smoother than a friar's,
Boy face, but grave with answerless desires,
Poet in all that poets have of best,
But foiled with riddles dark and cloudy aims,
  Who now hath found sure rest,
Not by still Isis or historic Thames,
Nor by the Charles he tried to love with me,   290
But, not misplaced, by Arno's hallowed brim,
Nor scorned by Santa Croce's neighboring fames,
 Haply not mindless, wheresoe'er he be,
Of violets that today I scattered over him.
  He, too, is there,
After the good centurion fitly named,
Whom learning dulled not, nor convention tamed,
Shaking with burly mirth his hyacinthine hair,
Our hearty Grecian of Homeric ways,
Still found the surer friend where least he hoped the praise.   300

6.

Yea truly, as the sallowing years
Fall from us faster, like frost-loosened leaves
Pushed by the misty touch of shortening days,
    And that unwakened winter nears,
'Tis the void chair our surest guest receives,
'Tis lips long cold that give the warmest kiss,
'Tis the lost voice comes oftenest to our ears;
We count our rosary by the beads we miss:
    To me, at least, it seemeth so,
An exile in the land once found divine,   310
    While my starved fire burns low,
And homeless winds at the loose casement whine
Shrill ditties of the snow-roofed Apennine.

IV

1.

Now forth into the darkness all are gone,
But memory, still unsated, follows on,
Retracing step by step our homeward walk,
With many a laugh among our serious talk,
Across the bridge where, on the dimpling tide,
The long red streamers from the windows glide,
        Or the dim western moon   320
Rocks her skiff's image on the broad lagoon,
And Boston shows a soft Venetian side
In that Arcadian light when roof and tree,
Hard prose by daylight, dream in Italy;
Or haply in the sky's cold chambers wide
Shivered the winter stars, while all below,
As if an end were come of human ill,
The world was wrapt in innocence of snow
And the cast-iron bay was blind and still;
These were our poetry; in him perhaps   330
Science had barred the gate that lets in dream,

And he would rather count the perch and bream
Than with the current's idle fancy lapse;
And yet he had the poet's open eye
That takes a frank delight in all it sees,
Nor was earth voiceless, nor the mystic sky,
To him the life-long friend of fields and trees:
Then came the prose of the suburban street,
Its silence deepened by our echoing feet,
And converse such as rambling hazard finds;   340
Then he who many cities knew and many minds,
And men once world-noised, now mere Ossian forms
Of misty memory, bade them live anew
As when they shared earth's manifold delight,
In shape, in gait, in voice, in gesture true,
And, with an accent heightening as he warms,
Would stop forgetful of the shortening night,
Drop my confining arm, and pour profuse
Much worldy wisdom kept for others' use,
Not for his own, for he was rash and free,   350
His purse or knowledge all men's, like the sea.
Still can I hear his voice's shrilling might
(With pauses broken, while the fitful spark
He blew more hotly rounded on the dark
To hint his features with a Rembrandt light)
Call Oken back, or Humboldt, or Lamarck,
Or Cuvier's taller shade, and many more
Whom he had seen, or knew from others' sight,
And make them men to me as ne'er before:
Not seldom, as the undeadened fibre stirred   360
Of noble friendships knit beyond the sea,
German or French thrust by the lagging word,
For a good leash of mother-tongues had he.
At last, arrived at where our paths divide,
"Good night!" and, ere the distance grew too wide,
"Good night!" again; and now with cheated ear
I half hear his who mine shall never hear.

2.

Sometimes it seemed as if New England air
For his large lungs too parsimonious were,
As if those empty rooms of dogma drear   370
Where the ghost shivers of a faith austere
    Counting the horns o'er of the Beast,
Still scaring those whose faith in it is least,
As if those snaps o' th' moral atmosphere
That sharpen all the needles of the East,
    Had been to him like death,
Accustomed to draw Europe's freer breath
        In a more stable element;
Nay, even our landscape, half the year morose,
Our practical horizon grimly pent,   380
Our air, sincere of ceremonious haze,
Forcing hard outlines mercilessly close,
Our social monotone of level days,
    Might make our best seem banishment;
        But it was nothing so;
    Haply his instinct might divine,
Beneath our drift of puritanic snow,
    The marvel sensitive and fine
Of sanguinaria over-rash to blow
And trust its shyness to an air malign;   390
Well might he prize truth's warranty and pledge
In the grim outcrop of our granite edge,
Or Hebrew fervor flashing forth at need
In the gaunt sons of Calvin's iron breed,
As prompt to give as skilled to win and keep;
But, though such intuitions might not cheer,
Yet life was good to him, and, there or here,
With that sufficing joy, the day was never cheap;
    Thereto his mind was its own ample sphere,
    And, like those buildings great that through the year   400
Carry one temperature, his nature large
Made its own climate, nor could any marge
Traced by convention stay him from his bent:

He had a habitude of mountain air;
He brought wide outlook where he went,
      And could on sunny uplands dwell
Of prospect sweeter than the pastures fair
      High-hung of viny Neufchâtel;
            Nor, surely, did he miss
            Some pale, imaginary bliss   410
Of earlier sights whose inner landscape still was Swiss.

V

1.

I cannot think he wished so soon to die
With all his senses full of eager heat,
And rosy years that stood expectant by
To buckle the winged sandals on their feet,
He that was friends with Earth, and all her sweet
Took with both hands unsparingly:
Truly this life is precious to the root,
And good the feel of grass beneath the foot;
To lie in buttercups and clover-bloom,   420
      Tenants in common with the bees,
And watch the white clouds drift through gulfs of trees,
Is better than long waiting in the tomb;
Only once more to feel the coming spring
As the birds feel it, when it bids them sing,
      Only once more to see the moon
Through leaf-fringed abbey-arches of the elms
      Curve her mild sickle in the West
Sweet with the breath of hay-cocks, were a boon
Worth any promise of soothsayer realms   430
Or casual hope of being elsewhere blest;
      To take December by the beard
And crush the creaking snow with springy foot,
While overhead the North's dumb streamers shoot,
Till Winter fawn upon the cheek endeared,

Then the long evening-ends
Lingered by cosy chimney-nooks,
With high companionship of books
Or slippered talk of friends
And sweet habitual looks,   440
Is better than to stop the ears with dust:
Too soon the spectre comes to say, "Thou must!"

2.

When toil-crooked hands are crost upon the breast,
They comfort us with sense of rest;
They must be glad to lie forever still;
Their work is ended with their day;
Another fills their room; 'tis the World's ancient way,
Whether for good or ill;
But the deft spinners of the brain,
Who love each added day and find it gain,   450
Them overtakes the doom
To snap the half-grown flower upon the loom
(Trophy that was to be of life-long pain),
The thread no other skill can ever knit again.
'Twas so with him, for he was glad to live,
'Twas doubly so, for he left work begun;
Could not this eagerness of Fate forgive
Till all the allotted flax were spun?
It matters not; for, go at night or noon,
A friend, whene'er he dies, has died too soon,   460
And, once we hear the hopeless *He is dead*,
So far as flesh hath knowledge, all is said.

VI

1.

I seem to see the black procession go:
That crawling prose of death too well I know,
The vulgar paraphrase of glorious woe;
I see it wind through that unsightly grove,

Once beautiful, but long defaced
With granite permanence of cockney taste
And all those grim disfigurements we love:
There, then, we leave him: Him? such costly waste   470
Nature rebels at: and it is not true
Of those most precious parts of him we knew:
    Could we be conscious but as dreamers be,
'Twere sweet to leave this shifting life of tents
    Sunk in the changeless calm of Deity;
Nay, to be mingled with the elements,
    The fellow-servant of creative powers,
Partaker in the solemn year's events,
    To share the work of busy-fingered hours,
    To be night's silent almoner of dew,   480
    To rise again in plants and breathe and grow,
    To stream as tides the ocean caverns through,
    Or with the rapture of great winds to blow
About earth's shaken coignes, were not a fate
      To leave us all-disconsolate;
Even endless slumber in the sweetening sod
      Of charitable earth
    That takes out all our mortal stains,
And makes us cleanlier neighbors of the clod,
      Methinks were better worth   490
Than the poor fruit of most men's wakeful pains,
      The heart's insatiable ache:
      But such was not his faith,
   Nor mine: it may be he had trod
Outside the plain old path of *God thus spake*,
      But God to him was very God,
      And not a visionary wraith
    Skulking in murky corners of the mind,
      And he was sure to be
Somehow, somewhere, imperishable as He,   500
Not with His essence mystically combined,
As some high spirits long, but whole and free,
    A perfected and conscious Agassiz.

And such I figure him: the wise of old
Welcome and own him of their peaceful fold,
    Not truly with the guild enrolled
    Of him who seeking inward guessed
    Diviner riddles than the rest,
    And groping in the darks of thought
    Touched the Great Hand and knew it not;   510
    Rather he shares the daily light,
    From reason's charier fountains won,
Of his great chief, the slow-paced Stagyrite,
And Cuvier clasps once more his long-lost son.

2.

The shape erect is prone: forever stilled
The winning tongue; the forehead's high-piled heap,
A cairn which every science helped to build,
Unvalued will its golden secrets keep:
He knows at last if Life or Death be best:
Wherever he be flown, whatever vest   520
The being hath put on which lately here
So many-friended was, so full of cheer
To make men feel the Seeker's noble zest,
We have not lost him all; he is not gone
To the dumb herd of them that wholly die;
The beauty of his better self lives on
In minds he touched with fire, in many an eye
He trained to Truth's exact severity;
He was a Teacher: why be grieved for him
Whose living word still stimulates the air?   530
In endless file shall loving scholars come
The glow of his transmitted touch to share,
And trace his features with an eye less dim
Than ours whose sense familiar wont makes numb.
1874   1874

THREE MEMORIAL POEMS

> "Coscienza fusca
> O della propria o dell' altrui vergogna
> Pur sentirà la tua parola brusca."

If I let a word of bitter mirth
When public shames more shameful pardon won,
Some have misjudged me, and my service done,
If small, yet faithful, deemed of little worth:
Through veins that drew their life from Western earth
Two hundred years and more my blood hath run
In no polluted course from sire to son;
And thus was I predestined ere my birth
To love the soil wherewith my fibres own
Instinctive sympathies; yet love it so
As honor would, nor lightly to dethrone
Judgment, the stamp of manhood, nor forego
The son's right to a mother dearer grown
With growing knowledge and more chaste than snow.

ODE

READ AT THE ONE HUNDREDTH ANNIVERSARY
OF THE FIGHT AT CONCORD BRIDGE

19TH APRIL, 1875

I

Who cometh over the hills,
  Her garments with morning sweet,
The dance of a thousand rills
  Making music before her feet?
Her presence freshens the air;
  Sunshine steals light from her face;
The leaden footstep of Care
  Leaps to the tune of her pace,
Fairness of all that is fair,
  Grace at the heart of all grace,   10

Sweetener of hut and of hall,
Bringer of life out of naught,
Freedom, oh, fairest of all
The daughters of Time and Thought!

II

She cometh, cometh today:
Hark! hear ye not her tread,
Sending a thrill through your clay,
Under the sod there, ye dead,
Her nurslings and champions?
Do ye not hear, as she comes,   20
The bay of the deep-mouthed guns,
The gathering rote of the drums?
The bells that called ye to prayer,
How wildly they clamor on her,
Crying, "She cometh! prepare
Her to praise and her to honor,
That a hundred years ago
Scattered here in blood and tears
Potent seeds wherefrom should grow
Gladness for a hundred years!"   30

III

Tell me, young men, have ye seen
Creature of diviner mien
For true hearts to long and cry for,
Manly hearts to live and die for?
What hath she that others want?
Brows that all endearments haunt,
Eyes that make it sweet to dare,
Smiles that cheer untimely death,
Looks that fortify despair,
Tones more brave than trumpet's breath;   40
Tell me, maidens, have ye known
Household charm more sweetly rare,

Grace of woman ampler blown,
Modesty more debonair,
Younger heart with wit full grown?
Oh for an hour of my prime,
The pulse of my hotter years,
That I might praise her in rhyme
Would tingle your eyelids to tears,
Our sweetness, our strength, and our star,   50
Our hope, our joy, and our trust,
Who lifted us out of the dust,
And made us whatever we are!

IV

Whiter than moonshine upon snow
Her raiment is, but round the hem
Crimson stained; and, as to and fro
Her sandals flash, we see on them,
And on her instep veined with blue,
Flecks of crimson, on those fair feet,
High-arched, Diana-like, and fleet,   60
Fit for no grosser stain than dew:
Oh, call them rather chrisms than stains,
Sacred and from heroic veins!
For, in the glory-guarded pass,
Her haughty and far-shining head
She bowed to shrive Leonidas
With his imperishable dead;
Her, too, Morgarten saw,
Where the Swiss lion fleshed his icy paw;
She followed Cromwell's quenchless star   70
Where the grim Puritan tread
Shook Marston, Naseby, and Dunbar:
Yea, on her feet are dearer dyes
Yet fresh, not looked on with untearful eyes.

V

Our fathers found her in the woods
  Where Nature meditates and broods,
    The seeds of unexampled things
Which Time to consummation brings
Through life and death and man's unstable moods;
They met her here, not recognized,   80
A sylvan huntress clothed in furs,
To whose chaste wants her bow sufficed,
Nor dreamed what destinies were hers:
She taught them bee-like to create
Their simpler forms of Church and State;
She taught them to endue
The past with other functions than it knew,
And turn in channels strange the uncertain stream of Fate;
Better than all, she fenced them in their need
With iron-handed Duty's sternest creed,   90
'Gainst Self's lean wolf that ravens word and deed.

VI

Why cometh she hither today
To this low village of the plain
Far from the Present's loud highway,
From Trade's cool heart and seething brain?
Why cometh she? She was not far away.
Since the soul touched it, not in vain,
With pathos of immortal gain,
'Tis here her fondest memories stay.
She loves yon pine-bemurmured ridge   100
Where now our broad-browed poet sleeps,
Dear to both Englands; near him he
Who wore the ring of Canace;
But most her heart to rapture leaps
Where stood that era-parting bridge,
O'er which, with footfall still as dew,
The Old Time passed into the New;

Where, as your stealthy river creeps,
He whispers to his listening weeds
Tales of sublimest homespun deeds.   110
Here English law and English thought
'Gainst the self-will of England fought;
And here were men (coequal with their fate),
Who did great things, unconscious they were great.
They dreamed not what a die was cast
With that first answering shot; what then?
There was their duty; they were men
Schooled the soul's inward gospel to obey,
Though leading to the lion's den.
They felt the habit-hallowed world give way   120
Beneath their lives, and on went they,
Unhappy who was last.
When Buttrick gave the word,
That awful idol of the unchallenged Past,
Strong in their love, and in their lineage strong,
Fell crashing: if they heard it not,
Yet the earth heard,
Nor ever hath forgot,
As on from startled throne to throne,
Where Superstition sate or conscious Wrong,   130
A shudder ran of some dread birth unknown.
Thrice venerable spot!
River more fateful than the Rubicon!
O'er those red planks, to snatch her diadem,
Man's Hope, star-girdled, sprang with them,
And over ways untried the feet of Doom strode on.

VII

Think you these felt no charms
In their gray homesteads and embowered farms?
In household faces waiting at the door
Their evening step should lighten up no more?   140
In fields their boyish feet had known?
In trees their fathers' hands had set,

And which with them had grown,
Widening each year their leafy coronet?
Felt they no pang of passionate regret
For those unsolid goods that seem so much our own?
These things are dear to every man that lives,
And life prized more for what it lends than gives.
Yea, many a tie, through iteration sweet,
Strove to detain their fatal feet;   150
And yet the enduring half they chose,
Whose choice decides a man life's slave or king,
The invisible things of God before the seen and known:
Therefore their memory inspiration blows
With echoes gathering on from zone to zone;
For manhood is the one immortal thing
Beneath Time's changeful sky,
And, where it lightened once, from age to age,
Men come to learn, in grateful pilgrimage,
That length of days is knowing when to die.   160

VIII

What marvellous change of things and men!
She, a world-wandering orphan then,
So mighty now! Those are her streams
That whirl the myriad, myriad wheels
Of all that does, and all that dreams,
Of all that thinks, and all that feels,
Through spaces stretched from sea to sea;
By idle tongues and busy brains,
By who doth right, and who refrains,
Hers are our losses and our gains;   170
Our maker and our victim she.

IX

Maiden half mortal, half divine,
We triumphed in thy coming; to the brinks
Our hearts were filled with pride's tumultuous wine;
Better today who rather feels than thinks.

Yet will some graver thoughts intrude,
And cares of sterner mood;
They won thee: who shall keep thee? From the deeps
Where discrowned empires o'er their ruins brood,
And many a thwarted hope wrings its weak hands and weeps,
I hear the voice as of a mighty wind   181
From all heaven's caverns rushing unconfined,
"I, Freedom, dwell with Knowledge: I abide
With men whom dust of faction cannot blind
To the slow tracings of the Eternal Mind;
With men by culture trained and fortified,
Who bitter duty to sweet lusts prefer,
Fearless to counsel and obey.
Conscience my sceptre is, and law my sword,
Not to be drawn in passion or in play,   190
But terrible to punish and deter;
Implacable as God's word,
Like it, a shepherd's crook to them that blindly err.
Your firm-pulsed sires, my martyrs and my saints,
Offshoots of that one stock whose patient sense
Hath known to mingle flux with permanence,
Rated my chaste denials and restraints
Above the moment's dear-paid paradise:
Beware lest, shifting with Time's gradual creep,
The light that guided shine into your eyes.   200
The envious Powers of ill nor wink nor sleep:
Be therefore timely wise,
Nor laugh when this one steals, and that one lies,
As if your luck could cheat those sleepless spies,
Till the deaf Fury comes your house to sweep!"
I hear the voice, and unaffrighted bow;
Ye shall not be prophetic now,
Heralds of ill, that darkening fly
Between my vision and the rainbowed sky,
Or on the left your hoarse forebodings croak   210
From many a blasted bough
On Yggdrasil's storm-sinewed oak,

That once was green, Hope of the West, as thou:
Yet pardon if I tremble while I boast;
For I have loved as those who pardon most.

x

Away, ungrateful doubt, away!
At least she is our own today.
Break into rapture, my song,
Verses, leap forth in the sun,
Bearing the joyance along   220
Like a train of fire as ye run!
Pause not for choosing of words,
Let them but blossom and sing
Blithe as the orchards and birds
With the new coming of spring!
Dance in your jollity, bells;
Shout, cannon; cease not, ye drums;
Answer, ye hillside and dells;
Bow, all ye people! She comes,
Radiant, calm-fronted, as when   230
She hallowed that April day.
Stay with us! Yes, thou shalt stay,
Softener and strengthener of men,
Freedom, not won by the vain,
Not to be courted in play,
Not to be kept without pain.
Stay with us! Yes, thou wilt stay,
Handmaid and mistress of all,
Kindler of deed and of thought,
Thou that to hut and to hall   240
Equal deliverance brought!
Souls of her martyrs, draw near,
Touch our dull lips with your fire,
That we may praise without fear
Her our delight, our desire,
Our faith's inextinguishable star,
Our hope, our remembrance, our trust,

Our present, our past, our to be,
Who will mingle her life with our dust
And makes us deserve to be free!   250
1875   1875

UNDER THE OLD ELM

POEM READ AT CAMBRIDGE ON THE HUNDREDTH ANNIVERSARY OF
WASHINGTON'S TAKING COMMAND OF THE AMERICAN ARMY,
3D JULY, 1775

I

1.

Words pass as wind, but where great deeds were done
A power abides transfused from sire to son:
The boy feels deeper meanings thrill his ear,
That tingling through his pulse life-long shall run,
With sure impulsion to keep honor clear,
When, pointing down, his father whispers, "Here,
Here, where we stand, stood he, the purely great,
Whose soul no siren passion could unsphere,
Then nameless, now a power and mixed with fate."
Historic town, thou holdest sacred dust,   10
Once known to men as pious, learnèd, just,
And one memorial pile that dares to last;
But Memory greets with reverential kiss
No spot in all thy circuit sweet as this,
Touched by that modest glory as it past,
O'er which yon elm hath piously displayed
These hundred years its monumental shade.

2.

Of our swift passage through this scenery
Of life and death, more durable than we,
What landmark so congenial as a tree   20
Repeating its green legend every spring,
And, with a yearly ring,

Recording the fair seasons as they flee,
Type of our brief but still-renewed mortality?
We fall as leaves: the immortal trunk remains,
Builded with costly juice of hearts and brains
Gone to the mould now, whither all that be
Vanish returnless, yet are procreant still
In human lives to come of good or ill,
And feed unseen the roots of Destiny.   30

II

1.

Men's monuments, grown old, forget their names
They should eternize, but the place
Where shining souls have passed imbibes a grace
Beyond mere earth; some sweetness of their fames
Leaves in the soil its unextinguished trace,
Pungent, pathetic, sad with nobler aims,
That penetrates our lives and heightens them or shames.
This insubstantial world and fleet
Seems solid for a moment when we stand
On dust ennobled by heroic feet   40
Once mighty to sustain a tottering land,
And mighty still such burthen to upbear,
Nor doomed to read the path of things that merely were:
Our sense, refined with virtue of the spot,
Across the mists of Lethe's sleepy stream
Recalls him, the sole chief without a blot,
No more a pallid image and a dream,
But as he dwelt with men decorously supreme.

2.

Our grosser minds need this terrestrial hint
To raise long-buried days from tombs of print: 50
"Here stood he," softly we repeat,
And lo, the statue shrined and still
In that gray minster-front we call the Past,

Feels in its frozen veins our pulses thrill,
Breathes living air and mocks at Death's deceit.
It warms, it stirs, comes down to us at last,
Its features human with familiar light,
A man, beyond the historian's art to kill,
Or sculptor's to efface with patient chisel-blight.

3.

Sure the dumb earth hath memory, nor for naught   60
Was Fancy given, on whose enchanted loom
Present and Past commingle, fruit and bloom
Of one fair bough, inseparably wrought
Into the seamless tapestry of thought.
So charmed, with undeluded eye we see
In history's fragmentary tale
Bright clues of continuity,
Learn that high natures over Time prevail,
And feel ourselves a link in that entail
That binds all ages past with all that are to be.   70

III

1.

Beneath our consecrated elm
A century ago he stood,
Famed vaguely for that old fight in the wood
Whose red surge sought, but could not overwhelm
The life foredoomed to wield our rough-hewn helm:—
From colleges, where now the gown
To arms had yielded, from the town,
Our rude self-summoned levies flocked to see
The new-come chiefs and wonder which was he.
No need to question long; close-lipped and tall,   80
Long trained in murder-brooding forests lone
To bridle others' clamors and his own,
Firmly erect, he towered above them all,
The incarnate discipline that was to free
With iron curb that armed democracy.

2.

A motley rout was that which came to stare,
In raiment tanned by years of sun and storm,
Of every shape that was not uniform,
Dotted with regimentals here and there;
An army all of captains, used to pray   90
And stiff in fight, but serious drill's despair,
Skilled to debate their orders, not obey;
Deacons were there, selectmen, men of note
In half-tamed hamlets ambushed round with woods,
Ready to settle Freewill by a vote,
But largely liberal to its private moods;
Prompt to assert by manners, voice, or pen,
Or ruder arms, their rights as Englishmen,
Nor much fastidious as to how and when:
Yet seasoned stuff and fittest to create   100
A thought-staid army or a lasting state:
Haughty they said he was, at first; severe;
But owned, as all men own, the steady hand
Upon the bridle, patient to command,
Prized, as all prize, the justice pure from fear,
And learned to honor first, then love him, then revere.
Such power there is in clear-eyed self-restraint
And purpose clean as light from every selfish taint.

3.

Musing beneath the legendary tree,
The years between furl off: I seem to see   110
The sun-flecks, shaken the stirred foliage through,
Dapple with gold his sober buff and blue
And weave prophetic aureoles round the head
That shines our beacon now nor darkens with the dead.
O man of silent mood,
A stranger among strangers then,
How art thou since renowned the Great, the Good,
Familiar as the day in all the homes of men!

The wingèd years, that winnow praise to blame,
Blow many names out: they but fan and flame   120
The self-renewing splendors of thy fame.

IV

1.

How many subtlest influences unite,
With spiritual touch of joy or pain,
Invisible as air and soft as light,
To body forth that image of the brain
We call our Country, visionary shape,
Loved more than woman, fuller of fire than wine,
Whose charm can none define,
Nor any, though he flee it, can escape!
All party-colored threads the weaver Time   130
Sets in his web, now trivial, now sublime,
All memories, all forebodings, hopes and fears,
Mountain and river, forest, prairie, sea,
A hill, a rock, a homestead, field, or tree,
The casual gleanings of unreckoned years,
Take goddess-shape at last and there is She,
Old at our birth, new as the springing hours,
Shrine of our weakness, fortress of our powers,
Consoler, kindler, peerless 'mid her peers,
A force that 'neath our conscious being stirs,   140
A life to give ours permanence, when we
Are borne to mingle our poor earth with hers,
And all this glowing world goes with us on our biers.

2.

Nations are long results, by ruder ways
Gathering the might that warrants length of days;
They may be pieced of half-reluctant shares
Welded by hammer-strokes of broad-brained kings,
Or from a doughty people grow, the heirs
Of wise traditions widening cautious rings;

At best they are computable things,   150
A strength behind us making us feel bold
In right, or, as may chance, in wrong;
Whose force by figures may be summed and told,
So many soldiers, ships, and dollars strong,
And we but drops that bear compulsory part
In the dumb throb of a mechanic heart;
But Country is a shape of each man's mind
Sacred from definition, unconfined
By the cramped walls where daily drudgeries grind;
An inward vision, yet an outward birth   160
Of sweet familiar heaven and earth;
A brooding Presence that stirs motions blind
Of wings within our embryo being's shell
That wait but her completer spell
To make us eagle-natured, fit to dare
Life's nobler spaces and untarnished air.

3.

You, who hold dear this self-conceived ideal,
Whose faith and works alone can make it real,
Bring all your fairest gifts to deck her shrine
Who lifts our lives away from Thine and Mine   170
And feeds the lamp of manhood more divine
With fragrant oils of quenchless constancy.
When all have done their utmost, surely he
Hath given the best who gives a character
Erect and constant, which nor any shock
Of loosened elements, nor the forceful sea
Of flowing or of ebbing fates, can stir
From its deep bases in the living rock
Of ancient manhood's sweet security:
And this he gave, serenely far from pride   180
As baseness, boon with prosperous stars allied,
Part of what nobler seed shall in our loins abide.

4.

No bond of men as common pride so strong,
In names time-filtered for the lips of song,
Still operant, with the primal Forces bound
Whose currents, on their spiritual round,
Transfuse our mortal will nor are gainsaid:
These are their arsenals, these the exhaustless mines
That give a constant heart in great designs;
These are the stuff whereof such dreams are made   190
As make heroic men: thus surely he
Still holds in place the massy blocks he laid
'Neath our new frame, enforcing soberly
The self-control that makes and keeps a people free.

V

1.

Oh, for a drop of that Cornelian ink
Which gave Agricola dateless length of days,
To celebrate him fitly, neither swerve
To phrase unkempt, nor pass discretion's brink,
With him so statue-like in sad reserve,
So diffident to claim, so forward to deserve!   200
Nor need I shun due influence of his fame
Who, mortal among mortals, seemed as now
The equestrian shape with unimpassioned brow,
That paces silent on through vistas of acclaim.

2.

What figure more immovably august
Than that grave strength so patient and so pure,
Calm in good fortune, when it wavered, sure,
That mind serene, impenetrably just,
Modelled on classic lines so simple they endure?
That soul so softly radiant and so white   210
The track it left seems less of fire than light,
Cold but to such as love distemperature?

And if pure light, as some deem, be the force
That drives rejoicing planets on their course,
Why for his power benign seek an impurer source?
His was the true enthusiasm that burns long,
Domestically bright,
Fed from itself and shy of human sight,
The hidden force that makes a lifetime strong,
And not the short-lived fuel of a song.   220
Passionless, say you? What is passion for
But to sublime our natures and control
To front heroic toils with late return,
Or none, or such as shames the conqueror?
That fire was fed with substance of the soul
And not with holiday stubble, that could burn,
Unpraised of men who after bonfires run,
Through seven slow years of unadvancing war,
Equal when fields were lost or fields were won,
With breath of popular applause or blame,   230
Nor fanned nor damped, unquenchably the same,
Too inward to be reached by flaws of idle fame.

                              3.

Soldier and statesman, rarest unison;
High-poised example of great duties done
Simply as breathing, a world's honors worn
As life's indifferent gifts to all men born;
Dumb for himself, unless it were to God,
But for his barefoot soldiers eloquent,
Tramping the snow to coral where they trod,
Held by his awe in hollow-eyed content;   240
Modest, yet firm as Nature's self; unblamed
Save by the men his nobler temper shamed;
Never seduced through show of present good
By other than unsetting lights to steer
New-trimmed in Heaven, nor than his steadfast mood
More steadfast, far from rashness as from fear;

Rigid, but with himself first, grasping still
In swerveless poise the wave-beat helm of will;
Not honored then or now because he wooed
The popular voice, but that he still withstood;   250
Broad-minded, higher-souled, there is but one
Who was all this and ours, and all men's,—WASHINGTON.

4.

Minds strong by fits, irregularly great,
That flash and darken like revolving lights,
Catch more the vulgar eye unschooled to wait
On the long curve of patient days and nights
Rounding a whole life to the circle fair
Of orbed fulfilment; and this balanced soul,
So simple in its grandeur, coldly bare
Of draperies theatric, standing there   260
In perfect symmetry of self-control,
Seems not so great at first, but greater grows
Still as we look, and by experience learn
How grand this quiet is, how nobly stern
The discipline that wrought through lifelong throes
That energetic passion of repose.

5.

A nature too decorous and severe,
Too self-respectful in its griefs and joys,
For ardent girls and boys
Who find no genius in a mind so clear   270
That its grave depths seem obvious and near,
Nor a soul great that made so little noise.
They feel no force in that calm-cadenced phrase,
The habitual full-dress of his well-bred mind,
That seems to pace the minuet's courtly maze
And tell of ampler leisures, roomier length of days.
His firm-based brain, to self so little kind
That no tumultuary blood could blind,
Formed to control men, not amaze,

Looms not like those that borrow height of haze: 280
It was a world of statelier movement then
Than this we fret in, he a denizen
Of that ideal Rome that made a man for men.

VI

1.

The longer on this earth we live
And weigh the various qualities of men,
Seeing how most are fugitive,
Or fitful gifts, at best, of now and then,
Wind-wavered corpse-lights, daughters of the fen,
The more we feel the high stern-featured beauty
Of plain devotedness to duty,   290
Steadfast and still, nor paid with mortal praise,
But finding amplest recompense
For life's ungarlanded expense
In work done squarely and unwasted days.
For this we honor him, that he could know
How sweet the service and how free
Of her, God's eldest daughter here below,
And choose in meanest raiment which was she.

2.

Placid completeness, life without a fall
From faith or highest aims, truth's breachless wall,   300
Surely if any fame can bear the touch,
His will say "Here!" at the last trumpet's call,
The unexpressive man whose life expressed so much.

VII

1.

Never to see a nation born
Hath been given to mortal man,
Unless to those who, on that summer morn,
Gazed silent when the great Virginian

Unsheathed the sword whose fatal flash
Shot union through the incoherent clash
Of our loose atoms, crystallizing them   310
Around a single will's unpliant stem,
And making purpose of emotion rash.
Out of that scabbard sprang, as from its womb,
Nebulous at first but hardening to a star,
Through mutual share of sunburst and of gloom,
The common faith that made us what we are.

2.

That lifted blade transformed our jangling clans,
Till then provincial, to Americans,
And made a unity of wildering plans;
Here was the doom fixed: here is marked the date   320
When this New World awoke to man's estate,
Burnt its last ship and ceased to look behind:
Nor thoughtless was the choice; no love or hate
Could from its poise move that deliberate mind,
Weighing between too early and too late
Those pitfalls of the man refused by Fate:
His was the impartial vision of the great
Who see not as they wish, but as they find.
He saw the dangers of defeat, nor less
The incomputable perils of success;   330
The sacred past thrown by, an empty rind;
The future, cloud-land, snare of prophets blind;
The waste of war, the ignominy of peace;
On either hand a sullen rear of woes,
Whose garnered lightnings none could guess,
Piling its thunder-heads and muttering "Cease!"
Yet drew not back his hand, but gravely chose
The seeming-desperate task whence our new nation rose.

3.

A noble choice and of immortal seed!
Nor deem that acts heroic wait on chance   340

Or easy were as in a boy's romance;
The man's whole life preludes the single deed
That shall decide if his inheritance
Be with the sifted few of matchless breed,
Our race's sap and sustenance,
Or with the unmotived herd that only sleep and feed.
Choice seems a thing indifferent; thus or so,
What matters it?   The Fates with mocking face
Look on inexorable, nor seem to know
Where the lot lurks that gives life's foremost place.   350
Yet Duty's leaden casket holds it still,
And but two ways are offered to our will,
Toil with rare triumph, ease with safe disgrace,
The problem still for us and all of human race.
He chose, as men choose, where most danger showed,
Nor ever faltered 'neath the load
Of petty cares, that gall great hearts the most,
But kept right on the strenuous up-hill road,
Strong to the end, above complaint or boast:
The popular tempest on his rock-mailed coast   360
Wasted its wind-borne spray,
The noisy marvel of a day;
His soul sate still in its unstormed abode.

VIII

Virginia gave us this imperial man
Cast in the massive mold
Of those high-statured ages old
Which into grander forms our mortal metal ran;
She gave us this unblemished gentleman:
What shall we give her back but love and praise
As in the dear old unestrangèd days   370
Before the inevitable wrong began?
Mother of States and undiminished men,
Thou gavest us a country, giving him,
And we owe alway what we owed thee then:

The boon thou wouldst have snatched from us agen
Shines as before with no abatement dim.
A great man's memory is the only thing
With influence to outlast the present whim
And bind us as when here he knit our golden ring.
All of him that was subject to the hours   380
Lies in thy soil and makes it part of ours:
Across more recent graves,
Where unresentful Nature waves
Her pennons o'er the shot-ploughed sod,
Proclaiming the sweet Truce of God,
We from this consecrated plain stretch out
Our hands as free from afterthought or doubt
As here the united North
Poured her embrownèd manhood forth
In welcome of our savior and thy son.   390
Through battle we have better learned thy worth,
The long-breathed valor and undaunted will,
Which, like his own, the day's disaster done,
Could, safe in manhood, suffer and be still.
Both thine and ours the victory hardly won;
If ever with distempered voice or pen
We have misdeemed thee, here we take it back,
And for the dead of both don common black.
Be to us evermore as thou wast then,
As we forget thou hast not always been,   400
Mother of States and unpolluted men,
Virginia, fitly named from England's manly queen!
1875   1875

AN ODE

FOR THE FOURTH OF JULY, 1876

I

1.

Entranced I saw a vision in the cloud
That loitered dreaming in yon sunset sky,

Full of fair shapes, half creatures of the eye,
Half chance-evoked by the wind's fantasy
In golden mist, an ever-shifting crowd:
There, 'mid unreal forms that came and went
In air-spun robes, of evanescent dye,
A woman's semblance shone preëminent;
Not armed like Pallas, not like Hera proud,
But as on household diligence intent,   10
Beside her visionary wheel she bent
Like Aretë or Bertha, nor than they
Less queenly in her port: about her knee
Glad children clustered confident in play:
Placid her pose, the calm of energy;
And over her broad brow in many a round
(That loosened would have gilt her garment's hem),
Succinct, as toil prescribes, the hair was wound
In lustrous coils, a natural diadem.
The cloud changed shape, obsequious to the whim   20
Of some transmuting influence felt in me,
And, looking now, a wolf I seemed to see
Limned in that vapor, gaunt and hunger-bold,
Threatening her charge: resolve in every limb,
Erect she flamed in mail of sun-wove gold,
Penthesilea's self for battle dight;
One arm uplifted braced a flickering spear,
And one her adamantine shield made light;
Her face, helm-shadowed, grew a thing to fear,
And her fierce eyes, by danger challenged, took   30
Her trident-sceptred mother's dauntless look.
"I know thee now, O goddess-born!" I cried,
And turned with loftier brow and firmer stride;
For in that spectral cloud-work I had seen
Her image, bodied forth by love and pride,
The fearless, the benign, the mother-eyed,
The fairer world's toil-consecrated queen.

2.

What shape by exile dreamed elates the mind
Like hers whose hand, a fortress of the poor,
No blood in vengeance spilt, though lawful, stains?   40
Who never turned a suppliant from her door?
Whose conquests are the gains of all mankind?
Today her thanks shall fly on every wind,
Unstinted, unrebuked, from shore to shore,
One love, one hope, and not a doubt behind!
Cannon to cannon shall repeat her praise,
Banner to banner flap it forth in flame;
Her children shall rise up to bless her name,
And wish her harmless length of days,
The mighty mother of a mighty brood,   50
Blessed in all tongues and dear to every blood,
The beautiful, the strong, and, best of all, the good.

3.

Seven years long was the bow
Of battle bent, and the heightening
Storm-heaps convulsed with the throe
Of their uncontainable lightning;
Seven years long heard the sea
Crash of navies and wave-borne thunder;
Then drifted the cloud-rack a-lee,
And new stars were seen, a world's wonder;   60
Each by her sisters made bright,
All binding all to their stations,
Cluster of manifold light
Startling the old constellations:
Men looked up and grew pale:
Was it a comet or star,
Omen of blessing or bale,
Hung o'er the ocean afar?

4.

Stormy the day of her birth:
Was she not born of the strong,   70
She, the last ripeness of earth,
Beautiful, prophesied long?
Stormy the days of her prime:
Hers are the pulses that beat
Higher for perils sublime,
Making them fawn at her feet.
Was she not born of the strong?
Was she not born of the wise?
Daring and counsel belong
Of right to her confident eyes: 80
Human and motherly they,
Careless of station or race:
Hearken! her children today
Shout for the joy of her face.

II

1.

No praises of the past are hers,
No fanes by hallowing time caressed,
No broken arch that ministers
To Time's sad instinct in the breast:
She has not gathered from the years
Grandeur of tragedies and tears,   90
Nor from long leisure the unrest
That finds repose in forms of classic grace:
These may delight the coming race
Who haply shall not count it to our crime
That we who fain would sing are here before our time.
She also hath her monuments;
Not such as stand decrepitly resigned
To ruin-mark the path of dead events
That left no seed of better days behind,

The tourist's pensioners that show their scars   100
And maunder of forgotten wars;
She builds not on the ground, but in the mind,
Her open-hearted palaces
For larger-thoughted men with heaven and earth at ease:
Her march the plump mow marks, the sleepless wheel,
The golden sheaf, the self-swayed commonweal;
The happy homesteads hid in orchard trees
Whose sacrificial smokes through peaceful air
Rise lost in heaven, the household's silent prayer;
What architect hath bettered these?   110
With softened eye the westward traveller sees
A thousand miles of neighbors side by side,
Holding by toil-worn titles fresh from God
The lands no serf or seigneur ever trod,
With manhood latent in the very sod,
Where the long billow of the wheatfield's tide
Flows to the sky across the prairie wide,
A sweeter vision than the castled Rhine,
Kindly with thoughts of Ruth and Bible-days benign.

2.

O ancient commonwealths, that we revere   120
Haply because we could not know you near,
Your deeds like statues down the aisles of Time
Shine peerless in memorial calm sublime,
And Athens is a trumpet still, and Rome;
Yet which of your achievements is not foam
Weighed with this one of hers (below you far
In fame, and born beneath a milder star),
That to Earth's orphans, far as curves the dome
Of death-deaf sky, the bounteous West means home,
With dear precedency of natural ties   130
That stretch from roof to roof and make men gently wise?
And if the nobler passions wane,
Distorted to base use, if the near goal
Of insubstantial gain

Tempt from the proper race-course of the soil
That crowns their patient breath
Whose feet, song-sandalled, are too fleet for Death,
Yet may she claim one privilege urbane
And haply first upon the civic roll,
That none can breathe her air nor grow humane.   140

3.

Oh, better far the briefest hour
Of Athens self-consumed, whose plastic power
Hid Beauty safe from Death in words or stone;
Of Rome, fair quarry where those eagles crowd
Whose fulgurous vans about the world had blown
Triumphant storm and seeds of polity;
Of Venice, fading o'er her shipless sea,
Last iridescence of a sunset cloud;
Than this inert prosperity,
This bovine comfort in the sense alone!   150
Yet art came slowly even to such as those,
Whom no past genius cheated of their own
With prudence of o'ermastering precedent;
Petal by petal spreads the perfect rose,
Secure of the divine event;
And only children rend the bud half-blown
To forestall Nature in her calm intent:
Time hath a quiver full of purposes
Which miss not of their aim, to us unknown,
And brings about the impossible with ease: 160
Haply for us the ideal dawn shall break
From where in legend-tinted line
The peaks of Hellas drink the morning's wine,
To tremble on our lids with mystic sign
Till the drowsed ichor in our veins awake
And set our pulse in tune with moods divine:
Long the day lingered in its sea-fringed nest,
Then touched the Tuscan hills with golden lance

And paused; then on to Spain and France
The splendor flew, and Albion's misty crest: 170
Shall Ocean bar him from his destined West?
Or are we, then, arrived too late,
Doomed with the rest to grope disconsolate,
Foreclosed of Beauty by our modern date?

III

1.

Poets, as their heads grow gray,
Look from too far behind the eyes,
Too long-experienced to be wise
In guileless youth's diviner way;
Life sings not now, but prophesies;
Time's shadows they no more behold,   180
But, under them, the riddle old
That mocks, bewilders, and defies:
In childhood's face the seed of shame,
In the green tree an ambushed flame,
In Phosphor a vaunt-guard of Night,
They, though against their will, divine,
And dread the care-dispelling wine
Stored from the Muse's vintage bright,
By age imbued with second-sight.
From Faith's own eyelids there peeps out,   190
Even as they look, the leer of doubt;
The festal wreath their fancy loads
With care that whispers and forebodes:
Nor this our triumph-day can blunt Megæra's goads.

2.

Murmur of many voices in the air
Denounces us degenerate,
Unfaithful guardians of a noble fate,
And prompts indifference or despair:
Is this the country that we dreamed in youth,

Where wisdom and not numbers should have weight,   200
Seed-field of simpler manner, braver truth,
Where shams should cease to dominate
In household, church, and state?
Is this Atlantis? This the unpoisoned soil,
Sea-whelmed for ages and recovered late,
Where parasitic greed no more should coil
Round Freedom's stem to bend awry and blight
What grew so fair, sole plant of love and light?
Who sit where once in crowned seclusion sate
The long-proved athletes of debate   210
Trained from their youth, as none thinks needful now?
Is this debating club where boys dispute,
And wrangle o'er their stolen fruit,
The Senate, erewhile cloister of the few,
Where Clay once flashed and Webster's cloudy brow
Brooded those bolts of thought that all the horizon knew?

3.

Oh, as this pensive moonlight blurs my pines,
Here while I sit and meditate these lines,
To gray-green dreams of what they are by day,
So would some light, not reason's sharp-edged ray,   220
Trance me in moonshine as before the flight
Of years had won me this unwelcome right
To see things as they are, or shall be soon,
In the frank prose of undissembling noon!

4.

Back to my breast, ungrateful sigh!
Whoever fails, whoever errs,
The penalty be ours, not hers!
The present still seems vulgar, seen too nigh;
The golden age is still the age that's past:
I ask no drowsy opiate   230
To dull my vision of that only state
Founded on faith in man, and therefore sure to last.

For, O my country, touched by thee,
The gray hairs gather back their gold;
Thy thought sets all my pulses free;
The heart refuses to be old;
The love is all that I can see.
Not to thy natal-day belong
Time's prudent doubt or age's wrong,
But gifts of gratitude and song: 240
Unsummoned crowd the thankful words,
As sap in spring-time floods the tree,
Foreboding the return of birds,
For all that thou hast been to me!

IV

1.

Flawless his heart and tempered to the core
Who, beckoned by the forward-leaning wave,
First left behind him the firm-footed shore,
And, urged by every nerve of sail and oar,
Steered for the Unknown which gods to mortals gave,
Of thought and action the mysterious door,   250
Bugbear of fools, a summons to the brave:
Strength found he in the unsympathizing sun,
And strange stars from beneath the horizon won,
And the dumb ocean pitilessly grave:
High-hearted surely he;
But bolder they who first off-cast
Their moorings from the habitable Past
And ventured chartless on the sea
Of storm-engendering Liberty:
For all earth's width of waters is a span,   260
And their convulsed existence mere repose,
Matched with the unstable heart of man,
Shoreless in wants, mist-girt in all it knows,
Open to every wind of sect or clan,
And sudden-passionate in ebbs and flows.

2.

They steered by stars the elder shipmen knew,
And laid their courses where the currents draw
Of ancient wisdom channelled deep in law,
The undaunted few
Who changed the Old World for the New,   270
And more devoutly prized
Than all perfection theorized
The more imperfect that had roots and grew.
They founded deep and well,
Those danger-chosen chiefs of men
Who still believed in Heaven and Hell,
Nor hoped to find a spell,
In some fine flourish of a pen,
To make a better man
Than long-considering Nature will or can,   280
Secure against his own mistakes,
Content with what life gives or takes,
And acting still on some fore-ordered plan,
A cog of iron in an iron wheel,
Too nicely poised to think or feel,
Dumb motor in a clock-like commonweal.
They wasted not their brain in schemes
Of what man might be in some bubble-sphere,
As if he must be other than he seems
Because he was not what he should be here,   290
Postponing Time's slow proof to petulant dreams:
Yet herein they were great
Beyond the incredulous lawgivers of yore,
And wiser than the wisdom of the shelf,
That they conceived a deeper-rooted state,
Of hardier growth, alive from rind to core,
By making man sole sponsor of himself.

3.

God of our fathers, Thou who wast,
Art, and shalt be when those eye-wise who flout
Thy secret presence shall be lost   300
In the great light that dazzles them to doubt,
We, sprung from loins of stalwart men
Whose strength was in their trust
That Thou wouldst make thy dwelling in their dust
And walk with those a fellow-citizen
Who build a city of the just,
We, who believe Life's bases rest
Beyond the probe of chemic test,
Still, like our fathers, feel Thee near,
Sure that, while lasts the immutable decree,   310
The land to Human Nature dear
Shall not be unbeloved of Thee.
1876   1876

AUSPEX

My heart, I cannot still it,
Nest that had song-birds in it;
And when the last shall go,
The dreary days, to fill it,
Instead of lark or linnet,
Shall whirl dead leaves and snow.

Had they been swallows only,
Without the passion stronger
That skyward longs and sings,—
Woe's me, I shall be lonely   10
When I can feel no longer
The impatience of their wings!

A moment, sweet delusion,
Like birds the brown leaves hover;

But it will not be long
Before their wild confusion
Fall wavering down to cover
The poet and his song.

1878

TO WHITTIER

ON HIS SEVENTY-FIFTH BIRTHDAY

New England's poet, rich in love as years,
Her hills and valleys praise thee, her swift brooks
Dance in thy verse; to her grave sylvan nooks
Thy steps allure us, which the wood-thrush hears
As maids their lovers', and no treason fears;
Through thee her Merrimacs and Agiochooks
And many a name uncouth win gracious looks,
Sweetly familiar to both Englands' ears:

Peaceful by birthright as a virgin lake,
The lily's anchorage, which no eyes behold   10
Save those of stars, yet for thy brother's sake
That lay in bonds, thou blewst a blast as bold
As that wherewith the heart of Roland brake,
Far heard across the New World and the Old.
1882   1882

TO HOLMES

ON HIS SEVENTY-FIFTH BIRTHDAY

Dear Wendell, why need count the years
    Since first your genius made me thrill,
If what moved then to smiles or tears,
    Or both contending, move me still?

What has the Calendar to do
    With poets? What Time's fruitless tooth

With gay immortals such as you
  Whose years but emphasize your youth?

One air gave both their lease of breath;
  The same paths lured our boyish feet;   10
One earth will hold us safe in death
  With dust of saints and scholars sweet.

Our legends from one source were drawn,
  I scarce distinguish yours from mine,
And *don't* we make the Gentiles yawn
  With "You remember?" o'er our wine!

If I, with too senescent air,
  Invade your elder memory's pale,
You snub me with a pitying "Where
  Were you in the September Gale?"   20

Both stared entranced at Lafayette,
  Saw Jackson dubbed with LL.D.
What Cambridge saw not strikes us yet
  As scarcely worth one's while to see.

Ten years my senior, when my name
  In Harvard's entrance-book was writ,
Her halls still echoed with the fame
  Of you, her poet and her wit.

'Tis fifty years from then to now:
  But your Last Leaf renews its green,   30
Though, for the laurels on your brow
  (So thick they crowd), 'tis hardly seen.

The oriole's fledglings fifty times
  Have flown from our familiar elms;
As many poets with their rhymes
  Oblivion's darkling dust o'erwhelms.

The birds are hushed, the poets gone
　　Where no harsh critic's lash can reach,
And still your wingèd brood sing on
　　To all who love our English speech.   40

Nay, let the foolish records be
　　That make believe you're seventy-five:
You're the old Wendell still to me,—
　　And that's the youngest man alive.

The gray-blue eyes, I see them still,
　　The gallant front with brown o'erhung,
The shape alert, the wit at will,
　　The phrase that stuck, but never stung.

You keep your youth as yon Scotch firs,
　　Whose gaunt line my horizon hems,   50
Though twilight all the lowland blurs,
　　Hold sunset in their ruddy stems.

You with the elders? Yes, 'tis true,
　　But in no sadly literal sense,
With elders and coevals too,
　　Whose verb admits no preterite tense.

Master alike in speech and song
　　Of fame's great antiseptic—Style,
You with the classic few belong
　　Who tempered wisdom with a smile.   60

Outlive us all! Who else like you
　　Could sift the seedcorn from our chaff,
And make us with the pen we knew
　　Deathless at least in epitaph?

1884   1884

CREDIDIMUS JOVEM REGNARE

(1887)

O days endeared to every Muse,
When nobody had any Views,
Nor, while the cloudscape of his mind
By every breeze was new designed,
Insisted all the world should see
Camels or whales where none there be!
O happy days, when men received
From sire to son what all believed,
And left the other world in bliss,
Too busy with bedevilling this!   10

Beset by doubts of every breed
In the last bastion of my creed,
With shot and shell for Sabbath-chime,
I watch the storming-party climb,
Panting (their prey in easy reach),
To pour triumphant through the breach
In walls that shed like snowflakes tons
Of missiles from old-fashioned guns,
But crumble 'neath the storm that pours
All day and night from bigger bores.   20
There, as I hopeless watch and wait
The last life-crushing coil of Fate,
Despair finds solace in the praise
Of those serene dawn-rosy days
Ere microscopes had made us heirs
To large estates of doubts and snares,
By proving that the title-deeds,
Once all-sufficient for men's needs,
Are palimpsests that scarce disguise
The tracings of still earlier lies,   30
Themselves as surely written o'er
An older fib erased before.

So from these days I fly to those
That in the landlocked Past repose,
Where no rude wind of doctrine shakes
From bloom-flushed boughs untimely flakes;
Where morning's eyes see nothing strange,
No crude perplexity of change,
And morrows trip along their ways
Secure as happy yesterdays.   40
Then there were rulers who could trace
Through heroes up to gods their race,
Pledged to fair fame and noble use
By veins from Odin filled or Zeus,
And under bonds to keep divine
The praise of a celestial line.
Then priests could pile the altar's sods,
With whom gods spake as they with gods,
And everywhere from haunted earth
Broke springs of wonder, that had birth   50
In depths divine beyond the ken
And fatal scrutiny of men;
Then hills and groves and streams and seas
Thrilled with immortal presences,
Not too ethereal for the scope
Of human passion's dream or hope.

Now Pan at last is surely dead,
And King No-Credit reigns instead,
Whose officers, morosely strict,
Poor Fancy's tenantry evict,   60
Chase the last Genius from the door,
And nothing dances any more.
Nothing? Ah, yes, our tables do,
Drumming the Old One's own tattoo,
And, if the oracles are dumb,
Have we not mediums? Why be glum?

Fly thither? Why, the very air
Is full of hindrance and despair!

Fly thither? But I cannot fly;
My doubts enmesh me if I try,   70
Each Liliputian, but, combined,
Potent a giant's limbs to bind.
This world and that are growing dark;
A huge interrogation mark,
The Devil's crook episcopal,
Still borne before him since the Fall,
Blackens with its ill-omened sign
The old blue heaven of faith benign.
Whence? Whither? Wherefore? How? Which? Why?
All ask at once, all wait reply.   80
Men feel old systems cracking under 'em;
Life saddens to a mere conundrum
Which once Religion solved, but she
Has lost—has Science found?—the key.

What was snow-bearded Odin, trow,
The mighty hunter long ago,
Whose horn and hounds the peasant hears
Still when the Northlights shake their spears?
Science hath answers twain, I've heard;
Choose which you will, nor hope a third;   90
Whichever box the truth be stowed in,
There's not a sliver left of Odin.
Either he was a pinchbrowed thing,
With scarcely wit a stone to fling,
A creature both in size and shape
Nearer than we are to the ape,
Who hung sublime with brat and spouse
By tail prehensile from the boughs,
And, happier than his maimed descendants,
The culture-curtailed *in*dependents,   100
Could pluck his cherries with both paws,
And stuff with both his big-boned jaws;
Or else the core his name enveloped
Was from a solar myth developed,

Which, hunted to its primal shoot,
Takes refuge in a Sanskrit root,
Thereby to instant death explaining
The little poetry remaining.

Try it with Zeus, 'tis just the same;
The thing evades, we hug a name;   110
Nay, scarcely that,—perhaps a vapor
Born of some atmospheric caper.
All Lempriere's fables blur together
In cloudy symbols of the weather,
And Aphrodite rose from frothy seas
But to illustrate such hypotheses.
With years enough behind his back,
Lincoln will take the selfsame track,
And prove, hulled fairly to the cob,
A mere vagary of Old Prob.   120
Give the right man a solar myth,
And he'll confute the sun therewith.

They make things admirably plain,
But one hard question *will* remain:
If one hypothesis you lose,
Another in its place you choose,
But, your faith gone, O man and brother,
Whose shop shall furnish you another?
One that will wash, I mean, and wear,
And wrap us warmly from despair?   130
While they are clearing up our puzzles,
And clapping prophylactic muzzles
On the Actæon's hounds that sniff
Our devious track through But and If,
Would they'd explain away the Devil
And other facts that won't keep level,
But rise beneath our feet or fail,
A reeling ship's deck in a gale!
God vanished long ago, iwis,
A mere subjective synthesis;   140

A doll, stuffed out with hopes and fears,
Too homely for us pretty dears,
Who want one that conviction carries,
Last make of London or of Paris.
He gone, I felt a moment's spasm,
But calmed myself with Protoplasm,
A finer name, and, what is more,
As enigmatic as before;
Greek, too, and sure to fill with ease
Minds caught in the Symplegades   150
Of soul and sense, life's two conditions,
Each baffled with its own omniscience.
The men who labor to revise
Our Bibles will, I hope, be wise,
And print it without foolish qualms
Instead of God in David's psalms:
Noll had been more effective far
Could he have shouted at Dunbar,
"Rise, Protoplasm!" No dourest Scot
Had waited for another shot.   160

And yet I frankly must confess
A secret unforgivingness,
And shudder at the saving chrism
Whose best New Birth is Pessimism;
My soul—I mean the bit of phosphorus
That fills the place of what that was for us—
Can't bid its inward bores defiance
With the new nursery-tales of science.
What profits me, though doubt by doubt,
As nail by nail, be driven out,   170
When every new one, like the last,
Still holds my coffin-lid as fast?
Would I find thought a moment's truce,
Give me the young world's Mother Goose
With life and joy in every limb,
The chimney-corner tales of Grimm!

Our dear and admirable Huxley
Cannot explain to me why ducks lay,
Or, rather, how into their eggs
Blunder potential wings and legs   180
With will to move them and decide
Whether in air or lymph to glide.
Who gets a hair's-breadth on by showing
That Something Else set all agoing?
Farther and farther back we push
From Moses and his burning bush;
Cry, "Art Thou there?" Above, below,
All Nature mutters *yes* and *no!*
'Tis the old answer: we're agreed
Being from Being must proceed,   190
Life be Life's source. I might as well
Obey the meeting-house's bell,
And listen while Old Hundred pours
Forth through the summer-opened doors,
From old and young. I hear it yet,
Swelled by bass-viol and clarinet,
While the gray minister, with face
Radiant, let loose his noble bass.
If Heaven it reached not, yet its roll
Waked all the echoes of the soul,   200
And in it many a life found wings
To soar away from sordid things.
Church gone and singers too, the song
Sings to me voiceless all night long,
Till my soul beckons me afar,
Glowing and trembling like a star.
Will any scientific touch
With my worn strings achieve as much?

I don't object, not I, to know
My sires were monkeys, if 'twas so;   210
I touch my ear's collusive tip
And own the poor-relationship.

That apes of various shapes and sizes
Contained their germs that all the prizes
Of senate, pulpit, camp, and bar win
May give us hopes that sweeten Darwin.
Who knows but from our loins may spring
(Long hence) some winged sweet-throated thing
As much superior to us
As we to Cynocephalus?   220

This is consoling, but, alas
It wipes no dimness from the glass
Where I am flattening my poor nose,
In hope to see beyond my toes.
Though I accept my pedigree,
Yet where, pray tell me, is the key
That should unlock a private door
To the Great Mystery, such no more?
Each offers his, but one nor all
Are much persuasive with the wall   230
That rises now, as long ago,
Between I wonder and I know,
Nor will vouchsafe a pin-hole peep
At the veiled Isis in its keep.
Where is no door, I but produce
My key to find it of no use.
Yet better keep it, after all,
Since Nature's economical,
And who can tell but some fine day
(If it occur to her) she may,   240
In her good-will to you and me,
Make door and lock to match the key?

1887

[Æt. 25]

TO C. F. BRIGGS
["ELMWOOD JUNIOR"; "DR. PRIMROSE"]

Elmwood, Sept. 18, 1844.

My dear Friend,—

... I have inherited from my father an intellectual temperament which would fain keep its hands soft. I feel the sorrows
of my friends and their joys with as much intensity as human
nature is capable of, but I too often remain satisfied with the
feeling. Partly from constitutional indolence and partly from
timidity, I sit in the corner with my heart full and let others
speak and act. But, with God's help, I am resolved to conquer
this. I am too ready to leave things undone, because I am never
satisfied with my manner of doing them. ...

You speak of our marriage as one of "convenience," by which
I suppose you mean that our means are such as to warrant us in
being married at any time. This is not the case. My *Pioneer*
debts will not be paid before January. ... My father would have
assisted me greatly, but he lost a great part of his own property
a few years ago, and his income will hardly keep pace with his
generosity. You will be glad to hear, however, that he has
offered, without any hint on my part, to build me a cottage on
a piece of his land here, if it can be done for a thousand dollars
or thereabout. I think that I can put up quite a comfortable
little nest for that sum, with a spare chamber for you and your
wife whenever you may be able to pay us "provincials" a
visit. ... I have already christened my new castle (though as
yet an atmospheric one) "Elmwood Junior," much to the
delight of my father, who is one of the men you would like to
know. He is Dr. Primrose in the comparative degree, the very
simplest and charmingest of sexagenarians, and not without a
great deal of the truest magnanimity. Nothing delights him
so much as any compliment paid to me, except the idea of build-

ing me a cottage. If you could see him criticising the strut or
crow of one of my chanticleers with a child's enthusiasm, or
reading a review of my poems which he does not think lauda-
tory enough (at the same time professing himself a disciple of
Pope and pretending that he can't understand more than a tithe
of what I write), or pointing out the advantages of the site he
has selected for planting the Colony from Elmwood Senior, or
talking of the efficacy of prayer, or praising "the old Federal
Party with Washington at its head," or speaking of Jefferson as
harshly as his kind heart will let him speak of anybody—in
short, if you had a more than Asmodeus-faculty and could take
the roof off his heart, you would fall in love with him. He has
had far more sorrow, too, than most men, and his wounds have
been in his tenderest part . . . but nothing could shake my
beloved and honored father's trust in God and his sincere
piety. . . .

Most affectionately your friend,

J. R. L.

[Æt. 26]

TO C. F. BRIGGS
[HIS DAUGHTER]

Wednesday, Feb. 5, 1846.

MY DEAR FRIEND,—

You must count this as two distinct letters, and give me credit
accordingly. To tell the truth, I am very much taken up with
the baby at present. It is true our enlarged means enable us to
keep a maid, but I do not think Blanche safe in any one's arms
but her mother's and mine, and Maria cannot bear the fatigue
of "tending" her a great deal. I belong to a class of philosophers
(unhappily, I believe, a small one) who do not believe that children are born into the world to subject their mothers to a diaper
despotism, and to be brought down to their fathers after dinner,
as an additional digestive to the nuts and raisins, to be bundled
up and hurried away at the least symptom of disaffection or disturbed digestion. Unlike many philanthropists, I endeavor to

put my principles into practice, and the result is that I find pretty steady employment and (to finish the quotations from the advertisements of serving-men's Elysian Fields) good wages. Blanche, already, with a perverted taste, prefers her father to any one else, and considers me (as the antiquaries do whatever they can't explain in the old mythologies, whether it be male or female) as "the personification of the maternal principle." She is a very good child, however, and only cries enough to satisfy us, as the old Greek said, that we have begotten a mortal. The only portentous thing she ever does is to sneeze, and as it would be quite supererogatory in her to do this in order to procure a hearty "God bless you!" from all present, I incline to interpret it by Sir Thomas Browne's theory, who, in his exposure of vulgar errors, after pulling to pieces the notion that there is anything ominous in it, proceeds to inform us that it is an effort of nature to expel any *humor* that may lurk in the brain. If this be so, I should imagine, from Miss Fuller's attempts at facetiousness, which now and then give a melancholy air to the *Tribune*, that she must be an unparalleled sternutator. . . .

[Æt. 29]

TO C. F. BRIGGS
[HIS "OLD GARRET"; "A FABLE FOR CRITICS"]

Elmwood, May 12, 1848.

MY DEAR FRIEND,—

. . . Here I am in my garret. I slept here when I was a little curly-headed boy, and used to see visions between me and the ceiling, and dream the so often recurring dream of having the earth put into my hand like an orange. In it I used to be shut up without a lamp—my mother saying that none of her children should be afraid of the dark—to hide my head under the pillows, and then not be able to shut out the shapeless monsters that thronged around me, minted in my brain. It is a pleasant room, facing, from the position of the house, almost equally towards the morning and the afternoon. In winter I can see the sunset, in summer I can see it only as it lights up the tall trunks of the English elms in front of the house, making them sometimes, when the sky behind them is lead-colored, seem of the most brilliant yellow. When the sun, towards setting, breaks out suddenly after a thunder-shower and I see them against an almost black sky, they have seemed of a most peculiar and dazzling green tint, like the rust on copper. In winter my view is a wide one, taking in a part of Boston. I can see one long curve of the Charles, and the wide fields between me and Cambridge, and the flat marshes beyond the river, smooth and silent with glittering snow. As the spring advances and one after another of our trees puts forth, the landscape is cut off from me piece by piece, till, by the end of May, I am closeted in a cool and rustling privacy of leaves. Then I begin to bud with the season. Towards the close of winter I become thoroughly wearied of closed windows and fires. I feel dammed up, and yet there is not flow enough in me to gather any head of water. When I can sit at my open window and my friendly leaves hold their hands before my eyes to prevent their wandering to the landscape, I can sit down and write.

I have begun upon the "Fable" again fairly, and am making some headway. I think with what I sent you (which I believe was about 500 lines) it will make something over a thousand. I have done, since I sent the first half, Willis, Longfellow, Bryant, Miss Fuller, and Mrs. Child. In Longfellow's case I have attempted no characterization. The same (in a degree) may be said of S. M. F. With her I have been perfectly good-humored, but I have a fancy that what I say will stick uncomfortably. It will make you laugh. So will L. M. C. After S. M. F. I make a short digression on bores in general, which has some drollery in it. Willis I think good. Bryant is funny, and as fair as I could make it, immitigably just. Indeed I have endeavored to be so in all. I am glad I did Bryant before I got your letter. The only verses I shall add regarding him are some complimentary ones, which I left for a happier mood after I had written the comic part. *I* steal from him indeed! If he knew me he would not say so. When I steal I shall go to a specie-vault, not to a till. Does he think that he *invented* the Past and has a prescription title to it? Do not think I am provoked. I am simply amused. If he had *riled* me, I might have knocked him into a cocked hat in my satire. But that, on second thought, would be no revenge, for it might make him President, a cocked hat being now the chief qualification. It would be more severe to knock him into the middle of next week, as that is in the future, and he has such a partiality towards the past. However, enough of him. My next volume will be enough revenge, for it will be better than my last. . . .

[Æt. 30]

TO CHARLES R. LOWELL[1]
["THE IMPORTANCE OF 'OBSERVING'"]

Elmwood, June 11, 1849.

MY DEAR CHARLIE,—

I have had so much to do in the way of writing during the past week that I have not had time sooner to answer your letter, which came to me in due course of mail, and for which I am much obliged to you.

I am very glad to hear that you are enjoying yourself so much, and also that the poor musquash dug faster than you did. I was not so long ago a boy as not to remember what sincere satisfaction there is in a good ducking, and how the spirit of maritime adventure is ministered to by a raft which will not float. I congratulate you on both experiences.

And now let me assume the privilege of my uncleship to give you a little advice. Let me counsel you to make use of all your visits to the country as opportunities for an education which is of great importance, which town-bred boys are commonly lacking in, and which can never be so cheaply acquired as in boyhood. Remember that a man is valuable in our day for what he *knows*, and that his company will always be desired by others in exact proportion to the amount of intelligence and instruction he brings with him. I assure you that one of the earliest

[1] At the age of fourteen. Killed at the Battle of Cedar Creek, 1864.

pieces of definite knowledge we acquire after we become men is this—that our company will be desired no longer than we honestly pay our proper share in the general reckoning of mutual entertainment. A man who knows more than another knows *incalculably* more, be sure of that, and a person with eyes in his head cannot look even into a pigsty without learning something that will be useful to him at one time or another. Not that we should educate ourselves for the mere selfish sake of that advantage of superiority which it will give us. But knowledge is power in this noblest sense, that it enables us to *benefit* others and to pay our way honorably in life by being of *use*.

Now, when you are at school in Boston you are furnishing your brain with what can be obtained from books. You are training and enriching your intellect. While you are in the country you should remember that you are in the great school of the senses. Train your eyes and ears. Learn to know all the trees by their bark and leaves, by their general shape and manner of growth. Sometimes you can be able to say positively what a tree is *not* by simply examining the lichens on the bark, for you will find that particular varieties of lichen love particular trees. Learn also to know all the birds by sight, by their notes, by their manner of flying; all the animals by their general appearance and gait or the localities they frequent.

You would be ashamed not to know the name and use of every piece of furniture in the house, and we ought to be as familiar with every object in the world—which is only a larger kind of house. You recollect the pretty story of Pizarro and the Peruvian Inca: how the Inca asked one of the Spaniards to write the word *Dio* (God) upon his thumb-nail, and then, showing it to the rest, found only Pizarro unable to read it! Well, you will find as you grow older that this same name of God is written all over the world in little phenomena that occur under our eyes every moment, and I confess that I feel very much inclined to hang my head with Pizarro when I cannot translate these hieroglyphics into my own vernacular.

Now, I write all this to you, my dear Charlie, not in the least because it is considered proper for uncles to bore their nephews with musty moralities and advice; but I should be quite willing that you should think me a bore, if I could only be the means of impressing upon you the importance of *observing*, and the great fact that we cannot properly observe till we have learned *how*. Education, practice, and especially a determination not to be satisfied with remarking that side of an object which happens to catch our eye first when we first see it—these gradually make an observer. The faculty, once acquired, becomes at length another sense which works mechanically.

I think I have sometimes noticed in you an *impatience* of mind which you should guard against carefully. Pin this maxim up in your memory—that Nature abhors the credit system, and that we never get anything in life till we have paid for it. Anything good, I mean; evil things we always pay for afterwards, and always when we find it hardest to do it. By paying for them, of course, I mean *laboring* for them. Tell me how much good solid *work* a young man has in him, and I will erect a horoscope for him as accurate as Guy Mannering's for young Bertram. Talents are absolutely nothing to a man except he have the faculty of work along with them. They, in fact, turn upon him and worry him, as Actæon's dogs did—these are the sails and the rudder even of genius, without which it is only a wretched hulk upon the waters.

It is not fair to look a gift horse in the mouth, unless, indeed, it be a wooden horse, like that which carried the Greeks into Troy; but my lecture on patience and *finish* was apropos of your letter, which was more careless in its chirography and (here and there) in its composition than I liked. Always make a thing as good as you can. Otherwise it was an excellent letter, because it told what you had seen and what you were doing—certainly better as a *letter* than this of mine, which is rather a sermon. But read it, my dear Charlie, as the advice of one who takes a sincere interest in you. I hope to hear from you again, and my answer to your next shall be more entertaining.

I remain your loving uncle,
J. R. LOWELL.

[Æt. 30]

TO C. F. BRIGGS

Elmwood, Jan. 23, 1850.

MY DEAR FRIEND,—

I have never thanked you for your gift of a box of cigars. I am smoking one of them at this very moment. I know not in what light to regard them other than as a kind of parishioner's gift to the Rev. Mr. Wilbur, though there may be a covert satire in thus throwing that gentleman's weakness into his very teeth. My great-grandfather, who was minister of Newbury, and who, being very much of a gentleman and scholar, held out against Whitefield and his extravagances, used to take (I have no doubt) the grocer's share of his salary in tobacco. He was a terrible smoker, and there is still extant in the house he lived in at Newbury a painted panel representing a meeting of the neighboring clergy, each with his pipe and his—pot.[1] I have a great regard for this excellent man's memory, strengthened by his notebooks and by his portrait in gown, bands, and wig, painted (alas!) by one of his parishioners. Therefore I scruple not to thank you for this compliance with my weakness, and feel that I have an ancestral right to pronounce the cigars excellent. . . .

. . . My "new book" is to be called "The Nooning." Maria invented the title for me, and is it not a pleasant one? My plan is this. I am going to bring together a party of half a dozen old friends at Elmwood. They go down to the river and bathe, and then one proposes that they shall go up into a great willow-tree (which stands at the end of the causey near our house, and has seats in it) to take their nooning. There they agree that each shall tell a story or recite a poem of some sort. In the tree they find a countryman already resting himself, who enters into the plan and tells a humorous tale, with touches of Yankee character and habits in it. *I* am to read my poem of the "Voyage of Leif" to Vinland, in which I mean to bring my hero straight into Boston Bay, as befits a Bay-state poet. Two of my

---

[1] This interesting old panel was afterwards transferred to Elmwood, and set above the mantelpiece in the study.

poems are already written—one "The Fountain of Youth" (no connection with any other firm), and the other an "Address to the Muse," by the Transcendentalist of the party. I guess I am safe in saying that the first of these two is the best thing I have done yet. But you shall judge when you see it. But "Leif's Voyage" is to be far better. I intend to confute my critics, not with another satire, but by writing better. It is droll that they should say I want variety. Between "Columbus" and Hosea Biglow I think there is some range and some variety of power shown. I cannot help thinking that my countrymen will wake up some day and find that they have got a poet. But no matter; do you keep on believing in me, and I shall justify you if I live. I feel that I am very young for a man of thirty, and that I have not by any means got my growth. My poems hitherto have been a true record of my life, and I mean that they shall continue to be. As Alcott said to me the other day, they contain a great deal of *history*. The public have not yet learned to look beyond the titles of them at their meaning. As soon as the wise world is satisfied that I am a poet, I think it will find more in them than it suspected. This is all as it ought to be, and I am writing about it to you as to one who thinks more of me than I do of myself—though, of course, if I did not believe that I was a poet, I should not write a line. The world is right, too, after its own fashion, for I am perfectly conscious that I have not yet got the best of my poetry out of me. What I have written will need to be carried down to posterity on the shoulders of better poems written hereafter, and strong enough to carry the ore in the stone which imbeds it. My dear friend—and you are very dear—I am *not* a fool, at any rate, and I know my own wants and faults a great deal better than any of my critics.

I begin to feel that I must enter on a new year of my apprenticeship. My poems have thus far had a regular and natural sequence. First, Love and the mere happiness of existence beginning to be conscious of itself, then Freedom—both being the sides which Beauty presented to me—and now I am going to try more *wholly* after Beauty herself. Next, if I live, I shall try to present Life as I have seen it. In the "Nooning" I shall have not even a glance towards Reform. If the poems I have already written are good for anything they are perennial, and it is tedious as well as foolish to repeat one's self. I have preached sermons enow, and now I am going to come down out of the pulpit and *go about among my parish*. I shall turn my barrel over and read my old discourses; it will be time to write new ones when my hearers have sucked all the meaning out of those old ones. Certainly I shall not grind for any Philistines, whether Reformers or Conservatives. I find that Reform cannot take up the whole of me, and I am quite sure that eyes were given us to look about us with sometimes, and not to be always looking forward. If some of my good red-hot friends were to see this they would call me a backslider, but there are other directions in which one may get away from people beside the rearward one. Thus I have taken an observation whereby to indicate to you my present mental and moral latitude and longitude. As well as I can judge, I am farther eastward or nearer morning than ever hitherto. Am I as tedious as a king?

I am not certain that my next appearance will not be in a pamphlet on the Hungarian question in answer to the *North American Review*. But I shall not write anything if I can help it. I am tired of controversy, and though I have cut out the oars with which to row up my friend Bowen, yet I have enough to do, and, besides, am not so well as usual, being troubled in my head as I was summer before last. I should like to play for a year, and after I have written and printed the "Nooning," I mean to *take* a nooning and lie under the trees looking at the sky.

Fredrika Bremer stayed three weeks with us, and I do not *like* her, I *love* her. She is one of the most beautiful persons I have ever known—so clear, so simple, so right-minded and -hearted, and so full of judgement. I believe she liked us, too, and had a good time. . . .

                                                    With all love,
                                                          J. R. L.

[Æt. 33]
              TO MRS. FRANCIS G. SHAW
              [LETTERS; THE SOULS OF HOUSES]
                                        Elmwood, Jan. 11, 1853.

MY DEAR SARAH,—

You know that I promised solemnly to write you a letter
from Switzerland, and therefore, of course, I didn't do it. These
epistolary promises to pay always do (or at least always ought
to) come back protested. A letter ought always to be the
genuine and natural flower of one's disposition—proper both
to the writer and the season—and none of your turnip japonicas
cut laboriously out of a cheap and flabby material. Then, when
you have sealed it up, it comes out fresh and fragrant. I do
not like shuttle-cock correspondences. What is the use of our
loving people if they can't let us owe them a letter? if they can't
be sure we keep on loving them if we don't keep sending an
acknowledgment under our hands and seals once a month? As
if there were a statute of limitations for affection! The moment
Love begins to think of Duty, he may as well go hang himself
with his own bow-string. All this means that if I should never
write you another letter (which is extremely likely), and we
should never meet again till I drop in upon you some day in
another planet, I shall give an anxious look at myself in the
mirror (while I am waiting for you to come down), and shall
hear the flutter of your descending wings with the same admiring expectation as I should now listen for your foot upon
the stairs. . . .

Now, the reason I am writing to you is this: I spent Sunday
with Edmund Quincey at Dedham, and, as I came back over
the rail yesterday, I was roused from a reverie by seeing "West
Roxbury Station" written up over the door of a kind of Italian
villa at which we stopped. I almost twisted my head off looking
for the house on the hill. There it stood in mourning still,
just as Frank painted it. The color suited my mood exactly.
The eyes of the house were shut, the welcoming look it had was
gone; it was dead. I am a Platonist about houses. They get to

my eye a shape from the souls that inhabit them. My friends' dwellings seem as peculiar to them as their bodies, looks, and motions. People have no right to sell their dead houses; they should burn them as they used to burn corpses. Suppose these bodies of ours could be reinhabited, and that our heirs could turn an honest penny (as American heirs certainly would) by disposing of them by auction. How could we endure to see Miss Amelia Augusta Smith's little soul giggling out of those sacred caves where we had been wont to catch glimpses of the shrinking Egeria of refined and noble womanhood? With what horror should we hear the voice that had thrilled us with song, startled us with ambushes of wit, or softened us with a sympathy that made us feel somehow as if our mother's tears were mixed with its tones—I say, with what horror' should we hear it using all its pathos and all its melodious changes for the cheapening of a tarlatan muslin or the describing the dress that Eliza Ann wore at her wedding! I was too far off, thank God, to see Mrs. Smith looking out of your dead house's windows, but I mused of these things as the train rolled on, and caught fragments of the vapid talk of a couple on the seat before me. I have buried that house now and flung my pious handful of earth over it and set up a head-stone—and I shall never look up to the hill-top again, let me pass it never so often. But I resolved to write a letter to its departed spirit.

. . . It is hard writing at such a distance. If one be in good spirits, and write a nice, pleasant, silly letter, it may find those to whom it goes on the other side of the world in the midst of a new sorrow, and will be as welcome as a half-tipsy wedding guest at a funeral. The thing which everybody here is talking about is the Tippers. The Rappers are considered quite *slow* nowadays. Tables speak as inspired, consolatory nothings are literally delivered *ex cathedrâ*. Bores whom we thought buried out of the way long ago revive in washstands and bedsteads. Departed spirits still rule us—but no longer metaphorically from their urns—they speak to us through the excited centre-table. I have heard of a particular teapoy that was vehement, slowly argumentative, blandly sympathetic, wildly romantic,

and all with its legs alone. Little did John Chinaman dream
what he was making, as little as John Shakespeare knew that he
had begotten the world's wonder William. A neighbor of ours
has an exhorting boot-jack, and I expect every day to hear of
the spirit of Diogenes in a wash-tub. Judge Wells (*Aunt* Wells,
as he is affectionately called by the Bar) is such a powerful
medium that he has to drive back the furniture from following
him when he goes out, as one might a pack of too-affectionate
dogs. I have no doubt I shall meet him some day with a foot-
stool gambolling at his side or leaping up on his reluctant
legs. . . .

[*Æt.* 35]

TO MISS NORTON
[BEVERLY A NEW ENGLAND SORRENTO]
[BEVERLY], SHIP "UNDERHILL," ELDREDGE, MISTRESS,
Lat. 40° 20′, Long. (bad observation),
Islands of Sirens bearing E. S. E. 2½ miles.

August 14, 1854.

. . . If I may trust a rather poor memory—without a book
to make a crutch of—I ought to thank you for having given
me so happy an example of the force of habit. Some four
thousand years ago the fountain of Arethusa went down near
Eleusis (?) and came up at Syracuse in Sicily, and now, translated to America and tolerably well bound, it has contrived to
do the same thing between Shady Hill and Newport. I am
quite content. I could not have a better minister resident, nor
one less intrusive, only reminding you of me when you choose
to give an audience, and then always saying better things than
I could. So pray do not give her her passports yet. I shall
bring the "Conversations" when I am happy enough to come
myself.

Now, in order that you may not fancy (as most persons who
go to Rhode Island do) that Newport is the only place in the
world where there is any virtue in salt water—I will say a word
or two of Beverly. Country and sea-shore are combined here

in the most charming way. Find the Yankee word for Sorrento, and you have Beverly—it is only the Bay of Naples translated into the New England dialect. The ocean and the forest are not estranged here, and the trees trust themselves down to the water's edge most confidingly. In some places the ivy plays in the air and the kelp in the water, like children of different ranks making shy advances to each other. Close behind us rises a rocky hill, and the pine woods begin—wonderful woods, called Witch Woods by the natives because it is so easy to lose your way in them. All through them strange rocks bulge out—amphibious-looking hybrids between sea-shore and inland—their upper edges fringed lightly with ferns that seem to entangle the sunshine and hold it fast, and their bases rough with queer lichens that look like water-weeds. I think there is more ocean than land in the blood of these rocks, and they always seem to me listening and waiting for the waves. If you leap down from one of them you sink ankle-deep in springy pine-tassel or moss. Somewhere in these woods is a visionary clearing and farm-house, which every one gets a glimpse of—but no man hath seen twice. You hear the crowing of cocks, the contented low of cattle rubbing their soft throats over the polished bars, and sometimes a muffled throb of flails; presently, through some wood-gap, you see the chimney and the blue breath of the hearth in the cool air, but when you have made your way through the next thicket, all is gone. I think it is the farm of one of the old Salem warlocks, and buy my vegetables warily, fearful of some ill thing. Here and there, climbing some higher rock, you get a gleam of sea through some scoop in the woods—a green cup filled half with potable gold.

We are in a little house close upon the road, with the sea just below, as seen through a fringe of cedar, wild cherry, and barberry. Beyond this fringe is a sand-beach where we bathe. . . . As I look out of my window I see the flicker of the sea's golden scales (which the moon will by and by touch with her long wand and turn to silver) stretching eastward forever. We are at the foot of a bay, across the mouth of which lies a line of islands—some bare rock, some shrubby, and some wooded.

These are the true islands of the Sirens. One has been disenchanted by a great hotel to which a steamboat runs innumerably every day with a band—the energetic *boong! boong!—boong! boong! boong!*—of the bass drum being all we hear. Our sunset is all in the southeast, and every evening the clouds and islands bloom and the slow sails are yellowed and the dories become golden birds swinging on the rosy water.

Well, well, after all, I am only saying that Nature is here as well as at Newport, and that she has not lost her knack at miracles. But at Newport you have no woods, and ours are so grand and deep and unconverted! They have those long pauses of conscious silence that are so fine, as if the spirit that inhabits them were hiding from you and holding its breath—and then all the leaves stir again, and the pines cheat the rocks with their mock surf, and that invisible bird that haunts such solitudes calls once and is answered, and then silence again. I would not have told you how much better this is than your Rhode Island glories—only that you Newport folks always seem a little (I must go to my Yankee) *stuck up*, as if Newport were all the world, and you the saints that had inherited it. But I hope to see you and Newport soon, and I will be lenient. You shall find in me the Beverly grandeur of soul which can acknowledge alien merit.

[Æt. 38]

TO C. E. NORTON
[MORNING WALKS]

Cambridge, Dec. 31, 1857.

MY DEAR CHARLES,—

At last! Like a true lazzarone as I am I have been waiting for sunshine before I wrote—I mean, for one of those moods that would make a letter worth sending; and such a mood is not dependent on mere cheerfulness, but almost altogether on having nothing to do, so that one can have time to hatch one's thoughts fairly out as one goes along. Pen and paper are never inspiring to me as conversation sometimes is,—and I was born to sit on a fence in the sun, and (if I had my own way) in those latter days of May, when the uneasy blue-bird shifts his freight of song from post to post, and the new green of spring is just passing from the miraculous into the familiar. . . .

For a lazy man I have a great deal to do. A magazine allows no vacations. What with manuscripts and proofs and what not, it either takes up or breaks up all one's time. . . .

But even the magazine has its compensations. First, it has almost got me out of debt, and next, it compels me into morning walks to the printing-office. There is a little foot-path which leads along the river-bank, and it is lovely; whether in clear, cold mornings, when the fine filaments of the bare trees on the horizon seem floating up like sea-masses in the ether sea, or when (as yesterday) a gray mist fills our Cambridge cup and gives a doubtful loom to its snowy brim of hills, while the silent gulls wheel over the rustling cakes of ice which the Charles is whirling seaward. So I get my bits of country and can feel like a rustic still, but I miss the winter-birds I used to see at home. I continue to think the marshes lovely, and this winter they are covered with plump ricks, whereof some half-dozen standing on my own amphibious territory give me a feeling of ownership and dignity, albeit the hay does not belong to me. This only strengthens a faith I have long held, that we are only metaphysically and imaginatively rich as far as mere possession goes, and only actually so in what we give away. . . .

[Æt. 39]

TO MISS NORTON
[GOUT]

Cambridge, Aug. 30, 1858.

. . . Since I got your Berkshire letter I have come into an inheritance—I have had my life insured for forty years—I have been chained by one leg—I have suffered the torture of the Boot—I have said disrespectful things of my great-grandfather —I have received no sympathy, but have been laughed at—I have laughed myself, sometimes on the wrong side of my mouth—in short, I have had an attack of the—no, I won't tell you what yet. I will prepare your mind. I will dignify it by poetic precedent. I may compare myself with Milton (in this respect). I may claim brotherhood with Gray and Walpole. In short I have had the *gout*. I cannot escape the conclusion that I am a middle-aged man. I even fear that I shall have to wear a special shoe on my left foot. My verses will no longer be admired by young ladies of sixteen. On the other hand, I have been thinking over the advantages. I find by the books that (if nothing happens) I shall live long. That it "relieves the system"—which seems to be true, for I have not been so well for a year. That in the course of time I shall be able to write my name and keep my milk-score with my knuckles. That I shall always have an excuse for being as testy as I please. On the whole, I think the odds are in favor of podagra. The worst danger is that the eyes are liable to be painfully affected with *iritis*—a comprehensive Greek term implying that the eye-wrong-is. But this is more than set off by the certainty that I shall never be subject to that *in-great-toe otio* to which Nereus, according to Horace, doomed the winds. (Since making these two puns I have carefully fumigated the paper, so that you need not fear infection.) As soon as my father heard of my trouble he came to see me, bringing a cyclopædia of medicine (from which he had selected a variety of choice complaints for himself), that my reading might be of an enlivening character. I do not find that there is any specific for the gout, but, on the *similia-similibus* principle, I eat "tomarters" daily. The disease derives its name (like *mons a non movendo*) from the patient's inability to *go out*. The ordinary derivation from *gutta* is absurd—for not only is the German form *Gicht* deduced from *gehen*, but the persons incident to the malady are precisely those who themselves (or their ancestors for them) have kept just this side of the gutter. I never heard that my great-grandfather died insolvent, but I am obliged to *foot* some of his bills for port. I can't help thinking that I shall be worse if I indulge any longer in this kind of thing—so I shall stop. . . .

[Æt. 39]
TO O. W. HOLMES
[THE "PROFESSOR"; "SAMSON'S WEAPON"]

Cambridge, Dec. 19, 1858.

MY DEAR WENDELL,—

Thank you ever so much for the "Autocrat," who comes at last drest like a gentleman. The color of the paper is just that which knowers love to see in old lace.

"Run out" indeed!—who has been suggesting the danger of that to you? I hope you will continue to run out in the style of the first "Professor." The comparison of the bung and the straw is excellent and touched a very tender spot in me, who was born between two cider-mills, and drew in much childish belly-ache from both, turned now by memory into something like the result that might follow nectar.

You have been holding-in all this while—*possumus omnes*, we all play the 'possum—and are now getting your second wind. I like the new Professor better than the old Autocrat. You have filled no ten pages so wholly to my liking as in the January number. I have just read it and am delighted with it. The "Old Boston" is an inspiration. You have never been so wise and witty as in this last number. I hold up my left foot in token of my unanimity.

The religious press (a true sour-cider press with belly-ache privileges attached) will be at you, but after smashing one of them you will be able to furnish yourself with a Samson's weapon for the rest of the Philisterei. Good-bye.

Always affectionately yours,

J. R. LOWELL.

[Æt. 41]
TO W. D. HOWELLS
["HOLD YOURSELF DEAR"]

Cambridge, Monday, Aug., 1860.

MY DEAR YOUNG FRIEND,—

Here is a note to Mr. Hawthorne, which you can use if you have occasion.

Don't print too much and too soon; don't get married in a hurry; read what will make you *think*, not *dream;* hold yourself dear, and more power to your elbow! God bless you!

> Cordially yours,
>
> J. R. Lowell.

A man may have ever so much in him, but ever so much depends on how he gets it out.

> *Finis, quoad* Biglow.

TO NATHANIEL HAWTHORNE
[WILLIAM DEAN HOWELLS]

> Cambridge, Aug. 5, 1860.

My dear Hawthorne,—

I have no masonic claim upon you except community of tobacco, and the young man who brings this does not smoke.

But he wants to look at you, which will do you no harm, and him a great deal of good.

His name is Howells, and he is a fine young fellow, and has written several *poems* in the *Atlantic*, which of course you have never read, because you don't do such things yourself, and are old enough to know better.

When I think how much you might have profited by the perusal of certain verses of somebody who shall be nameless— but, no matter! If my judgment is good for anything, this youth has more in him than any of our younger fellows in the way of rhyme.

Of course he can't hope to rival the *Consule Planco* men. Therefore let him look at you, and charge it

> To yours always,
>
> J. R. Lowell.

[Æt. 42]

TO MISS NORTON
[A MISDATED LETTER]

Elmwood, the day before you wrote
your last letter; viz., Sept. 28, 1861.

MY DEAR SIBYL,—

Will you kindly tell me what *has happened* next week, so that
I may be saved from this daily debauch of newspapers? How
many "heroic Mulligans" who "*meurent et ne se rendent pas*" to
the reporters, with the privilege of living and surrendering to
the enemy? How many "terrific conflicts" near Cheat Mountain (ominous name), with one wounded on our side, and
enemy's loss supposed to be heavy? How many times we are
to save Kentucky and lose our selfrespect? How many times
the Potomac is to be "hermetically sealed"? How often
Mr. Seward is to put newspaper correspondents on the level of
Secretaries of State? etc., etc. I ask all these questions because
your so-welcome letter, which I received on Wednesday the
25th, was dated to-morrow the 29th. There is something very
impressive to the imagination in a letter from the future, and to
be even a day in advance of the age is a good deal—how much
more five or six! How does it seem to come back? Is not
everything weary and stale? Or do you live all the time in a
balloon, thus seeing over the lines of Time, the old enemy of us
all? Pray tell me how much foolisher I shall be this day twelvemonth. Well, at any rate, you can't see far enough to find the
day when your friendship shall not be one of my dearest
possessions. . . .

Has it begun to be cold with you? I had a little Italian bluster
of brushwood fire yesterday morning, but the times are too
hard with me to allow of such an extravagance except on the
brink of gelation. The horror of my tax-bill has so infected my
imagination that I see myself and all my friends begging en-
trance to the P. H. (From delicacy I use initials.) I fancy all
of you gathering fuel on the Newport beaches. I hope you will
have lots of wrecks—Southern privateers, of course. Don't

ever overload yourself. I can't bear to think of you looking like the poor women I met in the Pineta at Ravenna just at dusk, having the air of moving druidical altars or sudden toadstools.

Our trees are beginning to turn—the maples are all ablaze, and even in our *ashes* live their wonted fires. The Virginia creeper that I planted against the old horse-chestnut stump trickles down in blood as if its support were one of Dante's living wood. The haze has begun, and the lovely mornings when one blesses the sun. I confess our summer weather too often puts one in mind of Smithfield and the Book of Martyrs.

I have had an adventure. I have dined with a prince. After changing my mind twenty times, I at last sat down desperately and "had the honor to accept." And I was glad of it—for H. I. H.'s resemblance to his uncle is something wonderful. I had always supposed the portraits of the elder Nap imperialized, but Jerome N. looks as if he had sat for that picture where the emperor lies reading on a sofa—you remember it. A trifle weaker about the mouth, suggesting loss of teeth; but it is not so, for his teeth are exquisite. He looks as you would fancy his uncle if he were *Empereur de Ste. Hélène, roi d'Yvetôt*. I sat next to colonel Ragon, who led the forlorn hope at the taking of the Malakoff and was at the siege of Rome. He was a very pleasant fellow. (I don't feel quite sure of my English yet— J'ai tant parlé Français que je trouve beaucoup de difficulté à m'y déshabituer.) Pendant—I mean during—the dinner Ooendel Homes récitait des vers vraiment jolis. Il arrivait déjà au bout, quand M. Ragon, se tournant vers moi d'un air mêlé d'intelligence et d'interrogation, et à la même fois d'un Colomb qui fait la découverte d'un monde tout nouveau, s'écria, "C'est en vers, Monsieur, n'est ce pas?" St'anegdot charmang j'ai rahcontay ah Ooendell daypwee, avec days eclah de reer. (See Bolmar.) Mr. Everett made a speech ou il y avait un soupçon de longueur. The prince replied most gracefully, as one

> "Who saying nothing yet saith all."

He speaks French exquisitely—foi de professeur. Ho parlato anche Italiano col Colonello, chi è stato sei anne in Italia, and I believe I should have tried Hebrew with the secretary of legation, who looked like a Jew, if I had had the chance. After dinner the prince was brought up and *presented to me!* Please remember that when we meet. The political part of our conversation of course I am not at liberty to repeat (!!), but he asked me whether I myself occupied of any work literary at present? to which I answered, no. Then he spoke of the factories at Lowell and Lawrence, and said how much the intelligence of the operatives had interested him, etc., etc. He said that Boston seemed to have much more movement intellectual than the rest of the country (to which I replied, *nous* le croyons, au moins); astonished himself at the freedom of opinion here, etc., at the absence of Puritanism and the like. I thought him very intelligent and thanked him for his bo deescoor o saynah Frongsay shure lays ahfair deetahlee. (See Bolmar again, which I took in my pocket.) . . .

> Ever yours,
> J. R. L.

[Æt. 46]

TO MISS NORTON
[HOT WEATHER; THE "COMMEMORATION ODE"]

Elmwood, July 25, 1865.

MY DEAR JANE,—

However statures and wits may degenerate, and we become, as Donne says, "our fathers' shadows cast at noon," July keeps his old force and is pleasing himself to-day with a noble display of it. It is so hot that the very locusts are dumb and cannot endure to carry on their own trade of spinning out "their long-drawn, red-hot wires of shrilly song," as they are called in a lost poem of Pindar's, from which I translate by direct inspiration of a scholiast turned table-tipper. Each under his cool leaf is taking his siesta. There is an unpleasing moisture even in the slender palms of the flies that fondle the restiff tip of my nose. The thin gray lives of mosquitoes are burnt up and evaporate. My anxious shirt-collar still stiffly holds its undiminished state, but with a damp foreboding of its doom. In short, dear Jane, it is just such a day as the Clerk of the Weather, abusing his opportunities, invariably appoints for public festivities— just such a day as were the Wednesday, Thursday, and Friday of last week. Nevertheless, I am here among my books and I am in a literal sense alive. I eat and smoke and sleep and go through all the nobler functions of a man mechanically still, and wonder at myself as at something outside of and alien to Me. For have I not worked myself lean on an "Ode for Commemoration"? Was I not so rapt with the fervor of conception as I have not been these ten years, losing my sleep, my appetite, and my flesh, those attributes to which I before alluded as nobly uniting us in a common nature with our kind? Did I not for two days exasperate everybody that came near me by reciting passages in order to try them on? Did I not even fall backward and downward to the old folly of hopeful youth, and think I had written something *really* good at last? And am I not now enduring those retributive dumps which ever follow such sinful exultations, the Erynnyes of Vanity? Did not I make John Holmes and William Story shed tears by my recitation of it (my ode) in the morning, both of 'em fervently declaring it was "noble"? Did not even the silent Rowse declare 'twas in a higher mood than much or most of later verse? Did not I think, in my nervous exhilaration, that 'twould be *the* feature (as reporters call it) of the day? And, after all, have I not a line in the *Daily Advertiser* calling it a "graceful poem" (or "some graceful verses," I forget which), which "was received with applause"? Why, Jane, my legs are those of grasshoppers, and my head is an autumn threshing-floor, still beating with the alternate flails of strophe and antistrophe, and an infinite virtue is gone out of me somehow—but it seems *not* into my verse as I dreamed. Well, well, Charles will like it—but then he always does, so what's the use? I am Icarus now with the cold salt sea over him instead of the warm exulting blue of ether. I am gone under, and I will never be a fool again. You read between the lines, don't you, my dear old friend, if I may dare to call a woman so? You know my foibles—women always know our foibles, confound them!—though they always wink at the right moment and seem not to see—bless them! Like a boy, I mistook my excitement for inspiration, and here I am in the mud. You see also I am a little disappointed and a little few (*un petit peu*) vexed. I did *not* make the hit I expected, and am ashamed at having been again tempted into thinking I could write poetry, a delusion from which I have been tolerably free these dozen years. . . .

26th.

The Storys have got home and look as young as ever. I first saw William on Commencement day, and glad enough I was. A friendship counting nearly forty years is the finest kind of shade-tree I know of. One is safe from thunder beneath it, as under laurel—nay, more safe, for the critical bolts do not respect the sacred tree any more than if it were so much theatrical green baize. To be sure, itself is of the harmless theatrical kind often enough. Well, he and two more came up hither after dinner, and we talked and laughed and smoked and drank Domdechanei till there wasn't a bald head nor a gray hair among us. Per Bacco and tobacco, how wisely silly we were! I forgot for a few blessed hours that I was a professor, and felt as if I were something real. But Phi Beta came next day, and *wasn't* I tired! Presiding from 9 A.M. till 6½ P.M. is no joke, and then up next morning at ½ past 4 to copy out and finish my ode. I have not got cool yet (I mean as to nerves), and lie awake at night thinking how much better my verses might have been, only I can't make 'em so. Well, I am printing fifty copies in 4to, and Charles will like it, as I said before, and I sha'nt, because I thought too well of it at first. . . .

Yours always,

J. R. L.

[Æt. 48]

TO C. E. NORTON
["SUCH STUFF·AS STARS ARE MADE OF"]

Elmwood, July 18, 1867.

. . . Emerson's oration was more disjointed than usual, even with *him*. It began nowhere and ended everywhere, and yet, as always with that divine man, it left you feeling that something beautiful had passed that way—something more beautiful than anything else, like the rising and setting of stars. Every possible criticism might have been made on it but one—that it was not noble. There was a tone in it that awakened all elevating associations. He boggled, he lost his place, he had to put on his glasses; but it was as if a creature from some fairer world had lost his way in our fogs, and it was *our* fault, not his. It was chaotic, but it was all such stuff as stars are made of, and and you couldn't help feeling that, if you waited awhile, all that was nebulous would be whirled into planets, and would assume the mathematical gravity of system. All through it I felt something in me that cried "Ha, ha, to the sound of the trumpets!". . .

[Æt. 50]

TO MISS NORTON
[ON LETTER-WRITING]

Elmwood, April 6th, 1869.

. . . Authors, my altogether dear woman, can't write letters. At best they squeeze out an essay now and then, burying every natural sprout in a dry and dreary *sand-flood*, as unlike as possible to those delightful freshets with which your heart overflows the paper. *They* are thinking of their punctuation, of crossing their *t*'s and dotting their *i*'s, and cannot forget themselves in their correspondent, which I take to be the true recipe for a letter. . . . Now, you know that the main excellence of Cambridge is that nothing ever happens there. Since the founding of the College, in 1636, there has been, properly speaking, no event till J. H. began to build his shops on the parsonage-lot.

. . . Elmwood is Cambridge at the fifth power, and indeed one of the great merits of the country is that it narcotizes instead of stimulating. Even Voltaire, who had wit at will, found Ferney an opiate, and is forced to apologize to *his* cleverest correspondent, Mme. du Deffand (do you remark the adroitness of the compliment in my italicized pronoun?) for the prolonged gaps, or yawns, in his letter-writing. Cowper, a first-rate epistolizer, was sometimes driven to the wall in the same way. There is something more than mere vacancy, there is a deep principle of human nature, in the first question of man to man when they meet—"What is the news?" A hermit has none. I fancy if I were suddenly snatched away to London, my brain would prickle all over, as a foot that has been asleep when the blood starts in it again. Books are good dry forage; we can keep alive on them; but, after all, men are the only fresh pasture. . . .

We have had a very long winter with very little snow. It is still cold, but the birds are come, and the impatient lovers among them insist on its being spring. I heard a blue-bird several weeks ago, but the next day came six inches of snow. The sparrows were the first persistent singers, and yesterday the robins were loud. I have no doubt the pines at Shady Hill are all a-creak with blackbirds by this time. . . .

I have nothing else in the way of novelty, except an expedient I hit upon for my hens who were backward with their eggs. On rainy days I set William to reading aloud to them the Lay-Sermons of Coleridge, and the effect was magical. Whether their consciences were touched or they wished to escape the preaching, I know not. . . .

[Æt. 50]

TO T. B. ALDRICH
["THE STORY OF A BAD BOY"]

Elmwood, Nov. 30, 1869.

MY DEAR ALDRICH,—

It is a capital little book—but I had read it all before, and liked it thoroughly. It has been pretty much all my novel reading all summer. I think it is wholesome, interesting, and above all, natural. The only quarrel I have with you is that I found in it that infamous word "transpired." E-pluribus-unum it! Why not "happened"? You are on the very brink of the pit. I read in the paper t'other day that some folks had "extended a dinner to the Hon." Somebody or other. There was something pleasing to the baser man in fancying it held out in a pair of tongs, as too many of our Hon'bles deserve—but consider where English is going!

I know something about Rivermouth myself; only before you were born. I remember in my seventh year opening a long red chest in the "mansion" of the late famous Dr. Brackett, and being confronted with a skeleton—the first I had ever seen. The "Mysteries of Udolpho" were nothing to it, for a child, somehow, is apt to think that these anatomies are always made so by foul means, a creed which I still hold to a certain extent.

However, I am not writing to tell you about myself—but merely to say how much I like your little book. I wish it had been twice as large! I shall send you a thin one of my own before long, and shall be content if it give you half the pleasure. Make my kind remembrances acceptable to Mrs. Aldrich, and tell the twins I wish they may both grow up Bad Boys.

Cordially yours,
J. R. Lowell.

[Æt. 53]

TO C. E. NORTON
["the idylls of the king" and "real arthurian romance"]

Hôtel de Lorraine, No. 7 Rue de Beaune,
Paris, Dec. 4, 1872.

. . . Oddly enough when I got your letter about Tennyson's poems I had just finished reading a *real* Arthurian romance— "Fergus"—not one of the best, certainly, but having that merit of being a genuine blossom for which no triumph of artifice can compensate; having, in short, that *woodsy* hint and tantalization of perfume which is so infinitely better than anything more defined. Emerson had left me Tennyson's book; so last night I took it to bed with me and finished it at a gulp—reading like a naughty boy till half-past one. The contrast between his pomp and my old rhymer's simpleness was very curious and even instructive. One bit of the latter (which I cannot recollect elsewhere) amused me a good deal as a Yankee. When Fergus comes to Arthur's court and Sir Kay "sarses" him (which, you know, is *de rigeur* in the old poems), Sir Gawain saunters up *whittling a stick* as a medicine against ennui. So afterwards, when Arthur is dreadfully bored by hearing no news of Fergus, he reclines at table without any taste for his dinner, and whittles to purge his heart of melancholy. I suppose a modern poet would not dare to come so near Nature as this lest she should fling up her heels. But I am not yet "af wi' the auld love," nor quite "on with the new." There are very fine childish things in Tennyson's poems and fine manly things, too, as it seems to me, but I conceive the theory to be wrong. I have the same feeling (I am not wholly sure of its justice) that I have when I see these modern-mediæval pictures. I am defrauded; I do not see reality, but a masquerade. The costumes are all that is genuine, and the people inside them are shams—which, I take it, is just the reverse of what ought to be. One special criticism I should make on Tennyson's new Idylls, and that is that the similes are so often dragged in by the hair. They seem to be taken (*à la* Tom Moore) from notebooks, and not suggested by the quickened sense of association in the glow of composition. Sometimes it almost seems as if the verses were made for the similes, instead of being the cresting of a wave that heightens as it rolls. This is analogous to the costume objection and springs perhaps from the same cause—the making of poetry with malice prepense. However, I am not going to forget the lovely things that Tennyson has written, and I think they give him rather hard measure now. However, it is the natural recoil of a too rapid fame. Wordsworth had the true kind—an unpopularity that roused and stimulated while he was strong enough to despise it, and honor, obedience, troops of friends, when the grasshopper would have been a burthen to the drooping shoulders. Tennyson, to be sure, has been childishly petulant; but what have these whipper-snappers, who cry "Go up, bald head," done that can be named with some things of his? He has been the greatest artist in words we have had since Gray—and remember how Gray holds his own with little fuel, but real fire. He had the secret of the inconsumable oil, and so, I fancy, has Tennyson.

I keep on picking up books here and there, but I shall be forced to stop, for I find I have got beyond my income. Still, I shall try gradually to make my Old French and Provençal collection tolerably complete, for the temptation is great where the field is definitely bounded. . . .

[Æt. 59]

TO MISS GRACE NORTON
[IMMORTALITY]

Madrid, March 7, 1878.

. . . I don't care where the notion of immortality came from. If it sprang out of a controlling necessity of our nature, some instinct of self-protection and preservation, like the color of some of Darwin's butterflies, at any rate it is there and as real as that, and I mean to hold it fast. Suppose we don't *know*, how much *do* we know after all? There are times when one doubts his own identity, even his own material entity, even the solidity of the very earth on which he walks. One night, the last time I was ill, I lost all consciousness of my flesh. I was dispersed through space in some inconceivable fashion, and mixed with the Milky Way. It was with great labor that I gathered myself again and brought myself within compatible limits, or so it seemed; and yet the very fact that I had a confused consciousness all the while of the Milky Way as something to be mingled with proved that I was there as much an individual as ever. . . .

[*Æt.* 63]

TO W. D. HOWELLS
[ADVICE TO AN AUTHOR]

Ashridge, Berkhampstead, Dec. 21, 1882.

DEAR HOWELLS,—

I was very glad to get your letter, though it put me under
bonds to be wiser than I have ever had the skill to be. If I
remember rightly, Panurge's doubts were increased by con-
sulting the Oracle, but how did the Oracle feel? Did it ever
occur to you that a certain share of our sympathy should go in
that direction?

My best judgment is this, and like all good judgment it is
to a considerable degree on both sides of the question. If you
are able now, without overworking mind or body, to keep the
wolf from the door and to lay by something for a rainy day—
and I mean, of course, without being driven to work with your
left hand because the better one is tired out—I should refuse the
offer, or should hesitate to accept it. If you are a systematic
worker, independent of moods, and sure of your genius whenever you want it, there might be no risk in accepting. You
would have the advantage of a fixed income to fall back on. Is
this a greater advantage than the want of it would be as a spur
to industry? Was not the occasion of Shakespeare's plays (I
don't say the motive of 'em) that he *had* to write? And are
any of us likely to be better inspired than he? Does not inspiration, in some limited sense at least, come with the exercise
thereof, as the appetite with eating? Is not your hand better
for keeping it in, as they say? A professorship takes a great
deal of time, and, if you teach in any more direct way than by
lectures, uses up an immense stock of nerves. Your inevitable
temptation (in some sort your duty) will be to make yourself
learned—which you haven't the least need to be as an author
(if you only have me at your elbow to correct your English
now and then, naughty boy!). If you can make your professorship a thing apart—but can you and be honest? I believe the
present generation doesn't think I was made for a poet, but I

think I could have gone nearer convincing 'em if I had not estranged the muse by donning a professor's gown. I speak of myself because you wanted my experience. I am naturally indolent, and being worked pretty hard in the College, was willing to be content with the amount of work that was squeezed out of me by my position, and let what my nature might otherwise have forced me into go. As I said before, if you can reckon on your own temperament, accept. If you have a doubt, *don't*. I think you will divine what I am driving at.

I find everybody here reading your books, and you know very well how much pleasure that gives me. They wish to see you, and I hope when you come back you will stay and let 'em do it. I wish you could know my hostess, for instance— noble in all senses of the word. I am staying here for a few days with a large party in a house as big as a small town, and a beautiful country of hill and dale and gray birch woods. Enough to say that there was once a convent here. The monks always had an eye for country.

You will have to be very fine when you show yourself in England, to look like the portrait I have painted of you—but I am willing to take the venture.

Inexorable lunch has sounded, and I must say good-by. I should say, on the whole—it is safe to ask my advice, but not to follow it. But then people never do.

. . . Love to all.

Affectionately yours,
J. R. L.

[Æt. 70]

TO MRS. LESLIE STEPHEN
[A GRAVE ROOK]

Whitby, Sept. 11, 1889.

. . . For the last few days we have been having American weather, except for the haze which softens and civilizes (perhaps I should say, artistically generalizes) all it touches, like the slower hand of time. It does in a moment what the other is too long about for the brevity of our lives. How I do love this unemphatic landscape, which suggests but never defines, in which so much license is left to conjecture and divination, as when one looks into the mysterious beyond. And how the robins and some other little minstrels whose names I don't know keep on pretending it is the very fresh of the year. I think few people are made as happy by the singing of birds as I, and this autumnal music (unknown at home), every bush a song, is one of the things that especially endear England to me. Even without song, birds are a perpetual delight, and the rooks alone are enough to make this country worth living in. I wish you could see a rook who every morning busies himself among the chimney-pots opposite my chamber window. For a good while I used to hear his chuckle, but thought he was only flying over. But one day I got out of bed and looked out. There he was on the top of a chimney opposite, perambulating gravely, and now and then cocking his head and looking down a flue. Then he would chuckle and go to another. Then to the next chimney and *da capo*. He found out what they were going to have for breakfast in every house, and whether he enjoyed an imaginary feast or reckoned on a chance at some of the leavings I know not, but he was evidently enjoying himself, and that is always a consoling thing to see. Even in the stingy back-yards of these houses too, wherever there is a disconsolate shrub, a robin comes every morning to cheer it up a bit and help it along through the day.

Since I wrote what I did about the weather (one should always let the Eumenides alone) it has begun to rain, but gently, like a rain that was trying to discriminate between the just and the unjust, and sympathized with those confiding enough to leave their umbrellas behind them (I hate to expose *mine* any more than I can help, for reasons of my own). So the rain let me get back dry from the beach, whither I had gone for a whiff of salt air and a few earfuls of that muffled crash of the surf which is so soothing—perpetual ruin with perpetual renewal.

I wonder if your moors have been as gracious as ours this year. I never know how deeply they impress me till long after

I have left them, and then I wonder at the store of images where-with they have peopled my memory. But what is the use of my asking you any questions when you tell me you could not read my last letter? Was it the blue paper with its ribs that made a corduroy road for my pen to jolt over, I wonder, or my failing eyesight, or—and this is saddest to think of—the dulness of the letter itself? Is this better? I am trying to write as well as I can for my dear and admirable friend, but what would you have? How should one write letters worth reading who has so many to write as I? But never mind. The true use of a letter is to let one know that one is remembered and valued, and as you are sure of that, perhaps I need not write at all! No, the true use of writing is that it brings your friend to you as you write, and so I have your sweet society for a while, and you need have only just as much of mine as you choose to give yourself. . . .

[Æt. 70]

TO THE MISSES LAWRENCE
[LIFE AT ELMWOOD]

Elmwood, Cambridge, Mass.,
Jan. 2, 1890.

. . . Here I am again in the house where I was born longer ago than you can remember, though I wish you more New Year's days than I have had. 'Tis a pleasant old house just about twice as old as I am, four miles from Boston, in what was once the country and is now a populous suburb. But it still has some ten acres of open about it, and some fine old trees. When the worst comes to the worst (if I live so long) I shall still have four and a half acres left with the house, the rest belonging to my brothers and sisters or their heirs. It is a square house with four rooms on a floor, like some houses of the Georgian era I have seen in English provincial towns, only they are of brick and this is of wood. But it is solid with its heavy oaken beams, the spaces between which in the four outer walls are filled in with brick, though you mustn't fancy a brick-

and-timber house, for outwardly it is sheathed with wood. Inside there is much wainscot (of deal) painted white in the fashion of the time when it was built. It is very sunny, the sun rising so as to shine (at an acute angle, to be sure) through the northern windows, and going round the other three sides in the course of the day. There is a pretty staircase with the quaint old twisted banisters—which they call balusters now, but mine are banisters. My library occupies two rooms opening into each other by arches at the sides of the ample chimneys. The trees I look out on are the earliest things I remember. There you have me in my new-old quarters. But you must not fancy a large house—rooms sixteen feet square and, on the ground floor, nine high. It was large, as things went here, when it was built, and has a certain air of amplitude about it as from some inward sense of dignity.

Now for out of doors. What do you suppose the thermometer is about on this second day of January? I was going to say he was standing on his head—at any rate he has forgotten what he's about and is marking sixty-three degrees Fahrenheit on the north side of the house and in the shade! Where is that sense of propriety that once belonged to the seasons? This is flat communism, January insisting on going halves with May. News I have none, nor other resources, as you see, save those of the special correspondent, who takes to description when events fail. Yes, I have one event. I dine to-night with Mr. R. C. Winthrop, who remembers your father very well nearly sixty years ago.

I have all my grandchildren with me, five of them, and the eldest boy is already conspiring with a beard! It is awful, this stealthy advance of Time's insupportable foot. There are two ponies for the children and two dogs, bull-terriers, and most amiable creatures. This is my establishment, and four of the weans have had the *grippe*. I remember it here in '31, I think it was. You see I make all I can of age's one privilege—that of having a drearier memory than other folks.

I forgot one thing. There are plenty of mice in the walls, and, now that I can't go to the play with you, I assist at their little tragedies and comedies behind the wainscot in the night-hours and build up plots in my fancy. 'Tis a French company, for I hear them distinctly say *wee, wee*, sometimes. My life, you see, is not without its excitements, and what are your London mice doing that is more important? I see you are to have a Parnell scandal at last, but I overheard an elopement the other night behind the wainscot, and the solicitors talking it over with the desolated husband afterwards. It was very exciting. Ten thousand grains of corn damaged!

Good-by, and take care of yourselves till I come with the daffodils. I wish you both many a happy New Year and a share for me in some of them. Poets seem to live long nowadays, and I, too, live in Arcadia after my own fashion.

Affectionately yours,

J. R. L.

JOURNALS

FROM LEAVES FROM MY JOURNAL IN ITALY

At Sea

(1854)

The sea was meant to be looked at from shore, as mountains are from the plain. Lucretius made this discovery long ago, and was blunt enough to blurt it forth, romance and sentiment— in other words, the pretence of feeling what we do not feel— being inventions of a later day. To be sure, Cicero used to twaddle about Greek literature and philosophy, much as people do about ancient art now-a-days; but I rather sympathize with those stout old Romans who despised both, and believed that to found an empire was as grand an achievement as to build an epic or to carve a statue. But though there might have been twaddle, (as why not, since there was a Senate?) I rather think Petrarch was the first choragus of that sentimental dance which so long led young folks away from the realities of life like the piper of Hamelin, and whose succession ended, let us hope, with Chateaubriand. But for them, Byron, whose real strength lay in his sincerity, would never have talked about the "sea bounding beneath him like a steed that knows his rider," and all that sort of thing. Even if it had been true, steam has been as fatal to that part of the romance of the sea as to handloom weaving. . . .

The fault of modern travellers is, that they see nothing out of sight. They talk of eocene periods and tertiary formations, and tell us how the world looked to the plesiosaur. They take science (or nescience) with them, instead of that soul of generous trust their elders had. All their senses are sceptics and doubters, materialists reporting things for other sceptics to doubt still further upon. Nature becomes a reluctant witness upon the stand, badgered with geologist hammers and phials of acid.

There have been no travellers since those included in Hakluyt
and Purchas, except Martin, perhaps, who saw an inch or two
into the invisible at the Western Islands. We have peripatetic lecturers, but no more travellers. Travellers' stories are no
longer proverbial. We have picked nearly every apple (wormy
or otherwise) from the world's tree of knowledge, and that without an Eve to tempt us. Two or three have hitherto hung luckily
beyond reach on a lofty bough shadowing the interior of Africa,
but there is a German Doctor at this very moment pelting them
with sticks and stones. It may be only next week, and these
too, bitten by geographers and geologists, will be thrown away.

Analysis is carried into everything. Even Deity is subjected
to chemic tests. We must have exact knowledge, a cabinet
stuck full of facts pressed, dried, or preserved in spirits, instead of the large, vague world our fathers had. With them
science was poetry; with us, poetry is science. Our modern
Eden is a *hortus siccus*. Tourists defraud rather than enrich us.
They have not that sense of æsthetic proportion which characterized the elder traveller. Earth is no longer the fine work of
art it was, for nothing is left to the imagination. Job Hortop,
arrived at the height of the Bermudas, thinks it full time to
indulge us in a merman. Nay, there is a story told by Webster, in his "Witchcraft," of a merman with a mitre, who, on
being sent back to his watery diocese of finland, made what advances he could toward an episcopal benediction by bowing
his head thrice. Doubtless he had been consecrated by St.
Antony of Padua. A dumb bishop would be sometimes no
unpleasant phenomenon, by the way. Sir John Hawkins is not
satisfied with telling us about the merely sensual Canaries, but
is generous enough to throw us in a handful of "certain flitting
islands" to boot. Henry Hawkes describes the visible Mexican
cities, and then is not so frugal but that he can give us a few invisible ones. Thus do these generous ancient mariners make
children of us again. Their successors show us an earth effete
and in a double sense past bearing, tracing out with the eyes of
industrious fleas every wrinkle and crowfoot.

The journals of the elder navigators are prose Odysseys.

The geographies of our ancestors were works of fancy and imagination. They read poems where we yawn over items. Their world was a huge wonder-horn, exhaustless as that which Thor strove to drain. Ours would scarce quench the small thirst of a bee. No modern voyager brings back the magical foundation-stones of a Tempest. No Marco Polo, traversing the desert beyond the city of Lok, would tell of things able to inspire the mind of Milton with

> "Calling shapes and beckoning shadows dire,
> And airy tongues that syllable men's names
> On sands and shores and desert wildernesses."

It was easy enough to believe the story of Dante, when two thirds of even the upper-world were yet untraversed and unmapped. With every step of the recent traveller our inheritance of the wonderful is diminished. Those beautifully pictured notes of the Possible are redeemed at a ruinous discount in the hard and cumbrous coin of the Actual. How are we not defrauded and impoverished? Does California vie with El Dorado? or are Bruce's Abyssinian kings a set-off for Prester John? A bird in the bush is worth two in the hand. And if the philosophers have not even yet been able to agree whether the world has any existence independent of ourselves, how do we not gain a loss in every addition to the catalogue of Vulgar Errors? Where are the fishes which nidificated in trees? Where the monopodes sheltering themselves from the sun beneath their single umbrella-like foot,—umbrella-like in everything but the fatal necessity of being borrowed? Where the Acephali, with whom Herodotus, in a kind of ecstasy, wound up his climax of men with abnormal top-pieces? Where the Roc whose eggs are possibly boulders, needing no far-fetched theory of glacier or iceberg to account for them? Where the tails of the men of Kent? Where the no legs of the bird of paradise? Where the Unicorn, with that single horn of his, sovereign against all manner of poisons? Where that Thessalian spring, which, without cost to the country, convicted and punished perjurers? Where the Amazons of Orellana? Where,

in short, the Fountain of Youth? All these, and a thousand
other varieties, we have lost, and have got nothing instead of
them. And those who have robbed us of them have stolen
that which not enriches themselves. It is so much wealth cast
into the sea beyond all approach of diving-bells. We owe no
thanks to Mr. J. E. Worcester, whose Geography we studied
enforcedly at school. Yet even he had his relentings, and in
some softer moment vouchsafed us a fine, inspiring print of
the Maelstrom, answerable to the twenty-four mile diameter
of its suction. Year by year, more and more of the world gets
disenchanted. Even the icy privacy of the arctic and antarctic
circles is invaded. Our youth are no longer ingenuous, as
indeed no ingenuity is demanded of them. Everything is accounted for, everything cut and dried, and the world may be
put together as easily as the fragments of a dissected map. The
Mysterious bounds nothing now on the North, South, East, or
West. We have played Jack Horner with our earth, till there
is never a plum left in it.

In the Mediterranean

The first sight of a shore so historical as that of Europe gives
an American a strange thrill. What we always feel the artistic
want of at home is background. It is all idle to say we are
Englishmen, and that English history is ours too. It is precisely in this that we are *not* Englishmen, inasmuch as we only
possess their history through our minds, and not by life-long
association with a spot and an idea we call England. History
without the soil it grew in is more instructive than inspiring,—
an acquisition, and not an inheritance. It is laid away in our
memories, and does not run in our veins. Surely, in all that
concerns æsthetics, Europeans have us at an immense advantage.
They start at a point which we arrive at after weary years, for
literature is not shut up in books, nor art in galleries: both are
taken in by unconscious absorption through the finer pores of
mind and character in the atmosphere of society. We are not
yet out of our Crusoe-hood, and must make our own tools as
best we may. Yet I think we shall find the good of it one of

these days, in being thrown back more wholly on nature; and our literature, when we have learned to feel our own strength, and to respect our own thought because it is ours, and not because the European Mrs. Grundy agrees with it, will have a fresh flavor and a strong body that will recommend it, especially as what we import is watered more and more liberally with every vintage.

My first glimpse of Europe was the shore of Spain. One morning a cream-colored blur on the now unwavering horizon's edge was pointed out to me as Cadiz. Since we got into the Mediterranean, we have been becalmed for some days within easy view of land. All along are fine mountains, brown all day, and with a bloom on them at sunset like that of a ripe plum. Here and there at their feet little white towns are sprinkled along the edge of the water, like the grains of rice dropped by the princess in the story. Sometimes we see larger buildings on the mountain slopes, probably convents. I sit and wonder whether the farther peaks may not be the Sierra Morena (the rusty saw) of Don Quixote. I resolve that they shall be, and am content. Surely latitude and longitude never showed me any particular respect, that I should be over-scrupulous with them.

But after all, Nature, though she may be more beautiful, is nowhere so entertaining as in man, and the best thing I have seen and learned at sea is our Chief Mate. My first acquaintance with him was made over my knife, which he asked to look at, and, after a critical examination, handed back to me, saying, "I shouldn't wonder if that was e'er a good piece o' stuff." Since then he has transferred a part of his regard for my knife to its owner. I like folks who like an honest bit of steel, and take no interest whatever in "your Raphaels, Correggios, and stuff." There is always more than the average human nature in a man who has a hearty sympathy with iron. It is a manly metal, with no sordid associations like gold and silver. My sailor fully came up to my expectation on further acquaintance. He might well be called an old salt who had been wrecked on Spitzbergen before I was born. He was not an American, but

I should never have guessed it by his speech, which was the
purest Cape Cod, and I reckon myself a good taster of dialects.
Nor was he less Americanized in all his thoughts and feelings,
a singular proof of the ease with which our omnivorous country assimilates foreign matter, provided it be Protestant, for he
was a grown man ere he became an American citizen. He used
to walk the deck with his hands in his pockets, in seeming abstraction, but nothing escaped his eye. *How* he saw, I could
never make out, though I had a theory that it was with his
elbows. After he had taken me (or my knife) into his confidence, he took care that I should see whatever he deemed of interest to a landsman. Without looking up, he would say, suddenly, "Ther's a whale blowin' clearn up to win'ard," or,
"Them's porpises to leeward: that means chănge o' wind." He
is as impervious to cold as a polar bear, and paces the deck
during his watch much as one of those yellow hummocks goes
slumping up and down his cage. On the Atlantic, if the wind
blew a gale from the northeast, and it was cold as an English
summer, he was sure to turn out in a calico shirt and trousers,
his furzy brown chest half bare, and slippers, without stockings.
But lest you might fancy this to have chanced by defect of
wardrobe, he comes out in a monstrous pea-jacket here in the
Mediterranean, when the evening is so hot that Adam would
have been glad to leave off his fig-leaves. "It's a kind o' damp
and unwholesome in these 'ere waters," he says, evidently regarding the Midland Sea as a vile standing-pool, in comparison
with the bluff ocean. At meals he is superb, not only for his
strengths, but his weaknesses. He has somehow or other come
to think me a wag, and if I ask him to pass the butter, detects
an occult joke, and laughs as much as is proper for a mate. For
you must know that our social hierarchy on shipboard is
precise, and the second mate, were he present, would only
laugh half as much as the first. Mr. X. always combs his hair,
and works himself into a black frock-coat (on Sundays he adds
a waistcoat) before he comes to meals, sacrificing himself nobly
and painfully to the social proprieties. The second mate, on
the other hand, who eats after us, enjoys the privilege of shirt-

sleeves, and is, I think, the happier man of the two. We do not have seats above and below the salt, as in old time, but above and below the white sugar. Mr. X. always takes brown sugar, and it is delightful to see how he ignores the existence of certain delicates which he considers above his grade, tipping his head on one side with an air of abstraction, so that he may seem not to deny himself, but to omit helping himself from inadvertence or absence of mind. At such times he wrinkles his forehead in a peculiar manner, inscrutable at first as a cuneiform inscription, but as easily read after you once get the key. The sense of it is something like this: "I, X., know my place, a height of wisdom attained by few. Whatever you may think, I do *not* see that currant jelly, nor that preserved grape. Especially, a kind Providence has made me blind to bowls of white sugar, and deaf to the pop of champagne corks. It is much that a merciful compensation gives me a sense of the dingier hue of Havana, and the muddier gurgle of beer. Are there potted meats? My physician has ordered me three pounds of minced salt-junk at every meal." There is such a thing, you know, as a ship's husband: X. is the ship's poor relation.

As I have said, he takes also a below-the-white-sugar interest in the jokes, laughing by precise point of compass, just as he would lay the ship's course, all *yawing* being out of the question with his scrupulous decorum at the helm. Once or twice I have got the better of him, and touched him off into a kind of compromised explosion, like that of damp fireworks, that splutter and simmer a little, and then go out with painful slowness and occasional relapses. But his fuse is always of the unwillingest, and you must blow your match, and touch him off again and again with the same joke. Or rather, you must magnetize him many times to get him *en rapport* with a jest. This once accomplished, you have him, and one bit of fun will last the whole voyage. He prefers those of one syllable, the *a-b abs* of humor. The gradual fattening of the steward, a benevolent mulatto with whiskers and ear-rings, who looks as if he had been meant for a woman, and had become a man by accident, as in some of those stories of the elder physiologists,

is an abiding topic of humorous comment with Mr. X. "That
'ere stooard," he says, with a brown grin like what you might
fancy on the face of a serious and aged seal, "'s agittin' as fat's a
porpis. He was as thin's a shingle when he come aboord last
v'yge. Them trousis 'll bust yit. He don't darst take 'em off
nights, for the whole ship's company couldn't git him into 'em
agin." And then he turns aside to enjoy the intensity of his
emotion by himself, and you hear at intervals low rumblings,
an indigestion of laughter. He tells me of St. Elmo's fires,
Marvell's *corposants*, though with him the original *corpos santos*
has suffered a sea change, and turned to *comepleasants*, pledges
of fine weather. I shall not soon find a pleasanter companion.
It is so delightful to meet a man who knows just what you do
not. Nay, I think the tired mind finds something in plump
ignorance like what the body feels in cushiony moss. Talk of
the sympathy of kindred pursuits! It is the sympathy of the
upper and nether millstones, both forever grinding the same
grist, and wearing each other smooth. One has not far to seek
for book-nature, artist-nature, every variety of superinduced
nature, in short, but genuine human-nature is hard to find.
And how good it is! Wholesome as a potato, fit company for
any dish. The freemasonry of cultivated men is agreeable,
but artificial, and I like better the natural grip with which manhood recognizes manhood. . . .

A Few Bits of Roman Mosaic

. . . It is not to be doubted that minds are of as many different orders as cathedrals, and that the Gothic imagination is
vexed and discommoded in the vain endeavor to flatten its
pinnacles, and fit itself into the round Roman arches. But if it
be impossible for a man to like everything, it is quite possible
for him to avoid being driven mad by what does not please him;
nay, it is the imperative duty of a wise man to find out what that
secret is which makes a thing pleasing to another. In approaching St. Peter's, one must take his Protestant shoes off his feet,
and leave them behind him, in the Piazza Rusticucci. Otherwise the great Basilica, with those outstretching colonnades of

Bramante, will seem to be a bloated spider lying in wait for him, the poor heretic fly. As he lifts the heavy leathern flapper over the door, and is discharged into the interior by its impetuous recoil, let him disburthen his mind altogether of stone and mortar, and think only that he is standing before the throne of a dynasty which, even in its decay, is the most powerful the world ever saw. Mason-work is all very well in itself, but it has nothing to do with the affair at present in hand.

Suppose that a man in pouring down a glass of claret could drink the South of France, that he could so disintegrate the wine by the force of imagination as to taste in it all the clustered beauty and bloom of the grape, all the dance and song and sunburnt jollity of the vintage. Or suppose that in eating bread he could transubstantiate it with the tender blade of spring, the gleam-flitted corn-ocean of summer, the royal autumn, with its golden beard, and the merry funerals of harvest. This is what the great poets do for us, we cannot tell how, with their fatally-chosen words, crowding the happy veins of language again with all the life and meaning and music that had been dribbling away from them since Adam. And this is what the Roman Church does for religion, feeding the soul not with the essential religious sentiment, not with a drop or two of the tincture of worship, but making us feel one by one all those original elements of which worship is composed; not bringing the end to us, but making us pass over and feel beneath our feet all the golden rounds of the ladder by which the climbing generations have reached that end; not handing us drily a dead and extinguished Q.E.D., but letting it rather declare itself by the glory with which it interfuses the incense-clouds of wonder and aspiration and beauty in which it is veiled. The secret of her power is typified in the mystery of the Real Presence. She is the only church that has been loyal to the heart and soul of man, that has clung to her faith in the imagination, and that would not give over her symbols and images and sacred vessels to the perilous keeping of the iconoclast Understanding. She has never lost sight of the truth, that the product human nature is composed of the sum of flesh and

spirit, and has accordingly regarded both this world and the
next as the constituents of that other world which we possess
by faith. She knows that poor Panza, the body, has his kitchen
longings and visions, as well as Quixote, the soul, his ethereal,
and has wit enough to supply him with the visible, tangible raw
material of imagination. She is the only poet among the
churches, and, while Protestantism is unrolling a pocket sur-
veyor's-plan, takes her votary to the pinnacle of her temple,
and shows him meadow, upland, and tillage, cloudy heaps of
forest clasped with the river's jewelled arm, hillsides white with
the perpetual snow of flocks, and, beyond all, the interminable
heave of the unknown ocean. Her empire may be traced upon
the map by the boundaries of races; the understanding is her
great foe; and it is the people whose vocabulary was incomplete
till they had invented the archword Humbug that defies her.
With that leaden bullet John Bull can bring down Sentiment
when she flies her highest. And the more the pity for John
Bull. One of these days some one whose eyes are sharp
enough will read in the Times a standing advertisement, "Lost,
strayed, or stolen from the farmyard of the subscriber the valuable horse Pegasus. Probably has on him part of a new plough-
harness, as that is also missing. A suitable reward, etc.

J. Bull."

Protestantism reverses the poetical process I have spoken of
above, and gives not even the bread of life, but instead of it the
alcohol, or distilled intellectual result. This was very well so
long as Protestantism continued to protest; for enthusiasm
sublimates the understanding into imagination. But now that
she also has become an establishment, she begins to perceive
that she made a blunder in trusting herself to the intellect alone.
She is beginning to feel her way back again, as one notices in
Puseyism, and other such hints. One is put upon reflection
when one sees burly Englishmen, who dine on beef and porter
every day, marching proudly through St. Peter's on Palm
Sunday, with those frightfully artificial palm-branches in their
hands. Romanism wisely provides for the childish in men.

Therefore I say again, that one must lay aside his Protestantism in order to have a true feeling of St. Peter's. Here in Rome is the laboratory of that mysterious enchantress, who has known so well how to adapt herself to all the wants, or, if you will, the weaknesses of human nature, making the retirement of the convent-cell a merit to the solitary, the scourge or the fast a piety to the ascetic, the enjoyment of pomp and music and incense a religious act in the sensual, and furnishing for the very soul itself a *confidante* in that ear of the dumb confessional, where it may securely disburthen itself of its sins and sorrows. And the dome of St. Peter's is the magic circle within which she works her most potent incantations. I confess that I could not enter it alone without a kind of awe. . . .

Shall I confess it? Michael Angelo seems to me, in his angry reaction against sentimental beauty, to have mistaken bulk and brawn for the antithesis of feebleness. He is the apostle of the exaggerated, the Victor Hugo of painting and sculpture. I have a feeling that rivalry was a more powerful motive with him than love of art, that he had the conscious intention to be original, which seldom leads to anything better than being extravagant. The show of muscle proves strength, not power; and force for mere force's sake in art makes one think of Milo caught in his own log. This is my second thought, and strikes me as perhaps somewhat niggardly toward one in whom you cannot help feeling there was so vast a possibility. And then his Eve, his David, his Sibyls, his Prophets, his Sonnets! Well, I take it all back, and come round to St. Peter's again just to hint that I doubt about domes. In Rome they are so much the fashion that I felt as if they were the *goitre* of architecture. Generally they look heavy. Those on St. Mark's in Venice are the only light ones I ever saw, and they look almost airy, like tents puffed out with wind. I suppose one must be satisfied with the interior effect, which is certainly noble in St. Peter's. But for impressiveness both within and without there is nothing like a Gothic cathedral for me, nothing that crowns a city so nobly, or makes such an island of twilight silence in the midst of its noonday clamors. . . .

I am not ashamed to confess a singular sympathy with what are known as the Middle Ages. I cannot help thinking that few periods have left behind them such traces of inventiveness and power. Nothing is more tiresome than the sameness of modern cities; and it has often struck me that this must also have been true of those ancient ones in which Greek architecture or its derivatives prevailed,—true at least as respects public buildings. But mediæval towns, especially in Italy, even when only fifty miles asunder, have an individuality of character as marked as that of trees. Nor is it merely this originality that attracts me, but likewise the sense that, however old, they are nearer to me in being modern and Christian. Far enough away in the past to be picturesque, they are still so near through sympathies of thought and belief as to be more companionable. I find it harder to bridge over the gulf of Paganism than of centuries. Apart from any difference in the men, I had a far deeper emotion when I stood on the *Sasso di Dante*, than at Horace's Sabine farm or by the tomb of Virgil. The latter, indeed, interested me chiefly by its association with comparatively modern legend; and one of the buildings I am most glad to have seen in Rome is the Bear Inn, where Montaigne lodged on his arrival.

I think it must have been for some such reason that I liked my Florentine better than my Roman walks, though I am vastly more contented with merely being in Rome. Florence is more noisy; indeed, I think it the noisiest town I was ever in. What with the continual jangling of its bells, the rattle of Austrian drums, and the street-cries, *Ancora mi raccapriccia*. The Italians are a vociferous people, and most so among them the Florentines. Walking through a back street one day, I saw an old woman higgling with a peripatetic dealer, who, at every interval afforded him by the remarks of his veteran antagonist, would tip his head on one side, and shout, with a kind of wondering enthusiasm, as if he could hardly trust the evidence of his own senses to such loveliness, *O, che bellezza! che belle-e-ezza!* The two had been contending as obstinately as the Greeks and Trojans over the body of Patroclus, and I was curious to know what was the object of so much desire on the one side and admiration on the other. It was a half-dozen of weazeny baked pears, beggarly remnant of the day's traffic. Another time I stopped before a stall, debating whether to buy some fine-looking peaches. Before I had made up my mind, the vender, a stout fellow, with a voice like a prize-bull of Bashan, opened a mouth round and large as the muzzle of a blunderbuss, and let fly into my ear the following pertinent observation: "*Belle pesche! belle pe-e-esche*" (*crescendo*). I stared at him in stunned bewilderment; but, seeing that he had reloaded and was about to fire again, took to my heels, the exploded syllables rattling after me like so many buckshot. A single turnip is argument enough with them till midnight; nay, I have heard a ruffian yelling over a covered basket, which, I am convinced, was empty, and only carried as an excuse for his stupendous vocalism. It never struck me before what a quiet people Americans are.

Of the pleasant places within easy walk of Rome, I prefer the garden of the Villa Albani, as being most Italian. One does not go to Italy for examples of Price on the Picturesque. Compared with landscape-gardening, it is Racine to Shakespeare, I grant; but it has its own charm, nevertheless. I like the balustraded terraces, the sun-proof laurel walks, the vases and statues. It is only in such a climate that it does not seem inhuman to thrust a naked statue out of doors. Not to speak of their incongruity, how dreary do those white figures look at Fountains Abbey in that shrewd Yorkshire atmosphere! To put them there shows the same bad taste that led Prince Polonia, as Thackeray calls him, to build an artificial ruin within a mile of Rome. But I doubt if the Italian garden will bear transplantation. Farther north, or under a less constant sunshine, it is but half-hardy at the best. Within the city, the garden of the French Academy is my favorite retreat, because little frequented; and there is an arbor there in which I have read comfortably (sitting where the sun could reach me) in January. By the way, there is something very agreeable in the way these people have of making a kind of fireside of the sunshine. With us it is either too hot or too cool, or we are too busy. But, on the other hand, they have no such thing as a chimney-corner.

Of course I haunt the collections of art faithfully; but my favorite gallery, after all, is the street. There I always find something entertaining, at least. The other day, on my way to the Colonna Palace, I passed the Fountain of Trevi, from which the water is now shut off on account of repairs to the aqueduct. A scant rill of soapsudsy liquid still trickled from one of the conduits, and, seeing a crowd, I stopped to find out what nothing or other had gathered it. One charm of Rome is that nobody has anything in particular to do, or, if he has, can always stop doing it on the slightest pretext. I found that some eels had been discovered, and a very vivacious hunt was going on, the chief Nimrods being boys. I happened to be the first to see a huge eel wriggling from the mouth of a pipe, and pointed him out. Two lads at once rushed upon him. One essayed the capture with his naked hands, the other, more provident, had armed himself with a rag of woollen cloth with which to maintain his grip more securely. Hardly had this latter arrested his slippery prize, when a ragged rascal, watching his opportunity, snatched it away, and instantly secured it by thrusting the head into his mouth, and closing on it a set of teeth like an ivory vice. But alas for ill-got gain! Rob Roy's

> "Good old plan,
> That he should take who has the power,
> And he should keep who can,"

did not serve here. There is scarce a square rood in Rome without one or more stately cocked hats in it, emblems of authority and police. I saw the flash of the snow-white cross-belts, gleaming through that dingy crowd like the *panache* of Henri Quatre at Ivry, I saw the mad plunge of the canvas-shielded head-piece, sacred and terrible as that of Gessler; and while the greedy throng were dancing about the anguilliceps, each taking his chance twitch at the undulating object of all wishes, the captor dodging his head hither and thither, (vulnerable, like Achilles, only in his 'eel, as a Cockney tourist

would say,) a pair of broad blue shoulders parted the assailants
as a ship's bows part a wave, a pair of blue arms, terminating in
gloves of Berlin thread, were stretched forth, not in benediction,
one hand grasped the slippery Briseis by the waist, the other
bestowed a cuff on the jaw-bone of Achilles, which loosened
(rather by its authority than its physical force) the hitherto
refractory incisors, a snuffy bandanna was produced, the
prisoner was deposited in this temporary watch-house, and the
cocked hat sailed majestically away with the property thus
sequestered for the benefit of the state.

> "Gaudeant anguillæ si mortuus sit homo ille,
> Qui, quasi morte reas, excruciabat eas!"

If you have got through that last sentence without stopping
for breath, you are fit to begin on the Homer of Chapman, who,
both as translator and author, has the longest wind, (especially
for a comparison,) without being long-winded, of all writers I
know anything of, not excepting Jeremy Taylor.

ESSAYS

From CAMBRIDGE THIRTY YEARS AGO
(1854)

A MEMOIR ADDRESSED TO THE EDELMANN STORG IN ROME.

In those quiet old winter evenings, around our Roman fire-side, it was not seldom, my dear Storg, that we talked of the advantages of travel, and in speeches not so long that our cigars would forget their fire (the measure of just conversation) debated the comparative advantages of the Old and New Worlds. You will remember how serenely I bore the imputation of provincialism, while I asserted that those advantages were reciprocal; that an orbed and balanced life would revolve between the Old and the New as opposite but not antagonistic poles, the true equator lying somewhere midway between them. . . . With this letter I propose to make you my fellow-traveller in one of those fireside voyages which, as we grow older, we make oftener and oftener through our own past. Without leaving your elbow-chair, you shall go back with me thirty years, which will bring you among things and persons as thoroughly preterite as Romulus or Numa. For so rapid are our changes in America that the transition from old to new, the shifting from habits and associations to others entirely different, is as rapid almost as the passing in of one scene and the drawing out of another on the stage. And it is this which makes America so interesting to the philosophic student of history and man. Here, as in a theatre, the great problems of anthropology —which in the Old World were ages in solving, but which are solved, leaving only a dry net result—are compressed, as it were, into the entertainment of a few hours. Here we have I know not how many epochs of history and phases of civilization contemporary with each other, nay, within five minutes of each other, by the electric telegraph. In two centuries we have seen rehearsed the dispersion of man from a small point over a whole continent; we witness with our own eyes the action of those forces which govern the great migration of the peoples now historical in Europe; we can watch the action and reaction of different races, forms of government, and higher or lower civilizations. Over there you have only the dead precipitate, demanding tedious analysis; but here the elements are all in solution, and we have only to look to know them all. History, which every day makes less account of governors and more of man, must find here the compendious key to all that picture-writing of the Past. Therefore it is, my dear Storg, that we Yankees may still esteem our America a place worth living in. But calm your apprehensions; I do not propose to drag you with me on such an historical circumnavigation of the globe, but only to show you that (however needful it may be to go abroad for the study of æsthetics) a man who uses the eyes of his heart may find here also pretty bits of what may be called the social picturesque, and little landscapes over which that Indian-summer atmosphere of the Past broods as sweetly and tenderly as over a Roman ruin. Let us look at the Cambridge of thirty years since.

The seat of the oldest college in America, it had, of course, some of that cloistered quiet which characterizes all university towns. Even now delicately-thoughtful A. H. C. tells me that he finds in its intellectual atmosphere a repose which recalls that of grand old Oxford. But, underlying this, it had an idiosyncrasy of its own. Boston was not yet a city, and Cambridge was still a country village, with its own habits and traditions, not yet feeling too strongly the force of suburban gravitation. Approaching it from the west by what was then called the New Road (it is called so no longer, for we change our names whenever we can, to the great detriment of all historical association), you would pause on the brow of Symonds' Hill to enjoy a view singularly soothing and placid. In front of you lay the town, tufted with elms, lindens, and horse-chestnuts, which had seen Massachusetts a colony, and were fortunately unable to emigrate with the Tories, by whom, or by whose fathers, they were planted. Over it rose the noisy belfry of the College, the square, brown tower of the church, and the slim, yellow spire of the parish meeting-house, by no means ungraceful, and then an invariable characteristic of New England religious architecture. On your right, the Charles slipped smoothly through green and purple salt-meadows, darkened here and there with the blossoming black-grass as with a stranded cloud-shadow. Over these marshes, level as water, but without its glare, and with softer and more soothing gradations of perspective, the eye was carried to a horizon of softly-rounded hills. To your left hand, upon the Old Road, you saw some half dozen dignified old houses of the colonial time, all comfortably fronting southward. If it were early June, the rows of horse-chestnuts along the fronts of these houses showed, through every crevice of their dark heap of foliage, and on the end of every drooping limb, a cone of pearly flowers, while the hill behind was white or rosy with the crowding blooms of various fruit-trees. There is no sound, unless a horseman clatters over the loose planks of the bridge, while his antipodal shadow glides silently over the mirrored bridge below, or unless,

> "O wingèd rapture, feathered soul of spring,
> Blithe voice of woods, fields, waters, all in one,
> Pipe blown through by the warm, mild breath of June
> Shepherding her white flocks of woolly clouds,
> The bobolink has come, and climbs the wind
> With rippling wings that quiver not for flight,
> But only joy, or, yielding to its will,
> Runs down, a brook of laughter, through the air."

Such was the charmingly rural picture which he who thirty years ago went eastward over Symonds' Hill had given him for nothing, to hang in the Gallery of Memory. But we are a city now, and Common Councils have yet no notion of the truth (learned long ago by many a European hamlet) that picturesqueness adds to the actual money value of a town. To save a few dollars in gravel, they have cut a kind of dry ditch through the hill, where you suffocate with dust in summer, or flounder through waist-deep snow-drifts in winter, with no prospect but the crumbling earth-walls on either side. The landscape was carried away cart-load by cart-load, and, dumped down on the roads, forms a part of that unfathomable pudding which has, I fear, driven many a teamster and pedestrian to the use of phrases not commonly found in English dictionaries.

We called it "the Village" then (I speak of Old Cambridge), and it was essentially an English village, quiet, unspeculative, without enterprise, sufficing to itself, and only showing such differences from the original type as the public school and the system of town government might superinduce. A few houses chiefly old, stood around the bare Common, with ample elbow-room, and old women, capped and spectacled, still peered through the same windows from which they had watched Lord Percy's artillery rumble by to Lexington, or caught a glimpse of the handsome Virginia General who had come to wield our homespun Saxon chivalry. People were still living who regretted the late unhappy separation from the mother island, who had seen no gentry since the Vassalls went, and who thought that Boston had ill kept the day of her patron saint, Botolph, on the 17th of June, 1775. The hooks were to be seen from which had swung the hammocks of Burgoyne's captive redcoats. If memory does not deceive me, women still washed clothes in the town spring, clear as that of Bandusia. One coach sufficed for all the travel to the metropolis. Commencement had not ceased to be the great holiday of the Puritan Commonwealth, and a fitting one it was,—the festival of Santa Scolastica, whose triumphal path one may conceive strewn with leaves of spelling-book instead of bay. The students (scholars they were called then) wore their sober uniform, not ostentatiously distinctive or capable of rousing democratic envy, and the old lines of caste were blurred rather than rubbed out, as servitor was softened into beneficiary. The Spanish king was sure that the gesticulating student was either mad or reading Don Quixote, and if, in those days, you met a youth swinging his arms and talking to himself, you might conclude that he was either a lunatic or one who was to appear in a "part" at the next Commencement. A favorite place for the rehearsal of these orations was the retired amphitheatre of the Gravel-pit, perched unregarded on whose dizzy edge, I have heard many a burst of *plusquam Ciceronian* eloquence, and (often repeated) the regular *saluto vos, præstantissimæ,* etc., which every year (with a glance at the gallery) causes a flutter among the fans innocent of Latin, and delights to applauses of conscious superiority the youth almost as innocent as they. It is curious, by the way, to note how plainly one can feel the pulse of self in the plaudits of an audience. At a political meeting, if the enthusiasm of the lieges hang fire, it may be exploded at once by an allusion to their intelligence or patriotism; and at a literary festival, the first Latin quotation draws the first applause, the clapping of hands being intended as a tribute to our own familiarity with that sonorous tongue, and not at all as an approval of the particular sentiment conveyed in it. For if the orator should say, "Well has Tacitus remarked, *Americani omnes quâdam vi naturæ furcâ dignissimi,*" it would be all the same. But the Gravel-pit was patient, if irresponsive; nor did the declaimer always fail to bring down the house, bits of loosened earth falling now and then from the precipitous walls, their cohesion perhaps overcome by the vibrations of the voice, and happily satirizing the effect of most popular discourses, which prevail rather with the earthy than the spiritual part of the hearer. Was it possible for us in those days to conceive of a greater potentate than the President of the University, in his square doctor's cap, that still filially recalled Oxford and Cambridge? If there was a doubt, it was suggested only by the Governor, and even by him on artillery-election days alone, superbly martial with epaulets and buckskin breeches, and bestriding the war-horse, promoted to that solemn duty for his tameness and steady habits.

Thirty years ago, the town had indeed a character. Railways and omnibuses had not rolled flat all little social prominences and peculiarities, making every man as much a citizen everywhere as at home. No Charlestown boy could come to our annual festival without fighting to avenge a certain traditional porcine

imputation against the inhabitants of that historic locality, and
to which our youth gave vent in fanciful imitations of the dialect
of the sty, or derisive shouts of "Charlestown hogs!" The
penny newspaper had not yet silenced the tripod of the barber,
oracle of news. Everybody knew everybody, and all about
everybody, and village wit, whose high 'change was around
the little market-house in the town square, had labelled every
more marked individuality with nicknames that clung like burs.
Things were established then, and men did not run through all
the figures on the dial of society so swiftly as now, when hurry
and competition seem to have quite unhung the modulating
pendulum of steady thrift and competent training. Some slow-
minded persons even followed their father's trade,—a humili-
ating spectacle, rarer every day. We had our established loafers,
topers, proverb-mongers, barber, parson, nay, postmaster,
whose tenure was for life. The great political engine did not
then come down at regular quadrennial intervals, like a nail-
cutting machine, to make all official lives of a standard length,
and to generate lazy and intriguing expectancy. Life flowed in
recognized channels,—narrower, perhaps, but with all the more
individuality and force.

There was but one white-and-yellow-washer, whose own
cottage, fresh-gleaming every June through grape-vine and
creeper, was his only sign and advertisement. He was said to
possess a secret, which died with him like that of Luca della
Robbia, and certainly conceived all colors but white and yellow
to savor of savagery, civilizing the stems of his trees annually
with liquid lime, and meditating how to extend that candent
baptism even to the leaves. His *pie-plants* (the best in town),
compulsory monastics, blanched under barrels, each in his little
hermitage, a vegetable Certosa. His fowls, his ducks, his geese,
could not show so much as a gray feather among them, and he
would have given a year's earnings for a white peacock. The
flowers which decked his little *door-yard* were whitest China-
asters and goldenest sunflowers, which last, back-sliding from
their traditional Parsee faith, used to puzzle us urchins not a
little by staring brazenly every way except towards the sun.

Celery, too, he raised, whose virtue is its paleness, and the silvery onion, and turnip, which, though outwardly conforming to the green heresies of summer, nourish a purer faith subterraneously, like early Christians in the catacombs. In an obscure corner grew the sanguine beet, tolerated only for its usefulness in allaying the asperities of Saturday's salt fish. He loved winter better than summer, because Nature then played the whitewasher, and challenged with her snows the scarce inferior purity of his overalls and neck-cloth. I fancy that he never rightly liked Commencement, for bringing so many black coats together. He founded no school. Others might essay his art, and were allowed to try their prentice hands on fences and the like coarse subjects, but the ceiling of every housewife waited on the leisure of Newman (*ichneumon* the students called him, for his diminutiveness), nor would consent to other brush than his. There was also but one brewer, Lewis, who made the village beer, both spruce and ginger,— a grave and amiable Ethiopian, making a discount always to the boys, and wisely, for they were his chiefest patrons. He wheeled his whole stock in a white-roofed handcart, on whose front a sign-board presented at either end an insurrectionary bottle; yet insurgent after no mad Gallic fashion, but soberly and Saxonly discharging itself into the restraining formulary of a tumbler, symbolic of orderly prescription. The artist had struggled manfully with the difficulties of his subject, but had not succeeded so well that we did not often debate in which of the twin bottles Spruce was typified, and in which Ginger. We always believed that Lewis mentally distinguished between them, but by some peculiarity occult to exoteric eyes. This ambulatory chapel of the Bacchus that gives the colic, but not inebriates, only appeared at the Commencement holidays, and the lad who bought of Lewis laid out his money well, getting respect as well as beer, three *sirs* to every glass,—"Beer, sir? Yes, sir: spruce or ginger, sir?" I can yet recall the innocent pride with which I walked away after that somewhat risky ceremony (for a bottle sometimes blew up), dilated not alone with carbonic acid gas, but with the more ethereal fixed air of that titular flattery. Nor was Lewis proud. When he tried his fortunes in the capital on Election-days, and stood amid a row of rival venders in the very flood of custom, he never forgot his small fellow-citizens, but welcomed them with an assuring smile, and served them with the first.

The barber's shop was a museum, scarce second to the larger one of Greenwood in the metropolis. The boy who was to be clipped there was always accompanied to the sacrifice by troops of friends, who thus inspected the curiosities *gratis*. While the watchful eye of R. wandered to keep in check these rather unscrupulous explorers, the unpausing shears would sometimes overstep the boundaries of strict tonsorial prescription, and make a notch through which the phrenological developments could be distinctly seen. As Michael Angelo's design was modified by the shape of his block, so R., rigid in artistic proprieties, would contrive to give an appearance of design to this aberration by making it the key-note to his work, and reducing the whole head to an appearance of premature baldness. What a charming place it was,—how full of wonder and delight! The sunny little room, fronting southwest upon the Common, rang with canaries and Java sparrows, nor were the familiar notes of robin, thrush, and bobolink wanting. A large white cockatoo harangued vaguely, at intervals, in what we believed (on R.'s authority) to be the Hottentot language. He had an unveracious air, but what inventions of former grandeur he was indulging in, what sweet South African Argos he was remembering, what tropical heats and giant trees by unconjectured rivers, known only to the wallowing hippopotamus, we could only guess at. The walls were covered with curious old Dutch prints, beaks of albatross and penguin, and whales' teeth fantastically engraved. There was Frederick the Great, with head drooped plottingly, and keen side-long glance from under the three-cornered hat. There hung Bonaparte, too, the long-haired, haggard general of Italy, his eyes sombre with prefigured destiny; and there was his island grave,—the dream and the fulfilment. Good store of sea-fights there was also; above all, Paul Jones in the Bonhomme Richard: the smoke rolling courteously to leeward, that we might see him dealing thunderous wreck to the two hostile vessels, each twice as large as his own, and the reality of the scene corroborated by streaks of red paint leaping from the mouth of every gun. Suspended over the fireplace, with the curling-tongs, were an Indian bow and arrows, and in the corners of the room stood New Zealand paddles and war-clubs, quaintly carved. The model of a ship in glass we variously estimated to be worth from a hundred to a thousand dollars, R. rather favoring the higher valuation, though never distinctly committing himself. Among these wonders, the only suspicious one was an Indian tomahawk, which had too much the peaceful look of a shingling-hatchet. Did any rarity enter the town, it gravitated naturally to these walls, to the very nail that waited to receive it, and where, the day after its accession, it seemed to have hung a lifetime. We always had a theory that R. was immensely rich (how could he possess so much and be otherwise?), and that he pursued his calling from an amiable eccentricity. He was a conscientious artist, and never submitted it to the choice of his victim whether he would be perfumed or not. Faithfully was the bottle shaken and the odoriferous mixture rubbed in, a fact redolent to the whole school-room in the afternoon. Sometimes the persuasive tonsor would impress one of the attendant volunteers, and reduce his poll to shoe-brush crispness, at cost of the reluctant ninepence hoarded for Fresh Pond and the next half-holiday. So purely indigenous was our population then that R. had a certain exotic charm, a kind of game flavor, by being a Dutchman. . . .

E PLURIBUS UNUM

(1861)

We do not believe that any government—no, not the Rump Parliament on its last legs—ever showed such pitiful inadequacy as our own during the past two months. Helpless beyond measure in all the duties of practical statesmanship, its members or their dependants have given proof of remarkable energy in the single department of peculation; and there, not content with the slow methods of the old-fashioned defaulter, who helped himself only to what there was, they have contrived to steal what there was going to be, and have peculated in advance by a kind of official post-obit. So thoroughly has the credit of the most solvent nation in the world been shaken, that an administration which still talks of paying a hundred millions for Cuba is unable to raise a loan of five millions for the current expenses of government. Nor is this the worst: the moral bankruptcy at Washington is more complete and disastrous than the financial, and for the first time in our history the Executive is suspected of complicity in a treasonable plot against the very life of the nation.

Our material prosperity for nearly half a century has been so unparalleled that the minds of men have become gradually more and more absorbed in matters of personal concern; and our institutions have practically worked so well and so easily that we have learned to trust in our luck, and to take the permanence of our government for granted. The country has been divided on questions of temporary policy, and the people have been drilled to a wonderful discipline in the manœuvres of party tactics; but no crisis has arisen to force upon them a consideration of the fundamental principles of our system, or to arouse in them a sense of national unity, and make them feel that patriotism was anything more than a pleasant sentiment,— half Fourth of July and half Eighth of January,—a feeble reminiscence, rather than a living fact with a direct bearing on the national well-being. We have had long experience of that unmemorable felicity which consists in having no history, so far as history is made up of battles, revolutions, and changes of dynasty; but the present generation has never been called upon to learn that deepest lesson of politics which is taught by a common danger, throwing the people back on their national instincts, and superseding party-leaders, the peddlers of chicane, with men adequate to great occasions and dealers in destiny. Such a crisis is now upon us; and if the virtue of the people make up for the imbecility of the Executive, as we have little doubt that it will, if the spirit of the whole country be awakened in time by the common peril, the present trial will leave the nation stronger than ever, and more alive to its privileges and the duties they imply. We shall have learned what is meant by a government of laws, and that allegiance to the sober will of the majority, concentrated in established forms and distributed by legitimate channels, is all that renders democracy possible, is its only conservative principle, the only thing that has made and can keep us a powerful nation instead of a brawling mob.

The theory that the best government is that which governs least seems to have been accepted literally by Mr. Buchanan, without considering the qualifications to which all general propositions are subject. His course of conduct has shown up its absurdity, in cases where prompt action is required, as effectually as Buckingham turned into ridicule the famous verse,—

"My wound is great, because it is so small,"

by instantly adding,—

"Then it were greater, were it none at all."

Mr. Buchanan seems to have thought, that, if to govern little was to govern well, then to do nothing was the perfection of policy. But there is a vast difference between letting well alone and allowing bad to become worse by a want of firmness at the outset. If Mr. Buchanan, instead of admitting the right of secession, had declared it to be, as it plainly is, rebellion, he would not only have received the unanimous support of the Free States, but would have given confidence to the loyal, reclaimed the wavering, and disconcerted the plotters of treason in the South.

Either we have no government at all, or else the very word implies the right, and therefore the duty, in the governing power, of protecting itself from destruction and its property from pillage. But for Mr. Buchanan's acquiescence, the doctrine of the right of secession would never for a moment have bewildered the popular mind. It is simply mob-law under a plausible name. Such a claim might have been fairly enough

urged under the old Confederation; though even then it would
have been summarily dealt with, in the case of a Tory colony,
if the necessity had arisen. But the very fact that we have a
National Constitution, and legal methods for testing, preventing, or punishing any infringement of its provisions, demon-
strates the absurdity of any such assumption of right now.
When the States surrendered their power to make war, did they
make the single exception of the United States, and reserve
the privilege of declaring war against them at any moment? If
we are a congeries of mediæval Italian republics, why should
the General Government have expended immense sums in
fortifying points whose strategic position is of continental
rather than local consequence? Florida, after having cost us
nobody knows how many millions of dollars and thousands of
lives to render the holding of slaves possible to her, coolly proposes to withdraw herself from the Union and take with her
one of the keys of the Mexican Gulf, on the plea that her slave-
property is rendered insecure by the Union. Louisiana, which
we bought and paid for to secure the mouth of the Mississippi,
claims the right to make her soil French or Spanish, and to cork
up the river again, whenever the whim may take her. The
United States are not a German Confederation, but a unitary
and indivisible nation, with a national life to protect, a national
power to maintain, and national rights to defend against any
and every assailant, at all hazards. Our national existence is all
that gives value to American citizenship. Without the respect
which nothing but our consolidated character could inspire,
we might as well be citizens of the toy-republic of San Marino,
for all the protection it would afford us. If our claim to a national existence was worth a seven years' war to establish, it is
worth maintaining at any cost; and it is daily becoming more
apparent that the people, so soon as they find that secession
means anything serious, will not allow themselves to be juggled
out of their rights, as members of one of the great powers of
the earth, by a mere quibble of Constitutional interpretation.

We have been so much accustomed to the Buncombe style
of oratory, to hearing men offer the pledge of their lives, for-

tunes, and sacred honor on the most trivial occasions, that we
are apt to allow a great latitude in such matters, and only smile
to think how small an advance any intelligent pawn-broker
would be likely to make on securities of this description. The
sporadic eloquence that breaks out over the country on the eve
of election, and becomes a chronic disease in the two houses of
Congress, has so accustomed us to dissociate words and things,
and to look upon strong language as an evidence of weak
purpose, that we attach no meaning whatever to declamation.
Our Southern brethren have been especially given to these
orgies of loquacity, and have so often solemnly assured us of
their own courage, and of the warlike propensities, power,
wealth, and general superiority of that part of the universe
which is so happy as to be represented by them, that, whatever
other useful impression they have made, they insure our never
forgetting the proverb about the woman who talks of her virtue.
South Carolina, in particular, if she has hitherto failed in the
application of her enterprise to manufacturing purposes of a
more practical kind, has always been able to match every yard
of printed cotton from the North with a yard of printed fustian,
the product of her own domestic industry. We have thought
no harm of this, so long as no Act of Congress required the
reading of the "Congressional Globe." We submitted to the
general dispensation of long-windedness and short-meaning-
ness as to any other providental visitation, endeavoring only to
hold fast our faith in the divine government of the world in the
midst of so much that was past understanding. But we lost
sight of the metaphysical truth, that, though men may fail to
convince others by a never so incessant repetition of sonorous
nonsense, they nevertheless gradually persuade themselves,
and impregnate their own minds and characters with a belief
in fallacies that have been uncontradicted only because not
worth contradiction. Thus our Southern politicians, by dint
of continued reiteration, have persuaded themselves to accept
their own flimsy assumptions for valid statistics, and at last
actually believe themselves to be the enlightened gentlemen, and
the people of the Free States the peddlers and sneaks they have

so long been in the habit of fancying. They have argued themselves into a kind of vague faith that the wealth and power of the
Republic are south of Mason and Dixon's line; and the Northern
people have been slow in arriving at the conclusion that treasonable talk would lead to treasonable action, because they could
not conceive that anybody should be so foolish as to think of
rearing an independent frame of government on so visionary
a basis. Moreover, the so often recurring necessity, incident
to our system, of obtaining a favorable verdict from the people
has fostered in our public men the talents and habits of jury-
lawyers at the expense of statesmanlike qualities; and the people
have been so long wonted to look upon the utterances of popular
leaders as intended for immediate effect and having no reference
to principles, that there is scarcely a prominent man in the
country so independent in position and so clear of any suspicion
of personal or party motives that they can put entire faith in
what he says, and accept him either as the leader or the exponent
of their thoughts and wishes. They have hardly been able to
judge with certainty from the debates in Congress whether
secession were a real danger, or only one of those political
feints of which they have had such frequent experience.

Events have been gradually convincing them that the peril
was actual and near. They begin to see how unwise, if nothing
worse, has been the weak policy of the Executive in allowing
men to play at Revolution till they learn to think the coarse
reality as easy and pretty as the vaudeville they have been acting. They are fast coming to the conclusion that the list of
grievances put forward by the secessionists is a sham and a
pretence, the veil of a long-matured plot against republican
institutions. And it is time the traitors of the South should
know that the Free States are becoming every day more united
in sentiment and more earnest in resolve, and that, so soon as
they are thoroughly satisfied that secession is something more
than empty bluster, a public spirit will be aroused that will be
content with no half-measures, and which no Executive, however unwilling, can resist.

The country is weary of being cheated with plays upon

words. The United States are a nation, and not a mass-meeting; theirs is a government, and not a caucus,—a government that was meant to be capable, and is capable, of something more than the helpless *please don't* of a village constable; they have executive and administrative officers that are not mere puppet-figures to go through the motions of an objectless activity, but arms and hands that become supple to do the will of the people so soon as that will becomes conscious and defines its purpose. It is time that we turned up our definitions in some more trust-worthy dictionary than that of avowed disunionists and their more dangerous because more timid and cunning accomplices. Rebellion smells no sweeter because it is called Secession, nor does Order lose its divine precedence in human affairs because a knave may nickname it Coercion. Secession means chaos, and Coercion the exercise of legitimate authority. You cannot dignify the one nor degrade the other by any verbal charlatanism. The best testimony to the virtue of coercion is the fact that no wrongdoer ever thought well of it. The thief in jail, the mob-leader in the hands of the police, and the murderer on the drop will be unanimous in favor of this new heresy of the unconstitutionality of constitutions, with its Newgate Calendar of confessors, martyrs, and saints. Falstaff's famous regiment would have volunteered to a man for its propagation or its defence. Henceforth let every unsuccessful litigant have the right to pronounce the verdict of a jury sectional, and to quash all proceedings and retain the property in controversy by seceding from the court-room. Let the planting of hemp be made penal, because it squints toward coercion. Why, the first great secessionist would doubtless have preferred to divide heaven peaceably, would have been willing to send commissioners, must have thought Michael's proceedings injudicious, and could probably even now demonstrate the illegality of hell-fire to any five-year-old imp of average education and intelligence. What a fine world we should have, if we could only come quietly together in convention, and declare by unanimous resolution, or even by a two-thirds vote, that edge-tools should hereafter cut everybody's fingers but his that played with them;

that, when two men ride on one horse, the hindmost shall always sit in front; and that, when a man tries to thrust his partner out of bed and gets kicked out himself, he shall be deemed to have established his title to an equitable division, and the bed shall be thenceforth his as of right, without detriment to the other's privilege in the floor!

If secession be a right, then the moment of its exercise is wholly optional with those possessing it. Suppose, on the eve of a war with England, Michigan should vote herself out of the Union and declare herself annexed to Canada, what kind of a reception would her commissioners be likely to meet in Washington, and what scruples should we feel about coercion? Or, to take a case precisely parallel to that of South Carolina, suppose that Utah, after getting herself admitted to the Union, should resume her sovereignty, as it is pleasantly called, and block our path to the Pacific, under the pretence that she did not consider her institutions safe while the other States entertained such unscriptural prejudices against her special weakness in the patriarchal line. Is the only result of our admitting a Territory on Monday to be the giving it a right to steal itself and go out again on Tuesday? Or do only the original thirteen States possess this precious privilege of suicide? We shall need something like a Fugitive Slave Law for runaway republics, and must get a provision inserted in our treaties with foreign powers, that they shall help us catch any delinquent who may take refuge with them, as South Carolina has been trying to do with England and France. It does not matter to the argument, except so far as the good taste of the proceeding is concerned, at what particular time a State may make her territory foreign, thus opening one gate of our national defences and offering a bridge to invasion. The danger of the thing is in her making her territory foreign under any circumstances; and it is a danger which the government must prevent, if only for self-preservation. Within the limits of the constitution two sovereignties cannot exist; and yet what practical odds does it make, if a State may become sovereign by simply declaring herself so? The legitimate consequence of secession is, not that a State becomes sovereign, but that, so far as the general government is concerned, she has outlawed herself, nullified her own existence as a State, and become an aggregate of riotous men who resist the execution of the laws.

We are told that coercion will be civil war; and so is a mob civil war, till it is put down. In the present case, the only coercion called for is the protection of the public property, and the collection of the federal revenues. If it be necessary to send troops to do this, they will not be sectional, as it is the fashion nowadays to call people who insist on their own rights and the maintenance of the laws, but federal troops, representing the will and power of the whole Confederacy. A danger is always great so long as we are afraid of it; and mischief like that now gathering head in South Carolina may soon become a danger, if not swiftly dealt with. Mr. Buchanan seems altogether too wholesale a disciple of the *laissez-faire* doctrine, and has allowed activity in mischief the same immunity from interference which is true policy only in regard to enterprise wisely and profitably directed. He has been naturally reluctant to employ force, but has overlooked the difference between indecision and moderation, forgetting the lesson of all experience, that firmness in the beginning saves the need of force in the end, and that forcible measures applied too late may be made to seem violent ones, and thus excite a mistaken sympathy with the sufferers by their own misdoing. The feeling of the country has been unmistakably expressed in regard to Major Anderson, and that not merely because he showed prudence and courage, but because he was the first man holding a position of trust who did his duty to the nation. Public sentiment unmistakably demands that, in the case of Anarchy *vs.* America, the cause of the defendant shall not be suffered to go by default. The proceedings in South Carolina, parodying the sublime initiative of our own Revolution with a Declaration of Independence that hangs the franchise of human nature on the kink of a hair, and substitutes for the visionary right of all men to the pursuit of happiness the more practical privilege of some men to pursue their own negro,—these proceedings would be merely ludicrous, were it not for the danger that the men engaged in them may so far commit themselves as to find the inconsistency of a return to prudence too galling, and to prefer the safety of their pride to that of their country.

It cannot be too distinctly stated or too often repeated that the discontent of South Carolina is not one to be allayed by any concessions which the Free States can make with dignity or even safety. It is something more radical and of longer standing than distrust of the motives or probable policy of the Republican party. It is neither more nor less than a disbelief in the very principles on which our government is founded. So long as they practically retained the government of the country, and could use its power and patronage to their own advantage, the plotters were willing to wait; but the moment they lost that control, by the breaking up of the Democratic party, and saw that their chance of ever regaining it was hopeless, they declared openly the principles on which they have all along been secretly acting. Denying the constitutionality of special protection to any other species of property or branch of industry, and in 1832 threatening to break up the Union unless their theory of the Constitution in this respect were admitted, they went into the late Presidential contest with a claim for extraordinary protection to a certain kind of property already the only one endowed with special privileges and immunities. Defeated overwhelmingly before the people, they now question the right of the majority to govern, except on their terms, and threaten violence in the hope of extorting from the fears of the Free States what they failed to obtain from their conscience and settled convictions of duty. Their quarrel is not with the Republican party, but with the theory of Democracy.

The South Carolina politicians have hitherto shown themselves adroit managers, shrewd in detecting and profiting by the weaknesses of men; but their experience has not been of a kind to give them practical wisdom in that vastly more important part of government which depends for success on common sense and business habits. The members of the South Carolina Convention have probably less knowledge of political economy than any single average Northern merchant whose success depends on an intimate knowledge of the laws of trade and the world-wide contingencies of profit and loss. Such a man would tell them, as the result of invariable experience, that the prosperity of no community was so precarious as that of one whose very existence was dependent on a single agricultural product. What divinity hedges cotton, that competition may not touch it,—that some disease, like that of the potato and the vine, may not bring it to beggary in a single year, and cure the overweening conceit of prosperity with the sharp medicine of Ireland and Madeira? But these South Carolina economists are better at vaporing than at calculation. They will find to their cost that the figures of statistics have little mercy for the figures of speech, which are so powerful in raising enthusiasm and so helpless in raising money. The eating of one's own words, as they must do, sooner or later, is neither agreeable nor nutritious; but it is better to do it before there is nothing else left to eat. The secessionists are strong in declamation, but they are weak in the multiplication-table and the ledger. They have no notion of any sort of logical connection between treason and taxes. It is all very fine signing Declarations of Independence, and one may thus become a kind of panic-price hero for a week or two, even rising to the effigial martyrdom of the illustrated press; but these gentlemen seem to have forgotten that, if their precious document should lead to anything serious, they have been signing promises to pay for the State of South Carolina to an enormous amount. It is probably far short of the truth to say that the taxes of an autonomous palmetto republic would be three times what they are now. To speak of nothing else, there must be a military force kept constantly on foot; and the ministers of King Cotton will find that the charge made by a standing army on the finances of the new empire is likely to be far more serious and damaging than can be compensated by the glory of a great many such "spirited charges" as that by which Colonel Pettigrew and his gallant rifles took Fort Pinckney, with its garrison of one engineer officer and its armament of no guns. Soldiers are the most costly of all toys or tools. The outgo for the army of the Pope, never amounting to ten thousand effective men, in the cheapest country in the world, has been half a million of dollars a month. Under the present system, it needs no argument to show that the non-slaveholding States, with a free population considerably more than double that of the slaveholding States, and with much more generally distributed wealth and opportunities of spending, pay far more than the proportion predicable on mere preponderance in numbers of the expenses of a government supported mainly by a tariff on importations. And it is not the burden of this difference merely that the new Cotton Republic must assume. They will need as large, probably a larger, army and navy than that of the present Union; as numerous a diplomatic establishment; a postal system whose large yearly deficit they must bear themselves; and they must assume the main charges of the Indian Bureau. If they adopt free trade, they will alienate the Border Slave States, and even Louisiana; if a system of customs, they have cut themselves off from the chief consumers of foreign goods. One of the calculations of the Southern conspirators is to render the Free States tributary to their new republic by adopting free trade and smuggling their imported goods across the border. But this is all moonshine; for, even if smuggling could not be prevented as easily as it now is from the British Provinces, how long would it be before the North would adapt its tariff to the new order of things? And thus thrown back upon direct taxation, how many years would it take to open the eyes of the poorer classes of Secessia to the hardship of their position and its causes? Their ignorance has been trifled with by men who cover treasonable designs with a pretence of local patriotism. Neither they nor their misleaders have any true conception of the people of the Free States, of those "white slaves" who in Massachusetts alone have a deposit in the Savings Banks whose yearly interest would pay seven times over the four hundred thousand dollars which South Carolina cannot raise.

But even if we leave other practical difficulties out of sight, what chance of stability is there for a confederacy whose very foundation is the principle that any member of it may withdraw at the first discontent? If they could contrive to establish a free trade treaty with their chief customer, England, would she consent to gratify Louisiana with an exception in favor of sugar? Some of the leaders of the secession movement have already become aware of this difficulty, and accordingly propose the abolition of all State lines,—the first step toward a military despotism; for, if our present system have one advantage greater than another, it is the neutralization of numberless individual ambitions by adequate opportunities of provincial distinction. Even now the merits of the Napoleonic system are put forward by some of the theorists of Alabama and Mississippi, who doubtless have as good a stomach to be emperors as ever Bottom had to a bottle of hay, when his head was temporarily transformed to the likeness of theirs,—and who, were they subjects of the government that looks so nice across the Atlantic, would, ere this, have been on their way to Cayenne, a spot where such red-peppery temperaments would find themselves at home.

The absurdities with which the telegraphic column of the newspapers has been daily crowded, since the vagaries of South Carolina finally settled down into unmistakable insanity, would give us but a poor opinion of the general intelligence of the country, did we not know that they were due to the necessities of "Our Own Correspondent." At one time, it is Fort Sumter that is to be bombarded with floating batteries mounted on rafts behind a rampart of cotton-bales; at another, it is Mr. Barrett, Mayor of Washington, announcing his intention that the President-elect shall be inaugurated, or Mr. Buchanan declaring that he shall cheerfully assent to it. Indeed! and who gave them any choice in the matter? Yesterday, it was General Scott who would not abandon the flag which he had illustrated with the devotion of a lifetime; to-day, it is General Harney or Commodore Kearney who has concluded to be true to the country whose livery he has worn and whose bread he has eaten for half a century; to-morrow, it will be Ensign Stebbins who has been magnanimous enough not to throw up his commission. What are we to make of the extraordinary confusion of ideas which such things indicate? In what other country would it be considered creditable to an officer that he merely did not turn traitor at the first opportunity? There can be no doubt of the honor both of the army and navy, and of their loyalty to their country. They will do their duty, if we do ours in saving them a country to which they can be loyal.

We have been so long habituated to a kind of local independence in the management of our affairs, and the central government has fortunately had so little occasion for making itself felt at home and in the domestic concerns of the States, that the idea of its relation to us as a power, except for protection from without, has gradually become vague and alien to our ordinary habits of thought. We have so long heard the principle admitted, and seen it acted on with advantage to the general weal, that the people are sovereign in their own affairs, that we must recover our presence of mind before we see the fallacy of the assumption, that the people, or a bare majority of them, in a single State, can exercise their right of sovereignty as against the will of the nation legitimately expressed. When such a contingency arises, it is for a moment difficult to get rid of our habitual associations, and to feel that we are not a mere partnership, dissolvable whether by mutual consent or on the demand of one or more of its members, but a nation, which can never abdicate its right, and can never surrender it while virtue enough is left in the people to make it worth retaining. It would seem to be the will of God that from time to time the manhood of nations, like that of individuals, should be tried by great dangers or by great opportunities. If the manhood be here, it makes the great opportunity out of the great danger; if it be not there, then the great danger out of the great opportunity. The occasion is offered us now of trying whether a conscious nationality and a timely concentration of the popular will for its maintenance be possible in a democracy, or whether it is only despotisms that are capable of the sudden and selfish energy of protecting themselves from destruction.

The Republican party has thus far borne itself with firmness and moderation, and the great body of the Democratic party in the Free States is gradually being forced into an alliance with it. Let us not be misled by any sophisms about conciliation and compromise. Discontented citizens may be conciliated and compromised with, but never open rebels with arms in their hands. If there be any concessions which justice may demand on the one hand and honor make on the other, let us try if we can adjust them with the Border Slave States; but a government has already signed its own death-warrant, when it consents to make terms with law-breakers. First re-establish the supremacy of order, and then it will be time to discuss terms; but do not call it a compromise, when you give up your purse with a pistol at your head. This is no time for sentimentalisms about the empty chair at the national hearth; all the chairs would be empty soon enough, if one of the children is to amuse itself with setting the house on fire, whenever it can find a match. Since the election of Mr. Lincoln, not one of the arguments has lost its force, not a cipher of the statistics has been proved mistaken, on which the judgment of the people was made up. Nobody proposes, or has proposed, to interfere with any existing rights of property; the majority have not assumed to decide upon any question of the righteousness or policy of certain social arrangements existing in any part of the Confederacy; they have not undertaken to constitute themselves the conscience of their neighbors; they have simply endeavored to do their duty to their own posterity, and to protect them from a system which, as ample experience has shown, and that of our present difficulty were enough to show, fosters a sense of irresponsibleness to all obligation in the governing class, and in the governed an ignorance and a prejudice which may be misled at any moment to the peril of the whole country.

But the present question is one altogether transcending all limits of party and all theories of party policy. It is a question of national existence; it is a question whether Americans shall govern America, or whether a disappointed clique shall nullify all government now, and render a stable government difficult hereafter; it is a question, not whether we shall have civil war under certain contingencies, but whether we shall prevent it

under any. It is idle, and worse than idle, to talk about Central
Republics that can never be formed. We want neither Central
Republics nor Northern Republics, but our own Republic and
that of our fathers, destined one day to gather the whole continent under a flag that shall be the most august in the world.
Having once known what it was to be members of a grand and
peaceful constellation, we shall not believe, without further
proof, that the laws of our gravitation are to be abolished, and
we flung forth into chaos, a hurlyburly of jostling and splinter-
ing stars, whenever Robert Toombs or Robert Rhett, or any
other Bob of the secession kite, may give a flirt of self-impor-
tance. The first and greatest benefit of government is that it
keeps the peace, that it insures every man his right, and not only
that, but the permanence of it. In order to this, its first requisite
is stability; and this once firmly settled, the greater the extent
of conterminous territory that can be subjected to one system
and one language and inspired by one patriotism, the better.
That there should be some diversity of interests is perhaps an
advantage, since the necessity of legislating equitably for all
gives legislation its needful safeguards of caution and largeness
of view. A single empire embracing the whole world, and controlling, without extinguishing, local organizations and na-
tionalities, has been not only the dream of conquerors, but the
ideal of speculative philanthropists. Our own dominion is of
such extent and power, that it may, so far as this continent is
concerned, be looked upon as something like an approach to the
realization of such an ideal. But for slavery, it might have succeeded in realizing it; and in spite of slavery, it may. One
language, one law, one citizenship over thousands of miles,
and a government on the whole so good that we seem to have
forgotten what government means,—these are things not to be
spoken of with levity, privileges not to be surrendered without
a struggle. And yet while Germany and Italy, taught by the
bloody and bitter and servile experience of centuries, are striving
toward unity as the blessing above all others desirable, we are
to allow a Union, that for almost eighty years has been the
source and the safeguard of incalculable advantages, to be

shattered by the caprice of a rabble that has outrun the intention of its leaders, while we are making up our minds what coercion means! Ask the first constable, and he will tell you that it is the force necessary for executing the laws. To avoid the danger of what men who have seized upon forts, arsenals, and other property of the United States, and continue to hold them by military force, may choose to call civil war, we are allowing a state of things to gather head which will make real civil war the occupation of the whole country for years to come, and establish it as a permanent institution. There is no such antipathy between the North and the South as men ambitious of a consideration in the new republic, which their talents and character have failed to secure them in the old, would fain call into existence by asserting that it exists. The misunderstanding and dislike between them is not so great as they were within living memory between England and Scotland, as they are now between England and Ireland. There is no difference of race, language, or religion. Yet, after a dissatisfaction of near a century and two rebellions, there is no part of the British dominion more loyal than Scotland, no British subjects who would be more loath to part with the substantial advantages of their imperial connection than the Scotch; and even in Ireland, after a longer and more deadly feud, there is no sane man who would consent to see his country irrevocably cut off from power and consideration to obtain an independence which would be nothing but Donnybrook Fair multiplied by every city, town, and village in the island. The same considerations of policy and advantage which render the union of Scotland and Ireland with England a necessity apply with even more force to the several States of our Union. To let one, or two, or half a dozen of them break away in a freak of anger or unjust suspicion, or, still worse, from mistaken notions of sectional advantage, would be to fail in our duty to ourselves and our country, would be a fatal blindness to the lessons which immemorial history has been tracing on the earth's surface, either with the beneficent furrow of the plough, or, when that was unheeded, the fruitless gash of the cannon ball.

When we speak of coercion, we do not mean violence, but

only the assertion of constituted and acknowledged authority. Even if seceding States could be conquered back again, they would not be worth the conquest. We ask only for the assertion of a principle which shall give the friends of order in the discontented quarters a hope to rally round, and the assurance of the support they have a right to expect. There is probably a majority, and certainly a powerful minority, in the seceding States, who are loyal to the Union; and these should have that support which the prestige of the General Government can alone give them. It is not to the North nor to the Republican party that the malcontents are called on to submit, but to the laws and to the benign intentions of the Constitution, as they were understood by its framers. What the country wants is a permanent settlement; and it has learned, by repeated trial, that compromise is not a cement, but a wedge. The Government did not hesitate to protect the doubtful right of property of a Virginian in Anthony Burns by the exercise of coercion, and the loyalty of Massachusetts was such that her own militia could be used to enforce an obligation abhorrent, and, as there is reason to believe, made purposely abhorrent, to her dearest convictions and most venerable traditions; and yet the same Government tampers with armed treason, and lets *I dare not* wait upon *I would*, when it is a question of protecting the acknowledged property of the Union, and of sustaining, nay, preserving even, a gallant officer whose only fault is that he has been too true to his flag. While we write, the newspapers bring us the correspondence between Mr. Buchanan and the South Carolina "Commissioners"; and surely never did a government stoop so low as ours has done, not only in consenting to receive these ambassadors from Nowhere, but in suggesting that a soldier deserves court-martial who has done all he could to maintain himself in a forlorn hope, with rebellion in his front and treachery in his rear. Our Revolutionary heroes had old-fashioned notions about rebels, suitable to the straightforward times in which they lived,—times when blood was as freely shed to secure our national existence as milk-and-water is now to destroy it. Mr. Buchanan might have profited by the example of men who knew nothing of the modern arts of Constitutional interpretation, but saw clearly the distinction between right and wrong. When a party of the Shays rebels came to the house of General Pomeroy, in Northampton, and asked if he could accommodate them,—the old soldier, seeing the green sprigs in their hats, the badges of their treason, shouted to his son, "Fetch me my hangar, and I'll *accommodate* the scoundrels!" General Jackson, we suspect, would have accommodated rebel commissioners in the same peremptory style.

While our Government, like Giles in the old rhyme, is wondering whether it is a government or not, emissaries of treason are cunningly working upon the fears and passions of the Border States, whose true interests are infinitely more on the side of the Union than of slavery. They are luring the ambitious with visionary promises of Southern grandeur and prosperity, and deceiving the ignorant into the belief that the principles and practice of the Free States were truly represented by John Brown. All this might have been prevented, had Mr. Buchanan in his Message thought of the interests of his country instead of those of his party. It is not too late to check and neutralize it now. A decisively national and patriotic policy is all that can prevent excited men from involving themselves so deeply that they will find "returning as tedious as go o'er," and be more afraid of cowardice than of consequences.

Slavery is no longer the matter in debate, and we must beware of being led off upon that side-issue. The matter now in hand is the reëstablishment of order, the reaffirmation of national unity, and the settling once for all whether there can be such a thing as a government without the right to use its power in self-defence. The Republican party has done all it could lawfully do in limiting slavery once more to the States in which it exists, and in relieving the Free States from forced complicity with an odious system. They can be patient, as Providence is often patient, till natural causes work that conviction which conscience has been unable to effect. They believe that the violent abolition of slavery, which would be sure to follow sooner or later the disruption of our Confederacy, would not

compensate for the evil that would be entailed upon both races
by the abolition of our nationality and the bloody confusion
that would follow it.   More than this, they believe that there
can be no permanent settlement except in the definite establishment of the principle, that this Government, like all others, rests
upon the everlasting foundations of just Authority,—that that
authority, once delegated by the people, becomes a common
stock of Power to be wielded for the common protection, and
from which no minority or majority of partners can withdraw
its contribution under any conditions,—that this power is what
makes us a nation, and implies a corresponding duty of submission, or, if that be refused, then a necessary right of self-
vindication.   We are citizens, when we make laws; we become
subjects, when we attempt to break them after they are made.
Lynch-law may be better than no law in new and half-organized
communities, but we cannot tolerate its application in the affairs
of government.   The necessity of suppressing rebellion by
force may be a terrible one, but its consequences, whatever
they may be, do not weigh a feather in comparison with those
that would follow from admitting the principle that there is no
social compact binding on any body of men too numerous to
be arrested by a United States marshal.

As we are writing these sentences, the news comes to us that
South Carolina has taken the initiative, and chosen the arbitra-
ment of war.   She has done it because her position was desperate, and because she hoped thereby to unite the Cotton States
by a complicity in blood, as they are already committed by a
unanimity in bravado.   Major Anderson deserves more than
ever the thanks of his country for his wise forbearance.   The
foxes in Charleston, who have already lost their tails in the trap
of Secession, wished to throw upon him the responsibility of
that second blow which begins a quarrel, and the silence of his
guns has balked them.   Nothing would have pleased them so
much as to have one of his thirty-two-pound shot give a taste of
real war to the boys who are playing soldier at Morris's Island.
But he has shown the discretion of a brave man.   South Carolina will soon learn how much she has undervalued the people

of the Free States. Because they prefer law to bowie-knives and revolvers, she has too lightly reckoned on their caution and timidity. She will find that, though slow to kindle, they are as slow to yield, and that they are willing to risk their lives for the defence of law, though not for the breach of it. They are beginning to question the value of a peace that is forced on them at the point of the bayonet, and is to be obtained only by an abandonment of rights and duties.

When we speak of the courage and power of the Free States, we do not wish to be understood as descending to the vulgar level of meeting brag with brag. We speak of them only as among the elements to be gravely considered by the fanatics who may render it necessary for those who value the continued existence of this Confederacy as it deserves to be valued to kindle a back-fire, and to use the desperate means which God has put into their hands to be employed in the last extremity of free institutions. And when we use the term coercion, nothing is farther from our thoughts than the carrying of blood and fire among those whom we still consider our brethren of South Carolina. These civilized communities of ours have interests too serious to be risked on a childish wager of courage, —a quality that can always be bought cheaper than day-labor on a railway-embankment. We wish to see the Government strong enough for the maintenance of law, and for the protection, if need be, of the unfortunate Governor Pickens from the anarchy he has allowed himself to be made a tool of by evoking. Let the power of the Union be used for any other purpose than that of shutting and barring the door against the return of misguided men to their allegiance. At the same time we think legitimate and responsible force prudently exerted safer than the submission, without a struggle, to unlawful and irresponsible violence.

Peace is the greatest of blessings, when it is won and kept by manhood and wisdom; but it is a blessing that will not long be the housemate of cowardice. It is God alone who is powerful enough to let His authority slumber; it is only His laws that are strong enough to protect and avenge themselves. Every hu-

man government is bound to make its laws so far resemble His
that they shall be uniform, certain, and unquestionable in their
operation; and this it can do only by a timely show of power,
and by an appeal to that authority which is of divine right, inasmuch as its office is to maintain that order which is the single
attribute of the Infinite Reason that we can clearly apprehend
and of which we have hourly example.

From NEW ENGLAND TWO CENTURIES AGO

(1865)

The history of New England is written imperishably on the
face of a continent, and in characters as beneficent as they are
enduring. In the Old World national pride feeds itself with the
record of battles and conquests;—battles which proved nothing
and settled nothing; conquests which shifted a boundary on the
map, and put one ugly head instead of another on the coin
which the people paid to the tax-gatherer. But wherever the
New-Englander travels among the sturdy commonwealths
which have sprung from the seed of the Mayflower, churches,
schools, colleges, tell him where the men of his race have been,
or their influence has penetrated; and an intelligent freedom is
the monument of conquests whose results are not to be measured in square miles. Next to the fugitives whom Moses led
out of Egypt, the little shipload of outcasts who landed at
Plymouth two centuries and a half ago are destined to influence
the future of the world. The spiritual thirst of mankind has
for ages been quenched at Hebrew fountains; but the embodiment in human institutions of truths uttered by the Son of Man
eighteen centuries ago was to be mainly the work of Puritan
thought and Puritan self-devotion. Leave New England out
in the cold! While you are plotting it, she sits by every fireside in the land where there is piety, culture, and free thought.

Faith in God, faith in man, faith in work,—this is the short
formula in which we may sum up the teaching of the founders
of New England, a creed ample enough for this life and the next.

If their municipal regulations smack somewhat of Judaism, yet there can be no nobler aim or more practical wisdom than theirs; for it was to make the law of man a living counterpart of the law of God, in their highest conception of it. Were they too earnest in the strife to save their souls alive? That is still the problem which every wise and brave man is lifelong in solving. If the Devil take a less hateful shape to us than to our fathers, he is as busy with us as with them; and if we cannot find it in our hearts to break with a gentleman of so much worldly wisdom, who gives such admirable dinners, and whose manners are so perfect, so much the worse for us.

Looked at on the outside, New England history is dry and unpicturesque. There is no rustle of silks, no waving of plumes, no clink of golden spurs. Our sympathies are not awakened by the changeful destinies, the rise and fall, of great families, whose doom was in their blood. Instead of all this, we have the homespun fates of Cephas and Prudence repeated in an infinite series of peaceable sameness, and finding space enough for record in the family Bible; we have the noise of axe and hammer and saw, an apotheosis of dogged work, where, reversing the fairy-tale, nothing is left to luck, and, if there be any poetry, it is something that cannot be helped,—the waste of the water over the dam. Extrinsically, it is prosaic and plebeian; intrinsically, it is poetic and noble; for it is, perhaps, the most perfect incarnation of an idea the world has ever seen. That idea was not to found a democracy, nor to charter the city of New Jerusalem by an act of the General Court, as gentlemen seem to think whose notions of history and human nature rise like an exhalation from the good things at a Pilgrim Society dinner. Not in the least. They had no faith in the Divine institution of a system which gives Teague, because he can dig, as much influence as Ralph, because he can think, nor in personal at the expense of general freedom. Their view of human rights was not so limited that it could not take in human relations and duties also. They would have been likely to answer the claim, "I am as good as anybody," by a quiet "Yes, for some things, but not for others; as good, doubtless, in your place, where all things are good." What the early settlers of Massachusetts *did* intend, and what they accomplished, was the founding here of a *new* England, and a better one, where the political superstitions and abuses of the old should never have leave to take root. So much, we may say, they deliberately intended. No nobles, either lay or cleric, no great landed estates, and no universal ignorance as the seed-plot of vice and unreason; but an elective magistracy and clergy, land for all who would till it, and reading and writing, will ye nill ye, instead. Here at last, it should seem, simple manhood is to have a chance to play his stake against Fortune with honest dice, uncogged by those three hoary sharpers, Prerogative, Patricianism, and Priestcraft. Whoever has looked into the pamphlets published in England during the Great Rebellion cannot but have been struck by the fact, that the principles and practice of the Puritan Colony had begun to react with considerable force on the mother country; and the policy of the retrograde party there, after the Restoration, in its dealings with New England, finds a curious parallel as to its motives (time will show whether as to its results) in the conduct of the same party towards America during the last four years.[1] This influence and this fear alike bear witness to the energy of the principles at work here.

We have said that the details of New England history were essentially dry and unpoetic. Everything is near, authentic, and petty. There is no mist of distance to soften outlines, no mirage of tradition to give characters and events an imaginative loom. So much downright work was perhaps never wrought on the earth's surface in the same space of time as during the first forty years after the settlement. But mere work is unpicturesque, and void of sentiment. Irving instinctively divined and admirably illustrated in his "Knickerbocker" the humorous element which lies in this nearness of view, this clear, prosaic daylight of modernness, and this poverty of stage properties, which make the actors and the deeds they were concerned in seem ludicrously small when contrasted with the semi-mythic grandeur in which we have clothed them, as we look backward

[1] Written in December, 1864.

from the crowned result, and fancy a cause as majestic as our conception of the effect. There was, indeed, one poetic side to the existence otherwise so narrow and practical; and to have conceived this, however partially, is the one original and American thing in Cooper. This diviner glimpse illumines the lives of our Daniel Boones, the man of civilization and old-world ideas confronted with our forest solitudes,—confronted, too, for the first time, with his real self, and so led gradually to disentangle the original substance of his manhood from the artificial results of culture. Here was our new Adam of the wilderness, forced to name anew, not the visible creation of God, but the invisible creation of man, in those forms that lie at the base of social institutions, so insensibly moulding personal character and controlling individual action. Here is the protagonist of our New World epic, a figure as poetic as that of Achilles, as ideally representative as that of Don Quixote, as romantic in its relation to our homespun and plebeian mythus as Arthur in his to the mailed and plumed cycle of chivalry. We do not mean, of course, that Cooper's "Leatherstocking" is all this or anything like it, but that the character typified in him is ideally and potentially all this and more.

But whatever was poetical in the lives of the early New Englanders had something shy, if not sombre, about it. If their natures flowered, it was out of sight, like the fern. It was in the practical that they showed their true quality, as Englishmen are wont. It has been the fashion lately with a few feeble-minded persons to undervalue the New England Puritans, as if they were nothing more than gloomy and narrow-minded fanatics. But all the charges brought against these large-minded and far-seeing men are precisely those which a really able fanatic, Joseph de Maistre, lays at the door of Protestantism. Neither a knowledge of human nature nor of history justifies us in confounding, as is commonly done, the Puritans of Old and New England, or the English Puritans of the third with those of the fifth decade of the seventeenth century. Fanaticism, or, to call it by its milder name, enthusiasm, is only powerful and active so long as it is aggressive. Establish it firmly in power, and it becomes conservatism, whether it will or no. A sceptre once put in the hand, the grip is instinctive; and he who is firmly seated in authority soon learns to think security, and not progress, the highest lesson of statecraft. From the summit of power men no longer turn their eyes upward, but begin to look about them. Aspiration sees only one side of every question; possession, many. And the English Puritans, after their revolution was accomplished, stood in even a more precarious position than most successful assailants of the prerogative of whatever *is* to continue in being. They had carried a political end by means of a religious revival. The fulcrum on which they rested their lever to overturn the existing order of things (as history always placidly calls the particular forms of *dis*order for the time being) was in the soul of man. They could not renew the fiery gush of enthusiasm when once the molten metal had begun to stiffen in the mould of policy and precedent. The religious element of Puritanism became insensibly merged in the political; and, its one great man taken away, it died, as passions have done before, of possession. It was one thing to shout with Cromwell before the battle of Dunbar, "Now, Lord, arise, and let thine enemies be scattered!" and to snuffle, "Rise, Lord, and keep us safe in our benefices, our sequestered estates, and our five per cent!" Puritanism meant something when Captain Hodgson, riding out to battle through the morning mist, turns over the command of his troop to a lieutenant, and stays to hear the prayer of a cornet, there was "so much of God in it." Become traditional, repeating the phrase without the spirit, reading the present backward as if it were written in Hebrew, translating Jehovah by "I was" instead of "I am,"—it was no more like its former self than the hollow drum made of Zisca's skin was like the grim captain whose soul it had once contained. Yet the change was inevitable, for it is not safe to confound the things of Cæsar with the things of God. Some honest republicans, like Ludlow, were never able to comprehend the chilling contrast between the ideal aim and the material fulfilment, and looked askance on the strenuous reign of Oliver,—that rugged boulder of primitive manhood lying lonely there on the dead level of the century,—as if some crooked changeling had been laid in the cradle instead of that fair babe of the Commonwealth they had dreamed. Truly there is a tide in the affairs of men, but there is no gulf-stream setting forever in one direction; and those waves of enthusiasm on whose crumbling crests we sometimes see nations lifted for a gleaming moment are wont to have a gloomy trough before and behind.

But the founders of New England, though they must have sympathized vividly with the struggles and triumphs of their brethren in the mother country, were never subjected to the same trials and temptations, never hampered with the same lumber of usages and tradition. They were not driven to win power by doubtful and desperate ways, nor to maintain it by any compromises of the ends which make it worth having. From the outset they were builders, without need of first pulling down, whether to make room or to provide material. For thirty years after the colonization of the Bay, they had absolute power to mould as they would the character of their adolescent commonwealth. During this time a whole generation would have grown to manhood who knew the Old World only by report, in whose habitual thought kings, nobles, and bishops would be as far away from all present and practical concern as the figures in a fairy-tale, and all whose memories and associations, all their unconscious training by eye and ear, were New English wholly. Nor were the men whose influence was greatest in shaping the framework and the policy of the Colony, in any true sense of the word, fanatics. Enthusiasts, perhaps, they were, but with them the fermentation had never gone further than the ripeness of the vinous stage. Disappointment had never made it acetous, nor had it ever putrefied into the turbid zeal of Fifth Monarchism and sectarian whimsey. There is no better ballast for keeping the mind steady on its keel, and saving it from all risk of *crankiness*, than business. And they were business men, men of facts and figures no less than of religious earnestness. The sum of two hundred thousand pounds had been invested in their undertaking,—a sum, for

that time, truly enormous as the result of private combination
for a doubtful experiment. That their enterprise might succeed,
they must show a balance on the right side of the counting-
house ledger, as well as in their private accounts with their own
souls. The liberty of praying when and how they would must
be balanced with an ability of paying when and as they ought.
Nor is the resulting fact in this case at variance with the *a priori*
theory. They succeeded in making their thought the life and
soul of a body politic, still powerful, still benignly operative,
after two centuries; a thing which no mere fanatic ever did or
ever will accomplish. Sober, earnest, and thoughtful men, it
was no Utopia, no New Atlantis, no realization of a splendid
dream, which they had at heart, but the establishment of the
divine principle of Authority on the common interest and the
common consent; the making, by a contribution from the free-
will of all, a power which should curb and guide the free-will of
each for the general good. If they were stern in their dealings
with sectaries, it should be remembered that the Colony was in
fact the private property of the Massachusetts Company, that
unity was essential to its success, and that John of Leyden had
taught them how unendurable by the nostrils of honest men is
the corruption of the right of private judgment in the evil and
selfish hearts of men when no thorough mental training has developed the understanding and given the judgment its needful
means of comparison and correction. They knew that liberty
in the hands of feeble-minded and unreasoning persons (and
all the worse if they are honest) means nothing more than the
supremacy of their particular form of imbecility; means nothing
less, therefore, than downright chaos, a Bedlam-chaos of mono-
maniacs and bores. What was to be done with men and
women, who bore conclusive witness to the fall of man by insisting on walking up the broad-aisle of the meeting-house in a
costume which that event had put forever out of fashion? About
their treatment of witches, too, there has been a great deal of
ignorant babble. Puritanism had nothing whatever to do with
it. They acted under a delusion, which, with an exception here
and there (and those mainly medical men, like Wierus and

Webster), darkened the understanding of all Christendom. Dr. Henry More was no Puritan; and his letter to Glanvil, prefixed to the third edition of the "Sadducismus Triumphatus," was written in 1678, only fourteen years before the trials at Salem. Bekker's "Bezauberte Welt" was published in 1693; and in the Preface he speaks of the difficulty of overcoming "the prejudices in which not only ordinary men, but the learned also, are obstinate." In Hathaway's case, 1702, Chief-Justice Holt, in charging the jury, expresses no disbelief in the possibility of witchcraft, and the indictment implies its existence. Indeed, the natural reaction from the Salem mania of 1692 put an end to belief in devilish compacts and demoniac possessions sooner in New England than elsewhere. The last we hear of it there is in 1720, when the Rev. Mr. Turell of Medford detected and exposed an attempted cheat by two girls. Even in 1692, it was the foolish breath of Cotton Mather and others of the clergy that blew the dying embers of this ghastly superstition into a flame; and they were actuated partly by a desire to bring about a religious revival, which might stay for a while the hastening lapse of their own authority, and still more by that credulous scepticism of feeble-minded piety which dreads the cutting away of an orthodox tumor of misbelief, as if the life-blood of faith would follow, and would keep even a stumbling-block in the way of salvation, if only enough generations had tripped over it to make it venerable. The witches were condemned on precisely the same grounds that in our day led to the condemnation of "Essays and Reviews."

But Puritanism was already in the decline when such things were possible. What had been a wondrous and intimate experience of the soul, a flash into the very crypt and basis of man's nature from the fire of trial, had become ritual and tradition. In prosperous times the faith of one generation becomes the formality of the next. "The necessity of a reformation," set forth by order of the Synod which met at Cambridge in 1679, though no doubt overstating the case, shows how much even at that time the ancient strictness had been loosened. The country had grown rich, its commerce was large, and wealth did its natural work in making life softer and more worldly, commerce in deprovincializing the minds of those engaged in it. But Puritanism had already done its duty. As there are certain creatures whose whole being seems occupied with an egg-laying errand they are sent upon, incarnate ovipositors, their bodies but bags to hold this precious deposit, their legs of use only to carry them where they may most safely be rid of it, so sometimes a generation seems to have no other end than the conception and ripening of certain germs. Its blind stirrings, its apparently aimless seeking hither and thither, are but the driving of an instinct to be done with its parturient function toward these principles of future life and power. Puritanism, believing itself quick with the seed of religious liberty, laid, without knowing it, the egg of democracy. The English Puritans pulled down church and state to rebuild Zion on the ruins, and all the while it was not Zion, but America, they were building. But if their millennium went by, like the rest, and left men still human; if they, like so many saints and martyrs before them, listened in vain for the sound of that trumpet which was to summon all souls to a resurrection from the body of this death which men call life,—it is not for us, at least, to forget the heavy debt we owe them. It was the drums of Naseby and Dunbar that gathered the minute-men on Lexington Common; it was the red dint of the axe on Charles's block that marked One in our era. The Puritans had their faults. They were narrow, ungenial; they could not understand the text, "I have piped to you and ye have not danced," nor conceive that saving one's soul should be the cheerfullest, and not the dreariest, of businesses. Their preachers had a way, like the painful Mr. Perkins, of pronouncing the word *damn* with such an emphasis as left a doleful echo in their auditors' ears a good while after. And it was natural that men who captained or accompanied the exodus from existing forms and associations into the doubtful wilderness that led to the promised land, should find more to their purpose in the Old Testament than in the New. As respects the New England settlers, however visionary some of their religious tenets may have been, their political ideas savored of the realty, and it was no Nephelococcygia of which they drew the plan, but of a commonwealth whose foundation was to rest on solid and familiar earth. If what they did was done in a corner, the results of it were to be felt to the ends of the earth; and the figure of Winthrop should be as venerable in history as that of Romulus is barbarously grand in legend.

I am inclined to think that many of our national characteristics, which are sometimes attributed to climate and sometimes to institutions, are traceable to the influences of Puritan descent. We are apt to forget how very large a proportion of our population is descended from emigrants who came over before 1660. Those emigrants were in great part representatives of that element of English character which was most susceptible of religious impressions; in other words, the most earnest and imaginative. Our people still differ from their English cousins (as they are fond of calling themselves when they are afraid we may do them a mischief) in a certain capacity for enthusiasm, a devotion to abstract principle, an openness to ideas, a greater aptness for intuitions than for the slow processes of the syllogism, and, as derivative from these, in minds of looser texture, a light-armed, skirmishing habit of thought, and a positive preference of the birds in the bush,—an excellent quality of character *before* you have your bird in the hand.

There have been two great distributing centres of the English race on this continent, Massachusetts and Virginia. Each has impressed the character of its early legislators on the swarms it has sent forth. Their ideas are in some fundamental respects the opposites of each other, and we can only account for it by an antagonism of thought beginning with the early framers of their respective institutions. New England abolished caste; in Virginia they still talk of "quality folks." But it was in making education not only common to all, but in some sense compulsory on all, that the destiny of the free republics of America was practically settled. Every man was to be trained, not only to the use of arms, but of his wits also; and it is these which alone make the others effective weapons for the maintenance of freedom. You may disarm the hands, but not the brains, of a people, and to know what should be defended is the first condition of successful defence. Simple as it seems, it was a great discovery that the key of knowledge could turn both ways, that it could open, as well as lock, the door of power to the many. The only things a New-Englander was ever locked out of were the jails. It is quite true that our Republic is the heir of the English Commonwealth; but as we trace events backward to their causes, we shall find it true also, that what made our Revolution a foregone conclusion was that act of the General Court, passed in May, 1647, which established the system of common schools. "To the end that learning may not be buried in the graves of our forefathers in Church and Commonwealth, the Lord assisting our endeavors, it is therefore ordered by this Court and authority thereof, that every township in this jurisdiction, after the Lord hath increased them to fifty householders, shall then forthwith appoint one within their towns to teach all such children as shall resort to him to write and read."

Passing through some Massachusetts village, perhaps at a distance from any house, it may be in the midst of a piece of woods where four roads meet, one may sometimes even yet see a small square one-story building, whose use would not be long doubtful. It is summer, and the flickering shadows of forest-leaves dapple the roof of the little porch, whose door stands wide, and shows, hanging on either hand, rows of straw hats and bonnets, that look as if they had done good service. As you pass the open windows, you hear whole platoons of high-pitched voices discharging words of two or three syllables with wonderful precision and unanimity. Then there is a pause, and the voice of the officer in command is heard reproving some raw recruit whose vocal musket hung fire. Then the drill of the small infantry begins anew, but pauses again because some urchin— who agrees with Voltaire that the superfluous is a very necessary thing—insists on spelling "subtraction" with an *s* too much.

If you had the good fortune to be born and bred in the Bay State, your mind is thronged with half-sad, half-humorous recollections. The a-b abs of little voices long since hushed in the mould, or ringing now in the pulpit, at the bar, or in the

Senate-chamber, come back to the ear of memory. You re-member the high stool on which culprits used to be elevated with the tall paper fool's-cap on their heads, blushing to the ears; and you think with wonder how you have seen them since as men climbing the world's penance-stools of ambition with-out a blush, and gladly giving everything for life's caps and bells. And you have pleasanter memories of going after pond-lilies, of angling for horn-pouts,—that queer bat among the fishes,—of nutting, of walking over the creaking snow-crust in winter, when the warm breath of every household was curl-ing up silently in the keen blue air. You wonder if life has any rewards more solid and permanent than the Spanish dollar that was hung around your neck to be restored again next day, and conclude sadly that it was but too true a prophecy and emblem of all worldly success. But your moralizing is broken short off by a rattle of feet and the pouring forth of the whole swarm,— the boys dancing and shouting,—the mere effervescence of the fixed air of youth and animal spirits uncorked,—the sedater girls in confidential twos and threes decanting secrets out of the mouth of one cape-bonnet into that of another. Times have changed since the jackets and trousers used to draw up on one side of the road, and the petticoats on the other, to salute with bow and curtsy the white neckcloth of the parson or the squire, if it chanced to pass during intermission.

Now this little building, and others like it, were an original kind of fortification invented by the founders of New England. They are the martello-towers that protect our coast. This was the great discovery of our Puritan forefathers. They were the first lawgivers who saw clearly and enforced practically the simple moral and political truth, that knowledge was not an alms to be dependent on the chance charity of private men or the precarious pittance of a trust-fund, but a sacred debt which the Commonwealth owed to every one of her children. The opening of the first grammar-school was the opening of the first trench against monopoly in church and state; the first row of trammels and pot-hooks which the little Shearjashubs and Elkanahs blotted and blubbered across their copybooks, was the preamble to the Declaration of Independence. The men who gave every man the chance to become a landholder, who made the transfer of land easy, and put knowledge within the reach of all, have been called narrow-minded, because they were intolerant. But intolerant of what? Of what they believed to be dangerous nonsense, which, if left free, would destroy the last hope of civil and religious freedom. They had not come here that every man might do that which seemed good in his own eyes, but in the sight of God. Toleration, moreover, is something which is won, not granted. It is the equilibrium of neutralized forces. The Puritans had no notion of tolerating mischief. They looked upon their little commonwealth as upon their own private estate and homestead, as they had a right to do, and would no more allow the Devil's religion of unreason to be preached therein, than we should permit a prize-fight in our gardens. They were narrow; in other words they had an edge to them, as men that serve in great emergencies must; for a Gordian knot is settled sooner with a sword than a beetle.

The founders of New England are commonly represented in the after-dinner oratory of their descendants as men "before their time," as it is called; in other words, deliberately prescient of events resulting from new relations of circumstances, or even from circumstances new in themselves, and therefore altogether alien from their own experience. Of course, such a class of men is to be reckoned among those non-existent human varieties so gravely catalogued by the ancient naturalists. If a man could shape his action with reference to what should happen a century after his death, surely it might be asked of him to call in the help of that easier foreknowledge which reaches from one day to the next,—a power of prophecy whereof we have no example. I do not object to a wholesome pride of ancestry, though a little mythical, if it be accompanied with the feeling that *noblesse oblige*, and do not result merely in a placid self-satisfaction with our own mediocrity, as if greatness, like righteousness, could be imputed. We can pardon it even in conquered races, like the Welsh and Irish, who make up to themselves for present degradation by imaginary empires in the past whose boundaries they can extend at will, carrying the bloodless conquests of fancy over regions laid down upon no map, and concerning which authentic history is enviously dumb. Those long beadrolls of Keltic kings cannot tyrannize over us, and we can be patient so long as our own crowns are uncracked by the shillalah sceptres of their actual representatives. In our own case, it would not be amiss, perhaps, if we took warning by the example of Teague and Taffy. At least, I think it would be wise in our orators not to put forward so prominently the claim of the Yankee to universal dominion, and his intention to enter upon it forthwith. If we do our duties as honestly and as much in the fear of God as our forefathers did, we need not trouble ourselves much about other titles to empire. The broad foreheads and long heads will win the day at last in spite of all heraldry, and it will be enough if we feel as keenly as our Puritan founders did that those organs of empire may be broadened and lengthened by culture.[1] That our self-complacency should not increase the complacency of outsiders is not to be wondered at. As *we* sometimes take credit to ourselves (since all commendation of our ancestry is indirect self-flattery) for what the Puritan fathers never were, so there are others who, to gratify a spite against their descendants, blame them for not having been what they could not be; namely, before their time in such matters as slavery, witchcraft, and the like. The view, whether of friend or foe, is equally unhistorical, nay, without the faintest notion of all that makes history worth having as a teacher. That our grandfathers shared in the prejudices of their day is all that makes them human to us; and that nevertheless they could act bravely and wisely on occasion makes them only the more venerable. If certain barbarisms and superstitions disappeared earlier in New England than else-

---

[1] It is curious, that, when Cromwell proposed to transfer a colony from New England to Ireland, one of the conditions insisted on in Massachusetts was that a college should be established. [Lowell. All footnotes in this and following essays are by Lowell, unless another author is indicated.]

where, not by the decision of exceptionally enlightened or
humane judges, but by force of public opinion, that is the fact
that is interesting and instructive for us.   I never thought it
an abatement of Hawthorne's genius that he came lineally from
one who sat in judgment on the witches in 1692; it was interesting rather to trace something hereditary in the sombre character of his imagination, continually vexing itself to account for
the origin of evil, and baffled for want of that simple solution
in a personal Devil. . . .

From ROUSSEAU AND THE SENTIMENTALISTS

(1867)

"We have had the great professor and founder of the philosophy of Vanity in England.   As I had good opportunities of
knowing his proceedings almost from day to day, he left no
doubt in my mind that he entertained no principle either to
influence his heart or to guide his understanding but vanity;
with this vice he was possessed to a degree little short of madness.   Benevolence to the whole species, and want of feeling
for every individual with whom the professors come in contact, form the character of the new philosophy.   Setting up for
an unsocial independence, this their hero of vanity refuses the
just price of common labor, as well as the tribute which opulence
owes to genius, and which, when paid, honors the giver and the
receiver, and then pleads his beggary as an excuse for his
crimes. He melts with tenderness for those only who touch
him by the remotest relation, and then, without one natural
pang, casts away, as a sort of offal and excrement, the spawn of
his disgustful amours, and sends his children to the hospital
of foundlings.   The bear loves, licks, and forms her young; but
bears are not philosophers."

This was Burke's opinion of the only contemporary who can
be said to rival him in fervid and sustained eloquence, to surpass him in grace and persuasiveness of style.   Perhaps we
should have been more thankful to him if he had left us instead

a record of those "proceedings almost from day to day" which he had such "good opportunities of knowing," but it probably never entered his head that posterity might care as much about the doings of the citizen of Geneva as about the sayings of even a British Right Honorable. Vanity eludes recognition by its victims in more shapes, and more pleasing, than any other passion, and perhaps had Mr. Burke been able imaginatively to translate Swiss Jean Jacques into Irish Edmund, he would have found no juster equivalent for the obnoxious trisyllable than "righteous self-esteem." For Burke was himself also, in the subtler sense of the word, a sentimentalist, that is, a man who took what would now be called an æsthetic view of morals and politics. No man who ever wrote English, except perhaps Mr. Ruskin, more habitually mistook his own personal likes and dislikes, tastes and distastes, for general principles, and this, it may be suspected, is the secret of all merely eloquent writing. He hints at madness as an explanation of Rousseau, and it is curious enough that Mr. Buckle was fain to explain *him* in the same way. It is not, I confess, a solution that we find very satisfactory in this latter case. Burke's fury against the French Revolution was nothing more than was natural to a desperate man in self-defence. It was his own life, or, at least, all that made life dear to him, that was in danger. He had all that abstract political wisdom which may be naturally secreted by a magnanimous nature and a sensitive temperament, absolutely none of that rough-and-tumble kind which is so needful for the conduct of affairs. Fastidiousness is only another form of egotism; and all men who know not where to look for truth save in the narrow well of self will find their own image at the bottom, and mistake it for what they are seeking. Burke's hatred of Rousseau was genuine and instinctive. It was so genuine and so instinctive as no hatred can be but that of self, of our own weaknesses as we see them in another man. But there was also something deeper in it than this. There was mixed with it the natural dread in the political diviner of the political logician,—in the empirical, of the theoretic statesman. Burke, confounding the idea of society with the form of it then existing, would have preserved that as the only specific against anarchy. Rousseau, assuming that society as it then existed was but another name for anarchy, would have reconstituted it on an ideal basis. The one has left behind him some of the profoundest aphorisms of political wisdom; the other, some of the clearest principles of political science. The one, clinging to Divine right, found in the fact that things were, a reason that they ought to be; the other, aiming to solve the problem of the Divine order, would deduce from that abstraction alone the claim of anything to be at all. There seems a mere oppugnancy of nature between the two, and yet both were, in different ways, the dupes of their own imaginations.

Now let us hear the opinion of a philosopher who *was* a bear, whether bears be philosophers or not. Boswell had a genuine relish for what was superior in any way, from genius to claret, and of course he did not let Rousseau escape him. "One evening at the Mitre, Johnson said sarcastically to me, 'It seems, sir, you have kept very good company abroad,— Rousseau and Wilkes!' I answered with a smile, 'My dear sir, you don't call Rousseau bad company; do you really think *him* a bad man?' JOHNSON. 'Sir, if you are talking jestingly of this, I don't talk with you. If you mean to be serious, I think him one of the worst of men, a rascal who ought to be hunted out of society, as he has been. Three or four nations have expelled him, and it is a shame that he is protected in this country. Rousseau, sir, is a very bad man. I would sooner sign a sentence for his transportation, than that of any felon who has gone from the Old Bailey these many years. Yes, I should like to have him work in the plantations.'" *We* were the plantations then, and Rousseau was destined to work there in another and much more wonderful fashion than the gruff old Ursa Major imagined. However, there is always a refreshing heartiness in his growl, a masculine bass with no snarl in it. The Doctor's logic is of that fine old crusted Port sort, the native manufacture of the British conservative mind. Three or four nations *have*, therefore England ought. A few years later, had the Doctor been living, if three or four nations had treated their kings as France did hers, would he have thought the *ergo* a very stringent one for England?

Mr. Burke, who could speak with studied respect of the Prince of Wales, and of his vices with that charity which thinketh no evil and can afford to think no evil of so important a living member of the British Constitution, surely could have had no unmixed moral repugnance for Rousseau's "disgustful amours." It was because they were *his* that they were so loathsome. Mr. Burke was a snob, though an inspired one. Dr. Johnson, the friend of that wretchedest of lewd fellows, Richard Savage, and of that gay man about town, Topham Beauclerk,—himself sprung from an amour that would have been disgustful had it not been royal,—must also have felt something more in respect of Rousseau than the mere repugnance of virtue for vice. We must sometimes allow to personal temperament its right of peremptory challenge. Johnson had not that fine sensitiveness to the political atmosphere which made Burke presageful of coming tempest, but both of them felt that there was something dangerous in this man. Their dislike has in it somewhat of the energy of fear. Neither of them had the same feeling toward Voltaire, the man of supreme talent, but both felt that what Rousseau was possessed by was genius, with its terrible force either to attract or repel.

> "By the pricking of my thumbs,
> Something wicked this way comes."

Burke and Johnson were both of them sincere men, both of them men of character as well as of intellectual force; and I cite their opinions of Rousseau with the respect due to an honest conviction which has apparent grounds for its adoption, whether we agree with it or no. But it strikes me as a little singular that one whose life was so full of moral inconsistency, whose character is so contemptible in many ways, in some one might almost say so revolting, should yet have exercised so deep and lasting an influence, and on minds so various, should still be an object of minute and earnest discussion,—that he should have had such vigor in his intellectual loins as to have been the father of Châteaubriand, Byron, Lamartine, George Sand, and many more in literature, in politics of Jefferson and Thomas Paine,—that the spots he had haunted should draw pilgrims so unlike as Gibbon and Napoleon, nay, should draw them still, after the lapse of near a century. Surely there must have been a basis of sincerity in this man seldom matched, if it can prevail against so many reasons for repugnance, aversion, and even disgust. He could not have been the mere sentimentalist and rhetorician for which the rough-and-ready understanding would at first glance be inclined to condemn him. In a certain sense he was both of these, but he was something more. . . .

It was not Rousseau's genius that was an impostor. It was the one thing in him that was always true. We grant that, in allowing that a man has genius. Talent is that which is in a man's power; genius is that in whose power a man is. That is the very difference between them. We might turn the tables on Moore, the man of talent, and say truly enough, What an impostor talent is! Moore talks of the mimetic power with a total misapprehension of what it really is. The mimetic power had nothing whatever to do with the affair. Rousseau had none of it; Shakespeare had it in excess; but what difference would it make in our judgment of Hamlet or Othello if a manuscript of Shakespeare's memoirs should turn up, and we should find out that he had been a pitiful fellow? None in the world; for he is not a professed moralist, and his life does not give the warrant to his words. But if Demosthenes, after all his Philippics, throws away his shield and runs, we feel the contemptibleness of the contradiction. With genius itself we never find any fault. It would be an over-nicety that would do that. We do not get invited to nectar and ambrosia so often that we think of grumbling and saying we have better at home. No; the same genius that mastered him who wrote the poem masters us in reading it, and we care for nothing outside the poem itself. How the author lived, what he wore, how he looked,—all that is mere gossip, about which we need not trouble ourselves. Whatever he was or did, somehow or other God let him be worthy to write *this*, and that is enough for us. We forgive everything to the genius; we are inexorable to the man. Shakespeare, Goethe, Burns,—what have their biographies to do with us? Genius is not a question of character. It may be sordid, like the lamp of Aladdin, in its externals; what care we, while the touch of it builds palaces for us, makes us rich as only men in dream-land are rich, and lords to the utmost bound of imagination? So, when people talk of the ungrateful way in which the world treats its geniuses, they speak unwisely. There is no work of genius which has not been the delight of mankind, no word of genius to which the human heart and soul have not, sooner or later, responded. But the man whom the genius takes possession of for its pen, for its trowel, for its pencil, for its chisel, *him* the world treats according to his deserts. Does Burns drink? It sets him to gauging casks of gin. For, remember, it is not to the practical world that the genius appeals; it *is* the practical world which judges of the man's fitness for its uses, and has a right so to judge. No amount of patronage could have made distilled liquors less toothsome to Robbie Burns, as no amount of them could make a Burns of the Ettrick Shepherd.

There is an old story in the *Gesta Romanorum* of a priest who was found fault with by one of his parishioners because his life was in painful discordance with his teaching. So one day he takes his critic out to a stream, and, giving him to drink of it, asks him if he does not find it sweet and pure water. The parishioner, having answered that it was, is taken to the source, and finds that what had so refreshed him flowed from between the jaws of a dead dog. "Let this teach thee," said the priest, "that the very best doctrine may take its rise in a very impure and disgustful spring, and that excellent morals may be taught by a man who has no morals at all." It is easy enough to see the fallacy here. Had the man known beforehand from what a carrion fountain-head the stream issued, he could not have drunk of it without loathing. Had the priest merely bidden him to *look* at the stream and see how beautiful it was, instead of tasting it, it would have been quite another matter. And this is precisely the difference between what appeals to our æsthetic or to our moral sense, between what is judged of by the taste or by the conscience.

It is when the sentimentalist turns preacher of morals that we investigate his character, and are justified in so doing. He may express as many and as delicate shades of feeling as he likes,—for this the sensibility of his organization perfectly fits him and no other person could do it so well,—but the moment he undertakes to establish his feeling as a rule of conduct, we ask at once how far are his own life and deed in accordance with what he preaches? For every man feels instinctively that all the beautiful sentiments in the world weigh less than a single lovely action; and that while tenderness of feeling and susceptibility to generous emotions are accidents of temperament, goodness is an achievement of the will and a quality of the life. Fine words, says our homely old proverb, butter no parsnips; and if the question be how to render those vegetables palatable, an ounce of butter would be worth more than all the orations of Cicero. The only conclusive evidence of a man's sincerity is that he give *himself* for a principle. Words, money, all things else, are comparatively easy to give away; but when a man makes a gift of his daily life and practice, it is plain that the truth, whatever it may be, has taken possession of him. From that sincerity his words gain the force and pertinency of deeds, and his money is no longer the pale drudge 'twixt man and man, but, by a beautiful magic, what erewhile bore the image and superscription of Cæsar seems now to bear the image and superscription of God. It is thus that there is a genius for goodness, for magnanimity, for self-sacrifice, as well as for creative art; and it is thus that by a more refined sort of Platonism the Infinite Beauty dwells in and shapes to its own likeness the soul which gives it body and individuality. But when Moore charges genius with being an impostor, the confusion of his ideas is pitiable. There is nothing so true, so sincere, so downright and forthright, as genius. It is always truer than the man himself is, greater than he. If Shakespeare the man had been as marvellous a creature as the genius that wrote his plays, that genius so comprehensive in its intelligence, so wise even in its play that its clowns are moralists and philosophers, so penetrative that a single one of its phrases reveals to us the secret of our own character, would his contemporaries have left us so wholly without record of him as they have done, distinguishing him in no wise from his fellow-players?

Rousseau, no doubt, was weak, nay, more than that, was sometimes despicable, but yet is not fairly to be reckoned among the herd of sentimentalists. It is shocking that a man whose preaching made it fashionable for women of rank to nurse their children should have sent his own, as soon as born, to the foundling hospital, still more shocking that, in a note to his *Discours sur l'Inégalité*, he should speak of this crime as one of the consequences of our social system. But for all that there was a faith and an ardor of conviction in him that distinguish him from most of the writers of his time. Nor were his practice and his preaching always inconsistent. He contrived to pay regularly, whatever his own circumstances were, a pension of one hundred *livres* a year to a maternal aunt who had been kind to him in childhood. Nor was his asceticism a sham. He might have turned his gift into laced coats and *châteaux* as easily as Voltaire, had he not held it too sacred to be bartered away in any such losing exchange.

But what is worthy of especial remark is this,—that in nearly all that he wrote his leading object was the good of his kind, and that, through all the vicissitudes of a life which illness, sensibility of temperament, and the approaches of insanity rendered wretched,—the associate of infidels, the foundling child, as it were, of an age without belief, least of all with any belief in itself,—he professed and evidently felt deeply a faith in the goodness both of man and of God. There is no such thing as scoffing in his writings. On the other hand, there is no stereotyped morality. He does not ignore the existence of scepticism; he recognizes its existence in his own nature, meets it frankly face to face, and makes it confess that there are things in the teaching of Christ that are deeper than its doubt. The influence of his early education at Geneva is apparent here. An intellect so acute as his, trained in the school of Calvin in a re-

public where theological discussion was as much the amusement of the people as the opera was at Paris, could not fail to be
a good logician. He had the fortitude to follow his logic where-
ever it led him. If the very impressibility of character which
quickened his perception of the beauties of nature, and made
him alive to the charm of music and musical expression, prevented him from being in the highest sense an original writer,
and if his ideas were mostly suggested to him by books, yet
the clearness, consecutiveness, and eloquence with which he
stated and enforced them made them his own. There was at
least that original fire in him which could fuse them and run
them in a novel mould. His power lay in this very ability of
manipulating the thoughts of others. Fond of paradox he
doubtless was, but he had a way of putting things that arrested
attention and excited thought.

It was, perhaps, this very sensibility to the surrounding atmosphere of feeling and speculation, which made Rousseau
more directly influential on contemporary thought (or perhaps
we should say sentiment) than any writer of his time. And this
is rarely consistent with enduring greatness in literature. It
forces us to remember, against our will, the oratorical character
of his works. They were all pleas, and he a great advocate,
with Europe in the jury-box. Enthusiasm begets enthusiasm,
eloquence produces conviction for the moment, but it is only
by truth to nature and the everlasting intuitions of mankind
that those abiding influences are won that enlarge from generation to generation. Rousseau was in many respects—as great
pleaders always are—a man of the day, who must needs become
a mere name to posterity, yet he could not but have had in him
some not inconsiderable share of that principle by which man
eternizes himself. . . .

But it would be sheer waste of time to hunt Rousseau through
all his doublings of inconsistency, and run him to earth in every
new paradox. His first two books attacked, one of them literature, and the other society. But this did not prevent him from
being diligent with his pen, nor from availing himself of his
credit with persons who enjoyed all the advantages of that in-

equality whose evils he had so pointedly exposed. Indeed, it is curious how little practical communism there has been, how few professors it has had who would not have gained by a general dividend. It is perhaps no frantic effort of generosity in a philosopher with ten crowns in his pocket when he offers to make common stock with a neighbor who has ten thousand of yearly income, nor is it an uncommon thing to see such theories knocked clean out of a man's head by the descent of a thumping legacy. But, consistent or not, Rousseau remains permanently interesting as the highest and most perfect type of the sentimentalist of genius. His was perhaps the acutest mind that was ever mated with an organization so diseased,[1] the brain most far-reaching in speculation that ever kept itself steady and worked out its problems amid such disordered tumult of the nerves. His letter to the Archbishop of Paris, admirable for its lucid power and soberness of tone, and his *Rousseau jugé de Jean Jacques*, which no man can read and believe him to have been sane, show him to us in his strength and weakness, and give us a more charitable, let us hope therefore a truer, notion of him than his own apology for himself. That he was a man of genius appears unmistakably in his impressibility by the deeper meaning of the epoch in which he lived. Before an eruption, clouds steeped through and through with electric life gather over the crater, as if in sympathy and expectation. As the mountain heaves and cracks, these vapory masses are seamed with fire, as if they felt and answered the dumb agony that is struggling for utterance below. Just such flashes of eager sympathetic fire break continually from the cloudy volumes of Rousseau, the result at once and the warning of that convulsion of which Paris was to be the crater and all Europe to feel the spasm. There are symptoms enough elsewhere of that want of faith in the existing order which made the Revolution inevitable,—even so shallow an observer as Horace Walpole could forebode it so early as 1765,—but Rousseau more than all others is the unconscious expression of the groping after something radically new, the instinct for a change

[1] Perhaps we should except Newton.

that should be organic and pervade every fibre of the social and political body. Freedom of thought owes far more to the jester Voltaire, who also had his solid kernel of earnest, than to the sombre Genevese, whose earnestness is of the deadly kind. Yet, for good or evil, the latter was the foster-father of modern democracy, and without him our Declaration of Independence would have wanted some of those sentences in which the immemorial longings of the poor and the dreams of solitary enthusiasts were at last affirmed as axioms in the manifesto of a nation, so that all the world might hear.

Though Rousseau, like many other fanatics, had a remarkable vein of common sense in him, (witness his remarks on duelling, on landscape-gardening, on French poetry, and much of his thought on education,) we cannot trace many practical results to his teaching, least of all in politics. For the great difficulty with his system, if system it may be called, is, that, while it professes to follow nature, it not only assumes as a starting-point that the individual man may be made over again, but proceeds to the conclusion that man himself, that human nature, must be made over again, and governments remodelled on a purely theoretic basis. But when something like an experiment in this direction was made in 1789, not only did it fail as regarded man in general, but even as regards the particular variety of man that inhabited France. The Revolution accomplished many changes, and beneficent ones, yet it left France peopled, not by a new race without traditions, but by Frenchmen. Still, there must have been a wonderful force in the words of a man who, above all others, had the secret of making abstractions glow with his own fervor; and his ideas, dispersed now in the atmosphere of thought, have influenced, perhaps still continue to influence, speculative minds, which prefer swift and sure generalization to hesitating and doubtful experience.

Rousseau has, in one respect, been utterly misrepresented and misunderstood. Even Châteaubriand most unfilially classes him and Voltaire together. It appears to me that the inmost core of his being was religious. Had he remained in the Catholic Church, he might have been a saint. Had he come

earlier, he might have founded an order. His was precisely
the nature on which religious enthusiasm takes the strongest
hold, a temperament which finds sensuous delight in spiritual
things, and satisfies its craving for excitement with celestial
debauch. He had not the iron temper of a great reformer and
organizer like Knox, who, true Scotchman that he was, found
a way to weld this world and the other together in a cast-iron
creed; but he had as much as any man ever had that gift of a
great preacher to make the oratorical fervor which persuades
himself while it lasts into the abiding conviction of his hearers.
That very persuasion of his, that the soul could remain pure
while the life was corrupt, is not unexampled among men who
have left holier names than he. His "Confessions," also,
would assign him to that class with whom the religious sentiment is strong and the moral nature weak. They are apt to
believe that they may, as special pleaders say, confess and
avoid. Hawthorne has admirably illustrated this in the penance
of Mr. Dimmesdale. With all the soil that is upon Rousseau, I
cannot help looking on him as one capable beyond any in his
generation of being divinely possessed; and if it happened otherwise, when we remember the much that hindered and the little
that helped in a life and time like his, we shall be much readier
to pity than to condemn. It was his very fitness for being something better that makes him able to shock us so with what in
too many respects he unhappily was. Less gifted, he had been
less hardly judged. More than any other of the sentimentalists,
except possibly Sterne, he had in him a staple of sincerity.
Compared with Châteaubriand, he is honesty, compared with
Lamartine, he is manliness, itself. His nearest congener in our
own tongue is Cowper.

In the whole school there is a sickly taint. The strongest
mark which Rousseau has left upon literature is a sensibility
to the picturesque in Nature, not with Nature as a strengthener
and consoler, a wholesome tonic for a mind ill at ease with
itself, but with Nature as a kind of feminine echo to the mood,
flattering it with sympathy rather than correcting it with rebuke or lifting it away from its unmanly depression, as in the

wholesomer fellow-feeling of Wordsworth. They seek in her an accessory, and not a reproof. It is less a sympathy with Nature than a sympathy with ourselves as we compel her to reflect us. It is solitude, Nature for her estrangement from man, not for her companionship with him; it is desolation and ruin, Nature as she has triumphed over man, with which this order of mind seeks communion and in which it finds solace. It is with the hostile and destructive power of matter, and not with the spirit of life and renewal that dwells in it, that they ally themselves. And in human character it is the same. St. Preux, René, Werther, Manfred, Quasimodo, they are all anomalies, distortions, ruins,—so much easier is it to caricature life from our own sickly conception of it than to paint it in its noble simplicity; so much cheaper is unreality than truth.

Every man is conscious that he leads two lives, the one trivial and ordinary, the other sacred and recluse; one which he carries to society and the dinner-table, the other in which his youth and aspiration survive for him, and which is a confidence between himself and God. Both may be equally sincere, and there need be no contradiction between them, any more than in a healthy man between soul and body. If the higher life be real and earnest, its result, whether in literature or affairs, will be real and earnest too. But no man can produce great things who is not thoroughly sincere in dealing with himself, who would not exchange the finest show for the poorest reality, who does not so love his work that he is not only glad to give himself for it, but finds rather a gain than a sacrifice in the surrender. The sentimentalist does not think of what he does so much as of what the world will think of what he does. He translates should into would, looks upon the spheres of duty and beauty as alien to each other, and can never learn how life rounds itself to a noble completeness between these two opposite but mutually sustaining poles of what we long for and what we must. . . .

From SHAKESPEARE ONCE MORE

(Hamlet)

(1868)

Goethe, in one of the most perfect of his shorter poems, tells us that a poem is like a painted window. Seen from without (and he accordingly justifies the Philistine, who never looks at them otherwise) they seem dingy and confused enough; but enter, and then

> "Da ist's auf einmal farbig helle,
> Geschicht' und Zierath glänzt in Schnelle."

With the same feeling he says elsewhere in prose, that "there is a destructive criticism and a productive. The former is very easy; for one has only to set up in his mind any standard, any model, however narrow" (let us say the Greeks), "and then boldly assert that the work under review does not match with it, and therefore is good for nothing,—the matter is settled, and one must at once deny its claim. Productive criticism is a great deal more difficult; it asks, What did the author propose to himself? Is what he proposes reasonable and comprehensible? and how far has he succeeded in carrying it out?" It is in applying this latter kind of criticism to Shakespeare that the Germans have set us an example worthy of all commendation. If they have been sometimes over-subtile, they at least had the merit of first looking at his works as wholes, as something that very likely contained an idea, perhaps conveyed a moral, if we could get at it. The illumination lent us by most of the English commentators reminds us of the candles which guides hold up to show us a picture in a dark place, the smoke of which gradually makes the work of the artist invisible under its repeated layers. Lessing, as might have been expected, opened the first glimpse in the new direction; Goethe followed with his famous exposition of Hamlet; A. W. Schlegel took a more comprehensive view in his Lectures, which Coleridge worked over into English, adding many fine criticisms of his own on

single passages; and finally, Gervinus has devoted four volumes
to a comment on the plays, full of excellent matter, though
pushing the moral exegesis beyond all reasonable bounds.[1]
With the help of all these, and especially of the last, I shall apply this theory of criticism to Hamlet, not in the hope of saying
anything new, but of bringing something to the support of the
thesis, that, if Shakespeare was skilful as a playwright, he was
even greater as a dramatist,—that, if his immediate business
was to fill the theatre, his higher object was to create something
which, by fulfilling the conditions and answering the requirements of modern life, should as truly deserve to be called a
work of art as others had deserved it by doing the same thing
in former times and under other circumstances. Supposing
him to have accepted—consciously or not is of little importance—the new terms of the problem which makes character
the pivot of dramatic action, and consequently the key of
dramatic unity, how far did he succeed?

Before attempting my analysis, I must clear away a little
rubbish. Are such anachronisms as those of which Voltaire
accuses Shakespeare in Hamlet, such as the introduction of
cannon before the invention of gunpowder, and making Christians of the Danes three centuries too soon, of the least bearing
aesthetically? I think not; but as they are of a piece with a
great many other criticisms upon the great poet, it is worth
while to dwell upon them a moment.

The first demand we make upon whatever claims to be a
work of art (and we have a right to make it) is that it shall be
in keeping. Now this propriety is of two kinds, either extrinsic
or intrinsic. In the first I should class whatever relates rather
to the body than the soul of the work, such as fidelity to the
facts of history (wherever that is important), congruity of costume, and the like,—in short, whatever might come under the
head of *picturesque* truth, a departure from which would shock
too rudely our preconceived associations. I have seen an Indian
chief in French boots, and he seemed to me almost tragic; but,

[1] I do not mention Ulrici's book, for it seems to me unwieldy and
dull—zeal without knowledge.

put upon the stage in tragedy, he would have been ludicrous.
Lichtenberg, writing from London in 1775, tells us that Garrick
played Hamlet in a suit of the French fashion, then commonly
worn, and that he was blamed for it by some of the critics; but,
he says, one hears no such criticism during the play, nor on
the way home, nor at supper afterwards, nor indeed till the
emotion roused by the great actor has had time to subside. He
justifies Garrick, though we should not be able to endure it now.
Yet nothing would be gained by trying to make Hamlet's costume true to the assumed period of the play, for the scene of it
is laid in a Denmark that has no dates.

In the second and more important category, I should put,
first, coördination of character, that is, a certain variety in harmony of the personages of a drama, as in the attitudes and
coloring of the figures in a pictorial composition, so that, while
mutually relieving and setting off each other, they shall combine in the total impression; second, that subordinate truth to
Nature which makes each character coherent in itself; and, third,
such propriety of costume and the like as shall satisfy the super-
historic sense, to which, and to which alone, the higher drama
appeals. All these come within the scope of *imaginative* truth.
To illustrate my third head by an example. Tieck criticises
John Kemble's dressing for Macbeth in a modern Highland
costume, as being ungraceful without any countervailing merit
of historical exactness. I think a deeper reason for his dissatisfaction might be found in the fact, that this garb, with its purely
modern and British army associations, is out of place on Forres
Heath, and drags the Weird Sisters down with it from their
proper imaginative remoteness in the gloom of the past to the
disenchanting glare of the foot-lights. It is not the antiquarian,
but the poetic conscience that is wounded. To this, exactness,
so far as concerns ideal representation, may not only not be
truth, but may even be opposed to it. Anachronisms and the
like are in themselves of no account, and become important
only when they make a gap too wide for our illusion to cross
unconsciously, that is, when they are anacoluthons to the imagination. The aim of the artist is psychologic, not historic

truth. It is comparatively easy for an author to *get up* any
period with tolerable minuteness in externals, but readers and
audiences find more difficulty in getting them down, though
oblivion swallows scores of them at a gulp. The saving truth
in such matters is a truth to essential and permanent characteristics. The Ulysses of Shakespeare, like the Ulysses of Dante
and Tennyson, more or less harmonizes with our ideal conception of the wary, long-considering, though adventurous son of
Laertes, yet Simon Lord Lovat is doubtless nearer the original
type. In Hamlet, though there be no Denmark of the ninth
century, Shakespeare has suggested the prevailing rudeness
of manners quite enough for his purpose. We see it in the
single combat of Hamlet's father with the elder Fortinbras, in
the vulgar wassail of the king, in the English monarch being expected to hang Rosencrantz and Guildenstern out of hand
merely to oblige his cousin of Denmark, in Laertes, sent to
Paris to be made a gentleman of, becoming instantly capable
of any the most barbarous treachery to glut his vengeance. We
cannot fancy Ragnar Lodbrog or Eric the Red matriculating at
Wittenberg, but it was essential that Hamlet should be a
scholar, and Shakespeare sends him thither without more ado.
All through the play we get the notion of a state of society in
which a savage nature has disguised itself in the externals of
civilization, like a Maori deacon, who has only to strip and he
becomes once more a tattooed pagan with his mouth watering
for a spare-rib of his pastor. Historically, at the date of Hamlet, the Danes were in the habit of burning their enemies alive
in their houses, with as much of their family about them as
might be to make it comfortable. Shakespeare seems purposely
to have dissociated his play from history by changing nearly
every name in the original legend. The motive of the play—
revenge as a religious duty—belongs only to a social state in
which the traditions of barbarism are still operative, but, with
infallible artistic judgment, Shakespeare has chosen, not untamed Nature, as he found it in history, but the period of transition, a period in which the times are always out of joint, and
thus the irresolution which has its root in Hamlet's own char-

acter is stimulated by the very incompatibility of that legacy of vengeance he has inherited from the past with the new culture and refinement of which he is the representative. One of the few books which Shakespeare is known to have possessed was Florio's Montaigne, and he might well have transferred the Frenchman's motto, *Que sçais je?* to the front of his tragedy; nor can I help fancying something more than accident in the fact that Hamlet has been a student at Wittenberg, whence those new ideas went forth, of whose results in unsettling men's faith, and consequently disqualifying them for promptness in action, Shakespeare had been not only an eye-witness, but which he must actually have experienced in himself.

One other objection let me touch upon here, especially as it has been urged against Hamlet, and that is the introduction of low characters and comic scenes in tragedy. Even Garrick, who had just assisted at the Stratford Jubilee, where Shakespeare had been pronounced divine, was induced by this absurd outcry for the proprieties of the tragic stage to omit the grave-diggers' scene from Hamlet. Leaving apart the fact that Shakespeare would not have been the representative poet he is, if he had not given expression to this striking tendency of the Northern races, which shows itself constantly, not only in their literature, but even in their mythology and their architecture, the grave-diggers' scene always impresses me as one of the most pathetic in the whole tragedy. That Shakespeare introduced such scenes and characters with deliberate intention, and with a view to artistic relief and contrast, there can hardly be a doubt. We must take it for granted that a man whose works show everywhere the results of judgment sometimes acted with forethought. I find the springs of the profoundest sorrow and pity in this hardened indifference of the grave-diggers, in their careless discussion as to whether Ophelia's death were by suicide or no, in their singing and jesting at their dreary work.

> "A pickaxe and a spade, a spade,
> For—and a shrouding-sheet:
> O, a pit of clay for to be made
> For such a guest is meet!"

We know who is to be the guest of this earthen hospitality,—
how much beauty, love, and heartbreak are to be covered in
that pit of clay. All we remember of Ophelia reacts upon us
with tenfold force, and we recoil from our amusement at the
ghastly drollery of the two delvers with a shock of horror.
That the unconscious Hamlet should stumble on *this* grave of
all others, that it should be *here* that he should pause to muse
humorously on death and decay,—all this prepares us for the
revulsion of passion in the next scene, and for the frantic confession,—

> "I loved Ophelia; forty thousand brothers
>   Could not with all *their* quantity of love
>   Make up my sum!"

And it is only here that such an asseveration would be true
even to the feeling of the moment; for it is plain from all we
know of Hamlet that he could not so have loved Ophelia, that
he was incapable of the self-abandonment of a true passion,
that he would have analyzed this emotion as he does all others,
would have peeped and botanized upon it till it became to him
a mere matter of scientific interest. All this force of contrast
and this horror of surprise were necessary so to intensify his
remorseful regret that he should believe himself for once in
earnest. The speech of the King, "O, he is mad, Laertes," recalls him to himself, and he at once begins to rave:—

> "Zounds! show me what thou'lt do!
>   Woul't weep? woul't fight? woul't fast? woul't tear thyself?
>   Woul't drink up eysil? eat a crocodile?"

It is easy to see that the whole plot hinges upon the character
of Hamlet, that Shakespeare's conception of this was the ovum
out of which the whole organism was hatched. And here let
me remark, that there is a kind of genealogical necessity in the
character,—a thing not altogether strange to the attentive
reader of Shakespeare. Hamlet seems the natural result of the
mixture of father and mother in his temperament, the resolution
and persistence of the one, like sound timber wormholed and

made shaky, as it were, by the other's infirmity of will and discontinuity of purpose. In natures so imperfectly mixed it is not uncommon to find vehemence of intention the prelude and counterpoise of weak performance, the conscious nature striving to keep up its self-respect by a triumph in words all the more resolute that it feels assured beforehand of inevitable defeat in action. As in such slipshod housekeeping men are their own largest creditors, they find it easy to stave off utter bankruptcy of conscience by taking up one unpaid promise with another larger, and at heavier interest, till such self-swindling becomes habitual and by degrees almost painless. How did Coleridge discount his own notes of this kind with less and less specie as the figures lengthened on the paper! As with Hamlet, so it is with Ophelia and Laertes. The father's feebleness comes up again in the wasting heartbreak and gentle lunacy of the daughter, while the son shows it in a rashness of impulse and act, a kind of crankiness, of whose essential feebleness we are all the more sensible as contrasted with a nature so steady on its keel, and drawing so much water, as that of Horatio,—the foil at once, in different ways, both to him and Hamlet. It was natural, also, that the daughter of self-conceited old Polonius should have her softness stiffened with a fibre of obstinacy; for there are two kinds of weakness, that which breaks, and that which bends. Ophelia's is of the former kind; Hero is her counterpart, giving way before calamity, and rising again as soon as the pressure is removed.

I find two passages in Dante that contain the exactest possible definition of that habit or quality of Hamlet's mind which justifies the tragic turn of the play, and renders it natural and unavoidable from the beginning. The first is from the second canto of the *Inferno:*—

> "E quale è quei che disvuol ciò che volle,
> E per nuovi pensier cangia proposta,
> Sì che dal cominciar tutto si tolle;
> Tal mi fec' io in quella oscura costa:
> Perchè pensando consumai la impresa
> Che fu nel cominciar cotanto tosta."

And like the man who unwills what he willed,
And for new thoughts doth change his first intent,
So that he cannot anywhere begin,
Such became I upon that slope obscure,
Because with thinking I consumed resolve,
That was so ready at the setting out.

Again, in the fifth of the *Purgatorio:*—

"Chè sempre l'uomo in cui pensier rampolla
Sopra pensier, da sè dilunga il segno,
Perchè la foga l'un dell'altro insolla."

For always he in whom one thought buds forth
Out of another farther puts the goal,
For each has only force to mar the other.

Dante was a profound metaphysician, and as in the first
passage he describes and defines a certain quality of mind, so
in the other he tells us its result in the character and life, namely,
indecision and failure,—the goal *farther* off at the end than at the
beginning. It is remarkable how close a resemblance of thought,
and even of expression, there is between the former of these
quotations and a part of Hamlet's famous soliloquy:—

"Thus conscience [i.e., consciousness] doth make
        cowards of us all:
And thus the native hue of resolution
Is sicklied o'er with the pale cast of thought,
And enterprises of great pith and moment
With this regard their currents turn awry,
And lose the name of action!"

It is an inherent peculiarity of a mind like Hamlet's that it
should be conscious of its own defect. Men of his type are
forever analyzing their own emotions and motives. They cannot do anything, because they always see two ways of doing it.
They cannot determine on any course of action, because they
are always, as it were, standing at the crossroads, and see too
well the disadvantages of every one of them. It is not that they
are incapable of resolve, but somehow the band between the

motive power and the operative faculties is relaxed and loose. The engine works, but the machinery it should drive stands still. The imagination is so much in overplus, that thinking a thing becomes better than doing it, and thought with its easy perfection, capable of everything because it can accomplish everything with ideal means, is vastly more attractive and satisfactory than deed, which must be wrought at best with imperfect instruments, and always falls short of the conception that went before it. "If to do," says Portia in the *Merchant of Venice*,—"if to do were as easy as to know what 't were good to do, chapels had been churches, and poor men's cottages princes' palaces." Hamlet knows only too well what 't were good to do, but he palters with everything in a double sense: he sees the grain of good there is in evil, and the grain of evil there is in good, as they exist in the world, and, finding that he can make those feather-weighted accidents balance each other, infers that there is little to choose between the essences themselves. He is of Montaigne's mind, and says expressly that "there is nothing good or ill, but thinking makes it so." He dwells so exclusively in the world of ideas that the world of facts seems trifling; nothing is worth the while; and he has been so long objectless and purposeless, so far as actual life is concerned, that, when at last an object and an aim are forced upon him, he cannot deal with them, and gropes about vainly for a motive outside of himself that shall marshal his thoughts for him and guide his faculties into the path of action. He is the victim not so much of feebleness of will as of an intellectual indifference that hinders the will from working long in any one direction. He wishes to will, but never wills. His continual iteration of resolve shows that he has no resolution. He is capable of passionate energy where the occasion presents itself suddenly from without, because nothing is so irritable as conscious irresolution with a duty to perform. But of deliberate energy he is not capable; for there the impulse must come from within, and the blade of his analysis is so subtile that it can divide the finest hair of motive 'twixt north and northwest side, leaving him desperate to choose between them. The very consciousness of his defect is an insuperable bar to his repairing it; for the unity of purpose, which infuses every fibre of the character with will available whenever wanted, is impossible where the mind can never rest till it has resolved that unity into its component elements, and satisfied itself which on the whole is of greater value. A critical instinct so insatiable that it must turn upon itself, for lack of something else to hew and hack, becomes incapable at last of originating anything except indecision. It becomes infallible in what *not* to do. How easily he might have accomplished his task is shown by the conduct of Laertes. When *he* has a death to avenge, he raises a mob, breaks into the palace, bullies the king, and proves how weak the usurper really was.

The world is the victim of splendid parts, and is slow to accept a rounded whole, because that is something which is long in completing, still longer in demonstrating its completion. We like to be surprised into admiration, and not logically convinced that we ought to admire. We are willing to be delighted with success, though we are somewhat indifferent to the homely qualities which insure it. Our thought is so filled with the rocket's burst of momentary splendor so far above us, that we forget the poor stick, useful and unseen, that made its climbing possible. One of these homely qualities is continuity of character, and it escapes present applause because it tells chiefly in the long run, in results. With his usual tact, Shakespeare has brought in such a character as a contrast and foil to Hamlet. Horatio is the only complete *man* in the play,— solid, well-knit, and true; a noble, quiet nature, with that highest of all qualities, judgment, always sane and prompt; who never drags his anchors for any wind of opinion or fortune, but grips all the closer to the reality of things. He seems one of those calm, undemonstrative men whom we love and admire without asking to know why, crediting them with the capacity of great things, without any test of actual achievement, because we feel that their manhood is a constant quality, and no mere accident of circumstance and opportunity. Such men are always sure of the presence of their highest self on demand. Hamlet is continually drawing bills on the future, secured by his promise of himself to himself, which he can never redeem. His own somewhat feminine nature recognizes its complement in Horatio, and clings to it instinctively, as naturally as Horatio is attracted by that fatal gift of imagination, the absence of which makes the strength of his own character, as its overplus does the weakness of Hamlet's. It is a happy marriage of two minds drawn together by the charm of unlikeness. Hamlet feels in Horatio the solid steadiness which he misses in himself; Horatio in Hamlet that need of service and sustainment to render which gives him a consciousness of his own value. Hamlet fills the place of a woman to Horatio, revealing him to himself not only in what he says, but by a constant claim upon his strength of nature; and there is great psychological truth in making suicide the first impulse of this quiet, undemonstrative man, after Hamlet's death, as if the very reason for his being were taken away with his friend's need of him. In his grief, he for the first and only time speaks of himself, is first made conscious of himself by his loss. If this manly reserve of Horatio be true to Nature, not less so are the communicativeness of Hamlet and his tendency to soliloquize. If self-consciousness be alien to the one, it is just as truly the happiness of the other. Like a musician distrustful of himself, he is forever tuning his instrument, first overstraining this cord a little, and then that, but unable to bring them into unison, or to profit by it if he could.

I do not believe that Horatio ever thought he "was not a pipe for Fortune's finger to play what stop she please," till Hamlet told him so. That was Fortune's affair, not his; let her try it, if she liked. He is unconscious of his own peculiar qualities, as men of decision commonly are, or they would not be men of decision. When there is a thing to be done, they go straight at it, and for the time there is nothing for them in the whole universe but themselves and their object. Hamlet, on the other hand, is always studying himself. This world and the other, too, are always present to his mind, and there in the corner is the little black kobold of a doubt making mouths at him. He breaks down the bridges before him, not behind him, as a man of action would do; but there is something more than this. He is an ingrained sceptic; though his is the scepticism, not of reason, but of feeling, whose root is want of faith in himself. In him it is passive, a malady rather than a function of the mind. We might call him insincere: not that he was in any sense a hypocrite, but only that he never was and never could be in earnest. Never could be, because no man without intense faith in something ever can. Even if he only believed in himself, that were better than nothing; for it will carry a man a great way in the outward successes of life, nay, will even sometimes give him the Archimedean fulcrum for moving the world. But Hamlet doubts everything. He doubts the immortality of the soul, just after seeing his father's spirit, and hearing from its mouth the secrets of the other world. He doubts Horatio even, and swears him to secrecy on the cross of his sword, though probably he himself has no assured belief in the sacredness of the symbol. He doubts Ophelia, and asks her, "Are you honest?" He doubts the ghost, after he has had a little time to think about it, and so gets up the play to test the guilt of the king. And how coherent the whole character is! With what perfect tact and judgment Shakespeare, in the advice to the players, makes him an exquisite critic! For just here that part of his character which would be weak in dealing with affairs is strong. A wise scepticism is the first attribute of a good critic. He must not believe that the fire-insurance offices will raise their rates of premium on the Charles, because the new volume of poems is printing at Riverside or the University Press. He must not believe so profoundly in the ancients as to think it wholly out of the question that the world has still vigor enough in its loins to beget some one who will one of these days be as good an ancient as any of them.

Another striking quality in Hamlet's nature is his perpetual inclination to irony. I think this has been generally passed over too lightly, as if it were something external and accidental, rather assumed as a mask than part of the real nature of the man. It seems to me to go deeper, to be something innate, and not merely factitious. It is nothing like the grave irony of Socrates, which was the weapon of a man thoroughly in earnest,—the *boomerang* of argument, which one throws in the opposite direction of what he means to hit, and which seems to be flying away from the adversary, who will presently find himself knocked down by it. It is not like the irony of Timon, which is but the wilful refraction of a clear mind twisting awry whatever enters it,—or of Iago, which is the slime that a nature essentially evil loves to trail over all beauty and goodness to taint them with distrust: it is the half-jest, half-earnest of an inactive temperament that has not quite made up its mind whether life is a reality or no, whether men were not made in jest, and which amuses itself equally with finding a deep meaning in trivial things and a trifling one in the profoundest mysteries of being, because the want of earnestness in its own essence infects everything else with its own indifference. If there be now and then an unmannerly rudeness and bitterness in it, as in the scenes with Polonius and Osrick, we must remember that Hamlet was just in the condition which spurs men to sallies of this kind: dissatisfied, at one neither with the world nor with himself, and accordingly casting about for something out of himself to vent his spleen upon. But even in these passages there is no hint of earnestness, of any purpose beyond the moment; they are mere cat's-paws of vexation, and not the deep-raking ground-swell of passion, as we see it in the sarcasm of Lear.

The question of Hamlet's madness has been much discussed and variously decided. High medical authority has pronounced, as usual, on both sides of the question. But the induction has been drawn from too narrow premises, being based on a mere diagnosis of the *case*, and not on an appreciation of the character in its completeness. We have a case of pretended madness in the Edgar of *King Lear* and it is certainly true that that is a charcoal sketch coarsely outlined, compared with the delicate drawing, the lights, shades, and half-tints of the portraiture in Hamlet. But does this tend to prove that the madness of the latter, because truer to the recorded observation of experts, is real, and meant to be real, as the other to be fictitious? Not in the least, as it appears to me. Hamlet, among all the characters

of Shakespeare, is the most eminently a metaphysician and psy-
chologist. He is a close observer, continually analyzing his
own nature and that of others, letting fall his little drops of acid
irony on all who come near him, to make them show what
they are made of. Even Ophelia is not too sacred, Osrick not
too contemptible for experiment. If such a man assumed madness, he would play his part perfectly. If Shakespeare himself,
without going mad, could so observe and remember all the
abnormal symptoms as to be able to reproduce them in Hamlet,
why should it be beyond the power of Hamlet to reproduce
them in himself? If you deprive Hamlet of reason, there is no
truly tragic motive left. He would be a fit subject for Bedlam,
but not for the stage. We might have pathology enough, but
no pathos. Ajax first becomes tragic when he recovers his
wits. If Hamlet is irresponsible, the whole play is a chaos.
That he is not so might be proved by evidence enough, were it
not labor thrown away.

This feigned madness of Hamlet's is one of the few points in
which Shakespeare has kept close to the old story on which he
founded his play; and as he never decided without deliberation,
so he never acted without unerring judgment. Hamlet *drifts*
through the whole tragedy. He never keeps on one tack long
enough to get steerage-way, even if, in a nature like his, with
those electric streamers of whim and fancy forever wavering
across the vault of his brain, the needle of judgment would
point in one direction long enough to strike a course by. The
scheme of simulated insanity is precisely the one he would have
been likely to hit upon, because it enabled him to follow his
own bent, and to drift with an apparent purpose, postponing
decisive action by the very means he adopts to arrive at its accomplishment, and satisfying himself with the show of doing
something that he may escape so much the longer the dreaded
necessity of really doing anything at all. It enables him to *play*
with life and duty, instead of taking them by the rougher side,
where alone any firm grip is possible,—to feel that he is on the
way towards accomplishing somewhat, when he is really paltering with his own irresolution. Nothing, I think, could be more

finely imagined than this. Voltaire complains that he goes mad without any sufficient object or result. Perfectly true, and precisely what was most natural for him to do, and, accordingly, precisely what Shakespeare meant that he should do. It was delightful to him to indulge his imagination and humor, to prove his capacity for something by playing a part: the one thing he could not do was to bring himself to *act*, unless when surprised by a sudden impulse of suspicion,—as where he kills Polonius, and there he could not see his victim. He discourses admirably of suicide, but does not kill himself; he talks daggers, but uses none. He puts by his chance to kill the king with the excuse that he will not do it while he is praying, lest his soul be saved thereby, though it be more than doubtful whether he believed himself that, if there were a soul to be saved, it could be saved by that expedient. He allows himself to be packed off to England, without any motive except that it would for the time take him farther from a present duty, the more disagreeable to a nature like his because it *was* present, and not a mere matter for speculative consideration. When Goethe made his famous comparison of the acorn planted in a vase which it bursts with its growth, and says that in like manner Hamlet is a nature which breaks down under the weight of a duty too great for it to bear, he seems to have considered the character too much from one side. Had Hamlet actually killed himself to escape his too onerous commission, Goethe's conception of him would have been satisfactory enough. But Hamlet was hardly a sentimentalist, like Werther; on the contrary, he saw things only too clearly in the dry north-light of the intellect. It is chance that at last brings him to his end. It would appear rather that Shakespeare intended to show us an imaginative temperament brought face to face with actualities, into any clear relation of sympathy with which it cannot bring itself. The very means that Shakespeare makes use of to lay upon him the obligation of acting—the ghost—really seems to make it all the harder for him to act; for the spectre but gives an additional excitement to his imagination and a fresh topic for his scepticism.

I shall not attempt to evolve any high moral significance from the play, even if I thought it possible; for that would be aside from the present purpose. The scope of the higher drama is to represent life, not every-day life, it is true, but life lifted above the plane of bread-and-butter associations, by nobler reaches of language, by the influence at once inspiring and modulating of verse, by an intenser play of passion condensing that misty mixture of feeling and reflection which makes the ordinary atmosphere of existence into flashes of thought and phrase whose brief, but terrible, illumination prints the outworn landscape of every-day upon our brains, with its little motives and mean results, in lines of tell-tale fire. The moral office of tragedy is to show us our own weaknesses idealized in grander figures and more awful results,—to teach us that what we pardon in ourselves as venial faults, if they seem to have but slight influence on our immediate fortunes, have arms as long as those of kings, and reach forward to the catastrophe of our lives; that they are dry-rotting the very fibre of will and conscience, so that, if we should be brought to the test of a great temptation or a stringent emergency, we must be involved in a ruin as sudden and complete as that we shudder at in the unreal scene of the theatre. But the primary *object* of a tragedy is not to inculcate a formal moral. Representing life, it teaches, like life, by indirection, by those nods and winks that are thrown away on us blind horses in such profusion. We may learn, to be sure, plenty of lessons from Shakespeare. We are not likely to have kingdoms to divide, crowns foretold us by weird sisters, a father's death to avenge, or to kill our wives from jealousy; but Lear may teach us to draw the line more clearly between a wise generosity and a loose-handed weakness of giving; Macbeth, how one sin involves another, and forever another, by a fatal parthenogenesis, and that the key which unlocks forbidden doors to our will or passion leaves a stain on the hand, that may not be so dark as blood, but that will not out; Hamlet, that all the noblest gifts of person, temperament, and mind slip like sand through the grasp of an infirm purpose; Othello, that the perpetual silt of some one weakness, the eddies of a suspicious temper depositing their one impalpable layer after another, may built up a shoal on which an heroic life and an otherwise mag- nanimous nature may bilge and go to pieces. All this we may learn, and much more, and Shakespeare was no doubt well aware of all this and more; but I do not believe that he wrote his plays with any such didactic purpose. He knew human nature too well not to know that one thorn of experience is worth a whole wilderness of warning,—that, where one man shapes his life by precept and example, there are a thousand who have it shaped for them by impulse and by circumstances. He did not mean his great tragedies for scarecrows, as if the nailing of one hawk to the barn-door would prevent the next from coming down souse into the hen-yard. No, it is not the poor bleaching victim hung up to moult its draggled feathers in the rain that he wishes to show us. He loves the hawk-nature as well as the hen-nature; and if he is unequalled in anything, it is in that sunny breadth of view, that impregnability of rea- son, that looks down on all ranks and conditions of men, all fortune and misfortune, with the equal eye of the pure artist.

Whether I have fancied anything into Hamlet which the author never dreamed of putting there I do not greatly concern myself to inquire. Poets are always entitled to a royalty on whatever we find in their works; for these fine creations as truly build themselves up in the brain as they are built up with deliberate forethought. Praise art as we will, that which the artist did not mean to put into his work, but which found itself there by some generous process of Nature of which he was as unaware as the blue river is of its rhyme with the blue sky, has somewhat in it that snatches us into sympathy with higher things than those which come by plot and observation. Goethe wrote his *Faust* in its earliest form without a thought of the deeper meaning which the exposition of an age of criticism was to find in it: without foremeaning it, he had impersonated in Mephistopheles the genius of his century. Shall this subtract from the debt we owe him? Not at all. If originality were con- scious of itself, it would have lost its right to be original. I believe that Shakespeare intended to impersonate in Hamlet not a mere metaphysical entity, but a man of flesh and blood: yet it is certainly curious how prophetically typical the character is of that introversion of mind which is so constant a phenomenon of these latter days, of that over-consciousness which wastes itself in analyzing the motives of action instead of acting.

The old painters had a rule, that all compositions should be pyramidal in form,—a central figure, from which the others slope gradually away on the two sides. Shakespeare probably had never heard of this rule, and, if he had, would not have been likely to respect it more than he has the so-called classical unities of time and place. But he understood perfectly the artistic advantages of gradation, contrast, and relief. Taking Hamlet as the keynote, we find in him weakness of character, which, on the one hand, is contrasted with the feebleness that springs from overweening conceit in Polonius and with frailty of temperament in Ophelia, while, on the other hand, it is brought into fuller relief by the steady force of Horatio and the impulsive violence of Laertes, who is resolute from thoughtlessness, just as Hamlet is irresolute from overplus of thought.

If we must draw a moral from Hamlet, it would seem to be, that Will is Fate, and that, Will once abdicating, the inevitable successor in the regency is Chance. Had Hamlet acted, instead of musing how good it would be to act, the king might have been the only victim. As it is, all the main actors in the story are the fortuitous sacrifice of his irresolution. We see how a single great vice of character at last draws to itself as allies and confederates all other weaknesses of the man, as in civil wars the timid and the selfish wait to throw themselves upon the stronger side.

> "In Life's small things be resolute and great
>   To keep thy muscles trained: know'st thou when Fate
>   Thy measure takes? or when she'll say to thee,
>   'I find thee worthy, do this thing for me'?"

I have said that it was doubtful if Shakespeare had any conscious moral intention in his writings. I meant only that he was purely and primarily poet. And while he was an English poet in a sense that is true of no other, his method was thoroughly Greek, yet with this remarkable difference,—that, while the Greek dramatists took purely national themes and gave them a universal interest by their mode of treatment, he took what may be called cosmopolitan traditions, legends of human nature, and nationalized them by the infusion of his perfectly Anglican breadth of character and solidity of understanding. Wonderful as his imagination and fancy are, his perspicacity and artistic discretion are more so. This country tradesman's son, coming up to London, could set high-bred wits, like Beaumont, uncopiable lessons in drawing gentlemen such as are seen nowhere else but on the canvas of Titian; he could take Ulysses away from Homer and expand the shrewd and crafty islander into a statesman whose words are the pith of history. But what makes him yet more exceptional was his utterly unimpeachable judgment, and that poise of character which enabled him to be at once the greatest of poets and so unnoticeable a good citizen as to leave no incidents for biography. His material was never far-sought; (it is still disputed whether the fullest head of which we have record were cultivated beyond the range of grammar-school precedent!) but he used it with a poetic instinct which we cannot parallel, identified himself with it, yet remained always its born and questionless master. He finds the Clown and Fool upon the stage,—he makes them the tools of his pleasantry, his satire, his wisdom, and even his pathos; he finds a facing rustic superstition, and shapes out of it ideal Pucks, Titanias, and Ariels, in whose existence statesmen and scholars believe forever. Always poet, he subjects all to the ends of his art, and gives in Hamlet the churchyard ghost, but with the cothurnus on,—the messenger of God's revenge against murder; always philosopher, he traces in Macbeth the metaphysics of apparitions, painting the shadowy Banquo only on the o'erwrought brain of the murderer, and staining the hand of his wife-accomplice (because she was the more refined and higher nature) with the disgustful blood-spot that is not there. I say he had no moral intention, for the reason, that, as artist, it was not his to deal with the realities, but only with the shows of things; yet, with a temperament so just, an insight so inevitable as his, it was impossible that the moral reality, which underlies the *mirage* of the poet's vision, should not always be suggested. His humor and satire are never of the destructive kind; what he does in that way is suggestive only,—not breaking bubbles with Thor's hammer, but puffing them away with the breath of a Clown, or shivering them with the light laugh of a genial cynic. Men go about to prove the existence of a God! Was it a bit of phosphorus, that brain whose creations are so real, that, mixing with them, we feel as if we ourselves were but fleeting magic-lantern shadows?

But higher even than the genius I rate the character of this unique man, and the grand impersonality of what he wrote. What has he told us of himself? In our self-exploiting nineteenth century, with its melancholy liver-complaint, how serene and high he seems! If he had sorrows, he has made them the woof of everlasting consolation to his kind; and if, as poets are wont to whine, the outward world was cold to him, its biting air did but trace itself in loveliest frost-work of fancy on the many windows of that self-centered and cheerful soul.

From MY GARDEN ACQUAINTANCE

(1869)

For many years I have been in the habit of noting down some of the leading events of my embowered solitude, such as the coming of certain birds and the like,—a kind of *memoires pour servir*, after the fashion of White, rather than properly digested natural history. I thought it not impossible that a few simple stories of my winged acquaintances might be found entertaining by persons of kindred taste.

There is a common notion that animals are better meteorologists than men, and I have little doubt that in immediate weather-wisdom they have the advantage of our sophisticated senses (though I suspect a sailor or shepherd would be their match), but I have seen nothing that leads me to believe their minds capable of erecting the horoscope of a whole season, and letting us know beforehand whether the winter will be severe or the summer rainless. I more than suspect that the clerk of the weather himself does not always know very long in advance whether he is to draw an order for hot or cold, dry or moist, and the musquash is scarce likely to be wiser. I have noted but two days' difference in the coming of the song-sparrow between a very early and a very backward spring. This very year I saw the linnets at work thatching, just before a snow-storm which covered the ground several inches deep for a number of days. They struck work and left us for a while, no doubt in search of food. Birds frequently perish from sudden changes in our whimsical spring weather of which they had no foreboding. More than thirty years ago, a cherry-tree, then in full bloom, near my window, was covered with humming-birds benumbed by a fall of mingled rain and snow, which probably killed many of them. It should seem that their coming was dated by the height of the sun, which betrays them into unthrifty matrimony:

"So priketh hem Nature in hir corages";

but their going is another matter. The chimney swallows leave us early, for example, apparently so soon as their latest fledglings are firm enough of wing to attempt the long rowing-match that is before them. On the other hand the wild-geese probably do not leave the North till they are frozen out, for I have heard their bugles sounding southward so late as the middle of December. What may be called local migrations are doubtless dictated by the chances of food. I have once been visited by large flights of cross-bills; and whenever the snow lies long and deep on the ground, a flock of cedar-birds comes in mid-winter to eat the berries on my hawthorns. I have never been quite able to fathom the local, or rather geographical partialities of birds. Never before this summer (1870) have the king-birds, handsomest of flycatchers, built in my orchard; though I always know where to find them within half a mile. The rose-breasted grosbeak has been a familiar bird in Brookline (three miles away), yet I never saw one here till last July, when I found a female busy among my raspberries and surprisingly bold. I hope she was *prospecting* with a view to settlement in our garden. She seemed, on the whole, to think well of my fruit, and I would gladly plant another bed if it would help to win over so delightful a neighbor.

The return of the robin is commonly announced by the newspapers, like that of eminent or notorious people to a watering-place, as the first authentic notification of spring. And such his appearance in the orchard and garden undoubtedly is. But, in spite of his name of migratory thrush, he stays with us all winter, and I have seen him when the thermometer marked 15 degrees below zero of Fahrenheit, armed impregnably within, like Emerson's Titmouse, and as cheerful as he. The robin has a bad reputation among people who do not value themselves less for being fond of cherries. There is, I admit, a spice of vulgarity in him, and his song is rather of the Bloomfield sort, too largely ballasted with prose. His ethics are of the Poor Richard school, and the main chance which calls forth all his energy is altogether of the belly. He never has these fine intervals of lunacy into which his cousins, the catbird and the mavis, are apt to fall. But for a' that and twice as muckle 's a' that, I would not exchange him for all the cherries that ever came out of Asia Minor. With whatever faults, he has not wholly forfeited that superiority which belongs to the children of nature. He has a finer taste in fruit than could be distilled from many successive committees of the Horticultural Society, and he eats with a relishing gulp not inferior to Dr. Johnson's. He feels and freely exercises his right of eminent domain. His is the earliest mess of green peas; his all the mulberries I had fancied mine. But if he get also the lion's share of the raspberries, he is a great planter, and sows those wild ones in the woods that solace the pedestrian, and give a momentary calm even to the jaded victims of the White Hills. He keeps a strict eye over one's fruit, and knows to a shade of purple when your grapes have cooked long enough in the sun. During the severe drought a few years ago the robins wholly vanished from my garden. I neither saw nor heard one for three weeks. Meanwhile a small foreign grape-vine, rather shy of bearing, seemed to find the dusty air congenial, and, dreaming, perhaps of its sweet Argos across the sea, decked itself with a score or so of fair bunches. I watched them from day to day till they should have secreted sugar enough from the sunbeams, and at last made up my mind that I would celebrate my vintage the next morning. But the robins, too, had somehow kept note of them. They must have sent out spies, as did the Jews into the promised land, before I was stirring. When I went with my basket at least a dozen of these winged vintagers bustled out from among the leaves, and alighting on the nearest trees interchanged some shrill remarks about me of a derogatory nature. They had fairly sacked the vine. Not Wellington's veterans made cleaner work of a Spanish town; not Federals or Confederates were ever more impartial in the confiscation of neutral chickens. I was keeping my grapes a secret to surprise the fair Fidele with, but the robins made them a profounder secret to her than I had meant. The tattered remnant of a single bunch was all my harvest-home. How paltry it looked at the bottom of my basket, —as if a humming-bird had laid her egg in an eagle's nest! I could not help laughing; and the robins seemed to join heartily in the merriment. There was a native grape-vine close by, blue with its less refined abundance, but my cunning thieves preferred the foreign flavor. Could I tax them with want of taste?

The robins are not good solo singers, but their chorus, as, like primitive fire-worshippers, they hail the return of light and warmth to the world, is unrivalled. There are a hundred singing like one. They are noisy enough then, and sing, as poets should, with no afterthought. But when they come after cherries to the tree near my window, they muffle their voices, and their faint *pip pip pop!* sounds far away at the bottom of the garden, where they know I shall not suspect them of robbing the great black-walnut of its bitter-rinded store.[1] They are

---

[1] The screech-owl, whose cry, despite his ill name, is one of the sweetest sounds in nature, softens his voice in the same way with the most beguiling mockery of distance. [Author's note. Each "Author's note" is by Lowell.]

feathered Pecksniffs, to be sure, but then how brightly their breasts, that look rather shabby in the sunlight, shine in a rainy day against the dark green of the fringe-tree! After they have pinched and shaken all the life out of an earthworm, as Italian cooks pound all the spirit out of a steak, and then gulped him, they stand up in honest self-confidence, expand their red waist-coats with the virtuous air of a lobby member, and outface you with an eye that calmly challenges inquiry. "Do *I* look like a bird that knows the flavor of raw vermin? I throw myself upon a jury of my peers. Ask any robin if he ever ate anything less ascetic than the frugal berry of the juniper, and he will answer that his vow forbids him." Can such an open bosom cover such depravity? Alas, yes! I have no doubt his breast was redder at that very moment with the blood of my rasp-berries. On the whole, he is a doubtful friend in the garden. He makes his dessert of all kinds of berries, and is not averse from early pears. But when we remember how omnivorous he is, eating his own weight in an incredibly short time, and that Nature seems exhaustless in her invention of new insects hostile to vegetation, perhaps we may reckon that he does more good than harm. For my own part, I would rather have his cheerfulness and kind neighborhood than many berries.

For his cousin, the catbird, I have a still warmer regard. Always a good singer, he sometimes nearly equals the brown thrush, and has the merit of keeping up his music later in the evening than any bird of my familiar acquaintance. Ever since I can remember, a pair of them have built in a gigantic syringa near our front door, and I have known the male to sing almost uninterruptedly during the evenings of early summer till twilight duskened into dark. They differ greatly in vocal talent, but all have a delightful way of crooning over, and, as it were, rehearsing their song in an undertone, which makes their nearness always unobtrusive. Though there is the most trustworthy witness to the imitative propensity of this bird, I have only once, during an intimacy of more than forty years, heard him indulge it. In that case, the imitation was by no means so close as to deceive, but a free reproduction of the notes of some other birds, especially of the oriole, as a kind of variation in his own song. The catbird is as shy as the robin is vulgarly familiar. Only when his nest or his fledglings are approached does he become noisy and almost aggressive. I have known him to station his young in a thick cornel-bush on the edge of the raspberry-bed, after the fruit began to ripen, and feed them there for a week or more. In such cases he shows none of the conscious guilt which makes the robin contemptible. On the contrary, he will maintain his post in the thicket, and sharply scold the intruder who ventures to steal *his* berries. After all, his claim is only for tithes, while the robin will bag your entire crop if he get a chance.

Dr. Watts's statement that "birds in their little nests agree," like too many others intended to form the infant mind, is very far from being true. On the contrary, the most peaceful relation of the different species to each other is that of armed neutrality. They are very jealous of neighbors. A few years ago I was much interested in the housebuilding of a pair of summer yellow-birds. They had chosen a very pretty site near the top of a tall white lilac, within easy eye-shot of a chamber window. A very pleasant thing it was to see their little home growing with mutual help, to watch their industrious skill interrupted only by little flirts and snatches of endearment, frugally cut short by the common-sense of the tiny housewife. They had brought their work nearly to an end, and had already begun to line it with fern-down, the gathering of which demanded more distant journeys and longer absences. But, alas! the syringa, immemorial manor of the catbirds, was not more than twenty feet away, and these "giddy neighbors" had, as it appeared, been all along jealously watchful, though silent, witnesses of what they deemed an intrusion of squatters. No sooner were the pretty mates fairly gone for a new load of lining, than

> "To their unguarded nest these weasel Scots
>   Came stealing."

Silently they flew back and forth, each giving a vengeful dab at the nest in passing. They did not fall-to and deliberately destroy it, for they might have been caught at their mischief. As it was, whenever the yellow-birds came back, their enemies were hidden in their own sight-proof bush. Several times their unconscious victims repaired damages, but at length, after counsel taken together, they gave it up. Perhaps, like other unlettered folk, they came to the conclusion that the Devil was in it, and yielded to the invisible persecution of witchcraft.

The robins, by constant attacks and annoyances, have succeeded in driving off the blue-jays who used to build in our pines, their gay colors and quaint, noisy ways making them welcome and amusing neighbors. I once had the chance of doing a kindness to a household of them, which they received with very friendly condescension. I had had my eye for some time upon a nest, and was puzzled by a constant fluttering of what seemed full-grown wings in it whenever I drew nigh. At last I climbed the tree, in spite of angry protests from the old birds against my intrusion. The mystery had a very simple solution. In building the nest, a long piece of packthread had been somewhat loosely woven in. Three of the young had contrived to entangle themselves in it, and had become full-grown without being able to launch themselves upon the air. One was unharmed; another had so tightly twisted the cord about its shank that one foot was curled up and seemed paralyzed; the third, in its struggles to escape, had sawn through the flesh of the thigh and so much harmed itself that I thought it humane to put an end to its misery. When I took out my knife to cut their hempen bonds, the heads of the family seemed to divine my friendly intent. Suddenly ceasing their cries and threats, they perched quietly within reach of my hand, and watched me in my work of manumission. This, owing to the fluttering terror of the prisoners, was an affair of some delicacy; but ere long I was rewarded by seeing one of them fly away to a neighboring tree, while the cripple, making a parachute of his wings, came lightly to the ground, and hopped off as well as he could with one leg, obsequiously waited on by his elders. A week later I had the satisfaction of meeting him in the pine-walk, in good spirits, and already so far recovered as to be able to balance himself with the lame foot. I have no doubt that in his old age he accounted for his lameness by some handsome story of a wound received at the famous Battle of the Pines, when our tribe, overcome by numbers, was driven from its ancient camping-ground. Of late years the jays have visited us only at intervals; and in winter their bright plumage, set off by the snow, and their cheerful cry, are especially welcome. They would have furnished Aesop with a fable, for the feathered crest in which they seem to take so much satisfaction is often their fatal snare. Country boys make a hole with their finger in the snow-crust just large enough to admit the jay's head, and, hollowing it out somewhat beneath, bait it with a few kernels of corn. The crest slips easily into the trap, but refuses to be pulled out again, and he who came to feast remains a prey.

Twice have the crow-blackbirds attempted a settlement in my pines, and twice have the robins, who claim a right of pre-emption, so successfully played the part of border-ruffians as to drive them away,—to my great regret, for they are the best substitute we have for rooks. At Shady Hill[1] (now, alas! empty of its so long-loved household) they build by hundreds, and nothing can be more cheery than their creaking clatter (like a convention of oldfashioned tavern-signs) as they gather at evening to debate in mass meeting their windy politics, or to gossip at their tent-doors over the events of the day. Their port is grave, and their stalk across the turf as martial as that of a second-rate ghost in Hamlet. They never meddled with my corn, so far as I could discover.

From DANTE

(1872)

Like all great artistic minds, Dante was essentially conservative, and, arriving precisely in that period of transition when Church and Empire were entering upon the modern epoch of

---

[1] The home of Charles Eliot Norton, in Cambridge, who was at the time of this paper in Europe.

thought, he strove to preserve both by presenting the theory
of both in a pristine and ideal perfection. The whole nature of
Dante was one of intense belief. There is proof upon proof
that he believed himself invested with a divine mission. Like
the Hebrew prophets, with whose writings his whole soul was
imbued, it was back to the old worship and the God of the
fathers that he called his people; and not Isaiah himself was
more destitute of that humor, that sense of ludicrous contrast,
which is an essential in the composition of a sceptic. In Dante's
time, learning had something of a sacred character; the line was
hardly yet drawn between the clerk and the possessor of supernatural powers; it was with the next generation, with the elegant Petrarch, even more truly than with the kindly Boccaccio,
that the purely literary life, and that dilettantism, which is the
twin sister of scepticism, began. As a merely literary figure,
the position of Dante is remarkable. Not only as respects
thought, but as respects æsthetics also, his great poem stands
as a monument on the boundary line between the ancient and
modern. He not only marks, but is in himself, the transition.
Arma virumque cano, that is the motto of classic song; the things
of this world and great men. Dante says, *subjectum est homo*,
not *vir;* my theme is man, not a man. The scene of the old
epic and drama was in this world, and its catastrophe here;
Dante lays his scene in the human soul, and his fifth act in the
other world. He makes himself the protagonist of his own
drama. In the *Commedia* for the first time Christianity wholly
revolutionizes Art, and becomes its seminal principle. But
æsthetically also, as well as morally, Dante stands between the
old and the new, and reconciles them. The theme of his poem
is purely subjective, modern, what is called romantic; but its
treatment is objective (almost to realism, here and there), and
it is limited by a form of classic severity. In the same way he
sums up in himself the two schools of modern poetry which had
preceded him, and, while essentially lyrical in his subject, is
epic in the handling of it. So also he combines the deeper and
more abstract religious sentiment of the Teutonic races with
the scientific precision and absolute systematism of the Romanic.

In one respect Dante stands alone. While we can in some sort account for such representative men as Voltaire and Goethe (nay, even Shakespeare) by the intellectual and moral fermentation of the age in which they lived, Dante seems morally isolated and to have drawn his inspiration almost wholly from his own internal reserves. Of his mastery in style we need say little here. Of his mere language, nothing could be better than the expression of Rivarol[1]: "His verse holds itself erect by the mere force of the substantive and verb, without the help of a single epithet." We will only add a word on what seems to us an extraordinary misapprehension of Coleridge, who disparages Dante by comparing his Lucifer with Milton's Satan. He seems to have forgotten that the precise measurements of Dante were not prosaic, but absolutely demanded by the nature of his poem. He is describing an actual journey, and his exactness makes a part of the verisimilitude. We read the *Paradise Lost* as a poem, the *Commedia* as a record of fact; and no one can read Dante without believing his story, for it is plain that he believed it himself. It is false æsthetics to confound the grandiose with the imaginative. Milton's angels are not to be compared with Dante's, at once real and supernatural; and the Deity of Milton is a Calvinistic Zeus, while nothing in all poetry approaches the imaginative grandeur of Dante's vision of God at the conclusion of the *Paradiso*. In all literary history there is no such figure as Dante, no such homogeneousness of life and works, such loyalty to ideas, such sublime irrecognition of the unessential; and there is no moral more touching than that the contemporary recognition of such a nature, so endowed and so faithful to its endowment, should be summed up in the sentence of Florence: *Igne comburatur sic quod moriatur.*[2]

[1] "Rivarol, who translated the *Inferno* in 1783, was the first Frenchman who divined the wonderful force and vitality of the *Commedia*." [Lowell, "Dante," pp. 143–144, Riverside Edition. This and following notes on the Dante text not marked as by "author" are by N. Foerster.]

[2] "Let him be burned with fire so that he die."

In order to fix more precisely in the mind the place of Dante in relation to the history of thought, literature, and events, we subjoin

The range of Dante's influence is not less remarkable than its intensity. Minds, the antipodes of each other in temper and endowment, alike feel the force of his attraction, the pervasive comfort of his light and warmth. Boccaccio and Lamennais are touched with the same reverential enthusiasm. The imaginative Ruskin is rapt by him, as we have seen, perhaps beyond the limit where critical appreciation merges in enthusiasm[1]; and the matter-of-fact Schlosser tells us that "he, who was wont to contemplate earthly life wholly in an earthly light, has made use of Dante, Landino, and Vellutello in his solitude to bring a heavenly light into his inward life." Almost all other poets have their seasons, but Dante penetrates to the moral core of those who once fairly come within his sphere, and possesses them wholly. His readers turn students, his students zealots, and what was a taste becomes a religion. The homeless exile finds a home in thousands of grateful hearts: *E da esilio venne a questa pace.*[2]

Every kind of objection, æsthetic and other, may be, and has been, made to the *Divina Commedia*, especially by critics who have but a superficial acquaintance with it, or rather with the *Inferno*, which is as far as most English critics go. Coleridge himself, who had a way of divining what was in books, may be justly suspected of not going further, though with Cary to help him. Mr. Carlyle, who has said admirable things of Dante the

---

a few dates: Dante born, 1265; end of Crusades, death of St. Louis, 1270; Aquinas died, 1274; Bonaventura died, 1274; Giotto born, 1276; Albertus Magnus died, 1280; Sicilian vespers, 1282; death of Ugolino and Francesca da Rimini, 1282; death of Beatrice, 1290; Roger Bacon died, 1292; death of Cimabue, 1302; Dante's banishment, 1302; Petrarch born, 1304; Fra Dolcino burned, 1307; Pope Clement V at Avignon, 1309; Templars suppressed, 1312; Boccaccio born, 1313; Dante died, 1321; Wycliffe born, 1324; Chaucer born, 1328. [Author's note.]

[1] "Perhaps no other man could have called forth such an expression as that of Ruskin, that 'the central man of all the world, as representing in perfect balance the imaginative, moral, and intellectual faculties, all at their highest, is Dante.'" [Lowell, "Dante," pp. 147–148, Riverside Edition.]

[2] "Out of exile he came into this peace."

man, was very imperfectly read in Dante the author, or he
would never have put Sordello in hell and the meeting with
Beatrice in paradise. In France it was not much better (though
Rivarol has said the best thing hitherto of Dante's parsimony of
epithet[1]) before Ozanam, who, if with decided ultramontane
leanings, has written excellently well of our poet, and after
careful study. Voltaire, though not without relentings toward
a poet who had put popes heels upward in hell, regards him on
the whole as a stupid monster and barbarian. It was no better
in Italy, if we may trust Foscolo, who affirms that "neither Pelli
nor others deservedly more celebrated than he ever read attentively the poem of Dante, perhaps never ran through it from
the first verse to the last."[2] Accordingly we have heard that
the *Commedia* was a sermon, a political pamphlet, the revengeful satire of a disappointed Ghibelline, nay, worse, of a turn-
coat Guelph. It is narrow, it is bigoted, it is savage, it is
theological, it is mediæval, it is heretical, it is scholastic, it is
obscure, it is pedantic, its Italian is not that of *la Crusca*,[3] its
ideas are not those of an enlightened eighteenth century, it is
everything, in short, that a poem should not be; and yet, singularly enough, the circle of its charm has widened in proportion
as men have receded from the theories of Church and State
which are supposed to be its foundation, and as the modes of
thought of its author have become more alien to those of his
readers. In spite of all objections, some of which are well
founded, the *Commedia* remains one of the three or four universal books that have ever been written.

We may admit, with proper limitations, the modern dis-

---

[1] Rivarol characterized only a single quality of Dante's style, who
knew how to spend as well as spare. Even the *Inferno*, on which he
based his remark, might have put him on his guard. Dante understood very well the use of ornament in its fitting place. *Est enim
exornatio alicujus convenientis additio*, he tells us in his *De Vulgari
Eloquio* (lib. ii. cap. i). His simile of the doves (*Inferno*, v, 82 et seq.),
perhaps the most exquisite in all poetry, quite oversteps Rivarol's
narrow limit of "substantive and verb." [Author's note.]

[2] *Discorso sul testo*, ec., § xviii. [Author's note.]

[3] A Florentine academy similar to the French Academy.

tinction between the Artist and the Moralist. With the one Form is all in all, with the other Tendency. The aim of the one is to delight, of the other to convince. The one is master of his purpose, the other mastered by it. The whole range of perception and thought is valuable to the one as it will minister to imagination, to the other only as it is available for argument. With the moralist use is beauty, good only as it serves an ulterior purpose; with the artist beauty is use, good in and for itself. In the fine arts the vehicle makes part of the thought, coalesces with it. The living conception shapes itself a body in marble, color, or modulated sound, and henceforth the two are inseparable. The results of the moralist pass into the intellectual atmosphere of mankind, it matters little by what mode of conveyance. But where, as in Dante, the religious sentiment and the imagination are both organic, something interfused with the whole being of the man, so that they work in kindly sympathy, the moral will insensibly suffuse itself with beauty as a cloud with light. Then that fine sense of remote analogies, awake to the assonance between facts seemingly remote and unrelated, between the outward and inward worlds, though convinced that the things of this life are shadows, will be persuaded also that they are not fantastic merely, but imply a substance somewhere, and will love to set forth the beauty of the visible image because it suggests the ineffably higher charm of the unseen original. Dante's ideal of life, the enlightening and strengthening of that native instinct of the soul which leads it to strive backward toward its divine source, may sublimate the senses till each becomes a window for the light of truth and the splendor of God to shine through. In him as in Calderón the perpetual presence of imagination not only glorifies the philosophy of life and the science of theology, but idealizes both in symbols of material beauty. Though Dante's conception of the highest end of man was that he should climb through every phase of human experience to that transcendental and supersensual region where the true, the good, and the beautiful blend in the white light of God, yet the prism of his imagination forever resolved the ray into color again, and he loved to show it also where, entangled and obstructed in matter, it became beautiful once more to the eye of sense. Speculation, he tells us, is the use, without any mixture, of our noblest part (the reason). And this part cannot in this life have its perfect use, which is to behold God (who is the highest object of the intellect), except inasmuch as the intellect considers and beholds him in his effects.[1] Underlying Dante the metaphysician, statesman, and theologian, was always Dante the poet,[2] irradiating and vivifying, gleaming through in a picturesque phrase, or touching things unexpectedly with that ideal light which softens and subdues like distance in the landscape. The stern outline of his system wavers and melts away before the eye of the reader in a mirage of imagination that lifts from beyond the sphere of vision and hangs in serener air images of infinite suggestion projected from worlds not realized, but substantial to faith, hope, and aspiration. Beyond the horizon of speculation floats, in the passionless splendor of the empyrean, the city of our God, the Rome whereof Christ is a Roman,[3] the citadel of refuge, even in this life, for souls purified by sorrow and self-denial, transhumanized[4] to the divine abstraction of pure contemplation. "And it is called Empyrean," he says in his letter to Can Grande, "which is the same as a heaven blazing with fire or ardor, not because there is in it a material fire or burning, but a spiritual one, which is blessed love or charity." But this

---

[1] *Convito*, Tr., IV, c. XXII. [Author's note.]

[2] It is remarkable that when Dante, in 1297, as a preliminary condition to active politics, enrolled himself in the guild of physicians and apothecaries, he is qualified only with the title *poeta*. The arms of the Alighieri (curiously suitable to him who *sovra gli altri come aquila vola*) were a wing of gold in a field of azure. His vivid sense of beauty even hovers sometimes like a *corposant* over the somewhat stiff lines of his Latin prose. For example, in his letter to the kings and princes of Italy on the coming of Henry VII: "A new day brightens, revealing the dawn which already scatters the shades of long calamity; already the breezes of morning gather; *the lips of heaven are reddening!*" [Author's note.]

[3] *Purgatorio*, XXXII, 100. [Author's note.]

[4] *Paradiso*, I, 70. [Author's note.]

splendor he bodies forth, if sometimes quaintly, yet always vividly and most often in types of winning grace.

Dante was a mystic with a very practical turn of mind. A Platonist by nature, an Aristotelian by training, his feet keep closely to the narrow path of dialectics, because he believed it the safest, while his eyes are fixed on the stars and his brain is busy with things not demonstrable, save by that grace of God which passeth all understanding, nor capable of being told unless by far-off hints and adumbrations. Though he himself has directly explained the scope, the method, and the larger meaning of his greatest work,[1] though he has indirectly pointed out the way to its interpretation in the *Convito,* and though everything he wrote is but an explanatory comment on his own character and opinions, unmistakably clear and precise, yet both man and poem continue not only to be misunderstood popularly, but also by such as should know better.[2] That those who confined their studies to the *Commedia* should have interpreted it variously is not wonderful, for out of the first or literal meaning others open, one out of another, each of wider circuit and purer abstraction, like Dante's own heavens, giving and receiving light.[3] Indeed, Dante himself is partly to blame for this. "The form or mode of treatment," he says, "is poetic, fictive, descriptive, digressive, transumptive, and withal definitive, divisive, probative, improbative, and positive of examples." Here are conundrums enough, to be sure! To Italians at home, for whom the great arenas of political and religious speculation were closed, the temptation to find a subtler meaning than the real one was irresistible. Italians in exile, on the

---

[1] In a letter to Can Grande (XI of the *Epistolæ*). [Author's note.]

[2] Witte, Wegele, and Ruth in German, and Ozanam in French, have rendered ignorance of Dante inexcusable among men of culture. [Author's note.]

[3] *Inferno,* VII, 75. "Nay, his style," says Miss Rossetti, "is more than concise: it is elliptical, it is recondite. A first thought often lies coiled up and hidden under a second; the words which state the conclusion involve the premises and develop the subject" (p. 3). [Author's note; the reference is to *The Shadow of Dante,* by Maria Francesca Rossetti.]

other hand, made Dante the stalking-horse from behind which they could take a long shot at Church and State, or at obscurer foes.[1] Infinitely touching and sacred to us is the instinct of intense sympathy which draws these latter toward their great forerunner, *exul immeritus*[2] like themselves.[3] But they have too often wrung a meaning from Dante which is injurious to the man and out of keeping with the ideas of his age. The aim in expounding a great poem should be, not to discover an endless variety of meanings often contradictory, but whatever it has of great and perennial significance; for such it must have, or it would long ago have ceased to be living and operative, would long ago have taken refuge in the Chartreuse of great libraries, dumb thenceforth to all mankind. We do not mean to say that this minute exegesis is useless or unpraiseworthy, but only that it should be subsidiary to the larger way. It serves to bring out more clearly what is very wonderful in Dante, namely, the omnipresence of his memory throughout the work, so that its intimate coherence does not exist in spite of the recondteness and complexity of allusion, but is woven out of them. The poem has many senses, he tells us, and there can be no doubt of it; but it has also, and this alone will account for its fascination, a living soul behind them all and informing

[1] A complete vocabulary of Italian billingsgate might be selected from Biagioli. Or see the concluding pages of Nannucci's excellent tract, *Intorno alle voci usate da Dante*, Corfù, 1840. Even Foscolo could not always refrain. Dante should have taught them to shun such vulgarities. See *Inferno*, xxx, 131-148. [Author's note.]

[2] "One unjustly exiled."

[3] "My Italy, my sweetest Italy, for having loved thee too much I have lost thee, and, perhaps, . . . ah, may God avert the omen! But more proud than sorrowful for an evil endured for thee alone, I continue to consecrate my vigils to thee alone. . . . An exile full of anguish, perchance, availed to sublime the more in thy Alighieri that lofty soul which was a beautiful gift of thy smiling sky; and an exile equally wearisome and undeserved now avails, perhaps, to sharpen my small genius so that it may penetrate into what he left written for thy instruction and for his glory." ([Gabriele] Rossetti, *Disamina*, etc., p. 405.) Rossetti is himself a proof that a noble mind need not be narrowed by misfortune. His *Comment* (unhappily incomplete) is one of the most valuable and suggestive. [Author's note.]

all, an intense singleness of purpose, a core of doctrine simple, human, and wholesome, though it be also, to use his own phrase, the bread of angels.

Nor is this unity characteristic only of the *Divina Commedia*. All the works of Dante, with the possible exception of the *De Vulgari Eloquio* (which is unfinished), are component parts of a Whole Duty of Man mutually completing and interpreting one another. They are also, as truly as Wordsworth's *Prelude*, a history of the growth of a poet's mind. Like the English poet he valued himself at a high rate, the higher no doubt after Fortune had made him outwardly cheap. *Sempre il magnanimo si magnifica in suo cuore; così lo pusillanimo per contrario sempre si tiene meno che non è.*[1] As in the prose of Milton, whose striking likeness to Dante in certain prominent features of character has been remarked by Foscolo, there are in Dante's minor works continual allusions to himself of great value as material for his biographer. Those who read attentively will discover that the tenderness he shows toward Francesca and her lover[2] did not spring from any friendship for her family, but was a constant quality of his nature, and that what is called his revengeful ferocity is truly the implacable resentment of a lofty mind and a lover of good against evil, whether showing itself in private or public life; perhaps hating the former manifestation of it the most because he believed it to be the root of the latter, —a faith which those who have watched the course of politics in a democracy, as he had, will be inclined to share. His gentleness is all the more striking by contrast, like that silken compensation which blooms out of the thorny stem of the cactus. His moroseness,[3] his party spirit, and his personal vindictive-

[1] The great-minded man ever magnifies himself in his heart, and in like manner the pusillanimous holds himself less than he is. (*Convito*, Tr. I, c. 11.) [Author's note.]

[2] *Inferno*, V, 73–141.

[3] Dante's notion of virtue was not that of an ascetic, nor has any one ever painted her in colors more soft and splendid than he in the *Convito*. She is "sweeter than the lids of Juno's eyes," and he dwells on the delights of her love with a rapture which kindles and purifies. So far from making her an inquisitor, he says expressly that she

ness are all predicated upon the *Inferno*, and upon a misapprehension or careless reading even of that. Dante's zeal was not of
that sentimental kind, quickly kindled and as soon quenched,
that hovers on the surface of shallow minds,

> "Even as the flame of unctuous things is wont
>   To move upon the outer surface only"[1];

it was the steady heat of an inward fire kindling the whole
character of the man through and through, like the minarets
of his own city of Dis.[2] He was, as seems distinctive in some
degree of the Latinized races, an unflinching *a priori* logician,
not unwilling to "syllogize invidious verities,"[3] wherever they
might lead him, like Sigier, whom he has put in paradise,
though more than suspected of heterodoxy. But at the same
time, as we shall see, he had something of the practical good
sense of that Teutonic stock whence he drew a part of his
blood, which prefers a malleable syllogism that can yield without breaking to the inevitable, but incalculable pressure of
human nature and the stiffer logic of events. His theory of
Church and State was not merely a fantastic one, but intended
for the use and benefit of men as they were; and he allowed accordingly for aberrations, to which even the law of gravitation
is forced to give place; how much more, then, any scheme whose
very starting-point is the freedom of the will!

*   *   *

The relation of Dante to literature is monumental, and marks
the era at which the modern begins. He is not only the first
great poet, but the first great prose writer who used a language
not yet subdued to literature, who used it moreover for scientific and metaphysical discussion, thus giving an incalculable
impulse to the culture of his countrymen by making the laity

"should be gladsome and not sullen in all her works." (*Convito*,
Tr. I, c. 8.) "Not harsh and crabbed as dull fools suppose"! [Au-
thor's note.]
  [1] *Inferno*, XIX, 28, 29. [Author's note.]
  [2] *Inferno*, VIII, 70–75. [Author's note.]
  [3] *Paradiso*, X, 138. [Author's note.]

free of what had hitherto been the exclusive guild of clerks.[1]
Whatever poetry had preceded him, whether in the Romance
or Teutonic tongues, is interesting mainly for its simplicity
without forethought, or, as in the *Nibelungen*, for a kind of
savage grandeur that rouses the sympathy of whatever of the
natural man is dormant in us. But it shows no trace of the
creative faculty either in unity of purpose or style, the proper
characteristics of literature. If it have the charm of wanting
artifice, it has not the higher charm of art. We are in the realm
of chaos and chance, nebular, with phosphorescent gleams here
and there, star-stuff, but uncondensed in stars. The *Nibelungen*
is not without far-reaching hints and forebodings of something
finer than we find in it, but they are a glamour from the vague
darkness which encircles it, like the whisper of the sea upon an
unknown shore at night, powerful only over the more vulgar
side of the imagination, and leaving no thought, scarce even
any image (at least of beauty) behind them. Such poems are
the amours, not the lasting friendships and possessions of the
mind. They thrill and cannot satisfy.

But Dante is not merely the founder of modern literature.
He would have been that if he had never written anything more
than his *Canzoni*, which for elegance, variety of rhythm, and
fervor of sentiment were something altogether new. They are
of a higher mood than any other poems of the same style in
their own language, or indeed in any other. In beauty of phrase
and subtlety of analogy they remind one of some of the Greek
tragic choruses. We are constantly moved in them by a noble-
ness of tone, whose absence in many admired lyrics of the kind
is poorly supplied by conceits. So perfect is Dante's mastery
of his material, that in compositions, as he himself has shown,

[1] See Wegele, *ubi supra*, p. 174 *et seq*. The best analysis of Dante's
opinions we have ever met with is Emil Ruth's *Studien über Dante
Alighieri*, Tübingen, 1853. Unhappily it wants an index, and accordingly loses a great part of its usefulness for those not already
familiar with the subject. Nor are its references sufficiently exact.
We always respect Dr. Ruth's opinions, if we do not wholly accept
them, for they are all the results of original and assiduous study.
[Author's note.]

so artificial,[1] the form seems rather organic than mechanical, which cannot be said of the best of the Provençal poets who led the way in this kind. Dante's sonnets also have a grace and tenderness which have been seldom matched. His lyrical excellence would have got him into the Collections, and he would have made here and there an enthusiast as Donne does in English, but his great claim to remembrance is not merely Italian. It is that he was the first Christian poet, in any proper sense of the word, the first who so subdued dogma to the uses of plastic imagination as to make something that is still poetry of the highest order after it has suffered the disenchantment inevitable in the most perfect translation. Verses of the kind usually called *sacred* (reminding one of the adjective's double meaning) had been written before his time in the vulgar tongue, such verses as remain inviolably sacred in the volumes of specimens, looked at with distant reverence by the pious, and with far other feelings by the profane reader. There were cycles of poems in which the physical conflict between Christianity and Paganism[2] furnished the subject, but in which the theological views of the authors, whether doctrinal or historical, could hardly be reconciled with any system of religion ancient or modern. There were Church legends of saints and martyrs versified, fit certainly to make any other form of martyrdom seem amiable to those who heard them, and to suggest palliative thoughts about Diocletian. Finally, there were the romances of Arthur and his knights, which later, by means of allegory, contrived to be both entertaining and edifying; every one who

[1] See the second book of the *De Vulgari Eloquio*. The only other Italian poet who reminds us of Dante in sustained dignity is Guido Guinicelli. Dante esteemed him highly, calls him maximus in the *De Vulgari Eloquio*, and "the father of me and of my betters," in the xxvi *Purgatorio*. See some excellent specimens of him in Mr. D. G. Rossetti's remarkable volume of translations from the early Italian poets. Mr. Rossetti would do a real and lasting service to literature by employing his singular gift in putting Dante's minor poems into English. [Author's note.]

[2] The old French poems confound all unbelievers together as pagans and worshippers of idols. [Author's note.]

listened to them paying the minstrel his money, and having his choice whether he would take them as song or sermon. In the heroes of some of these certain Christian virtues were typified, and around a few of them, as the Holy Grail, a perfume yet lingers of cloistered piety and withdrawal. Wolfram von Eschenbach, indeed, has divided his *Parzival* into three books, of Simplicity, Doubt, and Healing, which has led Gervinus to trace a not altogether fanciful analogy between that poem and the *Divina Commedia*. The doughty old poet, who says of himself,—

> "Of song I have some slight control,
> But deem her of a feeble soul
> That doth not love my naked sword
> Above my sweetest lyric word,"

tells us that his subject is the choice between good and evil;

> "Whose soul takes Untruth for its bride
> And sets himself on Evil's side,
> Chooses the Black, and sure it is
> His path leads down to the abyss;
> But he who doth his nature feed
> With steadfastness and loyal deed
> Lies open to the heavenly light
> And takes his portion with the White."

But Wolfram's poem has no system, and shows good feeling rather than settled conviction. Above all it is wandering (as he himself confesses), and altogether wants any controlling purpose. But to whatever extent Christianity had insinuated itself into and colored European literature, it was mainly as mythology. The Christian idea had never yet incorporated itself. It was to make its avatar in Dante. To understand fully what he accomplished we must form some conception of what is meant by the Christian idea. To bring it into fuller relief, let us contrast it with the Greek idea as it appears in poetry; for we are not dealing with a question of theology so much as with one of æsthetics.

Greek art at its highest point is doubtless the most perfect that we know. But its circle of motives was essentially limited; and the Greek drama in its passion, its pathos, and its humor is primarily Greek, and secondarily human. Its tragedy chooses its actors from certain heroic families, and finds its springs of pity and terror in physical suffering and worldly misfortune. Its best examples, like the *Antigone*, illustrate a single duty, or, like the *Hippolytus*, a single passion, on which, as on a pivot, the chief character, statuesquely simple in its details, revolves as pieces of sculpture are sometimes made to do, displaying its different sides in one invariable light. The general impression left on the mind (and this is apt to be a truer one than any drawn from single examples) is that the duty is one which is owed to custom, that the passion leads to a breach of some convention settled by common consent,[1] and accordingly it is an outraged society whose figure looms in the background, rather than an offended God. At most it was one god of many, and meanwhile another might be friendly. In the Greek epic, the gods are partisans, they hold caucuses, they lobby and log-roll for their candidates. The tacit admission of a revealed code of morals wrought a great change. The complexity and range of passion is vastly increased when the offence is at once both crime and sin, a wrong done against order and against conscience at the same time. The relation of the Greek tragedy to the higher powers is chiefly antagonistic, struggle against an implacable destiny, sublime struggle, and of heroes, but sure of defeat at last. And that defeat is final. Grand figures are those it exhibits to us, in some respects unequalled, and in their severe simplicity they compare with modern poetry as sculpture with painting. Considered merely as works of art, these products of the Greek imagination satisfy our highest conception of form. They suggest inevitably a feeling of perfect completeness, isolation, and independence, of something rounded and finished in itself. The secret of those old shapers died with them; their

[1] Dante is an ancient in this respect as in many others, but the difference is that with him society is something divinely ordained. He follows Aristotle pretty closely, but on his own theory crime and sin are identical. [Author's note.]

wand is broken, their book sunk deeper than ever plummet sounded. The type of their work is the Greek temple, which leaves nothing to hope for in unity and perfection of design, in harmony and subordination of parts, and in entireness of impression. But in this æsthetic completeness it ends. It rests solidly and complacently on the earth, and the mind rests there with it.

Now the Christian idea has to do with the human soul, which Christianity may be almost said to have invented. While all Paganism represents a few preëminent families, the founders of dynasties or ancestors of races, as of kin with the gods, Christianity makes every pedigree end in Deity, makes monarch and slave the children of one God. Its heroes struggle not against, but upward and onward *toward*, the higher powers who are always on their side. Its highest conception of beauty is not æsthetic, but moral. With it prosperity and adversity have exchanged meanings. It finds enemies in those worldly good-fortunes where Pagan and even Hebrew literature saw the highest blessing, and invincible allies in sorrow, poverty, humbleness of station, where the former world recognized only implacable foes. While it utterly abolished all boundary lines of race or country and made mankind unitary, its hero is always the individual man whoever and wherever he may be. Above all, an entirely new conception of the Infinite and of man's relation to it came in with Christianity. That, and not the finite, is always the background, consciously or not. It changed the scene of the last act of every drama to the next world. Endless aspiration of all the faculties became thus the ideal of Christian life, and to express it more or less perfectly the ideal of essentially Christian art. It was this which the Middle Ages instinctively typified in the Gothic cathedral,—no accidental growth, but the visible symbol of an inward faith,—which soars forever upward, and yearns toward heaven like a martyr-flame suddenly turned to stone.

It is not without significance that Goethe, who, like Dante, also absorbed and represented the tendency and spirit of his age, should, during his youth and while Europe was alive with the moral and intellectual longing which preluded the French Revolution, have loved the Gothic architecture. It is no less significant that in the period of reaction toward more positive thought which followed, he should have preferred the Greek. His greatest poem, conceived during the former era, is Gothic. Dante, endeavoring to conform himself to literary tradition, began to write the *Divina Commedia* in Latin, and had elaborated several cantos of it in that dead and intractable material. But that poetic instinct, which is never the instinct of an individual, but of his age, could not so be satisfied, and leaving the classic structure he had begun to stand as a monument of failure, he completed his work in Italian. Instead of endeavoring to manufacture a great poem out of what was foreign and artificial, he let the poem make itself out of him. The epic which he wished to write in the universal language of scholars, and which might have had its ten lines in the history of literature, would sing itself in provincial Tuscan, and turns out to be written in the universal dialect of mankind. Thus all great poets have been in a certain sense provincial,—Homer, Dante, Shakespeare, Goethe, Burns, Scott in the *Heart of Midlothian* and *Bride of Lammermoor*,—because the office of the poet is always vicarious, because nothing that has not been living experience can become living expression, because the collective thought, the faith, the desire of a nation or a race, is the cumulative result of many ages, is something organic, and is wiser and stronger than any single person, and will make a great statesman or a great poet out of any man who can entirely surrender himself to it.

As the Gothic cathedral, then, is the type of the Christian idea, so is it also of Dante's poem. And as that in its artistic unity is but the completed thought of a single architect, which yet could never have been realized except out of the faith and by the contributions of an entire people, whose beliefs and superstitions, whose imagination and fancy, find expression in its statues and its carvings, its calm saints and martyrs now at rest forever in the seclusion of their canopied niches, and its wanton grotesques thrusting themselves forth from every pinnacle and gargoyle, so in Dante's poem, while it is as personal and peculiar as if it were his private journal and autobiography, we can yet read the diary and the autobiography of the thirteenth century and of the Italian people. Complete and harmonious in design as his work is, it is yet no Pagan temple enshrining a type of the human made divine by triumph of corporeal beauty; it is not a private chapel housing a single saint and dedicate to one chosen bloom of Christian piety or devotion; it is truly a cathedral, over whose high altar hangs the emblem of suffering, of the Divine made human to teach the beauty of adversity, the eternal presence of the spiritual, not overhanging and threatening, but informing and sustaining the material. In this cathedral of Dante's there are sidechapels as is fit, with altars to all Christian virtues and perfections; but the great impression of its leading thought is that of aspiration, forever and ever. In the three divisions of the poem we may trace something more than a fancied analogy with a Christian basilica. There is first the ethnic forecourt, then the purgatorial middle space, and last the holy of holies dedicated to the eternal presence of the mediatorial God.[1]

* * *

Perhaps it seems little to say that Dante was the first great poet who ever made a poem wholly out of himself, but, rightly looked at, it implies a wonderful self-reliance and originality in his genius. His is the first keel that ever ventured into the silent sea of human consciousness to find a new world of poetry.

"L' acqua ch' io prendo giammai non si corse."[2]

[1] "The poem consists of three parts, Hell, Purgatory, and Paradise. . . . In the form of the verse (triple rhyme) we may find an emblem of the Trinity, and in the three divisions, of the threefold state of man, sin, grace, and beatitude. Symbolic meanings reveal themselves, or make themselves suspected, everywhere, as in the architecture of the Middle Ages." (Lowell, "Dante," Riverside Ed.

[2] "The water which I take was never coursed before." *Paradiso*, II, 7. Lucretius makes the same boast:—

"Avia Pieridum peragro loca nullius ante
    Trita solo." [Author's note.]

He discovered that not only the story of some heroic person, but that of any man might be epical; that the way to heaven was not outside the world, but through it. Living at a time when the end of the world was still looked for as imminent,[1] he believed that the second coming of the Lord was to take place on no more conspicuous stage than the soul of man; that his kingdom would be established in the surrendered will. A poem, the precious distillation of such a character and such a life as his through all those sorrowing but undespondent years, must have a meaning in it which few men have meaning enough in themselves wholly to penetrate. That its allegorical form belongs to a past fashion, with which the modern mind has little sympathy, we should no more think of denying than of whitewashing a fresco of Giotto. But we may take it as we may nature, which is also full of double meanings, either as picture or as parable, either for the simple delight of its beauty or as a shadow of the spiritual world. We may take it as we may history, either for its picturesqueness or its moral, either for the variety of its figures, or as a witness to that perpetual presence of God in his creation of which Dante was so profoundly sensible. He had seen and suffered much, but it is only to the man who is himself of value that experience is valuable. He had not looked on man and nature as most of us do, with less interest than into the columns of our daily newspaper. He saw in them the latest authentic news of the God who made them, for he carried everywhere that vision washed clear with tears which detects the meaning under the mask, and, beneath the casual and transitory, the eternal keeping its sleepless watch. The secret of Dante's power is not far to seek. Whoever can express *himself* with the full force of unconscious sincerity will be found to have uttered something ideal and universal. Dante intended a didactic poem, but the most picturesque of poets could not escape his genius, and his sermon sings and glows and charms in a manner that surprises more at the fiftieth reading than the first, such variety of freshness is in imagination.

[1] *Convito*, Tr. II, c. 15. [Author's note.]

There are no doubt in the *Divina Commedia* (regarded merely as poetry) sandy spaces enough both of physics and metaphysics, but with every deduction Dante remains the first of descriptive as well as moral poets. His verse is as various as the feeling it conveys; now it has the terseness and edge of steel, and now palpitates with iridescent softness like the breast of a dove. In vividness he is without a rival. He drags back by its tangled locks the unwilling head of some petty traitor of an Italian provincial town, lets the fire glare on the sullen face for a moment, and it sears itself into the memory forever. He shows us an angel glowing with that love of God which makes him a star even amid the glory of heaven, and the holy shape keeps lifelong watch in our fantasy, constant as a sentinel. He has the skill of conveying impressions indirectly. In the gloom of hell his bodily presence is revealed by his stirring something, on the mount of expiation by casting a shadow. Would he have us feel the brightness of an angel? He makes him whiten afar through the smoke like a dawn,[1] or, walking straight toward the setting sun, he finds his eyes suddenly unable to withstand a greater splendor against which his hand is unavailing to shield him. Even its reflected light, then, is brighter than the direct ray of the sun.[2] And how much more keenly do we feel the parched lips of Master Adam for those rivulets of the Casentino which run down into the Arno, "making their channels cool and soft"! His comparisons are as fresh, as simple, and as directly from nature as those of Homer.[3] Sometimes they show a more subtle observation, as where he compares the stooping of Antæus over him to the leaning tower of Carisenda, to which the clouds, flying in an opposite direction to its inclination, give away their motion.[4] His suggestions of in-

---

[1] *Purgatorio*, XVI, 142. Here is Milton's "Far off his coming shone." [Author's note.]

[2] *Purgatorio*, XV, 7, *et seq.* [Author's note.]

[3] See, for example, *Inferno*, XVII, 127–132; *ib.*, XXIV, 7–12; *Purgatorio* II, 124–129; *ib.*, III, 79–84; *ib.*, XXVII, 76–81; *Paradiso*, XIX, 91–93; *ib.*, XXI, 34–39; *ib.*, XXIII, 1–9. [Author's note.]

[4] *Inferno*, XXXI, 136–138.

dividuality, too, from attitude or speech, as in Farinata, Sordello, or Pia,[1] give in a hint what is worth acres of so-called character-painting. In straightforward pathos, the single and sufficient thrust of phrase, he has no competitor. He is too sternly touched to be effusive and tearful:

> "Io non piangeva, sì dentro impietrai." [2]

His is always the true coin of speech,

> "Sì lucida e sì tonda
> Che nel suo conio nulla ci s' inforsa," [3]

and never the highly ornamental promise to pay, token of insolvency.

No doubt it is primarily by his poetic qualities that a poet must be judged, for it is by these, if by anything, that he is to maintain his place in literature. And he must be judged by them absolutely, with reference, that is, to the highest standard, and not relatively to the fashions and opportunities of the age in which he lived. Yet these considerations must fairly enter into our decision of another side of the question, and one that has much to do with the true quality of the man, with his character as distinguished from his talent, and therefore with how much he will influence men as well as delight them. We may reckon up pretty exactly a man's advantages and defects as an artist; these he has in common with others, and they are

---

> "And those thin clouds above, in flakes and bars,
> That give away their motion to the stars."
> (Coleridge, "Dejection, an Ode.")

See also the comparison of the dimness of the faces seen around him in Paradise to "a pearl on a white forehead." (*Paradise*, III, 14.) [Author's note.]

[1] *Inferno*, X, 35–41; *Purgatorio*, VI, 61–66; *ib.*, X, 133. [Author's note.]

[2] "I did not weep: so strong grew I within" (*Inferno*, XXXIII, 49). For example, Cavalcanti's *Come dicesti egli ebbe?* (*Inferno*, X, 67, 68.) Anselmuccio's *Tu guardi sì, padre, che haio?* (*Inferno*, XXXIII, 51.) [Author's note.]

[3] "So bright and round that there is nothing dubious in its coining." (*Paradiso*, XXIV, 86–87.)

to be measured by a recognized standard; but there is something in his *genius* that is incalculable. It would be hard to define the causes of the difference of impression made upon us respectively by two such men as Æschylus and Euripides, but we feel profoundly that the latter, though in some respects a better dramatist, was an infinitely lighter weight. Æschylus stirs something in us far deeper than the sources of mere pleasurable excitement. The man behind the verse is far greater than the verse itself, and the impulse he gives to what is deepest and most sacred in us, though we cannot always explain it, is none the less real and lasting. Some men always seem to remain outside their work; others make their individuality felt in every part of it; their very life vibrates in every verse, and we do not wonder that it has "made them lean for many years." The virtue that has gone out of them abides in what they do. The book such a man makes is indeed, as Milton called it, "the precious lifeblood of a master spirit." Theirs is a true immortality, for it is their soul, and not their talent, that survives in their work. Dante's concise forthrightness of phrase, which to that of most other poets is as a stab[1] to a blow with a cudgel, the vigor of his thought, the beauty of his images, the refinement of his conception of spiritual things, are marvellous if we compare him with his age and its best achievement. But it is for his power of inspiring and sustaining, it is because they find in him a spur to noble aims, a secure refuge in that defeat which the present always seems, that they prize Dante who know and love him best. He is not merely a great poet, but an influence, part of the soul's resources in time of trouble. From him she learns that, "married to the truth, she is a mistress, but otherwise a slave shut out of all liberty."[2]

All great poets have their message to deliver us, from something higher than they. We venture on no unworthy comparison between him who reveals to us the beauty of this world's

---

[1] To the "bestiality" of certain arguments Dante says, "one would wish to reply, not with words, but with a knife." (*Convito*, Tr. IV, c. 14.) [Author's note.]

[2] *Convito*, Tr. IV, c. 2. [Author's note.]

love and the grandeur of this world's passion and him who shows that love of God is the fruit whereof all other loves are but the beautiful and fleeting blossom, that the passions are yet sublimer objects of contemplation, when, subdued by the will, they become patience in suffering and perseverance in the upward path. But we cannot help thinking that if Shakespeare be the most comprehensive intellect, so Dante is the highest spiritual nature that has expressed itself in rhythmical form. Had he merely made us feel how petty the ambitions, sorrows, and vexations of earth appear when looked down on from the heights of our own character and the seclusion of our own genius, or from the region where we commune with God, he had done much:

> "I with my sight returned through one and all
> The sevenfold spheres, and I beheld this globe
> Such that I smiled at its ignoble semblance." [1]

But he has done far more; he has shown us the way by which that country far beyond the stars may be reached, may become the habitual dwelling-place and fortress of our nature, instead of being the object of its vague aspiration in moments of indolence. At the Round Table of King Arthur there was left always one seat empty for him who should accomplish the adventure of the Holy Grail. It was called the perilous seat because of the dangers he must encounter who would win it. In the company of the epic poets there was a place left for whoever should embody the Christian idea of a triumphant life, outwardly all defeat, inwardly victorious, who should make us partakers of that cup of sorrow in which all are communicants with Christ. He who should do this would indeed achieve the perilous seat, for he must combine poesy with doctrine in such cunning wise that the one lose not its beauty nor the other its severity,— and Dante has done it. As he takes possession of it we seem to hear the cry he himself heard when Virgil rejoined the company of great singers,

> "All honor to the loftiest of poets!"

[1] *Paradiso*, XXII, 132–135; *ib.*, XXVII, 110. [Author's note.]

From WORDSWORTH

(1875)

A generation has now passed away since Wordsworth was laid with the family in the churchyard at Grasmere.[1] Perhaps it is hardly yet time to take a perfectly impartial measure of his value as a poet. To do this is especially hard for those who are old enough to remember the last shot which the foe was sullenly firing in that long war of critics which began when he published his manifesto as Pretender, and which came to a pause rather than to an end when they flung up their caps with the rest at his final coronation. Something of the intensity of the *odium theologicum* (if indeed the *aestheticum* be not in these days the more bitter of the two) entered into the conflict. The Wordsworthians were a sect, who, if they had the enthusiasm, had also not a little of the exclusiveness and partiality to which sects are liable. The verses of the master had for them the virtue of religious canticles stimulant of zeal and not amenable to the ordinary tests of cold-blooded criticism. Like the hymns of the Huguenots and Covenanters, they were songs of battle no less than of worship, and the combined ardors of conviction and conflict lent them a fire that was not naturally their own. As we read them now, that virtue of the moment is gone out of them, and whatever of Dr. Wattsiness there is gives us a slight shock of disenchantment. It is something like the difference between the "Marseillaise" sung by armed propagandists on the edge of battle, or by Brissotins in the tumbrel, and the words of it read coolly in the closet, or recited with the factitious frenzy of Thérèse. It was natural in the early days of Wordsworth's career to dwell most fondly on those profounder qualities to appreciate which settled in some sort the measure of a

[1] "I pay many little visits to the family in the churchyard at Grasmere," writes James Dixon (an old servant of Wordsworth) to Crabb Robinson, with a simple, one might almost say canine pathos, thirteen years after his wife's death. Wordsworth was always considerate and kind with his servants, Robinson tells us. [Author's note. The notes in this essay are all Lowell's.]

man's right to judge of poetry at all. But now we must admit the shortcomings, the failures, the defects, as no less essential elements in forming a sound judgment as to whether the seer and artist were so united in him as to justify the claim first put in by himself and afterwards maintained by his sect to a place beside the few great poets who exalt men's minds, and give a right direction and safe outlet to their passion through the imagination, while insensibly helping them toward balance of character and serenity of judgment by stimulating their sense of proportion, form, and the nice adjustment of means to ends. In none of our poets has the constant propulsion of an unbending will, and the concentration of exclusive, if I must not say somewhat narrow, sympathies done so much to make the original endowment of Nature effective, and in none accordingly does the biography throw so much light on the works, or enter so largely into their composition as an element whether of power or of weakness. Wordsworth never saw, and I think never wished to see, beyond the limits of his own consciousness and experience. He early conceived himself to be, and through life was confirmed by circumstances in the faith that he was, a "dedicated spirit,"[1] a state of mind likely to further an intense but at the same time one-sided development of the intellectual powers. The solitude in which the greater part of his mature life was passed, while it doubtless ministered to the passionate intensity of his musings upon man and nature, was, it may be suspected, harmful to him as an artist, by depriving him of any standard of proportion outside himself by which to test the comparative value of his thoughts, and by rendering him more and more incapable of that urbanity of mind which could be gained only by commerce with men more nearly on his own

---

[1] In the *Prelude* he attributes this consecration to a sunrise seen (during a college vacation) as he walked homeward from some village festival where he had danced all night:

> My heart was full; I made no vows, but vows
> Were then made for me; bond unknown to me
> Was given that I should be, else sinning greatly,
> A dedicated Spirit. (Bk. IV.)

level, and which gives tone without lessening individuality. Wordsworth never quite saw the distinction between the eccentric and the original. For what we call originality seems not so much anything peculiar, much less anything odd, but that quality in a man which touches human nature at most points of its circumference, which reinvigorates the consciousness of our own powers by recalling and confirming our own unvalued sensations and perceptions, gives classic shape to our own amorphous imaginings, and adequate utterance to our own stammering conceptions or emotions. The poet's office is to be a Voice, not of one crying in the wilderness to a knot of already magnetized acolytes, but singing amid the throng of men, and lifting their common aspirations and sympathies (so first clearly revealed to themselves) on the wings of his song to a purer ether and a wider reach of view. We cannot, if we would, read the poetry of Wordsworth as mere poetry; at every other page we find ourselves entangled in a problem of aesthetics. The world-old question of matter and form, of whether nectar *is* of precisely the same flavor when served to us from a Grecian chalice or from any jug of ruder pottery, comes up for decision anew. The Teutonic nature has always shown a sturdy preference of the solid bone with a marrow of nutritious moral to any shadow of the same on the flowing mirror of sense. Wordsworth never lets us long forget the deeply rooted stock from which he sprang—*vien ben dà lui.* . . .

The true rank of Wordsworth among poets is, perhaps, not even yet to be fairly estimated, so hard is it to escape into the quiet hall of judgment uninflamed by the tumult of partisanship which beset the doors.

Coming to manhood, predetermined to be a great poet, at a time when the artificial school of poetry was enthroned with all the authority of long succession and undisputed legitimacy, it was almost inevitable that Wordsworth, who, both by nature and judgment, was a rebel against the existing order, should become a partisan. Unfortunately, he became not only the partisan of a system, but of William Wordsworth as its representative. Right in general principle, he thus necessarily became wrong in particulars. Justly convinced that greatness only achieves its ends by implicitly obeying its own instincts, he perhaps reduced the following his instincts too much to a system, mistook his own resentments for the promptings of his natural genius, and, compelling principle to the measure of his own temperament or even of the controversial exigency of the moment, fell sometimes into the error of making naturalness itself artificial. If a poet resolve to be original, it will end commonly in his being merely peculiar.

Wordsworth himself departed more and more in practice, as he grew older, from the theories which he had laid down in his prefaces; but those theories undoubtedly had a great effect in retarding the growth of his fame. He had carefully constructed a pair of spectacles through which his earlier poems were to be studied, and the public insisted on looking through them at his mature works, and were consequently unable to see fairly what required a different focus. He forced his readers to come to his poetry with a certain amount of conscious preparation, and thus gave them beforehand the impression of something like mechanical artifice, and deprived them of the contented repose of implicit faith. To the child a watch seems to be a living creature; but Wordsworth would not let his readers be children, and did injustice to himself by giving them an uneasy doubt whether creations which really throbbed with the very heart's-blood of genius, and were alive with nature's life of life, were not contrivances of wheels and springs. A naturalness which we are told to expect has lost the crowning grace of nature. The men who walked in Cornelius Agrippa's visionary gardens had probably no more pleasurable emotion than that of a shallow wonder, or an equally shallow self-satisfaction in thinking they had hit upon the secret of the thaumaturgy; but to a tree that has grown as God willed we come without a theory and with no botanical predilections, enjoying it simply and thankfully; or the Imagination recreates for us its past summers and winters, the birds that have nested and sung in it, the sheep that have clustered in its shade, the winds that have visited it, the cloudbergs that have drifted over it, and the snows that have

ermined it in winter. The Imagination is a faculty that flouts
at foreordination, and Wordsworth seemed to do all he could
to cheat his readers of her company by laying out paths with a
peremptory *Do not step off the gravel!* at the opening of each,
and preparing pitfalls for every conceivable emotion, with
guide-boards to tell each when and where it must be
caught.

But if these things stood in the way of immediate appreciation, he had another theory which interferes most seriously with
the total and permanent effect of his poems. He was theoretically
determined not only to be a philosophic poet, but to be a *great*
philosophic poet, and to this end he must produce an epic.
Leaving aside the question whether the epic be obsolete or not,
it may be doubted whether the history of a single man's mind is
universal enough in its interest to furnish all the requirements
of the epic machinery, and it may be more than doubted whether
a poet's philosophy be ordinary metaphysics, divisible into
chapter and section. It is rather something which is more energetic in a word than in a whole treatise, and our hearts unclose
themselves instinctively at its simple *Open sesame!* while they
would stand firm against the reading of the whole body of
philosophy. In point of fact, the one element of greatness
which "The Excursion" possesses indisputably is heaviness. It
is only the episodes that are universally read, and the effect of
these is diluted by the connecting and accompanying lectures
on metaphysics. Wordsworth had his epic mould to fill, and,
like Benvenuto Cellini in casting his Perseus, was forced to
throw in everything, debasing the metal lest it should run short.
Separated from the rest, the episodes are perfect poems in their
kind, and without example in the language.

Wordsworth, like most solitary men of strong minds, was a
good critic of the substance of poetry, but somewhat niggardly
in the allowance he made for those subsidiary qualities which
make it the charmer of leisure and the employment of minds
without definite object. It may be doubted, indeed, whether
he set much store by any contemporary writing but his own,
and whether he did not look upon poetry too exclusively as an

exercise rather of the intellect than as a nepenthe of the imagination.[1] He says of himself, speaking of his youth:—

> In fine,
> I was a better judge of thoughts than words,
> Misled in estimating words, not only
> By common inexperience of youth,
> But by the trade in classic niceties,
> The dangerous craft of culling term and phrase
> From languages that want the living voice
> To carry meaning to the natural heart;
> To tell us what is passion, what is truth,
> What reason, what simplicity and sense.[2]

Though he here speaks in the preterite tense, this was always true of him, and his thought seems often to lean upon a word too weak to bear its weight. No reader of adequate insight can help regretting that he did not earlier give himself to "the trade of classic niceties." It was precisely this which gives to the blank verse of Landor the severe dignity and reserved force which alone among later poets recall the tune of Milton, and to which Wordsworth never attained. Indeed, Wordsworth's blank verse (though the passion be profounder) is always essentially that of Cowper. They were alike also in their love of outward nature and of simple things. The main difference between them is one of scenery rather than of sentiment, between the lifelong familiar of the mountains and the dweller on the plain.

It cannot be denied that in Wordsworth the very highest powers of the poetic mind were associated with a certain tendency to the diffuse and commonplace. It is in the understanding (always prosaic) that the great golden veins of his imagination are embedded.[3] He wrote too much to write always well; for it

[1] According to Landor, he pronounced all Scott's poetry to be "not worth five shillings."

[2] *Prelude*, bk. IV.

[3] This was instinctively felt, even by his admirers. Miss Martineau said to Crabb Robinson in 1839, speaking of Wordsworth's conversation: "Sometimes he is annoying from the pertinacity with which

is not a great Xerxes-army of words, but a compact Greek ten thousand, that march safely down to posterity. He set tasks to his divine faculty, which is much the same as trying to make Jove's eagle do the service of a clucking hen. Throughout "The Prelude" and "The Excursion" he seems striving to bind the wizard Imagination with the sand-ropes of dry disquisition, and to have forgotten the potent spell-word which would make the particles cohere. There is an arenaceous quality in the style which makes progress wearisome. Yet with what splendors as of mountain sunsets are we rewarded! what golden rounds of verse do we not see stretching heavenward with angels ascending and descending! what haunting harmonies hover around us deep and eternal like the undying barytone of the sea! and if we are compelled to fare through sands and desert wildernesses, how often do we not hear airy shapes that syllable our names with a startling personal appeal to our highest consciousness and our noblest aspiration, such as we wait for in vain in any other poet! Landor, in a letter to Miss Holford, says admirably of him, "Common minds alone can be ignorant what breadth of philosophy, what energy and intensity of thought, what insight into the heart, and what observation of nature are requisite for the production of such poetry."

Take from Wordsworth all which an honest criticism cannot but allow, and what is left will show how truly great he was. He had no humor, no dramatic power, and his temperament was of that dry and juiceless quality, that in all his published correspondence you shall not find a letter, but only essays. If we consider carefully where he was most successful, we shall find that it was not so much in description of natural scenery, or delineation of character, as in vivid expression of the effect produced by external objects and events upon his own mind, and of the shape and hue (perhaps momentary) which they in turn

---

he dwells on trifles; at other times he flows on in the utmost grandeur, leaving a strong impression of inspiration." Robinson tells us that he read *Resolution and Independence* to a lady who was affected by it even to tears, and then said, "I have not heard anything for years that so much delighted me; but, *after all, it is not poetry.*"

took from his mood or temperament. His finest passages are always monologues. He had a fondness for particulars, and there are parts of his poems which remind us of local histories in the undue relative importance given to trivial matters. He was the historian of Wordsworthshire. This power of particularization (for it is as truly a power as generalization) is what gives such vigor and greatness to single lines and sentiments of Wordsworth, and to poems developing a single thought or sentiment. It was this that made him so fond of the sonnet. That sequestered nook forced upon him the limits which his fecundity (if I may not say his garrulity) was never self-denying enough to impose on itself. It suits his solitary and meditative temper, and it was there that Lamb (an admirable judge of what was permanent in literature) liked him best. Its narrow bounds, but fourteen paces from end to end, turn into a virtue his too common fault of giving undue prominence to every passing emotion. He excels in monologue, and the law of the sonnet tempers monologue with mercy. In "The Excursion" we are driven to the subterfuge of a French verdict of extenuating circumstances. His mind had not that reach and elemental movement of Milton's, which, like the trade-wind, gathered to itself thoughts and images like stately fleets from every quarter; some deep with silks and spicery, some brooding over the silent thunders of their battailous armaments, but all swept forward in their destined track, over the long billows of his verse, every inch of canvas strained by the unifying breath of their common epic impulse. It was an organ that Milton mastered, mighty in compass, capable equally of the trumpet's ardors or the slim delicacy of the flute, and sometimes it bursts forth in great crashes through his prose, as if he touched it for solace in the intervals of his toil. If Wordsworth sometimes put the trumpet to his lips, yet he lays it aside soon and willingly for his appropriate instrument, the pastoral reed. And it is not one that grew by any vulgar stream, but that which Apollo breathed through, tending the flocks of Admetus, —that which Pan endowed with every melody of the visible universe,—the same in which the soul of the despairing nymph

took refuge and gifted with her dual nature,—so that ever and
anon, amid the notes of human joy or sorrow, there comes suddenly a deeper and almost awful tone, thrilling us into dim
consciousness of a forgotten divinity.

Wordsworth's absolute want of humor, while it no doubt
confirmed his self-confidence by making him insensible both
to the comical incongruity into which he was often led by his
earlier theory concerning the language of poetry and to the not
unnatural ridicule called forth by it, seems to have been indica-
tive of a certain dulness of perception in other directions.[1] We

[1] Nowhere is this displayed with more comic self-complacency than
when he thought it needful to rewrite the ballad of *Helen of Kir-
connel*,—a poem hardly to be matched in any language for swiftness
of movement and savage sincerity of feeling. Its shuddering com-
pression is masterly.

> "Curst be the heart that thought the thought,
>   And curst the hand that fired the shot,
>   When in my arms burd Helen dropt,
>   That died to succor me!
>
> O, think ye not my heart was sair
> When my love dropt down and spake na mair?"

Compare this with—

> "Proud Gordon cannot bear the thoughts
>   That through his brain are travelling,
>   And, starting up, to Bruce's heart
>   He launched a deadly javelin;
>
> Fair Ellen saw it when it came,
> And, *stepping forth to meet the same,*
>   Did with her body cover
>   The Youth, her chosen lover.
>
>   *   *   *
>
> And Bruce (*as soon as he had slain
> The Gordon*) sailed away to Spain,
>   And fought with rage incessant
>   Against the Moorish Crescent."

These are surely the verses of an attorney's clerk "penning a
stanza when he should engross." It will be noticed that Wordsworth
here also departs from his earlier theory of the language of poetry

cannot help feeling that the material of his nature was essentially prose, which, in his inspired moments, he had the power of transmuting, but which, whenever the inspiration failed or was factitious, remained obstinately leaden. The normal condition of many poets would seem to approach that temperature to which Wordsworth's mind could be raised only by the white heat of profoundly inward passion. And in proportion to the intensity needful to make his nature thoroughly aglow is the very high quality of his best verses. They seem rather the productions of nature than of man, and have the lastingness of such, delighting our age with the same startle of newness and beauty that pleased our youth. Is it his thought? It has the shifting inward lustre of diamond. Is it his feeling? It is as delicate as the impressions of fossil ferns. He seems to have caught and fixed forever in immutable grace the most evanescent and intangible of our intuitions, the very ripple-marks on the remotest shores of being. But this intensity of mood which insures high quality is by its very nature incapable of prolongation, and Wordsworth, in endeavoring it, falls more below

---

by substituting a javelin for a bullet as less modern and familiar. Had he written—

> And Gordon never gave a hint,
> But, having somewhat picked his flint,
> Let fly the fatal bullet
> That killed that lovely pullet,—

it would hardly have seemed more like a parody than the rest. He shows the same insensibility in a note upon the *Ancient Mariner* in the second edition of the *Lyrical Ballads:* "The poem of my friend has indeed great defects; first, that the principal person has no distinct character, either in his profession of mariner, or as a human being who, having been long under the control of supernatural impressions, might be supposed himself to partake of something supernatural; secondly, that he does not act, but is continually acted upon; thirdly, that the events, having no necessary connection, do not produce each other; and lastly, that the imagery is somewhat laboriously accumulated." Here is an indictment, to be sure, and drawn, plainly enough, by the attorney's clerk aforenamed. One would think that the strange charm of Coleridge's most truly original poems lay in this very emancipation from the laws of cause and effect.

himself, and is, more even than many poets his inferiors in imaginative quality, a poet of passages. Indeed, one cannot help having the feeling sometimes that the poem is there for the sake of these passages, rather than that these are the natural jets and elations of a mind energized by the rapidity of its own motion. In other words, the happy couplet or gracious image seems not to spring from the inspiration of the poem conceived as a whole, but rather to have dropped of itself into the mind of the poet in one of his rambles, who then, in a less rapt mood, has patiently built up around it a setting of verse too often ungraceful in form and of a material whose cheapness may cast a doubt on the priceless quality of the gem it encumbers.[1] During the most happily productive period of his life, Wordsworth was impatient of what may be called the mechanical portion of his art. His wife and sister seem from the first to have been his scribes. In later years, he had learned and often insisted on the truth that poetry was an art no less than a gift, and corrected his poems in cold blood, sometimes to their detriment. But he certainly had more of the vision than of the faculty divine, and was always a little numb on the side of form and proportion. Perhaps his best poem in these respects is the "Laodamia," and it is not uninstructive to learn from his own lips that "it cost him more trouble than almost anything of equal length he had ever written." His longer poems (miscalled epical) have no more intimate bond of union than their more or less immediate relation to his own personality. Of character other than his own he had but a faint conception, and all the personages of "The Excursion" that are not Wordsworth are the merest shadows of himself upon mist, for his self-concentrated nature was incapable of projecting itself into the consciousness of other men and seeing the springs of action at their source in the re-

---

[1] "A hundred times when, roving high and low,
    I have been harassed with the toil of verse,
    Much pains and little progress, and at once
    Some lovely Image in the song rose up,
    Full-formed, like Venus rising from the sea."
                                        Prelude, bk. IV.

cesses of individual character. The best parts of these longer poems are bursts of impassioned soliloquy, and his fingers were always clumsy at the *callida junctura*. The stream of narration is sluggish, if varied by times with pleasing reflections (*viridesque placido aequore sylvas*); we are forced to do our own rowing, and only when the current is hemmed in by some narrow gorge of the poet's personal consciousness do we feel ourselves snatched along on the smooth but impetuous rush of unmistakable inspiration. The fact that what is precious in Wordsworth's poetry was (more truly even than with some greater poets than he) a gift rather than an achievement should always be borne in mind in taking the measure of his power. I know not whether to call it height or depth, this peculiarity of his, but it certainly endows those parts of his work which we should distinguish as Wordsworthian with an unexpectedness and impressiveness of originality such as we feel in the presence of Nature herself. He seems to have been half conscious of this, and recited his own poems to all comers with an enthusiasm of wondering admiration that would have been profoundly comic[1] but for its simple sincerity and for the fact that William Wordsworth, Esquire, of Rydal Mount, was one person, and the William Wordsworth whom he so heartily reverenced quite another. We recognize two voices in him, as Stephano did in Caliban. There are Jeremiah and his scribe Baruch. If the prophet cease from dictating, the amanuensis, rather than be idle, employs his pen in jotting down some anecdotes of his master, how he one day went out and saw an old woman, and the next day did *not*, and so came home and dictated some verses on this ominous phenomenon, and how another day he saw a cow. These marginal annotations have been carelessly taken up into the text, have been religiously held by the pious

---

[1] Mr. Emerson tells us that he was at first tempted to smile, and Mr. Ellis Yarnall (who saw him in his eightieth year) says, "These quotations [from his own works] he read in a way that much impressed me; it seemed almost as if he were *awed by the greatness of his own power, the gifts with which he had been endowed*." (The italics are mine.)

to be orthodox scripture, and by dexterous exegesis have been made to yield deeply oracular meanings. Presently the real prophet takes up the word again and speaks as one divinely inspired, the Voice of a higher and invisible power. Wordsworth's better utterances have the bare sincerity, the absolute abstraction from time and place, the immunity from decay, that belong to the grand simplicities of the Bible. They seem not more his own than ours and every man's, the word of the inalterable Mind. This gift of his was naturally very much a matter of temperament, and accordingly by far the greater part of his finer product belongs to the period of his prime, ere Time had set his lumpish foot on the pedal that deadens the nerves of animal sensibility.[1] He did not grow as those poets do in whom the artistic sense is predominant. One of the most delightful fancies of the Genevese humorist, Toepffer, is the poet Albert, who, having had his portrait drawn by a highly idealizing hand, does his best afterwards to look like it. Many of Wordsworth's later poems seem like rather unsuccessful efforts to resemble his former self. They would never, as Sir John Harrington says of poetry, "keep a child from play and an old man from the chimney-corner."[2]

Chief Justice Marshall once blandly interrupted a junior coun-

[1] His best poetry was written when he was under the immediate influence of Coleridge. Coleridge seems to have felt this, for it is evidently to Wordsworth that he alludes when he speaks of "those who have been so well pleased that I should, year after year, flow with a hundred nameless rills into *their* main stream." (*Letters, Conversations, and Recollections of S. T. C.*, Vol. I, pp. 5, 6.) "Wordsworth found fault with the repetition of the concluding sound of the participles in Shakespeare's line about bees:

The singing masons building roofs of gold.

This, he said, was a line that Milton never would have written. Keats thought, on the other hand, that the repetition was in harmony with the continued note of the singers." (Leigh Hunt's *Autobiography*.) Wordsworth writes to Crabb Robinson in 1837, "My ear is susceptible to the clashing of sounds almost to disease." One cannot help thinking that his training in these niceties was begun by Coleridge.

[2] In the Preface to his translation of the *Orlando Furioso*.

sel who was arguing certain obvious points of law at needless length, by saying, "Brother Jones, there are *some* things which a Supreme Court of the United States sitting in equity may be presumed to know." Wordsworth has this fault of enforcing and restating obvious points till the reader feels as if his own intelligence were somewhat underrated. He is over-conscientious in giving us full measure, and once profoundly absorbed in the sound of his own voice, he knows not when to stop. If he feels himself flagging, he has a droll way of keeping the floor, as it were, by asking himself a series of questions sometimes not needing, and often incapable of answer. There are three stanzas of such near the close of the First Part of "Peter Bell," where Peter first catches a glimpse of the dead body in the water, all happily incongruous, and ending with one which reaches the height of comicality:—

> "Is it a fiend that to a stake
> Of fire his desperate self is tethering?
> Or stubborn spirit doomed to yell,
> In solitary ward or cell,
> Ten thousand miles from all his brethren?"

The same want of humor which made him insensible to incongruity may perhaps account also for the singular unconsciousness of disproportion which so often strikes us in his poetry. For example, a little farther on in "Peter Bell" we find:—

> "*Now*—like a tempest-shattered bark
> That overwhelmed and prostrate lies,
> And in a moment to the verge
> Is lifted of a foaming surge—
> Full suddenly the Ass doth rise!"

And one cannot help thinking that the similes of the huge stone, the sea-beast, and the cloud, noble as they are in themselves, are somewhat too lofty for the service to which they are put.[1]

The movement of Wordsworth's mind was too slow and his

---

[1] In *Resolution and Independence.*

mood too meditative for narrative poetry. He values his own
thoughts and reflections too much to sacrifice the least of them
to the interests of his story. Moreover, it is never action that
interests him, but the subtle motives that lead to or hinder it.
"The Wagoner" involuntarily suggests a comparison with
"Tam O'Shanter" infinitely to its own disadvantage. "Peter
Bell," full though it be of profound touches and subtle analysis,
is lumbering and disjointed. Even Lamb was forced to confess
that he did not like it. "The White Doe," the most Wordsworthian of them all in the best meaning of the epithet, is also
only the more truly so for being diffuse and reluctant. What
charms in Wordsworth and will charm forever is the

> "Happy tone
> Of meditation slipping in between
> The beauty coming and the beauty gone."

A few poets, in the exquisite adaptation of their words to the
tune of our own feelings and fancies, in the charm of their manner, indefinable as the sympathetic grace of woman, *are* everything to us without our being able to say that they are much in
themselves. They rather narcotize than fortify. Wordsworth
must subject our mood to his own before he admits us to his
intimacy; but, once admitted, it is for life, and we find ourselves
in his debt, not for what he has been to us in our hours of relaxation, but for what he has done for us as a reinforcement of
faltering purpose and personal independence of character. His
system of a Nature-cure, first professed by Dr. Jean Jacques
and continued by Cowper, certainly breaks down as a whole.
The Solitary of "The Excursion," who has not been cured of
his scepticism by living among the medicinal mountains, is, so
far as we can see, equally proof against the lectures of Pedler
and Parson. Wordsworth apparently felt that this would be
so, and accordingly never saw his way clear to finishing the
poem. But the treatment, whether a panacea or not, is certainly
wholesome, inasmuch as it inculcates abstinence, exercise, and
uncontaminate air. I am not sure, indeed, that the Nature-cure
theory does not tend to foster in constitutions less vigorous

than Wordsworth's what Milton would call a fugitive and cloistered virtue at a dear expense of manlier qualities. The ancients and our own Elizabethans, ere spiritual megrims had become fashionable, perhaps made more out of life by taking a frank delight in its action and passion and by grappling with the facts of this world, rather than muddling themselves over the insoluble problems of another. If they had not discovered the picturesque, as we understand it, they found surprisingly fine scenery in man and his destiny, and would have seen something ludicrous, it may be suspected, in the spectacle of a grown man running to hide his head in the apron of the Mighty Mother whenever he had an ache in his finger or got a bruise in the tussle for existence.

But when, as I have said, our impartiality has made all those qualifications and deductions against which even the greatest poet may not plead his privilege, what is left to Wordsworth is enough to justify his fame. Even where his genius is wrapped in clouds, the unconquerable lightning of imagination struggles through, flashing out unexpected vistas, and illuminating the humdrum pathway of our daily thought with a radiance of momentary consciousness that seems like a revelation. If it be the most delightful function of the poet to set our lives to music, yet perhaps he will be even more sure of our maturer gratitude if he do his part also as moralist and philosopher to purify and enlighten; if he define and encourage our vacillating perceptions of duty; if he piece together our fragmentary apprehensions of our own life and that larger life whose unconscious instruments we are, making of the jumbled bits of our dissected map of experience a coherent chart. In the great poets there is an exquisite sensibility both of soul and sense that sympathizes like gossamer sea-moss with every movement of the element in which it floats, but which is rooted on the solid rock of our common sympathies. Wordsworth shows less of this finer feminine fibre of organization than one or two of his contemporaries, notably than Coleridge or Shelley; but he was a masculine thinker, and in his more characteristic poems there is always a kernel of firm conclusion from far-reaching principles that stimulates thought and challenges meditation. Groping in the dark passages of life, we come upon some axiom of his, as it were a wall that gives us our bearings and enables us to find an outlet. Compared with Goethe we feel that he lacks that serene impartiality of mind which results from breadth of culture; nay, he seems narrow, insular, almost provincial. He reminds us of those saints of Dante who gather brightness by revolving on their own axis. But through this very limitation of range he gains perhaps in intensity and the impressiveness which results from eagerness of personal conviction. If we read Wordsworth through, as I have just done, we find ourselves changing our mind about him at every other page, so uneven is he. If we read our favorite poems or passages only, he will seem uniformly great. And even as regards "The Excursion" we should remember how few long poems will bear consecutive reading. For my part I know of but one,—the "Odyssey."

None of our great poets can be called popular in any exact sense of the word, for the highest poetry deals with thoughts and emotions which inhabit, like rarest sea-mosses, the doubtful limits of that shore between our abiding divine and our fluctuating human nature, rooted in the one, but living in the other, seldom laid bare, and otherwise visible only at exceptional moments of entire calm and clearness. Of no other poet except Shakespeare have so many phrases become household words as of Wordsworth. If Pope has made current more epigrams of worldly wisdom, to Wordsworth belongs the nobler praise of having defined for us, and given us for a daily possession, those faint and vague suggestions of other-worldliness of whose gentle ministry with our baser nature the hurry and bustle of life scarcely ever allowed us to be conscious. He has won for himself a secure immortality by a depth of intuition which makes only the best minds at their best hours worthy, or indeed capable, of his companionship, and by a homely sincerity of human sympathy which reaches the humblest heart. Our language owes him gratitude for the habitual purity and abstinence of his style, and we who speak it, for having emboldened us to take delight in simple things, and to trust ourselves to our own instincts. And he hath his reward. It needs not to bid

> "Renowned Spenser, lie a thought more nigh
> To learned Chaucer, and rare Beaumont lie
> A little nearer Spenser";—

for there is no fear of crowding in that little society with whom he is now enrolled as fifth in the succession of the great English poets.

DEMOCRACY

(1884)

He must be a born leader or misleader of men, or must have been sent into the world unfurnished with that modulating and restraining balance-wheel which we call a sense of humor, who, in old age, has as strong a confidence in his opinions and in the necessity of bringing the universe into conformity with them as he had in youth. In a world the very condition of whose being is that it should be in perpetual flux, where all seems mirage, and the one abiding thing is the effort to distinguish realities from appearances, the elderly man must be indeed of a singularly tough and valid fibre who is certain that he has any clarified residuum of experience, any assured verdict of reflection, that deserves to be called an opinion, or who, even if he had, feels that he is justified in holding mankind by the button while he is expounding it. And in a world of daily—nay, almost hourly—journalism, where every clever man, every man who thinks himself clever, or whom anybody else thinks clever, is called upon to deliver his judgment point-blank and at the word of command on every conceivable subject of human thought, or, on what sometimes seems to him very much the same thing, on every inconceivable display of human want of thought, there is such a spendthrift waste of all those commonplaces which furnish the permitted staple of public discourse that there is little chance of beguiling a new tune out of the one-stringed instrument on which we have been thrumming so long. In this desperate necessity one is often tempted to think that, if all the words of the dictionary were tumbled down in a heap and then all those fortuitous juxtapositions and combinations that made tolerable sense were picked out and pieced together, we might find among them some poignant suggestions towards novelty of thought or expression. But, alas! it is only the great poets who seem to have this unsolicited profusion of unexpected and incalculable phrase, this infinite variety of topic. For everybody else everything has been said before, and said over again after. He who has read his Aristotle will be apt to think that observation has on most points of general applicability said its last word, and he who has mounted the tower of Plato to look abroad from it will never hope to climb another with so lofty a vantage of speculation. Where it is so simple if not so easy a thing to hold one's peace, why add to the general confusion of tongues? There is something disheartening, too, in being expected to fill up not less than a certain measure of time, as if the mind were an hour-glass, that need only be shaken and set on one end or the other, as the case may be, to run its allotted sixty minutes with decorous exactitude. I recollect being once told by the late eminent naturalist, Agassiz, that when he was to deliver his first lecture as professor (at Zurich, I believe) he had grave doubts of his ability to occupy the prescribed three quarters of an hour. He was speaking without notes, and glancing anxiously from time to time at the watch that lay before him on the desk. "When I had spoken a half hour," he said, "I had told them everything I knew in the world, everything! Then I began to repeat myself," he added, roguishly, "and I have done nothing else ever since." Beneath the humorous exaggeration of the story I seemed to see the face of a very serious and improving moral. And yet if one were to say only what he had to say and then stopped, his audience would feel defrauded of their honest measure. Let us take courage by the example of the French, whose exportation of Bordeaux wines increases as the area of their land in vineyard is diminished.

To me, somewhat hopelessly revolving these things, the undelayable year has rolled round, and I find myself called upon to say something in this place, where so many wiser men have spoken before me. Precluded, in my quality of national guest, by motives of taste and discretion, from dealing with any question of immediate and domestic concern, it seemed to me wisest, or at any rate most prudent, to choose a topic of comparatively abstract interest, and to ask your indulgence for a few somewhat generalized remarks on a matter concerning which I had some experimental knowledge, derived from the use of such eyes and ears as Nature had been pleased to endow me withal, and such report as I had been able to win from them. The subject which most readily suggested itself was the spirit and the working of those conceptions of life and polity which are lumped together, whether for reproach or commendation, under the name of Democracy. By temperament and education of a conservative turn, I saw the last years of that quaint Arcadia which French travellers saw with delighted amazement a century ago, and have watched the change (to me a sad one) from an agricultural to a proletary population.[1] The testi-

---

[1] The participation of Frenchmen in the American Revolutionary War naturally led to considerable intercourse between the United States and France, and with the oncoming of the Revolution in the latter country interest there became especially keen as to the success of the new republic across the Atlantic. For these and other reasons, many French travellers visited our shores in the last part of the eighteenth and the first part of the nineteenth centuries, and owing to the political unrest at home, they were quite generally predisposed to favorable views of our institutions.

Brissot de Warville, who travelled in the United States in 1788, says, in the preface to the book which he published in 1791: "Is it not evident that private morals associate naturally with a rural life? ... The reason why the Americans possess such pure morals is because nine tenths of them live dispersed in the country.... O Frenchmen! Study the Americans of the present day. Open this book: you will here see to what degree of prosperity the blessings of freedom can elevate the industry of man." [All notes to this essay except those marked J. R. L. are by Norman Foerster.]

mony of Balaam[1] should carry some conviction. I have grown to manhood and am now growing old with the growth of this system of government in my native land; have watched its advances, or what some would call its encroachments, gradual and irresistible as those of a glacier; have been an ear-witness to the forebodings of wise and good and timid men, and have lived to see those forebodings belied by the course of events, which is apt to show itself humorously careless of the reputation of prophets. I recollect hearing a sagacious old gentleman say in 1840 that the doing away with the property qualification for suffrage twenty years before had been the ruin of the State of Massachusetts; that it had put public credit and private estate alike at the mercy of demagogues. I lived to see that Commonwealth twenty odd years later paying the interest on her bonds in gold, though it cost her sometimes nearly three for one to keep her faith, and that while suffering an unparalleled drain of men and treasure in helping to sustain the unity and self-respect of the nation.

If universal suffrage has worked ill in our larger cities, as it certainly has, this has been mainly because the hands that wielded it were untrained to its use. There the election of a majority of the trustees of the public money is controlled by the most ignorant and vicious of a population which has come to us from abroad, wholly unpracticed in self-government and incapable of assimilation by American habits and methods. But the finances of our towns, where the native tradition is still dominant and whose affairs are discussed and settled in a public assembly of the people, have been in general honestly and prudently administered. Even in manufacturing towns, where a majority of the voters live by their daily wages, it is not so often the recklessness as the moderation of public expenditure that surprises an old-fashioned observer. "The beggar is in the saddle at last," cried Proverbial Wisdom.[2] "Why, in the name

[1] That is, the testimony of one whose message is not what his hearers would most gladly receive, but who speaks the truth as it has been shown to him. See Numbers xxii–xxiv.

[2] "Beggars mounted run their horses to death."—*Old Proverb.*

of all former experience, doesn't he ride to the Devil?" Because in the very act of mounting he ceased to be a beggar and became part owner of the piece of property he bestrides. The last thing we need be anxious about is property. It always has friends or the means of making them. If riches have wings to fly away from their owner, they have wings also to escape danger.

I hear America sometimes playfully accused of sending you all your storms, and am in the habit of parrying the charge by alleging that we are enabled to do this because, in virtue of our protective system, we can afford to make better bad weather than anybody else. And what wiser use could we make of it than to export it in return for the paupers which some European countries are good enough to send over to us who have not attained to the same skill in the manufacture of them? But bad weather is not the worst thing that is laid at our door. A French gentleman, not long ago, forgetting Burke's monition of how unwise it is to draw an indictment against a whole people,[1] has charged us with the responsibility of whatever he finds disagreeable in the morals or manners of his countrymen. If M. Zola or some other competent witness would only go into the box and tell us what those morals and manners were before our example corrupted them! But I confess that I find little to interest and less to edify me in these international bandyings of "You're another."

I shall address myself to a single point only in the long list of offences of which we are more or less gravely accused, because that really includes all the rest. It is that we are infecting the Old World with what seems to be thought the entirely new disease of Democracy. It is generally people who are in what are called easy circumstances who can afford the leisure to treat themselves to a handsome complaint, and these experience an immediate alleviation when once they have found a sonorous Greek name to abuse it by. There is something consolatory

---

[1] In his speech on moving his resolution for conciliation with the American Colonies, in the House of Commons, March 22, 1775. See *Riverside Literature Series*, No. 100, p. 36.

also, something flattering to their sense of personal dignity, and to that conceit of singularity which is the natural recoil from our uneasy consciousness of being commonplace, in thinking ourselves victims of a malady by which no one had ever suffered before. Accordingly they find it simpler to class under one comprehensive heading whatever they find offensive to their nerves, their tastes, their interests, or what they suppose to be their opinions, and christen it Democracy, much as physicians label every obscure disease gout, or as cross-grained fellows lay their ill-temper to the weather. But is it really a new ailment, and, if it be, is America answerable for it? Even if she were, would it account for the phylloxera, and hoof-and-mouth disease, and bad harvests, and bad English, and the German bands, and the Boers,[1] and all the other discomforts with which these later days have vexed the souls of them that go in chariots? Yet I have seen the evil example of Democracy in America cited as the source and origin of things quite as heterogeneous and quite as little connected with it by any sequence of cause and effect. Surely this ferment is nothing new. It has been at work for centuries, and we are more conscious of it only because in this age of publicity, where the newspapers offer a rostrum to whoever has a grievance, or fancies that he has, the bubbles and scum thrown up by it are more noticeable on the surface than in those dumb ages when there was a cover of silence and suppression on the cauldron. Bernardo Navagero, speaking of the Provinces of Lower Austria in 1546, tells us that "in them there are five sorts of persons, Clergy, Barons, Nobles, Burghers, and Peasants. Of these last no account is made, *because they have no voice in the Diet.*"[2]

[1] A reference to the unsuccessful attempt of the English in 1880 to reduce the Boers of the Transvaal to submission.

[2] Below the Peasants, it should be remembered, was still another even more helpless class, the servile arm-laborers. The same witness informs us that of the extraordinary imposts the Peasants paid nearly twice as much in proportion to their estimated property as the Barons, Nobles, and Burghers together. Moreover, the upper classes were assessed at their own valuation, while they arbitrarily fixed that of the Peasants, who had no voice. (*Relazioni degli Ambasciatori Veneti,* Serie I, tomo i, pp. 378, 379, 389.)—J. R. L.

Nor was it among the people that subversive or mistaken doctrines had their rise. A Father of the Church[1] said that property was theft many centuries before Proudhon was born.[2] Bourdaloue reaffirmed it. Montesquieu was the inventor of national workshops, and of the theory that the State owed every man a living. Nay, was not the Church herself the first organized Democracy? A few centuries ago the chief end of man was to keep his soul alive, and then the little kernel of leaven that sets the gases at work was religious, and produced the Reformation. Even in that, far-sighted persons like the Emperor Charles V saw the germ of political and social revolution. Now that the chief end of man seems to have become the keeping of the body alive, and as comfortably alive as possible, the leaven also has become wholly political and social. But there had also been social upheavals before the Reformation and contemporaneously with it, especially among men of Teutonic race. The Reformation gave outlet and direction to an unrest already existing. Formerly the immense majority of men—our brothers—knew only their sufferings, their wants, and their desires. They are beginning now to know their opportunity and their power. All persons who see deeper than their plates are rather inclined to thank God for it than to bewail it, for the sores of Lazarus have a poison in them against which Dives has no antidote.

There can be no doubt that the spectacle of a great and prosperous Democracy on the other side of the Atlantic must react powerfully on the aspirations and political theories of men in the Old World who do not find things to their mind; but, whether for good or evil, it should not be overlooked that the

[1] St. Ambrose said: "For nature has given all things to all men in common; for God has ordained that all things shall be so produced that food shall be common to all, and the earth as it were the common possession of all. Nature therefore is the mother of common right, usurpation of private."

[2] Pierre Joseph Proudhon, a French publicist and a speculator on social and political subjects, published in 1840 his first book, "Qu'est-ce que la Propriété?" And his own answer was, "La propriété c'est le vol." (What is property? Property is theft.)

acorn from which it sprang was ripened on the British oak. Every successive swarm that has gone out from this *officina gentium*[1] has, when left to its own instincts—may I not call them hereditary instincts?—assumed a more or less thoroughly democratic form. This would seem to show, what I believe to be the fact, that the British Constitution, under whatever disguises of prudence or decorum, is essentially democratic. England, indeed, may be called a monarchy with democratic tendencies, the United States a democracy with conservative instincts. People are continually saying that America is in the air, and I am glad to think it is, since this means only that a clearer conception of human claims and human duties is beginning to be prevalent. The discontent with the existing order of things, however, pervaded the atmosphere wherever the conditions were favorable, long before Columbus, seeking the back door of Asia, found himself knocking at the front door of America. I say wherever the conditions were favorable, for it is certain that the germs of disease do not stick or find a prosperous field for their development and noxious activity unless where the simplest sanitary precautions have been neglected. "For this effect defective comes by cause," as Polonius said long ago.[2] It is only by instigation of the wrongs of men that what are called the Rights of Man become turbulent and dangerous. It is then only that they syllogize unwelcome truths. It is not the insurrections of ignorance that are dangerous, but the revolts of intelligence:—

> "The wicked and the weak rebel in vain,
> Slaves by their own compulsion."

Had the governing classes in France during the last century paid as much heed to their proper business as to their pleasures or manners, the guillotine need never have severed that spinal marrow of orderly and secular tradition through which in a normally constituted state the brain sympathizes with the extremities and sends will and impulsion thither. It is only when

---

[1] Workshop of the world.   [2] See *Hamlet*, Act II, Scene 2.

the reasonable and practicable are denied that men demand the unreasonable and impracticable; only when the possible is made difficult that they fancy the impossible to be easy. Fairy tales are made out of the dreams of the poor. No; the sentiment which lies at the root of democracy is nothing new. I am speaking always of a sentiment, a spirit, and not of a form of government; for this was but the outgrowth of the other and not its cause. This sentiment is merely an expression of the natural wish of people to have a hand, if need be a controlling hand, in the management of their own affairs. What is new is that they are more and more gaining that control, and learning more and more how to be worthy of it. What we used to call the tendency or drift—what we are being taught to call more wisely the evolution of things—has for some time been setting steadily in this direction. There is no good in arguing with the inevitable. The only argument available with an east wind is to put on your overcoat. And in this case also, the prudent will prepare themselves to encounter what they cannot prevent. Some people advise us to put on the brakes, as if the movement of which we are conscious were that of a railway train running down an incline. But a metaphor is no argument, though it be sometimes the gunpowder to drive one home and imbed it in the memory. Our disquiet comes of what nurses and other experienced persons call growing-pains, and need not seriously alarm us. They are what every generation before us—certainly every generation since the invention of printing— has gone through with more or less good fortune. To the door of every generation there comes a knocking, and unless the household, like the Thane at Cawdor[1] and his wife, have been doing some deed without a name, they need not shudder. It turns out at worst to be a poor relation who wishes to come in out of the cold. The porter always grumbles and is slow to open. "Who's there, in the name of Beelzebub?" he mutters. Not a change for the better in our human housekeeping has ever taken place that wise and good men have not opposed it,—have not prophesied with the alderman that the world

[1] See *Macbeth*, Act II, Scene 2.

would wake up to find its throat cut in consequence of it. The world, on the contrary, wakes up, rubs its eyes, yawns, stretches itself, and goes about its business as if nothing had happened. Suppression of the slave trade, abolition of slavery, trade unions,—at all of these excellent people shook their heads despondingly, and murmured "Ichabod."[1] But the trade unions are now debating instead of conspiring, and we all read their discussions with comfort and hope, sure that they are learning the business of citizenship and the difficulties of practical legislation.

One of the most curious of these frenzies of exclusion was that against the emancipation of the Jews. All share in the government of the world was denied for centuries to perhaps the ablest, certainly the most tenacious, race that had ever lived in it—the race to whom we owed our religion and the purest spiritual stimulus and consolation to be found in all literature— a race in which ability seems as natural and hereditary as the curve of their noses, and whose blood, furtively mingling with the bluest bloods in Europe, has quickened them with its own indomitable impulsion. We drove them into a corner, but they had their revenge, as the wronged are always sure to have it sooner or later. They made their corner the counter and banking-house of the world, and thence they rule it and us with the ignobler sceptre of finance. Your grandfathers mobbed Priestley[2] only that you might set up his statue and

[1] "And she named the child Ichabod, saying, 'The glory is departed from Israel.'" I Sam. iv. 21.

[2] Rev. Dr. Joseph Priestley, an English Dissenting minister who was also a scientist of repute, noted as the discoverer of oxygen. At the time of the French Revolution he was settled in Birmingham, where he became so unpopular on account of his theological and political doctrines that his church and dwelling-house were destroyed by a mob. He tells the story with much calmness in his *Memoirs:*—

"On occasion of the celebration of the French Revolution on July 14, 1791, by several of my friends, but with which I had little to do, a mob, encouraged by some persons in power, first burned the meeting-house in which I preached, then another meeting-house in the town, and then my dwelling-house, demolishing my library, apparatus, and, as far as they could, everything belonging to me. They

make Birmingham the headquarters of English Unitarianism. We hear it said sometimes that this is an age of transition, as if that made matters clearer; but can any one point us to an age that was not? If he could, he would show us an age of stagnation. The question for us, as it has been for all before us, is to make the transition gradual and easy, to see that our points are right so that the train may not come to grief. For we should remember that nothing is more natural for people whose education has been neglected than to spell evolution with an initial "*r*." A great man struggling with the storms of fate has been called a sublime spectacle; but surely a great man wrestling with these new forces that have come into the world, mastering them and controlling them to beneficent ends, would be a yet sublimer. Here is not a danger, and if there were it would be only a better school of manhood, a nobler scope for ambition. I have hinted that what people are afraid of in democracy is less the thing itself than what they conceive to be its necessary adjuncts and consequences. It is supposed to reduce all mankind to a dead level of mediocrity in character and culture, to vulgarize men's conceptions of life, and therefore their code of morals, manners, and conduct—to endanger the rights of property and possession. But I believe that the real gravamen of the charges lies in the habit it has of making itself generally disagreeable by asking the Powers that Be at the most inconvenient moment whether they are the powers that ought to be. If the powers that be are in a condition to give a satisfactory answer to this inevitable question, they need feel in no way discomfited by it.

Few people take the trouble of trying to find out what democracy really is. Yet this would be a great help, for it is

---

also burned, or much damaged, the houses of many Dissenters, chiefly my friends. . . . Being in some personal danger on this occasion, I went to London; and so violent was the spirit of party which then prevailed that I believe I could hardly have been safe in any other place."

Dr. Priestley spent the last years of his life in the United States, at Northumberland, Pa., on the Susquehanna River.

our lawless and uncertain thoughts, it is the indefiniteness of our impressions, that fill darkness, whether mental or physical, with spectres and hobgoblins. Democracy is nothing more than an experiment in government, more likely to succeed in a new soil, but likely to be tried in all soils, which must stand or fall on its own merits as others have done before it. For there is no trick of perpetual motion in politics any more than in mechanics. President Lincoln defined democracy to be "the government of the people by the people for the people." This is a sufficiently compact statement of it as a political arrangement. Theodore Parker said that "Democracy meant not 'I'm as good as you are,' but 'You're as good as I am.'" And this is the ethical conception of it, necessary as a complement of the other; a conception which, could it be made actual and practical, would easily solve all the riddles that the old sphinx of political and social economy who sits by the roadside has been proposing to mankind from the beginning, and which mankind have shown such a singular talent for answering wrongly. In this sense Christ was the first true democrat that ever breathed, as the old dramatist Dekker said he was the first true gentleman. The characters may be easily doubled, so strong is the likeness between them. A beautiful and profound parable of the Persian poet Jellaladeen[1] tells us that "One knocked at the Beloved's door, and a voice asked from within 'Who is there?' and he answered 'It is I.' Then the voice said, 'This house will not hold me and thee'; and the door was not opened. Then went the lover into the desert and fasted and prayed in solitude, and after a year he returned and knocked again at the door; and again the voice asked 'Who is there?' and he said 'It is thyself'; and the door was opened to him." But that is idealism, you will say, and this is an only too practical world. I grant it; but I am one of those who believe that the real will never find an irremovable basis till it rests on the ideal. It used to be thought that a democracy was possible only in a small territory,

[1] Jelál-ed-dín, Mohammed er-Rúmí, a famous Persian poet of the thirteenth century, who was at the head of a college of mystic theology.

and this is doubtless true of a democracy strictly defined, for in such all the citizens decide directly upon every question of public concern in a general assembly. An example still survives in the tiny Swiss canton of Appenzell. But this immediate intervention of the people in their own affairs is not of the essence of democracy; it is not necessary, nor indeed, in most cases, practicable. Democracies to which Mr. Lincoln's definition would fairly enough apply have existed, and now exist, in which, though the supreme authority reside in the people, yet they can act only indirectly on the national policy. This generation has seen a democracy with an imperial figurehead, and in all that have ever existed the body politic has never embraced all the inhabitants included within its territory: the right to share in the direction of affairs has been confined to citizens, and citizenship has been further restricted by various limitations, sometimes of property, sometimes of nativity, and always of age and sex.

The framers of the American Constitution were far from wishing or intending to found a democracy in the strict sense of the word, though, as was inevitable, every expansion of the scheme of government they elaborated has been in a democratical direction. But this has been generally the slow result of growth, and not the sudden innovation of theory; in fact, they had a profound disbelief in theory, and knew better than to commit the folly of breaking with the past. They were not seduced by the French fallacy that a new system of government could be ordered like a new suit of clothes.[1] They would as soon have thought of ordering a new suit of flesh and skin. It is only on the roaring loom of time that the stuff is woven for such a vesture of their thought and experience as they were meditating. They recognized fully the value of tradition and habit as the great allies of permanence and stability. They all had that distaste for innovation which belonged to their race, and many of them a distrust of human nature derived from

---

[1] No other nation of importance has ever made such frequent changes in its form of government as has France since the first Revolution.

their creed. The day of sentiment was over, and no dithy-
rambic affirmations or fine-drawn analyses of the Rights of
Man would serve their present turn. This was a practical question, and they addressed themselves to it as men of knowledge
and judgment should. Their problem was how to adapt English principles and precedents to the new conditions of American life, and they solved it with singular discretion. They put
as many obstacles as they could contrive, not in the way of the
people's will, but of their whim. With few exceptions they
probably admitted the logic of the then accepted syllogism,
democracy, anarchy, despotism. But this formula was framed
upon the experience of small cities shut up to stew within their
narrow walls, where the number of citizens made but an inconsiderable fraction of the inhabitants, where every passion was
reverberated from house to house and from man to man with
gathering rumor till every impulse became gregarious and
therefore inconsiderate, and every popular assembly needed but
an infusion of eloquent sophistry to turn it into a mob, all the
more dangerous because sanctified with the formality of law.[1]

Fortunately their case was wholly different. They were to
legislate for a widely scattered population and for States already practised in the discipline of a partial independence. They
had an unequalled opportunity and enormous advantages. The
material they had to work upon was already democratical by
instinct and habitude. It was tempered to their hands by more
than a century's schooling in self-government. They had but to
give permanent and conservative form to a ductile mass. In
giving impulse and direction to their new institutions, especially
in supplying them with checks and balances, they had a great
help and safeguard in their federal organization. The different,
sometimes conflicting, interests and social systems of the several
States made existence as a Union and coalescence into a nation
conditional on a constant practice of moderation and com-

---

[1] The effect of the electric telegraph in reproducing this trooping
of emotion and perhaps of opinion is yet to be measured. The effect
of Darwinism as a disintegrator of humanitarianism is also to be
reckoned with.—J. R. L.

promise. The very elements of disintegration were the best guides in political training. Their children learned the lesson of compromise only too well, and it was the application of it to a question of fundamental morals that cost us our civil war. We learned once for all that compromise makes a good umbrella but a poor roof; that it is a temporary expedient, often wise in party politics, almost sure to be unwise in statesmanship.

Has not the trial of democracy in America proved, on the whole, successful? If it had not, would the Old World be vexed with any fears of its proving contagious? This trial would have been less severe could it have been made with a people homogeneous in race, language, and traditions, whereas the United States have been called on to absorb and assimilate enormous masses of foreign population, heterogeneous in all these respects, and drawn mainly from that class which might fairly say that the world was not their friend, nor the world's law. The previous condition too often justified the traditional Irishman, who, landing in New York and asked what his politics were, inquired if there was a Government there, and on being told that there was, retorted, "Thin I'm agin it!" We have taken from Europe the poorest, the most ignorant, the most turbulent of her people, and have made them over into good citizens, who have added to our wealth, and who are ready to die in defence of a country and of institutions which they know to be worth dying for. The exceptions have been (and they are lamentable exceptions) where these hordes of ignorance and poverty have coagulated in great cities. But the social system is yet to seek which has not to look the same terrible wolf in the eyes. On the other hand, at this very moment Irish peasants are buying up the worn-out farms of Massachusetts, and making them productive again by the same virtues of industry and thrift that once made them profitable to the English ancestors of the men who are deserting them. To have achieved even these prosaic results (if you choose to call them so), and that out of materials the most discordant,— I might say the most recalcitrant,—argues a certain beneficent virtue in the system that could do it, and is not to be accounted for by mere luck. Carlyle said scornfully that America meant only roast turkey every day for everybody. He forgot that States, as Bacon said of wars, go on their bellies. As for the security of property, it should be tolerably well secured in a country where every other man hopes to be rich, even though the only property qualification be the ownership of two hands that add to the general wealth. Is it not the best security for anything to interest the largest possible number of persons in its preservation and the smallest in its division? In point of fact, far-seeing men count the increasing power of wealth and its combinations as one of the chief dangers with which the institutions of the United States are threatened in the not distant future. The right of individual property is no doubt the very corner-stone of civilization as hitherto understood, but I am a little impatient of being told that property is entitled to exceptional consideration because it bears all burdens of the State. It bears those, indeed, which can most easily be borne, but poverty pays with its person the chief expenses of war, pestilence, and famine. Wealth should not forget this, for poverty is beginning to think of it now and then. Let me not be misunderstood. I see as clearly as any man possibly can, and rate as highly, the value of wealth, and of hereditary wealth, as the security of refinement, the feeder of all those arts that ennoble and beautify life, and as making a country worth living in. Many an ancestral hall here in England has been a nursery of that culture which has been of example and benefit to all. Old gold has a civilizing virtue which new gold must grow old to be capable of secreting.

I should not think of coming before you to defend or to criticise any form of government. All have their virtues, all their defects, and all have illustrated one period or another in the history of the race, with signal services to humanity and culture. There is not one that could stand a cynical cross-examination by an experienced criminal lawyer, except that of a perfectly wise and perfectly good despot, such as the world has never seen, except in that white-haired king of Browning's, who

"Lived long ago
In the morning of the world,
When Earth was nearer Heaven than now."[1]

The English race, if they did not invent government by discussion, have at least carried it nearest to perfection in practice.
It seems a very safe and reasonable contrivance for occupying
the attention of the country, and is certainly a better way of
settling questions than by push of pike. Yet, if one should ask
it why it should not rather be called government by gabble,
it would have to fumble in its pocket a good while before it
found the change for a convincing reply. As matters stand,
too, it is beginning to be doubtful whether Parliament and
Congress sit at Westminster and Washington or in the editors'
rooms of the leading journals, so thoroughly is everything debated before the authorized and responsible debaters get on
their legs. And what shall we say of government by a majority
of voices? To a person who in the last century would have
called himself an Impartial Observer, a numerical preponderance seems, on the whole, as clumsy a way of arriving at truth
as could well be devised, but experience has apparently shown
it to be a convenient arrangement for determining what may be
expedient or advisable or practicable at any given moment.
Truth, after all, wears a different face to everybody, and it
would be too tedious to wait till all were agreed. She is said
to lie at the bottom of a well, for the very reason, perhaps, that
whoever looks down in search of her sees his own image at the
bottom, and is persuaded not only that he has seen the goddess,
but that she is far better-looking than he had imagined.

The arguments against universal suffrage are equally unanswerable. "What," we exclaim, "shall Tom, Dick, and
Harry have as much weight in the scale as I?" Of course,
nothing could be more absurd. And yet universal suffrage has
not been the instrument of greater unwisdom than contrivances
of a more select description. Assemblies could be mentioned

[1] See Browning's *Pippa Passes*. These lines occur in one of Pippa's
songs.

composed entirely of Masters of Arts and Doctors in Divinity which have sometimes shown traces of human passion or prejudice in their votes. Have the Serene Highnesses and Enlightened Classes carried on the business of Mankind so well, then, that there is no use in trying a less costly method? The democratic theory is that those Constitutions are likely to prove steadiest which have the broadest base, that the right to vote makes a safety-valve of every voter, and that the best way of teaching a man how to vote is to give him the chance of practice. For the question is no longer the academic one, "Is it wise to give every man the ballot?" but rather the practical one, "Is is prudent to deprive whole classes of it any longer?" It may be conjectured that it is cheaper in the long run to lift men up than to hold them down, and that the ballot in their hands is less dangerous to society than a sense of wrong in their heads. At any rate this is the dilemma to which the drift of opinion has been for some time sweeping us, and in politics a dilemma is a more unmanageable thing to hold by the horns than a wolf by the ears. It is said that the right of suffrage is not valued when it is indiscriminately bestowed, and there may be some truth in this, for I have observed that what men prize most is a privilege, even if it be that of chief mourner at a funeral. But is there not danger that it will be valued at more than its worth if denied, and that some illegitimate way will be sought to make up for the want of it? Men who have a voice in public affairs are at once affiliated with one or other of the great parties between which society is divided, merge their individual hopes and opinions in its safer, because more generalized, hopes and opinions, are disciplined by its tactics, and acquire, to a certain degree, the orderly qualities of an army. They no longer belong to a class, but to a body corporate. Of one thing, at least, we may be certain, that, under whatever method of helping things to go wrong man's wit can contrive, those who have the divine right to govern will be found to govern in the end, and that the highest privilege to which the majority of mankind can aspire is that of being governed by those wiser than they. Universal suffrage has in the United States sometimes been made the instrument of inconsiderate changes, under the notion of reform, and this from a misconception of the true meaning of popular government. One of these has been the substitution in many of the States of popular election for official selection in the choice of judges. The same system applied to military officers was the source of much evil during our civil war, and, I believe, had to be abandoned. But it has been also true that on all great questions of national policy a reserve of prudence and discretion has been brought out at the critical moment to turn the scale in favor of a wiser decision. An appeal to the reason of the people has never been known to fail in the long run. It is, perhaps, true that, by effacing the principle of passive obedience, democracy, ill understood, has slackened the spring of that ductility to discipline which is essential to "the unity and married calm of States." But I feel assured that experience and necessity will cure this evil, as they have shown their power to cure others. And under what frame of policy have evils ever been remedied till they became intolerable, and shook men out of their indolent indifference through their fears?

We are told that the inevitable result of democracy is to sap the foundations of personal independence, to weaken the principle of authority, to lessen the respect due to eminence, whether in station, virtue, or genius. If these things were so, society could not hold together. Perhaps the best forcing-house of robust individuality would be where public opinion is inclined to be most overbearing, as he must be of heroic temper who should walk along Piccadilly at the height of the season in a soft hat. As for authority, it is one of the symptoms of the time that the religious reverence for it is declining everywhere, but this is due partly to the fact that state-craft is no longer looked upon as a mystery, but as a business, and partly to the decay of superstition, by which I mean the habit of respecting what we are told to respect rather than what is respectable in itself. There is more rough and tumble in the American democracy than is altogether agreeable to people of sensitive nerves and refined habits, and the people take their political duties lightly and laughingly, as is, perhaps, neither unnatural nor unbecom-

ing in a young giant. Democracies can no more jump away
from their own shadows than the rest of us can. They no doubt
sometimes make mistakes and pay honor to men who do not
deserve it. But they do this because they believe them worthy
of it, and though it be true that the idol is the measure of the
worshipper, yet the worship has in it the germ of a nobler
religion. But is it democracies alone that fall into these errors?
I, who have seen it proposed to erect a statue to Hudson, the
railway king,[1] and have heard Louis Napoleon hailed as the
saviour of society by men who certainly had no democratic
associations or leanings, am not ready to think so. But democracies have likewise their finer instincts. I have also seen the
wisest statesman and most pregnant speaker of our generation,
a man of humble birth and ungainly manners, of little culture
beyond what his own genius supplied, become more absolute
in power than any monarch of modern times through the reverence of his countrymen for his honesty, his wisdom, his
sincerity, his faith in God and man, and the nobly humane
simplicity of his character. And I remember another whom
popular respect enveloped as with a halo, the least vulgar of
men, the most austerely genial, and the most independent of
opinion. Wherever he went he never met a stranger, but everywhere neighbors and friends proud of him as their ornament
and decoration. Institutions which could bear and breed such
men as Lincoln and Emerson had surely some energy for good.
No, amid all the fruitless turmoil and miscarriage of the world,
if there be one thing steadfast and of favorable omen, one thing
to make optimism distrust its own obscure distrust, it is the
rooted instinct in men to admire what is better and more beautiful than themselves. The touchstone of political and social
institutions is their ability to supply them with worthy objects

[1] George Hudson, an English railway director and speculator, who
was for a time immensely successful in his schemes. At the height
of his prosperity a statue to him was proposed, and £25,000 were sub-
scribed for it. But before the money could be collected he had been
exposed as dishonorable in his business affairs, and his fall was more
rapid than his rise.

of this sentiment, which is the very tap-root of civilization and progress. There would seem to be no readier way of feeding it with the elements of growth and vigor than such an organization of society as will enable men to respect themselves, and so to justify them in respecting others.

Such a result is quite possible under other conditions than those of an avowedly democratical Constitution. For I take it that the real essence of democracy was fairly enough defined by the First Napoleon when he said that the French Revolution meant "la carrière ouverte aux talents"—a clear pathway for merit of whatever kind. I should be inclined to paraphrase this by calling democracy that form of society, no matter what its political classification, in which every man had a chance and knew that he had it. If a man can climb, and feels himself encouraged to climb, from a coalpit to the highest position for which he is fitted, he can well afford to be indifferent what name is given to the government under which he lives. The Bailli[1] of Mirabeau, uncle of the more famous tribune of that name, wrote in 1771: "The English are, in my opinion, a hundred times more agitated and more unfortunate than the very Algerines themselves, because they do not know and will not know till the destruction of their over-swollen power, which I believe very near, whether they are monarchy, aristocracy, or democracy, and wish to play the part of all three." England has not been obliging enough to fulfil the Bailli's prophecy, and perhaps it was this very carelessness about the name, and concern about the substance of popular government, this skill in getting the best out of things as they are, in utilizing all the motives which influence men, and in giving one direction to many impulses, that has been a principal factor of her greatness and power. Perhaps it is fortunate to have an unwritten Constitution, for men are prone to be tinkering the work of their own hands, whereas they are more willing to let time and circumstance mend or modify what time and circumstance have made. All

---

[1] Jean Antoine Mirabeau, Bailli, or Bailiff. The founder of the family of Mirabeau was Honoré Riquete, who bought the estate of Mirabeau, whence the name.

free governments, whatever their name, are in reality governments by public opinion, and it is on the quality of this public
opinion that their prosperity depends. It is, therefore, their
first duty to purify the element from which they draw the breath
of life. With the growth of democracy grows also the fear, if
not the danger, that this atmosphere may be corrupted with
poisonous exhalations from lower and more malarious levels,
and the question of sanitation becomes more instant and pressing. Democracy in its best sense is merely the letting in of
light and air. Lord Sherbrooke, with his usual epigrammatic
terseness, bids you educate your future rulers.[1] But would this
alone be a sufficient safeguard? To educate the intelligence is
to enlarge the horizon of its desires and wants. And it is well
that this should be so. But the enterprise must go deeper and
prepare the way for satisfying those desires and wants in so far
as they are legitimate. What is really ominous of danger to the
existing order of things is not democracy (which, properly
understood, is a conservative force), but the Socialism which
may find a fulcrum in it. If we cannot equalize conditions and
fortunes any more than we can equalize the brains of men—and
a very sagacious person has said that "where two men ride of
a horse one must ride behind"—we can yet, perhaps, do something to correct those methods and influences that lead to enormous inequalities, and to prevent their growing more enormous. It is all very well to pooh-pooh Mr. George[2] and to
prove him mistaken in his political economy. I do not believe
that land should be divided because the quantity of it is limited

---

[1] Robert Lowe, Viscount Sherbrooke, (1811–1892). An English
politician who opposed the movements for the extenson of suffrage.
In an address on education, delivered in 1867, he said:—

"We are all aware that the Government of the country, the voice
potential in the Government, is placed in the hands of persons in a
lower position of life than has hitherto been the case. . . . I am most
anxious to educate the lower classes of this country, in order to
qualify them for the power that has passed, and perhaps will pass in
a still greater degree, into their hands. . . . The lower classes ought
to be educated to discharge the duties cast upon them."

[2] Henry George (1839–1897), author of *Progress and Poverty*.

by nature. Of what may this not be said? *A fortiori*, we might on the same principle insist on a division of human wit, for I have observed that the quantity of this has been even more inconveniently limited. Mr. George himself has an inequitably large share of it. But he is right in his impelling motive; right, also, I am convinced, in insisting that humanity makes a part, by far the most important part, of political economy; and in thinking man to be of more concern and more convincing than the longest columns of figures in the world. For unless you include human nature in your addition, your total is sure to be wrong and your deductions from it fallacious. Communism means barbarism, but Socialism means, or wishes to mean, coöperation and community of interests, sympathy, the giving to the hands not so large a share as to the brains, but a larger share than hitherto in the wealth they must combine to produce—means, in short, the practical application of Christianity to life, and has in it the secret of an orderly and benign reconstruction. State Socialism would cut off the very roots in personal character—self-help, forethought, and frugality—which nourish and sustain the trunk and branches of every vigorous Commonwealth.

I do not believe in violent changes, nor do I expect them. Things in possession have a very firm grip. One of the strongest cements of society is the conviction of mankind that the state of things into which they are born is a part of the order of the universe, as natural, let us say, as that the sun should go round the earth. It is a conviction that they will not surrender except on compulsion, and a wise society should look to it that this compulsion be not put upon them. For the individual man there is no radical cure, outside of human nature itself, for the evils to which human nature is heir. The rule will always hold good that you must

"Be your own palace or the world's your gaol."

But for artificial evils, for evils that spring from want of thought, thought must find a remedy somewhere. There has been no period of time in which wealth has been more sensible of its duties than now. It builds hospitals, it establishes missions among the poor, it endows schools. It is one of the advantages of accumulated wealth, and of the leisure it renders possible, that people have time to think of the wants and sorrows of their fellows. But all these remedies are partial and palliative merely. It is as if we should apply plasters to a single pustule of the small-pox with a view of driving out the disease. The true way is to discover and to extirpate the germs. As society is now constituted these are in the air it breathes, in the water it drinks, in things that seem, and which it has always believed, to be the most innocent and healthful. The evil elements it neglects corrupt these in their springs and pollute them in their courses. Let us be of good cheer, however, remembering that the misfortunes hardest to bear are those which never come. The world has outlived much, and will outlive a great deal more, and men have contrived to be happy in it. It has shown the strength of its constitution in nothing more than in surviving the quack medicines it has tried. In the scales of the destinies brawn will never weigh so much as brain. Our healing is not in the storm or in the whirlwind, it is not in monarchies, or aristocracies, or democracies, but will be revealed by the still small voice that speaks to the conscience and the heart, prompting us to a wider and wiser humanity.

From HARVARD ANNIVERSARY

(1886)

. . . I shall not attempt, even in brief, a history of the College. It has already been excellently done. A compendium of it would be mainly a list of unfamiliar names, and Coleridge has said truly that such names "are non-conductors; they stop all interest."

The fame and usefulness of all institutions of learning depend on the greatness of those who teach in them,

> "Queis arte benigna,
>   Et meliore luto finxit praecordia Titan,"

and great teachers are almost rarer than great poets. We can lay claim to none such (I must not speak of the living), unless it be Agassiz, whom we adopted, but we have had many devoted and some eminent. It has not been their fault if they have not pushed farther forward the boundaries of knowledge. Our professors have been compelled by the necessities of the case (as we are apt to call things which we ought to reform, but do not) to do too much work not properly theirs, and that of a kind so exacting as to consume the energy that might have been ample for higher service. They have been obliged to double the parts of professor and tutor. During the seventeenth century we have reason to think that the College kept pretty well up to the standard of its contemporary colleges in England, so far as its poverty would allow. It seems to have enjoyed a certain fame abroad among men who sympathized with the theology it taught, for I possess a Hebrew Accidence, dedicated some two hundred years ago to the "illustrious academy at Boston in New England," by a Dutch scholar whom I cannot help thinking a very discerning person. That the students of that day had access to a fairly good library may be inferred from Cotton Mather's "Magnalia," though he knew not how to make the best use of it, and is a very nightmare of pedantry. That the College had made New England a good market for books is proved by John Dunton's journey hither in the interests of his trade. During the eighteenth and first quarter of the nineteenth centuries, I fancy the condition of things here to have been very much what it was in the smaller English colleges of the period, if we may trust the verses which Gray addressed to the goddess Ignorance. Young men who were willing mainly to teach themselves might get something to their advantage, while the rest were put here by their parents as into a comfortable quarantine, where they could wait till the gates of life were opened to them, safe from any contagion of learning, except such as might be developed from previous infection. I am speaking of a great while ago. Men are apt, I know, in after life to lay the blame of their scholastic shortcomings at the door of their teachers. They are often wrong in this, and

I am quite aware that there are some pupils who are knowledge-proof; but I gather from tradition, which I believe to be trustworthy, that there have been periods in the history of the college when the students might have sung with Bishop Golias:—

> "Hi nos docent, sed indocti;
> Hi dos docent, et nox nocti
> Indicat scientiam."

Despite all this, it is remarkable that the two first American imaginative artists, Allston in painting and Greenough in sculpture, were graduates of Harvard. A later generation is justly proud of Story.

We have a means of testing the general culture given here towards the middle of the last century in the *Gratulatio* presented by Harvard College on the accession of George III. It is not duller than such things usually are on the other side of the water, and it shows a pretty knack at tagging verses. It is noteworthy that the Greek in it, if I remember rightly, is wholly or chiefly Governor Bernard's. A few years earlier, some of the tracts in the Whitfield controversy prove that the writers had got here a thorough training in English at least. They had certainly not read their Swift in vain.

But the chief service, as it was the chief office, of the College during all those years was to maintain and hand down the traditions of how excellent a thing Learning was, even if the teaching were not always adequate by way of illustration. And yet, so far as that teaching went, it was wise in this, that it gave its pupils some tincture of letters as distinguished from mere scholarship. It aimed to teach them the authors, that is, the few great ones,—the late Professor Popkin, whom the older of us remember, would have allowed that title only to the Greeks,—and to teach them in such a way as to enable the pupil to assimilate somewhat of their thought, sentiment, and style, rather than to master the minuter niceties of the language in which they wrote. It struck for their matter, as Montaigne advised, who would have men taught to love Virtue instead of learning to decline *virtus*. It set more store by the marrow than by the bone that encased it. It made language, as it should be, a ladder to literature, and not literature a ladder to language. Many a boy has hated, and rightly hated, Homer and Horace the pedagogues and grammarians, who would have loved Homer and Horace the poets, had he been allowed to make their acquaintance. The old method of instruction had the prime merit of enabling its pupils to conceive that there is neither ancient nor modern on the narrow shelves of what is truly literature. We owe a great debt to the Germans. No one is more indebted to them than I, but is there not danger of their misleading us in some directions into pedantry? In his preface to an Old French poem of the thirteenth century, lately published, the editor informs us sorrowfully that he had the advantage of listening only two years and a half to the lectures of Professor Gaston Paris, in which time he got no farther than through the first three vowels. At this rate, to master the whole alphabet, consonants and all, would be a task fitter for the centurial adolescence of Methuselah than for our less liberal ration of years. I was glad my editor had had this advantage, and I am quite willing that Old French should get the benefit of such scrupulosity, but I think I see a tendency to train young men in the languages as if they were all to be editors, and not lovers of polite literature. Education, we are often told, is a drawing out of the faculties. May they not be drawn out too thin? I am not undervaluing philology or accuracy of scholarship. Both are excellent and admirable in their places. But philology is less beautiful to me than philosophy, as Milton understood the word, and mere accuracy is to Truth as a plaster-cast to the marble statue; it gives the facts, but not their meaning. If I must choose, I had rather a young man should be intimate with the genius of the Greek dramatic poets than with the metres of their choruses, though I should be glad to have him on easy terms with both.

For more than two hundred years, in its discipline and courses of study, the College followed mainly the lines traced by its founders. The influence of its first half century did more than any other, perhaps more than all others, to make New England what it is. During the one hundred and forty years preceding our War of Independence it had supplied the schools of the greater part of New England with teachers. What was even more important, it had sent to every parish in Massachusetts one man, the clergyman, with a certain amount of scholarship, a belief in culture, and generally pretty sure to bring with him or to gather a considerable collection of books, by no means wholly theological. Simple and godly men were they, the truest modern antitypes of Chaucer's Good Parson, receiving much, sometimes all, of their scanty salary in kind, and eking it out by the drudgery of a cross-grained farm where the soil seems all backbone. If there was no regular practitioner, they practised without fee a grandmotherly sort of medicine, probably not much more harmful (*O, dura messorum ilia*) than the heroic treatment of the day. They contrived to save enough to send their sons through college, to portion their daughters, decently trained in English literature of the more serious kind, and perfect in the duties of household and dairy, and to make modest provision for the widow, if they should leave one. With all this, they gave their two sermons every Sunday of the year, and of a measure that would seem ruinously liberal to these less stalwart days, when scarce ten parsons together could lift the stones of Diomed which they hurled at Satan with the easy precision of lifelong practice. And if they turned their barrel of discourses at the end of the Horatian ninth year, which of their parishioners was the wiser for it? Their one great holiday was Commencement, which they punctually attended. They shared the many toils and the rare festivals, the joys and the sorrows, of their townsmen as bone of their bone and flesh of their flesh, for all were of one blood and of one faith. They dwelt on the same brotherly level with them as men, yet set apart from and above them by their sacred office. Preaching the most terrible of doctrines, as most of them did, they were humane and cheerful men, and when they came down from the pulpit seemed to have been merely twisting their "cast-iron logic" of despair, as Coleridge said of Donne, "into true-love-knots." Men of authority, wise in council, independent, for their settlement was a life-tenure, they were living lessons of piety, industry, frugality, temperance, and, with the magistrates, were a recognized aristocracy. Surely never was an aristocracy so simple, so harmless, so exemplary, and so fit to rule. I remember a few lingering survivors of them in my early boyhood, relics of a serious but not sullen past, of a community for which in civic virtue, intelligence, and general efficacy I seek a parallel in vain:—

> "rusticorum mascula militum
> Proles . . . docta . . .
> Versare glebas et severæ
> Matris ad arbitrium recisos
> Portare fustes."

I know too well the deductions to be made. It was a community without charm, or with a homely charm at best, and the life it led was visited by no muse even in dream. But it was the stuff out of which fortunate ancestors are made, and twenty-five years ago their sons showed in no diminished measure the qualities of the breed. In every household some brave boy was saying to his mother, as Iphigenia to hers,—

Πᾶσι γάρ μ' Ἕλλησι κοινὸν ἔτεκες οὐχὶ σοὶ μόνῃ.

Nor were Harvard's sons the last. This hall commemorates them, but their story is written in headstones all over the land they saved.

To the teaching and example of those reverend men whom Harvard bred and then planted in every hamlet as pioneers and outposts of her doctrine, Massachusetts owes the better part of her moral and intellectual inheritance. They, too, were the progenitors of a numerous and valid race. My friend Dr. Holmes was, I believe, the first to point out how large a proportion of our men of light and leading sprang from their loins. The illustrious Chief Magistrate of the Republic, who honors us with his presence here to-day, has ancestors italicized in our printed registers, and has shown himself worthy of his pedigree.

During the present century, I believe that Harvard received

and welcomed the new learning from Germany at the hands of
Everett, Bancroft, and Ticknor, before it had been accepted by
the more conservative universities of the Old Home. Everett's
translation of Buttmann's Greek Grammar was reprinted in
England, with the "Massachusetts" omitted after "Cambridge,"
at the end of the preface, to conceal its American origin. Emerson has told us how his intellectual life was quickened by the
eloquent enthusiasm of Everett's teaching. Mr. Bancroft made
strenuous efforts to introduce a more wholesome discipline
and maturer methods of study, with the result of a rebellion of
the Freshman Class, who issued a manifesto of their wrongs,
written by the late Robert Rantoul, which ended thus: "Shall
FREEMEN bear this? FRESHMEN are freemen!" They, too, remembered Revolutionary sires. Mr. Bancroft's translation of
Heeren was the first of its kind, and it is worth mention that the
earliest version from the prose of Henry Heine into English
was made here, though not by a graduate of Harvard. Ticknor
also strove earnestly to enlarge the scope of the collegiate
courses of study. The force of the new impulse did not last
long, or produce, unless indirectly, lasting results. It was
premature, the students were really school-boys, and the college was not yet capable of the larger university life. The conditions of American life, too, were such that young men looked
upon scholarship neither as an end nor as a means, but simply
as an accomplishment, like music or dancing, of which they
were to acquire a little more or a little less, generally a little less,
according to individual taste or circumstances. It has been
mainly during the last twenty-five years that the College, having already the name, but by no means all the resources, of a
university, has been trying to perform some, at least, of the
functions which that title implies.

> "Now half appears
>   The tawny lion, pawing to get free"

Let us, then, no longer look backwards, but forwards, as our
fathers did when they laid our humble foundations in the wilderness. The motto first proposed for the College arms was, as

you know, *Veritas*, written across three open books. It was a noble one, and, if the full bearing of it was understood, as daring as it was noble. Perhaps it was discarded because an *open* book seemed hardly the fittest symbol for what is so hard to find, and, if ever we fancy we have found it, so hard to decipher and to translate into our own language and life. Pilate's question still murmurs in the ear of every thoughtful, and Montaigne's in that of every honest man. The motto finally substituted for that, *Christo et Ecclesiæ*, is, when rightly interpreted, substantially the same, for it means that we are to devote ourselves to the highest conception we have of Truth and to the preaching of it. Fortunately, the Sphinx proposes her conundrums to us one at a time and at intervals proportioned to our wits.

Joseph de Maistre says that "un homme d'esprit est tenu de savoir deux choses: 1°, ce qu'il est; 2°, où il est." The questions for us are, In what sense are we become a university? And then, if we become so, What and to what end should a university aim to teach now and here in this America of ours whose meaning no man can yet comprehend? And, when we have settled what it is best to teach, comes the further question, How are we to teach it? Whether with an eye to its effect on developing character or personal availability, that is to say, to its effect in the conduct of life, or on the chances of getting a livelihood? Perhaps we shall find that we must have a care for both, and I cannot see why the two need be incompatible; but if they are, I should choose the former term of the alternative.

In a not remote past, society had still certain recognized, authoritative guides, and the college trained them as the fashion of the day required. But

> "Damnosa quid non imminuit dies?"

That ancient close corporation of official guides has been compelled to surrender its charter. We are pestered with as many volunteers as at Niagara, and, as there, if we follow any of them, may count on paying for it pretty dearly. The office of the higher instruction, nevertheless, continues to be as it always was, the training of such guides; only it must now try to fit them out with as much more personal accomplishment and authority as may compensate the loss of hierarchical prestige.

When President Walker, it must be now nearly thirty years ago, asked me in common with my colleagues what my notion of a university was, I answered, "A university is a place where nothing useful is taught; but a university is possible only where a man may get his livelihood by digging Sanscrit roots." What I meant was that the highest office of the somewhat complex thing so named was to distribute the true Bread of Life, the *pane 'degli angeli*, as Dante called it, and to breed an appetite for it; but that it should also have the means and appliances for teaching everything, as the mediæval universities aimed to do in their *trivium* and *quadrivium*. I had in mind the ideal and the practical sides of the institution, and was thinking also whether such an institution was practicable, and, if so, whether it was desirable, in a country like this. I think it eminently desirable, and, if it be, what should be its chief function? I choose rather to hesitate my opinion than to assert it roundly. But some opinion I am bound to have, either my own or another man's, if I would be in the fashion, though I may not be wholly satisfied with the one or the other. Opinions are "as handy," to borrow our Yankee proverb, "as a pocket in a shirt," and, I may add, as hard to come at. I hope, then, that the day will come when a competent professor may lecture here also for three years on the first three vowels of the Romance alphabet, and find fit audience, though few. I hope the day may never come when the weightier matters of a language, namely, such parts of its literature as have overcome death by reason of their wisdom and of the beauty in which it is incarnated, such parts as are universal by reason of their civilizing properties, their power to elevate and fortify the mind,—I hope the day may never come when these are not predominant in the teaching given here. Let the Humanities be maintained undiminished in their ancient right. Leave in their traditional pre-eminence those arts that were rightly called liberal; those studies that kindle the imagination, and through it irradiate the reason; those studies that manumitted the modern mind; those in which the brains of finest temper have found alike their stimulus and their repose, taught by them that the power of intellect is heightened in proportion as it is made gracious by measure and symmetry. Give us science, too, but give first of all, and last of all, the science that ennobles life and makes it generous. I stand here as a man of letters, and as a man of letters I must speak. But I am speaking with no exclusive intention. No one believes more firmly than I in the usefulness, I might well say the necessity, of variety in study, and of opening the freest scope possible to the prevailing bent of every mind when that bent shows itself to be so predominating as to warrant it. Many-sidedness of culture makes our vision clearer and keener in particulars. For after all, the noblest definition of Science is that breadth and impartiality of view which liberates the mind from specialties, and enables it to organize whatever we learn, so that it become real Knowledge by being brought into true and helpful relation with the rest.

By far the most important change that has been introduced into the theory and practice of our teaching here by the new position in which we find ourselves has been that of the elective or voluntary system of studies. We have justified ourselves by the familiar proverb that one man may lead a horse to water, but ten can't make him drink. Proverbs are excellent things, but we should not let even proverbs bully us. They are the wisdom of the understanding, not of the higher reason. There is another animal, which even Simonides could compliment only on the spindle-side of his pedigree, and which ten men could not lead to water, much less make him drink when they got him thither. Are we not trying to force university forms into college methods too narrow for them? There is some danger that the elective system may be pushed too far and too fast. There are not a few who think that it has gone too far already. And they think so because we are in process of transformation, still in the hobbledehoy period, not having ceased to be a college, nor yet having reached the full manhood of a university, so that we speak with that ambiguous voice, half bass, half treble, or mixed of both, which is proper to a certain stage of adolescence. We are trying to do two things with one tool, and that tool not specially adapted to either. Are our students old enough thoroughly to understand the import of the choice they are called on to make, and, if old enough, are they wise enough? Shall their parents make the choice for them? I am not sure that even parents are so wise as the unbroken experience and practice of mankind. We are comforted by being told that in this we are only complying with what is called the Spirit of the Age, which may be, after all, only a finer name for the mischievous goblin known to our forefathers as Puck. I have seen several Spirits of the Age in my time, of very different voices and summoning in very different directions, but unanimous in their propensity to land us in the mire at last. Would it not be safer to make sure first whether the Spirit of the Age, who would be a very insignificant fellow if we docked him of his capitals, be not a lying spirit, since such there are? It is at least curious that, while the more advanced teaching has a strong drift in the voluntary direction, the compulsory system, as respects primary studies, is gaining ground. Is it indeed so self-evident a proposition as it seems to many that "You may" is as wholesome a lesson for youths as "You must"? Is it so good a fore-schooling for Life, which will be a teacher of quite other mood, making us learn, rod in hand, precisely those lessons we should not have chosen? I have, to be sure, heard the late President Quincy (*clarum et venerabile nomen*) say that if a young man came hither and did nothing more than rub his shoulders against the college buildings for four years, he would imbibe some tincture of sound learning by an involuntary process of absorption. The founders of the College also believed in some impulsions towards science communicated *à tergo* but of sharper virtue, and accordingly armed their president with that *ductor dubitantium* which was wielded to such good purpose by the Reverend James Bowyer at Christ's Hospital in the days of Coleridge and Lamb. They believed with the old poet that whipping was "a wild benefit of nature," and, could they have read Wordsworth's exquisite stanza,—

> "One impulse from a vernal wood
>   Can teach us more of man,
>   Of moral evil and of good,
>   Than all the sages can,"

they would have struck out "vernal" and inserted "birchen" on the margin.

I am not, of course, arguing in favor of a return to those vapulatory methods, but the birch, like many other things that have passed out of the region of the practical, may have another term of usefulness as a symbol after it has ceased to be a reality.

One is sometimes tempted to think that all learning is as repulsive to ingenuous youth as the multiplication table to Scott's little friend Marjorie Fleming, though this is due in great part to mechanical methods of teaching. "I am now going to tell you," she writes, "the horrible and wretched plaege that my multiplication table gives me; you can't conceive it; the most Devilish thing is 8 times 8 and 7 times 7; it is what nature itself can't endure." I know that I am approaching treacherous ashes which cover burning coals, but I must on. Is not Greek, nay, even Latin, yet more unendurable than poor Marjorie's task? How many boys have not sympathized with Heine in hating the Romans because they invented Latin Grammar? And they were quite right, for we begin the study of languages at the wrong end, at the end which nature does not offer us, and are thoroughly tired of them before we arrive at them, if you will pardon the bull. But is that any reason for not studying them in the right way? I am familiar with the arguments for making the study of Greek especially a matter of choice or chance. I admit their plausibility and the honesty of those who urge them. I should be willing also to admit that the study of the ancient languages without the hope or the prospect of going on to what they contain would be useful only as a form of intellectual gymnastics. Even so they would be as serviceable as the higher mathematics to most of us. But I think that a wise teacher should adapt his tasks to the highest, and not the lowest, capacities of the taught. For those lower also they would not be wholly without profit. When there is a tedious sermon, says George Herbert,

> "God takes a text and teacheth patience,"

not the least pregnant of lessons. One of the arguments against the compulsory study of Greek, namely, that it is wiser to give our time to modern languages and modern history than to dead languages and ancient history, involves, I think, a verbal fallacy. Only those languages can properly be called dead in which nothing living has been written. If the classic languages are dead, they yet speak to us, and with a clearer voice than that of any living tongue.

> "Graiis ingenium, Graiis dedit ore rotundo
> Musa loqui, præter laudem nullius avaris."

If their language is dead, yet the literature it enshrines is rammed with life as perhaps no other writing, except Shakespeare's, ever was or will be. It is as contemporary with to-day as with the ears it first enraptured, for it appeals not to the man of then or now, but to the entire round of human nature itself. Men are ephemeral or evanescent, but whatever page the authentic soul of man has touched with her immortalizing finger, no matter how long ago, is still young and fair as it was to the world's gray fathers. Oblivion looks in the face of the Grecian Muse only to forget her errand. Plato and Aristotle are not names but things. On a chart that should represent the firm earth and wavering oceans of the human mind, they would be marked as mountain-ranges, forever modifying the temperature, the currents, and the atmosphere of thought, astronomical stations whence the movements of the lamps of heaven might best be observed and predicted. Even for the mastering of our own tongue, there is no expedient so fruitful as translation out of another; how much more when that other is a language at once so precise and so flexible as the Greek! Greek literature is also the most fruitful comment on our own. Coleridge has told us with what profit he was made to study Shakespeare and Milton in conjunction with the Greek dramatists. It is no sentimental argument for this study that the most justly balanced, the most serene, and the most fecundating minds since the revival of learning have been steeped in and saturated with Greek literature. We know not whither other studies will lead us, especially if dissociated from this; we do know to what summits, far above our lower region of turmoil, this has led, and what the many-sided outlook thence. Will such studies make anachronisms of us, unfit us for the duties and the business of to-day? I can recall no writer more truly modern than Montaigne, who was almost more at home in Athens and Rome than in Paris. Yet he was a thrifty manager of his estate and a most competent mayor of Bordeaux. I remember passing once in London where demolition for a new thoroughfare was going on. Many houses left standing in the rear of those cleared away bore signs with the inscription "Ancient Lights." This was the protest of their owners against being built out by the new improvements from such glimpse of heaven as their fathers had, without adequate equivalent. I laid the moral to heart.

I am speaking of the College as it has always existed and still exists. In so far as it may be driven to put on the forms of the university,—I do not mean the four Faculties, merely, but in the modern sense,—we shall naturally find ourselves compelled to assume the method with the function. Some day we shall offer here a chance, at least, to acquire the *omne scibile*. I shall be glad, as shall we all, when the young American need no longer go abroad for any part of his training, though that may not be always a disadvantage, if Shakespeare was right in thinking that

"Home-keeping youths have ever homely wits."

I should be still gladder if Harvard should be the place that offered the alternative. It seems more than ever probable that this will happen, and happen in our day. And whenever it does happen, it will be due, more than to any and all others, to the able, energetic, single-minded, and yet fair-minded man who has presided over the College during the trying period of transition, and who will by a rare combination of eminent qualities carry that transition forward to its accomplishment without

haste and without jar,—*ohne Hast, ohne Rast*. He more than
any of his distinguished predecessors has brought the university into closer and more telling relations with the national
life in whatever that life has which is most distinctive and most
hopeful.

But we still mainly occupy the position of a German Gym-
nasium. Under existing circumstances, therefore, and with the
methods of teaching they enforce, I think that special and advanced courses should be pushed on, so far as possible, as the
other professional courses are, into the post-graduate period.
The opportunity would be greater because the number would
be less, and the teaching not only more thorough, but more
vivifying through the more intimate relation of teacher and
pupil. Under those conditions the voluntary system will not
only be possible, but will come of itself, for every student will
know what he wants and where he may get it, and learning will
be loved, as it should be, for its own sake as well as for what it
gives. The friends of university training can do nothing that
would forward it more than the founding of post-graduate
fellowships and the building and endowing of a hall where
the holders of them might be commensals, remembering that
when Cardinal Wolsey built Christ Church at Oxford his first
care was the kitchen. Nothing is so great a quickener of the
faculties or so likely to prevent their being narrowed to a single
groove as the frequent social commingling of men who are
aiming at one goal by different paths. If you would have really
great scholars, and our life offers no prizes for such, it would
be well if the university could offer them. I have often been
struck with the many-sided versatility of the Fellows of English
colleges who have kept their wits in training by continual fence
one with another.

During the first two centuries of her existence, it may be affirmed that Harvard did sufficiently well the only work she was
called on to do, perhaps the only work it was possible for her to
do. She gave to Boston her scholarly impress, to the Commonwealth her scholastic impulse. To the clergy of her training was mainly intrusted the oversight of the public schools;

these were, as I have said, though indirectly, feeders of the College, for their teaching was of the plainest. But if a boy in any country village showed uncommon parts, the clergyman was sure to hear of it. He and the Squire and the Doctor, if there was one, talked it over, and that boy was sure to be helped onward to college; for next to the five points of Calvinism our ancestors believed in a college education, that is, in the best education that was to be had. The system, if system it should be called, was a good one, a practical application of the doctrine of Natural Selection. Ah! how the parents—nay, the whole family—moiled and pinched that their boy might have the chance denied to them! Mr. Matthew Arnold has told us that in contemporary France, which seems doomed to try every theory of enlightenment by which the fingers may be burned or the house set on fire, the children of the public schools are taught in answer to the question, "Who gives you all these fine things?" to say, "The State." Ill fares the State in which the parental image is replaced by an abstraction. The answer of the boy of whom I have been speaking would have been in a spirit better for the State and for the hope of his own future life: "I owe them, under God, to my own industry, to the sacrifices of my father and mother, and to the sympathy of good men." Nor was the boy's self-respect lessened, for the aid was given by loans, to be repaid when possible. The times have changed, and it is no longer the ambition of a promising boy to go to college. They are taught to think that a common-school education is good enough for all practical purposes. And so perhaps it is, but not for all ideal purposes. Our public schools teach too little or too much: too little if education is to go no further, too many things if what is taught is to be taught thoroughly; and the more they *seem* to teach, the less likely is education to go further, for it is one of the prime weaknesses of a democracy to be satisfied with the second-best if it appear to answer the purpose tolerably well, and to be cheaper—as it never is in the long run.

Our ancestors believed in education, but not in making it wholly eleemosynary. And they were wise in this, for men do not value what they get for nothing any more than they value air and light till deprived of them. It is quite proper that the cost of our public schools should be paid by the rich, for it is their interest, as Lord Sherbrooke said, "to educate their rulers." But it is to make paupers of the pupils to furnish them, as is now proposed, with text-books, slates, and the like at public cost. This is an advance towards that State Socialism which, if it ever prevail, will be deadly to certain homespun virtues far more precious than most of the book-knowledge in the world. It is to be hoped that our higher institutions of learning may again be brought to bear, as once they did, more directly on the lower, that they may again come into such closer and graduated relation with them as may make the higher education the goal to which all who show a clear aptitude shall aspire. I know that we cannot have ideal teachers in our public schools for the price we pay or in the numbers we require. But teaching, like water, can rise no higher than its source, and, like water again, it has a lazy aptitude for running down-hill unless a constant impulse be applied in the other direction. Would not this impulse be furnished by the ambition to send on as many pupils as possible to the wider sphere of the university? Would not this organic relation to the Higher Education necessitate a corresponding rise in the grade of intelligence, capacity, and culture demanded in the teachers?

Harvard has done much by raising its standard to force upwards that also of the preparatory schools. The leaven thus infused will, let us hope, filter gradually downwards till it raise a ferment in the lower grades as well. What we need more than anything else is to increase the number of our highly cultivated men and thoroughly trained minds; for these, wherever they go, are sure to carry with them, consciously or not, the seeds of sounder thinking and of higher ideals. The only way in which our civilization can be maintained even at the level it has reached, the only way in which that level can be made more general and be raised higher, is by bringing the influence of the more cultivated to bear with greater energy and directness on the less cultivated, and by opening more inlets to those indirect influences which make for refinement of mind and body. Democracy must show its capacity for producing not a higher average man, but the highest possible types of manhood in all its manifold varieties, or it is a failure. No matter what it does for the body, if it do not in some sort satisfy that inextinguishable passion of the soul for something that lifts life away from prose, from the common and the vulgar, it is a failure. Unless it know how to make itself gracious and winning, it is a failure. Has it done this? Is it doing this? Or trying to do it? Not yet, I think, if one may judge by that commonplace of our newspapers that an American who stays long enough in Europe is sure to find his own country unendurable when he comes back. This is not true, if I may judge from some little experience, but it is interesting as implying a certain consciousness, which is of the most hopeful augury. But we must not be impatient; it is a far cry from the dwellers in caves to even such civilization as we have achieved. I am conscious that life has been trying to civilize me for now nearly seventy years with what seem to me very inadequate results. *We* cannot afford to wait, but the Race can. And when I speak of civilization I mean those things that tend to develop the moral forces of Man, and not merely to quicken his æsthetic sensibility, though there is often a nearer relation between the two than is popularly believed.

The tendency of a prosperous Democracy—and hitherto we have had little to do but prosper—is towards an overweening confidence in itself and its home-made methods, an overestimate of material success, and a corresponding indifference to the things of the mind. The popular ideal of success seems to be more than ever before the accumulation of riches. I say "seems," for it may be only because the opportunities are greater. I am not ignorant that wealth is the great fertilizer of civilization, and of the arts that beautify it. The very names of civilization and politeness show that the refinement of manners which made the arts possible is the birth of cities where wealth earliest accumulated because it found itself secure. Wealth may be an excellent thing, for it means power, it means leisure, it means liberty.

But these, divorced from culture, that is, from intelligent purpose, become the very mockery of their own essence, not goods, but evils fatal to their possessor, and bring with them, like the Niblung hoard, a doom instead of a blessing. A man rich only for himself has a life as barren and cheerless as that of the serpent set to guard a buried treasure. I am saddened when I see our success as a nation measured by the number of acres under tillage or of bushels of wheat exported; for the real value of a country must be weighed in scales more delicate than the Balance of Trade. The garners of Sicily are empty now, but the bees from all climes still fetch honey from the tiny garden-plot of Theocritus. On a map of the world you may cover Judea with your thumb, Athens with a finger-tip, and neither of them figures in the Prices Current; but they still lord it in the thought and action of every civilized man. Did not Dante cover with his hood all that was Italy six hundred years ago? And, if we go back a century, where was Germany outside of Weimar? Material success is good, but only as the necessary preliminary of better things. The measure of a nation's true success is the amount it has contributed to the thought, the moral energy, the intellectual happiness, the spiritual hope and consolation, of mankind. There is no other, let our candidates flatter us as they may. We still make a confusion between huge and great. I know that I am repeating truisms, but they are truisms that need to be repeated in season and out of season.

The most precious property of Culture and of a college as its trustee is to maintain higher ideals of life and its purpose, to keep trimmed and burning the lamps of that pharos, built by wiser than we, which warns from the reefs and shallows of popular doctrine. In proportion as there are more thoroughly cultivated persons in a community will the finer uses of prosperity be taught and the vulgar uses of it become disreputable. And it is such persons that we are commissioned to send out with such consciousness of their fortunate vocation and such devotion to it as we may. We are confronted with unexampled problems. First of all is democracy, and that under conditions in great part novel, with its hitherto imperfectly tabulated results, whether we consider its effect upon national character, on popular thought, or on the functions of law and government; we have to deal with a time when the belief seems to be spreading that truth not only can but should be settled by a show of hands rather than by a count of heads, and that one man is as good as another for all purposes,—as, indeed, he is till a real man is needed; with a time when the press is more potent for good or for evil than ever any human agency was before, and yet is controlled more than ever before, by its interests as a business rather than by its sense of duty as a teacher, and must purvey news instead of intelligence; with a time when divers and strange doctrines touching the greatest human interests are allowed to run about unmuzzled in greater number and variety than ever before since the Reformation passed into its stage of putrefactive fermentation; with a time when the idols of the market-place are more devoutly worshipped than ever Diana of the Ephesians was; when the guilds of the Middle Ages are revived among us with the avowed purpose of renewing by the misuse of universal suffrage the class-legislation to escape which we left the Old World; when the electric telegraph, by making public opinion simultaneous, is also making it liable to those delusions, panics, and gregarious impulses which transform otherwise reasonable men into a mob; and when, above all, the better mind of the country is said to be growing more and more alienated from the highest of all sciences and services, the government of it. I have drawn up a dreary catalogue, and the moral it points is this: That the College, in so far as it continues to be still a college, as in great part it does and must, is and should be limited by certain pre-existing conditions, and must consider first what the more general objects of education are without neglecting special aptitudes more than cannot be helped. That more general purpose is, I take it, to set free, to supple, and to train the faculties in such wise as shall make them most effective for whatever task life may afterwards set them, for the duties of life rather than for its business, and to open windows on every side of the mind where thickness of wall does not prevent it.

Let our aim be as hitherto to give a good all-round education fitted to cope with as many exigencies of the day as possible. I had rather the college should turn out one of Aristotle's four-square men, capable of holding his own in whatever field he may be cast, than a score of lopsided ones developed abnormally in one direction. Our scheme should be adapted to the wants of the majority of under-graduates, to the objects that drew them hither, and to such training as will make the most of them after they come. Special aptitudes are sure to take care of themselves, but the latent possibilities of the average mind can only be discovered by experiment in many directions. When I speak of the average mind, I do not mean that the courses of study should be adapted to the average level of intelligence, but to the highest, for in these matters it is wiser to grade upwards than downwards, since the best is the only thing that is good enough. To keep the wing-footed down to the pace of the leaden-soled disheartens the one without in the least encouraging the other. "Brains," says Machiavelli, "are of three generations, those that understand of themselves, those that understand when another shows them, and those that understand neither of themselves nor by the showing of others." It is the first class that should set the stint; the second will get on better than if they had set it themselves; and the third will at least have the pleasure of watching the others show their paces.

In the College proper, I repeat, for it is the birthday of the College that we are celebrating, it is the College that we love and of which we are proud, let it continue to give such a training as will fit the rich to be trusted with riches, and the poor to withstand the temptations of poverty. Give to History, give to Political Economy, that ample verge the times demand, but with no detriment to those liberal Arts which have formed open-minded men and good citizens in the past, nor have lost the skill to form them. Let it be our hope to make a gentleman of every youth who is put under our charge; not a conventional gentleman, but a man of culture, a man of intellectual resource, a man of public spirit, a man of refinement, with that good taste which is the conscience of the mind, and that conscience which is the good taste of the soul. This we have tried to do in the past, this let us try to do in the future. We cannot do this for all, at best,—perhaps only for the few; but the influence for good of a highly trained intelligence and a harmoniously developed character is incalculable; for though it be subtle and gradual in its operation, it is as pervasive as it is subtle. There may be few of these, there must be few, but

> "That few is all the world which with a few
> Doth ever live and move and work and stirre."

If these few can best be winnowed from the rest by the elective system of studies, if the drift of our colleges towards that system be general and involuntary, showing a demand for it in the conditions of American life, then I should wish to see it unfalteringly carried through. I am sure that the matter will be handled wisely and with all forethought by those most intimately concerned in the government of the College.

They who, on a tiny clearing pared from the edge of the woods, built here, most probably with the timber hewed from the trees they felled, our earliest hall, with the solitude of ocean behind them, the mystery of forest before them, and all about them a desolation, must surely (*si quis animis celestibus locus*) share our gladness and our gratitude at the splendid fulfilment of their vision. If we could but have preserved the humble roof which housed so great a future, Mr. Ruskin himself would almost have admitted that no castle or cathedral was ever richer in sacred associations, in pathos of the past, and in moral significance. They who reared it had the sublime prescience of that courage which fears only God, and could say confidently in the face of all discouragement and doubt, "He hath led me forth into a large place; because he delighted in me He hath delivered me." We cannot honor them too much; we can repay them only by showing, as occasions rise, that we do not undervalue the worth of their example.

Brethren of the Alumni, it now becomes my duty to welcome in your name the guests who have come, some of them so far, to share our congratulations and hopes to-day. I cannot name them all and give to each his fitting phrase. Thrice welcome to them all, and, as is fitting, first to those from abroad, representatives of illustrious seats of learning that were old in usefulness and fame when ours was in its cradle; and next to those of our own land, from colleges and universities which, if not daughters of Harvard, are young enough to be so, and are one with her in heart and hope. I said that I should single out none by name, but I should not represent you fitly if I gave no special greeting to the gentleman who brings the message of John Harvard's College, Emmanuel. The welcome we give him could not be warmer than that which we offer to his colleagues, but we cannot help feeling that in pressing his hand our own instinctively closes a little more tightly, as with a sense of nearer kindred. There is also one other name of which it would be indecorous not to make an exception. You all know that I can mean only the President of our Republic. His presence is a signal honor to us all, and to us all I may say a personal gratification. We have no politics here, but the sons of Harvard all belong to the party which admires courage, strength of purpose, and fidelity to duty, and which respects, wherever he may be found, the

"Justum ac tenacem propositi virum,"

who knows how to withstand the

"Civium ardor prava jubentium."

He has left the helm of state to be with us here, and so long as it is intrusted to his hands we are sure that, should the storm come, he will say with Seneca's Pilot, "O Neptune, you may save me if you will; you may sink me if you will; but whatever happen, I shall keep my rudder true."

From THE PROGRESS OF THE WORLD[1]

(1886)

As at noon every day the captain of a ship tries to learn his whereabouts of the sun, that he may know how much nearer he is to his destined port, and how far he may have been pushed away from his course by the last gale or drifted from it by unsuspected currents, so on board this ship of ours, the Earth, in which that abstract entity we call the World is a passenger, we strive to ascertain, from time to time, with such rude instruments as we possess, what progress we have made and in what direction. It is rather by a kind of dead-reckoning than by taking the height of the Sun of Righteousness, which should be our sea-mark, that we accomplish this, for such celestial computations are gone somewhat out of fashion. It is only a few scholars and moralists in their silent and solitary observatories that any longer make account of them. We mostly put faith in our statisticians, and the longer they make their columns of figures, the bigger their sums of population, of exports and imports, and of the general output of fairy-gold, the more stupidly are we content. Nor are we over-nice in considering the direction of our progress, if only we be satisfied that to-day we are no longer where we were yesterday. Yet the course of this moral thing we call the World is controlled by laws as certain and immutable and by influences as subtle as those which govern with such exquisite precision that of the physical thing we call the Earth, could we only find them out. It has ever been the business of wise men to trace and to illustrate them, of prudent men to allow for and to seek an alliance with them, of good men to conform their lives with them.

Between those observations taken on shipboard and ours there is also this other difference, that those refer always to a fixed, external standard, while for these the standard is internal

[1] This paper was written for an introduction to a work entitled *The World's Progress* (published by Messrs. Gately & O'Gorman, Boston), in which the advance in various departments of intellectual and material activity was described and illustrated.

and fluctuating, so that the point toward which the World is making progress shall seem very different according to the temperament, the fortunes, nay, even the very mood or age of the observer. It may be remarked that Mr. Gladstone and Lord Tennyson are very far from being at one in their judgment of it. Old men in general love not change, and are suspicious of it; while young men are impatient of present conditions and of the slowness of movement to escape from them. Yet change is the very condition of our being and thriving, deliberation and choice that of all secure foothold on the shaky steppingstones by which we cross the torrent of Circumstances. Is it in the power of any man, whatever his age, to arrive at that equilibrium of temper and judgment without which no even probable estimate of where we are and whither we are tending is possible? Certainly no such trustworthy estimate can be deduced from our inward consciousness or from our outward environments; nor can we, with all our statistics, make ourselves independent of the inextinguishable lamps of heaven. We pile our figures one upon another, even as the builders of Babel their bricks, and the heaven we hope to attain is as far away as ever. It is moral forces that, more than all the others, govern the direction and regulate the advance of our affairs, and these forces are as calculable as the Trade-Winds or the Gulf-Stream.

And yet, though this be so, one of the greatest lessons taught by History is the close relation between the moral and the physical well-being of man. The case of the Ascetics makes but a seeming exception to this law, for they voluntarily denied themselves that bodily comfort which is the chief object of human endeavor, and renunciation is the wholesomest regimen of the soul. If we cannot strike a precise balance and say that the World is better because it is richer now than it was three centuries, or even half a century, ago, we may at least comfort ourselves with the belief that this, if not demonstrably true, is more than probable, and that there is less curable unhappiness, less physical suffering, and therefore less crime, than heretofore. Yet there is no gain without corresponding loss. If the sum of happiness be greater, yet the amount falling to each of us in the division of it seems to be less. It is noteworthy that literature, as it becomes more modern, becomes also more melancholy, and that he who keeps most constantly to the minor key of hopelessness, or strikes the deepest note of despair, is surest of at least momentary acclaim. Nay, do not some sources of happiness flow less full or cease to flow as settlement and sanitation advance, even as the feeders of our streams are dried by the massacre of our forests? We cannot have a new boulevard in Florence unless at sacrifice of those ancient city walls in which inspiring memories had for so many ages built their nests and reared their broods of song. Did not the plague, brooded and hatched in those smotherers of fresh air, the slits that thoroughfared the older town, give us the "Decameron"? And was the price too high? We cannot widen and ventilate the streets of Rome without grievous wrong to the city that we loved, and yet it is well to remember that this city too had built itself out of and upon the ruins of that nobler Rome which gave it all the wizard hold it had on our imagination. The Social Science Congress rejoices in changes that bring tears to the eyes of the painter and the poet. Alas! we cannot have a world made expressly for Mr. Ruskin, nor keep it if we could, more's the pity! Are we to confess, then, that the World grows less lovable as it grows more convenient and comfortable? that beauty flees before the step of the Social Reformer as the wild pensioners of Nature before the pioneers? that the lion will lie down with the lamb sooner than picturesqueness with health and prosperity? Morally, no doubt, we are bound to consider the Greatest Good of the Greatest Number, but there is something in us, *vagula, blandula*, that refuses, and rightly refuses, to be Benthamized; that asks itself in a timid whisper, "Is it so certain, then, that the Greatest Good is also the Highest? and has it been to the Greatest or to the Smallest Number than man has been most indebted?" For myself, while I admit, because I cannot help it, certain great and manifest improvements in the general well-being, I cannot stifle a suspicion that the Modern Spirit, to whose tune we are marching so cheerily, may have borrowed of the Pied Piper of Hamelin the instrument whence he draws such bewitching music. Having made this confession, I shall do my best to write in a becoming spirit the Introduction that is asked of me, and to make my antiquated portico as little unharmonious as I can with the modern building to which it leads.

But, before we enter upon a consideration of the Progress of the World, we must take a glance at that of the Globe on whose surface what we call the World came into being, rests, and has grown to what we see. This Globe is not, as we are informed, a perfect sphere, but slightly flattened at the poles; and in like manner this World is by no means a perfect world, though it be not quite so easy, as in the other case, to say where or why it is not. For it there is no moon-mirror in which to study its own profile. Perhaps it would be wise to ask ourselves now and then whether the fault may not be in the nature of man, after all, rather than anywhere else. So far as he is a social animal, that is, an animal liable in various ways to make his neighbor uncomfortable, it is certainly prudent to remember always that, though his natural impulses may be restrained, or guided, or even improved, yet that they are always there and ready to take the bit in their teeth at the first chance which offers. This might save us a pretty long bill for quack nostrums, since, though no astronomer has ever volunteered to rectify the Earth's outline, there is hardly a man who does not fancy that the World would become and continue just what it should be, if only his patent specific could once be fairly tried. Quacks of genius like Rousseau have sometimes persuaded to the experiment of their panaceas, but always with detriment to the patient's constitution. We are long in learning the lesson of Medea's cauldron.

The Earth, fortunately, is beyond the reach of our wisdom, and, like the other shining creatures of God, whirls her sphere and brings about her appointed seasons in happy obedience to laws for which she is not responsible and which she cannot tinker. Beginning as a nebulous nucleus of fiery gases, a luminous thistle-down blown about the barren wastes of space, then slowly shrinking, compacting, growing solid, and cooling at the rind, our planet was forced into a system with others like it, some smaller, some vastly greater than itself, and, in its struggle with over-mastering forces, having the Moon wrenched from it to be its night-lamp and the timer of its tides. Then slowly, slowly, it became capable of sustaining living organisms, rising by long and infinitesimal gradations, symbolically rehearsed again, it is said, by the child in embryo, from the simplest to the more complex, from merely animated matter to matter informed with Soul, and in Man, sometimes controlled by reason. The imagination grows giddy as it looks downwards along the rounds of the ladder lost, save a short stretch of it, in distance below, by which life has climbed from the zoophyte to Plato, to Newton, to Michael Angelo, to Shakespeare. During the inconceivable aeons implied in these processes, the Earth has gone through many vicissitudes, unrecorded save in the gigantic runes of Geology, the *graffiti* of Pluto and Neptune, which man, having painfully fashioned a key to them, is spelling out letter by letter, arranging as syllables, as words, as sentences, and at last reading as coherent narrative. Every one of these records is the mortuary inscription of an Epoch or a Cycle, but the last word of every one is *Resurgam*. They point backwards to such endless files of centuries that the poor six thousand years of our hieratic reckoning are dwindled to a hairbreadth, and our students of the rocks and stars, like the drunken man of Esdras, disdain the smaller change of temporal computation, and rattle off their millions as carelessly as Congress in dealing with our national strongbox. Nor has this sudden accession of secular wealth made them any more careful of the humbler interests of their neighbors than it is wont to make other *nouveaux riches*. A malignant astronomer has lately done his best to prove that the sun's stock of fuel cannot hold out more than seventeen millions of years. Is, then, that assurance of an earthly immortality which has hitherto sustained poets through cold and hunger and Philistine indifference, to be fobbed off at last with so beggarly a pittance as this? Let us hope for better things.

Though these memories of the rocks and mountains and

ocean-beds seem to belittle and abbreviate man, yet it is nothing
so; for, till he came, the universe, so far as we can explore and
know it, had neither eyes, nor ears, nor tongue, nor any dim-
mest consciousness of its own being. This antiquity has been
the gift of modern science; and the brain of man has been the
hour-glass that gave to these regardless sands of Time, running
to waste through the dreaming fingers of idle Oblivion, the
measure and standard of their own duration. It is the cunning
of man that has delineated the great dial-plate of the heavens;
his mind that looks before and after, and can tell the unwitting
stars where they were at any moment of the unmeasured past,
where they will be at any moment of the unmeasurable future.
Though he cannot loose the bands of Orion, he can weigh them
to the uttermost scruple; though he cannot bind the sweet influences of the Pleiades, he knows upon what eyes of mortal
men they are shed, and at what moment, though by himself
unseen. Shut in his study, he can look at the New Moon with
lovers at the Antipodes. If Science have made men seem
ephemeral as midges, she has conferred a great benefit on humanity by endowing collective Man with something of that
longaeval dignity which she has compelled the individual to
renounce. He is no longer the creature of yesterday, but the
crowning product and heir of ages so countless as to make Time a
sharer in the grandeur of that immensity to which Astronomy has
dilated the bounds of Space. And who shall reproach her with
having put far away from us the homely and neighborly heaven
of unlettered faith, when she has opened such a playground
for the outings of speculation, and noted in her guide-book
so many spacious inns for the refreshment of the disembod-
ied spirit on its travels, so many and so wondrous *magnalia*
for its curiosity and instruction? To me it seems not unreasonable to find a reinforcement of optimism, a renewal of courage and hope, in the modern theory that man has mounted to
what he is from the lowest step of potentiality, through toil-
some grades of ever-expanding existence, even though it have
been by a spiral stairway, mainly dark or dusty, with loop-holes
at long intervals only, and these granting but a narrow and one-

sided view. The protoplasmic germ to which it was incalculable promotion to become a stomach, has it not, out of the
resources with which God had endowed it, been able to develop
the brain of Darwin, who should write its biography? Even
Theology is showing signs that she is getting ready to exchange
a man who fell in Adam for a man risen out of nonentity and
still rising through that aspiring virtue in his veins which is
spurred onwards and upwards by the very inaccessibility of
what he sees above him.

From THE INDEPENDENT IN POLITICS

(1888)

It is time for lovers of their country to consider how much of
the success of our experiment in democracy has been due to such
favorable conditions as never before concurred to make such an
attempt plausible; whether those conditions have changed and
are still changing for the worse; how far we have been ac-
cessories in this degeneration, if such there be, and how far it
is in our power, with the means furnished by the very instruments of destruction, to stay its advance and to repair its
ravages. Till within a few years of our civil war, everything
conduced to our measuring the success of our institutions by
the evidence of our outward prosperity, and to our seeing the
future in rose-color. The hues of our dawn had scarcely faded
from the sky. Men were still living who had seen the face
and heard the voice of the most august personage in our history,
and of others scarce less august than he. The traditions of our
founders were fresh. Our growth in wealth and power was
without precedent. We had been so fortunate that we had
come to look upon our luck as partly due to our own merits
and partly to our form of government. When we met together it was to felicitate each other on our superiority to the
rest of mankind. Our ears caught from behind the horizon
the muffled thunders of war, only to be lulled, as with the
murmurs of the surf on a far-off shore. We heard of revolutions,

but for us Fortune forgot to turn her wheel. This was what may be called the Fourth of July period of our history. Among the peoples of the earth we were the little Jack Horner. We had put in our thumb, and pulled out a plum, and the rest of mankind thought that we were never tired of saying, "What a good little boy am I!" Here is a picture of our growth, drawn by a friendly, yet impartial hand: "Nothing in the history of mankind is like their progress. For my part, I never cast an eye on their flourishing commerce and their cultivated and commodious life but they seem to me rather ancient nations grown to perfection through a long series of fortunate events and a train of successful industry accumulating wealth in many centuries than the colonies of yesterday. Your children do not grow faster from infancy to manhood than they spread from families to communities, and from villages to nations." But for a certain splendor of style these words seem to be of yesterday, so pertinent are they still. They were uttered in the British Parliament more than a year before the battle of Lexington, by Edmund Burke. There is no exaggeration in them. They are a simple statement of fact. Burke, with his usual perspicacity, saw and stated one and a chief cause of this unprecedented phenomenon. He tells us that the colonies had made this marvelous growth because, "through a wise and salutary neglect, a generous nature has been suffered to take her own way to perfection." But by that "wise and salutary neglect," he meant freedom from the petty and short-sighted meddlesomeness of a paternal government; he meant being left to follow untrammelled the instincts of our genius under the guidance of our energy. The same causes have gone on ever since working the same marvels. Those marvels have been due in part to our political system. But there were other circumstances tending to stimulate personal energy and enterprise, especially land to be had for the taking, and free trade over a larger share of the earth's surface peopled by thriving and intelligent communities than had ever been enjoyed elsewhere. I think, however, that there was one factor more potent than any other, or than all others together. Before we broke away from the mother country politically, a century and a half of that "wise neglect" of which Burke spoke had thoroughly made over again and Americanized all the descendants of the earlier settlers, and these formed the great bulk of the population. The same process was rapidly going on in the more recent immigrants. So thorough had this process been that many, perhaps most, of the refugees who, during or after the Revolutionary War, went to England, or home, as they fondly called it, found themselves out of place and unhappy there. The home they missed was that humane equality, not of condition or station, but of being and opportunity, which by some benign influence of the place had overcome them here, like a summer cloud, without their special wonder. Yet they felt the comfort of it as of an air wholesome to breathe. I more than suspect that it was the absence of this inestimable property of the moral atmosphere that made them aliens in every other land, and convinced them that an American can no more find another country than a second mother. This equality had not then been proclaimed as a right; it had been incorporated in no constitution, but was there by the necessity of the case—a gift of the sky and of the forest, as truly there as it now is in that great West whose history was so admirably treated by Senator Hoar a few days ago, and whose singular good fortune it has been that no disparities except those of nature's making have ever been known there. Except in the cities of the seaboard, where the habits of the Old World had to some extent been kept alive by intercourse and importation, the defecation of the body politic and the body social of all purely artificial and arbitrary distinctions had been going on silently and surely among the masses of the people for generations. This was true (in a more limited sense) even of communities where slavery existed, for as that was based on complexion, every white, no matter what his condition, belonged to the privileged class, just as in Hungary every Magyar was a noble. This was the American novelty, no bantling of theory, no fruit of forethought, no trophy of insurgent violence, but a pure evolution from the nature of man in a perfectly free medium. The essential triumph was achieved in this tacit recognition of a certain privilege and adequacy in mere manhood, and democracy may be said to have succeeded before it was accepted as doctrine or embodied as a political fact. Our ancestors sought a new country. What they found was a new condition of mind. It is more than questionable whether the same conditions in as favorable combination of time and place will ever occur again, whether equality, so wholesome when a social evolution, as I have described it, may not become harmful as a sudden gift in the form of dogma, may not indeed prove dangerous when interpreted and applied politically by millions of newcomers alien to our traditions, unsteadied by lifelong training and qualifying associations. We have great and thus-far well-warranted faith in the digestive and assimilative powers of our system; but may not these be overtaxed?

The theory of equality was old, among men of English blood, as Jack Cade's rebellion, but it was not practically conceived even by the very men who asserted it. Here, on the edge of the forest, where civilized man was brought face to face again with nature and taught to rely mainly on himself, mere manhood became a fact of prime importance. That century and a half of apprenticeship in democracy stimulated self-help, while it also necessitated helpfulness for others and mutual dependence upon them. Not without reason did "help" take the place of "servant" in our vocabulary. But the conditions of life led to other results that left less salutary effects behind them. They bred a habit of contentment with what *would do*, as we say, rather than an impatience of whatever was not best; a readiness to put up with many evils or inconveniences, because they could not be helped; and this has, especially in our politics, conduced to the growth of the greatest weakness in our American character—the acquiescence in makeshifts and abuses which can and ought to be helped, and which, with honest resolution, might be helped.

Certainly never were the auguries so favorable as when our republic was founded, a republic sure from inherent causes to broaden into a more popular form. But while the equality of which I have been speaking existed in the instincts, the habits, and obscurely in the consciousness of all, it was latent and inert. It found little occasion for self-assertion, none for aggression, and was slow to invent one. A century ago there was still a great respect for authority in all its manifestations; for the law first of all, for age, for learning, and for experience. The community recognized and followed its natural leaders, and it was these who framed our Constitution, perhaps the most remarkable monument of political wisdom known to history. The convention which framed it was composed of the choicest material in the community, and was led astray by no theories of what *might* be good, but clave closely to what experience had demonstrated to *be* good. The late Mr. Guizot once asked me "how long I thought our republic would endure." I replied: "So long as the ideas of the men who founded it continue dominant," and he assented. I will not say that we could not find among us now the constituents of as able an assembly, but I doubt if there be a single person in this audience who believes that with our present political methods we should or could elect them. We have revived the English system of rotten boroughs, under which the electors indeed return the candidate, but it is a handful of men, too often one man, that selects the person to be so returned. If this be so, and I think it is so, it should give us matter for very serious reflection.

After our Constitution got fairly into working order it really seemed as if we had invented a machine that would go of itself, and this begot a faith in our luck which even the civil war itself but momentarily disturbed. Circumstances continued favorable, and our prosperity went on increasing. I admire the splendid complacency of my countrymen, and find something exhilarating and inspiring in it. We are a nation which has *struck ile,* but we are also a nation that is sure the well will never run dry. And this confidence in our luck with the absorption in material interests, generated by unparalleled opportunity, has in some respects made us neglectful of our political duties. I have long thought that the average men of our revolutionary period were better grounded in the elementary principles of government than their descendants. The town-meeting was then a better training-school than the caucus and the convention are now, and the smaller the community the greater the influence of the better mind in it. In looking about me, I am struck with the fact that while we produce great captains, financial and industrial leaders in abundance, and political managers in overabundance, there seems to be a pause in the production of leaders in statesmanship. I am still more struck with the fact that my newspaper often gives me fuller reports of the speeches of Prince Bismarck and of Mr. Gladstone than of anything said in Congress. If M. Thiers or M. Gambetta were still here, it would be the same with them; but France, like ourselves, has gone into the manufacture of small politicians. Why are we interested in what these men say? Because they are important for what they *are*, as well as for what they represent. They are Somebodies, and their every word gathers force from the character and life behind it. They stand for an idea as well as for a constituency. An adequate amount of small change will give us the equivalent of the largest piece of money, but what aggregate of little men will amount to a single great one, that most precious coinage in the mint of nature? It is not that we have lost the power of bringing forth great men. They are not the product of institutions, though these may help or hinder them. I am thankful to have been the contemporary of one and among the greatest, of whom I think it is safe to say that no other country and no other form of government could have fashioned him, and whom posterity will recognize as the wisest and most bravely human of modern times. It is a benediction to have lived in the same age and in the same country with Abraham Lincoln.

Had democracy borne only this consummate flower and then perished like the century-plant, it would have discharged its noblest function. It is the crown of a nation, one might almost say the chief duty of a nation, to produce great men, for without them its history is but the annals of ants and bees. Two conditions are essential: the man, and the opportunity. We must wait on Mother Nature for the one, but in America we ourselves can do much to make or mar the other. We cannot always afford to set our house on fire as we did for Lincoln, but we are certainly responsible if the door to distinction be made so narrow and so low as to admit only petty and crouching men. . . .

Our politicians are so busy studying the local eddies of prejudice or interest that they allow the main channel of our national energies to be obstructed by dams for the grinding of private grist. Our leaders no longer lead, but are as skilful as Indians in following the faintest trail of public opinion. I find it generally admitted that our moral standard in politics has been lowered, and is every day going lower. Some attribute this to our want of a leisure class. It is to a book of the Apocrypha that we are indebted for the invention of the Man of Leisure.[1] But a leisure class without a definite object in life, and without generous aims, is a bane rather than a blessing. It would end in the weariness and cynical pessimism in which its great Exemplar Ecclesiastes ended, without leaving us the gift which his genius left. What we want is an active class who will insist in season and out of season that we shall have a country whose greatness is measured, not only by its square miles, its number of yards woven, of hogs packed, of bushels of wheat raised, not only by its skill to feed and clothe the body, but also by its power to feed and clothe the soul; a country which shall be as great morally as it is materially; a country whose very name shall not only, as now it does, stir us as with the sound of a trumpet, but shall call out all that is best within us by offering us the radiant image of something better and nobler and more enduring than we, of something that shall fulfill our own thwarted aspiration, when we are but a handful of forgotten dust in the soil trodden by a race whom we shall have helped to make more worthy of their inheritance than we ourselves had the power, I might almost say, the means, to be.

[1] The wisdom of a learned man cometh by opportunity of leisure and he that hath little business shall become wise"—Ecclesiasticus, xxxviii. 24. [Lowell]

NOTES

Page 3.   TO THE SPIRIT OF KEATS

In writing of this sonnet to E. A. Duyckinck, December 5, 1841, Lowell spoke of Keats as "a poet whom I especially love and whom I consider to be one of the true old Titan brood." On Lowell's early interest in Keats, as well as in Tennyson and Spenser, see Scudder, *Biography*, I, 94–96. Also J. O. Eidson, *Tennyson in America* (1943), index. Keats is echoed in "Bobolink," "Ianthe," "Irene" (Lowell's tribute to Maria White, who became his bride), and "A Legend of Brittany" (cf. "Isabella, or the Pot of Basil"). Lowell's cool essay on Keats now in his collected works, originally an introduction to an edition of *Keats's Poems* (Boston, 1854), shows that his early enthusiasm for the romanticist has become considerably tempered by critical judgment.

Thirty-five sonnets by Lowell were collected in his first book, *A Year's Life* (1841), but of these he preserved only two in later collections. On the relation of these to the history of the sonnet in America see L. G. Sterner's Introduction to *The Sonnet in American Literature* (Philadelphia, 1930), and F. W. Powell's *The Sonnet in American Magazines before 1860* (a dissertation of 1932, available in manuscript at the library of the University of Virginia).

Page 6.   THE SHEPHERD OF KING ADMETUS

This is one of the many illustrations of the fact that Lowell could write simply and without the didactic "isms" which he recognized as his besetting sin. The primitivistic notion, however, that the mere "loveliness of things," of nature, taught the first poet all he knew, is typical of Lowell's general disregard of cultural tradition at this time.

Page 8.   AN INCIDENT IN A RAILROAD CAR

Note Lowell's early faith in goodness of "the primitive soul" as the basis of democracy, and his view that "all thought begins in feeling."

Page 12.   WENDELL PHILLIPS

On the work of this great abolitionist whom Lowell admired, especially during his early humanitarian period, see Carlos Martyn, *Wendell Phillips: the Agitator* (New York, 1890).

Page 12.   RHŒCUS

"This fairy legend of old Greece," telling the story of a mortal who lost his love because he wounded a bee, represents Lowell's early humanitarian view, especially in its moral:

> "he who scorns the least of Nature's works
> Is thenceforth exiled and shut out from all."

Cf. "The Ancient Mariner"—the episode of securing release from penance by blessing watersnakes, and the attendant moral in lines 614–617.

Page 17.   COLUMBUS

This spirited dramatic monologue embodies Lowell's early anti-traditionalism ("Europe's world / Reels on to judgment") and his ardent humanitarian utopianism.

Page 25.   THE PRESENT CRISIS

The "crisis" was the controversy regarding whether Texas should be annexed and the area of slavery extended. This poem probably represents the high-water mark in the sonorous and lofty expression of moral passion aimed at slavery. Lowell may have had the verse form of "Locksley Hall" in mind, although as a whole the poem has much greater intensity than Tennyson's has. A trumpet-call to fight wrong even if single-handed, the poem is built around the idea of progress ("Humanity sweeps onward") and the resultant conviction that the Past can teach us nothing but the necessity of revolt: "Time makes ancient good uncouth"; we must not "attempt the Future's portal with the Past's blood-rusted key." "For twenty years," says Greenslet (*Lowell*, p. 79), "the solemn monitory music of this poem never ceased to reëcho in public halls. In the Lowell Memorial Address which George William Curtis delivered before the Brooklyn Institute, February 22, 1892, he said in his heightened way of some passages of 'The Present Crisis': 'Wendell Phillips [the orator] winged with their music and tipped with their flame the darts of his fervid appeal and manly scorn. As he quoted them with suppressed emotion in his low, melodious, penetrating voice the white plume of the resistless Navarre of eloquence gained a loftier grace, that relentless sword of invective a more flashing edge.' And the stanza of 'The Present Crisis,' beginning, 'For humanity sweeps onward,' was made by Sumner the text and motif of that famous 'Crime against Speech' oration that provoked the assault of Preston Brooks."

Notes

Notes 469

Page 31.   THE BIGLOW PAPERS

In Lowell's "Introduction" to the collected second series of *The Biglow Papers* (1862) he explained his aims in part as follows: ". . . When, more than twenty years ago, I wrote the first of the series, I had no definite plan and no intention of ever writing another. Thinking the Mexican war, as I think it still, a national crime committed in behoof of Slavery, our common sin, and wishing to put the feeling of those who thought as I did in a way that would tell, I imagined to myself such an upcountry man as I had often seen at antislavery gatherings, capable of district-school English, but always instinctively falling back into the natural stronghold of his homely dialect when heated to the point of self-forgetfulness. When I began to carry out my conception and to write in my assumed character, I found myself in a strait between two perils. On the one hand, I was in danger of being carried beyond the limit of my own opinions, or at least of that temper with which every man should speak his mind in print, and on the other I feared the risk of seeming to vulgarize a deep and sacred conviction. I needed on occasion to rise above the level of mere *patois*, and for this purpose conceived the Rev. Mr. Wilbur, who should express the more cautious element of the New England character and its pedantry, as Mr. Biglow should serve for its homely common-sense vivified and heated by conscience. The parson was to be the complement rather than the antithesis of his parishioner, and I felt or fancied a certain humorous element in the real identity of the two under a seeming incongruity. Mr. Wilbur's fondness for scraps of Latin, though drawn from the life, I adopted deliberately to heighten the contrast. Finding soon after that I needed some one as a mouthpiece of the mere drollery, for I conceive that true humor is never divorced from moral conviction, I invented Mr. Sawin for the clown of my little puppet-show. I meant to embody in him that half-conscious *un*morality which I had noticed as the recoil in gross natures from a puritanism that still strove to keep in its creed the intense savor which had long gone out of its faith and life. In the three I thought I should find room enough to express, as it was my plan to do, the popular feeling and opinion of the time For the names of two of my characters, since I have received some remonstrances from very worthy persons who happen to bear them, I would say that they were purely fortuitous, probably mere unconscious memories of signboards or directories. Mr. Sawin's sprang from the accident of a rhyme at the end of his first epistle, and I purposely christened him by the impossible surname of Birdofredum not more to stigmatize him as the incarnation of 'Manifest Destiny,' in other words, of national recklessness as to right and wrong, than to avoid the chance of wounding any private sensitiveness.

"The success of my experiment soon began not only to astonish me, but to make me feel the responsibility of knowing that I held in my hand a weapon instead of the mere fencing-stick I had supposed. Very far from being a popular author under my own name, so far, indeed, as to be almost unread, I found the verses of my pseudonym copied everywhere; I saw them pinned up in workshops; I heard them quoted and their authorship debated; I once even, when rumor had at length caught up my name in one of its eddies, had the satisfaction of overhearing it demonstrated, in the pauses of a concert, that *I* was utterly incompetent to have written anything of the kind. I had read too much not to know the utter worthlessness of contemporary reputation, especially as regards satire, but I knew also that by giving a certain amount of influence it also had its worth, if that influence were used on the right side. I had learned, too, that the first requisite of good writing is to have an earnest and definite purpose, whether æsthetic or moral, and that even good writing, to please long, must have more than an average amount either of imagination or common-sense. The first of these falls to the lot of scarcely one in several generations; the last is within the reach of many in every one that passes; and of this an author may fairly hope to become in part the mouthpiece. If I put on the cap and bells and made myself one of the court-fools of King Demos, it was less to make his majesty laugh than to win a passage to his royal ears for certain serious things which I had deeply at heart. I say this because there is no imputation that could be more galling to any man's self-respect than that of being a mere jester. I endeavored, by generalizing my satire, to give it what value I could beyond the passing moment and the immediate application. How far I have succeeded I cannot tell, but I have had better luck than I ever looked for in seeing my verses survive to pass beyond their nonage.

"In choosing the Yankee dialect, I did not act without forethought. It had long seemed to me that the great vice of American writing and speaking was a studied want of simplicity, that we were in danger of coming to look on our mother-tongue as a dead language, to be sought in the grammar and dictionary rather than in the heart, and that our only chance of escape was by seeking it at its living sources among those who were, as Scottowe says of Major-General Gibbons, 'divinely illiterate' President Lincoln, the only really great public man whom these latter days have seen, was great also in this, that he was master—witness his speech at Gettysburg—of a truly masculine English, classic, because it was of no special period, and level at once to the highest and lowest of his countrymen. I learn from the highest authority that his favorite reading was in Shakespeare and Milton, to which, of course, the Bible should be added. But whoever should read the debates in Congress might fancy himself present at a meeting of the city council of some city of Southern Gaul in the decline of the Empire, where barbarians with a Latin varnish emulated each other in being more than Ciceronian. Whether it be want of culture, for the highest outcome of that is simplicity, or for whatever reason, it is certain that very few American writers or speakers wield their native language with the directness, precision, and force that are common as the day in the mother country. We use it like Scotsmen, not as if it belonged to us, but as if we wished to prove that we belonged to it, by showing our intimacy with its written rather than with its spoken dialect. And yet all the while our popular idiom is racy with life and vigor and originality, bucksome (as Milton used the word) to our new occasions, and proves itself no mere graft by sending up new suckers from the old root in spite of us. It is only from its roots in the living generations of men that a language can be reinforced with fresh vigor for its needs; what may be called a literate dialect grows ever more and more pedantic and foreign, till it becomes at last as unfitting a vehicle for living thought as monkish Latin. That we should all be made to talk like books is the danger with which we are threatened by the Universal Schoolmaster, who does his best to enslave the minds and memories of his victims to what he esteems the best models of English composition, that is to say, to the writers whose style is faultily correct and has no blood-warmth in it. No language after it has faded into *diction*, none that cannot suck up the feeding juices secreted for it in the rich mother-earth of common folk, can bring forth a sound and lusty book. True vigor and heartiness of phrase do not pass from page to page, but from man to man, where the brain is kindled and the lips suppled by downright living interests and by passion in its very throe. Language is the soil of thought, and our own especially is a rich leaf-mould, the slow deposit of ages, the shed foliage of feeling, fancy, and imagination, which has suffered an earth-change, that the vocal forest, as Howell called it, may clothe itself anew with living green. There is death in the dictionary; and, where language is too strictly limited by convention, the ground for expression to grow in is limited also; and we get a *potted* literature, Chinese dwarfs instead of healthy trees. . . .

"The quality of exaggeration has often been remarked on as typical of American character, and especially of American humor. In Dr. Petri's *Gedrängtes Handbuch der Fremdwörter*, we are told that the word *humbug* is commonly used for the exaggerations of the North-Americans. To be sure, one would be tempted to think the dream of Columbus half fulfilled, and that Europe had found in the West a nearer way to Orientalism, at least in diction. But it seems to me that a great deal of what is set down as mere extravagance is more fitly to be called intensity and picturesqueness, symptoms of the imaginative faculty in full health and strength, though producing, as yet, only the raw and formless material in which poetry is to work. By and by, perhaps, the world will see it fashioned into poem and picture, and Europe, which will be hard pushed for originality erelong, may have to thank us for a new sensation. The French continue to find Shakespeare exaggerated because he treated English just as our country-folk do when they speak of a 'steep price,' or say that they 'freeze to' a thing. The first postulate of an original literature is that a people should use their language instinctively and unconsciously, as if it were a lively part of their growth and personality, not as the mere torpid boon of education or inheritance."

In becoming "one of the court-fools of King Demos," Lowell said he had in mind "serious things." He used laughter as a weapon to modify public opinion of contemporary events. (These events, as they relate to *The Biglow Papers*, have been discussed in detail in notes—to which I am gratefully indebted—by F. B. Williams, printed in the Cambridge Edition of Lowell's *Poetical Works*, pp. 471–479.) As a satiric humorist Lowell carried on certain traditions embodied in earlier American humorists such as Seba Smith (author of Jack Downing's papers, collected as *My Thirty Years out of the Senate*) and Thomas Chandler Haliburton (Sam Slick). Hosea, like Downing and Slick, was a rustic and illiterate Yankee, who said wise and comical things in dialect about politics and who indulged in apt caricatures. Lowell himself refers in *The Biglow Papers*, First Series, No. VIII, to Enoch Timbertoes:

> "'Then you call me 'Timbertoes'—thet's wut the people likes,
>   Sutthin combinin' morril truth with phrases sech ez strikes.'"

(See Bibliography for scholarly studies of his relation to earlier humorists by Miss Jeanette Tandy, and of his use of the Yankee dialect by Grandgent, Heil, and Miss Kilheffer.) It is interesting to notice that Lowell, who is popularly regarded today as a snobbish and academic Brahmin of "The Genteel Tradition," actually gave us one of our best and most sympathetic portraits of rustic common sense in Hosea Biglow. In general Lowell's shift from sentiment to humor as a weapon in his humanitarian campaign is an index to his broadening perspective and masculinity.

Satire of contemporary political events seldom outlives the memory of the events satirized, and the continued popularity of *The Biglow Papers* is probably accounted for in part by the fact that in them Lowell departed from most of his predecessors by creating three characters and arranging them so as to produce a credible piece of fiction. For example, Birdofredum Sawin, a study in degeneration and disillusionment, is thrown into relief, in his delightful rascality, by the pedantic Parson Wilbur. The chief character, however, is of course Hosea Biglow, the embodiment of "homely common-sense vivified and heated by conscience." Whereas Jack Downing was a politician, Hosea is a farmer, with a farmer's homely illustrations at the tip of his tongue. As W. D. Howells, the novelist, concluded (*Atlantic*, XIX, 123, Jan., 1867), "It is not as mere satire, however, that the *Biglow Papers* are to be valued. The First and Second Series form a creative fiction of unique excellence." J. R. Dennet (*Nation*, III, 387, Nov., 1866) agreed that Lowell's characters are "so life-like and, in the main, so true to nature—so good as individuals and as types that we know not where in literature to look for . . . others that excel them." Incidentally Lowell not only illustrated himself his theory that our literature should be vivid and homely and strongly flavored with the soil, but he also, as editor of the *Atlantic*, encouraged writers such as Harriet Prescott Spofford and Rose Terry Cooke who heralded the realistic movement in American fiction.

Page 31. A LETTER FROM MR. EZEKIEL BIGLOW OF JAALAM TO THE HON. JOSEPH T. BUCKINGHAM

It should be noted here that Lowell in this humanitarian period (1846) advocates through Hosea both pacifism (l. 33) and disunion (l. 154), attitudes which he reversed in his next period. Hosea, riled at the attempt to recruit soldiers for the Mexican War to extend slavery, is created by Lowell to express his own views as opposed to those of Birdofredum Sawin, who enlists and reports his gradual disillusionment regarding the glory of war as a result of his manifold sufferings, including the loss of a leg, an arm, four fingers, one eye, etc. (See *Biglow Papers*, Series One, Nos. II and VIII.) Note Hosea's absolute appeal to the religious conscience of the inheritors of Puritanism and his constant reference to details of the farmer's life. His rusticity is thrown into relief by Parson Wilbur's pedantic introductory letter and his postscript.

Page 42. THE DEBATE IN THE SENNIT

Captain Drayton and his mate Sayres tried, in April, 1848, to kidnap seventy-seven slaves from Washington. The slaves were recaptured and returned to the South, and Drayton and Sayres, barely escaping from a mob, were sentenced to long terms of imprisonment. When Senator Hale of New Hampshire introduced a resolution (April 20, 1848) suggesting sympathy with the slaves, Senator Calhoun said he "would as soon argue with a maniac from Bedlam" as with Mr. Hale, and rested the case on the Constitution, which, in safeguarding property, was interpreted as sanctioning the right to slaves. Henry S. Foote, Senator from Mississippi from 1847

to 1852, said that Mr. Hale was "as guilty as if he had committed
highway robbery," and that he could not advance ten miles within
the state of Mississippi before "he would grace one of the tallest
trees of the forest with a rope around his neck, with the approbation
of all honest and patriotic citizens." These expressions illustrate
the heatedness with which the debate was then carried on in the
Senate. (For Calhoun's views see his *Disquisition on Government*
[1851], his *Discourse on the Constitution and the Government of the
United States* [1851], F. Bancroft's *Calhoun and the South Carolina
Nullification Movement* [Baltimore: 1928], and V. L. Parrington's
The Romantic Revolution [New York: 1927, pp. 69–82]. Briefly, it
may be said that Calhoun regarded the contract of the individual
states in entering into the union as revocable when their interests
were violated; Webster and Lincoln held this contract irrevocable,
and the abolitionists did not admit that property could rightfully
include a human being. The latter appealed to the "higher law"—
the moral law—as opposed to the Constitution.)

Note Lowell's dire irony in setting the debate to a nursery rime,
and his skill in making Calhoun's arguments seem ridiculous. See
Lowell's similar method in "What Mr. Robinson Thinks," *Biglow
Papers*, First Series, No. III.

During this humanitarian period when he scorned the past and
traditional restraints such as checks and balances, Lowell regarded
the Constitution as a "Sacred Parasol" to be interposed "wherever
there seemed danger from the hostile incursions of Light" (Lowell's
Anti-Slavery Papers, I, 85–92).

Page 49.   THE PIOUS EDITOR'S CREED

This poem was occasioned by the fact that although Southerners,
such as Senator Foote, glorified the revolution in France as marking
the downfall of "the age of tyranny and slavery," the attorney for
Drayton and Sayres who quoted these words in defence of his clients
was silenced by the judge for trying to "endanger our institutions"
with words which were "inflammatory."

Lowell himself wrote a great deal for anti-slavery journals, notably
the *Anti-Slavery Standard*, and he exalted the journalist's responsibility and power.

Page 53.   A LETTER FROM A CANDIDATE . . .

The colorless Zachary Taylor was nominated in 1848 for the presidency by the Whigs, who wished to draw votes from both North and
South through an avoidance of any statement as to policy. Early
in 1847, when the *Cincinnati Signal* inquired regarding Taylor's attitude toward the Wilmot Proviso, he stated his position in such a two-

faced manner that he was interpreted as being on both sides at once. (This Proviso was a measure for excluding slavery from Texas which passed the House but not the Senate.) The refusal of the Whigs to make the Wilmot Proviso a campaign issue resulted in many voters deserting the Whigs for the Free-Soil Party, which eventually evolved into the Republican Party.

This is one of the most satisfying satires on fence-straddling and hypocrisy in the English language.

Page 65.   ODE TO FRANCE

First published in *The Standard* for April 6, 1848, after Lowell had arranged (see letter to Briggs, March 26, 1848) to make a weekly contribution to this periodical at a salary of $500. a year. Lowell said he was "heartily in accord" with the committee which operated *The Standard* so far as concerned their "fundamental doctrine of opposition to slavery, morally and politically," but he told Briggs that he did "not agree with the abolitionists in their disunion and non-voting theories." See Scudder, I, 203–207, for further details regarding Lowell's admiration for the idealism of the French people in their overthrow of King Louis Philippe in order to form a republic. Also his editorial in *The Standard* (April 6, 1848) on "The French Republic of 1848," his poem "To Lamartine" (August 3, 1848), and his editorial "Shall We Ever Be a Republic?" in which he attacks American slavery.

Page 70.   THE FIRST SNOW-FALL

The poem refers to the death of Lowell's daughter Blanche, in March, 1847, at the age of fourteen months. Lowell's second child, Mabel, who outlived him, was born in September of the same year. The poem was published in *The Standard*, Dec. 27, 1849.

Page 72.   THE VISION OF SIR LAUNFAL

Lowell's first mention of this poem is in a letter to Briggs, dated February 1, 1848, where he speaks of it as "a sort of story, and more likely to be popular than what I write generally. Maria thinks very highly of it." It was published first in book form Dec. 17, 1848, after *The Biglow Papers, First Series*, and in the same year as *Poems, Second Series* and *A Fable for Critics*. It was the work of this Annus Mirabilis which determined his recognition as poet, political satirist, humorist, and critic. Shortly after the publication of "The Vision of Sir Launfal," Lowell wrote Briggs: "I walked to Watertown [to the wedding of Mrs. Lowell's sister] over the snow with the new moon before me and a sky exactly like that in Page's evening landscape. Orion was rising behind me, and, as I stood on the hill just before you enter the village, the stillness of the fields around me was delicious, broken only by the tinkle of a little brook which runs too swiftly for Frost to catch it. My picture of the brook in 'Sir Launfal' was drawn from it. But why do I send you this description—like the bones of a chicken I had picked? Simply because I was so happy as I stood there, and felt so sure of doing something that would justify my friends. But why do I not say that I *have* done something? I believe I have done better than the world knows yet, but the past seems so little compared with the future. . . . I am the first poet who has endeavored to express the American Idea, and I shall be popular by and by."—Norton, *Letters*, I, 148.

According to H. E. Scudder (*Biography*, I, 268): "As Tennyson threw into his retelling of Arthurian romance a moral sense, so Lowell, also a moralist in his poetic apprehension, made a parable of his tale, and, in the broadest interpretation of democracy, sang of the levelling of all ranks in a common divine humanity. There is a subterranean passage connecting the 'Biglow Papers' with 'Sir Launfal'; it is the holy zeal which attacks slavery issuing in this fable of a beautiful charity, Christ in the guise of a beggar." Mr. Scudder thinks the invention may "have been suggested by Tennyson's 'Sir Galahad,' but the verses in the poem which linger longest in the mind are not those connected with the fable, but rather the full-throated burst of song in praise of June."

For an able analysis of the technique of the poem, see Allen's *American Prosody*, pp. 256–258. Mr. Allen shows that "No American poet had hitherto achieved more varied and subtle effects with meter, and indeed Lowell scarcely ever succeeded so well again himself." Beginning with the idea of a "musing organist" who "lets his fingers wander as they list," Lowell begins with iambic pentameter, turns to octosyllabic couplets, shifts to irregular four-stress verse with frequent trisyllabic substitutions, and in certain places varies from four to ten syllables to the line. Lowell used double rhyme more than any of his predecessors. Mr. Allen regards this poem as the chief illustration of Lowell's distinctive skill as a prosodist in introducing into American poetry a greater metrical freedom, melody, and harmony, secured chiefly by a more varied placing of accents and the combining of different kinds of feet to produce a suggestiveness of tone and cadence.

Page 83.   A FABLE FOR CRITICS

Lowell's comment on his progress in composing this *Fable*, at first published anonymously, may be found in his letters of November 13, 1847, and March 26 and May 12, 1848. One of the earlier of our "surveys" of American literature, it illustrates his youthful contempt for tradition ("Forget Europe wholly") and also his gradual turn from sentimentalism to the critical temper which was to be developed so finely in his long series of mature critical essays. (On parallel contemporary "surveys" see E. C. Hassold *American Literary History before the Civil War*, Chicago, 1935.) Many of Lowell's thumbnail sketches show surprising critical insight, and many of his conclusions have been supported by recent exhaustive studies. Compare the somewhat similar *A Critical Fable* (1922), published anonymously by Amy Lowell.

ll. 73 ff., on Emerson. Note that, like Holmes, Lowell emphasizes Emerson's balance, his union of idealism and practicality: he is "Plotinus-Montaigne." See Lowell's essay on "Emerson the Lecturer," and his comparison and contrast of Carlyle and Emerson in his essay on Thoreau, *Writings*, I, 363–368, where he emphasizes "the tendency of the one toward Authority and of the other toward Independency."

ll. 165 ff., on Thoreau. For a scholarly discussion of Lowell's failure to do Thoreau justice (especially in his essay on Thoreau in *Writings*, I, and in his essay on Thoreau's *Week* in Lowell's *The Round Table*), see Austin Warren's "Lowell on Thoreau," *Studies in Philology*, XXVII, 442–461 (July, 1930).

ll. 181 ff., on Bryant. In a letter of May 12, 1848, Lowell wrote of this passage: "Bryant is funny, and as fair as I could make it, immitigably just. Indeed I have endeavored to be so in all." The curious discrepancy between Lowell's view of Bryant's "iceolation" and Bryant's own glorification of poetic "fire" in his poem "The Poet" may be accounted for in part by the fact that Lowell wrote in 1848 before Bryant had been stirred by the issues leading to the Civil War, while Bryant's poem recorded his feeling in 1860.

ll. 242 ff., on Whittier. As fellow-abolitionists Lowell and Whittier always had cordial relations, and when Lowell founded the *Atlantic* he published many of Whittier's poems, often suggesting improvements in phrasing, as, for example, in the case of "Skipper Ireson's Ride." Lowell not only recognized Whittier's genius as a balladist of local themes but he saw that he transcended his Quaker sect in his broad humanity and his treatment of the universal aspects of man's destiny.

ll. 278–303. Note the manner in which this poem represents Lowell's first humanitarian period not only in its contempt for European traditionalism but in its high tribute to abolitionists.

ll. 304 ff., on Hawthorne. For an able elaboration of the view that Hawthorne is "a Puritan Tieck," an unstable compound of stern moralist and fantastic romanticist, see W. C. Brownell's essay in *American Prose Masters*. Lowell regarded Hawthorne as having "the rarest creative imagination of the century, the rarest in some ideal respects since Shakespeare" (*Writings*, I, 365). He planned to write the biography of Hawthorne for the American Men of Letters Series.

ll. 321 ff., on Cooper. Elsewhere (*Writings*, II, 5) Lowell wrote with reference to American life and our literature: "There was, indeed, one poetic side to the existence otherwise so narrow and practical; and to have conceived this, however partially, is the one original and American thing in Cooper. This diviner glimpse illumines the lives of our Daniel Boones, the man of civilization and old-world ideas confronted with our forest solitudes,—confronted, too, for the first time, with his real self, and so led gradually to disentangle the original substance of his manhood from the artificial results of culture. Here was our new Adam of the wilderness, forced to name anew, not the visible creation of God, but the invisible creation of man, in those forms that lie at the base of social institutions, so sensibly moulding personal character and controlling individual action. Here is the protagonist of our New World epic, a figure as poetic as that of Achilles, as ideally representative as that of Don Quixote, as romantic in its relation to our homespun and plebian myths as Arthur in his to the mailed and plumed cycle of chivalry." See the admirable essay in H. S. Canby's *Classic Americans*, pp. 97–142.

l. 361. *Than Adams the parson or Primrose the vicar.* The reference is to Parson Adams in Joseph Fielding's *Joseph Andrews* and to Oliver Goldsmith's Dr. Primrose in *The Vicar of Wakefield*,—two of the most memorably humanized characters of English fiction.

l. 367. *truth in his strictures.* In Cooper's *American Democrat* and other books of social criticism he attacked the uncouthness and lack of individuality and distinction in equalitarian democracy. His point of view was essentially Federalistic. For full discussion see R. E. Spiller's Introduction to *Cooper* in the American Writers Series.

ll. 374 ff. Note Lowell's ardent nationalism and his contempt for European traditionalism.

ll. 436 ff., on Miranda (Margaret Fuller). Lowell had been much hurt by Margaret Fuller's belittling of him in her essay "American Literature," and he was tempted to retaliate, although in a letter of May 12, 1848, he said, "With her I have been perfectly good-humored, but I have a fancy that what I say will stick uncomfortably. It will make you laugh." Margaret Fuller was an ardent Transcendentalist, an editor of *The Dial*, and a disseminator of German philosophy. See her *Memoirs* (edited by Emerson, Channing, and Clarke, 1852) and Helen N. McMaster's *Margaret Fuller as a Literary Critic* (Buffalo: 1928).

ll. 463 ff., on Poe. For a more extended discussion see Lowell's essay on Poe in *Graham's Magazine*, XXVI, 49–53 (Feb., 1845). Poe reviewed *The Fable*, attacking its abolitionism. In many ways Lowell and Poe were antithetical: contrast their critical creeds as summarized in Foerster's *American Criticism*.

ll. 596 ff., on Holmes. Although eventually Lowell and Holmes, colleagues on the Harvard faculty, were good friends, being the wits of The Saturday Club, Lowell had originally tried as a humanitarian to reprimand Holmes, ten years his senior, for his apparent indifference to reforms. See Holmes's reply (Morse's *Life and Letters*, I, 295–303) to a letter from Lowell defending himself against the latter's criticism of his indifference to (1) pacifism, (2) abolition, (3) temperance, (4) the poor, and (5) reform in general. It should be noted that Lowell's characterization in *A Fable* was written ten years before Holmes's *Autocrat*, which Lowell persuaded him to contribute serially to his newly founded *Atlantic Monthly* in 1857.

ll. 618 ff. On Lowell and his "whole bale of *isms*." This self-criticism illustrates that as early as 1848 Lowell had begun to see the poetic perils of the didactic humanitarianism to which he had been addicted. In 1849 he severed his connection with the *Anti-Slavery Standard*, for which he had written steadily in favor of abolitionism. In a letter of January 23, 1850, he summarizes his "mental and moral latitude and longitude," convinced that he is "farther eastward and nearer morning than ever hitherto." "I begin to feel that I must enter on a new year of my apprenticeship. My poems have thus far had a regular and natural sequence. First, Love and the mere happiness of existence beginning to be conscious of itself, then Freedom—both being the sides of Beauty presented to me—and now I am going to try more *wholly* after Beauty herself. Next, if I live, I shall try to present Life as I have seen it. In the 'Nooning' I shall not even glance towards Reform. . . . Certainly I shall not grind for any Philistines, whether Reformers or Conservatives. I find that Reform cannot take up the whole of me, and I am sure that eyes were given us to look about us with sometimes, and not to be always looking forward." Lowell was coming to see life in broader perspective and to be indifferent to fanaticism and propaganda and an intolerance of the past. Travel and extended reading were soon to give him a greater responsiveness to what was excellent in the culture of other times and lands. And the death of his wife and his children was about to suggest to the hitherto complacent reformer that before the most profound of human sufferings and sorrows merely outward legislative reform stands impotent.

Page 104.   ODE TO HAPPINESS

This poem was not published until 1861 (*Atlantic Monthly*, VIII, 365 ff.), and should not be confused with Lowell's poem "Happiness"

(*Atlantic*, I, 685, April, 1858). The "Ode to Happiness" occupies a place in Lowell's intellectual development somewhat analogous to that of the "Ode to Duty" in Wordsworth's development: both embody a recantation of the poets' earlier philosophy, and a turn toward conservatism. Lowell, following his disillusionment with outward reform and his grief at the death of his two daughters and his wife, is confident that, although the capricious "half-earthly" happiness of boyhood has fled, Tranquillity, her "elder sister, . . . born of the immortals," will come to him who matches impulse with control: passion and sin, regarded as of inward origin, are to be matched by "culture wise" and renunciation. The poem marks Lowell's turn from an outward environmentalism and a contempt for traditionalism toward a reverence for traditionalism and an insistence upon inward control and self-mastery.

Page 108.   THE WASHERS OF THE SHROUD

This important poem, first published in the *Atlantic*, VIII, 641–643 (November, 1861), is comparable in its impassioned Unionism to Longfellow's "The Building of the Ship"—in fact both men use the same figure to represent the Union. Regarding the composition of this poem Lowell wrote his friend C. E. Norton (*Letters*, I, 318): "I had just two days allowed me by Fields for the November *Atlantic*, and I got it done. It had been in my head some time, and when you see it you will remember my having spoken to you about it. Indeed, I owe it to you, for the hint came from one of those books of Souvestre's you lent me—the Breton legends. The writing took hold of me enough to leave me tired out and to satisfy me entirely as to what was the original of my head and back pains. But whether it is good or not, I am not yet far enough off to say. But *do* like it, if you can. Fields says it is 'splendid,' with tears in his eyes—but then I read it to him, which is half the battle. I began it as a lyric, but it *would* be too aphoristic for that, and finally flatly refused to sing at any price. So I submitted, took to pentameters, and only hope the thoughts are good enough to be preserved in the ice of the colder and almost glacier-slow measure. I think I have done well—in some stanzas at least—and not wasted words."

This poem is much more philosophical than Longfellow's "The Building of the Ship," and its significance in the growth of Lowell's mind is thrown into sharper relief when we compare its ideas with his earlier democratic radicalism. First, the former pacifist who had said in 1846, "Ez fer war, I call it murder" (p. 33), now knows "the sheathed blade may rust with darker sin" (p. 111). This recoil from pacifism is also expressed in the "Commemoration Ode" (p. 139), and in *The Biglow Papers*, Second Series (*Works*, VIII, 264).

Second, the former equalitarian democrat who had sung of "levelling of all ranks in a common humanity" and who had tended to senti-mentalize religion (cf. "Rhœcus" and "The Vision of Sir Launfal"), now sees temporal law as sanctioned by eternal law—like Emerson's Over-Soul—whose violation invites our destruction. Nerved by his Puritan heritage (cf. "New England Two Centuries Ago," p. 314), Lowell concluded, "Every human government is bound to make its laws so far resemble His that they shall be uniform, certain, and un-questionable in their operation; and this it can do only by a timely show of power, and by an appeal to that authority which is of divine right, inasmuch as its office is to maintain that order which is the single attribute of the Infinite Reason" (*Works*, V, 74). This is the sublime mood, then, which inspired "The Washers of the Shroud" with its impassioned conviction that America's doom depends not on demo-cratic voting, on "Opinion's wind," but on an intelligent and pur-poseful obedience to "the Law before all time":

> "Three roots bear up Dominion: Knowledge, Will—
> These twain are strong, but stronger yet the third,—
> Obedience."

In the third place, the former radical who had urged revolt from the past, who had insisted that one cannot unlock "the Future's portal with the Past's blood-rusted key" (p. 29), now holds that "Time Was unlocks the riddle of Time Is" (l.81), showing an increasing respect for tradition. For full discussion see Bibliography under Jenkins and Clark.

Page 115.   JONATHAN TO JOHN

Parson Wilbur's letter introducing "Mason and Slidell: A Yankee Idyll" discusses the "idyll" as a form which involves rustic language and the description of real scenery and manners—illustrating Lowell's trend toward localism and nationalism in literary theory. This letter also contains a resentful discussion of England's tendency to favor the South in the Civil War, a tendency which culminated in England's preparation for war after the Unionist Captain Wilkes had removed from an English vessel Mason and Slidell who were going to England and France as commissioners to seek aid for the South. (For back-grounds see F. L. Owsley's *King Cotton Diplomacy*, Chicago, 1925, and L. M. Sears's *John Slidell*, Durham, N.C., 1925.) Note that Lowell's growing nationalism was accentuated by England's inso-lence at this time.

This letter by Parson Wilbur is followed by a poem, omitted here, describing Hosea Biglow's dream in which, while at the Concord Battle Ground, he overhears an argument between Concord Bridge (representing resentment against England) and the Bunker Hill

Monument (representing those who urge tolerance toward England). The argument is followed by an eloquent prophecy of America's greatness.

The poem "Jonathan to John" is effective in its mingled expression of outraged feelings (ll. 11–13), disdainful ridicule (ll. 96–97) of England's self-interest, advocacy of America's forgiveness, and insistence on the righteousness of her cause. Cf. Holmes's earlier poem on the estrangement between the North and South, "Brother Jonathan's Lament for Sister Caroline."

Page 119. A MESSAGE OF JEFF DAVIS IN SECRET SESSION

Mr. Wilbur's letter introducing this poem by Hosea Biglow was dated March 10, 1862. In this poem, an imaginary speech by the President of the Confederacy, Lowell satirizes the difficulty of the South in securing funds to preserve its status as a nation founded on the Secessionists' doctrine "Thet a Gov'ment's fust right is to tumble to pieces." Needless to say, he is grossly unfair to Davis in portraying him as an arch-hypocrite.

l. 92. *Once . . . my own Mississippi.* The chances of Davis in securing recognition of his confederate nation in England were lessened by the fact that in the period of 1830–1840 he had strongly advocated the repudiation of Mississippi's debt which was mainly owed to England.

l. 155. *But Roanoke, Bufort, Millspring.* These were strategic points whose capture by the North early in 1862 deprived the South of Port Royal, South Carolina, one of its finest harbors.

l. 163. *Oh, ef we hed on'y jes' gut Reecognition.* It is said that only the timely news of the defeat of the South at Gettysburg prevented England from recognizing the independence of the Confederacy.

Compare and contrast this poem with Freneau's poems ridiculing the pretensions of England in the Revolution.

Page 125.   SUNTHIN' IN THE PASTORAL LINE

Lines 1–107 illustrate the fact that, in keeping with Lowell's nationalism of this period, he opposed having poets draw on foreign countries (l. 16) in their use of nature. His practice of treating the flowers and birds of his native locality should be compared with the rich knowledge of nature which he reveals in his essay on "My Garden Acquaintance." (For full discussion see N. Foerster on Lowell in *Nature in American Literature.*) It will be recalled that this plea that our poets treat the American scene goes back at least as far as Freneau.

In Parson Wilbur's letter introducing this poem he had developed the idea that the New England Puritans "showed remarkable practical sagacity as statesmen and founders." In the poem Hosea dreams, while asleep in the schoolhouse, that a Pilgrim Father appeared and said that just as he had helped behead the tyrannical Charles I, so now Hosea, his descendant, must overthrow slavery as "the fangs an' thinkin' head" of tyranny. This portion of the poem should be read in the light of Lowell's essay "New England Two Centuries Ago," in which he traces his view of a coercive federated republic back to the Puritan tradition of civil liberty; conversely, in his essays on "Rebellion: Its Causes and Consequences" (1864) and "Rousseau and the Sentimentalists" (1867) he traces the doctrine of secession, which he identifies with anarchy, back to Jefferson, author of the Kentucky Resolutions (1799), and to Jefferson's "father," the French radical, Rousseau. Lowell says that the Puritans "knew that liberty in the hands of feeble-minded and unreasoning persons . . . means nothing less . . . than downright chaos." "Sober, earnest, and thoughtful men, it was no Utopia, no New Atlantis, no realization of a splendid dream, which they had at heart, but the establishment of the divine principle of Authority on the common interest and the common consent; the making, by a contribution from the free-will of all, a power which should curb and guide the free-will of each for the general good" (*Writings*, II, 9–10).

l. 303. *The trouble is to 'mancipate the white.* Cf. Emerson's "Ode, inscribed to W. H. Channing."

Page 134. LATEST VIEWS OF MR. BIGLOW

With this poem Lowell announced the death of Parson Wilbur. The unfinished letter which the Parson left, dated Dec. 24, 1862, contained the following passage, expressing Lowell's own views at that time: "Though I believe Slavery to have been the cause of it [the war], by so thoroughly demoralizing Northern politicks for its own purposes as to give opportunity and hope to treason, yet I would not have our thought and purpose diverted from their true object,— the maintenance of the idea of Government. We are not merely suppressing an enormous riot, but contending for the possibility of permanent order coexisting with democratical fickleness; and while I would not superstitiously venerate form to the sacrifice of substance, neither would I forget that an adherence to precedent and prescription can alone give that continuity and coherence under a democratical constitution which are inherent in the person of a despotick monarch and the selfishness of an aristocratical class. *Stet pro ratione voluntas* is as dangerous in a majority as in a tyrant."

At this time Lincoln and his policies were meeting with strong opposition. Horatio Seymour (l. 56) had been elected governor of New York on the Democratic Party's platform which denounced

practically all of Lincoln's measures.   Seymour's influence is supposed to have been partly responsible for the Draft Riot which took
place in New York in July, 1863.   Although Lincoln's first inaugural
address early in 1861 had disclaimed any intention of interfering with
slavery in its original stronghold, he became convinced that the
nation could not exist half slave and half free, and on September
22, 1862, he issued a proclamation (l. 122) giving warning that unless
certain conditions were fulfilled he would emancipate all the slaves
of the States in rebellion on the first day of the next year.   In the
ensuing election opposition to this policy was so strong that the
Republicans were defeated in New York, Pennsylvania, Ohio,
Indiana, and Illinois.   However, the support of New England, the
West, and the Border Slave States gave Lincoln a majority which
enabled him to emancipate the slaves.   In this great crisis Lowell's
"pep-talk" denouncing "Conciliation" (l. 42) and demanding "pison-
mad, pig-headed fightin'" (l. 96) in support of Lincoln's "grand"
policy, was particularly timely and effective.   The great popularity
of *The Biglow Papers* and their demand for decisive action must have
heartened Lincoln in those dark days when, as Lowell said, systems
and not parties were wrestling (l. 34).

ll. 145–148.   Note that Lowell's earlier a priori utopianism has
given way to a more sober recognition of the necessity of taking into
account not only theories but facts and concrete circumstances.   Cf.
also "Sunthin' in the Pastoral Line" (l. 274), where he says, "Th'
idees hev arms an' legs."   Compare this realistic, practical view with
that of Lowell's idol, Burke, who denounced the French Revolution-
ists because they were logical abstractionists who ignored expediency
and historical relativism and circumstances.

Page 139.   ODE RECITED AT THE HARVARD COMMEMORATION

Although this sublime "Ode" embodied thoughts which had been
growing slowly but steadily in Lowell's mind, it is possible that he
derived immediate inspiration for it from a poem read by George
Henry Boker before the Phi Beta Kappa Society at Harvard University on July 20, 1865, as Dr. A. H. Quinn has suggested ("George
Henry Boker—Playright and Patriot," *Scribner's Magazine*, LXXIII,
701 ff. June, 1923).

Since few casual readers grasp the full meaning of the poem, it may
not be amiss to note here the sequence of thought in the successive
stanzas:

    I. Compared to verse written in life-blood, "weak-winged is
       song," yet "feathered words" may preserve the memory of
       heroic deeds.

    II. The heroic deeds and the sacrifice of lives here commemorated were inspired by the passion for Truth for which Harvard stands.

III. Yet Truth not externalized, "made whole with deed," is futile. (Cf. Emerson on "Action" in "The American Scholar," and cf. Carlyle.)

IV. In a world of constant change, "What is there that abides . . .?" (Cf. Lowell's earlier celebration of change, progress, and revolt from the past.) Yet the life of man sacrificed for an ideal gives our life of change and oblivion "a high immunity from Night," a "noble permanence" which "haunts the soul."

V. Peace is not ignoble, but man should be ready when his Ideal is "foe-beset" to "front a lie in arms and not to yield," whether in the closet or the field. (Cf. Lowell's earlier pacifism—"Ez fer war, I call it murder.")

VI. Lincoln exemplified the ideal of the courageous, self-poised warrior against falsehood, molded by "the unexhausted West," the American frontier, with "nothing of Europe here."

VII. As long as man is loyal to "some more inspiring goal / Outside of Self," to "some ideal Good"—"Freedom, Law, Country" —man shall reverence sacrifice for its preservation.

VIII. Let us salute and honor "the sacred dead" who are "secure from change in their high-hearted ways."

IX. In the face of Oblivion and Change, the "Soul resents / Such short-lived service" and claims "a more divine investiture" in "a new imperial race." (Cf. stanza IV.)

X. Nobler than Europe's feudal rewards is "that plain civic wreath" given the brave by "a rescued Nation" which sets "her heel on treason."

XI. "Lift the heart," for " 'tis no Man we celebrate," but "the pith and marrow of a Nation." She is saved, and she "sends all her handmaid armies back to spin."

XII. He calls the country to "prayer and praise," for the preservation of the united nation.

Regarding the composition and form of this "Ode," Lowell wrote James B. Thayer: "But what I wished to say a word to you about (since you are so generous in your judgment) is the measures I have chosen in these [*Three Memorial Poems*] as well as the 'Commemoration Ode.' I am induced to this by reading in an article on Cowley copied into the *Living Age* from the *Cornhill* (and a very good article too, in the main) the following passage, 'As lately as our own day' (*my* ear would require '*So* lately as,' by the way) 'Mr. Lowell's "Commemoration Ode" is a specimen of the formless poem of unequal lines and broken stanzas supposed to be in the manner of Pindar, but

truly the descendant of our royalist poet's "majestick numbers."
Now, whatever my other shortcomings (and they are plenty, as none
knows better than I), want of reflection is not one of them. The
poems were all intended for public recitation. That was the first
thing to be considered. I suppose my ear (from long and painful
practice on ΦΒΚ poems) has more technical experience in this than
almost any. The least tedious measure is the rhymed heroic, but
this, too, palls unless relieved by passages of wit or even mere fun.
A long series of uniform stanzas (I am always speaking of public
recitation) with regularly recurring rhymes produces somnolence
among the men and a desperate resort to their fans on the part of the
women. No method has yet been invented by which the train of
thought or feeling can be shunted off from the epical to the lyrical
track. My ears have been jolted often enough over the sleepers on
such occasions to know that. I know *something* (of course an American can't know much) about Pindar. But *his* odes had the advantage
of being chanted. Now, my problem was to contrive a measure
which should not be tedious by uniformity, which should vary with
varying moods, in which the transitions (including those of the voice)
should be managed without jar. I at first thought of mixed rhymed
and blank verses of unequal measures, like those in the choruses of
Samson Agonistes, which are in the main masterly. Of course, Milton
deliberately departed from that stricter form of the Greek Chorus to
which it was bound quite as much (I suspect) by the law of its
musical accompaniment as by any sense of symmetry. I wrote some
stanzas of the 'Commemoration Ode' on this theory at first, leaving
some verses without a rhyme to match. But my ear was better
pleased when the rhyme, coming at a longer interval, as a far-off
echo rather than instant reverberation, produced the same effect
almost, and yet was grateful by unexpectedly recalling an association
and faint reminiscence of consonance. I think I have succeeded
pretty well, and if you try reading aloud I believe you would agree
with me. The sentiment of the 'Concord Ode' demanded a larger
proportion of lyrical movements, of course, than the others. Harmony, without sacrifice of melody, was what I had mainly in view."
—Norton, *Letters*, II, 189–190.

Page 152.   THE CATHEDRAL

The Cathedral, which first appeared in book form at Christmas,
1869, as well as in the *Atlantic* for January, 1870, was first entitled
A Day at Chartres. Lowell described it to Howells as having "a bit
of clean carving here and there, a solid buttress or two, and perhaps
a gleam through painted glass . . . (*Letters*, II, 35). Of the composition of the poem, Lowell said, "I wrote it in pencil, then copied it

out in ink, and worked over it as I never worked over anything before. I may fairly say that there is not a word in it which I have not thought, not an objection which I did not foresee and maturely consider." "I hope it is good," he wrote Miss Norton, "for it fairly trussed me at last and bore me up as high as my poor lungs will bear into the heaven of invention. I was happy writing it, and so steeped in it that if I had written to you it would have been in blank verse. It is a kind of religious poem . . ." (*Letters*, II, 38). Ruskin wrote of it, "The main substance of the poem is most precious to me, and its separate lines sometimes unbetterable." According to H. E. Scudder (*Biography*, II, 141-142), "Lowell here builds upon the foundation of human life a fane of worship, and in the speculations which discriminate between the conventional and the free aspirations of the soul, constructs out of living stones a house of prayer. Nor is there absent that capricious mood which carved grotesques upon the under side of the benches at which worshippers kneeled, so that when the reader, borne along by the high thought, stumbles over such lines as

> 'Who, meeting Caesar's self, would slap his back,
> Call him "Old Horse" and challenge to a drink,'

he may, if he will, console himself with the reflection that the most aspiring Gothic carries like grimacing touches within its majestic walls

> 'Imagination's very self in stone.'

That is the epithet Lowell bestows on Chartres Cathedral, and in the few spirited lines in which he contrasts the Greek with the Goth, and hints at the historic evolution of the latter, he is in a large way reflecting the native constitution of his own mind,

> 'Still climbing, luring fancy still to climb.'"

Devoted as Lowell was to the Greek tradition and to his native Puritanism, he confessed "a singular sympathy with what are known as the Middle Ages," finding it more difficult "to bridge over the gulf to Paganism." His study of the Middle Ages which crystallized in his great essay on Dante (*Works*, IV, 118-264) led him to recognize the values of Catholicism—"she has never lost sight of the truth" that man is "composed of the sum of flesh and spirit"; she is "the only church that has been loyal to the heart and soul of man, that has clung to her faith in the imagination," with a wholesome recognition of the perils of surrendering everything to "the iconoclast Understanding," the "blunder" of Protestantism. Nevertheless, in this scientific "age that blots out life with question marks," he confesses "'tis irrecoverable, that ancient faith," "its forms are weariness." Reluctantly, then, since "each age must worship its own thought of God," since the contemporary religion of nature has turned out to be "but our own conceit of what we see," Lowell takes refuge in the doctrine of immanence and he finds "inward surety" in faith in a depersonalized deity "so far above, yet in and of me," a deity revealed to the inward man in every impulse "that liberates and lifts, / In all that humbles, sweetens, and consoles."

The Cathedral should be compared with Tennyson's *In Memoriam* and especially with Arnold's "Stanzas from the Grande Chartreuse" (1855), which deals with much the same problem of the quest for religious certitude by those later nineteenth-century thinkers

> "Wandering between two worlds, one dead,
>   The other powerless to be born."

Compare also Longfellow's "The Golden Legend." For discussion see Bibliography under Shea, Strong, Quayle, and Bailey. The latter, p. 169, regards "The Cathedral" as "probably the most remarkable philosophic poem in American literature."

In form *The Cathedral* illustrates Lowell's mastery of "high seriousness" and "the grand style," although it contains bits of fun and some ornamentation as well as an occasional awkward line. The regularity and smoothness of the blank verse, in which Lowell wrote some twenty-five poems, is fairly typical in the limited variety of its cadences and pauses. Ferris Greenslet says in his chapter on "Lowell's Poetry" (*Lowell*, pp. 245–265) that "the quality of Lowell's poetic style at its very best is of a pithy and noble grandiloquence," and that this quality is especially represented in *The Cathedral*. The four other distinctive qualities Mr. Greenslet finds characteristic of Lowell's poetry are sincerity, a love of nature, a power of thought, and ideality.

Page 174.   AGASSIZ

Lowell wrote this poem while in Rome. On the circumstances of composition see his letter to Norton, Feb. 26, 1874 (*Letters*, II, 115–116). Agassiz interested Lowell not only because of his rare personal winsomeness but because he was loyal both to science and to traditional religion. On the conflict between science and religion, see B. J. Loewenberg's "The Controversy over Evolution in New England, 1859–1873," *New England Quarterly*, VIII, 232–257, and L. M. Shea's *Lowell's Religious Outlook*, pp. 100–113.

Note Lowell's attack (ll. 35 ff.) on the "public scandal, private fraud," associated with the Grant administration. On this subject consult V. L. Parrington's colorful analysis of "The Gilded Age," especially "The Great Barbecue," in *The Beginnings of Critical Realism in America*, pp. 7–47. Howells (*Literary Friends and Ac-*

quaintance, p. 219) testifies that originally Lowell had a line in this poem indicating "too bitterly his disappointment with his country," which he "left out of the printed version, at the fervent entreaty of his friends." Lowell was attacked for what he did say in criticism of America and materialism, both here and in "An Ode for the Fourth of July, 1876." It was charged that residence in Europe had made him hostile to democracy, a charge which is amply refuted in his chief address to Englishmen ("Democracy," 1884); "never," says the historian J. F. Jameson, "did American democracy receive a better defense."

Compare his comment on Holmes, Emerson, and Hawthorne at the Saturday Club with his own earlier comments in *A Fable for Critics* and with Holmes's comments in the poem "At the Saturday Club."

Page 191.   THREE MEMORIAL POEMS

These three poems appeared first in the *Atlantic Monthly* for June and August, 1875, and December, 1876. They were collected and published in book form in 1877 (really December, 1876) as *Three Memorial Poems*. Among contemporary reviews see those by W. D. Howells (*Atlantic Monthly*, March, 1877) and by J. V. Blake (*Radical Review*, May, 1877).

In the prefatory lines Lowell replied to those who attacked the second stanza of his poem on "Agassiz" (p. 175) as unpatriotic, showed his pride in his Puritan ancestry, and made clear his critical love of his country.

Page 191.   ODE READ AT THE ONE HUNDREDTH ANNIVERSARY OF
THE FIGHT AT CONCORD BRIDGE

For Lowell's explanation of the form of these poems see the portion of one of his letters to Thayer quoted in note on the "Commemoration Ode," above. It will be recalled that he said he wrote the poems primarily "for recitation," and that in this poem "harmony, without sacrifice of melody," was what he had "mainly in view." He used more three- and four-stress lines than in the other odes, and the last strophe is notable for the number of its anapestic substitutions. The first seven strophes embody Lowell's lyrical devotion to Freedom as evolved by our Puritan and Revolutionary ancestors, and they may well be read in the light of his lofty tribute to the Puritans and their heritage in his prose essay, "New England Two Centuries Ago" (*Works*, II, 1–76). Then Lowell turns to "graver thoughts"; he who had earlier exalted feeling at the expense of knowledge and traditional culture now hears the voice of Freedom saying (ll. 183–193) that she dwells only with Knowledge and "with

men by culture trained and fortified," with men who obey divine
law. (Cf. Freneau's "Rising Glory of America," Bryant's "The
Antiquity of Freedom," and Whitman's "Over the Carnage.")

Page 199.   UNDER THE OLD ELM

Lowell wrote J. B. Thayer, Jan. 14, 1877 (*Letters*, II, 188–189),
"I think the 'Old Elm' the best of the three [Memorial Poems],
mainly because it was composed after my college duties were over
. . ." He said earlier, "I took advantage of the occasion [praising
Washington] to hold out a hand of kindly reconciliation to Virginia.
I could do it with the profounder feeling, that no family lost more
than mine by the Civil War. Three nephews (the hope of our race)
were killed in one or other of the Virginia battles, and three cousins
on other of those bloody fields" (*Letters*, II, 141). On Lowell's
political views of the difficult problems presented by the South after
the war, see his essay on "Reconstruction" (1865), in his *Political
Essays*. The war was to him a sacrament and a consecration; it
abolished the sin of slavery and it proved that our people set the
ideals of democratic nationality above material prosperity. In this
essay, while he insisted on a peace which rested on a guarantee of
the equal rights of black and white, he insisted that "our duty is
not to punish but to repair. . . . Let us not harden our hearts against
our white brethren, from whom interest and custom, those slyer
knaves, whose fingers have felt about our own pockets, had stolen
away their conscience and their sense of brotherhood." He opposed
"any general confiscation of Rebel property" and "all irregular
modes of levying contributions." He favored "conceding all that
can be conceded without danger to the great principle [national
unity] which has been at stake," and he was confident that the
North and South would "live more harmoniously together in the
future than in the past, now that the one rock of offence has been
blasted out of the way."

The theme of the poem should be carefully compared and contrasted with that of the "Commemoration Ode" (p. 139, above).
They have much in common, including their lofty dignity and their
concern with communal thought and feeling and with civic responsibility. Yet the first, through its homage to Lincoln, exalts a disregard for traditionalism (strophe VI), while "Under the Old Elm,"
in viewing what Washington stood for through the memory of a
century, exalts a respect for traditionalism and for organic continuity
(strophes I and II) which were involved in the Federalistic spirit of
which Washington was one of the chief spokesmen. Furthermore,
while the "Commemoration Ode" emphasizes the nation, "Under
the Old Elm" emphasizes ultimately the influence of the self-con-

Notes

Notes

Notes   491

trolled and self-poised individual (strophes II, IV, V). Lines 257–
266, while applied to Washington, embody a noble expression of
Lowell's mature ideal of "orbed" and "balanced" development of
the individual "in perfect symmetry of self-control." Strophe VII
celebrates Washington as the man who "shot union" through the
chaotic colonies, and strophe VIII embodies Lowell's attempt at
reconciliation as mentioned above. On the whole, the poem is certainly one of the most impressive of all our poems devoted to the
tradition of political liberty and the good of all. On this important
aspect of Lowell's significance, see the essay by Bliss Perry listed in
the Bibliography.

Page 211.   AN ODE FOR THE FOURTH OF JULY, 1876

Although this poem may not have an artistic finish equal to that
of "Under the Old Elm," it probably represents the high-water
mark of Lowell's mature thought in poetry.

Section I deals with the Revolution and the achievement of independence. Section II compares and contrasts the civilization in
America which "the western traveller sees" with that of ancient
Greece and Rome. Lowell says that in the West equality of manhood is "latent in the very sod" (l. 115), that no one can breath its
air and not "grow humane." Incidentally, contrary to what some
unsympathetic interpreters imagine, Lowell was fully conscious of
the significance of the western frontier as the home of "distinctive
Americanism" (see *Works*, VI, 203–205; V, 192; X, 22, 55, 93–94;
Letters, I, 325; II, 169, 173, 248). Five years before F. J. Turner's
epoch-making address on "The Significance of the Frontier in American History" (1893), Lowell in "The Independent in Politics" (1888)
traced much of our distinctive equality, self-reliance, and optimism
to the western frontier, although he did not ignore the manner in
which these ideals were reinforced by European philosophies as well
as the dangers involved in these ideals. In this "Ode" (ll. 149–150)
he contrasts unfavorably our "inert prosperity, / This bovine comfort in the sense alone," with classical antiquity which "hid Beauty
safe from Death in words or stone"; yet he believes that American
potentialities are only partly developed, and that eventually America
may concern itself with Beauty. Section III records Lowell's disillusionment with a democratic reliance on numbers rather than wisdom; evidence of "parasitic greed" had caused Lowell to lose his
early faith in natural goodness, and to make him more realistic
(see Nevins, *The Emergence of Modern America, 1865–1878*, Chap.
VII). Section IV returns to a celebration of the Founders of the
nation who directed their courses by "ancient wisdom channelled
deep in law," who as Christian dualists "still believed in Heaven

and Hell." The Puritans, as he had illustrated in "New England Two Centuries Ago," were not utopians but practical statesmen whose central ideal of civil liberty involved making men not masterless but self-mastered—"making man sole sponsor of himself." Eventually, strengthened by his studies in the classics, in the mediaeval Dante, and in Puritanism, Lowell came to believe that the state, the whole, can be no stronger than the sum of its parts, the individuals composing it, and this poem, the crown of his development, emphasizes the need of self-conquest guided by tradition.

Page 225.   CREDIDIMUS JOVEM REGNARE

First published in *The Atlantic Monthly* for February, 1887, and collected in Lowell's *Heartsease and Rue* (1888). For discussion of his views of science see Introduction, p. lxxviii. It will be noted that in this poem, as well as in "The Cathedral," Lowell begins by touching on the possibility that in so far as science is merely materialistic it may lead to scepticism and pessimism, but that he ends with "hopes that sweeten Darwin" and the idea that if it is true that we have risen from "monkeys," our descendants may continue the rise and be

> "As much superior to us
> As we to Cynocephalus" (the dog-faced baboon).

Page 233.   LETTERS

Ferris Greenslet (p. 272) concludes that "the letters, a little more considerate than his talk, a little less elaborate than his essays, contain perhaps the very best of Lowell." And in the letter form Leslie Stephen said that "I don't think that Cowper or Gray or anyone could write better." It may be interesting, therefore, to note his theory of letter-writing. Greenslet (p. 271) quotes the following from the poems:

> "Letters, so it seems to me,
>   Our careless quintessence should be,
>   Our real nature's careless play
>   When Consciousness looks t'other way;
>   Not drop by drop, with watchful still,
>   Gathered in Art's deliberate skill,
>   But life's insensible completeness
>   Got as the ripe grape gets its sweetness,
>   As if it had a way to fuse
>   The golden sunlight into juice."

Lowell admired most as "real letters" those "of Gray, Cowper, Walpole, Howell, Lamb . . . (*New Letters*, xv). He doubted that "a pen that has once grown professional can limber itself to that free and easy kind of thing," and he told his daughter Mabel that "it takes a good while to secrete honey (or venom) for a good letter in my solitudes" (XV, 216). He remarked to Norton that "careless unconsciousness . . . is the life of a letter . . . I hold that a letter which is not mainly about the writer of it lacks the prime flavor. The wine must smack a little of the cask. You will recognize the taste of my old wood in this!" (XV, 277–278). And he thought that an "untrammelled mood of mind . . . is the main condition of agreeable letter-writing" (XV, 405). Into his letters are compressed, as M. A. DeWolfe Howe remarked, many of his distinctive merits such as "the breadth and zest of his reading, his equal appetite for litera- ture and life, the sympathy of his apprehensions, the wit of their ex- pressions" (*New Letters*, xiii). And, just as Emerson used his jour- nals as his "savings-bank," so Lowell put many of his best things as first thought of in his letters, and later re-worked them and polished them in his essays. If the latter at their best "are marked by extensive reading experience, a responsive humor, discrimination in taste, rich fancy, striking and stimulating allusions and figures, and the critic's own robust, vigorous, and brilliant personality," that fact is explained in part because his mind had "run a trial heat" in the letters. But they are perhaps most significant as illustrating Lowell's winsome capacity for deep and lasting friendships with such kindred spirits as Emerson, C. E. Norton, Leslie Stephen, Thomas Hughes, Henry Adams, F. J. Child, and Howells. In their ready sympathy and tact and understanding the letters illustrate Emer- son's remark that the only way to have a friend is to be one. Lowell was happy in being able to say that during his whole life he had never lost a friend.

Page 269.   LEAVES FROM MY JOURNAL IN ITALY

First printed in *Graham's Magazine*, April, May, July, 1854. In July, 1851, Lowell had sailed for Europe with his family and had spent the winter in Rome where his son Walter (born Dec. 22, 1850) died and was buried in April, 1852. They spent the summer of 1852 in England, met literary folk there, and returned home in October with Thackeray and A. H. Clough as shipmates.

Page 285.   CAMBRIDGE THIRTY YEARS AGO

First published in *Putnam's Magazine* (April and May, 1854) as "Fireside Travels." Lowell wrote the editor that this sketch of Cambridge "is done as nobody but I could do it, for nobody knows the old town so well" (Scudder, I, 354). See also his letter of 1862 (*New Letters*, 107–111) to E. R. Hoar of the Harvard Corporation in which Lowell favored unifying Harvard architecture around the ideal of the New England colonial type, with "a touch of archaism," simplicity, dignity, and "something that an association can love to cling round." As M. A. DeWolfe Howe remarks (p. 107) Lowell's tasteful "vision of the possibilities of Harvard architecture has met in recent years with a large measure of fulfillment."

Page 293.   E PLURIBUS UNUM

First published in *The Atlantic Monthly* (which Lowell founded in 1857 and edited until June, 1861) in February, 1861. This is perhaps the most earnest of Lowell's political essays of this period and centers on the idea that the major question is not abolition but the preservation of the Union in the face of the southern threat of Secession. Compare with the "Commemoration Ode," and notes on it (p. 484).

Page 314.   NEW ENGLAND TWO CENTURIES AGO

This is based on Lowell's article in *The North American Review* for January, 1865, on the Unitarian clergyman John Gorham Palfrey's "History of New England." This was a five-volume work of careful scholarship, the first volumes of which appeared in 1858, but which was not concluded until 1890. See Lowell's "Witchcraft" (III, 115–211) and Introduction, p. xlix.

Page 328.   ROUSSEAU AND THE SENTIMENTALISTS

First printed in the *North American Review* for July, 1867. The student may find it instructive to compare and contrast the view of Lowell (relating it to that of Irving Babbitt in *Rousseau and Romanticism*, Boston, 1919) with that of Ernest Hunter Wright in *The Meaning of Rousseau* (London, 1929). See also H. M. Jones, *America and French Culture, 1750–1848* (Chapel Hill, N.C., 1927) and Malcolm B. Jones, *French Literature and American Criticism, 1870–1900* (Cambridge, Mass., 1935).

Page 341.   SHAKESPEARE ONCE MORE (*Hamlet*)

This was first published in the *North American Review* for April, 1868. The portion in the present book is a selection from Lowell's longer essay, III, 215–320, pp. 215–289 being omitted. For orientation see Alfred Westfall, *Shakespearean Criticism in America, 1607–1865* (New York, 1939) especially useful on bibliographical data; and Esther C. Dunn, *Shakespeare in America* (New York, 1939). The latter (pp. 245 ff.) says that Lowell's lectures in 1855 on the English poets "were a means of injecting Shakespeare as a literary subject into the Harvard curriculum," although it was not until 1863 that Lowell "covered" Shakespeare in public University lectures.

In a speech before the Edinburgh Philosophical Institute in 1883 he said, "I never open my Shakespeare but what I find myself wishing that there might be professorships established for the study of his works." In 1889, in his talk as an early President of the Modern Language Association, when the advocates of ancient Greek and Latin literature disparaged less ancient studies, Lowell urged that the boredom of college boys could be overcome in part by allowing them to study the "modern" Shakespeare as "pastures new" in which they could "take a wholesome and vivifying interest in what was nearer to their habitual modes of thought and association." In *The Reading of Shakespeare in American Schools and Colleges* (New York, 1932), H. W. Simon says that "the beginning of the modern teaching of literature" came with F. J. Child (Lowell's close friend) who eventually made "a permanent place for the study of Shakespeare" in the college curriculum. G. L. Kittredge who took his A.B. at Harvard in 1882 was trained by Child, who retired from his professorship in 1896.

In general Lowell's criticism of Shakespeare followed the romantic tradition of idolizing him, for Lowell was influenced in this respect by Coleridge, Goethe, Lessing, and others. Dr. R. B. Falk's doctoral dissertation on *Representative American Criticism of Shakespeare, 1830–1885* (University of Wisconsin, 1940) treats R. H. Dana's unpublished criticism of Shakespeare and Henry Norman Hudson's *Lectures on Shakespeare*, 1848, as preceding and foreshadowing Lowell, whose contribution is followed by treatments of E. P. Whipple, Emerson, Jones Very. Dr. Falk illustrates realistic and social criticism of Shakespeare by analysis of Richard Grant White, Walt Whitman, and George Wilkes. It has been suggested that in Lowell's interpretation of Hamlet as a procrastinator, a thinker averse to action, Lowell (while following Coleridge) tended to read his own character into the hero.

In the earlier portions of the essay here omitted Lowell discussed the history of the language and Shakespeare's use of it and the necessity in criticism of accepting certain criteria, "certain principles as fixed beyond question. . . It is the Greeks who must furnish us with our standard of comparison. Their stamp is upon all the allowed measures and weights of aesthetic criticism" (III, 247, 252). It is possible, just as in matters of religion vs. science and political individualism vs. socialism, that Lowell was effective once more as a conciliator between advocates of the ancients vs. the moderns by suggesting that the study of the "modern" Shakespeare be approached in the light of the standards of ancient classical criticism, although he himself reflected in part the Coleridge-Goethe trend. See Augustus Ralli, *A History of Shakespearian Criticism* (London, 1932), for general orientation.

Page 367.   *From* DANTE

This essay, entitled "The Shadow of Dante," appeared first in
the *North American Review*, CXV, 139 ff. (July, 1872), and was reprinted in Lowell's *Among My Books*, Second Series, in 1876. Lowell
also deals with Dante in *Appleton's New American Encyclopedia*
(1870), and in the *Fifth Annual Report, Dante Society* (1886). Lowell
and C. E. Norton (who translated Dante) were invited by Longfellow
to constitute with him a Dante Club which met every Wednesday
evening in the winter of 1865–1866 to discuss Longfellow's translation of Dante then in progress. Lowell's course in Dante at Harvard
was his favorite, and his fresh, individual, and charming manner of
interpreting this poet to his students has been vividly recorded by
George E. Pond in an essay entitled "Lowell at Harvard," in *Liber
Scriptorum* (New York, 1893), pp. 456 ff. While Bryant and Emerson brought the classicism of Homer and Plato, respectively, to bear
on the American mind, Lowell and Longfellow were distinctive in
preferring, and in introducing to the descendants of the Puritans,
the Catholic medievalism of Dante. (For a brief discussion of attitudes toward Dante expressed by various Americans, see Emilio
Goggio's "Dante Interests in Nineteenth Century America," *Philological Quarterly*, I, 192–201 [July, 1922]; see also T. W. Koch's extensive study, "Dante in America," in *Fifteenth Annual Report of
the Dante Society* [Cambridge: 1896]. As early as 1854 in *Leaves
from My Journal in Italy* (*Works*, I, 195), Lowell recognized the
values of the dualism of Catholicism; see note on "The Cathedral,"
above.

Page 390.   .   *From* WORDSWORTH

Dated 1875, this essay was first published in *Among My Books*,
Second Series, 1876. See Lowell's "Introductory Essay" in *Wordsworth* in the series of *British Poets* (Boston, 1854 and 1859), and his discussion of Wordsworth in his lectures on the English Poets at the
Lowell Institute in 1855. For details on this and many miscellaneous
references to Wordsworth by Lowell, see Annabel Newton, *Wordsworth
in Early American Criticism* [1824–1860], Chicago, 1928 (index). See
also Lowell's second essay on Wordsworth (VII, 121–137) delivered on
May 10, 1884 while he was president (after Arnold) of the Wordsworth
Society. In this later essay he remarks that he has already said in
his earlier essay "what I thought good," but Dr. Knight's new edition of the poet's work does enable Lowell to see more clearly the
development of Wordsworth's thought from radicalism to conserva-
tivism. Scudder (II, 310) says that in Lowell's stress on this development one may read Lowell's own mind, more or less conscious
of change in its attitude, and finding in the mirror of another poet

some image of itself." In the essay of 1884 Lowell praises Words-worth's later tendency to rely less on outward nature and more on inward spiritual resources and on tradition and human institutions which have developed slowly and adapted themselves to time and place. The sections omitted (in Elmwood Edition, V, 177-219) are mainly biographical.

Page 407.   DEMOCRACY

While Ambassador to England from January, 1880, to June, 1885, Lowell delivered many public addresses, of which this one on "Democracy" given at Birmingham, October 6, 1884, is most noteworthy. In the opinion of the judicious historian J. F. Jameson (*Review of Reviews*, IV, 291), "Never did American democracy receive a better defence. Defences more sweeping it may often have had; it was not in Lowell's nature to indulge in uncritical laudation of all the traits and fruits of popular government in the United States. But with a wise and temperate, and therefore effective, championship, he set forth a high and reasonable faith in government by the people, a well-fortified confidence in their good sense and self-control. It was such a defence as should be made in behalf of a democracy no longer callow and vociferous, but adult, mellowed by time, and sobered by experience." Lowell's service in leading the British to understand and respect the United States and our democracy can hardly be overestimated. (See the chapter on Lowell in Beckles Willson's *America's Ambassadors to England*, New York, 1929.) Although during this period he was sympathetic toward Britain as "a monarchy with democratic tendencies" which had something in common with the United States as "a democracy with conservative instincts" (VII, 12), he had been sharply outspoken against the British for favoring the South during the Civil War and his essay "On A Certain Condescension in Foreigners" left no question of his Americanism. The British Leslie Stephen said that at the time Lowell was ambassador "Probably an offence to his patriotic sensibilities would have led to a retort, and he had powers of sarcasm which one could not have roused with impunity" (XVI, 336). Henry James, who knew Lowell well both as a student in 1862 and as a comrade of the London days, saw "his career as in the last analysis a tribute to the dominion of style," which included tact. (*Essays in London*, New York, 1893, p. 45).

Page 453.   THE PROGRESS OF THE WORLD

For orientation see J. B. Bury, *The Idea of Progress*, edited with an Introduction by C. A. Beard, New York, 1932; Arthur A. Ekirch, *The Idea of Progress in America, 1815–1860*, New York, 1944; Joyce

O. Hertzler, *Social Progress*, New York, 1928. Contrast Lowell's view of progress vs. science with that of his friend Henry Adams, who was much less optimistic because of the implications of the Second Law of Thermodynamics. See discussion of Lowell and science, Introduction, p. lxxviii.

Page 459.   THE INDEPENDENT IN POLITICS

First printed as a twenty-seven page pamphlet with sub-title, "An Address before the Reform Club of New York, April 13, 1888." [Reform Club Series, —I]. New York: The Reform Club, 1888. For discussion see Introduction, p. xcii. Further light on Lowell's political interests may be expected before long in a publication by Professor Leon Howard, based on some of Lowell's unpublished manuscripts.